# UNIVERSITY CASEBOOK SERIES

### EDITORIAL BOARD

**ROBERT C. CLARK**
*DIRECTING EDITOR*
Former Dean & Distinguished Service Professor
Harvard University

**DANIEL A. FARBER**
Sho Sato Professor of Law
University of California at Berkeley

**OWEN M. FISS**
Sterling Professor of Law
Yale University

**HERMA HILL KAY**
Dean & Barbara Nachtrieb Armstrong Professor of Law
University of California, Berkeley

**HAROLD HONGJU KOH**
Dean & Gerard C. & Bernice Latrobe Smith Professor of International Law
Yale Law School

**SAUL LEVMORE**
Dean & William B. Graham Professor of Law
University of Chicago

**THOMAS W. MERRILL**
Charles Keller Beekman Professor of Law
Columbia Law School

**ROBERT L. RABIN**
A. Calder Mackay Professor of Law
Stanford University

**CAROL M. ROSE**
Gordon Bradford Tweedy Professor of Law & Organization
Yale University

**DAVID L. SHAPIRO**
William Nelson Cromwell Professor of Law
Harvard University

**KATHLEEN M. SULLIVAN**
Stanley Morrison Professor of Law and
Former Dean of the School of Law
Stanford University

CASES AND MATERIALS

# FUNDAMENTALS OF PARTNERSHIP TAXATION

SEVENTH EDITION

_by_

STEPHEN A. LIND
Albert R. Abramson Distinguished Professor of Law,
University of California, Hastings College of the Law

STEPHEN SCHWARZ
Professor of Law Emeritus,
University of California, Hastings College of the Law

DANIEL J. LATHROPE
Professor of Law,
University of California, Hastings College of the Law

JOSHUA D. ROSENBERG
Professor of Law,
University of San Francisco School of Law

FOUNDATION PRESS
NEW YORK, NEW YORK
2005

THOMSON

WEST

MF

Foundation Press, of Thomson/West, has created this publication to provide you with accurate and authoritative information concerning the subject matter covered. However, this publication was not necessarily prepared by persons licensed to practice law in a particular jurisdiction. Foundation Press is not engaged in rendering legal or other professional advice, and this publication is not a substitute for the advice of an attorney. If you require legal or other expert advice, you should seek the services of a competent attorney or other professional.

© 1985, 1988, 1992, 1994, 1998, 2002 FOUNDATION PRESS
© 2005 By FOUNDATION PRESS
       395 Hudson Street
       New York, N.Y. 10014
       Phone Toll Free 1–877–888–1330
       Fax (212) 367–6799
       fdpress.com

Printed in the United States of America

**ISBN** 1–58778–832–2

*TEXT IS PRINTED ON 10% POST
CONSUMER RECYCLED PAPER*

*To our friend, Billy Hutton*

\*

# PREFACE

Even amidst the instability of the federal tax system that has marked the past several decades, the fundamental principles of partnership and S corporation taxation have remained intact since the First Edition of this text was published in 1984. The unrelenting pace of change continued during the brief shelf life of the Sixth Edition, as Congress reduced individual income tax rates, added to its patchwork quilt of partnership anti-abuse rules, and widened the eligibility gates for S corporations. These developments, along with the usual trickle of interesting rulings, justified this new Seventh Edition and offered another opportunity to cure a few viruses that may have infected our earlier efforts.

The constant barrage of tax legislation and complex regulations presents a challenge to instructors who seek to provide manageable coverage of an increasingly intricate subject matter. Although more detail has become unavoidable in a partnership tax course, we once again reaffirm our allegiance to teaching the "fundamentals" by the problem method. As we said in the Preface to the First Edition.

The pedagogical philosophy of this book is grounded in the problem oriented "fundamentals" approach to tax teaching that was pioneered by James J. Freeland, Stephen A. Lind and Richard B. Stephens in Fundamentals of Federal Income Taxation. For the uninitiated, the fundamentals approach involves selectivity of subject matter, an emphasis on basic concepts, avoidance of esoteric detail and realistic depth of coverage. It recognizes that the primary sources for any tax course are the Code and Regulations. Proceeding from these premises, this lean volume is a product of considerable self restraint by the authors. Cases have been selected and edited with care. Legislative history has been included but only when it is informative. Lengthy notes and voluminous citations to every case on a particular point have been scrupulously avoided. This is designed as a teaching text, not a treatise.

The book also contains a healthy dose of explanatory text and problems to accompany every topic. Partnership tax is a difficult course for law students. Although there are several fine treatises in the area, they are written primarily for practitioners. From our experience, even an abridged student edition of a professional treatise is simply too overwhelming and sophisticated to serve as an effective teaching tool. This volume attempts to fill the void by pro-

viding just enough explanation to provide a framework for the study of Subchapter K without getting bogged down in the details.

We also believe—almost as an article of faith—that the most productive method of teaching tax fundamentals is through a manageable set of problems that require the student to apply the Code and Regulations to discrete factual situations. Some of the problems in this book are intended to guide the student through the statutory maze; as such, they may even have specific answers. Others do not have definite solutions, reflecting the fact that much of Subchapter K remains unexplored territory. We have modestly attempted to confront students with some of the realities of practice by including a few problems with a planning orientation.

Turning to organization and coverage, the Seventh Edition retains the time-tested "cradle to grave" organization of its predecessors, with policy excerpts included selectively throughout the text. Chapter 1 introduces students to Subchapter K, examines the flexible "check-the-box" tax classification regime (without dwelling at great length on outdated concepts and cases), and provides a contemporary perspective on choice of entity issues. Chapter 2 covers partnership formations, including an introduction to partnership accounting and a preview of the impact of partnership liabilities on a partner's outside basis.

Chapters 3 through 5 address operational issues, moving systematically from the basic pass-through taxation scheme through partnership allocations, including allocations with respect to contributed property and partnership liabilities, and transactions between partners and partnerships. Our efforts at self restraint are continuously tested here by the intricacy and length of the regulations. Instructors who are pressed for time or concerned about a student meltdown should consider confining the assignments on allocations attributable to nonrecourse debt and partnership liabilities to the introductory material on each of those topics.

Chapter 6 through 8, covering sales and exchanges of partnership interests, operating and liquidating distributions, and partnership terminations, reflect the issuance of final regulations in a number of important areas, particularly sales and exchanges, elective basis adjustments, and partnership mergers and divisions, and have been updated to include coverage of several new anti-abuse rules designed to prevent the shifting of tax losses. Chapter 9 covers the special problems on the death of a partner.

Chapter 10 is a brief discussion of the partnership anti-abuse regulations. Our decision not to integrate this material into earlier chapters was based on the assumption that students had insufficient background to appreciate their meaning and scope. For those with the time and inclination, Chapter 10 offers an opportunity to review a few concepts studied in earlier chapters and to remind students that some tax planning maneuvers may be too good to be true.

Chapter 11 covers S corporations, which remain a popular alternative for businesses whose structure can accommodate to a simpler pass-through

taxing regime. Similar surveys of Subchapter S are included in our companion volume, Fundamentals of Corporate Taxation, and in Fundamentals of Business Enterprise Taxation, an alternative text for a combined course on corporate and partnership tax. Tax professors continue to debate whether S corporations are best covered in corporate tax, a course on taxation of pass-through entities, or a combined business enterprise taxation offering. Our books accommodate any of these approaches.

Turning to matters of style, we assume that the text will be assigned with the most recent edition of the Code and Regulations. Suggested assignments to these sources are provided for each topic. Instructors should review these assignments carefully, editing when necessary to ensure that they are consistent with the desired depth of coverage. Deletions from cases and other authorities have been made freely, with asterisks used to denote substantive omissions, but citations and internal cross references in excerpted materials have been deleted without so indicating. Editorial additions are in brackets. Footnotes to the original text are numbered consecutively within each section, and many footnotes have been deleted from cases without renumbering those that remain. Coverage is current through April 1, 2005.

We remain indebted to the late Richard B. Stephens of the University of Florida College of Law for his advice and support on the First Edition of this book. For their work as research assistants on prior editions, we thank former students Bob Appert, Steve Gee, Matt Richardson, Jim Berard, Thea Chester, Bill Goddard, and Jami Changaris Voge from Hastings College of the Law; Jay Katz, Dennis McGlothin and Chris Hanna from the University of Florida; and Francine Augustyn, Royda Krames and Piero Sallusolia from the University of San Francisco. Anthony Wan, a recent Hastings graduate, provided valuable research assistance on this new edition.

We also express our gratitude to Steve Lind and Josh Rosenberg, who have ended their active participation as co-authors, for their thoughtful contributions to the development of this text and to its many previous editions. And, as always, we are grateful to the administration of Hastings College of the Law for its support.

STEPHEN SCHWARZ
DANIEL J. LATHROPE

San Francisco, California
May, 2005

*

# ACKNOWLEDGEMENTS

We gratefully acknowledge the permission extended by the following author and publisher to reprint an excerpt from the material listed below.

William B. Brannan, "The Subchapter K Reform Act of 1997," 75 Tax Notes 121, 122-124 (April 7, 1997). Reprinted with permission. Copyright © 1997. Tax Analysts.

*

# SUMMARY OF CONTENTS

# TABLE OF CONTENTS

# TABLE OF INTERNAL REVENUE CODE SECTIONS

# TABLE OF TREASURY REGULATIONS

*

# TABLE OF REVENUE RULINGS

\*

# TABLE OF MISCELLANEOUS RULINGS

\*

# TABLE OF CASES

Principal cases are in bold type. Non-principal cases are in roman type. References are to Pages.

*

# TABLE OF AUTHORITIES

*

CASES AND MATERIALS

# FUNDAMENTALS OF PARTNERSHIP TAXATION

\*

# INTRODUCTION

1

CHAPTER 1

# An Overview of the Taxation of Partnerships and Partners

## A. Introduction to Subchapter K

The partnership has long served as a common business and investment vehicle, but for many years the taxation of partnerships was little more than a primitive backwater province in the Internal Revenue Code. Prior to 1954, only a small number of special sections dealt specifically with the taxation of partnerships.[1] It was not until the enactment of Subchapter K,[2] which at the time was lauded as one of the more "notable achievements of the 1954 Internal Revenue Code,"[3] that Congress provided a detailed statutory scheme to govern the federal income taxation of partnerships and partners. Both Congressional tax-writing committees explained the legislative objectives underlying the enactment of Subchapter K as follows:[4]

> The existing tax treatment of partners and partnerships is among the most confused in the entire income tax field. The present statutory provisions are wholly inadequate. The published regulations, rulings and court decisions are incomplete and frequently contradictory. As a result, partners today cannot form, operate or dissolve a partnership with any assurance as to tax consequences.
>
> This confusion is particularly unfortunate in view of the great number of business enterprises and ventures carried on in the partnership form. It should also be noted that the partnership form of organization is much more commonly employed by small businesses and in farming operations than the corporate form.
>
> Because of the vital need for clarification, your committee has undertaken the first comprehensive treatment of partners and partnerships in the history of the income tax laws. In establishing a broad pattern applicable to partnerships generally, the principal objectives have been simplicity, flexibility, and equity as between the partners.

**1.** I.R.C. (1939) Supplement F. See generally Little, Federal Income Taxation of Partnerships (1952).

**2.** I.R.C. §§ 701–761.

**3.** Jackson, Johnson, Surrey, Tenen & Warren, "The Internal Revenue Code of 1954: Partnerships," 54 Colum.L.Rev. 1183, 1235 (1954).

**4.** H.R.Rep. No. 1337, 83d Cong., 2d Sess. 65 (1954); S.Rep. No. 1622, 83d Cong., 2d Sess. 89 (1954).

A student encountering Subchapter K for the first time probably could read it in its entirety in a few hours time and emerge with an understanding of some general concepts of partnership taxation. But the brevity of the statute is deceptive, and the learning process becomes far more challenging when one digs beneath the surface and studies the statutory interrelationships in Subchapter K. As Judge Arnold Raum lamented in his now classic excerpt from Foxman v. Commissioner:[5]

> The distressingly complex and confusing nature of the provisions of subchapter K present a formidable obstacle to the comprehension of these provisions without the expenditure of a disproportionate amount of time and effort even by one who is sophisticated in tax matters with many years of experience in the tax field. Cf. Thomas G. Lewis, 35 T.C. 71, where we had occasion to comment (p. 76) upon the exasperating efforts required to deal with certain other provisions of the 1954 Code. * * * If there should be any lingering doubt on this matter one has only to reread section 736 in its entirety * * * and give an honest answer to the question whether it is reasonably comprehensible to the average lawyer or even to the average tax expert who has not given special attention and extended study to the tax problems of partners. Surely, a statute has not achieved "simplicity" when its complex provisions may confidently be dealt with by at most only a comparatively small number of specialists who have been initiated into its mysteries.

A major issue addressed by Congress in formulating Subchapter K was whether to treat a partnership as an entity or as an aggregate of its partners for federal tax purposes. The choice profoundly affects the tax consequences to the partnership and its partners. An entity approach would resemble the treatment of corporations in Subchapter C of the Code. A C corporation must determine and pay tax on its annual taxable income,[6] and transactions between corporations and shareholders generally are treated as if they were entered into by independent taxpayers. Since a corporation is a separate entity, distributions of corporate profits are taxable to the shareholders.[7] In comparison, under a pure aggregate approach, a partnership would not be recognized as an independent taxable entity. Instead, the partnership's income and deductions would be treated as directly earned or incurred by the partners. In keeping with this approach, partnership distributions generally would be nontaxable because the partners would be viewed as receiving income which was previously taxed.

The study of partnership taxation is challenging (some might even say fun) because Subchapter K does not exclusively employ either approach.

---

**5.** 41 T.C. 535, 551 n. 9 (1964). In a more recent but equally critical assessment, Professors Bittker and Lokken have acknowledged that Subchapter K was a notable achievement but only because "calamities are as worthy of note as good news." Bittker & Lokken, Federal Taxation of Income, Estates and Gifts ¶ 85.1.1 (3d ed. 2001).

**6.** I.R.C. § 11(a).

**7.** I.R.C. §§ 301(c)(1); 316. But compare the tax treatment of S corporations, which are considered in Chapter 11, infra.

Instead, partnerships are considered entities for some tax purposes and aggregates for others. On one hand, a partnership is a conduit through which income is taxed directly to the partners under an aggregate approach.[8] But partnerships are treated as entities for purposes of determining and characterizing partnership income, filing of informational returns and auditing by the Internal Revenue Service.[9] This mixture of approaches contributes to substantial complexities which are compounded by the fact that Subchapter K affords partners considerable flexibility in determining their individual tax consequences from partnership operations.[10]

As you study Subchapter K and the materials that follow in the text, pay careful attention to whether an entity or aggregate theory is being applied. As a preview of things to come and to test your understanding of the two approaches, consider the different potential tax consequences of the following transactions under an entity and aggregate approach:

(1) A partner contributes an asset in exchange for a partnership interest;

(2) A partnership asset is involuntarily converted and one of the partners wishes to take advantage of the nonrecognition provisions in Section 1033;

(3) A partner is compensated for services performed for the partnership;

(4) A partner sells his partnership interest;

(5) A partnership distributes property to a partner in an operating distribution;

(6) A partnership distributes property to a partner in a liquidating distribution;

(7) A partnership interest is sold or liquidated at a partner's death.

Reconsider your analysis as these topics are studied later in the course.

The rules in Subchapter K apply only to a business entity that is classified as a partnership for federal tax purposes. These enterprises include general and limited partnerships, limited liability partnerships, and limited liability companies. The next section of this chapter explores the threshold question of tax classification. In later chapters, it will be assumed that we are dealing with a business entity that is treated as a partnership for federal tax purposes.

## B.   Tax Classification of Business Enterprises

### 1.   In General

Code: §§ 761(a); 7701(a)(3).

---

**8.** I.R.C. §§ 701; 702.

**9.** See I.R.C. §§ 702(b); 703; 706(b); 6031; 6221–6233.

**10.** See, e.g., I.R.C. § 704.

The rules governing classification of a business enterprise for federal tax purposes have a rich and textured history as the stakes have changed over the years in response to shifting tax incentives to utilize one form of business entity over another. After decades of strife, much confusion, and reams of boilerplate classification opinion letters issued by high-priced counsel, there is good news. Beginning in 1997, the Internal Revenue Service simplified this topic considerably (and shortened your reading assignment) by adopting a classification system that permits a closely held unincorporated business to elect its taxing regime. The practical effect of these permissive rules is to enhance the ability of an unincorporated business to choose to be taxed as a partnership. Because of the importance of the classification issue, we begin with a brief overview of the historical standards and their background.

For tax purposes, Section 7701 defines a corporation to include "associations, joint-stock companies, and insurance companies." Thus, if an entity is an unincorporated "association," it will be classified as a corporation. The longstanding, pre–1997 classification regulations did not define the term "association." Instead, they listed six characteristics ordinarily found in a "pure" corporation: (1) associates (i.e., two or more persons joining together in shared control and ownership of the venture); (2) an objective to carry on business and divide the gains therefrom; (3) continuity of life (a corporation continues in existence despite the death or withdrawal of one or more shareholders); (4) centralization of management (i.e., management responsibility is vested in directors and is not exercised directly by the shareholders); (5) limited liability (shareholders are not personally liable for corporate debts); and (6) free transferability of interests (i.e., shareholders may dispose of their shares).[1] The regulations then explained that "an organization will be treated as an association if the corporate characteristics are such that the organization more nearly resembles a corporation than a partnership or trust."[2] Under those regulations, characteristics common to corporations and partnerships (associates and a business objective) were disregarded in classifying an entity as an association or a partnership. The remaining characteristics (continuity of life, centralized management, limited liability, and free transferability of interests) were then weighted equally and an organization was classified as an association only if it had three of the remaining corporate characteristics.[3]

The pre–1997 regulations were issued at a time when professional service providers (e.g., doctors and lawyers), forbidden from incorporating under state law, attempted to form entities that qualified as "associations" taxable as corporations. Their tax planning agenda was to qualify for tax advantages, such as qualified retirement plans and tax-free fringe benefits, that were then available to corporations and their employees but not to partnerships and partners.[4] The Treasury's mission was to make it more

---

**1.** Reg. § 301.7701–2(a)(1) (pre–1997).

**2.** Id.

**3.** Reg. § 1.7701–2(a) (pre–1997).

**4.** United States v. Kintner, 216 F.2d 418 (9th Cir.1954). Cf. Morrissey v. Commissioner, 296 U.S. 344, 56 S.Ct. 289 (1935). Virtually all of the advantages of corporate

difficult for unincorporated entities to qualify as corporations for federal tax purposes, but its efforts were undercut by the subsequent willingness of state legislators to permit the formation of professional corporations.[5]

One result of this early fray was that the old regulations reflected an anti-association, pro-partnership bias. This redounded to the benefit of high-income taxpayers seeking to shelter their compensation, dividends, or interest income with losses from strategically structured investment activities in real estate and other tax-favored industries. Limited partnerships became the vehicle of choice for these "tax shelters" because they permitted losses to pass through to investors, allowed the partners to maximize those losses by including their share of partnership debt in the basis of their partnership interests, and provided protection for the limited partners against personal liability for debts of the enterprise. These goals could not be achieved in a C or S corporation. The Service's effort to convince the courts that limited partnerships should be classified as "associations" was unsuccessful.[6] Even after tax shelters were derailed by the Tax Reform Act of 1986, the Service continued to issue stringent guidelines for limited partnerships seeking a favorable classification ruling.[7] Most tax advisors bypassed the ruling process, and the well informed easily were able to structure a limited partnership that would avoid "association" classification.

In the 1980's, limited liability companies (LLCs) emerged on the scene and quickly became touted as the "best of all worlds" alternative for conducting a closely held business. An LLC is an unincorporated entity in which the owners, called "members," have limited liability for the enterprise's debts and claims even if they participate in management. Members of an LLC have great flexibility in structuring the governance of their venture through the LLC's "operating agreement." The Internal Revenue Service gave a major boost to the LLC movement in 1988 by classifying a Wyoming LLC as a partnership for federal tax purposes.[8] That ruling was followed by others making it clear that an LLC could be structured as either an association or a partnership depending on the flexibility provided by state law and the desires of the members.[9] LLCs are now authorized in every state, and virtually all states permit single-member LLCs.[10]

---

classification in the retirement plan context have been eliminated.

**5.** See, e.g., West's Ann. Cal. Corp. Code §§ 13400–13410; Maryland Code, Corporations and Associations, Title 5, Subtitle 1 (1999); West's Florida Statutes Annotated, ch. 621.

**6.** See Larson v. Commissioner, 66 T.C. 159 (1976).

**7.** See, e.g., Rev. Proc. 89–12, 1989–1 C.B. 798; Rev. Proc. 91–13, 1991–1 C.B. 477.

**8.** Rev. Rul. 88–76, 1988–2 C.B. 360.

**9.** See Rev. Rul. 93–38, 1993–1 C.B. 233, where LLCs formed under the Delaware statute were classified as an association or a partnership depending on the terms of the LLC agreement.

**10.** See generally Bishop & Kleinberger, Limited Liability Companies: Tax and Business Law (2003).

## 2. CORPORATIONS AND PARTNERSHIPS

### a. "CHECK–THE–BOX" REGULATIONS

Code: § 7701(a)(3).

Regulations: §§ 301.7701–1(a)(1) & (2); –2(a), (b)(1)–(3), (c)(1) & (2); –3(a), (b)(1).

The pre–1997 classification regulations were based on the traditional state-law differences between a pure corporation and other types of organizations, such as partnerships.[1] State law developments, however, largely blurred the classic distinctions between corporations and the unincorporated forms for doing business. For example, the increasingly popular LLC offers all its investors (including those involved in management) limited liability for obligations of the venture—a characteristic traditionally available only in a corporation—along with classification as a partnership for federal tax purposes.

The Service eventually concluded that the state law differences between corporations and partnerships had narrowed to such a degree that the venerable corporate resemblance test for classifying unincorporated entities should be abandoned in favor of a simpler classification regime that is generally elective.[2] To that end, the regulations have discarded the four-factor classification system, which was de facto elective for individuals with skilled tax advisors, and replaced it with a "check-the-box" system in which most new unincorporated entities automatically will be classified as partnerships for federal tax purposes unless the entity elects to be an association taxable as a C corporation.

*General Classification Rules.* The regulations only apply to entities that are treated for federal tax purposes as being separate from their owners.[3] If an organization recognized as a separate entity for federal tax purposes is not a trust, it is a "business entity" under the regulations.[4] Certain business entities are automatically classified as corporations.[5] Most importantly, a business entity organized under a federal or state statute that refers to the entity as "incorporated" or as a "corporation," "body corporate," or "body politic," is treated as a corporation for federal tax purposes,[6] as are other business entities taxable as corporations under other Code provisions, such as publicly traded partnerships which are treated as corporations under Section 7704.[7]

Under the regulations, a noncorporate business entity (an "eligible entity") with at least two members is classified as a partnership unless an

---

**1.** Reg. § 301.7701–2(a)(1) (pre–1997).

**2.** Preamble to Final Regulations on Simplification of Entity Classification Rules, 61 Fed. Reg. 66584 (Dec. 18, 1986). The elective regime became effective as of January 1, 1997. Reg. § 301.7701–1(f).

**3.** See Section B2b of this chapter, infra.

**4.** Reg. § 301.7701–2(a).

**5.** Reg. § 301.7701–2(b)(1) through (8).

**6.** Reg. § 301.7701–2(b)(1).

**7.** Reg. § 301.7701–2(b)(7). See Section B2c of this chapter, infra, for a discussion of publicly traded partnerships.

election is made for the entity to be classified as an association. Thus, partnership status is the default classification for unincorporated entities with two or more members.[8]

*Single-Owner Organizations.* The regulations treat a noncorporate business entity that has a single owner as a "tax nothing." A single-owner entity is disregarded for tax purposes and treated as an extension of its owner unless the entity elects to be classified as an association and thus taxed as a C corporation.[9] Consequently, if no such election is made, the entity is treated for federal tax purposes as if it were a sole proprietorship (if owned by an individual), or a branch or division (if owned by another business entity, such as a C corporation)[10] This rule is particularly useful in the vast majority of states that permit single-member LLCs.

An entity that is solely owned by a husband and wife as community property may be treated by its owners as either a disregarded entity or a partnership unless the entity elects to be taxed as a C corporation.[11]

*Foreign Organizations.* The regulations list certain business entities formed in specific jurisdictions (e.g., a public limited company formed in Hong Kong) that will be automatically classified as a corporation.[12] In the absence of a contrary election, other foreign entities are classified as: (1) a partnership if the entity has two or more members and at least one member does not have limited liability, (2) an association if all members have limited liability, or (3) disregarded as an entity separate from its owner if the entity has a single owner that does not have limited liability.[13]

*Existing Entities.* Under the "check-the-box" system, an existing business entity generally retains the same classification that it claimed under the prior regulations unless it elects otherwise. An exception is provided for an entity with a single owner that claimed to be a partnership under the earlier regulations but which is disregarded as an entity separate from its owner under the current version.[14]

*Election.* A classification election under the regulations may be designated as effective up to 75 days before or twelve months after the election is filed.[15] The election generally must be signed either by (1) each member of the electing entity, including prior members affected by a retroactive election, or (2) by an officer, manager, or member authorized to make the election.[16] If an entity makes a classification election, a new classification

---

**8.** Reg. §§ 301.7701–2(c)(1); 301.7701–3(a); 301.7701–3(b)(1)(i).

**9.** Reg. §§ 301.7701–2(c)(2); 301.7701–3(a); 301.7701–3(b)(1)(ii).

**10.** Reg. § 1.301.7701–2(a). See Miller, "The Tax Nothing," 74 Tax Notes 619 (Feb. 3, 1997).

**11.** Rev. Proc. 2002–69, §§ 3.02, 4.01–4.02, 2002–2 C.B. 831. If such an entity changes its classification for tax purposes, the change is treated as a conversion of the entity. Id. at § 4.03.

**12.** Reg. § 301.7701–2(b)(8).

**13.** Reg. § 301.7701–3(b)(2)(i). Limited liability generally exists if the member has no personal liability for the debts of or claims against the entity by reason of being a member. Reg. § 301.7701–3(b)(2)(ii).

**14.** Reg. § 301.7701–3(b)(3).

**15.** Reg. § 301.7701–3(c)(1)(iii).

**16.** Reg. § 301.7701–3(c)(2).

election generally cannot be made for 60 months, unless the Service allows such an election and more than 50 percent of the ownership interests in the entity are owned by persons that did not own any interests when the first election was made.[17]

*Change in Number of Members of an Entity.* The regulations provide that the classification of an eligible entity as an association generally is not affected by any change in the numbers of members of the entity.[18] But if an eligible entity (such as a limited liability company) is classified as a partnership and its membership is reduced to one member, it becomes a disregarded entity.[19] A single-member disregarded entity also is classified as a partnership if it gains more than one member.[20]

*Elective Changes in Classification.* The regulations also prescribe the tax consequences when an entity makes a valid election to change its tax classification. If a partnership elects to be reclassified as an association, it is deemed to contribute all of its assets and liabilities to the association for stock and then to liquidate by distributing the stock to its partners.[21] If an association with more than one owner elects to be classified as a partnership, it is deemed to liquidate by distributing all of its assets and liabilities to its shareholders who then contribute the assets and liabilities to a newly formed partnership.[22] If an association with one owner elects to be classified as a disregarded entity, it is deemed to liquidate by distributing all of its assets and liabilities to the single owner.[23] Finally, if a disregarded entity elects to be classified as an association, the owner is deemed to contribute all of the assets and liabilities of the entity to the association for stock in the association.[24]

The tax treatment of a change in classification is determined under all relevant provisions of the Internal Revenue Code and general principles of tax law, including the step transaction doctrine.[25] An election to change the classification of an eligible entity is treated as occurring at the start of the day for which the election is effective.[26]

## b. EXISTENCE OF A SEPARATE ENTITY FOR FEDERAL TAX PURPOSES

Code: § 761(a).

Regulations: §§ 1.761–1(a); 301.7701–1(a)(1) & (2).

---

**17.** Reg. 301.7701–3(c)(1)(iv).

**18.** Reg. § 301.7701–3(f)(1).

**19.** Reg. § 301.7701–3(f)(2).

**20.** Id.

**21.** Reg. § 301.7701–3(g)(1)(i). See, e.g., Rev. Rul. 2004–59, 2004–1 C.B. 1050 (partnership that converts to a state law corporation under a local "formless conversion statute" is treated as having elected to be reclassified as an association).

**22.** Reg. § 301.7701–3(g)(1)(ii).

**23.** Reg. § 301.7701–3(g)(1)(iii). If an association is deemed to liquidate under Section 332 (relating to complete liquidations of

certain corporate subsidiaries), the election to change classification is considered to be the adoption of a plan of liquidation. Reg. § 301.7701–3(g)(2)(ii).

**24.** Reg. § 301.7701–3(g)(1)(iv).

**25.** Reg. § 301.7701–3(g)(2).

**26.** Reg. § 301.7701–3(g)(3)(i). Transactions deemed to occur as a result of the election are treated as occurring immediately before the close of the day before the election is effective. Id.

The check-the-box regulations only apply to an entity that is treated as separate from its owners. Whether a separate entity exists is a matter of federal tax law and does not depend on the organization's status under local law.[27] A joint venture or other contractual arrangement may create a separate entity for federal tax purposes if the participants carry on a trade, business, financial operation, or venture and divide the profits therefrom.[28] For example, because a separate entity is not created in an expense-sharing relationship or when mere co-owners maintain, repair, and rent their property, no classification issue is raised in those situations. But a separate entity does exist for federal tax purposes if co-owners of property lease space and also provide services to the tenants either directly or through an agent.[29] The two cases that follow illustrate the issues and tax stakes in deciding whether a separate tax entity exists.

## Podell v. Commissioner

United States Tax Court, 1970.
55 T.C. 429.

■ QUEALY, JUDGE.

\* \* \*

### OPINION

In this case, during each of the years 1964 and 1965, petitioner entered into an oral agreement with Young for the purchase, renovation, and sale of certain residential real estate. Profit and loss realized on the sale of such property was shared equally by petitioner and Young.

Section 1221, which defines "capital asset," provides in pertinent part: [Section 1221 is omitted. Ed.]

Petitioner maintains that the properties sold were capital assets and that any gains on those sales should be taxed as capital gains.

Respondent argues that the oral agreements between petitioner and Young established a partnership or joint venture for the purposes of purchasing, renovating, and selling real estate in the ordinary course of business, and that consequently, the gains arose from the sale of noncapital assets and are to be treated as ordinary income.

We have found as an ultimate fact that the agreement between petitioner and Young gave rise to a joint venture. Under section 761(a), a joint venture is included within the definition of a "partnership" for purposes of the internal revenue laws (henceforth in this opinion, the terms are used interchangeably). Section 761(a) provides:

27. Reg. § 301.7701–1(a)(1).          29. Id.
28. Reg. § 301.7701–1(a)(2).

(a) PARTNERSHIP.—For purposes of this subtitle, the term "partnership" *includes* a syndicate, group, pool, *joint venture* or other unincorporated organization through or by means of which any business, financial operation, or venture is carried on, and which is not, within the meaning of this title [subtitle], a corporation or a trust or estate. * * * [Emphasis supplied.]

A joint venture has been defined as a "special combination of two or more persons, where in some specific venture a profit is jointly sought without any actual partnership or corporate designation." * * *

The elements of a joint venture are: (a) A contract (express or implied) showing that it was the intent of the parties that a business venture be established; (b) an agreement for joint control and proprietorship; (c) a contribution of money, property, and/or services by the prospective joint venturers; and (d) a sharing of profits, but not necessarily of losses (although some jurisdictions require that there be a sharing of losses). * * *

In many respects, the concept of joint venture is similar to the concept of partnership, and many of the principles of partnership law are applicable to joint ventures. Blackner v. McDermott, 176 F.2d 498 (C.A.10, 1949). A primary distinction between the two concepts is that a joint venture is generally established for a single business venture (even though the business of managing the venture to a successful conclusion may continue for a number of years) while a partnership is formed to carry on a business for profit over a long period of time. Fishback v. United States, 215 F.Supp. 621 (D.S.Dak.1963).

It is undisputed that petitioner and Young joined in an agreement establishing a joint business venture to acquire, improve, and resell residential property at a profit, and it is immaterial that the petitioner was motivated, in part, by social objectives. There was a contribution to the business of property, services, or money by each of the parties involved. Petitioner and Young also agreed to share equally in any resulting gain or loss.

The fact that petitioner did not exercise as much managerial control over the day-to-day activities relating to the purchase, renovation, and sale of the real estate as Young is not sufficient reason for this Court to find against the existence of a joint venture. While petitioner gave Young discretion with respect to all aspects of the purchase, renovation, and sale of the real estate in question, petitioner retained the power to approve of the steps undertaken by Young to execute their agreement through his control over his continued contributions of funds to the venture. *Fishback v. United States*, supra; and *Flanders v. United States*, supra.

The real estate acquired by the joint venture is to be considered partnership property for purposes of taxation. [The court went on to conclude that the partnership's gains were ordinary income. See Chapter 3A. Ed.]

# Allison v. Commissioner

United States Tax Court, 1976.
35 T.C.M. 1069.

■ STERRETT, JUDGE.

\* \* \*

## OPINION

This consolidated case presents for our determination several issues involving the business relationships and practices of Acceptance, Mortgage, Allison, and Krikac. The first issue concerns the nature of the business relationship between Acceptance and Investment with respect to their Goose Lake activities and the attendant tax consequences of Acceptance's receipt of property in December, 1969.

Acceptance's position is that it entered into a joint venture with Investment to develop the property and that its receipt of the 75 lots represents a nontaxable distribution by a partnership to a partner. Respondent contends that the parties did not enter into a joint venture and that Acceptance's receipt of the 75 lots and the residual property represents ordinary income received for financial services rendered. We find the question a close one, but it is our responsibility to resolve the issue one way or the other.

A joint venture has been defined as a "special combination of two or more persons, where in some specific venture a profit is jointly sought without any actual partnership or corporate designation". The term "joint venture" is included within the definition of the term "partnership" as found in section 761(a) with the former to be considered under the same concepts as the latter.

The question of whether a joint venture has been created by the parties is essentially factual with special emphasis placed upon the intention of the parties. In sifting through the facts and circumstances of each case it is well established that they are to be applied against a framework of four basic attributes that are indicative of a joint venture. These attributes include: a contract, express or implied, that a joint venture be formed; the contribution of money, property and/or services by the venturers; an agreement for joint proprietorship and control; and an agreement to share profits.

Acceptance has recognized these principles and has argued that their application in this case leads to the conclusion that a joint venture was formed. Acceptance points to the October, 1969 agreement executed by the parties and the testimony of Allison and McCoy in support of its position. However, our interpretation of the agreement and the other related events leads us to come down on the respondent's side of the arguments.

In October, 1969 Acceptance and Investment entered into an agreement that established certain rights and obligations between them with respect to the Goose Lake property. Acceptance argues that this agreement

represents the intentions of the parties in that it memorializes the various discussions held during which the project was discussed. The agreement, which is reproduced in relevant part in the findings of fact, is entitled "Joint Venture Agreement" and does contain some indicia of a joint venture as that term is used in tax law. However, the form of the agreement is only one factor to be considered, and further we do not believe that it comports with the agreement's substance.

In the opening part the project is described as being limited to the purchase and subdivision of the property. There is no indication that the parties contemplated the subsequent joint sale of the lots or agreed to a procedure of dividing the possible profits. From the description of their endeavor and despite a "Pro Forma Profit and Loss Statement" attached to the agreement, it does not appear that the parties jointly sought a profit or that there was any agreement to pursue a business venture and to divide the profits as such therefrom. We believe that an analysis of the remaining portions of the agreement supports this conclusion.

In the next paragraph Acceptance was obligated to provide a $53,000 loan to Investment and to arrange for Investment the $80,000 secured loan from the Sierra National Bank. As noted previously, Acceptance was licensed as a property loan broker to deal in commercial finance. It appears that Acceptance's obligations with respect to this project fit within its primary business activity.

In a subsequent paragraph the agreement provides that the 75 lots were to be deeded to Acceptance "free and clear of any encumbrances * * * ". There is no indication that Investment would have any control over the ultimate disposition of these lots or that Acceptance would have any control over the property retained by Investment. This conclusion is supported by the method, which will be discussed infra, by which Acceptance attempted to dispose of these lots. Further, in the same paragraph it provides that these lots were to be deeded to Acceptance "for and in consideration of the efforts, services and liabilities specifically assumed by [Acceptance] * * * ". We find the specificity and certainty, as distinguished from a proportion of an unknown quantity, of the amount to be distributed significant. Between the parties Acceptance was entitled to the 75 lots in all events. Finally the agreement closed with the provision that it would terminate when the lots were distributed. The lack of a profit motive we find fatal to Acceptance's position.

The manner in which the agreement was implemented supports our conclusion. Acceptance fulfilled its obligations by providing and arranging for the financial requirements of the project. Pursuant to the agreements the loans were made directly to Investment. McCoy testified that his company, Investment, was directly liable for these loans. It is true that, when the venture terminated, Acceptance assumed and subsequently paid the outstanding indebtedness, but this fact indicates to us that Acceptance was merely financing Investment's project and was to receive part of the property for its trouble.

Acceptance did in fact, pursuant to the agreement, receive the 75 lots in December, 1969. Even before they were actually received, Acceptance or its subsidiaries had negotiated with Pacific States, Seckel, and the Starretts for the disposition of all but three of these lots. Even though these sales agreements did not mature, due to the inability to resell the lots at a predetermined price, we believe this clearly indicates that Acceptance had no intention of being in the real estate development business. Further, it appears these transactions were independently negotiated by Acceptance without any influence by Investment. Finally we do not agree that the president of McCoy testified that a joint venture had been formed.

Acceptance has cited several cases in support of its position, but we find that they only emphasize the distinctions upon which we are relying. In Hyman Podell, 55 T.C. 429 (1970), this Court found that a joint venture was created based upon an agreement to acquire, rehabilitate, and resell residential real estate. We have found the last element to be lacking in the case at bar. In Clarence A. Luckey, 41 T.C. 1 (1963), affd. 334 F.2d 719 (9th Cir.1964), we found the existence of a joint venture where the invested capital was to be repaid from the first profits of the business. In the case at bar we have found that Investment was primarily liable for the outstanding debts which apparently were intended to be repaid from its own profits.

We recognize that there are instances where Acceptance and Investment worked together towards the development of the property. However, when compared to the other elements in this case, they seem relatively insignificant. We find that the second agreement, executed by the parties in February, 1970, provides some insight into the nature and extent of these joint activities. From our review, the agreement appears merely to be a recitation of the rights and obligations of the parties with respect to the events that had transpired. Finally we note that neither partnership books were kept nor tax returns filed to record and report these events, an omission which can be fairly described as an admission against interest.

After a careful review of the evidence we hold that Acceptance and Investment did not enter into a joint venture to develop the Goose Lake property. We find that Acceptance received the 75 lots and its interest in the residual property on December 18, 1969 in return for financial services with respect to the property. Having made that determination we must now determine the fair market value of this property as of the above date so that Acceptance's income can be properly measured.

## NOTE

Section 761(a) permits all the members of an unincorporated organization to elect to be excluded from the application of Subchapter K if the organization is availed of: (1) for investment purposes only and not for the active conduct of a business; (2) for the joint production, extraction, or use of property but not for the purpose of selling services or property produced or extracted; or (3) by securities dealers who engage in a short-term joint

venture to underwrite, sell or distribute a particular issue of securities.[1] In all cases, the members of the organization must be able to determine their income adequately without the computation of "partnership taxable income." The regulations amplify the statutory requirements[2] and describe the time and method for making the Section 761 election.[3]

When might a Section 761 election be desirable? Co-owners of property held solely for investment purposes might make the election to assure that their arrangement is not governed by Subchapter K in the event the activity is classified as a partnership.[4] Members of joint operating arrangements also make Section 761 elections in order to make inconsistent tax elections to suit their individual tax situations.[5] For example, joint venturers engaged in drilling for oil may make a Section 761 election in order to permit inconsistent elections with respect to the tax treatment of intangible drilling and development costs.[6] Although a Section 761 election removes an unincorporated entity from the application of Subchapter K, the organization nonetheless is considered a partnership for purposes of other provisions of the Code.[7]

## PROBLEMS

**1.** Which of the following relationships are likely to constitute a separate entity for federal tax purposes?

   (a) A, B and C purchase a single parcel of land as tenants-in-common and hold the land as an investment. *not prtnsh*

   (b) Same as (a), above, except the land is subdivided and A, B and C sell the lots. *might be a prnsh*

   (c) Litigator and Negotiator are attorneys who share an office and a secretary. Each attorney services and bills his own individual clients. *not prnsh*

   (d) Doctor will locate and purchase a suitable four unit building. Architect will remodel it. When the work is done, the renovated building will be sold by the Doctor–Architect real estate company and Architect will receive 25% of the net profits. *prnsh -sharing profits*

   (e) Would the result in (d), above, be different if Doctor and Architect agreed that Doctor will retain three of the units as rental property and Architect will receive one unit to hold as rental property? *not prnsh – Allison case*

---

**1.** See generally McMahon, "The Availability and Effect of Election Out of Partnership Status Under Section 761(a)," 9 Va.Tax. Rev. 1 (1989).

**2.** Reg. § 1.761–2(a)(2) & (3).

**3.** Reg. § 1.761–2(b).

**4.** Willis, Pennell & Postlewaite, Partnership Taxation ¶ 1.02[8] (6th ed. 1997).

**5.** Cf. I.R.C. § 703(b).

**6.** Cf. Rev.Rul. 83–129, 1983–2 C.B. 105. See generally Burke and Meyer, "Federal Income Tax Classification of Natural Resource Ventures: Co–Ownership, Partnership or Association?," 37 S.W.L.J. 859, 865–72 (1984).

**7.** Cokes v. Commissioner, 91 T.C. 222 (1988).

(f) Fisher will purchase and operate a fishing boat. Lender will provide 10–year nonrecourse financing to Fisher. The arrangement will be evidenced by a note, secured by the boat, which will require repayment of the principal sum ratably over the 10–year period. In addition, Lender will receive 15% of Fisher's net profits from the fishing operation each year of the arrangement.

**2.** The provisions of Section 7701 that define corporations and partnerships do not explicitly describe an elective tax classification regime. The definition of a partnership in Section 7701(a)(2) provides that it "includes a syndicate, group, pool, joint venture, or other unincorporated organization, through or by means of which any business, financial operation, or venture is carried on, and which is not, within the meaning of [the Code], a trust or estate or a corporation." The statutory definition of a corporation (section 7701(a)(3)) provides that it "includes associations, joint-stock companies, and insurance companies." Moreover, in Morrissey v. Commissioner, 296 U.S. 344, 56 S.Ct. 289 (1935), the Supreme Court endorsed the corporate resemblance approach reflected in the prior classification regulations. Against this background, did the Treasury have the authority to issue the check-the-box regulations? See Section 7805. Is it likely that anyone would challenge the Treasury's authority? Should Congress codify the regulations by specific legislation?

### c.  PUBLICLY TRADED PARTNERSHIPS

Code: § 7704.

For a brief time after enactment of the Tax Reform Act of 1986, the publicly traded partnership ("PTP") surfaced as a refuge from the costly double tax regime of Subchapter C. Unlike an S corporation, a PTP could have an unlimited number of shareholders. It could register its limited partnership interests, known as "units," with the Securities and Exchange Commission, and the units were freely tradable on a securities exchange or in the over-the-counter market. A profitable PTP thus avoided the corporate income tax and passed through its income to noncorporate limited partners at the lower individual rates.

Alarmed at the proliferation of PTPs and the potential erosion of the corporate tax base, Congress responded by enacting Section 7704, which classifies certain PTPs as corporations for tax purposes. As defined, a "publicly traded partnership" is any partnership whose interests are: (1) traded on an established securities market, or (2) readily tradable on a secondary market (or its substantial equivalent).[1] An important exception from reclassification is provided for partnerships if 90 percent or more of their gross income consists of certain passive-type income items (e.g., interest, dividends, real property rents, gains from the sale of real property and income and gains from certain natural resources activities).[2]

---

**1.**  I.R.C. § 7704(b).

**2.**  I.R.C. § 7704(c).

The regulations generally provide that an interest is "readily tradable" if "taking into account all of the facts and circumstances, the partners are readily able to buy, sell, or exchange their partnership interests in a manner that is comparable, economically, to trading on an established securities market."[3]

## 3.  TRUSTS

Regulations: § 301.7701–4(a), (b).

Trusts, like corporations, may be taxpaying entities, but the income taxation of trusts differs from the taxation of corporations in several important respects. First, a corporation is taxed on its profits as they are earned under the relatively flat rates in Section 11. If it later distributes the remaining after-tax earnings as dividends, the shareholders are subject to a second tax. But there is no double tax on trust income. Under the complex rules of Subchapter J, trust income currently distributed to beneficiaries is generally not taxed to the trust. Rather, the income is taxed to the recipient beneficiaries to the extent of the trust's "distributable net income." If, however, trust income is accumulated, it is taxed to the trust when earned under the rates in Section 1(e) but normally not taxed again when distributed to the beneficiaries. Also, corporate shareholders who receive dividends are taxable at ordinary income rates, regardless of the character of the corporation's earnings. By contrast, trust income retains its tax character in the hands of the beneficiaries.

The regulations distinguish between "ordinary trusts" created to take title to property for the purpose of protecting and conserving it for the beneficiaries, and "business" or "commercial" trusts which are created to carry on a business for profit. An ordinary trust is classified as a "trust" and taxed under Subchapter J.[1] A business trust, on the other hand, is a business entity that is classified under the check-the-box regulations.[2] Because a business trust is an unincorporated entity, it will be classified as a partnership for federal tax purposes if it has two or more members and does not make an election to be classified as a corporation.[3]

## 4.  TAX POLICY CONSIDERATIONS

State law developments, particularly the increasing popularity of limited liability companies, along with the liberalized tax classification regime described above, have breathed new life into an ongoing policy debate over the appropriate business enterprise taxing model. These trends have prompted academics, other commentators and legislative staff to take a fresh look at the entity classification rules and other partnership tax issues

**3.** Reg. § 1.7704–1(c)(1).

**1.** Reg. § 301.7701–4(a).

**2.** Reg. § 301.7701–4(b).

**3.** Reg. § 301.7701–2(c)(1); –3(a), (b)(1)(i).

with the goal of identifying and correcting provisions that give rise to anomalous results, create problems in application, or are anachronistic.[1]

The excerpt below, from a study prepared by staff of the Joint Committee on Taxation, summarizes this policy debate by addressing the impact of the check-the-box regulations and the appropriate model of taxation for domestic business enterprises. Some of these questions will be revisited in connection with the study of S corporations.[2]

## Excerpt from Review of Selected Entity Classification and Partnership Tax Issues

Staff of Joint Committee on Taxation (JCS–6–97), April 8, 1997.

### 2. Impact of the Check-the-Box Regulations

*In general*

The advent of an affirmatively elective regime for determining whether an entity is a corporation or a partnership raises a number of issues. The principal impact is that taxpayers may now choose with greater simplicity and lower compliance costs whether they will pay two levels of tax on business income under the corporate tax rules, or whether they will pay only one level of tax under the partnership tax rules (or as a disregarded single-member entity). While it is argued that the entity classification regulations in effect prior to the check-the-box regulations were manipulable and were effectively elective for well-advised taxpayers, an affirmatively elective regime may make this choice much more broadly available for all businesses. At the same time, increased use of LLCs, a form of business entity that can provide limited liability to all owners yet be treated as a partnership for tax purposes, also makes the attractiveness of electing partnership status broader.

In addition, several other types of issues arise as a result of providing an affirmatively elective entity classification regime. One set of issues relates to whether the policy of many existing tax rules that depend on an entity's status is violated by making that status elective. A second group of issues stems from the increased importance of the present-law rules treating publicly traded partnerships as corporations, and the exception from such treatment that is provided to partnerships with a broad category of passive-type income. Thirdly, and more broadly, the check-the-box regula-

**1.** See Brannan, "The Subchapter K Reform Act of 1997," 75 Tax Notes 121 (April 7, 1997); Staff of Joint Committee on Taxation, Review of Selected Entity Classification and Partnership Tax Issues (JCS–6–97), April 8, 1997 (hereinafter "Joint Committee Review"); American Law Institute, Taxation of Private Enterprises—Reporter's Study (July, 1999); Burke, "Reassessing the Administration's Proposals for Reform of Subchapter K," 86 Tax Notes 1423 (March 6, 2000). For an analysis of the American Law Institute Reporter's Study and other commentary on the future of Subchapter K, see Lokken, "Taxation of Private Business Firms: Imagining a Future Without Subchapter K," 4 Fla. Tax Rev. 249 (1999); Postlewaite, "I Come to Bury Subchapter K, Not to Praise It," 54 Tax Lawyer 451 (2001).

**2.** See Chapter 11H1, infra.

tions call into question whether the tax law should continue to provide parallel, but differing, pass-through treatment for business entities that are partnerships and other entities, such as S corporations. Eliminating needlessly redundant rules could simplify the tax law. These issues are not the only ones raised by the check-the-box regulations, but represent some of the questions it may be appropriate for Congress to consider in the long term, in light of the current state of the entity classification rules.

*Impact on existing tax rules*

The check-the-box regulations make many other tax results, which depend on the tax status of an entity, also effectively elective for more taxpayers. In some cases under the prior regulations, well-advised taxpayers may have been able to achieve particular tax results, virtually by choice, that less sophisticated taxpayers may not have attained. In some cases, transaction costs for attaining a particular tax result may have been sufficiently high that attaining such a result was cost-effective only for especially large-scale transactions. The check-the-box regulations generally eliminate the need to meet the four-factor test of the Kintner regulations in order to achieve partnership status. Assuring that an entity lacks limited liability (one of the four factors) in order to have pass-through tax treatment, for example, no longer need hamper business arrangements where insulation of the owners from the entity's liabilities is central to the arrangement.

The check-the-box regulations facilitate transactions that could not usually be done (or could be done only in a convoluted or expensive manner) under prior law, but now may be accomplished more simply, efficiently or cheaply. The question is not whether efficiency is generally preferable to convolution. Rather, the question is whether the purpose of other tax rules that depend on the taxpayer's status as a partnership or corporation is violated by applying those rules only at the taxpayer's choice. The check-the-box regulations could have the long-term effect of drawing attention to rules that may have become elective (whether under the new regulations or under prior law), and of sparking a re-thinking of the rationale for such rules in some cases.

As described above in Part I of this pamphlet, the check-the-box regulations provide that single member entities may be disregarded, effectively providing for a classification of entity that has been called a "nothing." Disregarding an entity may serve as an alternative to partnership form as a means to achieve pass-through tax treatment. Treating an entity as a "nothing" may give a different tax result than would treating the entity as either a corporation or a partnership. At the same time, if the disregarded entity is an LLC, it may provide protection for the owner from the entity's liabilities. Similarly, a disregarded foreign entity may be treated for tax purposes like a branch rather than a separate corporation or partnership.

The check-the-box regulations may in some cases be more limiting than the prior entity classification regulations were. The list of foreign

entities that are now treated as *per se* corporations for Federal tax purposes may include some entities for which partnership tax status could have been achieved under the four-factor test of the prior regulations. For those foreign entities that are not included on the list of per se corporations, the check-the-box regulations may provide more flexibility or certainty than the prior regulations. [Discussion of the international implications of the regulations has been omitted. Ed.]

## C.   Introduction to Choice of Business Entity

The choice of entity for a business enterprise depends on a wide variety of tax and nontax considerations. In some instances, necessities of the particular business may drive the decision. For example, if public trading of ownership interests is desired, a C corporation almost always is the entity of choice.[1] Access to venture capital investors, a preference for executive compensation techniques such as stock options, or an exit strategy that anticipates a public offering or merger with a public company all may dictate use of the corporate form.

In many cases, however, the nontax objectives of the parties can be adequately satisfied in a variety of legal forms. For example, where limited liability is a critical concern, it can be achieved in a corporation, limited liability company, or limited partnership with a corporate general partner. In the many situations where state law provides flexibility to achieve these and other nontax goals, tax considerations often will be controlling or at least a paramount factor in deciding what legal form to select. In evaluating the choices, three critical questions are: (1) who will own the business and what type of economic relationship among them is contemplated, (2) how and when do the owners intend to realize a return on their investment, and (3) is the business initially expected to generate losses and for how long?[2] In making the choice, the threshold tax question often will be whether to use a C corporation or a pass-through entity and, if the latter, whether it should be a partnership, LLC or S corporation.

The choice of entity stakes and strategies have changed dramatically in recent years as the federal tax system has experienced a sustained period of instability. The discussion that follows provides an overview of the most significant tax considerations in making the decision, looking back briefly at tax history to place the current state of affairs into proper perspective. Throughout the discussion, remember that individuals, trusts and C corporations are separate taxable entities, while S corporations, partnerships and limited liability companies are generally not subject to an entity-level tax

---

**1.**  Except in a few specialized industries, such as natural resources, virtually all publicly traded partnerships are classified as corporations for tax purposes. As a result, there is rarely any tax incentive to use that legal form instead of a corporation. See I.R.C. § 7704 and Section B2c of this chapter, supra.

**2.**  See generally Bagley & Dauchy, The Entrepreneur's Guide to Business Law 62–67 (2d ed. 2003).

but pass through their income, losses, credits and other tax items to the owners of the business.

*Rates on Ordinary Income.* For C corporations with significant taxable income, the corporate income tax is essentially a 34 or 35 percent flat rate tax with no preferential rate for long-term capital gains.[3] Corporations with smaller amounts of income, however, can take advantage of lower rates (15 and 25 percent) on their first $75,000 of taxable income.[4] Individuals pay tax at graduated rates beginning at 10 percent of taxable income and peaking at a nominal rate of 35 percent.[5] And profits of C corporations are potentially taxed both at the corporate and shareholder levels when they are distributed as dividends or when the shareholders sell their stock.

At first glance, the highest individual and corporate rates appear to be the same, but a true comparison is a bit more complex. The effective marginal rate for some individuals may be higher than 35 percent on some income because of the disallowance of itemized deductions and the phase-out of personal exemptions for high-income taxpayers.[6] Beginning in 2003 and continuing until 2009, dividends received by noncorporate shareholders are taxed at the same preferential 15 percent maximum rate as long-term capital gains.[7] Other variables that may affect the overall tax burden include the corporate and individual alternative minimum taxes; a long list of corporate tax benefits, ranging from accelerated depreciation to targeted subsidies for particular industries, that lower the effective corporate tax rate; and employment taxes imposed on owners who also perform services for the business.

At one time, when the maximum individual tax rate on ordinary income peaked at 70 percent or higher and the top corporate rate was 46 percent, C corporations served as a refuge from the steeper individual rates. This rate differential prompted privately held firms to conduct their business and investment activities as C corporations rather than pass-through entities because their income was taxed at lower rates and could remain in corporate solution to compound at the these tax-preferred rates until the business was sold or liquidated. In the meantime, shareholders who wished to withdraw earnings utilized tax efficient strategies to avoid the sting of the double tax. For example, owner-employees of a C corporation typically have distributed profits in the form of salary and fringe benefits that are tax-deductible by the corporation and, in the case of many fringe benefits, excludable by the owner-employee. Shareholders also can loan funds or lease property to a C corporation and withdraw earnings in the form of tax-deductible interest or rent.

**3.** I.R.C. §§ 11; 1201(a).

**4.** I.R.C. 11(b). Certain corporations with major shareholders who render personal services, such as professional corporations of lawyers, accountants, architects, and the like, are not entitled to the lower marginal corporate rates. I.R.C. §§ 11(b)(2); 448(d)(2).

**5.** I.R.C. § 1.

**6.** See I.R.C. §§ 68; 151(d)(3). The phase-outs are themselves being phased out, however, and are scheduled for repeal by 2010, but just for one year unless Congress makes the repeal permanent.

**7.** I.R.C. § 1(h)(11).

To be sure, the Service had weapons to combat these self-help strategies. Payments of salary or interest could be attacked as unreasonable compensation or disguised dividends but usually these arguments were reserved for the most egregious cases. Congress also enacted penalty taxes to patrol against excessive accumulations or avoidance of the individual progressive rates.[8] With foresight and good planning, however, an active business that paid reasonable compensation and justified any accumulations of earnings on the basis of reasonable business judgment could avoid constructive dividends and the corporate penalty taxes with relative ease.

For many C corporations, these tax saving strategies have withstood the test of time. A study by the Joint Committee on Taxation revealed that in 1993, 61 percent of all C corporations reported no taxable income and another 37 percent reported taxable income of less than $355,000.[9] More recent data indicates that in 2001, 49 percent of all C corporations reported no taxable income, and only 35 percent of C corporations had any corporate tax liability after tax credits were taken into account.[10]

But some of the key variables have changed along with the tax rates. Today, with individuals and C corporations subject to the same top rate and with dividends and long-term capital gains taxed at a maximum rate of 15 percent, the C corporation earnings accumulation strategy is much less compelling than when corporations enjoyed a significant tax rate advantage over individuals. This rate parity, together with the prospect of two levels of tax when a C corporation is sold, provides a greater incentive to use a pass-through entity instead of a C corporation, particularly if the business intends to distribute its earnings currently, does not have owners who work for the firm, or holds assets that are likely to appreciate in value over a relatively short time horizon. It would be rare, for example, for a venture investing in real estate or financial assets for current income or capital appreciation (or both) to operate as a C corporation because the costs of doing so would be prohibitive in light of the double tax. In some cases, however, C corporations still offer tax savings, especially for businesses that are able to pay out most of their earnings as compensation to their high-income owners.

*Preferential Capital Gains Rates.* The decision to tax long-term capital gains at substantially lower rates than ordinary income is another feature of the tax system that historically eased the tax burden of conducting a business as a C corporation. Rather than paying dividends, tax advisors devised techniques to "bail out" earnings at capital gains rates. A "bailout" is a distribution of earnings in a transaction, such as a redemption of stock, that qualifies as a "sale or exchange," enabling the shareholder to recover all or part of her stock basis and to benefit from preferential capital gain

---

**8.**  See I.R.C. § 531 et seq. (accumulated earnings tax); § 541 (personal holding company tax).

**9.**  Joint Committee on Taxation, Impact of Small Business of Replacing the Federal Income Tax 5 (J.C.S., 3–96, April 23, 1996).

**10.**  Statistics of Income—2001, Corporation Income Tax Returns, Table 22 (2004).

treatment on any realized gain.[11] In some cases, such as where the shareholder has died and the basis of her stock has been stepped up to its date-of-death value, the bailout may be accomplished tax-free.[12] Over the years, Congress responded with complex anti-bailout provisions to ensure that distributions resembling dividends would be taxed as ordinary income.[13]

Now that dividends and capital gains are taxed at the same preferential rates, the traditional incentive for a bailout has just about disappeared. Under the new rate regime, the tax goal of a bailout will not be to convert dividend income to capital gain but rather to enable shareholders to recover all or part of the basis in their stock. It is unlikely that this will tip the scales in favor of using a C corporation, but this new type of bailout continues to raise challenging tax issues for the many closely held businesses that currently operate as C corporations.

*Pass-Through of Losses.* Investors often anticipate losses in the early years of a new venture and desire to deduct those losses against income from other sources as quickly as possible. A pass-through tax regime permits the losses to pass through to the owners who devote their time and energy to the business, but the ability of investors to deduct those losses is often delayed by an array of Code provisions designed to curtail tax shelters.[14]

A C corporation is not able to pass through start-up losses to its shareholders, but corporations may deduct losses against their taxable income and carry any excess back or forward as net operating losses.[15] For start-up companies that raise capital from outside investors, these tax rules are among several factors that may weigh in favor of a C corporation. Although the start-up losses do not pass through as they are realized, most taxable investors would be unable to deduct them currently in any event, and nontaxable investors, such as pension funds and charities, are indifferent. The losses may be used more efficiently as carryforwards to shelter income earned during the early years of a C corporation's profitability.[16]

*Subchapter K vs. Subchapter S.* If a pass-through tax regime is desired, the owners of the business must decide whether to employ a partnership (or LLC taxed as a partnership) or an S corporation. The ownership and capital structure restrictions imposed on S corporations may require use of a partnership or LLC. S corporations are limited to 100 shareholders (although members of a "family," broadly defined, are counted as one

---

**11.** Subchapter C includes many provisions to patrol against bailout transactions that are essentially equivalent to dividend distributions. See, e.g., I.R.C. §§ 302; 304; 306.

**12.** The date-of-death basis rule in Section 1014 is scheduled to be replaced by a carryover basis regime (with some exceptions) in 2010 (but for one year only) when the estate tax is repealed. See I.R.C. § 1022.

**13.** See, e.g., I.R.C. §§ 302; 304; 306.

**14.** See, e.g., I.R.C. §§ 465; 469; 704(d); 1366(d).

**15.** See I.R.C. § 172.

**16.** In some cases, however, the use of loss carryovers by a C corporation may be limited after a significant change of ownership. See I.R.C. § 382.

shareholder), and they may not have more than one class of stock.[17] Subchapter K is much more flexible. To accommodate different types of owners, partnerships and LLCs may make special allocations of partnership income and deduction items, while shareholders of an S corporation must include corporate income and loss on a pro rata share basis.[18] Thus, partners may agree to share certain income or deductions disproportionately, and the agreement will be respected for tax purposes if it reflects their economic business deal. In most cases, partnerships and LLCs (but not S corporations) also can distribute appreciated property in kind without immediate recognition of taxable gain.

Unlike S corporation shareholders, partners may increase the basis of their partnership interests by their allocable share of entity-level debts.[19] That additional "basis credit" may be important for maximizing the ability to deduct losses realized by the enterprise—e.g., in ventures that own leveraged real estate—or avoiding gain on distributions.[20] For these and other reasons, the conventional wisdom is that Subchapter K is more taxpayer-friendly than Subchapter S. In fact, much of the popularity of the LLC is attributable to the fact that LLCs offer limited liability to all investors combined with the more flexible partnership tax regime.

In some situations, however, the goals of business owners may be better achieved with an S corporation. For example, an S corporation may be the entity of choice for a business with only a few owners because the flexibility of Subchapter K is not necessary. Moreover, many entrepreneurs prefer to conduct their business as a state law corporation instead of a partnership or limited liability company because they (or their advisors) are more comfortable with the corporate governance structure. Subchapter S provides these owners with a relatively simple pass-through tax regime. As discussed below, S corporations also are often used by service providers to minimize their exposure to employment taxes.

On the other hand, S corporations are not a viable choice in many situations—for example, a business with foreign investors, who are not permissible S corporation shareholders. Many institutional investors (e.g., tax-exempt pension funds and charitable organizations) are discouraged by the tax system from investing in any type of active business that is operated as a pass-through entity.[21] Venture capital funds, which provide a large source of capital for start-up companies, appear to be more comfortable using the familiar C corporation capitalized with several classes of

---

**17.** I.R.C. § 1361(b).

**18.** Compare I.R.C. § 704(b)(2) with I.R.C. § 1366(a).

**19.** See I.R.C. §§ 722; 752(a).

**20.** See I.R.C. §§ 704(d); 731(a)(1); 1366(d)(1); 1368(b).

**21.** Stripped of detail, pension funds and other tax-exempt organizations are potentially subject to the "unrelated business income tax" on income passing through from an operating business conducted as a partnership or S corporation, but they are generally not taxable on income from "portfolio" investments, such as dividends and interest received from an equity or debt interest in a C corporation. See generally I.R.C. § 511 et seq.

stock, a structure not available in an S corporation.[22] These are just a few illustrations of the types of additional factors influencing the choice of entity decision.

*Employment Tax Considerations.* Where a principal owner also is a service provider for the business, employment taxes can be an influential factor. In addition to income taxes, social security and medicare taxes must be paid on income from self-employment and wages of employees.[23] Net earnings from self-employment include a sole proprietor or partner's gross income derived from any trade or business.[24] Assume, for example, that a trial lawyer has $500,000 of net earnings from self-employment. Her self-employment tax (using the 2005 wage base and rates) will be $25,660, consisting of 12.4 percent on the first $90,000 of self-employment income ($11,160) and 2.9 percent on the entire $500,000 ($14,500). Assume the trial lawyer incorporates her practice using an S corporation which nets the same $500,000, pays the lawyer a salary of $150,000, and either retains the $350,000 balance or distributes it as a dividend. Many tax advisors take the position that as long as the compensation paid by the S corporation is within a reasonable range, the 2.9 percent medicare tax can be avoided on any remaining S corporation income.[25] If this is correct, trial lawyer would save $10,150 (the 2.9 percent medicare tax on the $350,000). Whether or not this S corporation strategy should succeed is debatable, although anecdotal evidence suggests that it is widely used and often goes unchallenged. But the strategy clearly would fail if trial lawyer conducted her practice as a single member limited liability company (assuming state law allowed that form for lawyers) which, as a disregarded entity, would be treated as a sole proprietorship for tax purposes.

Employment taxes also may influence the choice between a limited partnership and an LLC. Unlike general partners, limited partners generally are not subject to self-employment tax on their distributive share of partnership income (apart from salary-like guaranteed payments), while the employment tax treatment of LLC members (who are classified as neither general nor limited partners under state law) is uncertain.[26] The unsettled state of the law has created an opportunity for abuse by LLC members who are active in the business. In 1997, the Service issued

---

**22.** See Bankman, "The Structure of Silicon Valley Start-ups," 42 UCLA L. Rev. 1737 (1994), which observes that venture capitalists are foregoing valuable tax benefits (e.g., current deductibility of start-up losses) by using C corporations rather than a business form eligible for pass-through tax treatment. See also Fleischer, "The Rational Exuberance of Structuring Venture Capital Start-ups," 57 Tax L. Rev. 137 (2003).

**23.** I.R.C. § 1401.

**24.** I.R.C. § 1402(a). Self-employment taxes include a 12.4 percent "social security" tax on self-employment income up to $90,000

(in 2005; the cap is indexed annually) and a 2.9 percent medicare tax on the entire amount of self-employment income. Self-employed taxpayers may take an above-the-line deduction for one-half of self-employment tax paid. I.R.C. § 164(f).

**25.** In egregious cases, such as where little or no compensation is paid and the S corporation distributes a large dividend to its sole owner, the Service likely will reclassify all or part of the dividend as wages for employment tax purposes. See Chapter 11H, infra.

**26.** I.R.C. § 1402(a)(13).

proposed regulations to clarify these issues,[27] but Congress imposed a moratorium[28] after a storm of protest and no final regulations had been issued as of early 2005.

*State Tax Issues.* State tax considerations may also play a role in the choice of entity decision. For example, in some states LLCs may be subject to taxes or charges that are not imposed on partnerships, or S corporations may be taxed adversely compared to partnerships.[29]

*Existing Entities: Change of Form.* If an existing entity wants to change its legal form or tax status, it may confront significant tax impediments. For example, converting a C corporation to a partnership or LLC will require the corporation to liquidate, which may trigger significant corporate and shareholder tax liability.[30] Alternatively, a C corporation may make an election to become an S corporation with no immediate tax consequences, but asset appreciation and other income accruing prior to the conversion still may be subject to a corporate-level tax when those gains are ultimately realized.[31] Incorporating a partnership or LLC, and converting a partnership into an LLC or an LLP, generally may be accomplished without adverse tax consequences.

*Choice of Entity Trends.* The choice of entity landscape continues to evolve, and some interesting trends are emerging. Despite the advent of limited liability companies, corporate formations outnumbered LLC formations in most jurisdictions during the 1990's by a healthy 2:1 margin.[32] Contrary to what had become the conventional wisdom, S corporations have shown surprising vitality. In 1997, for the first time, a majority of corporate tax returns were filed by S corporations,[33] and it was estimated that S corporations will be the fastest growing type of business entity from 1999 through 2005.[34] These predictions have proven true. Between 1997 and 2001, there was a 29.5 percent increase in S corporations and, by 2001, 58.2 percent of all corporations were S corporations.

Legislation increasing the number and type of permissible S corporation shareholders does not appear to have had much influence on this growth pattern. The available data confirms that S corporations are most

---

**27.**  Prop. Reg. § 1.1402(a)–2(h).

**28.**  Pub. L. No. 105–34, § 935, 111 Stat. 788 (1997).

**29.**  See generally Ely, Grissom & Houser, "State Tax Treatment of Limited Liability Companies and Limited Liability Partnerships," 106 Tax Notes 1557 (March 28, 2005).

**30.**  See I.R.C. §§ 331; 336.

**31.**  See I.R.C. § 1374, discussed in Chapter 11F, infra.

**32.**  See Lee, "Choice of Small Business Tax Entity: Facts and Fiction," 87 Tax Notes 417 (2000)(herein cited as "Lee I"), for data and analysis concerning the trends in formations of small business entities. See also Lee,

"A Populist Political Perspective of the Business Tax Entities Universe: Hey the Stars Might Lie But the Numbers Never Do," 78 Texas L. Rev. 885 (2000) (herein cited as Lee II).

**33.**  Treubert & Janquet, "Corporation Income Tax Returns, 1998," 21 SOI Bulletin 66, 67 (2001).

**34.**  Lee I, supra note 32, citing Zaffino, "Projections of Returns to be Filed in Calendar Years 1995–2005," 18 SOI Bulletin 178 (1999). For a view questioning this projection, see Alexander, "The Questionable Continued Flourishing of S Corporations," 87 Tax Notes 577 (April 24, 2000).

widely used by firms with very concentrated ownership. More than half of all S corporations filing returns in 2001 had only one shareholder, 98.8 percent of all S corporations had 10 or fewer shareholders, and only 2,300 S corporations (out of the approximately 3 million S corporations filing returns) had more than 30 shareholders.[35]

The number of businesses filing partnership tax returns has grown modestly, increasing at an average rate of 4.8 percent between 1994 and 2002, but the mix of entities within the partnership tax universe has changed dramatically.[36] The number of LLCs increased 400 percent between 1996 and 2002, from 221,498 to 946,130. LLCs now outnumber limited partnerships by more than 2:1, and in 2002, for the first time, the number of LLCs surpassed general and limited partnerships combined.[37] This data suggests that the explosive growth of LLCs is coming more at the expense of entities that would have been general or limited partnerships rather than from C or S corporations, which remain alive and well for closely held businesses.[38]

It is apparent from this introductory discussion that a good grounding in the fundamentals of business enterprise and individual taxation is essential to make a competent choice of entity decision. That study has just begun. When it ends, the many issues and options confronting the founders of a new business, which may seem quite intimidating at this point, should come into sharper focus.

**35.** Bennett, S Corporation Returns, 2001, 23 SOI Bulletin 53–54 (2004).

**36.** Wheeler & Persons, Partnership Returns, 2002, 23 SOI Bulletin 46 (2004).

**37.** Id. at 51–53.

**38.** See Lee I, supra note 32.

\*

# TAXATION OF PARTNERSHIPS AND PARTNERS

# CHAPTER 2

# FORMATION OF A PARTNERSHIP

## A. CONTRIBUTIONS OF PROPERTY

## 1. GENERAL RULES

Code: §§ 721; 722; 723. Skim §§ 453B(a), (b); 704(c)(1)(A); 724; 1223(1) & (2); 1245(b)(3).

Regulations: §§ 1.453–9(c)(2); 1.721–1; 1.722–1; 1.723–1; 1.1223–3(a), (b)(1).

Although the study of Subchapter K may become a "distressingly complex and confusing" enterprise,[1] it begins with a reassuring review of the fundamental tax concept of nonrecognition. Under general principles of Section 1001(a), a partner who contributes property to a newly formed partnership in exchange for a partnership interest would appear to *realize* gain or loss in an amount equal to the difference between the fair market value of the partnership interest and the adjusted basis of the transferred property.[2] But Section 721(a) comes to the rescue in a manner closely paralleling Section 351, its corporate tax counterpart, by providing that no gain or loss shall be *recognized* to a partnership or to any of its partners on a "contribution of property to the partnership in exchange for an interest in the partnership."[3] The rationale for nonrecognition is familiar. The transfer of property to a partnership is considered to be a mere change in the form of the partner's investment and is viewed as a business transaction that should not be impeded by the imposition of a tax. The general rule of Section 721, equally applicable whether the contribution is to a newly formed or preexisting partnership, is accompanied by the usual corollary provisions governing basis and holding period.[4]

---

**1.** See Judge Arnold Raum's gloomy appraisal of Subchapter K in Foxman v. Commissioner, 41 T.C. 535, 551 note 9 (1964), affirmed, 352 F.2d 466 (3d Cir.1965).

**2.** But see Helvering v. Walbridge, 70 F.2d 683 (2d Cir.1934), cert. denied, 293 U.S. 594, 55 S.Ct. 109 (1934), which held even prior to the enactment of Section 721, that a transfer of property to a partnership was not a taxable event.

**3.** This general nonrecognition rule is subject to a narrow exception in Section 721(b), which provides for recognition of gain when a partner transfers property to a

"partnership which would be treated as an investment company (within the meaning of Section 351) if the partnership were incorporated." See Section 351(e)(1) and Reg. § 1.351–1(c) for the definition of "investment company." This exception is designed to preclude the tax-free diversification of a portfolio by a group of taxpayers through the transfer of appreciated securities and certain other investment assets to a partnership.

**4.** Compare I.R.C. §§ 721, 722 and 723 with I.R.C. §§ 351, 1032(a), 358 & 362(a), and see I.R.C. § 1223(1) & (2).

The principal requirement for nonrecognition under Section 721 is that "property" must be contributed in exchange for an interest in the partnership. Since there is no statutory definition of property, the courts have been guided by analogous interpretations under Section 351, which provides for nonrecognition treatment on the transfer of property to a controlled corporation in exchange for stock. For purposes of both sections, the term is broadly defined to embrace money, goodwill, and even intangible service-flavored assets such as accounts receivable, patents, unpatented technical know-how and favorable loan or lease commitments embodied in a letter of intent secured through the efforts of the contributing partner.[5] But "property" does not include services rendered to the partnership,[6] and a partner who receives a partnership interest in exchange for services generally realizes ordinary income under Section 61.[7] While Section 721 and Section 351 are similar in many respects, the analogy is not perfect. Unlike Section 351, Section 721 does not require the transferors of property to be in "control" of the partnership immediately after the exchange.

If Section 721 applies to a transfer, any gain or loss realized by the partner is not currently recognized, but several related sections preserve to the contributing partner the amount and sometimes the character of any gain or loss inherent in the contributed property. The amount of gain initially is preserved by Section 723, which provides that the partner's basis in the contributed property is transferred to the partnership.[8] Section 1223(2) similarly provides that the partner's holding period in the property carries over to the partnership. The precontribution character of the contributed property sometimes is preserved by Section 724, which provides that, in certain situations, the partnership will recognize the same character of gain or loss that the contributing partner would have recognized on a sale of the property. Finally, Section 704(c)(1) generally prevents the precontribution gain or loss from being shifted to the other partners by requiring the partnership to allocate that gain or loss solely to the contributing partner when it subsequently disposes of the property or distributes it to another partner.[9]

---

**5.** For examples of this breadth, see Hempt Brothers, Inc. v. United States, 490 F.2d 1172 (3d Cir.1974), cert. denied, 419 U.S. 826, 95 S.Ct. 44 (1974) (a Section 351 case involving accounts receivable); United States v. Stafford, 727 F.2d 1043 (11th Cir. 1984) (a legally unenforceable "letter of intent" arranged by a developer to finance the construction of a hotel); and United States v. Frazell, 335 F.2d 487 (5th Cir.1964), rehearing denied, 339 F.2d 885 (5th Cir.1964), cert. denied, 380 U.S. 961, 85 S.Ct. 1104 (1965) (geophysical maps created by the personal efforts of the taxpayer).

**6.** See Reg. § 1.721–1(b)(1) and compare I.R.C. § 351(d)(1).

**7.** The timing of the income is governed by Section 83. These issues are discussed in Section C of this chapter.

**8.** See I.R.C. § 7701(a)(43)–(44) for the appropriate basis terminology ("transferred basis" and "exchanged basis"). The transferred basis is increased by any gain recognized by the partner on the transfer under Section 721(b).

**9.** Sections 724 and 704(c), both of which govern the tax consequences on a subsequent sale or distribution of the property, are discussed in Chapter 4C, infra.

To complete the statutory scheme, Section 722 provides that a partner's basis in his partnership interest is equal to the sum of the cash and adjusted basis of any property contributed to the partnership.[10] This ensures that the contributing partner may not avoid recognizing the gain that went unrecognized on the contribution by selling his interest before the partnership disposes of the contributed property. The partner's holding period in the partnership interest is determined by Section 1223(1), which permits the partner to tack his holding period for the contributed property if that property was a capital or Section 1231 asset. To the extent the contributed property consists of cash or ordinary income assets, the holding period begins on the date of the exchange. If a partner contributes a mix of assets (e.g., cash plus capital, Section 1231, and ordinary income assets), the holding period in the partnership interest is fragmented in proportion to the fair market value of the portion of the interest received for the property to which the holding period relates, divided by the fair market value of the entire interest.[11] For this purpose, recapture gain (e.g., under Section 1245) is treated as a separate asset which is not a capital or Section 1231 asset.[12]

A partner's basis in his partnership interest is commonly referred to as the "outside basis" and the partnership's basis in its assets is known as the "inside basis." These terms will be used throughout this book as shorthand references to distinguish the two concepts, which play an important role in the taxation of partnerships and partners.

The following Revenue Ruling illustrates the operation of the Code's general rules for determining the tax consequences of a contribution of property to a partnership.

## Revenue Ruling 99–5

1999–1 Cum.Bull. 434.

### ISSUE

What are the federal income tax consequences when a single member domestic limited liability company (LLC) that is disregarded for federal tax purposes as an entity separate from its owner under § 301.7701–3 of the Procedure and Administration Regulations becomes an entity with more than one owner that is classified as a partnership for federal tax purposes?

### FACTS

In each of the following two situations, an LLC is formed and operates in a state which permits an LLC to have a single owner. Each LLC has a single owner, A, and is disregarded as an entity separate from its owner for federal tax purposes under § 301.7701–3. In both situations, the LLC would not be treated as an investment company (within the meaning of

---

**10.** Once again, this basis is increased by any gain recognized by the partner on the transfer under Section 721(b).

**11.** Reg. §§ 1.1223–3(a)(2), (b)(1).

**12.** Reg. § 1.1223–3(e).

§ 351) if it were incorporated. All of the assets held by each LLC are capital assets or property described in § 1231. For the sake of simplicity, it is assumed that neither LLC is liable for any indebtedness, nor are the assets of the LLCs subject to any indebtedness.

*Situation 1.* B, who is not related to A, purchases 50% of A's ownership interest in the LLC for $5,000. A does not contribute any portion of the $5,000 to the LLC. A and B continue to operate the business of the LLC as co-owners of the LLC.

*Situation 2.* B, who is not related to A, contributes $10,000 to the LLC in exchange for a 50% ownership interest in the LLC. The LLC uses all of the contributed cash in its business. A and B continue to operate the business of the LLC as co-owners of the LLC.

After the sale, in both situations, no entity classification election is made under § 301.7701–3(c) to treat the LLC as an association for federal tax purposes.

LAW AND ANALYSIS

Section 721(a) generally provides that no gain or loss shall be recognized to a partnership or to any of its partners in the case of a contribution of property to the partnership in exchange for an interest in the partnership.

Section 722 provides that the basis of an interest in a partnership acquired by a contribution of property, including money, to the partnership shall be the amount of the money and the adjusted basis of the property to the contributing partner at the time of the contribution increased by the amount (if any) of gain recognized under § 721(b) to the contributing partner at such time.

Section 723 provides that the basis of property contributed to a partnership by a partner shall be the adjusted basis of the property to the contributing partner at the time of the contribution increased by the amount (if any) of gain recognized under § 721(b) to the contributing partner at such time.

Section 1001(a) provides that the gain or loss from the sale or other disposition of property shall be the difference between the amount realized therefrom and the adjusted basis provided in § 1011.

Section 1223(1) provides that, in determining the holding period of a taxpayer who receives property in an exchange, there shall be included the period for which the taxpayer held the property exchanged if the property has the same basis in whole or in part in the taxpayer's hands as the property exchanged, and the property exchanged at the time of the exchange was a capital asset or property described in § 1231.

Section 1223(2) provides that, regardless of how a property is acquired, in determining the holding period of a taxpayer who holds the property, there shall be included the period for which such property was held by any

other person if the property has the same basis in whole or in part in the taxpayer's hands as it would have in the hands of such other person.

HOLDING(S)

*Situation 1*. In this situation, the LLC, which, for federal tax purposes, is disregarded as an entity separate from its owner, is converted to a partnership when the new member, B, purchases an interest in the disregarded entity from the owner, A. B's purchase of 50% of A's ownership interest in the LLC is treated as the purchase of a 50% interest in each of the LLC's assets, which are treated as held directly by A for federal tax purposes. Immediately thereafter, A and B are treated as contributing their respective interests in those assets to a partnership in exchange for ownership interests in the partnership.

Under § 1001, A recognizes gain or loss from the deemed sale of the 50% interest in each asset of the LLC to B.

Under § 721(a), no gain or loss is recognized by A or B as a result of the conversion of the disregarded entity to a partnership.

Under § 722, B's basis in the partnership interest is equal to $5,000, the amount paid by B to A for the assets which B is deemed to contribute to the newly-created partnership. A's basis in the partnership interest is equal to A's basis in A's 50% share of the assets of the LLC.

Under § 723, the basis of the property treated as contributed to the partnership by A and B is the adjusted basis of that property in A's and B's hands immediately after the deemed sale.

Under § 1223(1), A's holding period for the partnership interest received includes A's holding period in the capital assets and property described in § 1231 held by the LLC when it converted from an entity that was disregarded as an entity separate from A to a partnership. B's holding period for the partnership interest begins on the day following the date of B's purchase of the LLC interest from A. See Rev. Rul. 66–7, 1966–1 C.B. 188, which provides that the holding period of a purchased asset is computed by excluding the date on which the asset is acquired. Under § 1223(2), the partnership's holding period for the assets deemed transferred to it includes A's and B's holding periods for such assets.

*Situation 2*. In this situation, the LLC is converted from an entity that is disregarded as an entity separate from its owner to a partnership when a new member, B, contributes cash to the LLC. B's contribution is treated as a contribution to a partnership in exchange for an ownership interest in the partnership. A is treated as contributing all of the assets of the LLC to the partnership in exchange for a partnership interest.

Under § 721(a), no gain or loss is recognized by A or B as a result of the conversion of the disregarded entity to a partnership.

Under § 722, B's basis in the partnership interest is equal to $10,000, the amount of cash contributed to the partnership. A's basis in the

partnership interest is equal to A's basis in the assets of the LLC which A was treated as contributing to the newly-created partnership.

Under § 723, the basis of the property contributed to the partnership by A is the adjusted basis of that property in A's hands. The basis of the property contributed to the partnership by B is $10,000, the amount of cash contributed to the partnership.

Under § 1223(1), A's holding period for the partnership interest received includes A's holding period in the capital and § 1231 assets deemed contributed when the disregarded entity converted to a partnership. B's holding period for the partnership interest begins on the day following the date of B's contribution of money to the LLC. Under § 1223(2), the partnership's holding period for the assets transferred to it includes A's holding period.

## NOTE

A partnership may acquire the capital it uses in its business ventures in a variety of ways. The simplest and most direct way is for the partners to contribute property in exchange for their partnership interests. In more complex transactions, the partnership may issue options that allow the holder to purchase an equity interest in the partnership. Similarly, a partnership may borrow funds in exchange for convertible debt that allows the holder to acquire an equity interest in the partnership through the instrument's conversion feature. How should Section 721 apply in these more complex transactions?

The Service has issued proposed regulations that govern the tax consequences of "noncompensatory" options to acquire a partnership interest—i.e., an option that is not issued in connection with the performance of services.[1] A noncompensatory option includes a call option or warrant to acquire a partnership interest, the conversion feature in a partnership debt instrument, and the conversion feature in a preferred equity interest in a partnership.[2] Under the regulations, Section 721 does not apply to the transfer of property to a partnership in exchange for a noncompensatory option, but it does apply to the exercise of the option.[3] For example, assume an individual transfers property with a basis of $600 and a fair market value of $1,000 to a partnership in exchange for an option to buy a one-third partnership interest for $5,000 at any time during the next three years. On the transfer for the option, the individual recognizes $400 of gain. If the individual later exercises the option by transferring property with a $3,000 basis and $5,000 fair market value to the partnership for a partnership interest, that transfer is protected by Section 721. The proposed regulations permit the partnership to use open transaction principles

---

**1.** Prop. Reg. § 1.721–2(d).

**2.** Prop. Reg. § 1.721–2(e)(1). For an extensive analysis of the proposed regulations, see Matthew P. Larvick, "Noncompensatory Partnership Options: The Proposed Regulations," 99 Tax Notes 271 (April 14, 2003).

**3.** Prop. Reg. § 1.721–2(a) & (b).

on the transfer of property for the option so it generally does not recognize any option income until the option is exercised or lapses and it takes a $1,000 basis in the property transferred for the option. Under Section 723 the partnership has a $3,000 basis in the property contributed for the partnership interest.[4] Section 721 does not apply to the lapse of a noncompensatory option.[5]

Generally, an individual holding a noncompensatory option to acquire a partnership interest is not treated as a partner for purposes of allocating partnership income but if the option provides the holder with rights substantially similar to the rights afforded a partner, then the option holder is treated as a partner in allocating income.[6]

PROBLEM

A, B, C and D (all individuals) form a general partnership in which they each have an equal interest in capital and profits. All the partners and the partnership are cash method taxpayers. In exchange for their respective partnership interests, each partner transfers the following assets, all of which have been held more than two years:

| Partner | Asset | Adjusted Basis | Fair Mkt. Value |
|---|---|---|---|
| A | Land | $ 30,000 | $ 70,000 |
| | Goodwill | 0 | 30,000 |
| B | Equipment (all § 1245 gain) | 25,000 | 45,000 |
| | Installment note from the sale of land | 20,000 | 25,000 |
| | Inventory | 5,000 | 30,000 |
| C | Building | 25,000 | 60,000 |
| | Land | 25,000 | 10,000 |
| | Receivables for services rendered to E | 0 | 30,000 |
| D | Cash | 100,000 | 100,000 |

(a) What are the tax consequences (consider only gain or loss realized and recognized, basis and holding period) to each of the partners?

(b) What are the tax consequences (consider only gain recognized, basis and holding period) to the partnership?

(c) Although each of the partners contributes property of equal value, D transfers only cash while the other partners transfer property.

---

**4.** This example is Prop. Reg. § 1.721–2(f) Example.

**5.** Prop. Reg. § 1.721–2(c). Thus, if the option in the example lapsed without being exercised, the partnership would have $1,000 of gross income and the individual would be entitled to a $1,000 loss deduction.

**6.** Prop. Reg. 1.761–3(a). Special rules also apply to capital account adjustments and allocations on the exercise of a noncompensatory option. Prop. Reg. §§ 1.704–1(b)(2)(iv)*(d)(4)*, 1.704–1(b)(2)(iv)*(s)*; see Prop. Reg. 1.704–1(b)(5) Examples 20–24. These rules are designed to account for any shifts in capital that result from the exercise of noncompensatory options.

Section 704(c)(1)(A) requires the partnership to allocate the pre-contribution gain or loss solely to the contributing partner when the partnership subsequently disposes of the property. What is the objective of that section? See also § 724.

## 2.  INTRODUCTION TO PARTNERSHIP ACCOUNTING

Regulations: § 1.704–1(b)(2)(iv)(b)–(d), (f), (h).

The partners' interests in the assets of the partnership, their responsibility for partnership liabilities, and their respective rights to profits and losses and to operating and liquidating distributions, are determined by the partnership agreement. The financial condition of a partnership on formation and each partner's ownership interest in the firm are depicted on an opening day "balance sheet" which lists the partnership's assets on the left side and the liabilities and partners' capital on the right side. Under the venerable accounting principle known as the "Fundamental Equation," the two sides always must be equal—that is, Assets = Liabilities + Net Worth. This makes sense because the partners' equity interest necessarily equates with the net worth of the partnership which in turn is the difference between the partnership's assets and its liabilities. Because this text often presents problems (or asks for answers) in the form of a partnership balance sheet, a basic introduction to partnership accounting is in order.

Assume that Alison ("A"), Bill ("B") and Carol ("C") join forces and agree to do business as the ABC Partnership. A contributes securities worth $60,000, B contributes land worth $30,000 and C contributes $10,000 cash. At the inception of the business, the ABC Partnership balance sheet is as follows:

| **Assets** | | **Liabilities and Partners' Capital** | |
|---|---|---|---|
| Cash | $ 10,000 | Liabilities: | |
| Securities | 60,000 | None | |
| Land | 30,000 | Capital: | |
| | | A | $ 60,000 |
| | | B | 30,000 |
| | | C | 10,000 |
| Total | $100,000 | | $100,000 |

Some elaboration is necessary. On the left side of the balance sheet, partnership assets are recorded at their "book value," which is sometimes called "historical cost." During the life of the partnership, book value is not necessarily the same as fair market value and, in some cases, it may differ from the tax basis of the asset. But book value is considered to be a more reliable figure for balance sheet purposes, and it will not change until some event occurs that warrants a revaluation of the partnership's assets. Moving to the right side, each partner's interest in partnership assets is reflected on the balance sheet by what is known in accounting lexicon as the partner's "capital account." The capital account represents a partner's equity in the firm. At any point in time during the life of a partnership, it

generally identifies what each partner would be entitled to receive upon liquidation of his or her interest in the partnership.[1] A partner's capital account begins with the amount of money and the fair market value of any property contributed to the partnership by the partner, is increased by the partner's share of the profits of the firm and is decreased by the partner's share of partnership losses and the amount of cash and the fair market value of any property distributed to the partner.[2]

The tax regulations governing partnership allocations provide detailed rules for the maintenance of capital accounts.[3] Capital accounts maintained in accordance with these requirements do not always accurately reflect the current fair market value of a partner's investment. In order to stay in balance with the asset side of the balance sheet, capital accounts must track the historical cost of assets as reported on the partnership's books; thus, they ordinarily do not take into account the appreciation or decline in value of partnership property until that gain or loss has been realized and recognized.[4]

The intrusion of tax concepts adds some complications to partnership accounting. Because the tax consequences of any disposition of property depend, in part, on the tax basis of that property, both the partnership's inside bases in its assets and the partners' outside bases in their partnership interests are important elements in the equation. To keep the example simple, assume that the land contributed by B has a tax basis equal to its value but that A has a $40,000 basis for the contributed securities. The "book/tax"[5] balance sheet of the partnership will be as follows:

**1.** A partner also may have an interest in partnership assets as a creditor. If so, the value of that interest will not be reflected in the partner's capital account. Rather, partner loans will be reflected as such on the partnership's books as a liability, along with the interests of the partnership's other creditors. Under the Uniform Partnership Act, debts to partners have a lower priority than debts to third party creditors if a partnership's assets are insufficient to discharge all of its liabilities. Uniform Partnership Act § 40(b).

**2.** Reg. § 1.704–1(b)(2)(iv)(*b*).

**3.** Reg. § 1.704–1(b)(2)(iv). See Chapter 4B2, infra.

**4.** In certain situations a partnership may restate its capital accounts at current value. See Reg. § 1.704–1(b)(2)(iv)(*f*). Moreover, in the case of depreciation or cost depletion, the balance sheet will reflect certain changes in the book value of assets (and corresponding changes to partners' capital accounts) prior to disposition of the asset. These changes are based on cost recovery principles and are not intended to mirror the real life changes in value of depreciable or depletable property.

**5.** "Book/Tax" balance sheet means a financial statement that shows both the book value of the partnership's assets and the

| Assets | A.B.[6] | Bk. Val. | Liabilities and Partners' Capital | A.B. | Bk. Val. |
|---|---|---|---|---|---|
| Cash | $10,000 | $ 10,000 | Liabilities: | | |
| Securities | 40,000 | 60,000 | None | | |
| Land | 30,000 | 30,000 | Capital: | | |
| | | | A | $40,000 | $ 60,000 |
| | | | B | 30,000 | 30,000 |
| | | | C | 10,000 | 10,000 |
| Total | $80,000 | $100,000 | | $80,000 | $100,000 |

Now that the ABC Partnership is off and running, the partners will become keenly interested in their share of partnership profits or losses—an amount that we will come to know as a partner's "distributive share."[7] Absent an agreement among the partners, the Uniform Partnership Act provides that profits will be shared equally,[8] but the flexibility of the partnership form allows partners to agree to share profits in any other manner they see fit. Partners frequently will agree to allocate profits in proportion to their respective interests in partnership capital. Other common approaches are to allocate to each partner a specific percentage of the overall profit or to assign a specific number of partnership "units."[9] No particular profit allocation method is required, and allocations in some partnerships may vary over the life of the enterprise.[10] Indeed, for both tax and business reasons, lawyers have concocted more profit sharing formulas than ever could be devised by the human mind (assuming, of course, that the legal community is an altogether different species).[11]

partners' capital accounts and the adjusted bases of those assets as used for tax purposes.

**6.** On the left side of the balance sheets in the text, "A.B." signifies the partnership's adjusted basis of an asset for tax purposes; on the right side, "A.B." signifies the partner's basis in his partnership interest. See I.R.C. §§ 722; 723.

**7.** The term "distributive" is somewhat misleading in that it suggests that a distribution may be imminent. Profits may or may not be distributed, depending on the agreement of the partners. For tax and accounting purposes, "distributive" connotes an allocation of the tax burdens and benefits arising from partnership operations which, to be respected for tax purposes, must correspond to the economic burdens and benefits that are reflected on the partners' capital accounts. See I.R.C. § 704(a), (b); Chapter 4B2, infra.

**8.** Uniform Partnership Act § 18(a).

**9.** The use of units to represent ownership and, correspondingly, profit sharing ratios, is typical in larger partnerships where the interests of the partners may vary frequently as new partners are admitted and others retire. For example, the profit share of a senior partner in a large law firm may be represented by eight units and a new junior partner may be assigned only two units. This method obviates the need to recalculate profit percentages and simplifies accounting for the entry or departure of partners and for the change in a partner's relative share of the firm. See Siegel & Siegel, Accounting and Financial Disclosure 90 (West, 1983).

**10.** For example, in more complex limited partnerships, the limited partner investors are often allocated virtually all of the losses and profits during the early years of the venture; but once the investors have recouped their initial contributions, the profit-sharing ratio often "flips" to a more equal division between the promoters (usually general partners) and the investors.

**11.** Because a partner's capital account represents the partner's equity investment, it would seem that when profits are shared in any manner other than in proportion to the relative capital account balances, any partner with a larger capital account is receiving a smaller percentage return on his investment and thus would be dissatisfied with the allocation. We will see, however, that there are many reasons, both tax and nontax, for "special allocations." See Chapter 4B, infra.

To observe the effects of ABC's operations on its balance sheet, assume that during year one it has a $10,000 net profit from its operations and sells the land for $40,000. Assume further that the partners have agreed to allocate profits according to their capital account balances. The $10,000 operating profit and the $10,000 gain on the sale of the land ($20,000 total income) will be allocated 60 percent ($12,000) to A, 30 percent ($6,000) to B and 10 percent ($2,000) to C. At the end of year one, the balance sheet will look like this:

| **Assets** | | | **Liabilities and Partners' Capital** | | |
|---|---|---|---|---|---|
| | **A.B.** | **Bk. Val.** | | **A.B.** | **Bk. Val.** |
| Cash | $ 60,000 | $ 60,000 [12] | Liabilities: | | |
| Securities | 40,000 | 60,000 | None | | |
| | | | Capital: | | |
| | | | A | $ 52,000 | $ 72,000 |
| | | | B | 36,000 | 36,000 |
| | | | C | 12,000 | 12,000 |
| Total | $100,000 | $120,000 | | $100,000 | $120,000 |

You may have noticed one strikingly unrealistic aspect of the ABC Partnership and therefore its balance sheet. It is devoid of any debt! Many partnerships, of course, need to borrow money to finance operations, either from the partners or outside lenders. To fill this gap in the liability column (and our knowledge of partnership accounting), assume that ABC borrows $30,000 from Bank at the beginning of year two. The bookkeeper will record this transaction by adding $30,000 to the asset side of the balance sheet and placing a corresponding entry on the right side under "Liabilities." The partners' capital accounts are unaffected by the loan,[13] but the bank's right to repayment takes priority over any return of capital to the partners. After the borrowing, ABC's balance sheet will look like this:

| **Assets** | | | **Liabilities and Partners' Capital** | | |
|---|---|---|---|---|---|
| | **A.B.** | **Bk. Val.** | | **A.B.**[14] | **Bk. Val.** |
| Cash | $ 90,000 | $ 90,000 | Liabilities: | | $ 30,000 |
| Securities | 40,000 | 60,000 | Capital: | | |
| | | | A | $ 70,000 | $ 72,000 |
| | | | B | 45,000 | 36,000 |
| | | | C | 15,000 | 12,000 |
| Total | $130,000 | $150,000 | | $130,000 | $150,000 |

**12.** This $60,000 of cash represents the original $10,000 cash contributed by C, the $40,000 proceeds from the sale of the land and the $10,000 of net profits earned during year one.

**13.** As we will see later in this chapter, however, each partner's *tax* basis in his partnership interest is increased by the partner's share of partnership liabilities on the theory that the partners ultimately will be responsible for paying that debt. I.R.C. § 752(a). The result is that the borrowed funds become an asset ($30,000 cash) having a basis of $30,000 to the partnership, and the resulting liability to repay that cash increases the partners' outside bases by that same amount in a ratio of 6:3:1, or $18,000 to A, $9,000 to B and $3,000 to C.

**14.** See note 13, supra.

The time will come when the partners wish to withdraw some funds from the business. As with the allocation of profits and losses, the timing and method of distributions is determined by the partnership agreement. Distributions may be made as profits are earned, before they are earned (in the form of "draws" against anticipated profits), or even in the absence of any profits (e.g., if the partners desire the return of some or all of their invested capital). Alternatively, the partners may elect to defer making any distributions until they dissolve the partnership or liquidate a particular partner's interest. Whatever the format, a distribution will affect the partnership balance sheet, and the distributee partner's capital account must be adjusted to reflect the removal of all or part of his or her investment in the firm.

To illustrate the effect of a distribution, assume that ABC realizes no net income or loss from operations during year two. But with its coffers still awash with cash from the land sale and bank loan, the partners agree to make a distribution of $60,000 in proportion to their respective capital account balances. A thus receives $36,000 (60%), B receives $18,000 (30%) and C receives $6,000 (10%). The balance sheet at the end of year two will then look like this:[15]

| Assets | | | Liabilities and Partners' Capital | | |
|---|---|---|---|---|---|
| | **A.B.** | **Bk. Val.** | | **A.B.** | **Bk. Val.** |
| Cash | $30,000 | $30,000 | Liabilities: | | $30,000 |
| Securities | 40,000 | 60,000 | Capital: | | |
| | | | A | $34,000 | $36,000 |
| | | | B | 27,000 | 18,000 |
| | | | C | 9,000 | 6,000 |
| Total | $70,000 | $90,000 | | $70,000 | $90,000 |

At this point, it is worth noting that the value of the securities may have changed from the time they were acquired. The securities nonetheless continue to be shown on the balance sheet at their historical cost ("book value").[16] When the securities are sold and the appreciation (or, in bear markets, the decline in value) is realized, any gain or loss will be reflected on the partnership balance sheet because, of course, the securities will have been converted into cash.

Assume, for example, that the partnership sells the securities for $160,000. Since the securities had appreciated in value between the time they were acquired by A and contributed to the partnership, Section 704(c)(1)(A) requires that the precontribution gain must be allocated solely to the contributing partner when the partnership sells the securities. Thus, the first $20,000 of tax gain will be allocated to A, but A's capital account is

**15.** Note that the distribution causes the cash to be reduced by $60,000 on the asset side of the balance sheet. The partners' capital accounts are reduced by a corresponding amount. Reg. § 1.704–1(b)(2)(iv)(b)(4).

**16.** The partners might wish to present a more accurate picture of the partnership's net worth to potential lenders or outside investors, and they are free to do so for that purpose.

not similarly adjusted[17] because the gain is already reflected in the value of the securities on the partnership's books and in A's capital account. The $100,000 of postcontribution gain, however, has not yet been reflected in the capital accounts and is allocated to the partners based on their capital account balances, which are increased accordingly.[18] The balance sheet after the sale would look like this:

| Assets | A.B. | Bk. Val. | Liabilities and Partners' Capital | A.B. | Bk. Val. |
|--------|------|----------|-----------------------------------|------|----------|
| Cash | $190,000 | $190,000 | Liabilities: | | $ 30,000 |
| | | | Capital: | | |
| | | | A | $114,000 | $ 96,000 |
| | | | B | 57,000 | 48,000 |
| | | | C | 19,000 | 16,000 |
| Total | $190,000 | $190,000 | | $190,000 | $190,000 |

Now assume the sale of securities does not occur and that, instead, a new partner arrives on the scene, or the relative interests of the partners change, or an asset is distributed to one of the partners. For example, assume that at the beginning of year three, the securities again are worth $160,000 and Dan ("D") desires to join the partnership as a 10 percent partner. If the parties simply look at the balance sheet, D might be expected to base his contribution on the $60,000 aggregate book value of the partnership.[19] In fact, however, the partnership has a net worth of $160,000 ($190,000 assets less $30,000 of liabilities) because the securities are worth $100,000 more than their reported book value. In this situation, the partners may wish to readjust their capital accounts to reflect the current economic condition of the partnership.[20] The securities (and any other partnership assets) then would be reflected on the partnership's books at their current fair market value ($160,000 for the securities), and each partner's capital account should be increased by his or her share of the unrealized postcontribution appreciation inherent in the securities.[21] After such a revaluation (and before D is admitted), the balance sheet would be as follows:

---

**17.** See Reg. § 1.704–1(b)(2)(iv)(b)(3); 1.704–1(b)(2)(iv)(d)(3); 1.704–1(b)(2)(iv)(g).

**18.** Reg. § 1.704–1(b)(2)(iv)(b)(3). Thus, A's capital account is increased by $60,000 to $96,000, B's is increased by $30,000 to $48,000, and C's is increased by $10,000 to $16,000. The partners' outside bases also are increased by their respective shares of tax gain—$80,000 to A, $30,000 to B and $10,000 to C. I.R.C. § 705(a)(1).

**19.** See the balance sheet accompanying note 15, supra.

**20.** Such a revaluation is permitted in this situation by the regulations governing partnership allocations. Reg. § 1.704–1(b)(2)(iv)(f). It may not be appropriate, however, under conventional accounting principles.

**21.** Similar adjustments are permitted if one or more existing partners changes his or her percentage interest in the partnership or if an asset is distributed to one of the partners. See, e.g., Reg. § 1.704–1(b)(2)(iv)(e)(1).

| Assets | | | Liabilities and Partners' Capital | | |
|---|---|---|---|---|---|
| | **A.B.** | **Bk. Val.** | | **A.B.** | **Bk. Val.** |
| Cash | $30,000 | $ 30,000 | Liabilities: | | $ 30,000 |
| Securities | 40,000 | 160,000 | Capital: | | |
| | | | A | $34,000 | $ 96,000 |
| | | | B | 27,000 | 48,000 |
| | | | C | 9,000 | 16,000 |
| Total | $70,000 | $190,000 | | $70,000 | $190,000 |

Finally, what happens when a partnership dissolves? Moving back to the original ABC partnership, assume that at the beginning of year three, the partnership sells the securities for $160,000, repays its $30,000 bank loan and liquidates. The $120,000 gain on the sale will be allocated to the partners in accordance with Section 704(c) and their interests in partnership profits and capital: $80,000 to A, $30,000 to B and $10,000 to C.[22] Immediately prior to the liquidation, the partnership balance sheet will look like this:

| Assets | | | Liabilities and Partners' Capital | | |
|---|---|---|---|---|---|
| | **A.B.** | **Bk. Val.** | | **A.B.** | **Bk. Val.** |
| Cash | $160,000 | $160,000 | Liabilities: | | |
| | | | None | | |
| | | | Capital: | | |
| | | | A | $ 96,000[23] | $ 96,000 |
| | | | B | 48,000 | 48,000 |
| | | | C | 16,000 | 16,000 |
| Total | $160,000 | $160,000 | | $160,000 | $160,000 |

Liquidating distributions of cash then will be made in accordance with the partners' final capital accounts.

## PROBLEM

A, B and C are equal general partners in the ABC Partnership. On formation of the partnership, A contributes $50,000 cash, B contributes land (Parcel #1) with a basis of $40,000 and a fair market value of $50,000, and C contributes securities with a basis and fair market value of $50,000. Prepare the partnership's opening balance sheet and then reconstruct the balance sheet to account for each of the following (cumulative) subsequent events:

(a) The partnership leases Parcel #1 for $15,000 and sells the securities for $50,000.

(b) The partnership borrows $300,000 and then buys more land (Parcel #2) for $330,000.

(c) The partnership distributes $20,000 each to A, B and C.

---

**22.** See notes 17 and 18, supra.

**23.** This figure represents A's adjusted basis of $34,000 at the beginning of year three decreased by his $18,000 (i.e., 60%) share of the liabilities (see I.R.C. §§ 752(b) and 733) and increased by his $80,000 share of the gain on the securities. Similar adjustments are made for B and C.

(d) The partnership sells Parcel #1 for $65,000.

(e) When Parcel #2 has a value of $420,000, the assets and capital accounts are restated to current value, and new partner D contributes $70,000 cash to the partnership in exchange for a 25% general partnership interest.

## B.   TREATMENT OF LIABILITIES: THE BASICS

### 1.   IMPACT OF LIABILITIES ON PARTNER'S OUTSIDE BASIS

Code: § 752(a)–(c). Skim §§ 705(a); 722; 733.

Regulations: § 1.752–1(a)(1) & (2), (b), (c); –2(a), (b); –3(a).

The general rules discussed in the preceding section closely parallel nonrecognition principles that recur throughout the study of the income tax. But they presuppose a world without debt—a fiscal utopia that has yet to be achieved. In reality, leverage pervades the partnership world, and many partnership formations involve the borrowing of money by the partnership or the contribution of encumbered property by a partner. These liabilities have a significant impact on a partner's outside basis.[1] Moreover, when property subject to a liability is transferred to a partnership or when a partnership incurs or pays off a liability, a mechanism must be found to allocate the liability among the partners and reflect that allocation in each partner's outside basis.

The solution adopted by Subchapter K to the treatment of partnership liabilities is intricate and requires an understanding of an amalgam of Code sections and complex regulations.[2] For these reasons, a detailed study of this topic is deferred until later in the text.[3] This early discussion will be confined to an overview of the general principles that relate to partnership formations. The starting point is Section 752, a broad provision that governs the treatment of partnership liabilities in many different contexts, including formations.[4] Section 752(a) treats any increase in a partner's share of partnership liabilities as if it were a cash contribution by the partner to the partnership, increasing the partner's outside basis under Section 722. Section 752(b) treats any decrease in a partner's share of liabilities, including the partnership's assumption of a partner's liability, as if it were a cash distribution to the partner, decreasing his outside basis under Sections 705(a) and 733. For purposes of Section 752, liabilities that would be deductible when paid (e.g., accounts payable of a cash basis

---

**1.** The outside basis is significant because, among other functions, it limits the amount of partnership losses which may be deducted by a partner and is used in determining the amount of gain or loss recognized by a partner on the receipt of certain partnership distributions and on the sale or liquidation of a partnership interest.

**2.** See Reg. § 1.752–2,–3.

**3.** See Chapter 4D, infra.

**4.** Section 752 applies, for example, when a partnership incurs or pays off a liability, distributes property subject to a liability, admits a new partner, or distributes property in liquidation of a partner's interest.

taxpayer) are disregarded.[5] This is consistent with the treatment of deductible liabilities in the corporate formation context under Section 357(c)(3)(A) and for purposes of cancellation of indebtedness under Section 108(e).

These rules are consistent with the teachings of the celebrated *Crane* case.[6] Under *Crane,* taxpayers who acquire property subject to a debt, whether or not there is personal liability, include the amount of the debt in their cost basis, just as if they had paid cash, on the assumption that the loan ultimately will be paid. Taxpayers who sell encumbered property must include the debt relief in the amount realized, just as if they had received additional cash. For the same reasons, a partner's outside basis includes his share of a partnership's liabilities on the assumption that the debt will be satisfied in due course and, similarly, the partner is treated as receiving the equivalent of cash when a partnership liability is extinguished. Also in keeping with *Crane,* Section 752(c) provides that a liability to which property is subject shall be treated as a liability of the owner, at least to the extent of the fair market value of the property.[7]

A partner's share of partnership liabilities for purposes of Section 752 generally depends on the status of the partner (general or limited) and the nature of the liability (recourse or nonrecourse). A partnership liability is a recourse liability to the extent that any partner bears the economic risk of loss for the liability.[8] If no partner bears the economic risk of loss, the liability is classified as nonrecourse.[9]

A partner's share of recourse liabilities equals the portion of the liability for which the partner bears the economic risk of loss.[10] A partner bears the economic risk of loss to the extent that the partner (or a person related to the partner) would be required to pay the liability if the partnership were unable to do so. This determination is made by asking who would be obligated to pay the liability if all of the partnership's liabilities are payable in full and all of the partnership's assets, including cash, are worthless.[11] Statutory and contractual obligations relating to the partnership liability, such as guarantees, obligations to restore a deficit capital account balance or obligations imposed by state law, are taken into account in deciding who bears the economic risk of loss.[12] Under these principles, equal partners in a general partnership ordinarily will share the economic risk of loss for a partnership recourse debt equally because that is

---

**5.** Rev.Rul. 88–77, 1988–2 C.B. 128.

**6.** Crane v. Commissioner, 331 U.S. 1, 67 S.Ct. 1047 (1947).

**7.** The fair market value limitation in Section 752(c) applies only to contributions to and distributions from a partnership. On the sale of a partnership interest, nonrecourse liabilities are included in the amount realized even if they exceed the fair market value of the property. See I.R.C. § 752(d); Commissioner v. Tufts, 461 U.S. 300, 103 S.Ct. 1826 (1983), rehearing denied, 463 U.S. 1215, 103 S.Ct. 3555 (1983).

**8.** Reg. § 1.752–1(a)(1).

**9.** Reg. § 1.752–1(a)(2).

**10.** Reg. § 1.752–2(a).

**11.** Reg. § 1.752–2(b)(1).

**12.** Reg. § 1.752–2(b)(3). The methodology employed by the regulations to determine who bears the economic risk of loss for a recourse liability is discussed in more detail in Chapter 4D, infra.

how they share the economic burden to pay the debt under state law. Since a limited partner ordinarily bears no risk of loss beyond his original capital contributions to the partnership and any additional contributions that he is committed to make under the partnership agreement, a limited partner's share of recourse liabilities generally may not exceed the amount which he is obligated to contribute to the partnership in the future.[13]

In the case of nonrecourse partnership liabilities, none of the partners has any personal liability. Since general and limited partners all enjoy limited liability with respect to nonrecourse debts, those liabilities generally are allocated among the partners in accordance with each partner's share of partnership profits rather than losses.[14]

PROBLEM

A, B, C and D each contribute $25,000 to the ABCD partnership, which then acquires a $1,000,000 building, paying $100,000 cash and borrowing $900,000 on a nonrecourse basis.

(a) If the parties are equal general partners, what is each partner's outside basis?

(b) What result if the partnership is a limited partnership, A is the sole general partner and all the partners share profits and losses equally?

(c) What result in (b), above, if the partnership were personally liable for the debt?

## 2.   CONTRIBUTIONS OF ENCUMBERED PROPERTY

Code: §§ 704(c)(1)(A); 731(a)(1); 752(a)–(c). Skim §§ 705(a); 722; 733; 734(b)(1)(A).

Regulations: § 1.752–1(b), (c) and (f); –2(a), (b); –3(a).

*General Rules.* Additional sections of the Code come into play in determining the tax consequences of a contribution of encumbered property to a partnership. The regulations under Section 722, incorporating the approach taken by Section 752, recharacterize such a contribution as a cash transaction.[1] To the extent that a contributing partner is relieved of a liability, he is treated as having received a distribution of cash from the partnership. This constructive distribution in turn triggers the rules governing operating distributions by a partnership.[2] Under Sections 731 and 733, a distribution of cash is considered a return of capital, which reduces the partner's outside basis (but not below zero) by the amount of the distribution. The portion of the debt from which the contributing partner is

---

**13.** Reg. § 1.752–2(b)(3)(ii).

**14.** Reg. § 1.752–3(a).

**1.** Reg. § 1.722–1; See Reg. § 1.752–1(b) and (c).

**2.** See I.R.C. §§ 731–734. These rules will be covered in depth in Chapter 7, infra.

relieved is then allocated to the other partners, who are considered to have contributed cash to the partnership, and the outside basis of each is increased accordingly. Section 752 works with the basic rules of Section 722 and the operating distribution provisions to reallocate the liabilities among the partners and properly adjust each partner's outside basis.

*Recourse Liabilities: In General.* The operation of these general rules is best illustrated by an example where the contributed property is encumbered by a recourse liability. Assume that Partner A contributes a parcel of land with a fair market value of $150,000, an adjusted basis of $50,000, and encumbered by a recourse mortgage of $30,000 in exchange for a 50 percent interest in the newly formed AB general partnership. B, the other partner, contributes $120,000 in cash. The partnership has a net worth of $240,000 and the value of each partner's interest is $120,000. If the partnership assumes the mortgage, A and B, as equal general partners, are each considered to bear the risk of loss for $15,000 of the $30,000 liability transferred by A.[3] A thus is considered to have $15,000 of debt relief and, under Section 752(b), is treated as receiving a $15,000 cash distribution from the partnership. A's outside basis would then be determined as follows:

| | |
|---|---:|
| Adjusted basis of parcel contributed by A | $ 50,000 |
| Less: Portion of liability treated under § 752(b) as cash distribution to A (½ of $30,000) | (15,000) |
| Equals: A's outside basis | $ 35,000 |

B's outside basis would be determined as follows:

| | |
|---|---:|
| Cash contributed by B | $120,000 |
| Plus: Portion of liability allocated to B and treated under § 752(a) as a cash contribution by B (½ of $30,000) | 15,000 |
| Equals: B's outside basis | $135,000 |

*Recourse Liabilities in Excess of Basis.* The plot thickens, however, if we assume the same facts except that the adjusted basis of the parcel contributed by A is $10,000 instead of $50,000 and the liability is recourse. A's outside basis under Section 722 initially is $10,000, the adjusted basis of the parcel. A's outside basis is then decreased (and B's is increased) by the net amount of debt that is allocated away from A and over to B.[4] Thus, $15,000 of the liability is reallocated from A to B,[5] and A is deemed to receive a constructive cash distribution of $15,000 (the net amount of the recourse debt that is allocated to B). A's outside basis under Section 722 initially is $10,000, the adjusted basis of the parcel. It then would appear to

---

**3.** Reg. § 1.752–2(b)(3)(iii). The example in the text assumes that A does not remain personally liable to the creditor. If A does remain personally liable, then B does not bear the economic risk of loss under state law.

**4.** See Reg. § 1.752–1(f).

**5.** In effect, A is relieved of $30,000 of debt and assumes as a general partner $15,000 of partnership debt, resulting in a net reduction of $15,000. See Reg. § 1.752–1(f).

be reduced by the $15,000 constructive distribution, seemingly yielding the impossible—a $5,000 negative basis. Section 733 precludes this tax taboo by providing that a distribution may not reduce a partner's basis below zero, and Section 731(a)(1) balances the books by treating the excess of the constructive cash distribution over A's outside basis as gain from the sale or exchange of A's newly acquired partnership interest.[6] This gain is treated as capital gain under Section 741.[7]

Returning to the example, A thus would recognize $5,000 of capital gain on the constructive cash distribution of $15,000. A's outside basis would be determined as follows:

| | |
|---|---|
| Adjusted basis of parcel (§ 722) | $10,000 |
| Less: Portion of liability treated as cash distribution to A (½ of $30,000) | (15,000) |
| Equals: A's outside basis (may not be less than zero under § 733) | –0– |

Keep in mind that any gain recognized because of the contribution of property with recourse liabilities in excess of basis results from the constructive cash distribution from the partnership—not from the contribution of property by the partner.[8] This point is significant in light of the language in both Sections 722 and 723 permitting an increase in basis "by the amount (if any) of gain recognized under Section 721(b) to the contributing partner *at such time*" (emphasis added). The clause "at such time" refers to the time of the contribution as distinguished from the time of the subsequent hypothetical cash distribution. Consequently, neither Partner A nor the AB Partnership in the example above is entitled to a basis increase for the $5,000 of gain recognized under Section 731.[9] An increase to outside and inside bases under Sections 722 and 723 is only allowed in the narrow situation where a partner recognizes gain under Section 721(b) on a contribution of an asset to a partnership that would be treated as an

---

**6.** See Reg. § 1.722–1 Example (2). This also is the result when a partner receives actual cash distributions in excess of his outside basis. The cited example predates the Section 752 regulations and does not accurately illustrate how partners share nonrecourse liabilities. See notes 11–20, infra, and accompanying text.

**7.** I.R.C. § 731(a), flush language. Reg. § 1.731–1(a)(3). Gain from the sale or exchange of a partnership interest generally is treated as capital gain under Section 741 except to the extent that the amount realized is attributable to certain ordinary income assets (known as "Section 751 assets"). See I.R.C. § 751 and Chapter 6A, infra. In addition, Section 751(b) treats certain distributions of partnership property (including cash) in exchange for Section 751 property as a

transaction resulting in ordinary income to the partner. See Chapter 7E, infra. Detailed consideration of these concepts is premature, other than to note that these rules appear not to apply to any Section 731(a)(1) gain recognized on the contribution of encumbered property to a partnership. See McKee, Nelson & Whitmire, Federal Taxation of Partnerships and Partners ¶ 4.03[3] at note 111 (3d ed. 1996). Cf. Rev.Rul. 84–102, 1984–2 C.B. 119.

**8.** But see Reg. § 1.1245–4(c)(4) Example (3), which inappropriately treats the gain as arising from a contribution of the property rather than a constructive distribution of cash by the partnership.

**9.** See Rev.Rul. 84–15, 1984–1 C.B. 158.

"investment company" within the meaning of Section 351 if the partnership were incorporated.[10]

*Nonrecourse Liabilities: In General.* In the basic example above, A contributes a parcel of land with a fair market value of $150,000, an adjusted basis of $50,000, and the property is encumbered by a $30,000 mortgage. In exchange for the property, A receives a 50 percent interest in the partnership. Assume now that the mortgage is a nonrecourse liability. Determining how the $30,000 debt is allocated in this case begins with the general principle that nonrecourse liabilities are allocated among the partners in proportion to their respective shares of partnership profits.[11] In the case of contributed property, however, the determination of the partners' profit-sharing ratios may become more complex.

Recall that when a partner contributes appreciated property to a partnership, precontribution gain is allocated to the contributing partner under section 704(c)(1)(A) to the extent it is realized by the partnership on a subsequent disposition. One difficulty in determining how future profits of the partnership will be shared is that it is impossible to know whether any of the potential built-in gain in the contributed property will ever be recognized. For example, if the parcel of land is only worth $30,000 when it is sold by the partnership, the result would be a $20,000 loss.[12] Perhaps because of this uncertainty, the regulations give partners a great deal of flexibility to determine their share of profits for purposes of allocating nonrecourse liabilities. Under the regulations, a partner's interest in partnership profits is determined by taking into account all facts and circumstances relating to the economic arrangement of the partners.[13] The partnership agreement for sharing profits and the partner's share of built-in gain in partnership property are factors to be considered in determining the partners' interests in profits.[14] The regulations also allow the partners to specify their interests in partnership profits for purposes of allocating nonrecourse liabilities, and those interests will be respected if they are reasonably consistent with allocations of other significant items of partnership income or gain that are respected for tax purposes.[15] Thus, in the example, if it is determined that A and B each have a 50 percent interest in partnership profits, A would be considered to have $15,000 of debt relief and a $15,000 cash distribution from the partnership. A's outside basis in the partnership interest would be $35,000. The other $15,000 of the liability would be allocated to B, and B's outside basis would be $135,000. A

---

**10.** See I.R.C. § 351(e)(1); Reg. § 1.351–1(c)(1).

**11.** Reg. § 1.752–3(a)(3).

**12.** In that case, the partnership's amount realized would consist of the $30,000 debt relief. Commissioner v. Tufts, 461 U.S. 300, 103 S.Ct. 1826 (1983), rehearing denied 463 U.S. 1215, 103 S.Ct. 3555 (1983).

**13.** Reg. § 1.752–3(a)(3).

**14.** Rev. Rul. 95–41, 1995–1 C.B. 132.

**15.** Reg. § 1.752–3(a)(3). The regulations also permit nonrecourse liabilities to be allocated (1) in accordance with the manner in which it is reasonably expected that the deductions attributable to those nonrecourse liabilities will be allocated, or (2) to a partner up to the amount of the built-in gain allocable to the partner on section 704(c) property that is in excess of any gain attributable to the liability exceeding the property's basis. Id. See Chapter 4D3, infra.

and B might want to specify that they share partnership profits equally for purposes of allocating the nonrecourse liability to ensure that result. Alternatively, A and B might want to specify some other profits-sharing arrangement (e.g., 60 percent to A and 40 percent to B) for purposes of allocating liabilities, and that arrangement will be respected if it is reasonably consistent with allocations of some other significant item of partnership income or gain that is respected for tax purposes.

*Nonrecourse Liabilities in Excess of Basis.* The analysis changes if contributed property is encumbered by nonrecourse liabilities that exceed the property's adjusted basis. Assume again that in the ongoing example Partner A contributes a parcel of land with a fair market value of $150,000, an adjusted basis of $10,000, and the property is encumbered by a $30,000 nonrecourse liability. Under the Supreme Court's decision in the *Tufts* case,[16] the amount realized by the partnership on the disposition of the land subject to nonrecourse debt includes at least the amount of the debt relief even if the debt exceeds the value of the property. As a result, whenever the partnership disposes of the land contributed by A, the amount realized at least will include the $30,000 of debt relief regardless of the actual value the land. On these facts, where the $30,000 nonrecourse debt exceeds the $10,000 basis of the land, the partnership is assured of recognizing at least $20,000 of gain when it sells the parcel even if its value should plummet, and under section 704(c)(1)(A) that gain must be allocated to contributing partner A. In keeping with the principle that nonrecourse debt is allocated in accordance with the partners' shares of partnership profits, the section 752 regulations provide that a partner who contributes property encumbered by nonrecourse debt is first allocated that portion of the liability equaling the gain that would be allocated to that partner under section 704(c) if the property were sold at the time of the contribution for an amount equal to the liability.[17] The balance of the liability is allocated under the flexible general rule—that is, in accordance with the partners' share of partnership profits.[18]

Applying these rules to the last example, when A contributes land with a basis of $10,000 subject to a $30,000 nonrecourse liability, $20,000 of that liability is allocated to A. The remaining $10,000 of liability is allocated according to A's and B's shares of partnership profits. Assuming they share partnership profits equally, the remaining $10,000 would be allocated $5,000 to each partner. The net effect is that $5,000 of the debt is reallocated from A to B. As a result, A's outside basis is decreased from $10,000 to $5,000,[19] and B's outside basis is increased by $5,000.[20]

## PROBLEMS

**1.** A and B each contribute $30,000 cash to the ABC partnership and C contributes land held for more than one year, worth $60,000 and subject to

---

**16.** Commissioner v. Tufts, supra note 12.

**17.** Reg. § 1.752–3(a)(2).

**18.** Reg. § 1.752–3(a)(3).

**19.** I.R.C. §§ 733; 752(b).

**20.** I.R.C. §§ 722; 752(a).

a recourse debt of $30,000. A, B and C are all general partners with a one-third interest in the profits and losses of ABC.

    (a) What are the tax consequences to A, B, C and ABC if the land has a basis to C of $40,000 and the partnership assumes the debt?

    (b) Same as (a), above, except that the land has a basis to C of $10,000. What could C do to avoid this result?

    (c) Same as (a), above, except that the debt is nonrecourse, and the partners agree that for purposes of allocating nonrecourse liabilities they each have a one-third interest in profits.

    (d) Same as (b), above, except that the debt is nonrecourse and the partners agree that for purposes of allocating nonrecourse liabilities they each have a one-third interest in profits.

**2**. Attorney, a cash method unincorporated sole practitioner, joins a cash method partnership of three other attorneys all of whom own an equal one-quarter interest in the partnership after Attorney joins the firm. Attorney transfers some accounts receivable for services with a zero basis and a $20,000 face value to the partnership as part of her contribution in exchange for her partnership interest. The partnership also assumes $6,000 of Attorney's accounts payable. What are the tax consequences of the transaction to attorney? See § 704(c)(3).

---

## C.  CONTRIBUTIONS OF SERVICES

## 1.  INTRODUCTION

    Section 721 provides nonrecognition of gain or loss only when a partner contributes "property" in exchange for an interest in the partnership. "Property" for this purpose does not include services—and properly so, because they are ephemeral and do not leave behind an identifiable continuing capital investment in the business. A partner who receives a partnership interest in exchange for services, whether they be past, present or future, is being compensated and should realize ordinary income under Section 61(a).[1] In that event, the partner takes a Section 1012 "tax cost" basis in the partnership interest equal to the amount that is included in income.

    The timing of the service partner's income, the valuation of the interest received and the tax consequences to the partnership raise more difficult questions. Because their resolution may turn on the nature of the interest received by the partner, a few definitions are in order at the outset. A service partner may receive a capital interest, which generally is defined as an interest in both the future earnings and the underlying assets (i.e., the "capital") of the partnership. A partner who has a capital interest will be entitled to a share of the partnership's net assets in the event the

---

    **1.**  Prop.Reg. § 1.721–1(b).

partner withdraws or the partnership is liquidated.[2] Alternatively, a partner may receive merely a profits interest, which entitles him to a share of future earnings (including, perhaps, gain on the sale of property) but gives him no current right to a distribution of a share of the partnership's capital in the event of a withdrawal or liquidation.

To illustrate, assume Proprietor, Investor and Manager join forces to form a partnership. Proprietor and Investor each contribute $60,000 but Manager contributes nothing except his agreement to provide needed expertise to the business. The partners agree to share profits and losses equally. If Manager also is credited with a one-third interest in the partnership's capital (⅓ of $120,000, or $40,000), he has received a capital interest, and the other partners have relinquished $20,000 each of their capital accounts—presumably to compensate Manager for his services. But if Manager's capital account is zero, he has received only a "profits interest" and would receive nothing on a subsequent liquidation apart from his share of undistributed earnings of the business.[3]

## 2. RECEIPT OF A CAPITAL INTEREST FOR SERVICES

Code: §§ 83(a)–(c), (h); 721. Skim §§ 706(d)(1); 707(a).

Regulations: § 1.83–6(b).

Proposed Regulations: § 1.721–1(b).

A service partner who receives a capital interest realizes ordinary income in an amount equal to the value of the interest received less the amount, if any, paid for the interest. The timing of that income is determined under Section 83, which broadly applies to all transfers of property in connection with the performance of services. If the interest is received without restrictions, income is realized upon its receipt. But if the interest is transferred subject to substantial restrictions, Section 83(a) provides that its fair market value is included in gross income when the restrictions lapse—i.e., in the first taxable year in which the service partner's rights are "transferable or are not subject to a substantial risk of forfeiture."[1] Thus, a partner whose interest will be forfeited unless he

---

**2.** See Rev.Proc. 93–27, 1993–2 C.B. 343, which defines a capital interest as "an interest that would give the holder a share of the proceeds if the partnership's assets were sold at fair market value and then the proceeds were distributed in a complete liquidation of the partnership." See also Reg. § 1.704–1(e)(1)(v) which, for purposes of the family partnership provisions, defines a "capital interest" as "an interest in the assets of the partnership, which is distributable to the owner of the capital interest upon his withdrawal from the partnership or upon liquidation of the partnership," as distinguished

from a "mere right to participate in the earnings and profits of a partnership * * *".

**3.** The example is no doubt oversimplified because many partnership agreements are ambiguous or silent as to the precise nature of the interest received by a service partner.

**1.** Section 83(c)(1) provides that a person's rights to property are subject to a substantial risk of forfeiture if their full enjoyment is "conditioned upon the future performance of substantial services by any individual." Section 83(c)(2) provides that "[t]he rights of a person in property are

continues to manage the partnership's business for five years may defer any inclusion of income until the interest is free of restrictions. The amount to be included in income is the excess of the fair market value of the interest at the time the partner's rights have vested over the amount, if any, paid for the interest.[2]

A transferee of restricted property is permitted to elect under Section 83(b) to include the value of the property in income at the time of its receipt.[3] If a Section 83(b) election is made, the transferee may not take any deduction (except for the amount actually paid) if the property is subsequently forfeited.[4] The service partner receiving a restricted interest is thus faced with a "gambler's choice." Where a partnership interest has minimal value upon receipt but is expected to appreciate by the time the restrictions lapse, service partners usually are motivated to make the election in the hope that the future appreciation in the property will be taxed at preferential capital gains rates at a later date when the property is sold.

The tax consequences to the service partner are only one side of the transaction. To return to our introductory example, assume that Proprietor and Investor each contribute $60,000 cash to the partnership and Manager, who contributes solely his expertise, receives an unrestricted one-third interest in capital and profits with a value of $40,000. Is the partnership entitled to deduct this $40,000?

One's initial reaction might be to permit the partnership to take a $40,000 ordinary and necessary business deduction, which would flow through to the partners (but which partners?),[5] reducing their distributive share of taxable income or increasing their loss, and in either event also reducing their outside bases under Section 705. But allowance of this deduction depends on the nature of Manager's services. If Manager is the company lawyer who received his interest for services rendered in connection with the formation of the partnership or the construction manager for the partnership's new hotel, an ordinary and necessary deduction for the entire $40,000 would be inappropriate.[6] Rather, the payment to Manager

transferable only if the rights in such property of any transferee are not subject to a substantial risk of forfeiture."

**2.** The Section 83 regulations also provide that property received with substantial restrictions is not regarded as owned by the transferee but rather by the person for whom the services are performed until the restrictions lapse. Reg. § 1.83–1(a)(1). Does that make the service partner a nonpartner until his rights have fully vested? For a discussion of the problems raised by this position, see McKee, Nelson & Whitmire, Federal Taxation of Partnerships and Partners ¶ 5.09 (3d ed. 1996).

**3.** The election must be made within thirty days of the transfer. I.R.C. § 83(b)(2).

**4.** I.R.C. § 83(b)(1), last sentence; Reg. § 1.83–2(a).

**5.** The logical result would be to pass through any deduction connected with the admission of a service partner to the other partners. This approach is supported by Section 706(d)(1) (a provision governing the computation of the partners' distributive shares when there is a change in partnership interests during the year; see Chapter 4E, infra), which would allocate the deduction to the other partners because the expense was incurred prior to the service partner's admission to the partnership. This result could be assured by a special allocation in the partnership agreement. See I.R.C. § 704(b).

**6.** The attorney's fee is an organiza-

would be a capital expenditure, and the partnership's deduction must be partially or totally deferred despite any realization of income by the partner.[7]

The transfer of a capital interest for services also may cause the partnership to recognize gain. Suppose, for example, that Manager receives a one-third capital interest in a partnership previously formed by Proprietor and Investor, and the partnership's sole asset is land with a value of $120,000 and an adjusted basis of $45,000. The transfer of the capital interest to Manager likely is viewed as a two-step transaction: (1) the transfer of a one-third undivided interest in the land from the partnership to Manager as compensation for his services and (2) the contribution of that interest back to the partnership by Manager. The first step involves the transfer of appreciated property (i.e., a one-third interest in the land, having a basis of $15,000 and a value of $40,000) in a Section 83 compensatory transfer to Manager and thus is a taxable event resulting in $25,000 of capital gain to the partnership (i.e., to Proprietor and Investor).[8] The second step is a tax-free contribution of Manager's $40,000 interest in the land back to the partnership under Section 721, and Manager's $40,000 "tax cost" basis is transferred to the partnership under Section 723.[9]

The preceding example involved the transfer of a capital interest to a partner in exchange for past or future services rendered to an ongoing partnership. The *McDougal* case, which follows, illustrates that the tax

tional expense, the first $5,000 of which could be deducted and the remainder of which would be amortizable over 180 months if the partnership so elects under Section 709(b). See Section D of this chapter, infra. Amounts paid to the construction manager would be capitalized and added to the partnership's basis in the building. Cf. Commissioner v. Idaho Power Co., 418 U.S. 1, 94 S.Ct. 2757 (1974).

**7.** This result is required by Reg. § 1.83–6(a)(4), which provides that no deduction is allowed under Section 83(h) to the extent that a transfer of property constitutes a capital expenditure or an item of deferred expense. If the service partner's interest is subject to substantial restrictions, any deduction allowable to the partnership is determined at the time the service partner recognizes income. See I.R.C. § 83(h); Reg. § 1.83–6(a)(4).

**8.** Reg. § 1.83–6(b); cf. United States v. Davis, 370 U.S. 65, 82 S.Ct. 1190 (1962), rehearing denied, 371 U.S. 854, 83 S.Ct. 14 (1962) (the transfer of property to satisfy an obligation constitutes a taxable disposition). The leading treatises agree that a partnership must recognize gain in this situation. McKee, Nelson & Whitmire, Federal Taxa-

tion of Partnerships and Partners ¶ 5.08[2][b] (3d ed. 1996); Willis, Pennell & Postlewaite, Partnership Taxation § 45.08 (4th ed. 1989). See also Gergen, "Pooling or Exchange: The Taxation of Joint Ventures Between Labor and Capital," 44 Tax L.Rev. 519 (1989). For a contrary view, see Gunn, "Partnership Interest for Services: Partnership Gain and Loss?" 47 Tax Notes 699 (May 7, 1990).

**9.** To preserve their equal one-third partnership arrangement and prevent the shifting of taxable gain to Manager, the partnership also should ensure that the remaining $50,000 appreciation in the land at the time Manager becomes a partner will be allocated to Proprietor and Investor when the property is sold. This may be accomplished by applying the principles of Section 704(c) in the context of a special allocation of the built-in gain under Section 704(b). Absent such an agreement, the gain would be shared equally among the three partners and would upset the equality of their capital accounts. See Reg. § 1.704–1(b)(2)(iv)*(f)(5)(iii)*, Reg. § 1.704–1(b)(5) Example (14)(i)–(iv), and Chapter 4C4, infra. The shifting of capital interests among the partners could have other tax consequences. See Reg. § 1.704–1(b)(1)(iii) & (iv).

consequences are similar when a partner receives a capital interest in a newly formed partnership in exchange for past services rendered. In reading *McDougal,* consider what steps the parties might have taken to minimize the adverse tax consequences that resulted upon the formation of the partnership.

# McDougal v. Commissioner

United States Tax Court, 1974.
62 T.C. 720.

■ FAY, JUDGE. * * *

FINDINGS OF FACT

Certain facts have been stipulated by the parties and are found accordingly. The stipulation of facts and exhibits attached thereto are incorporated herein by this reference.

F. C. and Frankie McDougal are husband and wife, as are Gilbert and Jackie McClanahan. Each couple filed joint Federal income tax returns for the years 1968 and 1969 with the district director of internal revenue in Austin, Tex. Petitioners were all residents of Berino, N. Mex., when they filed their petitions with this Court.

F. C. and Frankie McDougal maintained farms at Lamesa, Tex., where they were engaged in the business of breeding and racing horses. Gilbert McClanahan was a licensed public horse trainer who rendered his services to various horse owners for a standard fee. He had numbered the McDougals among his clientele since 1965.

On February 21, 1965, a horse of exceptional pedigree, Iron Card, had been foaled at the Anthony Ranch in Florida. Title to Iron Card was acquired in January of 1967 by one Frank Ratliff, Jr., who in turn transferred title to himself, M. H. Ratliff, and John V. Burnett (Burnett). The Ratliffs and Burnett entered Iron Card in several races as a 2–year-old; and although the horse enjoyed some success in these contests, it soon became evident that he was suffering from a condition diagnosed by a veterinarian as a protein allergy.

When, due to a dispute among themselves, the Ratliffs and Burnett decided to sell Iron Card for whatever price he could attract, McClanahan (who had trained the horse for the Ratliffs and Burnett) advised the McDougals to make the purchase. He made this recommendation because, despite the veterinarian's prognosis to the contrary, McClanahan believed that by the use of home remedy Iron Card could be restored to full racing vigor. Furthermore, McClanahan felt that as Iron Card's allergy was not genetic and as his pedigree was impressive, he would be valuable in the future as a stud even if further attempts to race him proved unsuccessful.

The McDougals purchased Iron Card for $10,000 on January 1, 1968. At the time of the purchase McDougal promised that if McClanahan trained and attended to Iron Card, a half interest in the horse would be his

once the McDougals had recovered the costs and expenses of acquisition. This promise was not made in lieu of payment of the standard trainer's fee; for from January 1, 1968, until the date of the transfer, McClanahan was paid $2,910 as compensation for services rendered as Iron Card's trainer.

McClanahan's home remedy proved so effective in relieving Iron Card of his allergy that the horse began to race with success, and his reputation consequently grew to such proportion that he attracted a succession of offers to purchase, one of which reached $60,000. The McDougals decided, however, to keep the horse and by October 4, 1968, had recovered out of their winnings the costs of acquiring him. It was therefore on that date that they transferred a half interest in the horse to McClanahan in accordance with the promise which McDougal had made to the trainer. A document entitled "Bill of Sale," wherein the transfer was described as a gift, was executed on the following day.

Iron Card continued to race well until very late in 1968 when, without warning and for an unascertained cause, he developed a condition called "hot ankle" which effectively terminated his racing career. From 1970 onward he was used exclusively for breeding purposes. That his value as a stud was no less than his value as a racehorse is attested to by the fact that in September of 1970 petitioners were offered $75,000 for him; but after considering the offer, the McDougals and McClanahan decided to refuse it, preferring to exploit Iron Card's earning potential as a stud to their own profit.

On November 1, 1968, petitioners had concluded a partnership agreement by parol to effectuate their design of racing the horse for as long as that proved feasible and of offering him out as a stud thereafter. Profits were to be shared equally by the McDougals and the McClanahans, while losses were to be allocated to the McDougals alone.

\* \* \*

OPINION

Respondent contends that the McDougals did not recognize a $25,000 gain on the transaction of October 4, 1968, and that they were not entitled to claim a $30,000 business expense deduction by reason thereof. He further contends that were Iron Card to be contributed to a partnership or joint venture under the circumstances obtaining in the instant case, its basis in Iron Card at the time of contribution would have been limited by the McDougals' cost basis in the horse, as adjusted. Respondent justifies these contentions by arguing that the transfer of October 4, 1968, constituted a gift.

In the alternative, respondent has urged us to find that at some point in time no later than the transfer of October 4, 1968, McDougal and McClanahan entered into a partnership or joint venture to which the McDougals contributed Iron Card and McClanahan contributed services. Respondent contends that such a finding would require our holding that the McDougals did not recognize a gain on the transfer of October 4, 1968,

by reason of section 721, and that under section 723 the joint venture's basis in Iron Card at the time of the contribution was equal to the McDougals' adjusted basis in the horse as of that time.

We dismiss at the outset respondent's contention that the transfer of October 4, 1968, constituted a gift, and we are undeterred in so doing by the fact that petitioners originally characterized the transfer as a gift, Bogardus v. Commissioner, 302 U.S. 34 (1937). A gift has been defined as a transfer motivated by detached and disinterested generosity, Commissioner v. Duberstein, 363 U.S. 278 (1960). The presence of such motivation is belied in this instance by two factors. The relationship of the parties concerned was essentially of a business nature, and the transfer itself was made conditional upon the outcome of an enterprise which McDougal had undertaken at McClanahan's suggestion and in reliance upon McClanahan's ability to render it profitable. These factors instead bespeak the presence of an arm's-length transaction.

With respect to respondent's alternative contention, we note firstly that the law provides no rule easy of application for making a determination as to whether a partnership or joint venture has been formed but rather directs our attention to a congeries of factors relevant to the issue, of which none is conclusive, Hubert M. Luna, 42 T.C. 1067 (1964).

A joint venture is deemed to arise when two or more persons agree, expressly or impliedly, to enter actively upon a specific business enterprise, the purpose of which is the pursuit of profit; the ownership of whose productive assets and of the profits generated by them is shared; the parties to which all bear the burden of any loss; and the management of which is not confined to a single participant, * * * .

While in the case at bar the risk of loss was to be borne by the McDougals alone, all the other elements of a joint venture were present once the transfer of October 4, 1968, had been effected. Accordingly, we hold that the aforesaid transfer constituted the formation of a joint venture to which the McDougals contributed capital in the form of the horse, Iron Card, and in which they granted McClanahan an interest equal to their own in capital and profits as compensation for his having trained Iron Card. We further hold that the agreement formally entered into on November 1, 1968, and reduced to writing in April of 1970, constituted a continuation of the original joint venture under section 708(b)(2)(A). Furthermore, that McClanahan continued to receive a fee for serving as Iron Card's trainer after October 4, 1968, in no way militates against the soundness of this holding. See sec. 707(c), and sec. 1.707–1(c), example 1, Income Tax Regs. However, this holding does not result in the tax consequences which respondent has contended would follow from it. See sec. 1.721–1(b)(1), Income Tax Regs.

When on the formation of a joint venture a party contributing appreciated assets satisfies an obligation by granting his obligee a capital interest in the venture, he is deemed first to have transferred to the obligee an undivided interest in the assets contributed, equal in value to the amount

of the obligation so satisfied. He and the obligee are deemed thereafter and in concert to have contributed those assets to the joint venture.

The contributing obligor will recognize gain on the transaction to the extent that the value of the undivided interest which he is deemed to have transferred exceeds his basis therein. The obligee is considered to have realized an amount equal to the fair market value of the interest which he receives in the venture and will recognize income depending upon the character of the obligation satisfied.[12] The joint venture's basis in the assets will be determined under section 723 in accordance with the foregoing assumptions. Accordingly, we hold that the transaction under consideration constituted an exchange in which the McDougals realized $30,000, United States v. Davis, 370 U.S. 65 (1962); Kenan v. Commissioner, 114 F.2d 217 (C.A.2, 1940), affirming 40 B.T.A. 824 (1939).

In determining the basis offset to which the McDougals are entitled with respect to the transfer of October 4, 1968, we note the following: that the McDougals had an unadjusted cost basis in Iron Card of $10,000; that they had claimed $1,390 in depreciation on the entire horse for the period January 1 to October 31, 1968; and that after an agreement of partnership was concluded on November 1, 1968, depreciation on Iron Card was deducted by the partnership exclusively.

Section 704(c) [pre–1984. Ed.] allows partners and joint venturers some freedom in determining who is to claim the deductions for depreciation on contributed property. As is permissible under the statute, petitioners clearly intended the depreciation to be claimed by the common enterprise once it had come into existence, an event which they considered to have occurred on November 1, 1968. Consistent with their intent and with our own holding that a joint venture arose on October 4, 1968, we now further hold that the McDougals were entitled to claim depreciation on Iron Card only until the transfer of October 4, 1968. Thereafter depreciation on Iron Card ought to have been deducted by the joint venture in the computation of its taxable income.

In determining their adjusted basis in the portion of Iron Card on whose disposition they are required to recognize gain, the McDougals charged all the depreciation which they had taken on the horse against their basis in the half in which they retained an interest. This procedure was improper. As in accordance with section 1.167(g)–1, Income Tax Regs., we have allowed the McDougals a depreciation deduction with respect to Iron Card for the period January 1 to October 4, 1968, computed on their entire cost basis in the horse of $10,000; so also do we require that the said deduction be charged against that entire cost basis under section 1016(a)(2)(A).

---

**12.** For example, if the obligation arose out of a loan, the obligee will recognize no income by reason of the transaction; if the obligation represents the selling price of a capital asset, he will recognize a capital gain to the extent that the amount he is deemed to have realized exceeds his adjusted basis in the asset; if the obligation represents compensation for services, the transaction will result in ordinary income to the obligee in an amount equal to the value of the interest which he received in the joint venture.

As the McDougals were in the business of racing horses, any gain recognized by them on the exchange of Iron Card in satisfaction of a debt would be characterized under section 1231(a) provided he had been held by them for the period requisite under section 1231(b) as it applies to livestock acquired before 1970. In that as of October 4, 1968, Iron Card had been used by the McDougals exclusively for racing and not for breeding, we do now hold that they had held him for a period sufficiently long to make section 1231(a) applicable to their gain on the transaction. This is the case although the McDougals may have intended eventually to use Iron Card for breeding purposes, Anderson Fowler, 37 T.C. 1124 (1962).

The joint venture's basis in Iron Card as of October 4, 1968, must be determined under section 723 in accordance with the principles of law set forth earlier in this opinion. In the half interest in the horse which it is deemed to have received from the McDougals, the joint venture had a basis equal to one-half of the McDougals' adjusted cost basis in Iron Card as of October 4, 1968, i.e., the excess of $5,000 over one-half of the depreciation which the McDougals were entitled to claim on Iron Card for the period January 1 to October 4, 1968. In the half interest which the venture is considered to have received from McClanahan, it can claim to have had a basis equal to the amount which McClanahan is considered to have realized on the transaction, $30,000. The joint venture's deductions for depreciation on Iron Card for the years 1968 and 1969 are to be determined on the basis computed in the above-described manner.

When an interest in a joint venture is transferred as compensation for services rendered, any deduction which may be authorized under section 162(a)(1) by reason of that transfer is properly claimed by the party to whose benefit the services accrued, be that party the venture itself or one or more venturers, sec. 1.721–1(b)(2), Income Tax Regs. Prior to McClanahan's receipt of his interest, a joint venture did not exist under the facts of the case at bar; the McDougals were the sole owners of Iron Card and recipients of his earnings. Therefore, they alone could have benefited from the services rendered by McClanahan prior to October 4, 1968, for which he was compensated by the transaction of that date. Accordingly, we hold that the McDougals are entitled to a business expense deduction of $30,000, that amount being the value of the interest which McClanahan received. Respondent has contended that a deduction of $30,000 would be unreasonable in amount in view of the nature of the services for which McClanahan was being compensated. But having found that the transaction under consideration was not a gift but rather was occasioned by a compensation arrangement which was entered upon at arm's length, we must reject this contention. See sec. 1.162–7(b)(2), Income Tax Regs.

* * *

## PROBLEM

C is offered a capital interest in a partnership whose sole asset is a commercial building with a fair market value of $150,000 and an adjusted

basis of $90,000. The building has been depreciated on the straight line method. A and B have $45,000 outside bases in their respective partnership interests. C has performed real estate management services for the partnership over the past year and has agreed to perform additional services in the future.

(a) What are the tax consequences to C and to the partnership (i.e., A and B) if in year one C receives a one-tenth capital interest in the partnership as compensation for his management services over the past year?

(b) What result in (a), above, if C receives his capital interest in exchange for legal services performed in connection with the acquisition of the building?

(c) What result in (a), above, if C receives his interest as compensation for services to be rendered in the succeeding three years provided, however, that if C ceases to render services before the end of year three, C or any transferee of C must relinquish his interest in the partnership. Assume for this problem that the building will have a value of $450,000 and an adjusted basis of $90,000 at the end of year three.

(d) What result in (a), above, if C is promised that if he renders services until the end of year three, the partnership interest will be transferred to him at that time? Again assume that the building will have a value of $450,000 and an adjusted basis of $90,000 at the end of year three.

## 3.   RECEIPT OF A PROFITS INTEREST FOR SERVICES

Regulations: § 1.83–3(e).

Proposed Regulations: § 1.721–1(b).

The principles considered above would seem to apply to the receipt of a profits interest for services. Returning to the example in the preceding section, if Manager receives only an interest in the future profits of the partnership, he nonetheless is being compensated for his services and theoretically has realized ordinary income. But what is the value of his interest, which measures the *amount* of his income? And should the income be considered realized at the time the interest is received, when the amount is speculative, or only when the profits are actually earned by the partnership? If the interest is taxed upon its receipt, will the service partner be taxed again when the profits are actually earned? And does it matter whether the service provider receives the interest for past or future services, or in what capacity (e.g., partner or employee) those services were performed? Because of the practical problems raised by these questions, it had long been assumed that the receipt of a profits interest was not a taxable event.[1] Rather, as the Tax Court suggests in footnote 3 of the *Hale*

---

**1.** See Gergen, "Pooling or Exchange: The Taxation of Joint Ventures Between Labor and Capital," 44 Tax L.Rev. 519 (1989), which analyzes the Code's treatment of exchanges of labor for capital.

case below, it seemed preferable to keep the transaction open and tax the service partner on his share of the profits as they were earned.

# Hale v. Commissioner

Tax Court of the United States, 1965.
24 T.C.M. 1497.

■ FAY, JUDGE. * * *

The first issue for decision involves the sale by Hale Co. of 90 percent of its partnership interest in Walnut Co. to D–K.

Hale Co. received for its contribution of future services to Walnut Co. a right as a partner to participate in Walnut Co.'s future profits.[3] Hale Co. sold 90 percent of said right or interest to D–K before receiving any income from Walnut Co.[4] The question before us concerns the nature of the amount received on the sale.

Petitioners argue that the gain received in the foregoing sale is a capital gain since (1) a right to share in income may constitute a partnership interest and (2) a partnership interest is generally a capital asset.

There is, however, authority for the proposition that a gain on the transfer of property technically qualifying as a capital asset (i.e., property) may be treated as ordinary income if it is in effect an anticipation of future income. See Hort v. Commissioner, 313 U.S. 28 (1941). We believe that this reasoning applies to deny capital gain treatment on Hale Co.'s sale of its partnership interest in Walnut Co.'s future profits.

Walnut Co. was created for the express purpose of developing a specific tract of land and selling the houses which it would construct thereon. Upon completion of the project and final sale of all the houses, Walnut Co. would cease to function. At the time of the sale, 111 of such houses were in existence, 39 of which were the subject of a deposit receipt or purchase agreement. Moreover, at such time the profit on each house could reasonably be estimated (although, of course, it could not be foreseen when the houses would be sold and how many would be sold).

The purposes of section 1221 were (1) "to relieve the taxpayer from * * * excessive burdens on gains resulting from a conversion of capital investments," and (2) "to remove the deterrent effect of those burdens on such conversions." See Commissioner v. P. G. Lake, Inc., 356 U.S. 260 (1958). This exception has always been narrowly construed. See Corn Products Co. v. Commissioner, 350 U.S. 46, 52 (1955).

We do not see here any conversion of a capital investment. The substance of what was assigned was the right to receive future income. The

---

**3.** Under the regulations, the mere receipt of a partnership interest in future profits does not create any tax liability. Sec. 1.721–(1)(b), Income Tax Regs.

**4.** At the time of the transaction involved herein, Walnut Co. had no profits.

lump sum consideration seems essentially the present value of income which the recipient, Hale Co., would otherwise obtain in the future as ordinary income. *Commissioner v. P. G. Lake, Inc.*, supra. Therefore, we are of the opinion that Hale Co. realized ordinary income on the transaction in issue as if it had received such income directly from Walnut Co. See *Commissioner v. P. G. Lake, Inc.*, supra.

\* \* \*

NOTE

Nine years after the *Hale* case was decided, along came Sol Diamond, whose clumsy attempt to convert ordinary income to capital gain on a routine real estate venture called the conventional wisdom into question. The Tax Court, affirmed by the Seventh Circuit in the opinion below, held that a service partner is currently taxable on receipt of a profits interest—provided that the interest is susceptible of valuation at the time of its receipt. In reading the *Diamond* opinion, consider whether Mr. Diamond was in fact a partner and whether the court might have reached the same result on narrower grounds.

# Diamond v. Commissioner

United States Court of Appeals, Seventh Circuit, 1974.
492 F.2d 286.

■ Fairchild, Circuit Judge.

This is an appeal from a decision of the Tax Court upholding the commissioner's assessment of deficiencies against Sol and Muriel Diamond for the years 1961 and 1962. The deficiencies for each year were consolidated for trial, but are essentially unrelated. The Tax Court concluded that Diamond realized ordinary income on the receipt of a right to a share of profit or loss to be derived from a real estate venture (the 1962 partnership case) \* \* \*. The facts in both cases appear in Diamond v. Commissioner, 56 T.C. 530 (1971). Unnecessary repetitions will be avoided.

*The 1962 Partnership Case*

During 1961, Diamond was a mortgage broker. Philip Kargman had acquired for $25,000 the buyer's rights in a contract for the sale of an office building. Kargman asked Diamond to obtain a mortgage loan for the full $1,100,000 purchase price of the building. Diamond and Kargman agreed that Diamond would receive a 60% share of profit or loss of the venture if he arranged the financing.

Diamond succeeded in obtaining a $1,100,000 mortgage loan from Marshall Savings and Loan. On December 15, 1961 Diamond and Kargman entered into an agreement which provided:

(1) The two were associated as joint venturers for 24 years (the life of the mortgage) unless earlier terminated by agreement or by sale;

(2) Kargman was to advance all cash needed for the purchase beyond the loan proceeds;

(3) Profits and losses would be divided, 40% to Kargman, 60% to Diamond;

(4) In event of sale, proceeds would be devoted first to repayment to Kargman of money supplied by him, and net profits thereafter would be divided 40% to Kargman, 60% to Diamond.

Early in 1962, Kargman and Diamond created an Illinois land trust to hold title to the property. The chief motivation for the land trust arrangement was apparently to insulate Diamond and Kargman from personal liability on the mortgage note.

The purchase proceeded as planned and closing took place on February 18, 1962. Kargman made cash outlays totalling $78,195.33 in connection with the purchase. Thus, under the terms of the agreement, the property would have to appreciate at least $78,195.33 before Diamond would have any equity in it.

Shortly after closing, it was proposed that Diamond would sell his interest and one Liederman would be substituted, except on a 50–50 basis. Liederman persuaded Diamond to sell his interest for $40,000. This sale was effectuated on March 8, 1962 by Diamond assigning his interest to Kargman for $40,000. Kargman in turn then conveyed a similar interest, except for 50–50 sharing, to Liederman for the same amount.

On their 1962 joint return, the Diamonds reported the March 8, 1962 $40,000 sale proceeds as a short term capital gain. This gain was offset by an unrelated short term capital loss. They reported no tax consequences from the February 18 receipt of the interest in the venture. Diamond's position is that his receipt of this type of interest in partnership is not taxable income although received in return for services. He relies on § 721 and Reg. § 1.721–1(b)(1). He further argues that the subsequent sale of this interest produced a capital gain under § 741. The Tax Court held that the receipt of this type of interest in partnership in return for services is not within § 721 and is taxable under § 61 when received. The Tax Court valued the interest at $40,000 as of February 18, as evidenced by the sale for that amount three weeks later, on March 8.

Both the taxpayer and the Tax Court treated the venture as a partnership and purported to apply partnership income tax principles. It has been suggested that the record might have supported findings that there was in truth an employment or other relationship, other than partnership, and produced a similar result, but these findings were not made. See Cowan, The Diamond Case, 27 Tax Law Review 161 (1972). It has also been suggested (and argued, alternatively, by the government) that although on the face of the agreement Diamond appeared to receive only a right to share in profit (loss) to be derived, the value of the real estate may well have been substantially greater than the purchase price, so that Diamond may really have had an interest in capital, if the assets were properly valued. This finding was not made. The Tax Court, 56 T.C. at 547, n. 16,

suggested the possibility that Diamond would not in any event be entitled to capital gains treatment of his sale of a right to receive income in the future, but did not decide the question.[3]

Taking matters at face value, taxpayer received, on February 18, an interest in partnership, limited to a right to a share of profit (loss) to be derived. In discussion we shall refer to this interest either as his interest in partnership or a profit-share.

The Tax Court, with clearly adequate support, found that Diamond's interest in partnership had a market value of $40,000 on February 18. Taxpayer's analysis is that under the regulations the receipt of a profit-share February 18, albeit having a market value and being conferred in return for services, was not a taxable event, and that the entire proceeds of the March 8 sale were a capital gain. The Tax Court analysis was that the interest in partnership, albeit limited to a profit-share, was property worth $40,000, and taxpayer's acquisition, thereof on February 18 was compensation for services and ordinary income. Assuming that capital gain treatment at sale would have been appropriate, there was no gain because the sale was for the same amount.

There is no statute or regulation which expressly and particularly prescribes the income tax effect, or absence of one, at the moment a partner receives a profit-share in return for services. The Tax Court's holding rests upon the general principle that a valuable property interest received in return for services is compensation, and income. Taxpayer's argument is predicated upon an implication which his counsel, and others, have found in Reg. § 1.721–1(1)(b), but which need not, and the government argues should not, be found there.

26 U.S.C. § 721 is entitled "Nonrecognition of gain or loss on contribution," and provides: "No gain or loss shall be recognized to a partnership or to any of its partners in the case of a contribution of property to the partnership in exchange for an interest in the partnership." Only if, by a strained construction, "property" were said to include services, would § 721 say anything about the effect of furnishing services. It clearly deals with a contribution like Kargman's of property, and prescribes that when he contributed his property, no gain or loss was recognized. It does not, of course, explicitly say that no income accrues to one who renders services and, in return, becomes a partner with a profit-share.

Reg. § 1.721–1 presumably explains and interprets § 721, perhaps to the extent of qualifying or limiting its meaning. Subsec. (b)(1), particularly relied on here, reads in part as follows:

> "Normally, under local law, each partner is entitled to be repaid
> his contributions of money or other property to the partnership (at
> the value placed upon such property by the partnership at the time
> of the contribution) whether made at the formation of the partner-
> ship or subsequent thereto. To the extent that any of the partners

---

**3.** Because of the decision we reach, it is also unnecessary for us to consider this possibility and we express no conclusions concerning it.

gives up any part of his right to be repaid his contributions (as distinguished from a share in partnership profits) in favor of another partner as compensation for services (or in satisfaction of an obligation), section 721 does not apply. The value of an interest in such partnership capital so transferred to a partner as compensation for services constitutes income to the partner under section 61. * * * ''

The quoted portion of the regulation may well be read, like § 721, as being directly addressed only to the consequences of a contribution of money or other property. It asserts that when a partner making such contributions transfers to another some part of the contributing partner's right to be repaid, in order to compensate the other for services or to satisfy an obligation to the other, § 721 does not apply, there is recognition of gain or loss to the contributing partner, and there is income to the partner who receives, as compensation for services, part of the right to be repaid.

The regulation does not specify that if a partner contributing property agrees that, in return for services, another shall be a partner with a profit-share only, the value of the profit-share is not income to the recipient. An implication to that effect, such as is relied on by taxpayer, would have to rest on the proposition that the regulation was meant to be all inclusive as to when gain or loss would be recognized or income would exist as a consequence of the contribution of property to a partnership and disposition of the partnership interests. It would have to appear, in order to sustain such implication, that the existence of income by reason of a creation of a profit-share, immediately having a determinable market value, in favor of a partner would be inconsistent with the result specified in the regulation.

We do not find this implication in our own reading of the regulation. It becomes necessary to consider the substantial consensus of commentators in favor of the principle claimed to be implied and to look to judicial interpretation, legislative history, administrative interpretation, and policy considerations to determine whether the implication is justified.

*The Commentators:* There is a startling degree of unanimity that the conferral of a profit-share as compensation for services is not income at the time of the conferral, although little by way of explanation of why this should be so, or analysis of statute or regulation to show that it is prescribed. See publications cited pp. 181–2 of Cowan, The Diamond Case.[4]

One of the most unequivocal statements, with an explanation in terms of practicality or policy, was made by Arthur Willis in a text:

"However obliquely the proposition is stated in the regulations, it is clear that a partner who receives only an interest in future profits of the partnership as compensation for services is

---

**4.** See also Halperin & Tucker, Low Income Housing (FHA 236) Programs: One of Few Tax Shelter Opportunities Left, 36 J. Taxation 2, 5–6 (1972); Research Institute of America, Tax Coordinator B–1210.1, Developments 15,010; Surrey & Warren, Federal Income Taxation: Cases and Materials (1964 Supp. to 1960 ed.), p. 146.

not required to report the receipt of his partnership interest as taxable income. The rationale is twofold. In the first place, the present value of a right to participate in future profits is usually too conjectural to be subject to valuation. In the second place, the service partner is taxable on his distributive share of partnership income as it is realized by the partnership. If he were taxed on the present value of the right to receive his share of future partnership income, either he would be taxed twice, or the value of his right to participate in partnership income must be amortized over some period of time."[5]

*Judicial Interpretation:* Except for one statement by the Tax Court no decision cited by the parties or found by us appears squarely to reach the question, either on principle in the absence of the regulations, or by application of the regulations. In a footnote in Herman M. Hale, 24 T.C.M. 1497, 1502 (1965) the Tax Court said: "Under the regulations, the mere receipt of a partnership interest in future profits does not create any tax liability. Sec. 1.721–1(b), Income Tax Regs." There was no explanation of how this conclusion was derived from the regulations.

*Legislative History:* The legislative history is equivocal.

An advisory group appointed in 1956 to review the regulations evidently felt concern about whether the provision of Reg. § 1.721–1 that the value of an interest in capital transferred to a partner in compensation for services constitutes income had a statutory basis in the light of § 721 providing that there shall be no recognition of gain or loss in the case of a contribution of property. The group proposed enactment of a new section to provide such basis, and legislation introduced into the 86th Congress in 1959 incorporated this recommendation. The bill, H.R. 9662, would have created a new § 770 providing specifically for the taxation of a person receiving an interest in partnership capital in exchange for the performance of services for the partnership. However, neither proposed § 770 nor anything else in H.R. 9662 dealt with the receipt merely of a profit-share. The lack of concern over an income tax impact when only a profit-share was conferred might imply an opinion that such conferring of a profit-share would not be taxable under any circumstances, or might imply an opinion that it would be income or not under § 61 depending upon whether it had a determinable market value or not.

Several statements in the course of the hearings and committee reports paralleled the first parenthetical phrase in Reg. § 1.721–1(b) and were to the effect that the provision did not apply where a person received only a profit-share.[6] There was, however, at least one specific statement by the chairman of the advisory group (Mr. Willis) that if the service partner "were to receive merely an interest in future profits in exchange for his services, he would have no immediate taxable gain because he would be

---

**5.** Willis on Partnership Taxation 84–85 (1971). See Cowan, The Diamond Case, 27 Tax Law Review 181 n. 56 (1972).

**6.** See, e.g., Senate Rep. No. 1616, 86th Cong., 2d Sess. 117 (1960).

taxed on his share of income as it was earned."[7] H.R. 9662 passed the House of Representatives, and was favorably reported to the Senate by its finance committee, but never came to a vote in the Senate. Even had the bill become law, it would not have dealt expressly with the problem at hand.

*Administrative Interpretation:* We are unaware of instances in which the Commissioner has asserted delinquencies where a taxpayer who received a profit-share with determinable market value in return for services failed to report the value as income, or has otherwise acted consistently with the Tax Court decision in *Diamond*. Although the consensus referred to earlier appears to exist, the Commissioner has not by regulation or otherwise acted affirmatively to reject it, and in a sense might be said to have agreed by silence.

*Consideration of partnership principles or practices:* There must be wide variation in the degree to which a profit-share created in favor of a partner who has or will render service has determinable market value at the moment of creation. Surely in many if not the typical situations it will have only speculative value, if any.

In the present case, taxpayer's services had all been rendered, and the prospect of earnings from the real estate under Kargman's management was evidently very good. The profit-share had determinable market value.

If the present decision be sound, then the question will always arise, whenever a profit-share is created or augmented, whether it has a market value capable of determination. Will the existence of this question be unduly burdensome on those who choose to do business under the partnership form?

Each partner determines his income tax by taking into account his distributive share of the taxable income of the partnership. 26 U.S.C. § 702. Taxpayer's position here is that he was entitled to defer income taxation on the compensation for his services except as partnership earnings were realized. If a partner is taxed on the determinable market value of a profit-share at the time it is created in his favor, and is also taxed on his full share of earnings as realized, there will arguably be double taxation, avoidable by permitting him to amortize the value which was originally treated as income. Does the absence of a recognized procedure for amortization militate against the treatment of the creation of the profit-share as income?

Do the disadvantages of treating the creation of the profit-share as income in those instances where it has a determinable market value at that time outweigh the desirability of imposing a tax at the time the taxpayer has received an interest with determinable market value as compensation for services?

7. See Hearings on Advisory Group Recommendations on Subchapters C, J, and K of the Internal Revenue Code before the House Comm. on Ways and Means, 86th Cong., 1st Sess. 53 (1959).

We think, of course, that the resolution of these practical questions makes clearly desirable the promulgation of appropriate regulations, to achieve a degree of certainty. But in the absence of regulation, we think it sound policy to defer to the expertise of the Commissioner and the Judges of the Tax Court, and to sustain their decision that the receipt of a profit-share with determinable market value is income.

\* \* \*

NOTE

*The Scope of Diamond.* The scope of *Diamond* has been widely debated. Although the decision reasonably can be read to apply whenever a service partner receives a profits interest that is readily susceptible of valuation, the facts of the case suggest a narrower holding. The Seventh Circuit assumed that Diamond received an interest in future partnership profits. Several weeks after receiving the interest, however, Diamond sold it for $40,000. This indicates that whatever he received was initially worth $40,000—that is, it was really a *capital* interest, which everyone agrees is taxable. It is likely that the building was worth more than the $1,100,000 option price, and what Diamond actually received was an interest of 60 percent of any amount realized in excess of that $1,100,000 plus Kargman's $80,000 cash investment. It also is significant that Diamond received his interest for past services rendered for Kargman, not future services to be performed for the partnership. Indeed, there is some question whether Diamond was even a partner.

*Subsequent Developments.* Since the opinion in *Diamond* was far from narrow, the case shocked the tax bar, which routinely had been advising clients that the receipt of a profits interest for services was not a taxable event. After making the obligatory calls to their malpractice carriers, partnership tax specialists authored reams of commentary urging the Service to reconsider its position, or at least narrow the *Diamond* holding.[1] In the ensuing debate, Section 83 assumed center stage. Recall that Section 83, which was enacted after the taxable year in *Diamond,* applies to any transfer of "property" (whether or not subject to restrictions) in connection with the performance of services. For this purpose, the regulations define "property" to include all real and personal property, excluding only money or "an unfunded and unsecured promise to pay money or property in the future."[2] The Section 83 regulations make no reference to partnership interests, or to property received in a partner capacity. But in view of the sweeping definition of "property" and the Congressional policy to include all forms of nonmonetary compensation within the scope of Section 83, it seemed theoretically correct, albeit impractical and unwise from a policy

**1.** The leading article was Cowan, "Receipt of an Interest in Partnership Profits in Consideration for Services: The *Diamond* Case," 27 Tax L.Rev. 161 (1972). See also Lane, "Sol Diamond: The Tax Court Upsets the Service Partner," 46 S.Cal.L.Rev. 239 (1973).

**2.** Reg. § 1.83–3(e).

standpoint, to treat a profits interest as Section 83 "property."[3] The pro-taxpayer commentators argued that a profits interest, being contingent on the future economic success of the partnership, is tantamount to an "unfunded and unsecured promise to pay money or property in the future." They pointed to the practical problems of timing and valuation that would result from extending Section 83 to service partners and urged that the revenue would be adequately protected by taxing the service partner on the profits as they are earned.[4]

The Service's initial response to *Diamond* was a mix of ambiguity and ambivalence. While the case was pending, it issued proposed regulations under Section 721 which obliquely imply that the receipt of a profits interest may not be a taxable event by providing that transfers of *capital* interests for services do come within Section 83 while remaining silent on the status of a profits interest as Section 83 "property."[5]

The Service later intimated, in an internal Chief Counsel's legal memorandum, that it would not follow *Diamond* to the extent that it held that the receipt of an interest in future partnership profits as compensation was a taxable event.[6] Tax advisors also were reassured by the few cases decided after *Diamond*, where the courts generally held that, whether or not Section 83 applied, a profits interest received for services had no value for tax purposes because the taxpayer would not be entitled to any interest in partnership capital on liquidation and the future profits of the partnership were speculative.[7]

This period of calm was abruptly interrupted in 1990 when the Tax Court held in Campbell v. Commissioner[8] that the receipt of profits interests in real estate limited partnerships by a taxpayer who had performed services for the syndicator of the ventures was taxable even though the taxpayer would not have been entitled to receive anything of value on an immediate liquidation of his interest. The court valued the interests by looking to the present value of the projected future tax benefits and cash distributions of the partnerships. On appeal, the Eighth Circuit reversed, holding that the profits interests had no value because the projected future benefits were wholly speculative.[9] The court of appeals decision in *Campbell*

---

**3.** But see McKee, Nelson & Whitmire, Federal Taxation of Partnerships and Partners ¶ 5.02[1] (3d ed. 1996). The authors argue that when the Section 721 and Section 83 regulations are read together, transfers of a profits interest are not directly covered by Section 83.

**4.** See generally Willis, Pennell & Postlewaite, Partnership Taxation § 46.04 (4th ed. 1989).

**5.** Prop.Reg. § 1.721–1(b)(1). These proposed regulations were issued in 1971 and have neither been adopted nor withdrawn since that time.

**6.** G.C.M. 36346 (July 25, 1977).

**7.** See, e.g., St. John v. United States, 84–1 USTC ¶ 9158 (C.D.Ill.1983); Kenroy, Inc. v. Commissioner, 47 T.C.M. 1749 (1984).

**8.** 59 T.C.M. 236 (1990).

**9.** Campbell v. Commissioner, 943 F.2d 815 (8th Cir.1991). On appeal, the *Campbell* case was complicated by the government's argument that the taxpayer had received the profits interest in his capacity as an employee of his corporate employer rather than as a partner. The court declined to consider this argument because it was raised for the first time on appeal.

was principally a valuation holding. In the course of its opinion, however, the court appeared to leave open the possibility that a profits interest received by a service partner acting in a partner capacity would be taxable if it were susceptible of valuation. At the same time, it suggested that, irrespective of valuation concerns, the receipt of a profits interest by a partner might not be taxable as a matter of law because Sections 61 and 83 were preempted by other provisions of Subchapter K that govern the taxation of compensatory payments to partners for services rendered in their partner and nonpartner capacities.[10]

The Eighth Circuit decision in *Campbell* settled the jangled nerves of tax advisors, but students of Subchapter K continued to debate the scope of the decision and its conceptual basis.[11] In the midst of this discussion, the Service finally announced a formal position on the taxation of profits interests in Revenue Procedure 93–27, which follows.

## Revenue Procedure 93–27

1993–2 Cum.Bull. 343.

### Sec. 1. Purpose

This revenue procedure provides guidance on the treatment of the receipt of a partnership profits interest for services provided to or for the benefit of the partnership.

### Sec. 2. Definitions

The following definitions apply for purposes of this revenue procedure.

.01 A capital interest is an interest that would give the holder a share of the proceeds if the partnership's assets were sold at fair market value and then the proceeds were distributed in a complete liquidation of the partnership. This determination generally is made at the time of receipt of the partnership interest.

.02 A profits interest is a partnership interest other than a capital interest.

### Sec. 3. Background

Under section 1.721–1(b)(1) of the Income Tax Regulations, the receipt of a partnership capital interest for services provided to or for the benefit of

---

**10.** See, e.g., I.R.C. § 707, which governs transactions between partners and partnerships and provides in effect that a partner may not receive taxable compensation from a partnership while acting in a *partner* capacity unless it is in the form of a fixed "guaranteed payment." See I.R.C. § 707(c). Other forms of compensatory payments to partners are included in the partner's distributive share of partnership profits and generally are taxed

when those profits are realized. Section 707 is examined in detail in Chapter 5, infra.

**11.** See, e.g., Cunningham, "Taxing Partnership Interests Exchanged for Services," 47 Tax L.Rev. 247 (1991); Castleberry, "*Campbell*—A Simpler Solution," 47 Tax L.Rev. 277 (1991); Schmolka, "Taxing Partnership Interests Exchanged for Services: Let *Diamond/Campbell* Quietly Die," 47 Tax L.Rev. 287 (1991).

the partnership is taxable as compensation. On the other hand, the issue of whether the receipt of a partnership profits interest for services is taxable has been the subject of litigation. Most recently, in Campbell v. Commissioner, 943 F.2d 815 (8th Cir.1991), the Eighth Circuit in dictum suggested that the taxpayer's receipt of a partnership profits interest received for services was not taxable, but decided the case on valuation. Other courts have determined that in certain circumstances the receipt of a partnership profits interest for services is a taxable event under section 83 of the Internal Revenue Code. See, e.g., Campbell v. Commissioner, T.C.M. 1990–236, rev'd, 943 F.2d 815 (8th Cir.1991); St. John v. United States, No. 82–1134 (C.D.Ill. Nov.16, 1983). The courts have also found that typically the profits interest received has speculative or no determinable value at the time of receipt. See Campbell, 943 F.2d at 823; St. John. In Diamond v. Commissioner, 56 T.C. 530 (1971), aff'd, 492 F.2d 286 (7th Cir.1974), however, the court assumed that the interest received by the taxpayer was a partnership profits interest and found the value of the interest was readily determinable. In that case, the interest was sold soon after receipt.

Sec. 4.  Application

.01 Other than as provided below, if a person receives a profits interest for the provision of services to or for the benefit of a partnership in a partner capacity or in anticipation of being a partner, the Internal Revenue Service will not treat the receipt of such an interest as a taxable event for the partner or the partnership.

.02 This revenue procedure does not apply:

(1) If the profits interest relates to a substantially certain and predictable stream of income from partnership assets, such as income from high-quality debt securities or a high-quality net lease;

(2) If within two years of receipt, the partner disposes of the profits interest; or

(3) If the profits interest is a limited partnership interest in a "publicly traded partnership" within the meaning of section 7704(b) of the Internal Revenue Code.

## NOTE

Revenue Procedure 93–27 goes a long way toward clarifying the tax treatment of a partner who receives a profits interest for services. In a typical situation, where a partner with managerial or technical expertise receives a share of future profits upon joining a partnership, the receipt of the profits interest will not be a taxable event as long as the three exceptions in Revenue Procedure 93–27 are avoided.

The Service's tolerant policy applies, however, only if the services are performed for the partnership "in a partner capacity or in anticipation of being a partner." Thus, if a profits interest is received for services performed in a nonpartner capacity (e.g., as an independent contractor or

employee), the service provider is taxable. Section 707(a), which is covered in Chapter 5, provides principles for determining the capacity in which a partner is acting in a particular transaction with the partnership.[1]

The exceptions in Revenue Procedure 93–27 raise a few additional issues. For example, when will a service partner be taxable because the stream of income from partnership assets is sufficiently "certain and predictable?" Does *every* disposition of a profits interest within two years of receipt trigger taxation? What if the partner disposes of the interest by gift, at death, or exchanges the interest for stock in a newly formed corporation in a nonrecognition transaction under Section 351? These and other lingering issues may need to be addressed in the future.[2]

If a partner is taxable under one of the exceptions in Revenue Procedure 93–27, several more thorny questions are raised. For example, is the profits interest taxable as "property" received in connection with the performance of services under Section 83? If so, what are the consequences to the partnership? If Section 83 applies, a profits interest that is freely transferable and not subject to a substantial risk of forfeiture would be taxable on receipt in an amount equal to the fair market value of the interest. After Revenue Procedure 93–27, the rare taxable profits interest would be susceptible of valuation, presumably based on the present value of the predictable income stream. The partner's outside basis in the profits interest would be the amount included in income.

As for the partnership, recall that upon transfer of a capital interest for services, the partnership may take an ordinary and necessary business deduction or must capitalize the expenditure, depending on the nature of the services rendered. The transfer of a capital interest also was a taxable event to the partnership—i.e., the other partners—on the theory that they were transferring an undivided interest in partnership assets that in turn was recontributed by the service partner to the partnership. A similar approach may apply if the transfer of a profits interest is taxable. First, the partnership would either deduct or capitalize an amount equal to the value of the profits interest transferred. Then, the transaction could be treated as the partnership's transfer of a right to future profits which, under the assignment of income doctrine, should result in immediate taxation of the other partners on the value of this assigned interest in future income.[3] Since the service partner is treated as transferring the right to future profits back to the partnership, the partnership should take a transferred inside basis equal to the amount that the service partner included in gross income upon receipt.[4] Finally, to avoid double taxation of the same profits, the partnership should be able to amortize this basis and reduce its taxable income in the future. To claim this deduction, however, the partnership

**1.** See Chapter 5A, infra.

**2.** See Lockhart, "IRS Concedes Tax Treatment of a Partnership Profits Interest Received for Services," 10 J.P'ship Tax'n 283 (1993) for a discussion of these and other issues raised by Revenue Procedure 93–27.

**3.** Cf. Stranahan's Estate v. Commissioner, 472 F.2d 867 (6th Cir.1973).

**4.** I.R.C. § 723.

would be required to demonstrate that the profits interest has a determinable useful life. This amortization deduction should be allocated to the service partner, who was already taxed when he received the profits interest and should not be taxed again.[5]

Still more questions would arise if a service provider received a taxable profits interest that was not substantially vested upon receipt. For example, unless the partner makes a Section 83(b) election, he would not be considered as the owner of the property until the restrictions lapse.[6] That may mean that the service provider is not a partner until the interest vests, but in that case it is unclear how the service provider and the other partners would be taxed in the meantime. Having raised all of these technical teasers, it is important to remember that they only arise when a partner is taxable on the receipt of a profits interest.

Revenue Procedure 2001–43[7]clarifies Revenue Procedure 93–27 on a few technical points. First, it provides that the determination of whether an interest granted to a service provider is a profits interest is tested at the time the interest is granted, even if that interest is not substantially vested under Section 83. Second, the Service will not treat the grant of a nontaxable profits interest, or the event that causes the interest to be substantially vested under Section 83, as a taxable event. Thus, a Section 83(b) election would not be needed if such a partnership interest were not substantially vested at the time it was granted. For these rules to apply, Revenue Procedure 2001–43 requires that: (1) the partnership and the service provider must treat the service provider as the owner of the interest from the date of its grant, and the service provider must take into account the distributive share of all items associated with the interest for the entire period during which the service provider has the interest, (2) neither the partnership nor any partner may deduct any amount for the fair market value of the interest either upon the grant of the interest or when it becomes substantially vested, and (3) all the other requirements of Revenue Procedure 93–27 must be satisfied.

## PROBLEMS

**1.** The AB partnership is a law firm. C, an associate in the firm, is offered a one-third partnership interest in the future profits of the partnership. C is not required to make any capital contribution. Is C taxable upon his *nontaxed* admission to the partnership?

---

**5.** This type of allocation could be made under Section 704(b). See Chapter 4B, infra. Alternatively, the regulations permit a revaluation of partnership property, adjustments to capital accounts, and application of Section 704(c) principles when a partnership interest (that is not de minimis) is transferred to a partner as consideration for the provision of services. See Reg. § 1.704–1(b)(2)(iv)*(f)(5)(iii)*.

**6.** Reg. § 1.83–1(a)(1).

**7.** 2001–2 C.B. 191. For an analysis of Rev. Proc. 2001–43, see Kalinka, "Rev. Proc. 2001–43 and the Transfer of a Nonvested Partnership Profits Interest," 79 Taxes 11 (2001).

**2.** C, an experienced real estate manager, receives a nonforfeitable one-tenth profits interest in the AB general partnership, whose sole asset is a commercial building with a value of $1,000,000 in return for his agreement to render management services in his capacity as a partner. Net rentals from the building recently have been averaging $100,000 per year. C has been asked to manage the building in the hope that his expertise will increase the rental income and ultimately lead to a profitable sale of the property.

(a) What are the tax consequences to C upon receipt of the profits interest?

(b) What are the tax consequences to C upon receipt of the profits interest if C, prior to becoming a partner, rendered services to the partnership in connection with obtaining financing and soliciting tenants for the building?

(c) What result in (a), above, if C sells his profits interest for $50,000 within one year of acquiring the interest and prior to receiving any profits?

(d) What results in (c), above, to the partnership (and to A and B)?

(e) What result to C and to the partnership in (a), above, if C's profits interest was subject to forfeiture until C rendered services for the partnership for a period of five years?

## D.   ORGANIZATION AND SYNDICATION EXPENSES

Code: § 709.

Regulations: § 1.709–1,–2.

A wide variety of expenses is incurred on the organization of a partnership. In keeping with the approach in the corporate area,[1] Section 709(a) provides that organizational expenses and expenses in connection with the promotion and sale of partnership interests (i.e., syndication fees) are not deductible. Under Section 709(b), however, a partnership may elect to deduct up to $5,000 of organizational expenses in the taxable year in which it begins business. The $5,000 amount is reduced (but not below zero) by the amount of the partnership's organizational expenses in excess of $50,000.[2] Organizational expenses that are not deducted in the year in which the partnership begins business may be amortized ratably over the 180–month period beginning with the month in which the business begins.[3] If the partnership liquidates before the end of the 180–month amortization period, it may deduct the unamortized portion of its organizational ex-

---

**1.**  See I.R.C. § 248.

**2.**  I.R.C. § 709(b)(1)(A).

**3.**  I.R.C.   § 709(b)(1)(B).   The   180–month period corresponds to the amortization period for intangibles in Section 197.

penses (but not capitalized syndication expenses) as a loss under Section 165.[4]

"Organizational expenses" are defined in Section 709(b)(3) as expenditures that are: (1) incident to the creation of the partnership; (2) chargeable to capital account; and (3) of a character which, if expended to create a partnership having an ascertainable life, would be amortizable over that life. Examples are legal fees incident to the organization of the partnership, including negotiation and preparation of the partnership agreement; fees for establishing an accounting system; and filing fees.[5] Specifically excluded are expenses connected with acquiring assets or transferring assets to the partnership; expenses connected with a contract relating to the operation of the partnership's trade or business; and syndication expenses.[6]

The flat ban against deducting or amortizing syndication expenses is intended to preclude the typical investment limited partnership from deducting payments made for services rendered with respect to the promotion of the venture. "Syndication expenses" are defined broadly to include brokerage and registration fees; legal fees of the underwriter and the general partner for securities advice; accounting fees for preparation of representations to be included in the offering materials; and printing costs of all selling and promotional material.[7] The Service also has ruled that fees paid by a syndicated limited partnership for the tax opinion used in its prospectus is a syndication expense that is neither deductible under Section 212(3) nor amortizable under Section 709(b).[8]

## PROBLEM

Napa Hotel Associates is a limited partnership that was organized in December of the current year to construct and operate a luxury hotel. Developer will serve as general partner and contribute $100 cash for his interest. Limited partnership interests of $100,000 each have been sold by Broker to twenty investors, each of whom has been furnished with a voluminous prospectus describing the offering. All the investors are clients of Financial Planner, an affiliate of Broker, who acts as an investment advisor to wealthy individuals.

To what extent are the following expenses, all of which are to be paid in the current year out of the $2,000,000 contributed by the limited partners, properly classified as "organizational expenses" under Section 709(b)(3)?

---

**4.** I.R.C. § 709(b)(2). If the partnership did not elect to amortize its organizational expenses, it may not deduct those costs on liquidation under Section 165. Rev.Rul. 87–111, 1987–2 C.B. 160. But because the costs ordinarily are reflected in the partners' outside bases, they should decrease the capital gain, increase the capital loss, or increase the basis of distributed property when the partnership liquidates. See Chapter 8D, infra.

**5.** Reg. § 1.709–2(a).

**6.** Id.

**7.** Reg. § 1.709–2(b). See Flowers v. Commissioner, 80 T.C. 914 (1983); Rev.Rul. 85–32, 1985–1 C.B. 186.

**8.** Rev.Rul. 88–4, 1988–1 C.B. 264. See Surloff v. Commissioner, 81 T.C. 210 (1983).

(a) A $100,000 "placement fee" paid to Broker for his efforts in selling the limited partnership interests?

(b) A $50,000 "organizational fee" paid to Developer for his services in connection with the organization of the partnership and negotiating the terms of the partnership agreement?

(c) $40,000 paid to Attorney for drafting the partnership agreement, filing the necessary papers and preparing the offering documents?

(d) $10,000 paid to Accountant for preparing the financial projections included in the offering documents?

(e) $10,000 paid to Printer for printing the limited partnership offering prospectus?

(f) $20,000 paid to Tax Attorney for tax advice to the prospective investors and for preparation of a tax opinion letter concerning issues affecting the partnership?

(g) $40,000 as an initial fee to Financial Planner for services to be rendered by her in reviewing partnership tax returns, assisting in the preparation of financial information to be furnished to the limited partners and for acting as liaison between the general partner and the limited partners?

# CHAPTER 3

# OPERATIONS OF A PARTNERSHIP: GENERAL RULES

## A. TAX CONSEQUENCES TO THE PARTNERSHIP: AGGREGATE AND ENTITY PRINCIPLES

### 1. THE PARTNERSHIP AS AN ENTITY

Code: §§ 701; 702(b); 703. Skim §§ 179(d)(8); 442; 702(a); 6031.

Regulations: §§ 1.701–1; 1.702–1(b); 1.703–1(a), (b)(1); 1.6031–1(e)(2).

The rules in Subchapter K for the taxation of partnership operations are a mixture of aggregate and entity principles. Section 701 adopts an aggregate approach by providing that a partnership is not a taxable entity. Instead, it is a conduit through which the income, deductions, credits and other tax attributes generated by partnership activities flow to the partners, who separately report their distributive shares of these items. But imagine a pure pass-through approach where each partner would independently determine partnership accounting methods, the availability of deductions, tax elections affecting the computation of taxable income and the many other issues that arise in computing the tax liability of a business enterprise. If each partner were left to his own devices, the results would be chaotic.

To bring order and uniformity to the taxation of partnership operations, Congress wisely chose to treat partnerships as entities for purposes of reporting and determining partnership income or loss. A partnership thus is required to file an informational tax return[1] and is essentially treated as an entity for purposes of administrative and judicial procedures.[2] Section 703(a) requires a partnership to determine its own taxable income and provides rules designed to preserve the character of capital gains, charitable contributions, foreign taxes and other items that may be subject to special treatment in the hands of the partners.[3] Section 702(b) similarly

---

**1.** I.R.C. § 6031. The return is to be filed on or before the 15th day of the fourth month after the close of the partnership's taxable year. Reg. § 1.6031–1(e)(2). Failure to file can lead to civil or criminal penalties. I.R.C. §§ 6698; 7203. Rev.Proc. 84–35, 1984–1 C.B. 509, provides that in certain limited situations, partnerships with 10 or fewer

partners will not be penalized for failing to file partnership tax returns.

**2.** I.R.C. §§ 6221–6233.

**3.** Section 702(a) lists certain items which must be separately stated so that they are properly reflected on the partners' returns, and Section 703(a)(2) disallows certain deductions in computing partnership taxable income. The mechanics of these computations

provides that the character of a partnership item taxed to the partners is to be determined "as if such item were realized directly from the source from which realized by the partnership, or incurred in the same manner as incurred by the partnership." As a result, questions involving the holding period of property[4] or the characterization of gains and losses[5] are determined at the partnership level.

In harmony with the entity approach, Section 703(b) provides, with limited exceptions, that the partnership will select its accounting method[6] and make various elections affecting the computation of taxable income. The partnership also will have its own taxable year, which may be separate from the taxable years of some of its partners.[7] The ruling and case that follow illustrate Subchapter K's application of entity principles to the characterization of partnership income and loss and partnership tax elections.

## Revenue Ruling 68–79

1968–1 Cum.Bull. 310.

Advice has been requested whether a partner's distributive share of partnership capital gains resulting under the circumstances described below is long-term capital gain. [Under the 1954 Code, as applicable to the years involved in this ruling, the required holding period for long-term capital gain or loss treatment was more than six months. Eds.]

*A, B* and *C* were equal partners in *ABC* partnership. On June 1, 1966, the partnership acquired 300 shares of *X* corporation stock as an investment. On February 1, 1967, *A* sold his partnership interest to new partner *D*. On May 1, 1967, the partnership sold at a gain the 300 shares of *X* stock (at which time *D*'s holding period for his partnership interest was not more than six months).

Section 1222(1) of the Internal Revenue Code of 1954 defines the term "short-term capital gain" as gain from the sale or exchange of a capital asset held for not more than six months, if and to the extent such gain is taken into account in computing gross income.

Section 1222(3) of the Code defines the term "long-term capital gain" as gain from the sale or exchange of a capital asset held for more than six months, if and to the extent that such gain is taken into account in computing gross income.

Section 702(a) of the Code provides that in determining his income tax, each partner shall take into account separately his distributive share of the

---

and their impact on the partners is discussed in Section B of this chapter.

**4.** See Rev.Rul. 68–79, below.

**5.** McManus v. Commissioner, 65 T.C. 197 (1975), affirmed 583 F.2d 443 (9th Cir. 1978), cert. denied, 440 U.S. 959, 99 S.Ct.

1501 (1979); Podell v. Commissioner, 55 T.C. 429 (1970).

**6.** Reg. § 1.703–1(b)(1). But see I.R.C. § 448(a)(2), (b).

**7.** See Section A3 of this chapter, infra.

partnership's gains and losses from sales or exchanges of capital assets held for more than six months.

Section 702(b) of the Code provides that the character of any item of income, gain, loss, deduction, or credit included in a partner's distributive share under paragraphs (1) through (8) of subsection (a) shall be determined as if such item were realized directly from the source from which realized by the partnership, or incurred in the same manner as incurred by the partnership.

The character of any item of income, gain, loss, deduction, or credit included in a partner's distributive share under paragraphs (1) through (8) of section 702(a) of the Code is determined at the partnership level. Compare Revenue Ruling 67–188, C.B. 1967–1, 216.

Since the *ABC* partnership held the *X* stock for more than six months, the gain realized by the partnership is long-term capital gain.

Accordingly, in computing his gross income, *D* should take into account separately in his return, as long-term capital gain, his distributive share of the partnership's long-term capital gain arising from the sale by the partnership of *X* corporation stock held by it as an investment for more than six months, notwithstanding that *D* has a holding period for his partnership interest of not more than six months.

## Demirjian v. Commissioner

United States Court of Appeals, Third Circuit, 1972.
457 F.2d 1.

■ VAN DUSEN, CIRCUIT JUDGE.

The petitioning taxpayers, Anne and Mabel Demirjian, have filed a timely petition for review of an adverse decision of the Tax Court affirming a finding of tax deficiencies for 1962 by the Commissioner of Internal Revenue. The tax deficiencies were based on the failure to report $54,835.00 in gain for the taxable year 1962. Plaintiffs maintain that the gain in question is covered by the nonrecognition provisions of Code Section 1033. As pointed out below, we agree with the ruling of the Tax Court that § 703 of the Internal Revenue Code requires that the nonrecognition of gain election and replacement under § 1033 be made by Kin–Bro Realty, a partnership, and that the replacements by plaintiffs individually were thus ineffective.

The facts, as stipulated in the proceedings before the Tax Court, show that Anne and Mabel Demirjian each owned 50% of the stock of Kin–Bro Realty Corporation, which had acquired title to a three-story office building in Newark, New Jersey, in October 1944. On November 3, 1960, the corporation was dissolved and its chief asset, the office building, was conveyed by deed to "Anne Demirjian * * * and Mabel Demirjian * * * partners trading as Kin–Bro Real Estate Company." Although no formal partnership agreement was executed, Anne and Mabel did file a trade name certificate indicating that they intended to conduct a real estate investment

business at the Newark office building under the name of Kin–Bro Real Estate Company. The office building, which constituted Kin–Bro's sole operating asset, was conveyed to the Newark Housing Authority on September 12, 1962, after an involuntary condemnation proceeding. In the deed of conveyance the grantors are listed as "Anne Demirjian and Mabel Demirjian, partners trading as Kin–Bro Real Estate Company." The net proceeds of the sale were distributed to Anne and Mabel in amounts equal to approximately 50% of the total sale price. At this point, both Anne and Mabel apparently elected to replace the property with equivalent property in order to take advantage of the nonrecognition of gain provision contained in § 1033 of the Internal Revenue Code. Normally gain resulting from the sale or exchange of investment real property is taxable, but § 1033 provides that if property is involuntarily converted and the proceeds are used to replace it with substantially equivalent property within one year [now two years, Ed.] then gain is recognized only to the extent that the amount received due to the conversion exceeds the purchase price of the replacement property. The reinvestments, however, were made by Anne and Mabel as individuals and not through the partnership. On April 15, 1963, Anne invested $40,934.05 of her share of the proceeds in property which was similar to the condemned property. Mabel was unable to find suitable replacement property within the one-year replacement period, and, by letter of October 17, 1963, she made a written application to the District Director of Internal Revenue, Newark, New Jersey, for an extension of time in which to make such a replacement. In a letter dated January 16, 1964, the District Director stated:

> "In a letter dated October 17, 1963 received from Mr. Ralph Niebart and subsequent correspondence, an extension of time was requested for the purpose of replacing your share of the partnership property that was owned by Kin–Bro Real Estate Company (a partnership). The property was sold to the Housing Authority of the City of Newark on September 12, 1962 under threat of condemnation.

> "You have stated that although you have made a continued effort to replace the converted property, you have not been successful to date.

* * *

> "Based on the information submitted, together with the data already in our file, extension is hereby granted until December 31, 1964, within which to complete the replacement of the converted property."

On February 7, 1964, Mabel invested $45,711.17 in similar real estate. Neither Anne nor Mabel reported any portion of the gain realized on the condemnation sale in their initial returns for the 1962 tax year. In 1964 Anne and Mabel filed amended 1962 joint returns with their husbands, reporting the excess of their distributive share from the condemnation sale over the cost of their respective replacement property as long-term capital

gains. The Commissioner of Internal Revenue disagreed with these computations and assessed deficiencies, reasoning that the § 1033 election for nonrecognition of gain and replacement with equivalent property could only be made by the partnership under the terms of § 703(b) of the Code. The Tax Court affirmed the Commissioner's finding of deficiencies and plaintiffs here appeal that decision.

In reviewing a decision of the Tax Court, this court is normally limited in its scope of review by the clearly erroneous test of Rule 52(a), F.R.Civ.P. However, in cases such as the instant action, where the facts have been fully stipulated and no testimony was taken, the Court of Appeals may, within certain limits, substitute its factual conclusions and inferences for those of the Tax Court.

Petitioners' first contention on this appeal is that the Newark office building was owned by Anne and Mabel as tenants in common, not as partners, and that, therefore, the § 1033 nonrecognition of gain election and replacement was properly made by them in their individual capacities as co-tenants. On the basis of the record before the Tax Court, we find that the property in question was owned by Kin–Bro Realty, a partnership, composed of Anne and Mabel Demirjian. It is noted that several federal cases have ruled that taxpayers such as petitioners who represent, in their dealings with the Internal Revenue Service, that property is owned by a partnership are bound by such representations.

Petitioners next contend that even if the office building was owned by the partnership, the election and replacement with equivalent property under 26 U.S.C. § 1033[(a)(2)(A), Ed.] were properly made by them in their capacity as individual partners. We agree with the Tax Court's determination that 26 U.S.C. § 703(b) requires that the election and replacement under § 1033 be made by the partnership and that replacement by individual partners of property owned by the partnership does not qualify for nonrecognition of the gain. Section 703(b) provides, with exceptions not relevant here, that any election which affects the computation of taxable income derived from a partnership must be made by the partnership. The election for nonrecognition of gain on the involuntary conversion of property would affect such computation and is the type of election contemplated by § 703(b). The partnership provisions of the Internal Revenue Code treat a partnership as an aggregate of its members for purposes of taxing profits to the individual members and as an entity for purposes of computing and reporting income. In light of this entity approach to reporting income, Congress included § 703(b) to avoid the possible confusion which might result if each partner were to determine partnership income separately only on his own return for his own purposes. To avoid the possible confusion which could result from separate elections under § 1033(a), the election must be made by the partnership as an entity, and the failure of the partnership to so act results in the recognition of the gain on the sale of partnership property.

Petitioners' final contention is that the Commissioner is estopped from denying that a valid election and replacement were made under § 1033.

Two separate grounds for estoppel are alleged. The first ground, that the petitioners have conformed their conduct to existing interpretations of the law and the Commissioner may not "invoke a retroactive interpretation to the taxpayer's detriment," is clearly without merit. The second alleged ground is that the Commissioner is estopped by the implicit approval of the individual partner's election and replacement by the District Director for Newark in his letter of January 16, 1964. Even if we were to accept the letter as a justifiable basis for detrimental reliance, petitioners have demonstrated no such reliance and, furthermore, the doctrine of estoppel does not prevent the Commissioner from correcting errors of law.

For the foregoing reasons, the September 1, 1970, orders of the Tax Court, in accordance with its opinion of that date, will be affirmed.

## 2.   ASSIGNMENT OF INCOME

## Schneer v. Commissioner

United States Tax Court, 1991.
97 T.C. 643.

■ GERBER, JUDGE: * * *

[The taxpayer, Mr. Schneer, was an associate in a law firm ("BSI"). BSI paid Schneer a salary and a percentage of fees generated by the clients he referred to the firm. When Schneer resigned from BSI, he was entitled to receive a percentage of the fees from clients he had referred to that firm and fees for other consulting services that he was obligated to perform for BSI with respect to those clients. Schneer subsequently became a partner in two different law firms ("B & K" and "SSG & M"). Under the partnership agreements of those firms, he was required to turn over the fees that he received from BSI. The new firms treated the fees as partnership income and allocated them to each partner, including Schneer, according to the partners' respective share of partnership profits. Ed.]

We consider here basic principles of income taxation. There is agreement that the amounts paid to petitioner by his former employer-law firm are income in the year of receipt. The question is whether petitioner (individually) or the partners of petitioner's partnerships (including petitioner) should report the income in their respective shares.

The parties have couched the issue in terms of the anticipatory assignment-of-income principles. See Lucas v. Earl, 281 U.S. 111 (1930). Equally important to this case, however, is the viability of the principle that partners may pool their earnings and report partnership income in amounts different from their contribution to the pool. See sec. 704(a) and (b). The parties' arguments bring into focus potential conflict between these two principles and compel us to address both.

First, we examine the parties' arguments with respect to the assignment-of-income doctrine. Respondent argues that petitioner earned the income in question before leaving BSI, despite the fact that petitioner did not receive that income until he was a partner in B & K and, later, SSG &

M. According to respondent, by entering into partnership agreements requiring payment of all legal fees to his new partnerships, petitioner anticipatorily assigned to those partnerships the income earned but not yet received from BSI. * * *

Petitioner contends that the income in question was not earned until after he left BSI and joined B & K and SSG & M. He argues that the income received from BSI is reportable by the partners of the B & K and SSG & M partnerships (including petitioner) in their respective shares. Petitioner also points out that partnership agreements, which like the ones in issue allocate and redistribute partners' income, have received the approval of respondent in Rev.Rul. 64–90, 1964–1 (Part 1) C.B. 226. Petitioner argues that he was obligated to consult with BSI in order to be entitled to the BSI fees. Petitioner concedes that, for some of the income in question, no consultation was performed or requested. He emphasizes, however, that a substantial amount (about 90 percent) of the fees involved clients of BSI for whom consultation was performed. Finally, petitioner believes that his failure to consult would have resulted in loss of the fees.

The principle of assignment of income, in the context of Federal taxation, first arose in Lucas v. Earl, supra, where the Supreme Court, interpreting the Revenue Act of 1918, held that income from a husband-taxpayer's legal practice was taxable to him, even though he and his wife had entered into a valid contract under State law to split all income earned by each of them. In so holding, Justice Holmes, speaking for the Court, stated:

> There is no doubt that the statute could tax salaries to those who
> earned them and provide that the tax could not be escaped by
> anticipatory arrangements and contracts however skillfully devised
> to prevent the salary when paid from vesting even for a second in
> the man who earned it. [281 U.S. at 114–115.]

From that pervasive and simply stated interpretation, a plethora of cases and learned studies have sprung forth. Early cases reflected the use of the assignment-of-income principle only with respect to income not yet earned. The theory behind those interpretations was that income not yet earned is controlled by the assignor, even if assigned to another. Such income is necessarily generated by services not yet performed. Because the assignor may refuse to perform services, he necessarily has control over income yet to be earned. * * * This early rationale left open the possibility of successful assignments, for tax purposes, of income already earned. That possibility was foreclosed in Helvering v. Eubank, 311 U.S. 122 (1940), where the Supreme Court held that income already earned would also fall within the assignment-of-income doctrine of Lucas v. Earl, supra.

* * *

In this case, petitioner was not entitled to the referral fees unless the work for the referred clients had been successfully completed. On the other hand, petitioner would be entitled to the fees if the work was completed or if at the time of the assignment there was nothing contingent in petition-

er's right to collect his percentage of the fees. Additionally, the majority of the services had not been performed prior to petitioner's leaving BSI. In this regard services had been performed with respect to $1,250 prior to 1984. With respect to $3,325 of the $21,329 of fees received in 1984, petitioner did not consult and was not required to do anything subsequent to leaving BSI to be entitled to those fees. With respect to the remainder of the $21,329 for 1984 and all of the 1985 fees, petitioner was called upon to and did consult while he was a partner of B & K or SSG & M.

We must decide whether petitioner had earned the fees in question prior to assigning them to the B & K or the SSG & M partnerships. Although petitioner was on the cash method, the principles that control use of the cash method are not suited to this inquiry. For purposes of the assignment-of-income doctrine, it must be determined whether the income was earned prior to an assignment. * * *

The record in this case reflects that, with the exception of $1,250 of services performed in prior years, the billings and payments in question were performed and collected subsequent to the time of assignment of the income. * * *

With these principles as our guide, we hold that petitioner had not earned the fees in question prior to leaving BSI, with the exception of the $1,250 received for services performed in an earlier year. More specifically, we hold that petitioner earned the income in question while a partner of a partnership to which he had agreed to pay such income. With respect to substantially all of the fees in issue, BSI records reflect that clients were billed and payment received during the years in issue. Moreover, if petitioner had refused a request for his consultation, it was, at the very least, questionable whether he would have received his share of the fee if the work had been successfully completed without him. Petitioner was requested to and did provide further services with regard to clients from which about 90 percent of the fees were generated. We note that BSI did not request consultation with respect to $3,325 remitted during 1984. However, that amount was not earned as of the time of the assignment because the work had not yet been performed for the BSI clients (irrespective of whether or not petitioner would be called upon to consult). Accordingly, with the exception of $1,250 for petitioner's 1984 taxable year, we hold that petitioner had not earned the income in question prior to leaving BSI and did not make an anticipatory assignment of income which had been earned.

Two additional related questions remain for our consideration. First, respondent argues that irrespective of when petitioner earned the income from BSI, "there was no relationship * * * [between] the past activity of introducing a client to * * * [BSI], and the petitioner's work as a partner with * * * [B & K or SSG & M]." According to respondent, petitioner should not be allowed to characterize as partnership income fees that did not have a requisite or direct relationship to a partnership's business. In making this argument, respondent attempts to limit and modify his long-standing and judicially approved position in Rev.Rul. 64–90, 1964–1 C.B. (Part 1) 226. * * * Second, while we generally hold that petitioner did not

make an assignment of income already earned, the possibility that this was an assignment of unearned income was not foreclosed.

These final two questions bring into focus the true nature of the potential conflict in this case—between respondent's revenue ruling and the assignment-of-income doctrine. Both questions, in their own way, ask whether any partnership agreement—under which partners agree in advance to turn over to the partnership all income from their individual efforts—can survive scrutiny under the assignment-of-income principles.

Rev.Rul. 64–90, 1964–1 (Part 1) C.B. at 226–227, in pertinent part, contains the following:

> Federal income tax treatment of compensation received by a partner and paid over to a partnership where the partner, who uses the cash receipts and disbursements method of accounting, files his returns on a calendar year basis and the partnership, which also uses the cash method, files its returns on a fiscal year basis. * * *

> Advice has been requested regarding the Federal income tax consequences of a change in the terms of a partnership agreement to provide that all compensation received by the partners will be paid over to the partnership immediately upon receipt.

> In the instant case, several individuals formed a partnership for the purpose of engaging in the general practice of law. Aside from the partnership business, each of the partners has performed services from time to time in his individual capacity and not as a partner. The several partners have always regarded the fees received for such services as compensation to the recipient as an individual.

> The partnership which was formed in 1954 and uses the cash receipts and disbursements method of accounting files its Federal income tax returns for fiscal years ending January 31, and the partners file their individual returns on the cash method for calendar years. Each partner reports his distributive share of the partnership income, gain, loss, deduction or credit for the partnership fiscal year ending within the calendar year for which his individual return is filed. All compensation received by each partner for services performed in his individual capacity is reported in that partner's return for the calendar year when received.

> It is proposed to amend the partnership agreement as of the beginning of the partnership's next fiscal year to provide that all compensation received by the partners be paid over to the partnership immediately upon receipt.

> The question in the instant case is whether compensation remitted to the partnership pursuant to this provision will constitute partnership income.

Similar inquiries were previously considered by the Internal Revenue Service. * * * In both instances, it was pointed out that a partnership could not exist for the purpose of performing the services for which the compensation and allowances were received, and, thus, the recipient partner would be required to report the taxable portion of the compensation and allowances in his individual return, even though these items were pooled with partnership earnings. * * *

*In the instant case, the general practice of the partnership consists of rendering legal advice and services. Consequently, fees received by a partner for similar services performed in his individual return capacity will be considered as partnership income if paid to the partnership in accordance with the agreement. Those fees need not be reported separately by the partner on his individual return. However, the partner's distributive share of the partnership's taxable income which he must report on his individual return will include a portion of such fees.* [Emphasis supplied.]

A key requirement of this ruling is that the services for which fees are received by individual partners must be SIMILAR to those normally performed by the partnership. * * * Respondent now attempts to add to this requirement by arguing that the fees here in question were earned through activity, which was admittedly legal work, but was not sufficiently related to the work of petitioner's new partnerships. In other words, respondent argues that the income here was earned in BSI's business activity and not B & K's or SSG & M's business activity.

\* \* \*

There is no need for us to adopt a broader view of petitioner's partnership in this case. His referral fee income was clearly earned through activities "within the ambit" of the business of his new partnerships. Their business was the practice of law as was petitioner's consulting activity for BSI. His work was incident to the conduct of the business of his partnerships. We decline to adopt respondent's more narrow characterization of the business of petitioner's new partnerships. Neither the case law nor respondent's rulings support such a characterization.

Thus, we arrive at the final question in this case. We have already held that petitioner had not yet earned the majority of the income in question when he joined his new partnerships. Additionally, petitioner's fee income from his BSI clients qualifies, under the case law and respondent's rulings, as income generated by services sufficiently related to the business conducted by petitioner's new partnerships. If we decide that petitioner's partnerships should report the income in question, petitioner would be taxable only to the extent of his respective partnership share. This would allow petitioner, through his partnership agreements with B & K and SSG & M, to assign income not yet earned from BSI. Thus, the case law and respondent's rulings permit (without explanation), in a partnership setting, the type of assignment addressed by Lucas v. Earl, 281 U.S. 111 (1930). We

must reconcile the principle behind Rev.Rul. 64–90, 1964–1 C.B. (Part 1) 226, with Lucas v. Earl, supra. The question is whether income not yet earned and anticipatorily assigned under certain partnership agreements are without the reach of the assignment-of-income principle.

The Internal Revenue Code of 1954 provided the first comprehensive statutory scheme for the tax treatment of partners and partnerships. No section of the 1954 Code, successive amendments or acts, nor the legislative history specifically addresses the treatment of income earned by partners in their individual capacity but which is pooled with other partnership income. It is implicit in subchapter K, however, that the pooling of income and losses of partners was intended by Congress. This question is more easily answered where the partnership contracts with the client for services which are then performed by the partner. The question becomes more complex where the partner contracts and performs the services when he is a partner.

Moreover, no opinion contains a satisfactory rationale as to why partnership pooling agreements do not come within the holding of Lucas v. Earl, supra. * * *

The fundamental theme penned by Justice Holmes provides that the individual who earns income is liable for the tax. It is obvious that the partnership, as an abstract entity, does not provide the physical and mental activity that facilitates the process of "earning" income. Only a partner can do so. The income earned is turned over to the partnership due solely to a contractual agreement, i.e., an assignment, in advance, of income.

The pooling of income is essential to the meaningful existence of subchapter K. If partners were not able to share profits in an amount disproportionate to the ratio in which they earned the underlying income, the partnership provisions of the Code would, to some extent, be rendered unnecessary. * * *

The provisions of subchapter K tacitly imply that the pooling of income is permissible. Said implication may provide sufficient reason to conclude that a partnership should be treated as an entity for the purpose of pooling the income of its partners. Under an entity approach, the income would be considered that of the partnership rather than the partner, even though the partner's individual efforts may have earned the income. If the partnership is treated as an entity earning the income, then assignment-of-income concepts would not come into play.

In this regard, an analysis of personal service corporations (PSC's) may provide, by way of analogy, some assistance in reconciling the principles inherent in Rev.Rul. 64–90, 1964–1 C.B. (Part 1) at 226, with those underlying Lucas v. Earl, supra. Keeping in mind Justice Holmes' desire to tax the "earner" of the income, we consider the assignment-of-income doctrine in the context of personal service corporation cases. In partnerships and personal service corporations an individual performs the services that earn income. In both, a separate entity—the partnership or personal service corporation—is cast as the "earner" for tax purposes. That charac-

terization in both situations is, in essence, an assignment of income.[9] If, in either situation, the transfer to the entity is of income earned before an agreement to turn it over is entered into, the assignment-of-income doctrine will serve to invalidate the transfer.[10] In both the context of a PSC or partnership, transfers prior to the performance of a partner's services may be subject to the partner's or employee's control—in that either may refuse to perform.

In analyzing the status of personal service corporations, courts have relied upon the rationale that:

> the realities of the business world present an overly simplistic application of the Lucas v. Earl rule whereby the true earner may be identified by merely pointing to the one actually turning the spade or dribbling the ball. Recognition must be given to corporations as taxable entities which, to a great extent, rely upon the personal services of their employees to produce corporate income. When a corporate employee performs labors which give rise to income, it solves little merely to identify the actual laborer. Thus, a tension has evolved between the basic tenets of Lucas v. Earl and recognition of the nature of the corporate business form. [Fn. ref. omitted.]

Johnson v. Commissioner, 78 T.C. 882, 890 (1982). * * * Thus, an employee of a personal service corporation, or other corporate entity, is outside the holding of Lucas v. Earl, supra, to some degree because of the "entity concept." The business entity is cast as the earner of the income, obviating the need to analyze whether there has been an assignment of income.[11]

The same type of approach may be used with respect to partners of a partnership. In the same manner that a corporation is considered the earner of income gained through the labor of its employees, a partnership, with an appropriate partnership agreement, may be considered the earner

---

**9.** The same could be said of the normal corporate entity as well. The analogy only to PSC's, however, is slightly more apt because, as discussed below, the influence of the assignment-of-income doctrine depends to a large extent on the presence and status of the business form as an entity. In this regard, the corporate form and the partnership are at opposite ends of the spectrum. PSC's fall somewhere in between. This becomes clear through an analysis of the cases where the issue is whether the business form should be disregarded for tax purposes. Compare Moline Properties, Inc. v. Commissioner, 319 U.S. 436, 438–439 (1943) (regular corporation remains separate taxable entity so long as business activity conducted); Keller v. Commissioner, 77 T.C. 1014 (1981), affd. 723 F.2d 58 (10th Cir.1983) (PSC entity form respect-ed because of contractual employment agreement); United States v. Basye, 410 U.S. 441, 448 (1973) (partnership an "independently recognizable entity" for reporting purposes but entity disregarded when determining partner's own tax liabilities).

**10.** Note that in some cases the act of incorporation itself will ostensibly act as the agreement to turn over all income earned.

**11.** It should be noted that in all of these cases, the assignment to the corporation was of income not yet earned. That is, in situations where the entity was validly cast as the earner of the income, the factual pattern involved an incorporation and subsequent earnings by the incorporator. Situations involving contrary facts are usually considered assignments of income.

of income.[12] Income earned prior to such an agreement, of course, remains within the principles and holding of Lucas v. Earl, supra. The link between respondent's Rev. Rul. 64–90, 1964–1 C.B. (Part 1) 226, and Lucas v. Earl, supra, must be the entity concept as it relates to partnerships.

The theory concerning partnerships as entities is not easily defined. It is well established that the partnership form is a hybrid—part separate entity, part aggregate. * * * The difficulty lies in deciding whether a particular set of circumstances relate to one end or the other of the partnership hybrid spectrum. The Supreme Court in *Basye* stated that "partnerships are entities for purposes of calculating and filing informational returns but * * * they are conduits through which the taxpaying obligation passes to the individual partners in accord with their distributive shares." 410 U.S. at 448 n. 8. This analysis provides some foundation for the idea that partners should report their distributive share, rather than the fruits of their personal labors. But it does not provide any guidance concerning the type of income or service that should be brought within the entity concept as it relates to partnerships.

The principle we must analyze in this case involves the role of the partnership with respect to the function of earning income. A general partnership[13] is "an association of two or more persons to carry on as co-owners a business for profit." Uniform Partnership Act sec. 6(1). Either a partnership or a corporation may enter into a contract with clients to perform services. In a partnership, however, either the entity or the individual may enter into contracts. The question we seek to answer is whether this distinction should be treated differently.

For purposes of an entity concept approach to partnerships, we must consider the type and source of income which should be included. Because we have already determined that the type of activity generating the income is relevant to an assignment-of-income analysis in the partnership setting, we focus our analysis of partnerships as entities on situations where the income is of a type normally earned by the partnership. Only in such situations has a partner acted as part of the partnership entity.

The entity concept as it relates to partnerships is based, in part, on the concept that a partner may further the business of the partnership by performing services in the name of the partnership or individually. The

---

**12.** We recognize that in a personal service corporation setting the person performing the service is an employee and that the contract to perform may be with the corporate entity. In a general partnership, the partners are principals and agents and not generally considered employees of the partnership. Partnerships, in the same manner as corporations, however, have employees who perform services contracted for by the partnership. That aspect draws a closer parallel between partnerships and personal service corporations for purposes of our analogy. This aspect does not answer the question concerning income of a partner becoming income of the partnership, but is concerned with the partnership's being treated as an entity for purposes of this issue.

**13.** Our discussion focuses upon professional partnerships composed of general partners who are actively engaged in a business venture. The principles here may not apply to limited or general partners who are mere passive investors and are not involved in the income earning process of the partnership.

name and reputation of a professional partnership plays a role in the financial success of the partnership business. If the partners perform services in the name of the partnership or individually they are, nonetheless, associated with the partnership as a partner. This is the very essence of a professional service partnership, because each partner, although acting individually, is furthering the business of the partnership. * * * The lack of structure inherent in the partnership form does not lend itself to easy resolution of the assignment-of-income question. A partnership's characteristics do, however, militate in favor of treating a partner's income from services performed in an individual capacity, which are contractually obligated to the partnership for allocation in accord with the pre-established distributive shares, in the same manner as income earned through partnership engagement.

Accordingly, in circumstances where individuals are not joining in a venture merely to avoid the effect of Lucas v. Earl, supra, it is appropriate to treat income earned by partners individually, as income earned by the partnership entity, i.e., partnership income, to be allocated to partners in their respective shares.[14] To provide the essential continuity necessary for the use of an entity concept in the partnership setting, the income should be earned from an activity which can reasonably be associated with the partnership's business activity. In the setting of this case, with the exception of $1,250 in 1984, petitioner was a partner of B & K or SSG & M when the fees were earned. Additionally, about 90 percent of the fees were, in part, earned through petitioner's efforts while he was a partner of B & K or SSG & M.

There is no apparent attempt to avoid the incidence of tax by the formation or operation of the partnerships in this case. Petitioner, in performing legal work for clients of another firm, was a partner with the law firms of B & K and SSG & M. In view of the foregoing, we hold that, with the exception of $1,250 for 1984, the fee income from BSI was correctly returned by the two partnerships in accord with the respective partnership agreements. * * *

■ BEGHE, J., concurring: I generally try to apply Occam's razor to the solution of legal problems as well as logic problems. In this case, however, I believe a two-step journey along the right-angle sides of the triangle follows a clearer path to the correct result. The path along the hypotenuse is beset with the obstacles and pitfalls of the assignment-of-income doctrine, if it isn't led to a dead-end by the disquisition on the law of agency.

---

**14.** In following this approach we can also look to the safeguards that are observed in the corporate setting where the entity is being misused. "The assignment of income doctrine * * * continues to be an essential tool * * * where the corporation is not respected by the taxpayer/shareholders as a separate entity which carries on business activities." Keller v. Commissioner, 77 T.C. at 1033. (Fn. ref. omitted.) Moreover, while geared primarily toward the family partnership area, there is a body of partnership-oriented case law involving safeguards which may be similarly applicable to the type of circumstances considered here. See Commissioner v. Culbertson, 337 U.S. 733, 742 (1949), where a facts and circumstances approach was used to determine the intent of parties in forming a partnership.

I reach the majority result in the following two steps. Even if the assignment-of-income doctrine requires petitioner to include in his gross income the amounts of the fees he earned and received from BSI after he became a partner in B & K and in SSG & M, his payments of those amounts to B & K and SSG & M, pursuant to his agreements with those firms, entitled him to equivalent concurrent deductions as ordinary and necessary business expenses under section 162(a). * * * Those amounts thereby became partnership income distributable to all the partners, including petitioner, in accordance with the partnership agreements.

■ JACOBS, J., agrees with this concurring opinion.

■ WELLS, J., dissenting: With due respect, I cannot agree with the majority's analysis and conclusion with respect to the primary issue to be decided in the instant case. Consequently, I must dissent.

The critical threshold issue framed by the majority is whether the fees were paid to petitioner for services he performed prior to leaving BSI or for services he performed after he left BSI. If the fees were for services performed by petitioner prior to the time he left BSI, they are "past services" which should be taxed to petitioner under the rule of Helvering v. Eubank, 311 U.S. 122 (1940).[1] On the other hand, if the fees were paid to petitioner for services to be performed by him after he left BSI, they are future services, Eubank does not apply, and the income should be taxed to the partners of petitioner's subsequent law firms.

To decide the issue, we must ask what petitioner did to earn the fees in question. The analysis necessary to such an inquiry should be made by examining the agreement and course of dealing between petitioner and BSI. * * * When the agreement and course of dealing between petitioner and BSI are examined closely, I am impelled to conclude that the fees in question actually were paid on account of petitioner's services in bringing or referring the clients to BSI, or at the very least, that petitioner failed to carry his burden of proving that the fees were not paid for such services.

* * *

Petitioner must show that the subsequent performance of services was the act giving rise to his right to the fees in order to put his case beyond the scope of *Eubank*. In my view, not only has he failed to do so, the majority's findings concerning the nature of the relationship between petitioner and BSI shows that the actual event giving rise to the right to the fees was the past services of petitioner in securing the clients for BSI. Accordingly, I would hold that the fee income was taxable to petitioner under assignment of income principles, as required by *Eubank*.

**1.** Helvering v. Eubank, 311 U.S. 122 (1940), involved an insurance agent who assigned the right to receive future renewal commissions paid on account of services he had rendered in selling insurance policies. The Supreme Court held that the commission income should be taxed to the agent, reasoning that an assignment of the right to receive income paid on account of past services was insufficient to shift the incidence of taxation on such income from the earner.

■ HALPERN, J., dissenting. The majority perceives a conflict between the anticipatory assignment-of-income doctrine, see Lucas v. Earl, 281 U.S. 111 (1930), and the principle that partners may pool their earnings and report partnership income in amounts different from their contribution to the pool. With respect, I believe the conflict to be illusory, except insofar as the majority here today creates one where heretofore none existed.

According to the majority, the mere redistribution of income within a partnership is inconsistent with the assignment-of-income doctrine. "In partnerships and personal service corporations an individual performs the services that earn income. In both, a separate entity—the partnership or personal service corporation—is cast as the 'earner' for tax purposes. That characterization in both situations is, in essence, an assignment of income." * * *

This analysis wholly ignores the doctrine of agency. When a partner, *acting as agent for the partnership,* performs services for a client, the partnership is the earner of the income: the instrumentality (in this case the partner) through which the partnership has earned its fee is of no consequence. Therefore, the focus of the anticipatory assignment-of-income analysis ought to be on whether the partner acted for himself individually or as agent of the partnership. This is entirely consistent with the latitude accorded partnerships to disproportionately distribute partnership income: the pertinent requirement is merely that the partnership income so distributed have been earned *by the partnership.* In this case, it is quite clear that petitioner earned the fees in question pursuant to an agreement he entered into, on his own behalf, with [BSI]—an agreement that was consummated before petitioner's relationship with [B & K].[2] Consequently, petitioner is the true earner of the income and should not escape taxation by means of an anticipatory assignment. Lucas v. Earl, 281 U.S. 111 (1930).

The majority's "resolution" of the perceived conflict is unsatisfactory, The majority considers the determinative question to be whether the income is "of a type normally earned by the partnership. Only in such situations has the partner acted as part of the partnership entity." * * * The majority requires merely that income "be earned from an activity which can reasonably be associated with the partnership's business activity." * * * Thus, the majority would allow a partner to assign fees to the partnership if the work performed for such fees is similar to that performed by the partnership, but not if the work is different. * * *

The majority's distinction is unprincipled.[3] The majority observes that "The name and reputation of a professional partnership plays a role in the

---

**2.** Had there been a novation, substituting the partnership for petitioner, then the partnership could properly be considered the earner of the income. In this case, however, there is no basis set forth in the majority opinion for concluding that a novation has taken place or that a substitution of [B & K] for petitioner had been even discussed with

[BSI]. We are not privileged to simply assume a novation, since petitioner bears the burden of proof. Rule 142(a).

**3.** The majority fails to explain why the similarity of the work done by the partner to earn the fees to the work of the partnership is determinative. That failure not only casts doubt upon the correctness of this decision,

financial success of a partnership business" suggesting that partners, even acting individually, can further the business of the partnership by adding to its reputation. * * * But, that may be so even if the partner acts individually, doing work entirely dissimilar to that normally performed by the partnership. In any event, the majority fails to explain why such an obviously incidental benefit to the partnership should permit us to frustrate the assignment-of-income doctrine. The majority asserts that "The lack of structure inherent in the partnership form does not lend itself to easy resolution of the assignment-of-income question." * * * I must respectfully disagree. The lack of structure of the partnership form is irrelevant. All that matters is whether the partner has acted on his own behalf or on behalf, and as agent of, the partnership. Moreover, even if the lack of structure were relevant, the majority fails to explain why such would mandate the distinction between the type of income normally earned by the partnership and the type of income that is not. It would make far more sense to ask, with agency principles in mind, whether the income in question was earned by the partnership or by the partner acting as an individual.

Furthermore, I must disagree with Judge Beghe's concurring opinion on several grounds. First, section 721 would seem to prohibit any deduction for petitioner's contribution of money to the partnership. Second, the issue of a deduction under section 162 was not raised by the parties and thus is an inappropriate basis for decision. Third, the majority opinion does not set forth sufficient facts to determine, under the theory of the concurring opinion, the timing of any available deduction.

For the foregoing reasons, I respectfully dissent.

## NOTE

The Tax Court's opinion in *Schneer* sparked a great deal of controversy, with the commentators being split in as many directions as the judges on the Tax Court. One observer labeled the decision "exquisitely wrong, so misguided at every turn, that it becomes a wayward sort of achievement."[1] Subscribing to Judge Halpern's view, this writer concludes that the critical fact for assignment of income purposes was that Schneer earned the income in his individual capacity and not as a partner of B & K and SSG & M. Further, when Schneer earned the fees he was not jointly carrying on a business enterprise with the new partnerships. Rather, he was conducting a separate business of servicing former clients and that enterprise should not have been pooled with B & K and SSG & M.

---

but foreshadows the difficulty future courts will have in resolving the question: how similar is similar enough? Without any inkling of why similarity has been deemed important, future courts will lack any effective guidelines for answering that question.

1. Sheppard, "Partnership Mysticism and the Assignment of Income Doctrine," 54 Tax Notes 8 (Jan. 6, 1992).

Defenders of the result in *Schneer* have offered varying alternative rationales to support the decision.[2] One commentator suggests that *Schneer* represents a proper compromise between the assignment of income doctrine and the policy of Section 721 against impeding the formation of partnerships.[3] The purpose of the assignment of income doctrine is to preserve the integrity of the progressive rates by preventing easy tax avoidance through income shifting strategies. The transaction in *Schneer* is fairly common among law partners, who typically agree to pool all of their income from the practice of law, including royalties from writings and other related earnings. Further, it is reasonable to assume that the partners of B & K and SSG & M were taxed at the same marginal tax rate as Mr. Schneer. Since the arrangement in *Schneer* posed no real abuse, the writer concludes that assignment of income doctrine is inapplicable. And if the doctrine does not apply because the transaction is not tax motivated, related issues, such as whether the income-generating activity is sufficiently similar to the business of the partnership, are no longer relevant.[4]

## 3.   THE TAXABLE YEAR

Code: § 706(b). Skim § 444.

Regulations: § 1.706–1(b)(1), (2) & (3)(i).

Section 706(a) requires a partner to include his share of partnership income, losses and other items in his tax return for the taxable year in which the partnership's year ends. To preclude partnerships from using fiscal years to achieve a deferral of the partners' tax liability, Section 706(b)(1)(B) generally requires a partnership to determine its taxable year by reference to a series of mechanical rules related to the taxable years of its partners unless the partnership can establish a "business purpose" for using a different taxable year.[1] Under the mechanical rules, if one or more partners having a majority (i.e., greater than 50 percent) interest in partnership profits and capital have the same taxable year, the partnership also must use that year.[2] Thus, if a partnership has two 30 percent individual partners who use a calendar year and a 40 percent corporate partner which uses a June 30 fiscal year, the partnership must adopt a calendar year. If partners owning a majority interest in partnership profits

---

**2.** See Asimow, "Applying the Assignment of Income Principle Correctly," 54 Tax Notes 607 (Feb. 3, 1992); Cowan, "Tax Court Leaves Confusion in Wake of Decision on Assignment of Income to Partnership," 55 Tax Notes 1535 (June 15, 1992); Raby, "Outside Income of Professionals in Practice," 54 Tax Notes 423 (Jan. 27, 1992); Raby, "More on Assignment of a Partner's Outside Income," 54 Tax Notes 991 (Feb. 24, 1992).

**3.** Asimow, supra note 2.

**4.** Id. at 608.

**1.** I.R.C. § 706(b)(1)(C). See infra notes 5–7 and accompanying text. Even more restrictive rules apply to S corporations and personal service corporations. See I.R.C. §§ 441(i); 1378.

**2.** I.R.C. § 706(b)(1)(B)(i) & (b)(4)(A)(i). Except as provided by regulations, any partnership forced to change to a "majority interest taxable year" by Section 706(b)(1)(B)(i) can not be required to change to another year for either of the two taxable years following the year of change. I.R.C. § 706(b)(4)(B).

and capital do not have the same taxable year, the partnership must use the same taxable year as all of its "principal partners" (i.e., those having a 5 percent or more interest in profits or capital).[3] If neither of these first two rules applies, the regulations require the partnership to use the taxable year that results in the least aggregate deferral of income to the partners.[4]

Alternatively, a partnership may use a year not prescribed by the mechanical tests described above if it establishes to the satisfaction of the Treasury a "business purpose" for doing so.[5] Deferral of income to partners, however, is not treated as a business purpose.[6] A business purpose for a different year may be established under either of two different tests. First, there is a business purpose for a partnership to use a natural business year if it satisfies a 25–percent test.[7] Under the test, a natural business year exists if 25 percent or more of the partnership's gross receipts for the selected year are earned in the last two months. The 25–percent test must be satisfied in each of the preceding three 12–month periods that correspond to the requested fiscal year.

If a taxpayer cannot satisfy the 25–percent test, the business purpose for a year must be established under an all facts and circumstances test, which considers the tax consequences of the proposed year.[8] Congress has identified certain nontax factors that ordinarily will not be sufficient to satisfy the business purpose requirement. Those factors are: (1) the use of a particular year for regulatory or accounting purposes; (2) the seasonal hiring patterns of a business; (3) the use of a particular year for administrative purposes, such as retirements, promotions, or salary increases; and (4) the fact that a business involves the use of price lists, a model year, or other items that change annually.[9] Because these factors all relate to taxpayer convenience, the Service has concluded that a taxpayer must demonstrate compelling reasons in order to establish a business purpose for a requested year.[10] For example, the Service found that a taxpayer established a business purpose to use a June 30 tax year, where the taxpayer could not satisfy the 25–percent test for a June 30 natural business year because a labor strike had closed the business during its normal peak season. The taxpayer also had data from prior years that demonstrated that the 25–percent test would have been met if the strike had not occurred.[11]

When the mechanical rules in Section 706(b)(1)(B) were enacted, adversely affected fiscal year entities and their tax advisors greeted the

---

**3.** I.R.C. § 706(b)(1)(B)(ii) & (b)(3). Note that this rule does not apply unless all of the "principal partners" have the same taxable year.

**4.** I.R.C. § 706(b)(1)(B)(iii). Reg. § 1.706–1(b)(2)(C). For a formula to determine "the least aggregate deferral," see Reg. § 1.706–1(b)(3)(i).

**5.** I.R.C. § 706(b)(1)(C). For a critique of the business purpose taxable year, see Hanna, "A Partnership's Business Purpose Taxable Year: A Deferred Provision Whose Time Has Passed," 45 Tax Lawyer 685 (1992).

**6.** I.R.C. § 706(b)(1)(C).

**7.** Rev. Proc. 2002–38; §§ 2.02, 2.06, 5.05; 2002–1 C.B. 1037.

**8.** Rev. Rul. 87–57, 1987–2 C.B. 117.

**9.** H.R. Rep. No. 99–841, 99th Cong., 2d Sess. II–319 (1986).

**10.** Rev. Rul. 87–57, 1987–2 C.B. 117.

**11.** Id. (Situation 6).

more restrictive taxable year rules with cries of outrage. In an effort to reduce the calendar year tax return preparation workload of the accounting industry without reopening the door to deferral, Congress agreed to permit some flexibility. Under Section 444, partnerships may elect a taxable year other than the year required by the mechanical tests in Section 706(b)(1)(B) under certain conditions, including the payment of an entity-level tax designed to eliminate the benefits of deferral at the partner level.[12] When elected, Section 444 thus provides an escape from the Section 706(b)(1)(B) mechanical rules, but the election does not apply to partnerships using a taxable year for which they have established a business purpose under Section 706(b)(1)(C).[13] Thus, a partnership which has established a business purpose for a fiscal year may continue to use that year without having to make a Section 444 election or to pay an entity-level tax under Section 7519.[14]

Although Section 444 is hardly a model of clarity, it was intended to permit a newly formed partnership that does not come within the business purpose exception to elect to use a taxable year other than that required by Section 706(b)(1)(B) provided that the year elected results in no more than a three-month deferral of income to the partners.[15] Reconfirming the adage that there is no free lunch, Congress provided that partnerships (and S corporations) making the Section 444 election would be subject to a new tax imposed by Section 7519.[16] Computation of this "required payment" is highly complex and we will dispense with many of the details,[17] but at least the concept should be understood. Congress is attempting to require an electing partnership to pay (and in effect keep "on deposit") an amount of tax roughly approximating the tax that the partners would have paid on their income for any deferral period if a Section 444 election had not been made. Thus, if a partnership whose partners all used calendar years elected a fiscal year ending September 30, it would be required to pay a tax that supposedly equalled the benefit of three months' deferral received by the

---

**12.**   I.R.C. §§ 444(a), (e); 7519. Similar relief was provided to S corporations and personal service corporations.

**13.**   I.R.C. § 444(a), (e).

**14.**   Although the statute is not crystal clear on this point, the legislative history suggests this is what Congress intended (see H.R.Rep. No. 100–495, 100th Cong., 1st Sess. 938 (1987)), and the Service has announced that it concurs with this interpretation (I.R.S. Notice 88–10, 1988–1 C.B. 478). But if the only business purpose for a previously approved fiscal year was an automatic three-month deferral, which was permitted prior to 1987, a Section 444 election will be required to retain that fiscal year.

**15.**   I.R.C. § 444(a), (b)(1). Thus, if the mechanical rules would have required a calendar year, the partnership nonetheless may

elect a fiscal year ending September 30 because the "deferral period" (I.R.C. § 444(b)(4)) does not exceed three months.

**16.**   I.R.C. § 444(c)(1).

**17.**   In general, the "required payment" under Section 7519(b) is an amount equal to the highest individual tax rate plus one percent multiplied by the partnership's "net base year income" (generally defined by Section 7519(d)(1) as the net income of the partnership for the year preceding the election multiplied by a "deferral ratio" based on the relationship of the number of months in the deferral period of the preceding taxable year to the total number of months in that year) less the amount of any "required" payment for the preceding election year. So much for reducing the accountants' workload.

partners.[18] Under a de minimis rule, no payment is required if the amount due is less than $500.[19]

## PROBLEM

What taxable year must Partnership adopt under § 706(b) in each of the following alternatives? Unless stated to the contrary, assume Partnership is a newly formed partnership.

(a) All partners of Partnership are calendar year taxpayers? If the partners believe that the partnership will have substantial income and they are free to choose, what taxable year should they select for the partnership? What if they expect the partnership to have substantial losses?

(b) Partnership has a 20% corporate general partner which uses a July 31 fiscal year and 20 individual 4% limited partners all of whom are on a calendar year?

(c) What result in (b), above, if, on the first day of year four, 10 of the limited partners sell their interests to the corporate general partner?

(d) What result in (b), above, if 10 of the limited partners use a September 30 fiscal year and the other 10 use a calendar year?

(e) What result in (b), above, if Partnership wants to adopt a September 30 fiscal year under § 706(b) in order to have sufficient time to gather tax information for its calendar year partners? May Partnership adopt a September 30 fiscal year in some other manner? If so, with what cost?

(f) What result in (b), above, if over the prior five years Partnership has been in the retail business and does 20% of its annual business in December and 10% of its business in January in post-Christmas sales. Partnership has been using a calendar year. It wishes to change to a January 31 fiscal year. May it do so? If so, is a § 444 election and a § 7519 "required payment" necessary?

---

## B.   TAX CONSEQUENCES TO THE PARTNERS

## 1.   GENERAL RULES

Code: §§ 701; 702; 703(a); 705; 706(a).

Regulations: §§ 1.702–1(a), (c); 1.705–1(a); 1.706–1(a).

---

**18.** We say "supposedly" because the Section 7519 required payment is determined mechanically, without regard to amounts actually deferred by the partners. If the partnership receives income evenly throughout its taxable year, the required payment eventually will approximate what the partners would have paid without the deferral. But if the partnership's income is bunched in a particular period (e.g., the first or last three months of the taxable year), the payment may be greater or lesser than the actual deferral benefits enjoyed by the partners.

**19.** I.R.C. § 7519(a)(2).

Under the aggregate theory of Section 701, each partner is taxed on his or her share of partnership income or loss,[1] but the entity approach requires that the income, deductions and other tax items must be computed at the partnership level in order to determine the amounts that flow through to the partners. For this purpose, Section 703(a) provides that a partnership computes its "taxable income" in the same manner as an individual except that certain items described in Section 702(a) must be separately stated and certain deductions are disallowed.

The items listed in Section 702(a) must be separately stated because they may have potentially varying tax consequences to the different partners. The most common separately stated items are capital and Section 1231 gains and losses,[2] tax-exempt interest, dividends taxed as net capital gain, charitable contributions, and foreign taxes. Each partner's share of items subject to special treatment at the partner level (e.g., income or losses from passive activities, alternative minimum tax adjustment and preference items) also must be separately stated. The character of these items must be preserved so that they can be passed through and combined with any similar items derived by the partners from other activities for purposes of applying various special rules and limitations on the partner's tax return.

To illustrate, assume that the equal ABC partnership has a $30,000 Section 1231 gain[3] in the current year. If the partnership simply netted its Section 1231 gains and losses and then determined the ultimate result as if it were an individual, each partner would report his one-third share of the $30,000 gain, or $10,000 of long-term capital gain each. But if each partner were required to report his one-third share of the Section 1231 gain, preserving its character as such, the results might differ substantially. One partner might have a $20,000 Section 1231 loss from another source, winding up with a net ordinary loss from Section 1231 transactions, while another partner might have no Section 1231 gains or losses and end up with simply a $10,000 long-term capital gain. Because the tax treatment of the partnership's Section 1231 gains and losses may have varying effects among the partners, depending upon each partner's individual Section 1231 gains and losses, the Subchapter K pass-through scheme requires the

---

**1.** Section 702(c) provides that where it is necessary to determine a partner's gross income (e.g., for purposes of determining the need to file a return) that amount will include the partner's distributive share of the partnership's gross income. See the examples in Reg. § 1.702–1(c)(1) and (2).

**2.** The different capital gains rates for individuals have expanded the list of separately stated items. Section 1(h)(9) authorizes the Service to issue regulations implementing the capital gains regime in the case of sales and exchanges by partnerships. See Reg. § 1.1(h)–1. Form 1065, Schedule K–1 (see

Appendix) now includes separate lines for reporting long-term capital gains, Section 1231 gains, and collectible gains that are subject to a 28 percent maximum rate. See infra note 5.

**3.** For convenience, assume that all long-term capital gains and Section 1231 gains in this and later illustrations are from the sale of assets held for more than one year and qualify for the 15 percent maximum long-term capital gains rate applicable to noncorporate taxpayers. See I.R.C. § 1(h).

partnership's Section 1231 gains and losses (among other items) to be separately reported by the partners.[4] Any items of partnership income or loss which may have potentially different tax consequences to the partners, or any other person, are commonly referred to as "separately stated" or "variable effect" items, and each partner must separately take into account his or her distributive share of such items.[5] The regulations also require that any specially allocated items under Sections 704(b) or (c)[6] must be separately stated by the partners.[7] All the remaining partnership items of income or loss (i.e., the nonseparately stated items) are combined into one aggregate income or loss amount, and each partner reports his or her distributive share of that lump sum amount.[8]

A partner is taxed on his distributive share of partnership income or loss in his taxable year in which the partnership's tax year ends. Consequently, Section 705(a) requires that adjustments be made to the partner's outside basis to reflect the tax results from partnership operations. In general, a partner's outside basis is *increased* by his share of the partnership's (1) taxable income,[9] and (2) tax-exempt income,[10] and *decreased* (but not below zero) by (1) distributions from the partnership as provided in Section 733,[11] (2) the partner's share of partnership loss,[12] and (3) his share of partnership expenditures which are not deductible in arriving at taxable income and are not properly capitalized.[13]

The rationale for most of the Section 705 adjustments is straightforward. A partner is taxed on partnership income whether or not it is currently distributed to him, and he is permitted an upward basis adjustment for his share of partnership income to prevent that income from being taxed again on a subsequent distribution or sale of his partnership interest.[14] When the income is distributed, the statute logically requires a corresponding downward basis reduction.[15] When a partner deducts his share of partnership losses, Section 705 requires a downward basis adjustment to prevent the partner from effectively recognizing the loss a second

---

**4.** I.R.C. § 702(a)(3); Reg. § 1.702–1(a)(3).

**5.** I.R.C. § 702(a)(1)–(7); Reg. § 1.702–1(a)(8)(i), (ii). For example, Rev. Rul. 92–97, 1992–2 C.B. 124, holds that cancellation of indebtedness income is a separately stated item under Section 702(a). In preparing its information return (Form 1065), the partnership is required to complete and send to each partner a schedule known as a "K–1," on which the partners are advised of their respective shares of income and loss items, separately stated deductions, credits, tax preference items, investment interest, foreign taxes and a few other specialized items. See Appendix, infra.

**6.** See Chapter 4, infra.

**7.** Reg. § 1.702–1(a)(8)(i).

**8.** I.R.C. § 702(a)(8).

**9.** I.R.C. § 705(a)(1)(A).

**10.** I.R.C. § 705(a)(1)(B).

**11.** I.R.C. § 705(a)(2).

**12.** I.R.C. § 705(a)(2)(A).

**13.** I.R.C. § 705(a)(2)(B). The regulations provide that the Section 705(a)(2)(B) decrease in basis for nondeductible expenses is made before any Section 705(a)(2)(A) decrease for the partner's share of losses. Reg. § 1.704–1(d)(2). Section 705(b) adds an alternative rule under which, in limited circumstances, a partner's outside basis will be determined by his share of the inside bases of partnership assets upon a termination of the partnership. See Reg. § 1.705–1(b).

**14.** See Chapters 6 and 7, infra.

**15.** I.R.C. § 733.

time in the form of less gain or more loss on a subsequent disposition of his partnership interest.

The rationale for the basis adjustments for tax-exempt income and nondeductible noncapitalized items is less obvious. Even though a partner is not taxed on his share of the partnership's tax-exempt income, the Section 705(a)(1)(B) upward adjustment is necessary to prevent the partner from being taxed on the income when it is distributed or when the partner sells his partnership interest. For example, assume that a partner has a $1,000 outside basis and his share of the partnership's tax-exempt interest for the year is $200. The partner will not be taxed on the exempt interest. But if the $200 of interest is not distributed to the partner, his partnership interest will be worth $200 more than it was at the beginning of the year. Without a $200 upward basis adjustment, the partner would recognize $200 of additional income attributable to the tax-exempt interest on a subsequent sale of his partnership interest because the partner's outside basis would remain $1,000. The same rationale underlies the Section 705(a)(2)(B) downward basis adjustment for nondeductible or noncapitalized items. Without this adjustment, a partner would realize less gain or more loss on a subsequent sale of his partnership interest because the nondeductible item would have decreased the value of his interest (also decreasing his amount realized on disposition of the interest) without changing his outside basis.

## PROBLEM

A and B, both calendar year noncorporate taxpayers, are equal partners in the AB Partnership, which had the following income and expenses during its (business purpose) taxable year that ended on July 31 of the current year:

| | |
|---|---:|
| Gross receipts from inventory sales | $100,000 |
| Cost of goods sold | 30,000 |
| Salaries paid to nonpartners | 10,000 |
| Depreciation | 12,000 |
| Advertising expenses | 8,000 |
| Interest expense paid on investment margin account maintained by AB (see § 163(d)) | 6,000 |
| Gain from the sale of machine held for two years: | |
| § 1245 gain | 8,000 |
| § 1231 gain | 2,000 |
| Dividends | 7,000 |
| Charitable contributions | 800 |
| Tax-exempt interest | 500 |
| STCG on a sale of stock | 6,000 |
| LTCG on a sale of stock held for two years | 4,000 |
| LTCL on a sale of stock held for two years | 2,000 |
| § 1231 gain on casualty to machine held for two years | 1,000 |

(a) How and when will AB, A and B report the income and who will be liable for the taxes?

(b) Assume this is the first year of partnership operations, A's basis in his partnership interest is $70,000 and B's basis in her partnership interest is $40,000. What will be the tax consequences of AB's first year of operations to A and B?

(c) What would be the result in (b), above, if the partnership distributed $20,000 in cash to each partner at the end of the year?

(d) Would it matter if the § 1231 gain on the sale of the machine would have been ordinary income if A had sold it individually?

## 2. ELECTING LARGE PARTNERSHIPS

Code: §§ 771; 772(a), (b), (c)(1); 773(a), (b); 775.

The Subchapter K pass-through rules are simple enough to apply in most situations, but they can become an accounting and paperwork nightmare for a partnership with a large number of passive investors. In connection with its ongoing study of tax simplification, the staff of the Joint Committee on Taxation described the problems confronting a large partnership:[1]

> The requirement that each partner take into account separately his distributive share of a partnership's income, gain, loss, deduction and credit can result in the reporting of a large number of items to each partner. The Schedule K–1, on which such items are reported, contains space for more than 40 items. Reporting so many separately stated items is burdensome for individual investors with relatively small, passive interests in large partnerships. In many respects such investments are indistinguishable from those made in corporate stock or mutual funds, which do not require reporting of numerous separate items.

> In addition, the number of items reported under the current regime makes it difficult for the Internal Revenue Service to match items reported on the K–1 against the partner's income tax return. Matching is also difficult because items on the K–1 are often modified or limited at the partner level before appearing on the partner's tax return.

The Joint Committee's proposed solution was to ease the reporting and audit burden by reducing the number of separately stated items and to develop a simpler Form K–1 for certain large partnerships. The proposals were trapped in legislative gridlock for several years but finally were added to Subchapter K in 1997.

The large partnership regime applies to an electing large partnership ("ELP") and its partners. An ELP generally is any partnership with 100 or more partners in the preceding taxable year that makes an election to apply the simplified rules.[2] The number of partners is determined by counting

---

**1.** Staff of the Joint Committee on Taxation, Technical Explanation of the Tax Simplification Act of 1993 (H.R. 13)(J.C.S–1–93) 55–56 (Jan. 8, 1993).

**2.** I.R.C. §§ 771; 775(a). The Service

only persons directly holding partnership interests in the taxable year, including persons holding through nominees, but persons holding interests indirectly (e.g., through another partnership) are not counted.[3] Once made, an ELP election applies to all subsequent taxable years unless it is revoked with the consent of the Service.[4] Significantly, service partnerships, such as law and accounting firms, may not make an ELP election.[5]

Each partner in an ELP separately takes into account his or her distributive share of the partnership's: (1) taxable income or loss from passive loss limitation activities, (2) taxable income or loss from other activities (e.g., portfolio income or loss), (3) net capital gain or loss separated into amounts allocable to passive activities and other activities,[6] (4) tax-exempt interest, (5) a net alternative minimum tax adjustment separately computed for passive activities and other activities, (6) various general and specialized tax credits, (7) foreign income taxes, and (8) other items to the extent the Treasury determines that separate treatment is appropriate.[7] The taxable income of an ELP generally is computed in the same manner as an individual except that the items identified above must be separately stated.[8] An ELP is not allowed deductions for personal exemptions, net operating losses, or certain itemized deductions other than Section 212 expenses (e.g., investment expenses).[9] All elections affecting the computation of an ELP's taxable income or tax credits generally are made by the partnership.[10] Similarly, all limitations and other provisions affecting the computation of the taxable income or tax credits of an ELP are applied at the partnership level, other than: (1) the Section 68 overall limitation on itemized deductions, (2) the at-risk limitations, (3) the passive activity loss limitations, and (4) any other provision specified in the regulations.[11] Finally, the Service is given broad regulatory authority to prescribe regulations necessary to carry out the purposes of the new ELP rules.[12]

Two special rules apply to an ELP's deductions. First, miscellaneous itemized deductions are not separately reported to the partners. At the partnership level, the two percent floor in Section 67 does not apply, but 70

---

may issue regulations under which a partnership will cease to be treated as an ELP in any taxable year in which it has fewer than 100 partners. I.R.C. § 775(a)(1).

**3.**  H.R. Rep. No. 105–148, 105th Cong., 1st Sess. 576 (1997).

**4.**  I.R.C. § 775(a)(2).

**5.**  I.R.C. § 775(b)(2).

**6.**  For example, if an ELP has an excess of net short-term capital gain over net long-term capital loss, the excess is consolidated with the ELP's other taxable income and is not separately stated. Also, Section 1231 gains and losses are netted at the partnership level and any net gain is treated as long-term capital gain. Net Section 1231 loss is treated

as ordinary loss and consolidated with the ELP's other taxable income. H.R. Rep. No. 105–148, supra note 3, at 573.

**7.**  I.R.C. § 772(a). See Notice 2004–5, 2004–1 C.B. 489, which requires a partner in a ELP to take into account separately the partner's distributive share of qualified dividend income under Section 1(h)(11)(B).

**8.**  I.R.C. § 773(a)(1)(A).

**9.**  I.R.C. §§ 773(b)(1).

**10.**  I.R.C. § 773(a)(2). Elections under Sections 901 (the foreign tax credit) and 108 (discharge of indebtedness) are made individually by the partners. Id.

**11.**  I.R.C. § 773(a)(3).

**12.**  I.R.C. § 777.

percent of such deductions are disallowed as a form of rough justice "payback."[13] Second, an ELP's charitable contributions are not separately stated, but a charitable deduction is allowed at the partnership level in determining taxable income, subject to the ten-percent-of-taxable income limitation applicable to C corporations.[14] Several other special provisions are either industry specific or designed to prevent abuse.[15] For example, if an ELP has discharge of indebtedness income, such income is separately reported to the partners and the provisions of Section 108 are applied at the partner level.[16] Finally, ELPs are subject to a special procedural regime which includes an audit system and accelerated due date (March 15 for calendar year partnerships) for providing tax information to the partners.[17]

## C.   LIMITATIONS ON PARTNERSHIP LOSSES

### 1.   BASIS LIMITATIONS

Code: § 704(d).

Regulations: § 1.704–1(d).

Section 704(d) provides that a partner's distributive share of partnership loss, including capital loss, is allowable as a deduction only to the extent of the partner's outside basis at the end of the partnership's taxable year in which the loss occurred. This is appropriate because the partner's outside basis is reduced by his share of partnership losses under Section 705(a)(2)(A) and may not be reduced below zero. Section 704(d) merely defers deductions; if the limitation applies, any excess loss may be carried forward indefinitely and utilized when the partner acquires additional outside basis. For example, assume that a partner's basis in his partnership interest is $1,000 and his share of partnership loss is $1,200. Section 704(d) will limit the partner's allowable loss to $1,000, unless the partner somehow obtains an increase in his outside basis (for example, by contributing cash or property, or by increasing his share of partnership liabilities).[1] The $200 of disallowed loss will be suspended and may be used in later years when the partner has additional basis. If the partnership has both ordinary and capital losses, the regulations provide that the partner's loss is allocated to reflect the composition of the partnership's loss.[2] In the example, if the $1,200 of loss consists of $900 of ordinary loss and $300 of short-term capital loss, the partner's $1,000 allowable loss will be characterized as follows:

**13.**   I.R.C. § 773(b)(3).

**14.**   I.R.C. § 773(b)(2).

**15.**   See, e.g., I.R.C. § 776 (special rules for partnerships holding oil and gas properties).

**16.**   I.R.C. § 773(c). Computations at the partnership level disregard reductions in tax attributes under Section 108(b), but the partners' distributive shares are adjusted to reflect such reductions. I.R.C. § 774(a).

**17.**   I.R.C. §§ 6031(b), 6240 et seq.

**1.**   I.R.C. § 752(a). The allocation of partnership liabilities is introduced in Chapter 2B, supra, and discussed in depth in Chapter 4D infra.

**2.**   Reg. § 1.704–1(d)(4) Example (3).

$$\frac{\$900}{\$1,200} \times \$1,000 = \$750 \text{ ordinary loss}$$

$$\frac{\$300}{\$1,200} \times \$1,000 = \$250 \text{ short-term capital loss}$$

The $200 of carryover loss will consist of $150 of ordinary loss and $50 of short-term capital loss.

While not free from doubt, it is likely that the carryover loss is generally personal to each individual partner. Thus, if a partner sells his partnership interest, the seller's previously deferred losses will disappear and not carry over to the buyer.[3] The carryover loss also apparently terminates if a partner dies,[4] but it is not totally certain whether a carryover loss may be used by a donee partner.[5]

## PROBLEM

C and D are partners who share income and losses equally. C has an outside basis of $5,000 in his partnership interest and D has an outside basis of $15,000 in her partnership interest.

(a) During the current year the partnership has gross income of $40,000 and expenses of $60,000. What are the tax results to C and D?

(b) What are the results to C and D in the succeeding year when the partnership has $20,000 of net profits?

(c) How might C have alleviated his problem in the first year?

(d) What result in (a), above, if the net $20,000 loss consists of $15,000 of ordinary loss and $5,000 of long-term capital loss?

(e) What result to S, C's son, in (a), above, if C gives his interest in the partnership to S on the first day of a year in which the partnership has profits of $20,000?

## 2. AT-RISK LIMITATIONS

Code: §§ 49(a)(1)(D)(iv) & (v); 465(a)(1) & (2), (b), (c)(1) & (3), (d), (e).

Individuals (including individual partners) and certain closely held corporations are subject to the Section 465 at-risk rules, which seek to limit

---

**3.** Cf. Sennett v. Commissioner, 80 T.C. 825 (1983), where the Tax Court held that Section 704(d) contemplates that a taxpayer will be a partner at the end of the year in which the carryover loss is utilized. In that case, a partner who sold his partnership interest to the partnership was not allowed to utilize suspended losses when he repaid the losses to the partnership in a later year pur-suant to a sale contract. Instead, the payment was treated as a reduction in gain from the sale of the partnership interest.

**4.** Capital loss carryovers also terminate at death. Rev.Rul. 74–175, 1974–1 C.B. 52.

**5.** Problem (e), below, raises this issue.

a taxpayer's deductible losses from a broad range of business and investment activities to the amount that the taxpayer is "at risk"[1] with respect to those activities. In the partnership setting, the at-risk rules are applied on a partner-by-partner basis rather than at the partnership level.[2] In general, the rules are applied separately to each "activity" in which a partnership is engaged,[3] but exceptions may require certain trade or business activities to be aggregated.[4]

A taxpayer's initial at-risk amount generally includes: (1) his cash contributions to the activity; (2) the adjusted basis of other property contributed by the taxpayer to the activity; and (3) amounts borrowed for use in the activity for which the taxpayer is personally liable or which are secured by property of the taxpayer (not otherwise used in the activity) to the extent of the fair market value of the encumbered property.[5] The most important distinction between the Section 704(d) basis limitation and the at-risk limitation is that nonrecourse liabilities of the partnership will increase a partner's outside basis[6] but, except with respect to certain real estate activities,[7] a taxpayer is not considered at risk with respect to nonrecourse loans and similar arrangements where the taxpayer has no economic risk.[8] As a result, a loss allowable after application of Section 704(d) nonetheless may be disallowed (or, more accurately, deferred) by Section 465. Any loss disallowed by Section 465 may be carried over and deducted when either the taxpayer becomes at risk, the partnership disposes of the activity, or the taxpayer disposes of his partnership interest.[9] If a partner's loss is deferred by Section 465, the partner's outside basis is nonetheless reduced by the amount of the loss.[10]

A partner is considered at risk with respect to his share of partnership recourse debt.[11] For a debt to be considered "recourse," the regulations require that a creditor must be able to sue the partner under state law, and the funds must be borrowed from a person who has no interest (other than as a creditor) in the activity in which those funds are used.[12]

---

**1.**  See I.R.C. § 465(b)(1) & (2).

**2.**  I.R.C.   § 465(a)(1);   Prop.Reg. § 1.465–41 Example (1). Cf. Prop.Reg. § 1.465–42(c)(2).

**3.**  I.R.C. § 465(c)(2)(A) & (3)(A).

**4.**  I.R.C. § 465(c)(2)(B), (3)(B), and (C). See McKee, Nelson & Whitmire, Federal Taxation of Partnerships and Partners ¶ 10.06[2][c] (3d ed. 1996).

**5.**  Id. The initial at-risk amount is generally increased by the taxpayer's share of income and decreased by the taxpayer's share of losses and distributions from the activity. I.R.C. § 465(b)(5). But see I.R.C. § 465(b)(3), which provides that a taxpayer is not at risk with respect to recourse borrowings if the lender or a person related to the lender has

an interest in the activity other than as a creditor.

**6.**  I.R.C. §§ 722; 752(a).

**7.**  See   I.R.C.   §§ 465(b)(6); 49(a)(1)(D)(iv) & (v) and infra notes 13–20 and accompanying text.

**8.**  I.R.C. § 465(b)(2) & (4).

**9.**  I.R.C.   § 465(a)(1);   Prop.Reg. § 1.465–66.

**10.**  Prop.Reg. § 1.465–1(e).

**11.**  I.R.C. § 465(b)(1)(B), (b)(2)(A). See Prop.Reg.   § 1.465–24.   Compare   Reg. § 1.752–2, discussed in Chapter 4D, infra.

**12.**  Reg.   § 1.465–8(a);   Prop.   Reg. § 1.465–24(a)(2);   I.R.C.   § 465(b)(3)(A)   & (B)(i).

Although Congress extended the at-risk rules to real estate activities in the 1986 Code, it included an important escape hatch. Taxpayers are still considered at risk with respect to certain nonrecourse loans secured by real property which constitute "qualified nonrecourse financing."[13] In broad outline, this exception is available for nonrecourse financing obtained from commercial lenders or the government but not with respect to seller or promoter-financed debt. Nonrecourse financing is "qualified" if it is non-convertible debt[14] for which no person is personally liable[15] and which is incurred by the taxpayer with respect to the holding of real estate[16] and is borrowed from a "qualified person" or from certain government instrumentalities. A "qualified person" is any person actively and regularly engaged in the business of lending money who is not related to the borrower and is not the seller of the property, a relative of the seller or a person who receives a fee (e.g., a promoter or a broker) with respect to the taxpayer's investment in the real property, or a relative of such a fee recipient.[17] A typical qualified person would be a bank, savings and loan association, insurance company or pension fund. These distinctions arose out of Congress's effort to limit the opportunity for taxpayers to inflate deductions by overvaluing depreciable real estate.[18] Unrelated lenders were viewed as less likely to make loans which exceed the true value of the encumbered property, while sellers, promoters and lenders related to the borrower were assumed to have little incentive to limit the financing to the value of the property.[19] Even related persons (other than sellers or promoters) will be treated as qualified, however, if they are regular money lenders and the loan is commercially reasonable and on substantially the same terms as loans to unrelated persons.[20]

In the case of a partnership, a partner's share of any qualified nonrecourse financing is determined on the basis of the partner's share of partnership liabilities under Section 752,[21] provided the financing is qualified nonrecourse financing with respect to both the partner and the

**13.** I.R.C. § 465(b)(6)(A); Reg. § 1.465–27.

**14.** I.R.C. § 465(b)(6)(B)(iv).

**15.** I.R.C. § 465(b)(6)(B)(iii). Congress authorized the Treasury to set forth circumstances in which guaranties, indemnities, or personal liability of a person other than the taxpayer will not prevent the debt from being treated as qualified nonrecourse financing. Staff of the Joint Committee on Taxation, General Explanation of the Tax Reform Act of 1986 (hereinafter "1986 Act General Explanation"), 100th Cong., 1st Sess. 258 (1987).

**16.** I.R.C. § 465(b)(6)(B)(i).

**17.** I.R.C. § 49(a)(1)(D)(iv). For this purpose, "related persons" are defined by a chain of statutory cross-references, beginning in Section 49(a)(1)(D) and snake dancing

through Section 465(b)(3)(C) and on to Sections 267(b) and 707(b)(1). In general, related persons include certain family members, trusts and corporations or partnerships in which a person has at least a 10 percent interest. Relationships are determined at the close of the taxable year. I.R.C. § 49(a)(1)(D)(v).

**18.** 1986 Act General Explanation, supra note 15, at 256.

**19.** Id. at 257.

**20.** I.R.C. § 465(b)(6)(D)(ii). For when the terms of a nonrecourse loan are considered commercially reasonable, see 1986 Act General Explanation, supra note 15, at 258–259.

**21.** I.R.C. § 465(b)(6)(C). See Reg. § 1.752–3 and Chapter 4D, infra.

partnership. The amount for which partners may be treated at risk, however, may not exceed the total amount of qualified nonrecourse financing at the partnership level.[22]

## PROBLEMS

**1.** LP is a limited partner in a newly formed partnership which is engaged in the following activities:

    (i) A research and development activity to which LP contributed $10,000 cash; LP's share of partnership nonrecourse liability attributable to this activity is $10,000. LP's share of loss from the research and development activity is $12,000 for the current year.

    (ii) A motion picture production activity to which LP contributed $20,000 cash; LP's share of income from this activity for the current year is $25,000.

LP's outside basis at the beginning of the year was $40,000, and his share of net gain for the year was $13,000. What are the tax consequences to LP under § 465.

**2.** The ABC equal limited partnership (in which A is a general partner and B and C are limited partners) purchased an apartment building for $540,000, paying $90,000 of cash (contributed equally by the partners to the partnership) and financing the balance with a $450,000 nonrecourse loan secured by the building. Assume that A, B and C are all unrelated and that the partnership holds no other assets. To what extent are each of the partners at risk if the loan is:

    (a) From a commercial bank in which none of the parties owns an interest.

    (b) From the seller of the apartment complex.

    (c) From B's brother, who is in the money lending business and makes the loan at a rate of interest 25% below comparable rates charged to unrelated borrowers.

    (d) The same as (c), above, except the loan is at regular commercial rates of interest.

    (e) Personally guaranteed equally by A, B and C.

## 3. PASSIVE LOSS LIMITATIONS

Code: § 469(a), (b), (c), (d)(1), (e)(1)(A), (g)(1), (h)(1), (2) and (5), (i)(1), (2), (3) and (6), (k); 772(a)(1) & (2), (c)(2) & (3), (d)(1), (f).

Temporary Regulations: § 1.469–5T(a), (b)(2), (c), (d), (e), (f)(1) & (4).

    *Overview.* Just as the Section 704(d) basis limitation was demoted upon the arrival of the at-risk rules, so it is that both those curbs on allowable losses were largely pushed to the sidelines with the enactment of

---

**22.** 1986 Act General Explanation, supra note 15, at 260.

the Section 469 passive loss limitations in the Tax Reform Act of 1986. Section 469 is broadly applicable and is likely to have been studied in a basic income tax course. Our coverage here will be selective, beginning with an overview and then focusing on the application of the passive loss limitations to partnerships and their interaction with Sections 704(d) and 465.

Section 469 was enacted to restrict taxpayers from using deductions and other losses generated from certain passive investment activities to "shelter" income from other sources (e.g., a taxpayer's regular business income, compensation, dividends and interest).[1] The Section 704(d) basis and Section 465 at-risk limitations are bottomed on similar objectives, but they were ineffective in curbing the proliferation of tax shelters. The ability of limited partners to include nonrecourse debt in their outside bases contributed to the impotence of Section 704(d). Although the at-risk rules were successful in limiting the pass-through of losses from some of the more exotic tax avoidance vehicles, the pre–1987 exemption of real estate from Section 465 permitted that most conventional of tax shelters to flourish. By 1986, Congress concluded that decisive action was needed to curb the tax shelter market and restore public confidence in the fairness of the tax system.

Section 469 goes well beyond its earlier counterparts by disallowing the current deductibility of losses and the use of credits from "passive activities."[2] The income and losses from each of a taxpayer's passive activities are first computed and then all are combined; in any taxable year, passive activity losses can be deducted only to the extent of the taxpayer's income from passive activities for that year.[3] To the extent that losses from passive activities for the taxable year exceed the taxpayer's passive income, that excess may be carried forward and deducted (subject to the same limitation) against future net income from passive activities.[4] Similar rules are applicable to credits from passive activities.[5] Disallowed losses from a particular activity (but not credits)[6] may be deducted in full on a taxable disposition of the entire activity.[7] In short, Section 469 does not forever

---

**1.** See generally Staff of the Joint Committee on Taxation, General Explanation of the Tax Reform Act of 1986 (hereinafter "1986 Act General Explanation"), 100th Cong., 1st Sess. 209–254 (1987). For another detailed discussion of Section 469, see Freeland, Lathrope, Lind & Stephens, Fundamentals of Federal Income Taxation 525–537 (Foundation Press, 13th ed. 2004).

**2.** I.R.C. § 469(a)(1).

**3.** I.R.C. § 469(a)(1)(A) & (d)(1).

**4.** I.R.C. § 469(b).

**5.** I.R.C. § 469(a)(1)(B). The limitation applies to the extent that credits from passive activities for the year exceed tax liability for the year attributable to such activities. I.R.C.

§ 469(d)(2). Credits also may be carried forward. I.R.C. § 469(b).

**6.** Disallowed credits are not allowed on the sale of a passive activity. Cf. I.R.C. § 469(g). See 1986 Act General Explanation, supra note 1, at 228.

**7.** I.R.C. § 469(g)(1)(A). This rule applies to a disposition of a limited partnership interest. The loss is allowed on the disposition by the partnership of a passive activity or on the disposition of the partnership interest, whichever occurs first. See 1986 Act General Explanation, supra note 1, at 227–229 and McKee, Nelson & Whitmire, Federal Taxation of Partnerships and Partners ¶ 10.08[3][a] (3d ed. 1996). Special rules ap-

disallow excess passive losses; it merely postpones them. This delayed gratification is enough to destroy any after-tax economic benefits of the typical leveraged tax shelter.

Section 469 applies to individuals (including partners), estates, trusts, personal service corporations and certain other closely held corporations.[8] As in the case of the at-risk rules, the passive loss limitations are applied on a partner-by-partner basis, not at the partnership level. The limitations are applied only after application of the Section 704(d) and Section 465 limitations.[9]

*The "Material Participation" Standard.* In considering the proper form of attack and the appropriate targets of reform, Congress determined that limitations should not be imposed on taxpayers who were actively involved in a business activity. Rather, the restrictions are aimed squarely at tax shelters by focusing on the passive investor, who is viewed as less likely to approach an activity with a significant nontax economic motive.[10] In keeping with these objectives, "passive activity" is defined by reference to a "material participation" standard. A "passive activity" is any activity involving the conduct of any trade or business (including nonbusiness profit-motivated activities within the ambit of Section 212) in which the taxpayer does not "materially participate."[11] Under the statute, a taxpayer materially participates in an activity only if he is involved on a regular, continuous and substantial basis in the operation of the activity.[12]

The regulations elaborate on the material participation standard by defining "participation" and setting forth seven separate situations in which a taxpayer's participation in an activity will be considered material. "Participation" generally includes work done by the taxpayer in all capacities except as an investor in the activity unless the taxpayer is directly involved in day-to-day management or operations.[13] A taxpayer is treated as materially participating in an activity for a taxable year[14] if any one of these tests is met:[15] (1) the taxpayer participates in the activity for more than 500 hours during the year; (2) the taxpayer's participation in the

---

ply to installment sale dispositions (I.R.C. § 469(g)(3)), dispositions to related parties (I.R.C. § 469(g)(1)(B)), dispositions at death (I.R.C. § 469(g)(2)), and dispositions by gift (I.R.C. § 469(j)(6)).

**8.** I.R.C. § 469(a)(2).

**9.** Temp.Reg. § 1.469–2T(d)(6). As in the case of the at-risk limitations (see Prop. Reg. § 1.465–1(e)), a partner's outside basis is reduced for losses which are allowed under Section 704(d) even though such losses are disallowed by Section 469. Id.

**10.** 1986 Act General Explanation, supra note 1, at 211–212.

**11.** I.R.C. § 469(c)(1) & (6). For the Service's flexible facts and circumstances approach to defining an "activity," see Prop.

Reg. § 1.469–4. Section 469 does not apply to working interests in oil and gas properties, ostensibly in order to attract investors to this beleaguered industry, at least if they are willing to accept the financial risk of a working interest. I.R.C. § 469(c)(3)(A). See 1986 Act General Explanation, supra note 1, at 213–214.

**12.** I.R.C. § 469(h)(1). See 1986 Act General Explanation, supra note 1, at 235–245.

**13.** Temp.Reg. § 1.469–5T(f)(2)(ii).

**14.** Where the taxpayer is a partner, the "taxable year" is the partnership's year rather than the partner's if the two are different. Temp.Reg. § 1.469–2T(e)(1).

**15.** Temp.Reg. § 1.469–5T(a)(1)–(7).

activity constitutes substantially all of the participation in the activity by any individual for the year; (3) the taxpayer devotes more than 100 hours to the activity during the year and his participation is not less than that of any other person; (4) the activity is a "significant participation" activity—that is, a trade or business activity in which the taxpayer participates for more than 100 hours and the taxpayer does not satisfy any of the other tests for material participation[16]—and the individual's aggregate participation in all "significant participation" activities for the year exceeds 500 hours; (5) the taxpayer materially participated in the activity for any five of the ten taxable years immediately preceding the taxable year; (6) the activity is a "personal service activity"—that is, an activity principally involving the performance of services in fields such as health, law, engineering, architecture and accounting[17]—and the taxpayer materially participated in the activity for any three taxable years preceding the taxable year; or (7) based on all the facts and circumstances, the taxpayer's participation in the activity during the taxable year is regular, continuous and substantial.[18] Notably, the regulations do not impose any particular recordkeeping requirements, but they suggest that appointment books, calendars and narrative summaries may help establish the approximate hours devoted to an activity.[19]

*Rental Activities.* Congress concluded that the material participation standard was inappropriate in the case of most rental activities, which were historically used as tax shelters and generally require less personal involvement than other business pursuits. For example, a taxpayer engaged full-time in one profession easily might provide all the necessary management activities for a rental property in her spare time and still meet the material participation test because she was the only person involved in managing the property.[20] With a few limited exceptions, Section 469 presumes that all rental activities are "passive" regardless of the extent of participation by the taxpayer.[21] Modest relief is provided for middle-income taxpayers who invest in rental property—for example, "Mom and Pop," who own and manage one duplex apartment to provide financial security rather than to shelter a substantial amount of other income. Under Section 469(i), these individual taxpayers may deduct up to $25,000 of losses attributable to rental real estate activities if they "actively participate"[22] and own at least

---

**16.** Temp.Reg. § 1.469–5T(c).

**17.** Temp.Reg. § 1.469–5T(d).

**18.** The regulations do not yet identify what facts and circumstances may be relevant, but they state that taxpayers will not meet this fallback test unless they participate in the activity for more than 100 hours. Temp.Reg. § 1.469–5T(b)(2)(iii).

**19.** Temp.Reg. § 1.469–5T(f)(4).

**20.** Temp.Reg. § 1.469–5T(a)(2). See S.Rep. No. 99–313, 99th Cong., 2d Sess. 718 (1986).

**21.** I.R.C. § 469(c)(2). "Rental activity" is broadly defined by Section 469(j)(8) as any activity where payments are made for the use of tangible property.

**22.** "Active" participation requires something less than "material" participation. Except as provided in regulations (not yet issued), limited partners are not treated as actively participating. I.R.C. § 469(i)(6)(C).

a 10 percent interest in the activity.[23] Beginning in 1994, the real estate rental activities of taxpayers other than closely held C corporations are treated as active trades or businesses if more than half of the personal services performed by the taxpayer in all trades or businesses during the year, and more than 750 hours, are in real property trades or businesses in which the taxpayer materially participates.[24] This rule, which was intended to provide relief to developers and other active real estate entrepreneurs, generally does not apply to limited partnership interests.[25]

*Working Interests.* Regardless of the taxpayer's material participation, a passive activity does not include a working interest in any oil or gas well which the taxpayer holds directly or through an entity that does not limit the taxpayer's liability with respect to the drilling or operation of the property.[26] Even though passive investors commonly have owned working interests, this exception was included in Section 469 at the behest of legislators from oil producing states.[27] The exception does not apply to a limited partnership in which the taxpayer is not a general partner.[28]

*Portfolio Income.* Without some refinement, the broad definition of passive activity would embrace all of a taxpayer's portfolio investments, such as stocks and bonds. As a result, a taxpayer could shelter the classic forms of investment income (dividends, interest, capital gains from the sales of securities) with passive losses. The Senate Finance Committee recognized that "[t]o permit portfolio income to be offset by passive losses or credits would create the inequitable result of restricting sheltering by individuals dependent for support on wages or active business income, while permitting sheltering by those whose income is derived from an investment portfolio."[29] Section 469 thus provides that "portfolio income" (interest, dividends, annuities, royalties not derived in the ordinary course of a trade or business and gains or losses from assets that produce such income, less related expenses) shall not be considered as arising from a passive activity.[30] To prevent investors from skirting these rules by investing in limited partnerships that generate dividends, interest, and capital gains, portfolio income earned by a partnership is separately stated and retains its character when it passes through to the partners.[31] Moreover, Section 469(*l*)(3) authorizes the Treasury to prescribe regulations to re-

---

**23.** I.R.C. § 469(i)(1), (2) and (6). The $25,000 allowance is phased out by 50 percent of the amount by which the taxpayer's adjusted gross income (without regard to this deduction) exceeds $100,000. I.R.C. § 469(i)(3).

**24.** I.R.C. § 469(c)(7).

**25.** I.R.C. § 469(c)(7)(A). For some other narrowing exceptions and safe harbors from the rental activity rule, see Temp.Reg. § 1.469–1T(e)(3)(ii).

**26.** I.R.C. § 469(c)(3).

**27.** See Birnbaum & Murray, Showdown at Gucci Gulch 229–232 (1987).

**28.** Temp.Reg. § 1.469–1T(e)(4)(v)(A)(*i*).

**29.** S.Rep. No. 99–313, supra note 20, at 728.

**30.** I.R.C. § 469(e)(1).

**31.** Temp.Reg. § 1.469–2T(c)(3)(i), 1.469–2T(c)(3)(iv) Example (2). Cf. Temp. Reg. § 1.469–2T(e)(1). See also Form 1065, Schedule K–1, reproduced in Appendix A, infra.

quire certain income from limited partnerships or from other passive activities to be reclassified as not arising from a passive activity.[32]

*General Partners.* Whether or not a *general* partner's share of income or loss is treated as derived from a passive activity requires a separate analysis of each general partner and of each separate activity in which the partnership engages. The critical issues narrow to: (1) when are different pursuits of the partnership classified as separate "activities" in which a partner must materially participate in order to avoid the passive loss limitations, and (2) what degree of participation by a partner in an activity is "material?"

The legislative history states that "[t]he determination of what constitutes a separate activity is intended to be made in a realistic economic sense" by looking to whether the "undertakings consist of an integrated and interrelated economic unit, conducted in coordination with or reliance upon each other, and constituting an appropriate unit for the measurement of gain or loss."[33] The regulations make it clear that a single partnership may engage in more than one activity.[34] When a partnership's separate activities are identified, the partner's participation in each activity must be analyzed to determine whether or not it is "material," employing the seven tests discussed above.[35] Apart from material participation, the definition of "activity" is significant because previously suspended losses from a passive activity become currently deductible upon the taxpayer's disposition of his entire interest in the activity.[36]

*Limited Partners.* Congress was aware of the widespread use of syndicated limited partnerships as tax shelters, and it also recognized that limited partners were restricted in their ability to manage partnership activities. Section 469 thus presumes, except as may be provided otherwise in regulations, that all limited partnership interests are activities in which a taxpayer does not materially participate.[37] Under the regulations, limited partners are considered to materially participate only if: (1) they participate in the activity for more than 500 hours during the taxable year, (2) they materially participated in the activity for any five tax years during the ten years preceding the taxable year, or (3) the activity is a "personal service activity" and the limited partner materially participated in the activity for any three tax years (whether or not consecutive) preceding the taxable year.[38] A limited partner who is also a general partner and who meets one of the seven tests for material participation is treated as materially partici-

---

**32.** For examples of the Treasury's exercise of this regulatory authority, see Temp. Reg. § 1.469–2T(f).

**33.** S.Rep. No. 99–313, supra note 20, at 739.

**34.** See generally Reg. § 1.469–4, especially 4(c), which adopts a flexible facts and circumstances approach to define an "activity."

**35.** See supra notes 13–19 and accompanying text.

**36.** I.R.C. § 469(g)(1)(A).

**37.** I.R.C. § 469(h)(2).

**38.** Temp.Reg. § 1.469–5T(e)(1) and (2).

pating with respect to both the limited and general partnership interests.[39] A limited partner's share of income received for the performance of services (e.g., by way of salary, guaranteed payment or allocation of partnership income) is not treated as income from a passive activity.[40]

*Electing Large Partnerships.* A partner in an electing large partnership takes into account separately the partner's share of taxable income or loss from (1) passive loss limitation activities, and (2) other activities.[41] A passive loss limitation activity is any partnership activity which involves the conduct of a trade or business and any rental activity.[42] A partner's distributive share of an ELP's taxable income or loss from passive loss limitation activities is treated as being from a single passive activity.[43] Thus, an ELP generally does not have to separately report items from its different activities.

A partner's distributive share of an ELP's taxable income or loss from activities that are not passive loss limitation activities is treated as income or expense from property held for investment.[44] Thus, an ELP's portfolio income is reported separately and reduced by portfolio deductions.[45]

A special rule applies to the passive loss limitation in the case of a general partner in an ELP. If a partner holds an interest in an ELP other than a limited partnership interest, the partner's distributive share of any items are taken into account separately to the extent necessary to comply with the passive loss rules.[46] For example, income from an ELP is not treated as passive income to a general partner who materially participates in the partnership's trade or business.[47]

*Publicly Traded Partnerships.* As soon as the passive limitations were enacted, taxpayers began maneuvering to avoid their impact by seeking out sources of passive income against which passive losses might be deducted. Because a limited partner's share of partnership income is presumptively passive,[48] the publicly traded partnership ("PTP") emerged as a promising passive income generator. Although the Treasury might have attacked this strategy with regulations classifying a PTP's income as "portfolio income,"[49] Congress concluded that specific legislation was preferable to ensure that income from a PTP would be treated on a par with other investment income for purposes of the passive loss limitations.[50]

We have seen that Congress first addressed the broader classification problem by enacting Section 7704, which provides that a PTP generally is

---

**39.** Temp.Reg. § 1.469–5T(e)(3)(ii).

**40.** I.R.C. § 469(e)(3). See 1986 Act General Explanation, supra note 1, at 236–237.

**41.** I.R.C. §§ 772(a)(1), 772(a)(2).

**42.** I.R.C. § 772(d)(1).

**43.** I.R.C. § 772(c)(2).

**44.** I.R.C. § 772(c)(3)(A).

**45.** H.R. Rep. No. 105–148, 105th Cong., 1st Sess. 574 (1997).

**46.** I.R.C. § 772(f).

**47.** H.R. Rep. No. 105–148, supra note 45, at 574–75.

**48.** I.R.C. § 469(h)(2).

**49.** I.R.C. § 469(*l*).

**50.** See S.Rep. No. 100–76, 100th Cong., 1st Sess. 185–186 (1987).

taxed as a corporation.[51] A PTP is defined for this purpose as a partnership whose interests are traded on an established securities market or are readily tradable on a secondary market.[52] If, however, 90 percent of the gross income of a PTP is "qualifying income" (generally passive investment income, such as dividends, interest, real property rents and natural resources royalties[53]), the PTP is not taxed as a corporation.[54]

For those PTPs still taxed as partnerships, net income that passes through to partners is treated as portfolio income which may not be offset by losses from passive activities.[55] A partner's passive losses from a PTP that is taxed as a partnership may be deducted only against passive income from the same PTP. Unused losses are suspended and carried forward until that PTP has passive income or until the partner completely disposes of his interest in the partnership.

## PROBLEMS

**1**. Producer owns both a 40% interest as a general partner and a 20% interest as a limited partner in PG–13 Associates, a motion picture production partnership which also pays Producer a $100,000 annual salary for her services as a full-time (1,500 hours per year) producer. After deducting Producer's salary, the partnership has a $300,000 net loss in the current year. Producer's aggregate outside basis for her partnership interests at the beginning of the year is $350,000. Producer's outside basis is attributable to cash contributed to PG–13 Associates.

   (a) What are the tax consequences to Producer from her interests in PG–13 Associates for the current year?

   (b) What result in (a), above, if Producer spends most of her time farming and only devotes 300 hours during the year to PG–13?

   (c) What result in (b), above, if Producer had devoted 1,500 hours to PG–13 during each of the previous five years?

   (d) What result in (b), above, if the partnership's loss for the year is only $200,000 because it also realizes $60,000 of dividend income and $40,000 of net gains from sales of marketable securities?

   (e) What result in (b), above, if Producer also has $75,000 of income from an interest in a "burned out" real estate limited partnership interest?

   (f) What result in (b), above, if Producer also has a $25,000 loss from a rental real estate limited partnership interest?

**51.**  I.R.C. § 7704(a). See Chapter 1B2c, supra.

**52.**  I.R.C. § 7704(b).

**53.**  I.R.C. § 7704(d).

**54.**  I.R.C. § 7704(c). The 90 percent test must be met for each year beginning after December 31, 1987 during which the partnership is in existence. I.R.C. § 7704(c)(1).

**55.**  I.R.C. § 469(k). See S.Rep. No. 100–76, supra note 50, at 186–187.

(g) What result in (b), above, if Producer also has a $50,000 loss from an investment in a general partnership that owns a working interest in an oil and gas property?

(h) Same as (g), above, except Producer holds her interest in the oil and gas partnership as a limited partner?

**2.** During the current year LP has investments in four limited partnerships as follows:

(i) A motion picture production limited partnership in which LP has an outside basis of $10,000 attributable to LP's cash contribution to the partnership. LP's distributive share of loss in this partnership for the current year is $25,000.

(ii) An equipment leasing limited partnership in which LP has a $100,000 outside basis (attributable to a $15,000 cash contribution and an $85,000 nonrecourse liability). LP's share of loss for the year is $20,000.

(iii) A real estate limited partnership in which LP has a positive outside basis and his share of partnership income is $30,000 for the year.

(iv) A research and development limited partnership in which LP has an outside basis of $60,000, attributable to his $60,000 cash contribution to the partnership. LP's share of the partnership's loss for the year is $40,000.

Consider to what extent LP may deduct his share of losses from these partnerships for the current year, assuming he has no carryovers under Sections 704(d), 465 or 469.

CHAPTER 4

# PARTNERSHIP ALLOCATIONS

## A. INTRODUCTION

One of the critical nontax differences between partnerships and corporations is the greater flexibility for partners to custom tailor their economic arrangements. Through their partnership agreement, partners have considerable latitude to structure allocations of profits and losses (both generally and as to specific income and expense items), the amount and timing of distributions of cash or property, and the compensation paid to partners who render services to the enterprise. The partnership agreement can provide priority returns to partners on their invested capital or for services, and it can specify how much each partner is entitled to receive on a liquidation of the firm.

Despite what this chapter may come to suggest, the vast majority of allocation provisions in partnership agreements are not tax driven. Rather, they are influenced by economic considerations that would be present even without an income tax system. Consider, for example, a typical "money and brains" partnership where investor partners contribute cash and other forms of capital, and manager partners contribute their expertise and entrepreneurial skills. With or without the intrusion of an income tax, a manager partner ordinarily will demand some form of base compensation for her efforts, while the investors may seek a preferred return on their invested capital and an allocation mechanism that provides for a recovery of their investment before profits are shared with the manager partners. If and when the enterprise becomes profitable, the managers usually will insist upon a priority allocation of a stated percentage of net profits (e.g., the first 20 percent), with the remaining profits to be shared among all partners in proportion to their capital investments. Additional allocation provisions may address such matters as the amount and timing of operating distributions of cash, payments to partners who retire, and distributions on liquidation.

Since its enactment, Subchapter K has largely accommodated for tax purposes the flexible economic arrangements that long have been the hallmark of the partnership under state law. The Code itself is remarkably terse on this important topic. Section 704(a) provides that a partner's "distributive share" of income, gain, loss, deduction or other tax items shall be determined by the partnership agreement, and Section 761(c) defines the partnership agreement as including any modifications up to the time for filing the partnership's tax return. This permits partners to make what are called "special allocations," which are allocations that differ from

the partners' respective interests in partnership capital. If there is no allocation agreement, Section 704(b) provides that distributive shares are determined for tax purposes "in accordance with the partner's interest in the partnership," taking into account "all facts and circumstances."

Without more, this permissive special allocation regime would offer taxpayers the opportunity to engage in a variety of tax saving maneuvers that might not be attainable outside the partnership setting. For example, the partnership could be used to shift income or losses between partners in high and low marginal income tax brackets and to allocate the character of income or losses among partners with different tax profiles. These arrangements, all scrupulously memorialized in the partnership agreement, might or might not be related to the partners' economic bargain.

As previewed in Chapter 2, additional income and character shifting opportunities are presented when a partner makes a tax-free contribution of an asset with a built-in gain or loss to a newly formed or ongoing partnership, and the contributed property is later sold or distributed, or where the contributed asset is depreciable. And because of the relationship between partnership liabilities and outside basis, the plot thickens even further when a partnership seeks to allocate its liabilities among the partners to inflate the outside bases of partners who may be seeking to increase their distributive shares of partnership losses. Still more temptations to exploit the system are presented by partnerships that consist primarily of members of the same family.

It took a while for Congress and the Treasury to appreciate these problems.[1] The statutory provisions governing partnership allocations are still brief—but with brevity comes ambiguity. Many of the gaps have been filled by a complex regulatory scheme that is the primary subject of this chapter. The starting point is Section 704(b) which, in addition to governing allocations where the partnership agreement fails to do so, provides that particular items or the entire amount of partnership income or loss will be allocated in accordance with the partners' interests in the partnership if an agreed allocation lacks substantial economic effect. The *Orrisch* case, which follows, sets the stage with a homely but fairly typical fact pattern illustrating the type of tax avoidance that Section 704(b) seeks to regulate.

## B. SPECIAL ALLOCATIONS UNDER SECTION 704(b)

### 1. BACKGROUND: THE SUBSTANTIAL ECONOMIC EFFECT CONCEPT

Code: § 704(b).

**1.** Commentators continue to debate whether Congress got it right. For a provocative argument to abolish all special alloca- tions, see Gergen, "Reforming Subchapter K: Special Allocations," 46 Tax L.Rev. 1 (1990).

# Orrisch v. Commissioner

United States Tax Court, 1970.
55 T.C. 395, affirmed per curiam in unpublished opinion (9th Cir.1973).

■ Featherston, Judge. * * *

[The Crisafis and the Orrisches formed a partnership to purchase and rent two apartment houses. The purchases were financed principally by approximately $385,000 in secured loans. In addition, from 1963 to 1965 the Orrisches contributed $35,300 cash and the Crisafis contributed $21,300. The parties had an oral partnership agreement in which they initially agreed to share profits and losses equally.

From 1963 to 1965, the partnership realized ordinary losses, principally as a result of accelerated depreciation deductions taken on the apartment buildings. As the partners had agreed, the losses were divided equally. The Orrisches were able to deduct their share of partnership losses against income that they realized from other business sources. The Crisafis, on the other hand, did not report any taxable income during the years in question because of large losses generated by their other real estate holdings. As a result, they did not receive any current tax benefit from their share of losses from the partnership with the Orrisches. It was against this background that, in early 1966, the partners agreed that for 1966 and subsequent years all the partnership's depreciation deductions would be allocated to the Orrisches, and any other gain or loss would be divided equally. They agreed further that, if the partnership sold the buildings, any gain attributable to the specially allocated depreciation deductions would be allocated ("charged back") to the Orrisches, and any remaining gain would be divided equally.

In 1966 and 1967, the partnership allocated all its depreciation deductions to the Orrisches. This special allocation, along with the original cash contributions of the partners and other partnership income and loss, was reflected in the partners' capital accounts. By the end of 1967, the Orrisches had a $25,187 capital account deficit, and the Crisafis had a positive capital account of $406.

The Service, applying a test imposed by the pre–1976 version of Section 704(b), determined that the special allocation of depreciation deductions to the Orrisches should be disregarded because it "was made with the principal purpose of avoidance of income." Ed.]

## OPINION

The only issue presented for decision is whether tax effect can be given the agreement between petitioners and the Crisafis that, beginning with 1966, all the partnership's depreciation deductions were to be allocated to petitioners for their use in computing their individual income tax liabilities. In our view, the answer must be in the negative, and the amounts of each of the partners' deductions for the depreciation of partnership property must be determined in accordance with the ratio used generally in computing their distributive shares of the partnership's profits and losses.

Among the important innovations of the 1954 Code are limited provisions for flexibility in arrangements for the sharing of income, losses, and deductions arising from business activities conducted through partnerships. The authority for special allocations of such items appears in section 704(a), which provides that a partner's share of any item of income, gain, loss, deduction, or credit shall be determined by the partnership agreement. That rule is coupled with a limitation in [pre–1976] section 704(b),[4] however, which states that a special allocation of an item will be disregarded if its "principal purpose" is the avoidance or evasion of Federal income tax. See Smith v. Commissioner, 331 F.2d 298 (C.A.7, 1964), affirming a Memorandum Opinion of this Court; Jean V. Kresser, 54 T.C. 1621 (1970). In case a special allocation is disregarded, the partner's share of the item is to be determined in accordance with the ratio by which the partners divide the general profits or losses of the partnership. Sec. 1.704–1(b)(2), Income Tax Regs.

The report of the Senate Committee on Finance accompanying the bill finally enacted as the 1954 Code (S.Rept. No. 1622, to accompany H.R. 8300 (Pub.L. No. 591), 83d Cong., 2d Sess., p. 379 (1954)) explained the tax-avoidance restriction prescribed by section 704(b) as follows:

> Subsection (b) * * * provides that if the principal purpose of any provision in the partnership agreement dealing with a partner's distributive share of a particular item is to avoid or evade the Federal income tax, the partner's distributive share of that item shall be redetermined in accordance with his distributive share of partnership income or loss described in section 702(a)(9) [i.e., the ratio used by the partners for dividing general profits or losses]. * * *

> Where, however, a provision in a partnership agreement for a special allocation of certain items has substantial economic effect and is not merely a device for reducing the taxes of certain partners without actually affecting their shares of partnership income, then such a provision will be recognized for tax purposes. * * *

This reference to "substantial economic effect" did not appear in the House Ways and Means Committee report (H.Rept. No. 1337, to accompany H.R. 8300 (Pub.L. No. 591), 83d Cong., 2d Sess., p. A223 (1954)) discussing section 704(b), and was apparently added in the Senate Finance Committee

---

**4.** SEC. 704 [prior to 1976 amendment Ed.]. PARTNER'S DISTRIBUTIVE SHARE.

(b) DISTRIBUTIVE SHARE DETERMINED BY INCOME OR LOSS RATIO.—A partner's distributive share of any item of income, gain, loss, deduction, or credit shall be determined in accordance with his distributive share of taxable income or loss of the partnership, as described in section 702(a)(9), for the taxable year, if—

(1) the partnership agreement does not provide as to the partner's distributive share of such item, or

(2) the principal purpose of any provision in the partnership agreement with respect to the partner's distributive share of such item is the avoidance or evasion of any tax imposed by this subtitle.

to allay fears that special allocations of income or deductions would be denied effect in every case where the allocation resulted in a reduction in the income tax liabilities of one or more of the partners. The statement is an affirmation that special allocations are ordinarily to be recognized if they have business validity apart from their tax consequences. Driscoll, "Tax Problems of Partnerships—Special Allocation of Specific Items," 1958 So. Cal. Tax Inst. 421, 426.

In resolving the question whether the principal purpose of a provision in a partnership agreement is the avoidance or evasion of Federal income tax, all the facts and circumstances in relation to the provision must be taken into account. Section 1.704–1(b)(2), Income Tax Regs., lists the following as relevant circumstances to be considered:

> Whether the partnership or a partner individually has a business purpose for the allocation; whether the allocation has "substantial economic effect", that is, whether the allocation may actually affect the dollar amount of the partners' shares of the total partnership income or loss independently of tax consequences; whether related items of income, gain, loss, deduction, or credit from the same source are subject to the same allocation; whether the allocation was made without recognition of normal business factors and only after the amount of the specially allocated item could reasonably be estimated; the duration of the allocation; and the overall tax consequences of the allocation. * * *

Applying these standards, we do not think the special allocation of depreciation in the present case can be given effect.

The evidence is persuasive that the special allocation of depreciation was adopted for a tax-avoidance rather than a business purpose. Depreciation was the only item which was adjusted by the parties; both the income from the buildings and the expenses incurred in their operation, maintenance, and repair were allocated to the partners equally. Since the deduction for depreciation does not vary from year to year with the fortunes of the business, the parties obviously knew what the tax effect of the special allocation would be at the time they adopted it. Furthermore, as shown by our Findings, petitioners had large amounts of income which would be offset by the additional deduction for depreciation; the Crisafis, in contrast, had no taxable income from which to subtract the partnership depreciation deductions, and, due to depreciation deductions which they were obtaining with respect to other housing projects, could expect to have no taxable income in the near future. On the other hand, the insulation of the Crisafis from at least part of a potential capital gains tax was an obvious tax advantage. The inference is unmistakably clear that the agreement did not reflect normal business considerations but was designed primarily to minimize the overall tax liabilities of the partners.

Petitioners urge that the special allocation of the depreciation deduction was adopted in order to equalize the capital accounts of the partners, correcting a disparity ($14,000) in the amounts initially contributed to the partnership by them ($26,500) and the Crisafis ($12,500). But the evidence

does not support this contention. Under the special allocation agreement, petitioners were to be entitled, in computing their individual income tax liabilities, to deduct the full amount of the depreciation realized on the partnership property. For 1966, as an example, petitioners were allocated a sum ($18,904) equal to the depreciation on the partnership property ($18,412) plus one-half of the net loss computed without regard to depreciation ($492). The other one-half of the net loss was, of course, allocated to the Crisafis. Petitioners' allocation ($18,904) was then applied to reduce their capital account. The depreciation specially allocated to petitioners ($18,412) in 1966 alone exceeded the amount of the disparity in the contributions. Indeed, at the end of 1967, petitioners' capital account showed a deficit of $25,187.11 compared with a positive balance of $405.65 in the Crisafis' account. By the time the partnership's properties are fully depreciated, the amount of the reduction in petitioners' capital account will approximate the remaining basis for the buildings as of the end of 1967. The Crisafis' capital account will be adjusted only for contributions, withdrawals, gain or loss, without regard to depreciation, and similar adjustments for these factors will also be made in petitioners' capital account. Thus, rather than correcting an imbalance in the capital accounts of the partners, the special allocation of depreciation will create a vastly greater imbalance than existed at the end of 1966. In the light of these facts, we find it incredible that equalization of the capital accounts was the objective of the special allocation.[5]

Petitioners rely primarily on the argument that the allocation has "substantial economic effect" in that it is reflected in the capital accounts of the partners. Referring to the material quoted above from the report of the Senate Committee on Finance, they contend that this alone is sufficient to show that the special allocation served a business rather than a tax-avoidance purpose.

According to the regulations, an allocation has economic effect if it "may actually affect the dollar amount of the partners' shares of the total partnership income or loss independently of tax consequences." The agreement in this case provided not only for the allocation of depreciation to petitioners but also for gain on the sale of the partnership property to be "charged back" to them. The charge back would cause the gain, for tax purposes, to be allocated on the books entirely to petitioners to the extent of the special allocation of depreciation, and their capital account would be correspondingly increased. The remainder of the gain, if any, would be

---

**5.** We recognize that petitioners had more money invested in the partnership than the Crisafis and that it is reasonable for the partners to endeavor to equalize their investments, since each one was to share equally in the profits and losses of the enterprise. However, we do not think that sec. 704(a) permits the partners' prospective tax benefits to be used as the medium for equalizing their investments, and it is apparent that the eco-

nomic burden of the depreciation (which is reflected by the allowance for depreciation) was not intended to be the medium used.

This case is to be distinguished from situations where one partner contributed property and the other cash; in such cases sec. 704(c) may allow a special allocation of income and expenses in order to reflect the tax consequences inherent in the original contributions.

shared equally by the partners. If the gain on the sale were to equal or exceed the depreciation specially allocated to petitioners, the increase in their capital account caused by the charge back would exactly equal the depreciation deductions previously allowed to them and the proceeds of the sale of the property would be divided equally. In such circumstances, the only effect of the allocation would be a trade of tax consequences, i.e., the Crisafis would relinquish a current depreciation deduction in exchange for exoneration from all or part of the capital gains tax when the property is sold, and petitioners would enjoy a larger current depreciation deduction but would assume a larger ultimate capital gains tax liability. Quite clearly, if the property is sold at a gain, the special allocation will affect only the tax liabilities of the partners and will have no other economic effect.

To find any economic effect of the special allocation agreement aside from its tax consequences, we must, therefore, look to see who is to bear the economic burden of the depreciation if the buildings should be sold for a sum less than their original cost. There is not one syllable of evidence bearing directly on this crucial point. We have noted, however, that when the buildings are fully depreciated, petitioners' capital account will have a deficit, or there will be a disparity in the capital accounts, approximately equal to the undepreciated basis of the buildings as of the beginning of 1966.[6] Under normal accounting procedures, if the building were sold at a gain less than the amount of such disparity petitioners would either be required to contribute to the partnership a sum equal to the remaining deficit in their capital account after the gain on the sale had been added back or would be entitled to receive a proportionately smaller share of the partnership assets on liquidation. Based on the record as a whole, we do not think the partners ever agreed to such an arrangement. On dissolution, we think the partners contemplated an equal division of the partnership assets which would be adjusted only for disparities in cash contributions or withdrawals.[7] Certainly there is no evidence to show otherwise. That being true, the special allocation does not "actually affect the dollar amount of the partners' share of the total partnership income or loss independently of tax consequences" within the meaning of the regulation referred to above.

Our interpretation of the partnership agreement is supported by an analysis of a somewhat similar agreement, quoted in material part in our Findings, which petitioners made as part of a marital property settlement agreement in 1968. Under this agreement, Orrisch was entitled to deduct all the depreciation for 1968 in computing his income tax liability, and his wife was to deduct none; but on the sale of the property they were to first reimburse Orrisch for "such moneys as he may have advanced," and then divide the balance of the "profits or proceeds" of the sale equally, each party to report one-half of the capital gain or loss on his income tax return.

---

6. This assumes, of course, that all partnership withdrawals and capital contributions will be equal.

7. We note that, in the course of Orrisch's testimony, petitioners' counsel made a distinction between entries in the taxpayer's capital accounts which reflect actual cash transactions and those relating to the special allocation which are "paper entries relating to depreciation."

In the 1969 amendment to this agreement the unequal allocation of the depreciation deduction was discontinued, and a provision similar to the partnership "charge back" was added, i.e., while the proceeds of the sale were to be divided equally, only Orrisch's basis was to be reduced by the depreciation allowed for 1968 so that he would pay taxes on a larger portion of the gain realized on the sale. Significantly, in both this agreement and the partnership agreement, as we interpret it, each party's share of the sales proceeds was determined independently from his share of the depreciation deduction.

In the light of all the evidence we have found as an ultimate fact that the "principal purpose" of the special allocation agreement was tax avoidance within the meaning of section 704(b). Accordingly, the deduction for depreciation for 1966 and 1967 must be allocated between the parties in the same manner as other deductions.

Decision will be entered for the respondent.

## NOTE

Although the *Orrisch* case is not a model of clarity, it is regarded as a major milestone in the interpretation of Section 704(b). The litigated allocations occurred in a year prior to 1977, at a time when Section 704(b) required special allocations to be tested by determining whether the principal purpose of the allocation was the avoidance or evasion of income tax.[1] As *Orrisch* illustrates, the regulations interpreting that test looked to whether the allocation had "substantial economic effect"—i.e., "whether the allocation may actually affect the dollar amount of the partners' shares of the total partnership income or loss independently of tax consequences."[2] In the Tax Reform Act of 1976,[3] Congress incorporated the "substantial economic effect" test in Section 704(b), in effect codifying the prior regulations.[4]

Under prior law, there was authority that Section 704(b) applied to "*items*" of income, loss, etc., but not to allocations of total or "bottom line" income or loss.[5] Nevertheless, the courts had applied a test to determine the propriety of bottom line allocations which is virtually identical to the Section 704(b) test.[6] As a second amendment in the 1976 Act, Congress provided that the propriety of bottom line allocations also would be

**1.** Reg. § 1.704–1(b)(2) (pre–1977).

**2.** Id.

**3.** Pub.L. No. 94–455, 90 Stat. 1520, reprinted in 1976–3 C.B. (Vol. 1) 1.

**4.** See generally Cowan, "Substantial Economic Effect—The Outer Limits for Partnership Allocations," 39 N.Y.U.Inst. on Fed. Tax'n 23–1 (1981); McKee, "Partnership Allocations: The Need for an Entity Approach," 66 Va.L.Rev. 1039 (1980); Weidner, "Partnership Allocations and Capital Account Analysis," 42 Ohio St. L.Rev. 467 (1981).

**5.** Holladay v. Commissioner, 72 T.C. 571 (1979).

**6.** Hamilton v. United States, 687 F.2d 408 (Ct.Cl.1982). At page 414 of the opinion, the Court states: "that standard [for bottom line items] differs only slightly from the standard found in section 704(b)(2) and the use of one rather than the other should have little effect on the outcome of [a] case."

evaluated under the substantial economic effect test. Both of the 1976 amendments were essentially house-cleaning measures to conform the statute to the approach being taken by the courts. The Joint Committee General Explanation of amended Section 704(b) describes the 1976 changes as follows:[7]

*Prior law*

> A limited (or a general) partnership agreement may allocate income, gain, loss, deduction, or credit (or items thereof) among the partners in a manner that is disproportionate to the capital contributions of the partners. These are sometimes referred to as "special allocations" and, with respect to any taxable year, may be made by amendment to the partnership agreement at any time up to the initial due date of the partnership tax return for that year (sec. 761(c)).

> A special allocation was not recognized under prior law (sec. 704(b)(2)) if its principal purpose was to avoid or evade a Federal tax. In determining whether a special allocation had been made principally for the avoidance of tax, the regulations focused upon whether the special allocation had "substantial economic effect," that is, whether the allocation may actually affect the dollar amount of the partner's share of the total partnership income or loss independently of tax consequences (Regs. § 1.704–1(b)(2)). The regulations also inquired as to whether there was a business purpose for this special allocation, whether related items from the same source were subject to the same allocation, whether the allocation ignored normal business factors and was made after the amount of the specially allocated item could reasonably be estimated, the duration of the allocation, and the overall tax consequences of the allocation.

> By its terms, the tax avoidance provisions of prior law section 704(b)(2) applied to allocations of *items* of income, gain, loss, deduction, or credit. It was thus argued that these provisions did not apply to and would not preclude allocations of taxable income or loss, as opposed to specific items of income, gain, deduction, loss, or credit.

* * *

*Reasons for change*

> Congress believed that an overall allocation of the taxable income or loss for a taxable year (described under section 702(a) [8]) should be subject to disallowance in the same manner as allocations of items of income or loss.

---

**7.**  Staff of the Joint Comm. on Internal Revenue Taxation, 94th Cong., 2d Sess., General Explanation of the Tax Reform Act of 1976 at 94, reprinted in 1976–3 C.B. (Vol. 2) 106.

Also, allocations of special items and overall allocations should be restricted to those situations where the allocations have substantial economic effect.

*Explanation of provisions*

The Act provides that an allocation of overall income or loss (described under Section 702(a) [8]), or of any item of income, gain, loss, deduction, or credit (described under section 702(a)(1)– [7]), shall be controlled by the partnership agreement if the partner receiving the allocation can demonstrate that it has "substantial economic effect", i.e., whether the allocation may actually affect the dollar amount of the partners' share of the total partnership income or loss, independent of tax consequences.* Other factors that could possibly relate to the determination of the validity of an allocation are set forth under the present regulations (Regs. § 1.704–1(b)(2)).

If an allocation made by the partnership is set aside, a partner's share of the income, gain, loss, deduction or credit (or item thereof) will be determined in accordance with his interest in the partnership.

In determining a "partner's interest in the partnership", all the relevant facts and circumstances are to be taken into account. Among the relevant factors to be taken into account are the interest of the respective partners in profits and losses (if different from that in taxable income or loss), cash flow, and their rights to distributions of capital upon liquidation.

As amended by the 1976 legislation, Section 704(b) is deceptively brief, stating merely that a special allocation will not be respected if it lacks "substantial economic effect." Congress delegated to the Treasury the arduous task of formulating guidelines for the application of the substantial economic effect concept to the innumerable and intricate partnership arrangements emanating from the business, investment and tax shelter communities.

Building upon the Tax Court's primitive analysis in *Orrisch* and other cases,[8] the Section 704(b) regulations are a lengthy and sophisticated response to the ingenuity of the tax advisors. They have been accurately described by one leading commentator as "a creation of prodigious complexity * * * essentially impenetrable to all but those with the time, talent

* The determination of whether an allocation may actually affect the dollar amount of the partners' shares of total partnership income or loss, independent of tax consequences, will to a substantial extent involve an examination of how these allocations are treated in the partners' capital accounts for financial (as opposed to tax) accounting purposes; this assumes that these accounts actually reflect the dollar amounts to which the partners would be entitled upon the liquidation of the partnership.

**8.** See, e.g., Ogden v. Commissioner, 84 T.C. 871 (1985), affirmed per curiam, 788 F.2d 252 (5th Cir.1986); Allison v. United States, 701 F.2d 933 (Fed.Cir.1983); Holladay v. Commissioner, 72 T.C. 571 (1979), affirmed, 649 F.2d 1176 (5th Cir.1981).

and determination to become thoroughly prepared experts on the subject."[9] Such a gloomy characterization prompts one to ask: is mastering these regulations worth the trouble, especially considering that one of the Treasury's principal targets—tax shelters—has been rendered virtually extinct?

It would be tempting to gloss over Section 704(b) but for the fact that drafters of partnership agreements have continued spawning diverse profit and loss sharing arrangements as the economy adapts to the altered tax landscape. In keeping with the philosophy of this text, the focus will be on the fundamentals, looking first at the basic rules for special partnership allocations under Section 704(b) and the consequences if an allocation is set aside,[10] and then turning to allocations attributable to nonrecourse debt.[11]

## 2. THE SECTION 704(b) REGULATIONS: BASIC RULES

Code: § 704(b).

Regulations: § 1.704–1(b)(1)(i), (iii) & (vii); –1(b)(2)(i)–(iii), (iv)(a)–(c), (f), (h), (n); –1(b)(3); –1(b)(5) Examples (1), (2), (3), (5), (6), (7), & (15)(i), (ii).

### a. INTRODUCTION

At the heart of the Section 704(b) regulations is a two-part test to determine if a partnership allocation has substantial economic effect. To be respected for tax purposes, an allocation first must have "economic effect," meaning generally that the allocation must be consistent with the economic business deal of the partners.[1] The economic effect test is objective and is satisfied if the partnership agreement complies with a series of mechanical requirements to be described below. The "substantiality" test is more subjective and thus harder to apply. In general, for the economic effect of an allocation to be substantial, there must be a reasonable possibility that the allocation will affect substantially the dollar amounts to be received by the partners from the partnership apart from tax consequences; insubstantiality results when the economic effect of an allocation is likely to be eliminated by one or more contemporaneous or later allocations and the overall tax liability of the partners is reduced.[2]

If the partnership agreement is silent as to the partners' distributive shares of income, losses and other tax items, or if a special allocation is found wanting because it lacks substantial economic effect, then the partners' respective shares of income, loss and other items are determined in accordance with the partners' respective "interests in the partnership."[3]

---

**9.** Lokken, "Partnership Allocations," 41 Tax L.Rev. 545, 621 (1986). See also Close & Kusnetz, "The Final Section 704(b) Regulations: Special Allocations Reach New Heights of Complexity," 40 Tax Lawyer 307 (1987).

**10.** See Reg. § 1.704–1(b)(1), (2), (3) & (5) and Section B2 of this chapter, infra.

**11.** See Reg. § 1.704–1(b)(4)(iv) and Section B3 of this chapter, infra.

**1.** Reg. § 1.704–1(b)(2)(ii)(a).

**2.** Reg. § 1.704–1(b)(2)(iii)(a).

**3.** I.R.C. § 704(b). See Reg. §§ 1.704–1(b)(1)(i), 1.704–1(b)(3).

A partner's interest in the partnership is determined by taking into account "all the facts and circumstances;" the regulations elaborate by providing a few broad rules and examples for making this essentially factual (and often elusive) determination.[4]

The Section 704(b) regulations have a broad scope. They apply to all allocations of specific items of income, gain, loss, deductions and credits (e.g., depreciation, tax-exempt income) as well as to allocations of partnership net (i.e., "bottom line") taxable income and loss.[5] The substantial economic effect test is applied on an annual basis to determine the validity of an allocation for the year involved.[6] An allocation that is valid in one year may fail to pass muster in a subsequent year, and in any one year, a portion of an allocation may be valid while other portions are invalid.[7]

The regulations include 19 examples illustrating practical applications of the rules.[8] In the explanation to follow, we borrow generously from these examples, but this discussion is not intended to relieve students from the obligation of reading and engaging in direct combat with the language of the regulations.

## b.   MAINTENANCE OF PARTNERS' CAPITAL ACCOUNTS

A critical precept of the substantial economic effect test is that an allocation is valid for tax purposes only if it is "consistent with the underlying economic arrangement of the partners."[9] The reference point employed by the regulations for testing whether allocations are sufficiently linked to the partners' economic deal is the capital account. Recall[10] that a capital account essentially represents a partner's equity in the partnership; at any point during the life of the firm, it identifies the amounts the partners would be entitled to receive if and when their interests in the partnerships were liquidated. The regulations go to great lengths to ensure that the capital accounts employed to test partnership allocations are an accurate measure of these economic entitlements. In so doing, the rules depart in some respects from generally accepted accounting principles. Our coverage here will be limited to the basic capital account maintenance rules; discussion of certain other capital account adjustments will be deferred until the transactions that trigger those adjustments are examined.[11]

From the standpoint of an attorney drafting a partnership agreement, the message of the regulations is that the capital account rules must be incorporated in the partnership agreement if an allocation is to have

---

**4.**   Reg. § 1.704–1(b)(3).

**5.**   Reg. § 1.704–1(b)(1)(vii).

**6.**   Reg. § 1.704–1(b)(2)(i).

**7.**   See, e.g., Reg. § 1.704–1(b)(5) Examples (1)(iv), (v), (vi) & (15)(ii).

**8.**   See Reg. § 1.704–1(b)(5).

**9.**   Reg. § 1.704–1(b)(2)(ii)(*a*).

**10.**   See Chapter 2A2, supra.

**11.**   See, e.g., Chapters 4C (contributed property), 6B (sales of partnership interests), 7C (operating distributions) and 8A (liquidating distributions).

economic effect. At the very least, a typical broad definition of "capital account" in an agreement would read:[12]

> The "Capital Account" of a partner shall mean the capital account of that partner from the inception of the partnership as determined in accordance with Section 1.704–1(b)(2)(iv) of the Treasury Regulations or any successor provision.

For this purpose, the "partnership agreement" includes all agreements among the partners, or between one or more partners and the partnership, whether oral or written and whether or not embodied in a document referred to by the partners as their "agreement."[13] Once the magic words are inserted in the document, it is primarily up to the partnership's accountant to ensure that capital accounts are properly maintained in accordance with the regulations throughout the life of the partnership.[14]

Capital accounts are considered properly determined and maintained only if each partner's capital account is increased by:[15]

(1) the amount of money contributed to the partnership by the partner;[16]

(2) the fair market value of property contributed by the partner to the partnership (net of liabilities securing the property that the partnership is considered to assume or take subject to under Section 752);[17] and

(3) allocations to the partner of partnership income and gain, including tax-exempt income;

and is decreased by:[18]

(1) the amount of money distributed to the partner by the partnership;

(2) the fair market value of property distributed to the partner by the partnership (net of liabilities secured by the property that the partner is considered to assume or take subject to under Section 752);[19]

---

**12.** This and later sample clauses have been adapted from partnership agreements made available to the authors by practitioners.

**13.** Reg. § 1.704–1(b)(2)(ii)(*h*). If a partner has more than one type of interest in the partnership—e.g., as both a general and a limited partner—the regulations require that one single capital account must be maintained reflecting all of those interests, whenever they were acquired. Reg. § 1.704–1(b)(2)(iv)(*b*).

**14.** Reg. § 1.704–1(b)(2)(iv)(*a*).

**15.** See Reg. § 1.704–1(b)(2)(iv)(*b*).

**16.** For this purpose, "money" includes the amount of any partnership liabilities as-

sumed by the partner to the extent that the assuming partner is primarily and personally liable with respect to the obligation and the creditor is aware of the assumption and can directly enforce the assuming partner's obligation. Reg. § 1.704–1(b)(2)(iv)(*b*), (*c*).

**17.** See Reg. § 1.704–1(b)(2)(iv)(*c*). Special rules are provided for contributions of promissory notes. See Reg. § 1.704–1(b)(2)(iv)(*d*)(2).

**18.** Reg. § 1.704–1(b)(2)(iv)(*b*).

**19.** Special rules are provided for distributions of promissory notes. See Reg. § 1.704–1(b)(2)(iv)(*e*)(2).

(3) allocations to the partner of partnership expenditures that are neither deductible in computing taxable income nor properly chargeable to capital account, including Section 705(a)(2)(B) items (e.g., gambling losses, bribes, charitable contributions), Section 709 organizational and syndication expenses that are not amortized under Section 709(b) and losses disallowed under Section 267(a)(1);[20] and

(4) allocations of partnership loss and deduction (excluding the items listed in (3), above).

Stepping back from the detail for a moment, it should be apparent that these rules are designed to determine, throughout the life of the partnership, the "book value" of each partner's interest in the firm. Thus, a partner's capital account may differ markedly from his outside basis, especially where the partnership has liabilities.[21] Moreover, the regulations seek a truer measure of a partner's equity by reflecting all contributions and distributions of property in the partners' capital accounts at their fair market value when contributed or distributed rather than at their adjusted tax basis. In the case of contributed property with built-in gain or loss, this treatment often will create a "book/tax" disparity—i.e., a difference between the adjusted basis of the asset for tax purposes and its value as reported on the partnership's books (and reflected in the partners' capital accounts).[22] These book/tax differences raise challenging issues, some of which will be examined in more detail later in this chapter.[23] For now, it is important to keep in mind that because capital accounts reflect the *value* of contributed property rather than its tax basis,[24] further adjustments may be required to ensure that capital accounts are adjusted by book income rather than taxable income.[25]

To patrol against inflated valuations, the regulations provide that a fair market value reasonably agreed to among the partners in arm's length negotiations will control if the partners have sufficiently adverse interests.[26] The theory is that if the valuation is hammered out between genuinely adverse parties, abuse is unlikely.[27] Fair market value is otherwise determined under "general tax principles," which in theory means a "willing buyer/willing seller" test and in practice degenerates into a battle

---

**20.** Reg. § 1.704–1(b)(2)(iv)(*i*).

**21.** For example, Section 752(a) treats an increase in a partner's share of partnership liabilities as a contribution of money, which results in an increase to the partner's outside basis under Section 705. Similarly, Section 752(b) treats a decrease of a partner's share of partnership liabilities as a distribution of money, resulting in a decrease in the partner's outside basis. See Section D of this chapter, infra. Neither of these adjustments is appropriate for capital account purposes, however, because liabilities obviously are not "capital" and they do not represent what the

partners would be entitled to receive on liquidation. See Reg. § 1.704–1(b)(2)(iv)(*c*).

**22.** See I.R.C. § 723 and Chapter 2A, supra.

**23.** See Section C of this chapter, infra.

**24.** Reg. § 1.704–1(b)(2)(iv)(*g*).

**25.** See, e.g., Reg. § 1.704–1(b)(2)(iv)(*d*)(*1*).

**26.** Reg. § 1.704–1(b)(2)(iv)(*h*).

**27.** Query whether valuation agreements among members of the same family will be respected?

of expert appraisers followed by a Solomonic compromise. If these conditions are not met, the capital account rules are considered to have been violated if "the value assigned to such property is overstated or understated (by more than an insignificant amount)."[28] The effect of a valuation error could be potentially devastating because, if capital accounts are improperly maintained, all allocations in the partnership agreement will be set aside and result in a reallocation in accordance with the partners' interests in the partnership.[29]

The regulations also allow partnerships to restate assets at their current fair market value on certain occasions, such as the admission of a new partner to the partnership, a distribution in complete or partial liquidation of a partner's interest in the firm, or the grant of a partnership interest as consideration for the provision of services to the partnership, provided the adjustments are made for a "substantial non-tax business purpose."[30] In these circumstances, restatements are permissible only if the partnership agreement so provides and a set of detailed rules are followed in making the adjustments.[31]

### c.   ECONOMIC EFFECT

*The Big Three.* In providing that an allocation will have economic effect only if it is consistent with the underlying economic arrangement of the partners, the regulations mean that if there is an economic benefit or burden corresponding to the allocation, the partner to whom the allocation is made must receive the benefit or bear the burden.[32] Fortunately, this standard is not as vague as it first appears. The regulations test "economic effect" mechanically, first providing a three-pronged primary test, then a more flexible alternate test and finally a narrowly applicable fallback test of "economic effect equivalence."

Under the primary test, an allocation will have economic effect if, and only if, throughout the life of the partnership, the partnership agreement provides that:

> (1) Capital accounts must be determined and maintained in accordance with the rules of Section 1.704–1(b)(2)(iv) of the regulations;[33]

---

**28.**   Reg. § 1.704–1(b)(2)(iv)(*h*).

**29.**   See Reg. § 1.704–1(b)(2)(ii)(*b*). But see Reg. § 1.704–1(b)(2)(ii)(*i*) and infra p. 140 for situations where an allocation nonetheless will be respected if it has "economic effect equivalence."

**30.**   Reg. § 1.704–1(b)(2)(iv)(*f*). A fourth situation where an optional restatement is permitted is where "substantially all of the partnership's property (excluding money)" consists of marketable securities. Reg. § 1.704–1(b)(2)(iv)(*f*)(*5*)(*iv*). In these circumstances, periodic "mark-ups to market" are permitted provided that "generally accepted industry accounting practices" are observed. Id.

**31.**   See Reg. § 1.704–1(b)(2)(iv)(*f*). See Section C of this chapter and Chapter 7C, infra, for circumstances in which a restatement of capital accounts may be desirable.

**32.**   Reg. § 1.704–1(b)(2)(ii)(*a*).

**33.**   Reg. § 1.704–1(b)(2)(ii)(*b*)(*1*). Only minor, accidental departures made in good faith will be tolerated. Reg. § 1.704–1(b)(2)(iv)(*p*).

(2) Upon a liquidation of the partnership, or of any partner's interest, liquidating distributions must be made in accordance with the positive capital account balances of the partners;[34]

(3) If a partner has a deficit balance in his capital account following the liquidation of his interest in the partnership, he must be unconditionally obligated to restore the deficit by the later of: (a) the end of the taxable year of the liquidation of the partner's interest, or (b) 90 days after the date of the liquidation.[35]

Because we will mention these three parts of the primary test frequently in the ensuing discussion, they collectively will be referred to for convenience as "The Big Three."

From a mechanical standpoint, satisfying The Big Three is a straightforward matter. The requirements are easily met simply by including the requisite provisions relating to maintenance of capital accounts, distributions on liquidation and restoration of deficit capital accounts in the partnership agreement and by adhering to them for the duration of the partnership.[36] Provisions that would satisfy the second and third requirements might read as follows:

*Distributions on Liquidation.* All distributions in liquidation of the partnership or of any partner's interest in the partnership shall be in an amount equal to the positive balance in the Capital Account of each partner whose interest is being liquidated as that account is determined after all adjustments to such account for the taxable year of the partnership during which the liquidation occurs as are required by Treasury Regulations § 1.704–1(b). Such adjustments shall be made within the time specified in such Regulations.

*Restoration of Deficit Capital Account.* Any partner whose Capital Account has a deficit balance after the liquidation of such partner's partnership interest shall restore such deficit to the partnership no later than the end of the partnership taxable year in which such liquidation occurs, or, if later, within 90 days after the date of such liquidation.

The rationale for The Big Three should be apparent. Unless tax allocations of income or loss are accompanied by increases or decreases to the partner's capital accounts, there is no way to assure that the tax consequences ever will reflect the partners' economic business deal. For

---

**34.** Reg. § 1.704–1(b)(2)(ii)(*b*)(2). This determination is made after taking into account all capital account adjustments for the partnership taxable year during which the liquidation occurs. Id. For when a "liquidation" occurs, see Reg. § 1.704–1(b)(2)(ii)(*g*). A liquidation may include a constructive termination of the partnership under Section 708(b)(1)—e.g., where there are sales and exchanges of 50 percent or more of the interests of the partnership with-

in a 12–month period. See Close & Kusnetz, "The Final Section 704(b) Regulations," 40 Tax Lawyer 307, 312–313 (1987) and Chapter 8D2, infra.

**35.** Reg. § 1.704–1(b)(2)(ii)(*b*)(3). Any amounts restored must be paid to creditors of the partnership or distributed to other partners in accordance with their positive capital account balances. Id.

**36.** Reg. § 1.704–1(b)(2)(ii)(*b*).

example, a special allocation of $100 of extra income can be respected for tax purposes only if the partners eventually will receive the economic benefit of that income. And since the partners' ultimate economic stakes in the partnership are measured by their capital accounts, all allocations (and other significant financial events in the life of the partnership) must be reflected in those capital accounts. The second and third requirements ensure the validity of this premise by requiring that the amounts partners will receive on liquidation are determined by their positive capital accounts. Because a negative capital account indicates that the partner is in debt to the partnership (i.e., to creditors or the other partners), the regulations require that the partner must satisfy that debt (by restoring the deficit) on or before a liquidation.

An example or two (adapted from the regulations)[37] may be helpful at this point. Assume a situation very similar to the *Orrisch* case, where A and B, each contributing $40,000 cash, form the AB general partnership to purchase and lease depreciable equipment. A and B thus each begin with a $40,000 capital account. The partnership agreement provides that: (1) the partners equally will share taxable income (without regard to Section 168 cost recovery deductions) and cash flow except that all cost recovery deductions are specially allocated to A; (2) capital accounts will be maintained in accordance with the regulations; and (3) on liquidation all distributions will be made equally between A and B. Neither partner, however, has any obligation to restore a deficit in his capital account. Something is awry here! Although A and B assiduously maintain capital accounts, they agree to ignore them upon liquidation. More facts are necessary to identify the flaw.

For convenience, assume that apart from cost recovery deductions, AB breaks even (i.e., operating income equals operating expenses) for its first taxable year, but a $20,000 cost recovery deduction is allocated to A pursuant to the agreement.[38] A's capital account is thus reduced to $20,000 while B's stays at $40,000. Assume further, as the regulations generally require,[39] that the fair market value of the equipment (the partnership's only asset) equals its adjusted basis ($60,000 here, after the first year's cost recovery deductions). In that event, if the partnership were to sell the equipment for $60,000 and liquidate, the agreement would require the proceeds to be divided equally ($30,000 each). The flaw thus is revealed because, if the special allocation of cost recovery deductions to A is to have economic effect, A must bear the full risk of economic loss corresponding to that allocated deduction. A does not bear that loss if the capital account balances—which are designed to reflect the economic entitlements of the partners—are ignored on liquidation. For this allocation to have economic effect, the agreement should have provided for distributions in liquidation

---

**37.**  See Reg. § 1.704–1(b)(5) Example (1)(i).

**38.**  Section 168 technicians should not be distracted by our computation of cost recovery deductions. Like the example in the regulations, we conveniently assume for illustration a four-year straight line recovery period, with no half-year convention or other complications.

**39.**  See Reg. § 1.704–1(b)(2)(iii)(*c*).

to be made in accordance with the positive capital accounts of the partners—i.e., $20,000 to A and $40,000 to B. Only then would the tax allocation match the economics. Because the allocation lacks economic effect, the $20,000 cost recovery deduction must be reallocated in accordance with the partners' interests in the partnership—50/50 in this example.[40]

Now assume the same basic facts except that A and B agreed from the outset to make distributions in accordance with the partners' positive capital account balances, but their agreement still fails to include a deficit restoration requirement. Assume further that apart from cost recovery deductions the partnership continues to break even in years two and three, and $20,000 of cost recovery deductions are allocated to A in each of those three years. Again assuming that the economic decline in value matches tax depreciation, the equipment is now presumed to be worth $20,000 ($80,000 cost less $60,000 cost recovery deductions for years one through three). The capital accounts of the partners are thus:

|  | **A** | **B** |
|---|---|---|
| On formation | $40,000 | $40,000 |
| Less: cost recovery deductions (years 1–3) | (60,000) | 0 |
| Capital account at end of year 3 | ($20,000) | $40,000 |

If the partnership sells the equipment for $20,000 and liquidates at the end of year three, the agreement would entitle B to the entire $20,000, which is all there is to distribute. Shouldn't that be enough for the allocation to have economic effect? The regulations answer "No!" because B—who enjoyed none of the cost recovery deductions associated with the equipment—should be entitled to fully recover her $40,000 investment, while A, whose $60,000 of cost recovery deductions ostensibly were coupled with an equivalent economic burden, has only lost $40,000 under the arrangement described above. For A's economic burden to correspond to the allocation, A must be obligated to restore the $20,000 deficit balance in his capital account so that B is not short-changed.[41] After such a restoration, the economics are respected because A will have lost $60,000 and B will have recouped her entire $40,000 investment—satisfying the command that "in the event there is an economic benefit or an economic burden that corresponds to an allocation, the partner to whom the allocation is made must receive such economic benefit or bear such economic burden."[42] Consequently, without such a deficit restoration obligation, the allocation fails The Big Three for all the years involved and must be reallocated in accordance with the partners' interests in the partnership.

The deficit restoration requirement is the most troublesome of The Big Three in the case of limited partnerships and limited liability companies

**40.** See Reg. § 1.704–1(b)(5) Example (1)(i).

**41.** But why should the absence of a deficit restoration obligation cause allocations to lack economic effect in the earlier years when A did *not* have a negative capital account? See infra pp. 134–140 for a possible answer.

**42.** Reg. § 1.704–1(b)(2)(ii)(a).

because investors with limited liability (limited partners and members of an LLC) invariably are unwilling to make such an open-ended commitment. As we are about to see, however, the regulations provide an alternate test to avoid this problem and preserve special allocations of losses as long as they do not reduce a partner's capital account below zero.

*Alternate Economic Effect: Basic Rules.* If a partnership agreement satisfies the first two requirements of The Big Three but fails to include an unconditional deficit make-up provision, the regulations provide an alternate test for economic effect. This more flexible standard looks to both the effect of an allocation on a partner's capital account and the extent of any partial obligation by the partner to restore a deficit or make additional capital contributions to the partnership. An allocation will have economic effect under the alternate test to the extent that it does not create or increase a deficit in the partner's capital account (in excess of any limited deficit restoration obligation that the partner may have)[43] and the agreement includes a provision known as a "qualified income offset."[44] The test makes sense because, even without an unlimited obligation to restore a deficit, a partner who receives an allocation of losses still suffers a corresponding economic burden as long as the allocation does not create a capital account deficit or exceed any additional amounts that the partner has agreed to contribute to the partnership in the future. If an allocation of loss does create or increase a deficit (in excess of any limited deficit make-up obligation), the loss will be reallocated in accordance with the partners' interests in the partnership.[45]

In the revenue ruling that follows, the Service illustrates the operation of the alternate test for economic effect in a situation where a partner has a limited deficit restoration obligation.

**43.** This test thus recognizes a partner's *limited* obligation to restore a deficit. For this purpose, the regulations provide that a partner will be treated as obligated to restore a deficit to the extent of: (1) the outstanding principal balance of any promissory note contributed by the partner to the partnership (Reg. § 1.704–1(b)(2)(ii)(*c*)(*1*)) and (2) the amount of any unconditional obligation (whether imposed by the partnership agreement or local law) of the partner to make subsequent contributions to the partnership (Reg. § 1.704–1(b)(2)(ii)(*c*)(*2*)). The note or obligation must have economic substance and payment must not be unduly deferred. Reg. § 1.704–1(b)(2)(ii)(*c*). See Reg. § 1.704–1(b)(2)(ii)(*g*). Despite the location of these rules in the regulations, it is clear from later examples that they do not apply to The Big Three primary test but are applicable only to the alternate test for economic effect. See, e.g., Reg. § 1.704–1(b)(5) Examples (1)(viii) and (ix). See also Rev. Rul. 92–97, 1992–2 C.B. 124, for a situation where the partners' limited deficit restoration obligation under a recourse liability of the partnership supported allocations under the alternate test for economic effect.

**44.** Reg. § 1.704–1(b)(2)(ii)(*d*).

**45.** See Reg. §§ 1.704–1(b)(3)(iii) & 1.704–1(b)(5) Example (1)(iv)–(vi).

# Revenue Ruling 97–38

1997–2 Cum.Bull. 69.

## ISSUE

If a partner is treated as having a limited deficit restoration obligation under § 1.704–1(b)(2)(ii)(c) of the Income Tax Regulations by reason of the partner's liability to the partnership's creditors, how is the amount of that obligation calculated?

## FACTS

In year 1, GP and LP, general partner and limited partner, each contribute $100x to form limited partnership LPRS. In general, GP and LP share LPRS's income and loss 50 percent each. However, LPRS allocates to GP all depreciation deductions and gain from the sale of depreciable assets up to the amount of those deductions. LPRS maintains capital accounts according to the rules set forth in § 1.704–1(b)(2)(iv), and the partners agree to liquidate according to positive capital account balances under the rules of § 1.704–1(b)(2)(ii)(*b*)(*2*).

Under applicable state law, GP is liable to creditors for all partnership recourse liabilities, but LP has no personal liability. GP and LP do not agree to unconditional deficit restoration obligations as described in § 1.704–1(b)(2)(ii)(*b*)(*3*) (in general, a deficit restoration obligation requires a partner to restore any deficit capital account balance following the liquidation of the partner's interest in the partnership); GP is obligated to restore a deficit capital account only to the extent necessary to pay creditors. Thus, if LPRS were to liquidate after paying all creditors and LP had a positive capital account balance, GP would not be required to restore GP's deficit capital account to permit a liquidating distribution to LP. In addition, GP and LP agree to a qualified income offset, thus satisfying the requirements of the alternate test for economic effect of § 1.704–1(b)(2)(ii)(*d*). GP and LP also agree that no allocation will be made that causes or increases a deficit balance in any partner's capital account in excess of the partner's obligation to restore the deficit.

LPRS purchases depreciable property for $1,000x from an unrelated seller, paying $200x in cash and borrowing the $800x balance from an unrelated bank that is not the seller of the property. The note is recourse to LPRS. The principal of the loan is due in 6 years; interest is payable semi-annually at the applicable federal rate. GP bears the entire economic risk of loss for LPRS's recourse liability, and GP's basis in LPRS (outside basis) is increased by $800x. See § 1.752–2.

In each of years 1 through 5, the property generates $200x of depreciation. All other partnership deductions and losses exactly equal income, so that in each of years 1 through 5 LPRS has a net loss of $200x.

## LAW AND ANALYSIS

Under § 704(b) of the Internal Revenue Code and the regulations thereunder, a partnership's allocations of income, gain, loss, deduction, or

credit set forth in the partnership agreement are respected if they have substantial economic effect. If allocations under the partnership agreement would not have substantial economic effect, the partnership's allocations are determined according to the partners' interests in the partnership. The fundamental principles for establishing economic effect require an allocation to be consistent with the partners' underlying economic arrangement. A partner allocated a share of income should enjoy any corresponding economic benefit, and a partner allocated a share of losses or deductions should bear any corresponding economic burden. See § 1.704–1(b)(2)(ii)(*a*).

To come within the safe harbor for establishing economic effect in § 1.704–1(b)(2)(ii), partners must agree to maintain capital accounts under the rules of § 1.704–1(b)(2)(iv), liquidate according to positive capital account balances, and agree to an unconditional deficit restoration obligation for any partner with a deficit in that partner's capital account, as described in § 1.704–1(b)(2)(ii)(*b*)(*3*). Alternatively, the partnership may satisfy the requirements of the alternate test for economic effect provided in § 1.704–1(b)(2)(ii)(*d*). LPRS's partnership agreement complies with the alternate test for economic effect.

The alternate test for economic effect requires the partners to agree to a qualified income offset in lieu of an unconditional deficit restoration obligation. If the partners so agree, allocations will have economic effect to the extent that they do not create a deficit capital account for any partner (in excess of any limited deficit restoration obligation of that partner) as of the end of the partnership taxable year to which the allocation relates. Section 1.704–1(b)(2)(ii)(*d*)(*3*) (flush language).

A partner is treated as having a limited deficit restoration obligation to the extent of: (1) the outstanding principal balance of any promissory note contributed to the partnership by the partner, and (2) the amount of any unconditional obligation of the partner (whether imposed by the partnership agreement or by state or local law) to make subsequent contributions to the partnership. Section 1.704–1(b)(2)(ii)(c).

LP has no obligation under the partnership agreement or state or local law to make additional contributions to the partnership and, therefore, has no deficit restoration obligation. Under applicable state law, GP may have to make additional contributions to the partnership to pay creditors. However, GP's obligation only arises to the extent that the amount of LPRS's liabilities exceeds the value of LPRS's assets available to satisfy the liabilities. Thus, the amount of GP's limited deficit restoration obligation each year is equal to the difference between the amount of the partnership's recourse liabilities at the end of the year and the value of the partnership's assets available to satisfy the liabilities at the end of the year.

To ensure consistency with the other requirements of the regulations under § 704(b), where a partner's obligation to make additional contributions to the partnership is dependent on the value of the partnership's assets, the partner's deficit restoration obligation must be computed by reference to the rules for determining the value of partnership property contained in the regulations under § 704(b). Consequently, in computing

GP's limited deficit restoration obligation, the value of the partnership's assets is conclusively presumed to equal the book basis of those assets under the capital account maintenance rules of § 1.704–1(b)(2)(iv). See § 1.704–1(b)(2)(ii)(*d*) (value equals basis presumption applies for purposes of determining expected allocations and distributions under the alternate test for economic effect); § 1.704–1(b)(2)(iii) (value equals basis presumption applies for purposes of the substantiality test); § 1.704–1(b)(3)(iii) (value equals basis presumption applies for purposes of the partner's interest in the partnership test); § 1.704–2(d) (value equals basis presumption applies in computing partnership minimum gain).

The LPRS agreement allocates all depreciation deductions and gain on the sale of depreciable property to the extent of those deductions to GP. Because LPRS's partnership agreement satisfies the alternate test for economic effect, the allocations of depreciation deductions to GP will have economic effect to the extent that they do not create a deficit capital account for GP in excess of GP's obligation to restore the deficit balance. At the end of year 1, the basis of the depreciable property has been reduced to $800x. If LPRS liquidated at the beginning of year 2, selling its depreciable property for its basis of $800x, the proceeds would be used to repay the $800 principal on LPRS's recourse liability. All of LPRS's creditors would be satisfied and GP would have no obligation to contribute to pay them. Thus, at the end of year 1, GP has no obligation to restore a deficit in its capital account.

Because GP has no obligation to restore a deficit balance in its capital account at the end of year 1, an allocation that reduces GP's capital account below $0 is not permitted under the partnership agreement and would not satisfy the alternate test for economic effect. An allocation of $200x of depreciation deductions to GP would reduce GP's capital account to negative $100x. Because the allocation would result in a deficit capital account balance in excess of GP's obligation to restore, the allocation is not permitted under the partnership agreement, and would not satisfy the safe harbor under the alternate test for economic effect. Therefore, the deductions for year 1 must be allocated $100x each to GP and LP (which is in accordance with their interests in the partnership).

The allocation of depreciation of $200x to GP in year 2 has economic effect. Although the allocation reduces GP's capital account to negative $200x, while LP's capital account remains $0, the allocation to GP does not create a deficit capital account in excess of GP's limited deficit restoration obligation. If LPRS liquidated at the beginning of year 3, selling the depreciable property for its basis of $600x, the proceeds would be applied toward the $800x LPRS liability. Because GP is obligated to restore a deficit capital account to the extent necessary to pay creditors, GP would be required to contribute $200x to LPRS to satisfy the outstanding liability. Thus, at the end of year 2, GP has a deficit restoration obligation of $200x, and the allocation of depreciation to GP does not reduce GP's capital account below its obligation to restore a deficit capital account.

This analysis also applies to the allocation of $200x of depreciation to GP in years 3 through 5. At the beginning of year 6, when the property is fully depreciated, the $800x principal amount of the partnership liability is due. The partners' capital accounts at the beginning of year 6 will equal negative $800x and $0, respectively, for GP and LP. Because value is conclusive presumed to equal basis, the depreciable property would be worthless and could not be used to satisfy LPRS's $800x liability. As a result, GP is deemed to be required to contribute $800x to LPRS. A contribution by GP to satisfy this limited deficit restoration obligation would increase GP's capital account balance to $0.

## HOLDING

When a partner is treated as having a limited deficit restoration obligation by reason of the partner's liability to the partnership's creditors, the amount of that obligation is the amount of money that the partner would be required to contribute to the partnership to satisfy partnership liabilities if all partnership property were sold for the amount of the partnership's book basis in the property.

## NOTE

*Alternate Economic Effect: Special Rules.* The drafters of the regulations were mindful that partners might attempt to manipulate the alternate test for economic effect by careful timing of distributions and other events that could be anticipated at the time of the allocation under scrutiny. To prevent such gambits, the regulations require that, for purposes of the alternate test, partners must reduce their capital accounts by distributions that are reasonably expected (to the extent those distributions exceed reasonably expected offsetting increases, other than recognized gains) as of the end of the partnership year in which the loss allocation was made.[1]

A return to the earlier example will illustrate the purpose of these rules. Recall that A and B each contributed $40,000 to the AB general partnership, which used the funds to acquire $80,000 of depreciable equipment. Assume that the first two prongs of The Big Three are satisfied, but the agreement does not include a deficit restoration requirement. A and B share all profits and losses equally, except all cost recovery deductions are allocated to A. As before, the partnership breaks even apart from the $20,000 annual cost recovery deduction. Finally, the partnership agreement contains a "qualified income offset" and neither distributions nor the other items specified in the regulations are expected to cause or increase a deficit balance in A's capital account.

In these circumstances, the $20,000 cost recovery deduction allocated to A for year one will have economic effect under the alternate test.[2]

---

**1.**  Reg. § 1.704–1(b)(2)(ii)(*d*).

**2.**  See Reg. § 1.704–1(b)(5) Example (1)(iii).

Assuming the partnership otherwise continues to break even apart from cost recovery deductions, a $20,000 allocation to A in year two also has economic effect because A's capital account has not yet fallen below zero. But if the cost recovery deduction allocated to A in year two were $25,000, only $20,000 (A's remaining capital account) would have economic effect; the $5,000 balance would be reallocated to B, who bears the economic burden in the absence of any deficit restoration agreement by A.[3] In short, under the alternate test, an allocation will be sustained to the extent of a partner's positive capital account plus any limited obligation to restore a deficit. That principle is simple enough to absorb, but students who are still conscious and the least bit inquisitive may be asking where the "reasonably anticipated distributions" and "qualified income offset" fit into this scheme.

Returning to the basic facts, assume it is near the end of year two. The partners need cash, and the partnership—holding only the equipment (presumed to be worth $40,000)—raises the funds by borrowing $40,000, using the equipment as security. The plan is to distribute the cash equally to the partners, but when? If $20,000 cash were distributed to A before the end of year two, it would reduce his capital account to zero and A would not be entitled to any further cost recovery deductions under the alternate test. But if the partnership waited until early in year three to make the distribution, A's capital account at the end of year two still would be $20,000, enabling the $20,000 special allocation to pass muster for that year. To preclude this maneuver, the regulations require A's capital account to be reduced by distributions that are reasonably expected to be made in future years to the extent they exceed reasonably expected capital account increases during the same period.[4] On these facts, then, with the partnership expected to break even in year three, the allocation to A must be tested under the alternate test by first reducing A's capital account by the $20,000 anticipated year three distribution. As a result, his capital account falls to zero, and the $20,000 year two cost recovery deduction will be reallocated to B.

Finally, return to the end of year two and assume no distributions are on the horizon. In that event, the $20,000 special allocation to A in year two will be respected under the alternate test. What happens if in year three, the partnership *unexpectedly* distributes cash to A, driving his capital account below zero, without any corresponding increase? Here is where the "qualified income offset" assumes center stage. A qualified income offset ("QIO") is a provision in the partnership agreement stating that any partner who has a deficit capital account as a result of unexpectedly receiving a distribution (or the other specialized adjustments listed in the regulations) must be allocated items of future income or gain in an amount

---

**3.** Reg. § 1.704–1(b)(3)(iii). See Reg. § 1.704–1(b)(5) Example (1)(iv).

**4.** If the partnership reasonably expected $10,000 of operating income over operating expenses for year two, A's $5,000 share of the resulting capital account increase could be taken into account and the anticipatory reduction to his capital account at the end of year two would only be $15,000 ($20,000 distribution less $5,000 anticipated income).

and manner sufficient to eliminate any remaining deficit balance as quickly as possible.[5] The allocation triggered by a QIO must consist of a pro rata share of each item of partnership income and gain for the taxable year;[6] the regulations deem such an allocation to be in accordance with the partner's interest in the partnership.[7] A QIO is only needed, then, when an event such as an unexpected distribution pushes a partner's capital account below zero. To preserve the economic effect of prior allocations, it requires partners with positive capital accounts to shift income otherwise allocable to them to the partners with deficit capital accounts until those deficits are eliminated.

*Economic Effect Equivalence.* If an allocation fails to meet either the primary or alternate tests for economic effect, the regulations offer relief if the allocation has "economic effect equivalence." Under this final fallback, allocations are deemed to have economic effect if the partnership agreement, interpreted by reference to applicable state law, ensures that a liquidation of the partnership as of the end of each partnership taxable year will produce the same economic results as if The Big Three were satisfied.[8] To illustrate, assume the partnership agreement commits a technical foot fault by failing to provide for the maintenance of capital accounts. The agreement allocates all income, losses, deductions and distributions among the partners in specified percentages and the partners are liable under state law in the same ratios for partnership debts. In these circumstances, the result on liquidation will be the same as if capital accounts were maintained and thus the allocations will be considered to have economic effect.[9]

### d.  SUBSTANTIALITY

*In General.* The second major test under the regulations looks to whether the economic effect of an allocation is "substantial," both in the year of the allocation[1] and over the life of the partnership.[2] The economic effect of an allocation is considered to be substantial if there is a reasonable possibility that the allocation will affect substantially the dollar amounts to

---

**5.** Reg. § 1.704–1(b)(2)(ii)(*d*). A typical qualified income offset provision would read:

> In the event that at the end of any partnership taxable year any partner's capital account is adjusted for, or such partner is allocated, or there is distributed to such partner, any item described in § 1.704–1(b)(2)(ii)(*d*)(*4*), (*5*) or (*6*) in an amount not reasonably expected at the end of such year, and such treatment creates a deficit balance in that partner's capital account, then such partner shall be allocated all items of income and gain of the partnership for such year and for all subsequent taxable years of the partnership until such deficit balance has been eliminated.

**6.** A qualified income offset seemingly requires an allocation of gross income in situations where the partnership has no taxable income—e.g., in a real estate partnership that realizes gross rental income but has no taxable income because of offsetting deductions.

**7.** Reg. § 1.704–1(b)(2)(ii)(*d*).

**8.** Reg. § 1.704–1(b)(2)(ii)(*i*).

**9.** See Reg. § 1.704–1(b)(5) Examples (4)(ii) & (iii).

**1.** Reg. § 1.704–1(b)(2)(i).

**2.** Cf. Reg. § 1.704–1(b)(2)(iii)(*c*).

be received by the partners from the partnership, independent of tax consequences.[3] Perhaps recognizing that this general rule is not very informative, the regulations elaborate by stating that, notwithstanding the above rule, the economic effect of an allocation is not substantial if, at the time the allocation becomes part of the partnership agreement:[4]

(1) the after-tax economic consequences of at least one partner may, in present value terms, be enhanced compared to such consequences if the allocation were not contained in the partnership agreement; and

(2) there is a strong likelihood that the after-tax economic consequences of no partner will, in present value terms, be substantially diminished compared to such consequences if the allocation were not contained in the partnership agreement.

In other words, an allocation fails the substantiality test if its effect is to benefit one or more partners after taxes and not to affect adversely any partner—in both cases, comparing the effect of the allocation to the result if no allocation had been contained in the agreement. In determining the after-tax economic benefit or detriment to a partner, tax consequences that result from the interaction of the allocation with other tax attributes of the partner unrelated to the partnership must be taken into account.[5]

To illustrate the general rule, assume the AB general partnership invests in income-producing securities. Partner A expects to be in the 30 percent marginal tax bracket in the current year[6] and Partner B expects to be in the 15 percent marginal bracket. Assume further that the partnership faithfully satisfies The Big Three and thus all of its allocations will have economic effect. Finally, assume that the partnership structures its investments so that it will earn relatively equal amounts of tax-exempt interest and taxable dividends and the partnership agreement allocates the tax-exempt interest 90% to A and 10% to B and the dividends 100% to B. Although the allocation has economic effect, the substantiality test is failed at the time the allocation is made because A is expected to enhance his after-tax economic consequences as a result of the allocation, and there is a strong likelihood that neither A nor B will substantially diminish his after-tax consequences.[7]

To illustrate more precisely, assume the partnership earns $10,000 each of tax-exempt interest and taxable dividends. The interest is allocated $9,000 to A and $1,000 to B; the dividends are allocated $10,000 to B. Before taxes are considered, A is allocated a total of $9,000 and B is allocated $11,000. After taxes, and taking the partners' individual tax brackets into account, the results are as follows:

---

**3.** Reg. § 1.704–1(b)(2)(iii)(*a*).

**4.** Id.

**5.** Id.

**6.** We adopt this fictional tax bracket for computational convenience.

**7.** This illustration is adapted from Reg. § 1.704–1(b)(5) Example (5).

|  | **A** | **B** |
|---|---|---|
| Interest | $9,000 | $ 1,000 |
| Dividends | 0 | 10,000 |
| Pre–Tax Income | $9,000 | $11,000 |
| Tax on Dividends | 0 | (1,500) |
| After–Tax | $9,000 | $9,500 |

If there had been no special allocation and the equal partners had shared the interest and dividends 50/50, the results would be as follows:

|  | **A** | **B** |
|---|---|---|
| Interest | $ 5,000 | $ 5,000 |
| Dividends | 5,000 | 5,000 |
| Pre–Tax Income | $10,000 | $10,000 |
| Tax on Dividends | (1,500) | (750) |
| After–Tax | $ 8,500 | $ 9,250 |

The effect of the special allocation is to benefit both partners after-taxes (A nets $9,000 rather than $8,500; B nets $9,500 rather than $9,250). The allocation thus fails the substantiality test because the after-tax consequences of at least one partner are enhanced relative to the consequences if there had been no such allocation, and there is a strong likelihood that the after-tax consequences of no partner will be substantially diminished. Under the partnership agreement, A's capital account is increased by $9,000 (45 percent of total partnership income) and B's is increased by $11,000 (55 percent). Since the special allocation fails the substantial test, the dividends and tax-exempt interest are reallocated 45 percent to A and 55 percent to B.[8]

*Shifting and Transitory Allocations.* The regulations elaborate on the general "substantiality" standard by highlighting two special situations where the economic effect of an allocation will be considered insubstantial: shifting allocations and transitory allocations.[9] In each case, the Treasury's concern is that an initial allocation will be offset by one or more later allocations, resulting in no significant economic consequences to the partners (i.e., no net impact on their capital accounts) but reducing their total tax liability. The effect of offsetting allocations is "shifting" if they occur within the same taxable year; it is "transitory" if the allocations span two or more taxable years.

Consider first a "shifting" allocation. The regulations provide that the economic effect of an allocation (or allocations) within one partnership taxable year is not substantial if, at the time the allocation becomes part of the partnership agreement, there is a "strong likelihood" that the capital accounts of the partners will be unaffected by the allocation (normally

**8.** Reg. § 1.704–1(b)(3). See Reg. § 1.704–1(b)(5) Example (5)(ii).

**9.** Reg. § 1.704–1(b)(2)(iii)(*b*), (*c*).

because of an equal and offsetting allocation in the same year),[10] and the total tax liability of the partners will be less than if there had been no such allocations, taking into account any tax consequences that result from the interaction of the allocation with tax attributes of the partner that are unrelated to the partnership.[11] It should be apparent that this is but an illustration of the general insubstantiality scenario discussed above—i.e., the partners know that the allocation will benefit one or more of them (after taxes) and nobody will suffer.

To illustrate,[12] assume that the AB equal general partnership acquires and leases Section 1231 real property and invests in marketable securities. The partnership agreement faithfully adheres to The Big Three. At the beginning of the current year, the partnership anticipates incurring a $100,000 loss on the sale of Section 1231 property, and it is in a position to realize a $100,000 capital loss on the sale of stock. It otherwise expects to break even. Partner A expects to have $500,000 of ordinary income and no Section 1231 gains for the same taxable year. Partner B expects to have $300,000 of ordinary income and a $200,000 Section 1231 gain from a sale unrelated to the partnership.[13] To maximize tax benefits resulting from the interaction of the partnership's expected losses with the individual tax attributes of the partners, A and B amend their partnership agreement and allocate up to $100,000 of Section 1231 loss to A and an equivalent amount of capital loss to B; all other losses in excess of these allocations will be divided equally between the partners.

Since each partner is allocated a total of $100,000 of partnership losses, their respective capital accounts at the end of the year are the same as if the Section 1231 loss and capital loss had been divided equally between A and B. The partners' agenda is revealed by comparing the after-tax consequences of the special allocation with the results in the current year if there had been an equal division of the two $100,000 losses:

**10.** For this purpose, "unaffected" means that the net increases and decreases to the respective capital accounts of the partners as a result of the allocation do not differ significantly from the net increases and decreases that would have been recorded without the special allocations. Reg. § 1.704–1(b)(2)(iii)(b)(1).

**11.** Reg. § 1.704–1(b)(2)(iii)(b). Thus, items such as a partner's net operating losses and Section 1231 gains and losses outside the partnership are taken into account.

**12.** This example is adapted from Reg. § 1.704–1(b)(5) Example (6).

**13.** To understand this example, you may need to review the operation of Section 1231. Keep in mind that Section 1231 gains and losses retain their character as they are passed through from the partnership to the partners (see Chapter 3A1, supra), and that net Section 1231 losses are treated as ordinary losses which may offset ordinary income without limitation (see I.R.C. § 1231(a)). But see I.R.C. § 1231(c).

|  | Special Allocation | Equal Division |
|---|---|---|
| **Partner A** | | |
| Ordinary income | $500,000 | $500,000 |
| Partnership losses: | | |
| § 1231 loss | (100,000) | (50,000) |
| Capital loss | 0 | (3,000) [14] |
| Net taxable income | $400,000 | $447,000 |
| **Partner B** | | |
| Ordinary income | $300,000 | $300,000 |
| § 1231 Gain | 200,000 | 200,000 |
| Partnership losses: | | |
| § 1231 loss | 0 | (50,000) |
| Capital loss | (100,000) | (50,000) [15] |
| Net taxable income | $400,000 | $400,000 |

Because of A's ability to fully utilize the Section 1231 loss in the current year to offset ordinary income, A's net income is reduced by $47,000 as a result of the allocation, while B's net income is unaffected. In addition, there was a strong likelihood[16] that these results would occur at the time the allocation became part of the agreement. Consequently, the economic effect of the allocation is insubstantial, and the losses must be reallocated in accordance with the partners' 50/50 interests in the partnership.[17]

Transitory allocations are simply a variation on the same theme. They lack substantial economic effect if the partnership agreement provides for the "possibility," over two or more taxable years, that an "original allocation" will be largely offset by one or more "offsetting allocations" and, at the time the allocations became part of the agreement, there is a "strong likelihood" that the partners' capital accounts will emerge unaffected by the allocations (relative to what would have occurred had there been no allocations) and the partners enjoy a reduction in their total tax liability for the period involved.[18] Once again, to relieve the Service from proving that the partners knew all of this was likely to occur when they agreed on the allocation, the regulations presume the requisite "strong likelihood" if the allocations in fact resulted in no material change to the partners' capital accounts and taxes were reduced relative to what would have occurred if there had been no special allocation.[19]

---

**14.** Only $3,000 of the capital loss passed through to A from the partnership is available to offset ordinary income in the current year. The $47,000 balance must be carried forward. See I.R.C. §§ 1211(b); 1212(b).

**15.** Both with and without the special allocation, B uses the capital loss and the Section 1231 loss in the same manner—i.e., they may be deducted against B's $200,000 Section 1231 gain. I.R.C. §§ 1231(a); 1211(b).

**16.** Keep in mind that the regulations, recognizing the problems of proving the requisite "strong likelihood," presume that if the conditions for a shifting allocation are in fact met, there was a strong likelihood that they would occur. Reg. § 1.704–1(b)(2)(iii)(*b*).

**17.** For what would happen in a more complex situation where the losses were not exactly equal, see supra note 8 and accompanying text. Reg. § 1.704–1(b)(5) Example (6).

**18.** Reg. § 1.704–1(b)(2)(iii)(*c*). In determining whether there is a reduction in tax liability, tax consequences resulting from the interaction of the allocation with partner tax attributes that are unrelated to the partnership, such as net operating losses and Section 1231 gains and losses, are taken into account. Reg. § 1.704–1(b)(2)(iii)(*c*)(2).

**19.** Reg. § 1.704–1(b)(2)(iii)(*c*).

To illustrate,[20] assume the equal three-person ABC partnership has a reliable and relatively fixed flow of income (e.g., its only activity is the rental of property subject to a long-term lease). At the beginning of year one, Partner A knows for certain that he has an expiring net operating loss deduction from activities unrelated to the partnership, while B and C are in the highest marginal tax brackets. To help A but burden neither B nor C, the partners agree to allocate 100 percent of the partnership income to A in year one; the trade-off is that 100 percent of the income will be divided equally between B and C in the succeeding two years, after which the partners will revert back to an equal three-way division of profits. At all times, the partnership agreement adheres to The Big Three so that all allocations have economic effect. But is the economic effect of this allocation substantial? Viewing year one in isolation, it is substantial because A benefits economically from the allocation and the other partners suffer.[21] But viewing all three years together, the economic effect of the deal is a "wash" because the partners are well aware from the start that the net increases and decreases in their capital accounts resulting from the allocations will be the same at the end of year three as they would have been in the absence of the allocations. Moreover, because the allocation enables A to apply his expiring net operating loss deduction against the year one partnership income, the total taxes of A, B and C over the three-year period are reduced.

The regulations contain an additional rule which is helpful to taxpayers in situations where an offsetting allocation is likely but will not occur for a while. An allocation and a subsequent offsetting allocation will not be considered transitory (and thus will not fail the substantiality test) if there is a strong likelihood that the offsetting allocation will not, in large part, be made within five years from the original allocation.[22] In addition, the regulations presume for purposes of the substantiality test that the adjusted tax basis of partnership property will be equal to its fair market value and that adjustments to the tax basis of the property will be matched by corresponding changes in its fair market value.[23] This presumption may be helpful in validating special allocations of cost recovery deductions to one partner (or partners) in situations where subsequent gains on the sale of the property are allocable to that partner in an amount equal to the prior cost recovery deductions.[24] As the problems below will illustrate, this type of special allocation scheme would be "transitory" were it not for the presumption that fair market value always equals adjusted basis. Using that assumption, even if it is plainly wrong, there cannot be a strong likelihood that the original cost recovery deductions will be offset in large part by the later offsetting allocations of gain on sale.[25]

**20.** This example is adapted from Reg. § 1.704–1(b)(5) Example (8)(i).

**21.** For example, if the partnership were liquidated at the end of year one, A would come out ahead because the allocation of 100 percent of the year one income would increase his capital account (and thus his share on liquidation) relative to the capital accounts of B and C.

**22.** Reg. § 1.704–1(b)(2)(iii)(c).

**23.** Reg. § 1.704–1(b)(2)(iii)(c).

**24.** This type of provision is known as a "gain chargeback" and was illustrated in the *Orrisch* case supra at page 118.

**25.** See Reg. § 1.704–1(b)(5) Example (1)(xi) and Problem 1(c), infra.

# Revenue Ruling 99–43

1999–2 Cum.Bull. 506.

ISSUE

Do partnership allocations lack substantiality under § 1.704–1(b)(2)(iii) of the Income Tax Regulations when the partners amend the partnership agreement to create offsetting special allocations of particular items after the events giving rise to the items have occurred?

FACTS

A and B, both individuals, formed a general partnership, PRS. A and B each contributed $1,000 and also agreed that each would be allocated a 50–percent share of all partnership items. The partnership agreement provides that, upon the contribution of additional capital by either partner, PRS must revalue the partnership's property and adjust the partners' capital accounts under § 1.704–1(b)(2)(iv)(*f*).

PRS borrowed $8,000 from a bank and used the borrowed and contributed funds to purchase nondepreciable property for $10,000. The loan was nonrecourse to A and B and was secured only by the property. No principal payments were due for 6 years, and interest was payable semi-annually at a market rate.

After one year, the fair market value of the property fell from $10,000 to $6,000, but the principal amount of the loan remained $8,000. As part of a workout arrangement among the bank, PRS, A, and B, the bank reduced the principal amount of the loan by $2,000, and A contributed an additional $500 to PRS. A's capital account was credited with the $500, which PRS used to pay currently deductible expenses incurred in connection with the workout. All $500 of the currently deductible workout expenses were allocated to A. B made no additional contribution of capital. At the time of the workout, B was insolvent within the meaning of § 108(a) of the Internal Revenue Code. A and B agreed that, after the workout, A would have a 60–percent interest and B would have a 40–percent interest in the profits and losses of PRS.

As a result of the property's decline in value and the workout, PRS had two items to allocate between A and B. First, the agreement to cancel $2,000 of the loan resulted in $2,000 of cancellation of indebtedness income (COD income). Second, A's contribution of $500 to PRS was an event that required PRS, under the partnership agreement, to revalue partnership property and adjust A's and B's capital accounts. Because of the decline in value of the property, the revaluation resulted in a $4,000 economic loss that must be allocated between A's and B's capital accounts.

Under the terms of the original partnership agreement, PRS would have allocated these items equally between A and B. A and B, however, amend the partnership agreement (in a timely manner) to make two special allocations. First, PRS specially allocates the entire $2,000 of COD income to B, an insolvent partner. Second, PRS specially allocates the book loss from the revaluation $1,000 to A and $3,000 to B.

While A receives a $1,000 allocation of book loss and B receives a $3,000 allocation of book loss, neither of these allocations results in a tax loss to either partner. Rather, the allocations result only in adjustments to A's and B's capital accounts. Thus, the cumulative effect of the special allocations is to reduce each partner's capital account to zero immediately following the allocations despite the fact that B is allocated $2,000 of income for tax purposes.

## LAW

Section 61(a)(12) provides that gross income includes income from the discharge of indebtedness.

Rev. Rul. 91–31, 1991–1 C.B. 19, holds that a taxpayer realizes COD income when a creditor (who was not the seller of the underlying property) reduces the principal amount of an under-secured nonrecourse debt.

Under § 704(b) and the regulations thereunder, allocations of a partnership's items of income, gain, loss, deduction, or credit provided for in the partnership agreement will be respected if the allocations have substantial economic effect. Allocations that fail to have substantial economic effect will be reallocated according to the partners' interests in the partnership (as defined in § 1.704–1(b)(3)).

Section 1.704–1(b)(2)(iv)(*f*) provides that a partnership may, upon the occurrence of certain events (including the contribution of money to the partnership by a new or existing partner), increase or decrease the partners' capital accounts to reflect a revaluation of the partnership property.

Section 1.704–1(b)(2)(iv)(*g*) provides that, to the extent a partnership's property is reflected on the books of the partnership at a book value that differs from the adjusted tax basis, the substantial economic effect requirements apply to the allocations of book items. Section 704(c) and § 1.704–1(b)(4)(*i*) govern the partners' distributive shares of tax items.

Section 1.704–1(b)(2)(i) provides that the determination of whether an allocation of income, gain, loss, or deduction (or item thereof) to a partner has substantial economic effect involves a two-part analysis that is made at the end of the partnership year to which the allocation relates. In order for an allocation to have substantial economic effect, the allocation must have both economic effect (within the meaning of § 1.704–1(b)(2)(ii)) and be substantial (within the meaning of § 1.704–1(b)(2)(iii)).

Section 1.704–1(b)(2)(iii)(a) provides that the economic effect of an allocation (or allocations) is substantial if there is a reasonable possibility that the allocation (or allocations) will substantially affect the dollar amounts to be received by the partners from the partnership independent of the tax consequences. However, the economic effect of an allocation is not substantial if, at the time the allocation becomes part of the partnership agreement, (1) the after-tax economic consequences of at least one partner may, in present value terms, be enhanced compared to the consequences if the allocation (or allocations) were not contained in the partnership agreement, and (2) there is a strong likelihood that the after-tax

economic consequences of no partner will, in present value terms, be substantially diminished compared to the consequences if the allocation (or allocations) were not contained in the partnership agreement. In determining the after-tax economic benefit or detriment to a partner, tax consequences that result from the interaction of the allocation with the partner's tax attributes that are unrelated to the partnership will be taken into account.

Section 1.704–1(b)(2)(iii)(*b*) provides that the economic effect of an allocation (or allocations) in a partnership taxable year is not substantial if the allocations result in shifting tax consequences. Shifting tax consequences result when, at the time the allocation (or allocations) becomes part of the partnership agreement, there is a strong likelihood that (1) the net increases and decreases that will be recorded in the partners' respective capital accounts for the taxable year will not differ substantially from the net increases and decreases that would be recorded in the partners' respective capital accounts for the year if the allocations were not contained in the partnership agreement, and (2) the total tax liability of the partners (for their respective tax years in which the allocations will be taken into account) will be less than if the allocations were not contained in the partnership agreement.

Section 1.704–1(b)(2)(iii)(*c*) provides that the economic effect of an allocation (or allocations) in a partnership taxable year is not substantial if the allocations are transitory. Allocations are considered transitory if a partnership agreement provides for the possibility that one or more allocations (the "original allocation(s)") will be largely offset by other allocations (the "offsetting allocation(s)"), and, at the time the allocations become part of the partnership agreement, there is a strong likelihood that (1) the net increases and decreases that will be recorded in the partners' capital accounts for the taxable years to which the allocations relate will not differ substantially from the net increases and decreases that would be recorded in such partners' respective capital accounts for such years if the original and offsetting allocation(s) were not contained in the partnership agreement, and (2) the total tax liability of the partners (for their respective tax years in which the allocations will be taken into account) will be less than if the allocations were not contained in the partnership agreement.

Section 761(c) provides that a partnership agreement includes any modifications made prior to, or at, the time prescribed for filing a partnership return (not including extensions) which are agreed to by all partners, or which are adopted in such other manner as may be provided by the partnership agreement.

ANALYSIS

PRS is free to allocate partnership items between A and B in accordance with the provisions of the partnership agreement if the allocations have substantial economic effect under § 1.704–1(b)(2). To the extent that

the minimum gain chargeback rules do not apply,[1] COD income may be allocated in accordance with the rules under § 1.704–1(b)(2). This is true notwithstanding that the COD income arises in connection with the cancellation of a nonrecourse debt.

The economic effect of an allocation is not substantial if, at the time that the allocation becomes part of the partnership agreement, the allocation fails each of two tests. The allocation fails the first test if the after-tax consequences of at least one partner may, in present value terms, be enhanced compared to the consequences if the allocation (or allocations) were not contained in the partnership agreement. The allocation fails the second test if there is a strong likelihood that the after-tax economic consequences of no partner will, in present value terms, be substantially diminished compared to such consequences if the allocation (or allocations) were not contained in the partnership agreement.

A and B amended the PRS partnership agreement to provide for an allocation of the entire $2,000 of the COD income to B. B, an insolvent taxpayer, is eligible to exclude the income under § 108, so it is unlikely that the $2,000 of COD income would increase B's immediate tax liability. Without the special allocation, A, who is not insolvent or otherwise entitled to exclude the COD income under § 108, would pay tax immediately on the $1,000 of COD income allocated under the general ratio for sharing income. A and B also amended the PRS partnership agreement to provide for the special allocation of the book loss resulting from the revaluation. Because the two special allocations offset each other, B will not realize any economic benefit from the $2,000 income allocation, even if the property subsequently appreciates in value.

The economics of PRS are unaffected by the paired special allocations. After the capital accounts of A and B are adjusted to reflect the special allocations, A and B each have a capital account of zero, Economically, the situation of both partners is identical to what it would have been had the special allocations not occurred. In addition, a strong likelihood exists that the total tax liability of A and B will be less than if PRS had allocated 50 percent of the $2,000 of COD income and 50 percent of the $4,000 book loss to each partner. Therefore, the special allocations of COD income and book loss are shifting allocations under § 1.704–1(b)(2)(iii)(b) and lack substantiality. (Alternatively, the allocations could be transitory allocations under § 1.704–1(b)(2)(iii)(c) if the allocations occur during different partnership taxable years).

---

**1.** Under certain circumstances, the COD income would be allocated between the partners in accordance with their shares of partnership minimum gain because the cancellation of the nonrecourse debt would result in a decrease in partnership minimum gain. See § 1.704–2(d). However, in this situation, there is no minimum gain because the principal amount of the debt never exceeded the property's book value. Therefore, the minimum gain charge-back requirement does not govern the manner in which the COD income is allocated between A and B, and PRS's special allocation of COD income must satisfy the substantial economic effect standard. See Rev. Rul. 92–97, 1992–2 C.B. 124.

This conclusion is not altered by the "value equals basis" rule that applies in determining the substantiality of an allocation. See § 1.704–1(b)(2)(iii)(c)(2). Under that rule, the adjusted tax basis (or, if different, the book value) of partnership property will be presumed to be the fair market value of the property. This presumption is appropriate in most cases because, under § 1.704–1(b)(2)(iv), property generally will be reflected on the books of the partnership at its fair market value when acquired. Thus, an allocation of gain or loss from the disposition of the property will reflect subsequent changes in the value of the property that generally cannot be predicted.

The substantiality of an allocation, however, is analyzed "at the time the allocation becomes part of the partnership agreement," not the time at which the allocation is first effective. See § 1.704–1(b)(2)(iii)(a). In the situation described above, the provisions of the PRS partnership agreement governing the allocation of gain or loss from the disposition of property are changed at a time that is after the property has been revalued on the books of the partnership, but are effective for a period that begins prior to the revaluation. See § 1.704–1(b)(2)(iv)(f).

Under these facts, the presumption that value equals basis does not apply to validate the allocations. Instead, PRS's allocations of gain or loss must be closely scrutinized in determining the appropriate tax consequences. Cf. § 1.704–1(b)(4)(vi). In this situation, the special allocations of the $2,000 of COD income and $4,000 of book loss will not be respected and, instead, must be allocated in accordance with the A's and B's interests in the partnership under § 1.704–1(b)(3).

Close scrutiny also would be required if the changes were made at a time when the events giving rise to the allocations had not yet occurred but were likely to occur or if, under the original allocation provisions of a partnership agreement, there was a strong likelihood that a disproportionate amount of COD income earned in the future would be allocated to any partner who is insolvent at the time of the allocation and would be offset by an increased allocation of loss or a reduced allocation of income to such partner or partners.

HOLDING

Partnership special allocations lack substantiality when the partners amend the partnership agreement to specially allocate COD income and book items from a related revaluation after the events creating such items have occurred if the overall economic effect of the special allocations on the partners' capital accounts does not differ substantially from the economic effect of the original allocations in the partnership agreement.

e.   DEFAULT REALLOCATIONS: THE PARTNERS' INTEREST IN THE PARTNERSHIP

If a partnership agreement is silent as to the partners' distributive shares or an allocation lacks substantial economic effect, then the partners' share of gain, loss, deduction or credit is determined in accordance with

"the partners' interest in the partnership."[1] Once again, the standard here is the economic arrangement of the partners. The term "partners' interest in the partnership" refers to "the manner in which the partners have agreed to share the economic benefit or burden * * * corresponding to the [item] that is allocated," taking into account all the facts and circumstances relating to the economic arrangement of the partners.[2] The regulations open the bidding with a presumption of equality—i.e., all the partners' interests are presumed to be equal, determined on a per capita basis.[3] In practice, this arbitrary presumption is little more than a last resort. It is rebuttable by either the taxpayer or the Service by establishing facts and circumstances that show that the partners' interest in the partnership are otherwise.[4] Among the factors to be considered in making this determination are:[5]

(1) The relative contributions of the partners to the partnership;

(2) The interests of the partners in economic profits and losses if they differ from their interests in taxable income or loss;

(3) The interests of the partners in cash flow and other nonliquidating distributions; and

(4) The rights of the partners to distributions of capital upon liquidation.

These factors are simple enough to apply if the agreement clearly specifies one method of sharing profits and losses throughout the life of the partnership. Thus, if a two-person partnership agreement provides for an equal division of profits and losses and liquidating distributions (without regard to capital accounts), but allocates cost recovery deductions only to one partner, we know that the special allocation lacks economic effect.[6] Because the arrangement clearly demonstrates that the partners intended to equally share risk and rewards, the cost recovery deduction would be split equally between the two partners. In more complex cases, however, the partners may have varying profit and loss sharing arrangements over the life of the partnership. Despite their length, the regulations offer little guidance as to how the partners' interests would be determined in such cases, an uncertainty which makes it all the more important to ensure that special allocations are structured to comply with the substantial economic effect safe harbor.

The regulations include a special rule if an allocation is upset because the partnership agreement fails to include an unlimited deficit make-up provision.[7] If the first two requirements of The Big Three are met and the substantiality rules have not been breached, this rule provides that the

---

**1.** I.R.C. § 704(b); Reg. § 1.704–1(b)(3)(i).

**2.** Reg. § 1.704–1(b)(3)(i).

**3.** Id.

**4.** Id.

**5.** Reg. § 1.704–1(b)(3)(ii).

**6.** See, e.g., Reg. § 1.704–1(b)(5) Example (1)(i).

**7.** Reg. § 1.704–1(b)(3)(iii).

partners' interests in the partnership with respect to the disallowed portion of the allocation are to be determined by comparing:

(1) the manner in which distributions (and contributions) would be made if all partnership property were sold at book value and the partnership were liquidated following the end of the taxable year in which the allocation relates with,

(2) the manner in which distributions (and contributions) would be made if all partnership property were sold at book value and the partnership were liquidated immediately following the end of the prior taxable year.[8]

The purpose of this formula is to reallocate items lacking economic effect to the partner who bears the economic loss corresponding to the item. Several examples in the regulations illustrate the application of this special rule.[9]

## f.  ALLOCATIONS OF DEPRECIATION RECAPTURE

Allocations of depreciation recapture cannot have substantial economic effect because classifying a portion of the gain as recapture merely changes its tax character. Also, if depreciation recapture can be allocated in the same manner as total gain, it is more likely that a partner may receive an allocation of recapture gain in excess of the partner's share of depreciation from the property.[10] For example, if a partner acquires an interest in a partnership that has fully depreciated a property and the partnership later sells that property at a gain, the partner may be allocated a portion of the total gain and a portion of the recapture gain, despite the fact that the partnership did not pass through any depreciation deductions from the property to the partner.[11]

The regulations attempt to minimize the mismatching of depreciation and recapture allocations.[12] Under the regulations, a partner's share of recapture gain generally is equal to the lesser of (1) the partner's share of the total gain from the disposition of the property, or (2) the total amount of depreciation previously allocated to the partner with respect to the property.[13] For example, assume A and B each contribute $5,000 to form the AB partnership. A and B agree that depreciation deductions will be allocated 90 percent to A and 10 percent to B. Gain on the sale of depreciable property will first be allocated as necessary to equalize the

**8.**  Id. The result then must be adjusted for the reasonably expected future distributions (in excess of anticipated offsetting positive capital account adjustments) and the other specialized items that are taken into account in determining a partner's capital account for purposes of the alternate test for economic effect. See Reg. § 1.704–1(b)(2)(i)(d).

**9.**  See Reg. § 1.704–1(b)(5) Examples (1)(iv)–(vi), (15)(i)–(ii).

**10.**  61 Fed. Reg. 65371 (Dec. 12, 1996).

**11.**  Id. But if the partnership had made a Section 754 election, this distortion would be eliminated. See Chapter 6B, infra.

**12.**  See Reg. §§ 1.704–3(a)(11); 1.1245–1(e)(2); 1.1250–1(f). See Kalinka, "In Light of Depreciation Recapture Regs, Plan Allocations Carefully," 77 Tax Notes 1387 (Dec. 22, 1997).

**13.**  Reg. §§ 1.1245–1(e)(2)(i) & (ii); 1.1250–1(f).

partners' capital accounts, and any remaining gain will be allocated equally between A and B. In its first year, AB purchases depreciable equipment for $5,000. Assume that AB depreciates the equipment over a 5–year recovery period using the straight-line method and has $1,000 of depreciation on the equipment each year.[14] Assume further that except for depreciation, AB's operating income equals its expenses in the first year. Under the partnership agreement, $900 of the depreciation is allocated to A and $100 is allocated to B. If at the end of the year the partnership sells the equipment for $5,200, there will be a total gain of $1,200 ($5,200 amount realized less $4,000 basis), of which $1,000 is Section 1245 recapture gain. Under the partnership agreement, the first $800 of gain is allocated to A to equalize the partner's capital accounts, and the remaining $400 of gain is allocated $200 each to A and B. Under the regulations, each partner's share of the Section 1245 gain is the lesser of the partner's share of total gain recognized on the sale of the equipment or the partner's share of total depreciation with respect to the equipment. Thus, A's share of Section 1245 gain is $900 (A's share of total gain is $1,000 and A's share of depreciation is $900) and B's share of Section 1245 gain is $100 (B's share of total gain is $200 and B's share of depreciation is $100).[15]

Under the regulations, a partner's allocation of recapture gain may be limited by that partner's share of total gain. Returning to the example, assume the same facts except that the partners agree that gains from the sale of depreciable property will be allocated equally between them. On the sale of the equipment for $5,200, the $1,200 gain would be allocated $600 each to A and B. A's share of the Section 1245 gain would be limited to $600 (the total gain allocated to A) even though A's share of depreciation from the equipment was $900. The remaining $400 of Section 1245 gain therefore must be allocated to B. Thus, all $600 of A's total gain is characterized as ordinary income and $400 of B's $600 of total gain is characterized as ordinary income.[16]

## g.  ALLOCATIONS OF TAX CREDITS

Allocations of tax credits are generally not reflected in the partners' capital accounts and, therefore, they cannot have economic effect.[17] As a result, tax credits and recapture of tax credits generally must be allocated in accordance with the partners' interests in the partnership. With respect to credits other than the investment tax credit, which wanders in and out of the Code,[18] the regulations provide that if a partnership expenditure (whether or not deductible) that gives rise to a tax credit also gives rise to valid tax allocations of loss or deduction, then the partners' interests in the

---

**14.**  For convenience, the example disregards the first-year depreciation convention.

**15.**  See Reg. § 1.1245–1(e)(2)(iii) Example 1.

**16.**  See Reg. § 1.1245–1(e)(2)(iii) Example 2(i) & (ii).

**17.**  Reg. § 1.704–1(b)(4)(ii).

**18.**  As of this writing, the "ITC" is essentially "out," having been repealed in large part by the Tax Reform Act of 1986.

partnership with respect to such credit shall be in the same proportion as the partner's distributive share of the loss or deduction.[19]

## PROBLEMS

**1.** A and B each contribute $100,000 upon formation of a limited partnership. A is a general partner and B is a limited partner. The partnership purchases an office building on leased land for $200,000 and elects straight-line cost recovery. Assume (for simplicity) that the property has a 10–year recovery period. The partnership agreement allocates all items of income and loss equally with the exception of the cost recovery deductions, which are allocated entirely to B. Assume (perhaps unrealistically) that both partners are unconditionally obligated to restore a deficit to their capital accounts upon a liquidation of the partnership.

(a) Assume that apart from cost recovery deductions, the partnership's rental income is equal to its operating expenses. What must the partners' respective capital account balances be at the end of year one if the allocation of cost recovery deductions is to have economic effect?

(b) Assume the partnership sells the building on January 1 of year two and immediately liquidates. Again, with an eye toward qualifying the allocation, how must the proceeds be distributed if the building is sold for $180,000? For $200,000?

(c) Assume the agreement further provides that gain on disposition will be allocated to B to the extent of the cost recovery deductions specially allocated to her. What result when the partnership sells the building on January 1 of year two for $200,000?

(d) Assume that B is not required to restore a deficit in her capital account, but the partnership agreement includes a "qualified income offset." If the partnership continues to operate the building, what is the result to A and B in year one? In year six?

(e) What results in both years under the facts of (d), above, if in addition B has contributed her promissory note for $100,000 to the partnership?

(f) What results under the facts in (e), above, if in year six the building has a $400,000 fair market value, and A and B, acting as partners, agree that they will borrow $200,000 on a recourse basis, using the building as security, and distribute the proceeds equally to themselves early in year seven?

(g) What result under the facts in (e), above, if in year six the value of the building is $300,000, and A and B, acting as partners, agree that when its value reaches $400,000 they will take out a $200,000 recourse mortgage and distribute the proceeds equally?

**19.**  Reg. § 1.704–1(b)(4)(ii). See Reg. § 1.704–1(b)(5) Example (11), illustrating   this principle in the context of the targeted jobs credit.

(h) Assume that B is not required to restore a deficit in her capital account and that the partnership agreement does not contain a "qualified income offset." If the partnership continues to operate the building, what is the result to A and B in year one? In year six?

(i) What results in both years under the facts of (h), above, if in addition B has contributed her promissory note for $100,000 to the partnership?

**2**. C and D are equal partners in a general partnership formed to design and produce clothing for sale to retailers located throughout Europe and the United States. D is a nonresident alien. At the beginning of the tax year, the relative dollar amounts of United States and foreign source income cannot be predicted. Any foreign source income allocated to D is exempt from United States taxation. Assume that all of the following allocations have economic effect.

(a) What result if the partnership agreement provides that all U.S. source income will be allocated to C, and all foreign source income will be allocated to D?

(b) What result if the agreement provides that all income will be shared equally but that D will be allocated all the foreign source income up to the dollar amount of her 50% share of income?

(c) Assume, instead, that at the beginning of the tax year it can be predicted that the relative dollar amounts of U.S. and foreign source income will be roughly equal. What result if the agreement provides, as in (a), above, that all U.S. source income shall be allocated to C, and all foreign source income shall be allocated to D?

**3**. E and F form a limited partnership to purchase and lease a computer for $1,000,000. E, the limited partner, contributes $990,000, and F, the general partner, contributes $10,000. The agreement provides that § 168 cost recovery deductions will be allocated entirely to E and that all other items of income or loss will be allocated 99% to E until he has been allocated income equal to his share of cost recovery deductions and partnership losses. Thereafter, E and F will share income and loss equally. Assuming the capital account, liquidating distribution, and deficit restoration tests are met, will the allocations be respected? See Reg. § 1.704–1(b)(5) examples (2) and (3).

## 3.   ALLOCATIONS ATTRIBUTABLE TO NONRECOURSE DEBT

Regulations: §§ 1.704–2(b), (c), (d)(1), (e), (f)(1)–(3) & (6), (g), (j)(2) & (m) Examples 1(i)–(iv) & 3(i).

*Overview.* The preceding discussion was limited to situations where partnership activities were financed with partner contributions of cash or property, or with recourse borrowings. Many partnerships, however, finance their acquisitions of property largely with nonrecourse debt. Although the *Crane* case has long permitted taxpayers to include the amount of a nonrecourse mortgage acquisition debt in the cost basis of the encum-

bered property,[1] the economic risk of those taxpayers is limited to their cash investment and any loans for which they are personally liable. If the value of the property declines below the amount of the debt, the owner is free to walk away, leaving the creditor to bear the economic loss to the extent that the property does not satisfy the debt.[2]

It follows that when a partnership finances depreciable property with nonrecourse debt, the economic burden of the resulting cost recovery deductions is borne by the partners only to the extent of their investments of cash and other property or their shares of recourse debt. Cost recovery deductions in excess of the partnership's equity and recourse borrowings are attributable to the nonrecourse debt, and the economic risk resulting from any equivalent decline in value of the property is borne by the lender. Because an allocation of deduction or loss lacks economic effect unless it reflects a corresponding economic burden to the partner, the regulations properly acknowledge that no allocation of deductions attributable to nonrecourse debt can have substantial economic effect.[3] To illustrate, assume that the AB partnership finances the purchase of a $100,000 building (on leased land) by borrowing the entire $100,000 on a nonrecourse basis from Lender. Assume further that the partnership's first year cost recovery deduction is $5,000. In these circumstances, no allocation of the deduction has substantial economic effect because, if the property declines in value by $5,000, the partnership could default on the loan and Lender would sustain the $5,000 economic loss.

Although borrowers can avoid the economic burden of repaying nonrecourse debt, they cannot escape the *tax* burden of including the full amount of the debt in their amount realized on a disposition (including a foreclosure) of the encumbered property. Under the Supreme Court's holding in Commissioner v. Tufts,[4] a taxpayer recognizes gain on a disposition at least to the extent that the nonrecourse debt exceeds the adjusted basis of the property, regardless of the actual value of the asset. For example, on a disposition of the building in the example above at the end of year one, the partnership's minimum amount realized would be $100,000 (the debt relief), and it would recognize at least $5,000 of gain (the excess of the $100,000 amount realized over the $95,000 adjusted basis of the building). Under the regulations, the gain represented by this excess of nonrecourse debt over basis is known as "partnership minimum gain." This is the amount of gain that the partnership would realize if it disposed of partnership property subject to a nonrecourse liability in full satisfaction of the debt and for no other consideration.[5] Deductions that create or increase

---

**1.** Crane v. Commissioner, 331 U.S. 1, 67 S.Ct. 1047 (1947). See also Parker v. Delaney, 186 F.2d 455 (1st Cir.1950), cert. denied, 341 U.S. 926, 71 S.Ct. 797 (1951).

**2.** On dispositions of property in these circumstances, the taxpayer recognizes gain to the extent that the outstanding indebtedness exceeds the taxpayer's adjusted basis in the property regardless of the fair market value of the property. See Commissioner v. Tufts, 461 U.S. 300, 103 S.Ct. 1826 (1983), rehearing denied, 463 U.S. 1215, 103 S.Ct. 3555 (1983).

**3.** Reg. § 1.704–2(b)(1).

**4.** See note 2, supra.

**5.** Reg. § 1.704–2(d)(1).

partnership minimum gain (e.g., by reducing the adjusted basis of an asset that secures nonrecourse debt below the amount of the debt) are called "nonrecourse deductions."[6] Although an allocation of nonrecourse deductions cannot have economic effect, the regulations nonetheless generally permit a partnership to allocate those deductions to partners to whom the related minimum gain will be allocated. This tax payback is accomplished by a "minimum gain chargeback,"[7] which is a provision in the partnership agreement that requires the partnership to allocate minimum gain to those partners to whom the nonrecourse deductions were previously allocated. These matching allocations of nonrecourse deductions and partnership minimum gain eventually neutralize each other in the partners' capital accounts.[8] And since an allocation of nonrecourse deductions must be accompanied by a minimum gain chargeback, the regulations treat a partner's share of partnership minimum gain as an increase to the partner's obligation to restore a deficit capital account balance for purposes of the alternate test for economic effect.[9] That deficit restoration obligation will be made up when partnership minimum gain is reduced—for example, on a disposition of the property or a repayment of the liability.

The regulations incorporate these concepts into a four-part safe harbor test. If the test is satisfied, allocations of nonrecourse deductions are deemed to be made in accordance with the partners' interests in the partnership.[10] If an allocation fails to meet the test, nonrecourse deductions are allocated "according to the partners' overall economic interests in the partnership."[11] For planning purposes, it is highly desirable to draft a partnership agreement that complies with the safe harbor.

Before examining the four-part test, it is necessary to master the technical vocabulary employed by the regulations. Those who are successful in this endeavor can reasonably add a new foreign language skill to their resumes. The critical terms of art are: "partnership minimum gain;" "nonrecourse deductions;" "distribution of nonrecourse liability proceeds allocable to an increase in minimum gain;" "partner's share of partnership minimum gain;" and "minimum gain chargeback."

*Partnership Minimum Gain.* "Partnership minimum gain" is the amount of gain that a partnership would realize if it disposed of each of its properties that is subject to a nonrecourse liability for no consideration other than satisfaction of the debt—i.e., the excess of the nonrecourse liability over the adjusted basis of the property securing the debt.[12] Clients

---

**6.** Reg. § 1.704–2(c).

**7.** Reg. § 1.704–2(f)(1).

**8.** Nonrecourse deductions generally may be allocated to any partner provided that the allocations are "reasonably consistent with allocations that have substantial economic effect of some other significant partnership item attributable to the property securing the nonrecourse liabilities * * *." Reg. § 1.704–2(e)(2). See infra notes 31–33 and accompanying text.

**9.** Reg. § 1.704–2(g)(1). See Reg. § 1.704–1(b)(2)(ii)(*d*).

**10.** Reg. § 1.704–2(b)(1) & (e).

**11.** Id. See Reg. § 1.704–1(b)(3).

**12.** Reg. § 1.704–2(d)(1). If a partnership has more than one nonrecourse liability, total partnership minimum gain is the aggregate of minimum gain on all properties of the partnership encumbered by nonrecourse debt. Id.

and others who do not understand the economics of leveraged transactions often describe this income as "phantom gain." Partnership minimum gain is created in two situations: (1) as the adjusted basis of the encumbered property is reduced below the amount of the nonrecourse liability (e.g., by cost recovery deductions), or (2) as the amount of the nonrecourse liability is increased in excess of the adjusted basis of the property (e.g., on a refinancing).

To illustrate, assume that Developer (the general partner) and Investor (the limited partner) form a limited partnership to acquire and rent out a $100,000 commercial building on leased land. Developer contributes $1,000 and Investor contributes $9,000 to the partnership, which finances the balance of the purchase price with a $90,000 nonrecourse loan secured by the building. No principal payments on the loan are due for ten years. The partnership agreement requires capital accounts to be maintained in accordance with the Section 704(b) regulations, and liquidating distributions must be made in accordance with the positive capital account balances of the partners. Developer is obligated to restore a deficit. Investor has no such obligation, but the partnership agreement contains a qualified income offset and a minimum gain chargeback provision. The partnership allocates all partnership income, deductions and losses 90 percent to Investor and 10 percent to Developer until aggregate partnership income offsets previously incurred losses, at which time all further items (except as otherwise provided by a qualified income offset or minimum gain chargeback provision) will be divided equally between the partners. Assume that the expenses of operating the building always equal the rental income; the partnership is entitled to straight-line cost recovery deductions of $5,000 per year[13] and the value of the building always equals its adjusted basis.

On these facts, the partnership will take $10,000 of cost recovery deductions in the first two years, reducing its adjusted basis in the building to $90,000. The losses, allocated 90 percent to Investor and 10 percent to Developer, reduce each partner's capital account to zero.[14] By the end of year three, the adjusted basis of the building is reduced to $85,000 (below the $90,000 nonrecourse debt), and the partners each have negative capital accounts ($4,500 for Investor and $500 for Developer) as a result of the allocation of year three cost recovery deductions. If the partnership disposed of the building at the end of year three in full satisfaction of the debt, the amount realized would include the $90,000 of debt relief, and the partnership would realize $5,000 of gain ($90,000 amount realized less $85,000 adjusted basis). That $5,000 is "partnership minimum gain"—i.e., the amount of gain that the partnership would realize if it disposed of property subject to a nonrecourse liability in full satisfaction of the debt.[15] There was no minimum gain at the end of years one or two because, if the

---

**13.** This simplified cost recovery system has been adopted for convenience.

**14.** Investor's initial capital account of $9,000 (his cash contribution) is reduced by his $9,000 share of cost recovery deductions.

Similarly, Developer's initial capital account of $1,000 is reduced by his $1,000 share of cost recovery deductions.

**15.** Reg. § 1.704–2(d)(1).

partnership had disposed of the building for no consideration other than full satisfaction of the nonrecourse debt in either of those years, its $90,000 amount realized would not have exceeded the building's adjusted basis—hence, no gain and no minimum gain. In year three, there was a $5,000 increase in partnership minimum gain.

An increase in partnership minimum gain also results when a partnership incurs a nonrecourse liability that exceeds the adjusted basis of the property encumbered by the new debt.[16] Returning to the example, assume it is the first day of year four, and the building (with an adjusted basis of $85,000 and subject to a nonrecourse liability of $90,000) has increased in value to $150,000. If the partnership then incurs an additional $20,000 nonrecourse loan secured by the property, partnership minimum gain would increase by $20,000, from $5,000 to $25,000.

*Nonrecourse Deductions.* Generally speaking, "nonrecourse deductions" are deductions that relate to a net increase[17] in partnership minimum gain.[18] They most commonly are cost recovery deductions that reduce the adjusted basis of depreciable property below the amount of nonrecourse debt secured by the property.[19] In our example with Developer and Investor, the partnership had no nonrecourse deductions in years one and two because there was no net increase in partnership minimum gain in those years. In year three, however, there was a $5,000 net increase in partnership minimum gain and thus nonrecourse deductions of $5,000.

Nonrecourse deductions also can arise on a refinancing where the proceeds of a nonrecourse liability that increase partnership minimum gain are not distributed (or treated as not distributed) by the partnership.[20] Since these proceeds are not distributed, the regulations assume that they will be spent by the partnership and generate deductions that are attributable to the additional nonrecourse borrowing.[21] To illustrate, if our real

---

**16.** Reg. § 1.704–2(b)(2). Such subsequent borrowing is not a currently taxable event. See Woodsam Associates, Inc. v. Commissioner, 198 F.2d 357 (2d Cir.1952). The *Woodsam* case held that a taxpayer does not realize income on incurring an additional liability on property because he has a corresponding obligation to repay the loan, and no upward basis adjustment is allowed unless the taxpayer uses the loan proceeds to make capital improvements to the property.

**17.** All of a partnership's increases and decreases in minimum gain during a taxable year are netted to determine if there is a net increase in minimum gain. Both nonrecourse deductions and nonrecourse distributions only arise if there is a *net* increase in partnership minimum gain during the year. See Reg. §§ 1.704–2(d)(1), (g)(1).

**18.** Reg. § 1.704–2(c).

**19.** Reg. § 1.704–2(b)(2).

**20.** Reg. § 1.704–2(c).

**21.** Id. Nonrecourse deductions are treated as consisting first of cost recovery or depreciation deductions attributable to the properties triggering the increase in "minimum gain" and then of a pro rata share of other partnership deductions and losses. Id. If cost recovery deductions exceed the net increase in minimum gain, a proportional share of those deductions constitutes a nonrecourse deduction. See Reg. § 1.704–2(m) Example (4). If the net increase in minimum gain exceeds total partnership deductions for a given year—e.g., as a result of a refinancing—the excess deductions are carried forward and treated as nonrecourse deductions in subsequent years. Reg. § 1.704–2(j)(1)(iii). If the carryover results from nondistributed nonrecourse liability proceeds, the carryover is treated as an increase in partnership minimum gain attributable to such proceeds in

estate partnership borrows an additional $20,000 on the first day of year four (when the adjusted basis of the building is $85,000 and the outstanding nonrecourse debt is $90,000), the new nonrecourse loan increases partnership minimum gain by $20,000. If the partnership does not distribute the proceeds, the regulations treat the first $20,000 of partnership deductions for the year as nonrecourse deductions, and each partner's share of partnership minimum gain is increased by his or her allocable share of those deductions.[22] Those whose intellectual curiosity compels them to ask what happens when the proceeds *are* distributed will be rewarded by reading onward.

*Distribution of Nonrecourse Liability Proceeds Allocable to An Increase in Minimum Gain.* During the gestation period of the Section 704(b) regulations, the Treasury discovered that a special rule was needed to handle certain cases where the proceeds of a nonrecourse loan are distributed. Recall that a partnership distribution may cause a partner to wind up with a deficit capital account that exceeds the partner's obligation to restore a deficit. If the partnership agreement complies with the alternate test for economic effect, such a distribution would trigger an allocation of gross income to the distributee partner under a qualified income offset provision. The partnership tax bar persuaded the Treasury that this was a harsh result. The complex cure provided by the regulations is best explained by returning to our example.

Assume once again that on the first day of year four the Developer–Investor partnership just generated $20,000 of minimum gain by borrowing an additional $20,000 without recourse and securing the debt with a second mortgage on the building. This time, however, the partnership distributes the $20,000 proceeds—$18,000 to Investor and $2,000 to Developer. The regulations call this a "distribution of nonrecourse liability proceeds allocable to an increase in minimum gain."[23] Since there are no nonrecourse deductions in this scenario,[24] the partnership is unable to allocate the minimum gain to a partner to whom the corresponding nonrecourse deductions were allocated. The solution is to allocate ("charge back" in the argot of the trade) the minimum gain generated by the borrowing to the partners to whom the loan proceeds are distributed.[25] This chargeback mechanism avoids triggering a qualified income offset and an undesired current tax liability for distributees who have negative capital accounts that exceed their deficit restoration obligations. In the case of Investor, whose capital account before the distribution was negative $4,500 and who

---

the succeeding year. Reg. § 1.704–2(c) and § 1.704–2(m) Example (1)(vi). Got it?

**22.** See Reg. § 1.704–2(m) Example (1)(vi). In effect, the regulations assume that the borrowed funds will be spent on a pro rata share of each deduction incurred in the year the partnership borrows the funds, or in the succeeding year if there are insufficient deductions in the year the loan is incurred. Reg. § 1.704–2(c). See Reg. § 1.704–2(j)(1).

**23.** Reg. § 1.704–2(h)(1).

**24.** Reg. § 1.704–2(c). Unlike the previous examples in the text, the partnership has neither taken deductions (e.g., depreciation) that trigger minimum gain nor spent the loan proceeds in a manner that will generate nonrecourse deductions.

**25.** Reg. § 1.704–2(g)(1) & (h)(1).

has a deemed deficit restoration obligation of $4,500 resulting from his share of minimum gain, the distribution of $18,000 of loan proceeds increases his capital account deficit to $22,500. Since Investor is subject to the qualified income offset provision in the partnership agreement, it appears that he must be allocated at least $18,000 of gross income in order to bring his capital account back up to negative $4,500 as quickly as possible. The regulations avoid this result by allocating $18,000 of the minimum gain generated by the borrowing to Investor. This, in turn, allows Investor's capital account to be reduced to negative $22,500 without triggering the qualified income offset because the deficit does not exceed Investor's $22,500 share of minimum gain ($4,500 from years 1–3 and $18,000 from the distribution).[26]

*A Partner's Share of Partnership Minimum Gain.* A central premise of the regulations is that, even in the absence of a deficit restoration provision, nonrecourse deductions may reduce a partner's capital account below zero to the extent of a partner's share of partnership minimum gain. This is because those deductions will be "recaptured" and charged back to the partner to whom they were allocated and increase that partner's capital account when the partnership disposes of the property. Consistent with this policy, partners must keep track of their respective shares of partnership minimum gain in order to: (1) determine the extent to which they may have a capital account deficit without triggering a qualified income offset; (2) ensure that they are allocated their appropriate share of partnership minimum gain when it is recognized by the partnership; and (3) properly determine their share of partnership nonrecourse liabilities under Section 752.[27]

A partner's share of partnership minimum gain at the end of any taxable year is equal to the sum of the nonrecourse deductions allocated to the partner throughout the life of the partnership and the partner's share of distributions of nonrecourse liability proceeds allocable to an increase in minimum gain, reduced by the partner's share of any prior net decreases in partnership minimum gain.[28]

*Minimum Gain Chargeback.* We have seen that the regulations permit an allocation of nonrecourse deductions and certain other events to reduce a partner's capital account below zero to the extent of that partner's share

---

**26.** The partnership may use any reasonable method to determine whether a distribution is allocable to the proceeds of a nonrecourse debt and, if so, to whom the proceeds are distributed. Reg. § 1.704–2(h)(2). If the partnership has no need to allocate minimum gain to any partner, it may elect to treat a distribution as not allocable to the proceeds of a nonrecourse debt (thus not carrying with it an allocation of minimum gain) provided that the distribution itself does not create or increase a current capital account deficit for the distributee that the distributee is not otherwise obligated to re-store. Reg. § 1.704–2(h)(3), last sentence. In that event the loan will be treated as generating nonrecourse deductions. See supra notes 20–22 and accompanying text. In contrast to allocations of nonrecourse deductions, a distribution of loan proceeds does not have to be "reasonably consistent" with allocations having substantial economic effect. Compare infra notes 37–39 and accompanying text.

**27.** See Reg. § 1.752–3(a)(1) and Section D of this chapter, infra.

**28.** Reg. § 1.704–2(g)(1).

of minimum gain. This is permitted, even though the allocations do not have economic effect, because at some time in the future the partner will be taxable on his share of that minimum gain, and the partner's capital account will be increased accordingly. That point may be best described as "payback time." It follows that if there is a decrease in a partner's share of minimum gain, something must be done to allocate gain to the partner and to make a corresponding increase in that partner's capital account. To that end, the regulations generally require that, for any taxable year in which there is a net decrease in a partner's share of minimum gain, that partner must be allocated, by a provision in the partnership agreement known as a "minimum gain chargeback," income and gain in an amount equal to the net decrease in the partner's share of minimum gain.[29]

The most obvious transaction that triggers a decrease in partnership minimum gain is the disposition of property subject to nonrecourse debt. Returning to the example, assume that it is the beginning of year four. The partnership's adjusted basis in the property is now $85,000 ($100,000 original cost less $15,000 of cost recovery deductions in years 1–3), and the minimum gain is thus $5,000 ($90,000 of total nonrecourse debt less $85,000 adjusted basis). Assume that the partners have the following shares of minimum gain and capital accounts:

|  | Developer | Investor |
| --- | --- | --- |
| Cash Investment | $1,000 | $ 9,000 |
| Cost Recovery Deductions | ($1,500) | ($13,500) |
| Capital Account (and Min. Gain) | ($  500) | ($  4,500) |

If during year four the property is foreclosed without the receipt of any cash, the partnership nonetheless recognizes a taxable gain of $5,000 ($90,000 debt relief less $85,000 adjusted basis). The foreclosure also triggers a $5,000 net decrease in partnership minimum gain because the partnership no longer holds any property with minimum gain potential.[30] The minimum gain chargeback requires the partnership to allocate the $5,000 net decrease in minimum gain on the foreclosure to the partners to the extent of their respective shares of partnership minimum gain. In the example, that means that $500 (10 percent) of the gain is allocated to Developer and $4,500 (90 percent) is allocated to Investor.[31] In keeping

**29.** Reg. § 1.704–2(f)(1). A partner's share of the net decrease in partnership minimum gain is the partner's percentage share of the partnership minimum gain at the end of the immediately preceding year multiplied by the total net decrease in partnership minimum gain. Reg. § 1.704–2(g)(2).

**30.** The minimum gain was $5,000 at the beginning of the year and zero at the end of the year.

**31.** Reg. § 1.704–2(g)(2). The regulations provide that any minimum gain chargeback consists first of gains recognized from the disposition of partnership property subject to a nonrecourse liability. Only where the gain from the disposition of the property is less than the decrease in partnership minimum gain for the year does the partnership need to allocate income or gain from other sources as part of an allocation of partnership minimum gain. Reg. § 1.704–2(f)(6). If the amount of the minimum gain chargeback exceeds the partnership's income and gain for the year, the excess carries over. Id. See Reg. § 1.704–2(j)(2)(i) & (iii).

with the principle of the *Tufts* case, the purpose of the minimum gain chargeback is to "balance the books" by recapturing, for tax purposes, the nonrecourse deductions previously allocated to a partner that did not result in a corresponding economic burden.

A decrease in partnership minimum gain also can occur when the principal amount due on a nonrecourse liability is reduced or when a partnership liability is converted from nonrecourse to recourse. In those situations, the minimum gain chargeback rule operates differently.

If a partner contributes capital to the partnership that is used to pay all or part of the partnership's nonrecourse debt, that partner's share of partnership minimum gain will decrease, but the partner's capital contribution increases his capital account in an amount equal to the total decrease in minimum gain. In that event, there is no need to allocate additional income to the partner in order to make an appropriate restoration of his negative capital account. The regulations reflect these realities by providing that a partner is not subject to a minimum gain chargeback to the extent that the decrease in the partner's share of minimum gain is attributable to the partner's own capital contribution that is used to pay the partnership's nonrecourse debt.[32]

A similar policy applies when partnership debt is converted in whole or in part from nonrecourse to recourse as a result of a guarantee, refinancing or a comparable arrangement. In that case, there is no minimum gain chargeback to a partner to the extent that the partner bears the economic risk of loss[33] for the new recourse liability.[34]

Under a final exception, a minimum gain chargeback is not triggered if it would cause a distortion in the economic arrangement among the partners and there is insufficient other income to correct the distortion.[35]

*Safe Harbor Test.* Having mastered the glossary, we finally can turn to the safe harbor test—an experience that gives new definition to the term "anticlimax." Allocations of "nonrecourse deductions" will be respected if the following four requirements are satisfied:

(1) Throughout the life of the partnership, the partnership agreement must satisfy the requirements of either The Big Three test or the alternative test for economic effect.[36]

(2) Beginning in the first taxable year in which the partnership has nonrecourse deductions and thereafter for the life of the partnership, nonrecourse deductions must be allocated in a manner that is reasonably consistent with allocations (having substantial economic effect) of some other significant partnership item attributable to

---

**32.** Reg. § 1.704–2(f)(3). See Reg. § 1.704–2(m) Example (1)(iv).

**33.** Reg. § 1.752–2.

**34.** Reg. § 1.704–2(f)(2).

**35.** Reg. § 1.704–2(f)(4). For an example of such a situation, see Reg. § 1.704–2(f)(7) Example 1. The Commissioner is authorized to provide additional exceptions to the minimum gain chargeback rule. Reg. § 1.704–2(f)(5).

**36.** Reg. § 1.704–2(e)(1).

the property securing the nonrecourse liabilities of the partnership (other than allocation of minimum gain).[37]

The second part of the test requires allocation of nonrecourse deductions to be "reasonably consistent" with allocations of some other "significant partnership item" attributable to the property. The agreement in our example provides that all income, deductions and losses are allocated 90 percent to Investor and 10 percent to Developer until aggregate profits from the venture exceed previously incurred losses, at which time all profits are split 50:50. In that situation, the regulations sanction either a 90:10 allocation or a 50:50 allocation of the nonrecourse deductions (or any ratio between 90:10 and 50:50), because either allocation would be "reasonably consistent" with the allocation of a different partnership item attributable to the property.[38] On the other hand, an allocation of 99 percent of nonrecourse deductions to Investor would not be treated as reasonably consistent with a 90:10 or 50:50 division of other partnership items.[39]

> (3) Beginning in the first year in which the partnership has nonrecourse deductions or makes a distribution of proceeds of a nonrecourse liability allocable to an increase in partnership minimum gain, the partnership agreement must contain a minimum gain chargeback.[40]

Although the concept is complex, it is simple enough to include a minimum gain chargeback provision in a partnership agreement. Moreover, the application of a minimum gain chargeback is usually quite routine because the partnership likely will realize enough gain on a disposition (including a foreclosure) of the encumbered property to eliminate the deficit capital accounts of partners who enjoyed the tax benefits flowing from nonrecourse deductions or who receive distributions of nonrecourse liability proceeds.[41]

At the conceptual level, remember that two principles are at work here. First, allocations of nonrecourse deductions will be respected, even though they reduce a partner's capital account below zero, if the partnership agreement requires a subsequent allocation of partnership income or gain, consisting of either the partner's proportionate share of the minimum gain realized on a later disposition of the property or, if partnership minimum gain is decreased without a disposition of the property, of sufficient items of partnership income to offset the earlier deductions and bring the partner's capital account back up to zero. Second, distributions of nonrecourse loan proceeds can reduce a partner's capital account below

---

**37.** Reg. § 1.704–2(e)(2).

**38.** Reg. § 1.704–2(m) Example (1)(i). The example in the regulations assumes that, at the time of the agreed allocation, there was a reasonable likelihood that the partnership would recognize amounts of income and gain significantly in excess of amounts of loss and deduction (other than nonrecourse deductions). Reg. § 1.704–2(m) Example (1).

**39.** Reg. § 1.704–2(m) Example (1)(iii).

**40.** Reg. § 1.704–2(e)(3).

**41.** It is important to remember that any tax benefits from allocations of nonrecourse deductions also are subject to the at-risk and passive loss limitations, which in many cases may postpone the deduction until the property is sold. See Chapter 3C, supra.

zero without triggering a qualified income offset, at least to the extent of the minimum gain to be charged back to the partner.

(4) All other material allocations and capital account adjustments under the partnership agreement must comply with the basic Section 704(b) regulations.[42]

The fourth and final prong of the safe harbor test is purely mechanical. It simply requires that allocations of other material items (other than nonrecourse deductions) must have substantial economic effect. Because limited partners are averse to unlimited deficit restoration obligations, limited partnerships typically will seek to validate allocations of other partnership items under the alternate economic effect test.[43] As a result, a properly drafted agreement for a partnership with nonrecourse debt should include both a qualified income offset for the limited partners and a minimum gain chargeback that complies with the regulations governing nonrecourse deductions.[44]

## PROBLEM

G and L form a limited partnership. G, the general partner, contributes $80,000 and L, the limited partner, contributes $320,000. The partnership purchases commercial real estate on leased land, paying $400,000 cash and borrowing $1,600,000 on a nonrecourse basis from a commercial lender. The terms of the loan require payment of interest only for the first five years. The GL partnership agreement allocates all income, gain, loss and deductions 20% to G and 80% to L until the first time that the partnership has recognized items of income and gain that exceed the items of loss and deduction recognized over its life, and then all further partnership items are to be allocated equally between G and L. At the time the partnership agreement is entered into, there is a reasonable likelihood that, over the partnership's life, it will recognize amounts of income and gain significantly in excess of losses and deductions. The partnership agreement requires that all allocations are to be reflected in appropriate adjustments to the partners' capital accounts and liquidation proceeds are to be distributed in accordance with positive capital account balances. Only G is required to restore a capital account deficit. The partnership agreement contains a qualified income offset for L and a minimum gain chargeback provision. Finally, the agreement provides that all nonliquidating distributions will be made 20% to G and 80% to L until a total of $400,000 (equal to the partners' original cash contributions) has been distributed, and thereafter such distributions will be made equally to G and L. The partnership depreciates its property using the straight-line method over a valid (you may assume) 10–year recovery period.

---

**42.** Reg. § 1.704–2(e)(4).

**43.** Reg. § 1.704–1(b)(2)(ii)(*d*).

**44.** See, e.g., Reg. § 1.704–2(m) Example (1)(i).

(a) Assume that rental income from the property of $150,000 equals operating expenses (including interest on the nonrecourse debt) of $150,000. Determine the allocation of the partnership's cost recovery deductions in each of the first three years of operations and determine the partners' capital accounts at the end of each year.

(b) Same as (a), above, except the partnership agreement provides that L will be allocated 99% and G 1% of all the partnership's cost recovery deductions.

(c) Same as (a), above, except that the partnership agreement provides that L will be allocated 70% and G 30% of all the partnership nonrecourse deductions.

(d) Is there an allocation under the minimum gain chargeback in (a), above, if at the end of year four G contributes $80,000 and L contributes $320,000 to the partnership, which uses the funds to pay down $400,000 of the liability.

(e) Is there an allocation under the minimum gain chargeback in (a), above, if during year four the partnership converts $600,000 of the $1,600,000 nonrecourse liability to a recourse liability? Determine the partners' capital accounts at the end of years four and five.

(f) What results under the facts of (a), above, in year four if in that year, when the property has appreciated in value, the partnership incurs an additional $300,000 of nonrecourse liability and it distributes the proceeds $60,000 to G and $240,000 to L?

## 4. POLICY CONSIDERATIONS

The Section 704(b) regulations are among the most complex rules that a student (or practitioner) will ever encounter. Anyone with the fortitude and perspective to master the technical details will discover that the allocation rules are quite permissive. It is relatively easy to anchor a partnership allocation within the liberal safe harbors if the partnership agreement includes certain magic language and the partners maintain their capital accounts properly throughout the life of their enterprise. The regulations even provide some guidance for those who fail to satisfy the safe harbors. If flexibility and certainty of result are desirable goals, the Section 704(b) regulations have much to offer.

But are the regulations too permissive? The excerpt below addresses these questions, focusing on allocations attributable to nonrecourse debt and the substantiality requirement. The author provides helpful insights on the deficiencies of the partnership allocation regulations and offers possible legislative solutions. The discussion is presented in the form of a congressional committee report on a hypothetical Subchapter K Reform Act. Keep in mind that this proposal has not yet been enacted into law, but it may be influential if Congress ever should engage in a comprehensive review of Subchapter K.

## Excerpt from William B. Brannan, The Subchapter K Reform Act of 1997

75 Tax Notes 121, 122–124 (April 7, 1997).

### 1.  Partnership Tax Allocation Provisions

### a.  Prohibit Special Allocations Attributable to Nonrecourse Debt

**Present Law**

Under section 704(b) and Treasury regulation section 1.704–1(b), partnerships have great flexibility in allocating income and loss among their partners. In general, partnership tax allocations will be respected if either (i) such allocations have substantial economic effect by complying with the detailed rules set forth in Treasury regulation section 1.704–1(b)(2) regarding the maintenance of capital accounts (as described below) or (ii) such allocations are in accordance with the economic interests of the partners in the partnership (as determined under the facts and circumstances test set forth in Treasury regulation section 1.704–1(b)(3)).

It appears that in practice most partnerships now rely on the capital account rules to validate their tax allocations. Under those rules, allocations of partnership tax items generally will be respected if such allocations satisfy the following three mechanical requirements that are intended to cause allocations to have economic effect: (i) the partnership maintains capital accounts for its partners in accordance with the principles of Treasury regulation section 1.704–1(b)(2)(ii) so as to reflect all partnership tax allocations, (ii) distributions upon liquidation of the partnership (or upon the liquidation of a partner's interest in the partnership) are made in accordance with such capital accounts, and (iii) any partner with a deficit balance in his capital account upon the liquidation of the partnership (or upon the liquidation of his interest in the partnership) must make a capital contribution to the partnership to eliminate such deficit balance. In addition to the foregoing mechanical requirements, the economic effect of the partnership's tax allocations must be "substantial" within the meaning of Treasury regulation section 1.704–1(b)(2)(iii).

As indicated by Treasury regulation section 1.704–2(b)(1), allocations of losses, deductions, or section 705(a)(2)(B) expenditures attributable to the nonrecourse debt of a partnership cannot have economic effect through capital account adjustments, because the economic risk of loss associated with such tax items is borne by the nonrecourse lender.[6] Thus, the normal substantial economic effect rules do not apply to such allocations. Instead, Treasury regulation section 1.704–2(b) generally allows a partnership to

---

**6.** As a broad generalization, tax items attributable to nonrecourse debt arise in any taxable year in which the ending debt balance exceeds the section 704(b) book value of the property securing such debt and such items usually consist of the depreciation or amortization deductions attributable to such property for such year (reduced by the amount of any amortization of the debt balance, or the amount of any capitalized expenditures with respect to such property, during such year). See Treas. reg. sections 1.704–2(c) and 1.704–2(i)(2). If such deductions were matched by a corresponding decline in the economic value of such property, the lender would bear such loss on a foreclosure.

allocate tax items attributable to nonrecourse debt however the partnership chooses, provided that such allocation corresponds to the allocation of some other significant partnership tax item that itself has substantial economic effect and the partnership agreement contains a so-called "minimum gain chargeback" to ensure that such allocations will be reversed by income allocations when the property securing the debt is sold or the debt is paid down.[7] The one important exception to that rule is for tax items attributable to nonrecourse debt where the lender is a partner or an affiliate of a partner, in which case such tax items generally must be allocated exclusively to that partner.[8]

Since most partnership agreements provide for "flips" in their allocations over time, special allocations of particular tax items or other complexities in their allocations, the above-stated limitation on allocations of tax items attributable to third-party nonrecourse debt often leaves a partnership with a wide range of choices in making such allocations. Even if the desired allocation of tax items attributable to third-party nonrecourse debt is not supported by the other allocations that naturally would occur by reason of the business arrangement of the partners, it is possible in many circumstances to provide for a special allocation of a significant partnership tax item in order to support the desired allocation of tax items attributable to third-party nonrecourse debt.

The foregoing discussion has focused on allocations of the items attributable to nonrecourse debt in the context of partnerships that rely on the capital account rules to validate their tax allocations. It should be noted that it is not clear how much latitude partnerships that rely upon the alternative test based upon the economic interests of the partners have to allocate tax items attributable to nonrecourse debt, since there is no regulation that specifically addresses that issue. In the case of third-party nonrecourse debt, the spirit of the section 704(b) regulations appears to be that such allocations should be based upon the overall economic interests of the partners in the partnership.[9] In the case of partner nonrecourse debt, it is arguable that the fact that the partner (or its affiliate) bears the economic risk of loss on the debt should be taken into account in allocating

---

**7.** In the parlance of the section 704(b) regulations, such allocations of tax items attributable to nonrecourse debt are "deemed" to be in accordance with economic interests of the partners.

**8.** See Treas. reg. section 1.704–2(i). Such debt is referred to in the section 704(b) regulation as "partner nonrecourse debt." See Treas. reg. section 1.704–2(b)(4). In the discussion below, the term "third-party nonrecourse debt" is used to distinguish partner nonrecourse debt from nonrecourse debt that is not subject to Treas. reg. section 1.704–2(i). * * *

**9.** The general approach of the alternate test in the section 704(b) regulations is to treat the overall economic interests of the partners as the basis for tax allocations, except where there is a special arrangement for sharing the economic benefit or burden corresponding to a particular item, in which event that tax item should be specially allocated to reflect such arrangement. See Treas. reg. section 1.704–1(b)(3)(i). Cf. Treas. reg. section 1.704–2(b)(1) (tax items attributable to the nonrecourse debt of a partnership that is attempting to follow the capital account rules must be allocated in accordance with "the partners' overall economic interests" if the requirements of that regulation are not satisfied).

tax items attributable to that debt, although it is by no means clear that economic risk of loss borne in a lender capacity (particularly if the lender is not a partner) is relevant for that purpose.

### Reasons for Change

The committee generally believes that partnerships should have the flexibility in allocating tax items to reflect the economic arrangement of their partners and that section 704(b) should provide as much certainty as possible regarding the validity of such allocations, which objectives are facilitated by the mechanical capital account rules under section 704(b). However, the committee believes that it is inappropriate to allow partnerships to specially allocate losses, deductions and section 705(a)(2)(B) expenditures attributable to third-party nonrecourse debt as permitted under current law. As indicated above, such allocations, by definition, have no economic effect on the partners. While it is true that other partnership tax allocations may not, in practice, have actual economic effect in many circumstances because of offsetting allocations or other events that occur later, there is at least a potential for actual economic effect that usually necessitates that such allocations follow the economic arrangement of the partners. In contrast, allocations of tax items attributable to third-party nonrecourse debt often are highly tax-motivated.

The current system imposes no meaningful limitation on the ability of partnerships to make tax-motivated allocations of tax items attributable to third-party nonrecourse debt. Indeed, one professional group has equated the ability to shift tax benefits among partners afforded by the current rules governing the allocation of tax items attributable to non-recourse debt with the old safe harbor leasing rules.[10]

### Explanation of Provision

Under the act, section 704(b) is amended to provide that partnership tax [items] attributable to third-party nonrecourse debt, as determined under the principles of Treasury regulation section 1.704–2, generally must be allocated in accordance with the overall economic interests of the partners in the partnership. The overall economic interests of the partners in the partnership shall be determined in accordance with the principles of Treasury regulations section 1.704–1(b)(3). However, to provide some certainty in making this determination, partnerships generally may elect to determine the economic interests of the partners based on the partners' relative capital contributions.[11] The foregoing provisions apply to both

---

**10.** New York State Bar Association Tax Section, Report on Proposed Treasury Regulations Under Internal Revenue Code Section 704(b) (May 12, 1983) at 36–7. That comment was made with reference to the original 1983 proposed section 704(b) regulations, which did not even include the requirement that the allocation of tax items attributable to nonrecourse debt be consistent with

the allocation of some other partnership tax item that does have substantial economic effect. * * * However, as indicated above, the committee does not view that as an adequate limitation.

**11.** The determination of the economic interests of the partners based on relative capital contributions may be challenged by

partnerships that rely on capital accounts to validate their tax allocations and to partnerships that rely on the partners' economic interests in the partnership approach.

The provisions of the act do not affect the current rules regarding allocations of losses, deductions, or section 705(a)(2)(B) expenditures attributable to so-called "partner nonrecourse liabilities" set forth in Treasury regulation section 1.704–2(i). Accordingly, such items generally must continue to be allocated to the partner that bears the economic risk of loss with respect to such tax items. However, the act expressly provides that this rule also applies to partnerships that rely on the economic interests of the partners approach to validate their tax allocations.

### b.   Strengthen the Substantiality Requirement

### Present Law

As indicated above, the substantial economic effect test in Treasury regulations section 1.704–1(b)(2) is not satisfied unless the economic effect of that allocation is "substantial."

The basic test for determining whether the economic effect of an allocation is substantial is set forth in Treasury regulation section 1.704–1(b)(2)(iii). Under that test, the economic effect of an allocation is not substantial if, at the time the allocation becomes part of the partnership agreement, (i) the economic consequences to at least one partner, as determined on a present value, after-tax basis, may be enhanced as compared to the case where such allocation is not made, and (ii) there is a strong likelihood that the economic consequences to no partner, as so determined, will be substantially diminished as compared to the case where such allocation is not made. To provide certainty in applying the test, the fair market value of partnership property is presumed to be equal to its adjusted book value as determined for section 704(b) purposes. As a result, the substantiality of allocations is tested on the assumption that there will be no gain on the sale of partnership property that might reverse the effect of prior allocations.

In addition to the basic substantiality test, Treasury regulation section 1.704–1(b)(2)(iii) contains specific rules preventing shifting and transitory allocations.

### Reasons for Change

The committee believes the "value equals basis" presumption that applies in testing the substantiality of an allocation, while often economically unrealistic, generally is appropriate for two reasons. First, it makes the substantiality test relatively simple to apply, thereby avoiding the

the Service in any case where (i) the capital contributions by the partners represent an insubstantial part of the total capitalization of the partnership or (ii) the partners expect that the partnership will earn substantial profits in excess of a reasonable return on such capital contributions and such residual profits will be shared on a basis that is substantially different from the relative capital contributions of the partners.

burdensome financial forecasting that would be necessary if partnerships were required to use a more economically realistic model. Second, it provides a reasonable degree of certainty in testing allocations, thereby facilitating taxpayer planning and minimizing controversies on audit.[12]

However, at the same time, the "value equals basis" presumption usually makes it fairly easy for a partnership to satisfy the substantiality test, even in a tax-motivated situation. That follows because the "value equals basis" presumption effectively means that each dollar of loss or deduction specially allocated to a partner generally will reduce the amount such partner will receive on liquidation of the partnership, and so the only question is whether the present value of the tax benefit created by that allocation is fully offset by the present value of the lost dollar of liquidating distributions. At the same time, it is perfectly rational for the parties to make such special allocations if, as is often the case, the economic value of partnership property is not expected to decline at the same rate as its adjusted book basis declines to reflect book depreciation or amortization. In such cases, the potential economic effect of the special allocation can be offset by specially allocating gain on the sale of the property (or other partnership income).

In some extreme cases, it is possible that an allocation would be vulnerable to challenge under the anti-abuse rule in Treasury regulation section 1.701–2 or some general principle of law.[13] However, as a practical matter, it is very unlikely that any such general principle would be used to attack an abusive partnership tax allocation. First, the audit rate for partnerships is extremely low.[14] Second, it is unlikely that an auditor would seek to apply general principles to situations that facially seem to satisfy the capital account rules, since auditors usually have difficulty just understanding complex partnership tax allocations and there is no decided case or ruling that applies general principles in the section 704(b) context. Third, it is quite possible that a court would conclude that the extremely detailed capital account rules occupy the field (except in cases involving a total sham), thereby precluding the application of general principles.[15]While

**12.** The substantiality test does involve some uncertainties, such as what the allocations of the partnership would be in the absence of the special allocation being tested (an issue that is considerably more difficult than might first appear) and how to make assumptions about asset holding periods, annual operating income, and other relevant facts.

**13.** The section 704(b) regulations actually contain an express statement that allocations that satisfy the mechanical rules of the regulations may still be vulnerable to challenge under general tax principles. See Treas. reg. section 1.704–1(b)(1)(iii).

**14.** According to a recent General Accounting Office report, the audit rate for

partnerships, which has never been high, has been dropping steadily in recent years and is now about 0.5 percent (versus 2.89 percent for corporations). See General Accounting Office, Report to the Joint Committee on Taxation, GGD–95–151 (June 16, 1995).

**15.** With respect to the section 701 anti-abuse rule [discussed in Chapter 10, infra, Ed.], the regulations contain examples that strongly suggest that the anti-abuse rule may not be used to challenge allocations that satisfy the section 704(b) rules (see Treasury reg. section 1.701–2(d) (Examples 5 and 6)). In addition, it may be significant that the Treasury did not amend the section 704(b) regulation referred to in note 13, supra, to

Congress wants to maintain the basic framework of the current rules, it does not want the substantiality test to be easily satisfied in cases of tax-motivated allocations where there is some objective indication that the allocations are not expected to have economic effect.

### Explanation of Provision

Under the act, a special allocation of income or loss will be treated as not having substantial economic effect if the parties believe that there is only a remote possibility that such allocation will actually have economic effect. Whether a special allocation is expected to have economic effect for this purpose is to be evaluated on a present value, after-tax basis.

The Service shall have the burden of proof under this provision, and must satisfy that burden with clear and convincing evidence. Such burden of proof generally will be satisfied if the offering documents or other promotional materials for the transaction do not disclose the potential economic effect of the special allocation or, if they do disclose the potential economic effect, they characterize the risk of such effect actually occurring in a manner such that a reasonable person would conclude that the risk is not significant.

---

## C.   ALLOCATIONS WITH RESPECT TO CONTRIBUTED PROPERTY

## 1.   INTRODUCTION

Code: §§ 704(a), (c)(1)(A) & (3).

Regulations:  §§ 1.704–3(a)(1)–(5)  &  (10),–3(e)(1);  1.704–1(b)(1)(vi),–1(b)(2)(iv)(*d*)(*1*) & (*3*).

*Background.* When partners contribute property to a partnership in exchange for an interest in the firm,[1] they recognize neither gain nor loss[2] and their basis in the contributed property carries over to the partnership.[3] If the general rule in Section 704(a) applied to this transaction, gain or loss on the disposition of the contributed property would be allocated in accordance with the partnership agreement. This approach would provide a convenient method for shifting precontribution gains or losses among the partners. For example, assume the AB equal partnership is formed with A contributing Gainacre, a capital asset, with an adjusted basis of $12,000 and a fair market value of $20,000, and B contributing $20,000 in cash. Although Gainacre is recorded on the partnership's books at its fair market value,[4] the partnership takes over A's $12,000 adjusted basis for tax purposes.[5] If A and B agree to allocate profits according to their equal 50 percent interests in the partnership, any gain or loss on a subsequent sale

---

provide a specific cross-reference to the antiabuse rule.

**1.**  See Chapter 2A, supra.

**2.**  I.R.C. § 721. See I.R.C. § 722.

**3.**  I.R.C. § 723.

**4.**  Reg. §§ 1.704–1(b)(2)(iv)(*b*), (*d*)(*1*); 1.704–1(b)(5) Example (13)(i).

**5.**  I.R.C. § 723. The effect is to create a book/tax disparity of $8,000.

of Gainacre would be allocated equally to A and B under Section 704(a). Thus, if the partnership sold Gainacre for $20,000, it would not realize any book gain and the capital accounts of the partners would be unaffected,[6] but $4,000 of the $8,000 *tax* gain realized on the sale would be allocated to B even though that entire gain is attributable to the period when A held the property. Half of the precontribution gain would be shifted to B simply because the AB partnership, rather than A, sold the property. Similarly, a tax loss could be shifted if A contributed property with an adjusted basis exceeding its fair market value.

The shift of precontribution gain to B is not permanent, but it may last for many years—perhaps as long as the AB partnership remains in existence. After the partnership's $8,000 tax gain is allocated equally to A and B, their outside bases are increased to $16,000 and $24,000, respectively.[7] If the partnership then were liquidated with A and B each receiving $20,000 in cash, A would recognize his remaining $4,000 gain and B would recognize a $4,000 loss. Even though B eventually recognizes a $4,000 loss to offset his earlier gain on the sale of Gainacre, substantial time may have elapsed before the loss is recognized. Moreover, if the contributed property were depreciable, the character of the gain and the later offsetting loss may differ. B's loss on a liquidation or sale of his partnership interest would be a capital loss[8] while the gain on the sale of the depreciable property might be ordinary as a result of depreciation recapture.[9]

The example illustrates a problem with applying the general allocation rule in Section 704(a) to gain or loss on the disposition of contributed property. That rule would enable partners to shift income or loss for tax purposes without any corresponding economic benefit or burden,[10] and cause distortions in the timing and character of future income or loss.[11] Similar distortions would result from depreciation deductions with respect to contributed property.

A tempting solution to the income shifting problem might be for the partnership to make a special allocation of the $8,000 of tax gain to contributing partner A under Section 704(b). But remember that the property was recorded on the books of the partnership at its $20,000 fair market value when it was contributed by A. As a result, there is no book gain (or capital account adjustment) on its sale for $20,000, and a special allocation of the $8,000 tax gain thus would not have substantial economic effect under the now familiar principles of Section 704(b).

---

**6.** Reg. §§ 1.704–1(b)(2)(iv)(*b*)(*3*); 1.704–1(b)(4)(i).

**7.** I.R.C. § 705(a)(1)(A).

**8.** I.R.C. §§ 731(a); 741. See Chapters 6 & 8, infra.

**9.** I.R.C. §§ 1245; 1250.

**10.** Even when marginal tax rates are compressed, incentives remain for shifting in-come and losses in the partnership setting. For example, it might be desirable to shift taxable income to a tax-exempt partner or to a partner with an expiring net operating loss carryover.

**11.** In the event of a partner's death, even the amount of loss could be affected. I.R.C. § 1014.

*General Section 704(c) Allocation Principles.* The Congressional response to these and related concerns is Section 704(c)(1)(A), which provides, under regulations promulgated by the Service,[12] that items of income, gain, loss and deduction with respect to property contributed by a partner to a partnership shall be shared among the partners "so as to take account of the variation between the basis of the property to the partnership and its fair market value at the time of contribution."[13] Because this is a tax allocation that lacks substantial economic effect, it is not accompanied by any change to the partners' capital accounts.

Typically, Congress did not grovel in the details of how these tax allocations would be made, delegating that arduous task to the regulations writers at the Treasury. The regulations apply to allocations with respect to "Section 704(c) property," which is defined as property that at the time of its contribution to the partnership has a fair market (book) value that differs from contributing partner's adjusted tax basis.[14] If the property's book value is greater than its adjusted basis, the difference is a "built-in gain," and if the adjusted basis exceeds the book value, the difference is a "built-in loss."[15] In determining whether property has a built-in gain or loss, the Service generally will accept the valuation determined by the arm's lengths dealings of the partners as reflected in their capital accounts if the parties have sufficiently adverse interests.[16]

In keeping with the Service's policy to "simplify" and provide "flexibility" to taxpayers, the regulations permit a partnership to make allocations using any reasonable method that is consistent with the purpose of Section 704(c).[17] The regulations give their blessing to three methods: the "traditional method,"[18] the "traditional method with curative allocations,"[19] and the "remedial method."[20] Each is subject to a general anti-abuse rule under which an allocation method is not reasonable if the contribution of property and the corresponding allocation of tax items are made with a view to shifting the tax consequences of the built-in gain or loss among the partners in a manner that substantially reduces the present value of their aggregate tax liability.[21]

**12.** See Reg. § 1.704–3.

**13.** Section 704(c)(1)(A) is patterned after its predecessor, Section 704(c)(2), which was wholly or partially elective by the partners. It also applies to contributions by cash method taxpayers of accounts payable and other accrued but unpaid cash basis items, such as zero basis accounts receivable. I.R.C. § 704(c)(3); Reg. § 1.704–3(a)(4). See Chapter 2B, supra, and Problem 2 at page 51 supra.

**14.** Reg. § 1.704–3(a)(3)(i).

**15.** Reg. § 1.704–3(a)(3)(ii). Built-in gains and losses are determined at the time of the contribution. They are reduced thereafter by any decreases in the difference between the property's adjusted basis and book value. Id.

**16.** This determination will be respected except in abuse cases. See Staff of the Joint Committee on Taxation, General Explanation of the Revenue Provisions of the Deficit Reduction Act of 1984 (hereinafter "1984 Act General Explanation"), 98th Cong., 2d Sess. 213 (1984). Cf. Reg. § 1.704–1(b)(2)(iv)(h).

**17.** Reg. § 1.704–3(a)(1).

**18.** Reg. § 1.704–3(b).

**19.** Reg. § 1.704–3(c).

**20.** Reg. § 1.704–3(d).

**21.** Reg. § 1.704–3(a)(10). For examples of unreasonable allocations, see Reg.

No more than one allocation method may be used with respect to each item of Section 704(c) property and, although a different method may be used with respect to different items of property, a partner and partnership must use a method or combination of methods that is reasonable under the facts and circumstances.[22] In general, Section 704(c) must be applied on a property-by-property basis except that property with identical tax characteristics (e.g., depreciable property, inventory) may be aggregated for purposes of determining whether built-in gains and losses exist.[23]

A partnership may disregard or defer the application of Section 704(c) in a single year if there is a "small disparity" between the book value and the adjusted basis of the contributed property.[24] A "small disparity" exists if the total fair market value of all property contributed by a partner during the taxable year does not differ from the total adjusted basis of the property by more than 15 percent of the adjusted basis, and the total gross disparity does not exceed $20,000.[25] To illustrate, assume that the AB partnership is formed with A contributing $100,000 cash and B contributing land with an adjusted basis of $90,000 and a fair market value of $100,000. The partnership may disregard Section 704(c) with respect to the land because the $10,000 difference between its fair market value and basis does not differ from the adjusted basis by more than 15 percent of that basis (i.e., 15% × $90,000 = $13,500, which is more than $10,000), and the disparity does not exceed $20,000.

Against the background of these general rules and exceptions, we turn next to the application of the three allocation methods to the two most typical situations that arise under Section 704(c): sales and exchanges, and depreciation of contributed property.

## 2. SALES AND EXCHANGES OF CONTRIBUTED PROPERTY

### a. SECTION 704(c) ALLOCATION METHODS

Code: § 704(c)(1)(A).

Regulations: § 1.704–3(b)(1); –3(c)(1)–(3); –3(d)(1), (3), (4), (5), and (7) Example 2.

*The Traditional Method.* The "traditional method" is based on the approach used when Section 704(c) allocations were elective and during the period between the enactment of current Section 704(c)(1)(A) in 1984 and the effective date of the regulations. As applied to sales of contributed

§§ 1.704–3(b)(2) Example 2 and 1.704–3(c)(4) Example 1(iii). The abuses identified in the examples are reminiscent of the types of manipulation that may violate the "substantiality" test of the Section 704(b) regulations. See Reg. § 1.704–1(b)(2)(iii).

**22.** Reg. § 1.704–3(a)(2). The regulations indicate that it may be unreasonable to use one method for appreciated property and another method for depreciated property.

Whatever method is elected must be consistently applied by both the partner and the partnership in each year. Id.

**23.** Reg. §§ 1.704–3(a)(2) & (e)(2).

**24.** Reg. § 1.704–3(e)(1)(i).

**25.** Reg. § 1.704–3(e)(1)(ii). In determining whether a disparity is "small," the partner can aggregate properties with similar tax characteristics. Id.

property, the traditional method generally requires a partnership to allocate any built-in gain or loss to the contributing partner.[1]

Return again to the example in which A and B form the AB partnership with A contributing Gainacre (basis—$12,000, value—$20,000), and B contributing $20,000 cash. If the partnership sells Gainacre for $20,000, the traditional method allocates the entire $8,000 of built-in gain to A.[2] If the partnership sells Gainacre for $35,000, resulting in $23,000 of taxable gain, of which $8,000 accrued prior to A's contribution and $15,000 accrued while Gainacre was held by the partnership, the $8,000 precontribution gain is allocated to A under Section 704(c)(1)(A), and the $15,000 postcontribution gain is divided equally between A and B.[3]

The Section 704(b) regulations elaborate on the relationship between Section 704(c) allocations and the rules governing maintenance of capital accounts. The difference between the tax basis and the fair market (book) value of contributed property at the time of the contribution requires a partnership to keep two sets of accounts—one for "book" (including capital account) purposes and the other for "tax" purposes. The "book" items, which reflect the economic arrangement of the partners, are used in testing the substantial economic effect of an allocation. The "tax" items—i.e., the amounts reported on the partnership's tax return that pass through to the partners—must be determined with reference to the partners' distributive shares of the corresponding book items.[4]

In the example, Gainacre would be recorded on the partnership's books at its $20,000 fair market value,[5] but the partnership takes over A's $12,000 adjusted basis for tax purposes,[6] creating an initial book/tax disparity of $8,000. A and B each have a $20,000 capital account upon formation of the partnership,[7] but A's initial outside basis for tax purposes is $12,000 while B's outside basis is $20,000.[8] When Gainacre is sold for $35,000 (and assuming the partnership otherwise breaks even), the bookkeeper must do double duty, separately computing a $15,000 book gain ($35,000 amount realized less $20,000 book value) and a $23,000 tax gain ($35,000 amount realized less $12,000 adjusted basis). Under the partnership agreement, the book gain is allocated $7,500 each to A and B, and their capital accounts are adjusted accordingly.[9] For tax purposes, the partners are allocated their respective shares of this book gain and, in addition, the traditional method allocates the $8,000 difference between the

---

**1.** Reg. § 1.704–3(b)(1). If the partnership disposes of Section 704(c) property in a nonrecognition transaction, such as a like-kind exchange, the new property is treated as Section 704(c) property with the same built-in gain or loss as the property disposed of by the partnership. Reg. § 1.704–3(a)(8).

**2.** The same rule would apply to any successor in interest to A (e.g., a donee). See I.R.C. § 704(c)(3), last sentence.

**3.** Cf. Reg. § 1.704–1(b)(5) Example (13)(i).

**4.** Reg. § 1.704–1(b)(1)(vi).

**5.** Reg.         § 1.704–1(b)(2)(iv)(b),–1(b)(2)(iv)(d)(1),–1(b)(5) Example (13)(i).

**6.** I.R.C. § 723.

**7.** Reg. § 1.704–1(b)(2)(iv)(b).

**8.** I.R.C. § 722.

**9.** The allocation of the book gain has substantial economic effect under Section 704(b). See Reg. § 1.704–1(b)(5) Example (13)(i).

book and tax gains to A, the contributing partner, to take into account the variation between the tax basis and the fair market value of Gainacre at the time of the contribution and to eliminate to the extent possible any book/tax disparity.[10] After recovering from this computational binge, the bookkeeper will be gratified to discover that the book and tax capital accounts of the partners are back in balance:

|  | **A** | | **B** | |
|  | **Tax** | **Book** | **Tax** | **Book** |
|---|---|---|---|---|
| On Formation | $12,000 | $20,000 | $20,000 | $20,000 |
| Gain on Sale | 15,500 | 7,500 | 7,500 | 7,500 |
| Balance | $27,500 | $27,500 | $27,500 | $27,500 |

*The Ceiling Rule.* Suppose that the partnership sells Gainacre for $15,000—an amount less than its $20,000 book value but more than its $12,000 adjusted tax basis. On the sale, the partnership has a tax gain of $3,000 but a book loss of $5,000. Under the partnership agreement, the partners share the book loss equally, but what about the tax gain? A sensible approach might be to allocate the $8,000 precontribution gain to A and then to allocate the $5,000 postcontribution loss equally to A and B so that A ends up with a $5,500 net taxable gain and B ends up with a $2,500 tax loss. Each partner's outside basis then would be reconciled with his share of inside basis, and any book/tax disparity would be eliminated.[11]

The traditional method, however, imposes a "ceiling rule," under which the total gain or loss allocated to the partners may not exceed the tax gain or loss realized by the partnership.[12] As a result, no tax loss can be allocated to B despite his economic loss of $2,500 because the partnership did not realize a loss for tax purposes. And although A has a precontribution gain of $8,000 and a postcontribution loss of $2,500, for a net gain of $5,500, the ceiling rule allows only $3,000 of tax gain to be allocated to A because that is all of the tax gain recognized by the partnership. This deprives B of his rightful share of the loss on Gainacre while it was held by the partnership and understates the gain accruing to A during the entire time he held Gainacre—the very shifting of income or loss that Section 704(c)(1)(A) was designed to prevent! As the following summary of the partners' book (capital) and tax accounts reveals, the ceiling rule perpetuates the partnership's book/tax disparities:[13]

**10.**  Reg. § 1.704–1(b)(4)(i).

**11.**  A's outside basis under this approach would be $17,500 ($12,000 on formation + $8,000 allocable gain − $2,500 allocable loss); B's outside basis also would be $17,500 ($20,000 on formation − $2,500 allocable loss). I.R.C. §§ 722; 705. The partners' outside bases would equal their respective shares of the inside bases of the partnership's assets (the $35,000 cash, representing B's $20,000 initial cash contribution plus the $15,000 proceeds on the sale of Gainacre).

The outside bases of the partners also would equal their $17,500 capital accounts after the sale ($20,000 minus $2,500 book loss).

**12.**  Reg. § 1.704–3(b)(1).

**13.**  This distortion is not necessarily permanent. Assume, for example, that the partnership liquidates after the sale, distributing $35,000 of cash equally to A and B. On the liquidation, A would recognize $2,500 gain and B would recognize $2,500 loss. I.R.C. § 731. As discussed earlier, however,

|  | A | | B | |
|---|---|---|---|---|
|  | **Tax** | **Book** | **Tax** | **Book** |
| On Formation | $12,000 | $20,000 | $20,000 | $20,000 |
| Tax Gain on Sale |  | 3,000 |  |  |
| Book Loss on Sale |  | (2,500) |  | (2,500) |
| Balance | $15,000 | $17,500 | $20,000 | $17,500 |

Apart from a nostalgic adherence to tradition, it is not clear why the Service continues to sanction an allocation method that incorporates the ceiling rule and its resulting distortions. The regulations authorize two additional methods, however, that use different approaches to cure (or remedy) the ceiling rule malady.

*Traditional Method With Curative Allocations.* The traditional method with curative allocations permits a partnership to make reasonable "curative allocations" of other partnership tax items of income, gain, loss or deduction to correct ceiling rule distortions.[14] A curative allocation is an allocation made solely for tax purposes that differs from the partnership's allocation of the corresponding book item. As such, a curative allocation has no economic effect and is not reflected in the partners' capital accounts.

A curative allocation is reasonable only if (1) it does not exceed the amount necessary to offset the effect of the ceiling rule[15] and (2) the income or loss allocated is of the same character and has the same tax consequences as the tax item affected by the ceiling rule.[16] Curative allocations may be made to correct ceiling rule distortions from a prior taxable year if they are made over a "reasonable period of time" (e.g., the economic life of the property) and were authorized by the partnership agreement in effect for the year that the property was contributed.[17]

Curative allocations are best explained by returning to the example, where the AB partnership sells Gainacre for $15,000, realizing a $5,000 book loss ($20,000 book value less $15,000 amount realized) and a $3,000 tax gain ($15,000 amount realized less $12,000 tax basis). As before, the book loss is allocated equally to A and B, and the tax gain is allocated entirely to A. Assume further that the partnership invested the $20,000 cash contributed by B in stock that it has held long-term and the partnership sells the stock for $30,000, realizing a book and tax gain of $10,000. The book gain is allocated $5,000 to each partner. In addition, since the gain on the sale of Gainacre and the stock are of the same character (long-term capital gain), the partnership may make a curative allocation of $2,500 of B's tax gain on the stock to A. Thus, instead of allocating to A $5,000 capital gain on the stock sale to match his book gain, A is allocated a $7,500 capital gain, and B is allocated only a $2,500 capital gain. The net

this adjustment still results in distortions of timing or character.

**14.** Reg. § 1.704–3(c)(1).

**15.** Reg. § 1.704–3(c)(3)(i). Cf. Reg. § 1.704–3(c)(4) Examples 1(ii) & (iii).

**16.** Reg. § 1.704–3(c)(3)(ii).

**17.** Reg. § 1.704–3(c)(3)(ii).

result cures the ceiling rule distortion that caused not enough gain to be allocated to A and not enough loss to be allocated to B on the sale of Gainacre. And all is well. After these allocations, the partners' tax and book (capital) accounts would be as follows:

|  | **A** | | **B** | |
|---|---|---|---|---|
|  | **Tax** | **Book** | **Tax** | **Book** |
| On Formation | $12,000 | $20,000 | $20,000 | $20,000 |
| Gainacre—Tax Gain | 3,000 | | | |
| Gainacre—Book Loss | | (2,500) | | (2,500) |
| Stock—Tax Gain | 7,500 | | 2,500 | |
| Stock—Book Gain | | 5,000 | | 5,000 |
| Balance | $22,500 | $22,500 | $22,500 | $22,500 |

*Remedial Method.* The traditional method with curative allocations cures ceiling rule distortions only if the partnership has enough recognized tax gain or loss of the appropriate type from another source. If the partnership had not sold the stock in the example, there would have been no tax gain to allocate to A, and the pernicious impact of the ceiling rule would linger. The remedial allocation method allows the partnership to restore its books to good health by creating the tax gain or loss of the appropriate type needed to offset ceiling rule distortions. Like their curative cousins, remedial allocations are solely tax allocations that have no effect on the partnership's book capital accounts.[18]

Under the remedial method, if the ceiling rule results in a book allocation to a noncontributing partner that differs from the partner's corresponding tax allocation, the partnership may make a remedial allocation to the noncontributing partner equal to the full amount of the disparity and a simultaneous offsetting remedial allocation to the contributing partner.[19] A remedial allocation must have the same effect on each partner's tax liability as the item limited by the ceiling rule—for example, if the tax item limited by the ceiling rule is a loss from the sale of a contributed capital asset, the offsetting remedial allocation to the contributing partner must be capital gain.[20]

Returning to the example, assume again that the partnership sells Gainacre for $15,000 and has no other taxable transactions during the year. If it adopts the remedial allocation method, it may create and then allocate $2,500 of capital gain to A, and make an offsetting remedial allocation of $2,500 of capital loss to B.[21] Note that this has the same effect as allocating to A the entire $8,000 precontribution gain on Gainacre less A's share ($2,500) of postcontribution loss (for a net gain of $5,500), and of allocating to B his rightful $2,500 share of postcontribution loss.

*Planning Aspects.* Although the remedial method assures that ceiling rule distortions are corrected regardless of other income or loss realized by

---

**18.**  Reg. § 1.704–3(d)(4)(ii).

**19.**  Reg. § 1.704–3(d)(1).

**20.**  Reg. § 1.704–3(d)(3).

**21.**  See Reg. § 1.704–3(d)(7) Example 2.

the partnership, the regulations do not make it mandatory. The partnership may adopt any reasonable method in making Section 704(c) allocations, including the traditional method with its potential for book/tax disparities. The regulations thus offer taxpayers some flexibility in dealing with contributed property. They even permit the partnership to use different methods for different properties. What method would A and B prefer in our continuing example? The answer may depend on the tax profiles of the partners outside the partnership. In the case where the partnership sells Gainacre for $15,000, the method of choice might be the traditional method and its ceiling rule (which understates A's gain and delays B's use of his $2,500 economic loss for tax purposes) if A were in a high tax bracket and B had no use for the deduction, perhaps because he had an expiring net operating loss from another source or was subject to the $3,000 limitation on capital losses. This assumes that use of the traditional method is reasonable on these facts. If it were not, the allocation would violate the anti-abuse rule of the regulations and cause the Service to intervene.[22] Alternatively, if B were in a high tax bracket relative to A, the partners might prefer to use the traditional method with curative allocations or the remedial method so that B could use the loss more rapidly.

### b.  CHARACTERIZATION OF GAIN OR LOSS ON DISPOSITION OF CONTRIBUTED PROPERTY

Code: §§ 724; 751(c), (d). Skim §§ 7701(a)(42)–(44).

We must take a brief detour from Section 704(c) to address the related issue of characterization of the gain or loss when a partnership disposes of contributed property. In addition to income shifting, taxpayers historically have sought to alter the tax character of gain or loss—converting ordinary income into capital gains and capital losses into ordinary losses. Partnerships were useful vehicles for this pastime because the character of income or loss from the disposition of partnership property was generally determined at the partnership level, without regard to the prior status of the property in the hands of the contributing partner. For example, a partner who was a dealer in land might transfer an appreciated parcel to a partnership with no prior real estate dealings and cause the partnership to sell the property at some later time. If the partnership aged the real estate sufficiently to withstand scrutiny under the step transaction doctrine or other judicially created barriers to tax avoidance, it might successfully contend that it realized a capital gain on the sale. Similarly, a taxpayer might attempt to convert a built-in capital loss on contributed property (e.g., securities) into an ordinary loss. We have seen how Section 704(c)(1)(A) prevents income *shifting* in this context by allocating any built-in gain or loss to the contributing partner. Section 724 seeks to prevent the *conversion* of gain or loss through contributions of property to a new or existing partnership.[1]

---

**22.** See, e.g., Reg. § 1.704–3(b)(2) Example 2.

**1.** Congress also has acted to prevent altering the character of gain or loss through

Section 724 applies to three categories of contributed property: unrealized receivables, inventory items and capital loss property. Different rules are provided for each category. "Unrealized receivables" are generally defined in Section 751(c) as rights (contractual or otherwise) to payment for goods or services that have not been previously included in income, provided in the case of goods that the sales proceeds would be treated as received from the sale or exchange of noncapital assets.[2] Because unrealized receivables essentially represent ripe transactions that will produce ordinary income or loss, Section 724(a) provides that any gain or loss recognized by the partnership on the disposition of unrealized receivables will be ordinary.[3]

The term "inventory items" is broadly defined in Section 751(d)(2) to include not only the familiar category of noncapital assets described in Section 1221(1) (i.e., inventory and other dealer property) but also any other property which, upon sale by the contributing partner, would not be considered as a capital or Section 1231 asset.[4] Inventory items retain their ordinary income taint under Section 724(b) for five years after their contribution to the partnership.[5] After that period, the character of contributed inventory items is determined at the partnership level.

"Capital loss property" includes any capital asset held by the contributing partner which had an adjusted basis in excess of its fair market value immediately before it was contributed to the partnership.[6] If the partnership sells capital loss property at a loss, Section 724(c) requires the built-in loss at the time of the contribution to retain its character as a capital loss for a period of five years from the date of the contribution. Any additional loss accruing while the property is held by the partnership is characterized at the partnership level.

A partnership might attempt to remove the taint inflicted by Section 724 by exchanging the contributed asset for other property in a nonrecognition transaction (e.g., a like-kind exchange). Section 724(d)(3) prevents this

---

distributions in kind by a partnership followed by a sale by the distributee partner. See I.R.C. § 735 and Chapter 7A2, infra.

**2.**  I.R.C. §§ 724(d)(1); 751(c). For certain other purposes, "unrealized receivables" also include certain assets to the extent that their disposition at fair market value would result in recapture of depreciation. But the Section 751(c) definition of unrealized receivables does not include recapture income for purposes of Section 724. See I.R.C. § 751(c), last paragraph, which applies only to Sections 731 and 741.

**3.**  It is not necessary for Section 724 to apply to recapture income because the lurking recapture gain on contributed property carries over to the partnership, which recognizes ordinary income to that extent on a subsequent disposition of the property. This

is accomplished through the definitions of "recomputed basis," (I.R.C. § 1245(a)(2)) and "depreciation adjustments" (I.R.C. § 1250(b)(3)).

**4.**  I.R.C. §§ 724(d)(2); 751(d). In determining whether an asset is Section 1231 property, the Section 1231(b) holding period requirement is disregarded. I.R.C. § 724(d)(2). The definitions of both unrealized receivables and inventory items are considered in more depth in connection with sales of partnership interests. See Chapter 6A, infra.

**5.**  For purposes of measuring the five-year time period, the holding period of the partner does not tack.

**6.**  I.R.C. § 724(c).

opportunity by making it clear that the Section 724 taint applies to any "substituted basis property"[7] resulting from such a transaction, whether held by the transferor-partnership or a transferee[8] unless that property is stock of a C corporation[9] acquired in an exchange governed by Section 351 (relating to certain transfers of property to 80 percent or more controlled corporations). In the case of substituted basis property, the five-year taint period commences as of the date that the original property was contributed to the partnership.[10]

## 3. DEPRECIATION OF CONTRIBUTED PROPERTY

Regulations: § 1.704–3(b)(1), (2) Examples 1(i) and 2; –3(c)(1)–(3), (4) Example 1; –3(d)(1)–(5), (7) Example 1.

Section 704(c)(1)(A) also applies to the allocation of depreciation, amortization, and depletion deductions with respect to contributed property. In the typical case where a partner contributes depreciable property with a tax basis that is less than the property's book value, a general goal of Section 704(c) is to ensure that the noncontributing partners are not deprived of their legitimate share of the partnership's tax depreciation. As with sales or exchanges, this policy (and students of partnership tax) can be frustrated by the ceiling rule.

*Traditional Method.* Under the traditional method, tax depreciation on contributed property is allocated first to the noncontributing partner in an amount equal to his share of book depreciation, and the balance of tax depreciation is allocated to the contributing partner.[1] Book and tax depreciation must be computed using the same depreciation method and recovery period.[2] To illustrate, assume that the AB partnership is formed by A contributing depreciable equipment with an adjusted basis of $12,000 and a fair market value of $20,000, and B contributing $20,000 cash. Assume that the equipment, which is 10–year property and depreciable under the straight line method, was purchased by A for $24,000 and has five years remaining on its recovery period.[3] The equipment is recorded on the books of the partnership at its $20,000 fair market value, and each partner has a

---

**7.** See I.R.C. § 7701(a)(42)–(44).

**8.** See Staff of the Joint Committee on Taxation, General Explanation of the Tax Reform Act of 1984 (hereinafter "1984 Act General Explanation"), 98th Cong., 2d Sess. 235 (1984).

**9.** A "C corporation" is any corporation which is not an "S corporation." See I.R.C. § 1361(a)(2) and Chapter 11, infra.

**10.** 1984 Act General Explanation, supra note 8, at 235.

**1.** Reg. § 1.704–3(b)(1) and–3(b)(2) Example 1(ii).

**2.** The Section 704(b) regulations require that book depreciation be an amount which bears the same relationship to the book value of the property as the tax depreciation bears to the adjusted basis of the property. This relationship can be maintained only if the book and tax depreciation are computed in similar fashion. Reg. § 1.704–1(b)(2)(iv)(*g*)(*3*). If the property has a zero adjusted basis, book depreciation may be determined under any reasonable method. Id.

**3.** The depreciation methods, which ignore the half-year convention prescribed by Section 168, are being made for convenience of illustration.

$20,000 capital account,[4] but the partnership takes over A's $12,000 adjusted tax basis and remaining five-year recovery period.[5]

The partnership is entitled to $4,000 of book depreciation each year, allocated $2,000 each to A and B. Tax depreciation is $2,400 per year, of which $2,000 is allocated to B (the amount equal to his book depreciation) and the balance of $400 is allocated to A. Note that the tax depreciation is allocated so as to reduce to the extent possible the disparity between the partners' book and tax accounts. If the equipment is held for its entire remaining recovery period, the $8,000 built-in gain at the time of the contribution results in an $8,000 reduction of depreciation deductions for A. At the end of the recovery period, the tax and capital accounts are brought into balance:

|  | A | | B | |
|---|---|---|---|---|
|  | **Tax** | **Book** | **Tax** | **Book** |
| On Formation | $12,000 | $20,000 | $20,000 | $20,000 |
| Depreciation | (2,000) | (10,000) | (10,000) | (10,000) |
| Balance | $10,000 | $10,000 | $10,000 | $10,000 |

Allocation of depreciation under Section 704(c)(1)(A) using the traditional method also can be affected by the ceiling rule. Assume that A contributes $20,000 of equipment with an adjusted basis of $8,000 and 5–year remaining recovery period, and B contributes $20,000 cash to the AB partnership. Because B's share of book depreciation is still $2,000, B should be allocated $2,000 of tax depreciation, but the ceiling rule limits the partnership's tax depreciation to $1,600 per year, all of which is allocated to B.[6] At the end of the first year, the book value of the equipment is $16,000 ($20,000 less the $4,000 book depreciation), its adjusted tax basis is $6,400 ($8,000 less the $1,600 tax depreciation), and A's built-in gain decreases from $12,000 to $9,600 ($16,000 book value less $6,400 tax basis).

If the partnership sells the equipment at the beginning of AB's second year for $16,000, the partnership realizes tax gain of $9,600 ($16,000 amount realized less $6,400 adjusted basis), but no book gain. Under the traditional method, the entire tax gain is allocated to A because the contributed equipment has that much built-in gain remaining. If the tax gain had exceeded the remaining built-in gain, the excess would be allocated equally to A and B under the partnership agreement. If the tax gain had been less than the remaining built-in gain (e.g., on sale for $14,000, yielding tax gain of only $7,600), the ceiling rule again would intervene by limiting the gain allocable to A to the partnership's tax gain.[7]

*Traditional Method With Curative Allocations.* In the example where A contributes equipment with an adjusted basis of $8,000, a fair market value of $20,000, and a 5–year remaining straight-line recovery period, the ceiling rule limited B's tax depreciation to $1,600 per year even though his book

---

**4.**  Reg. § 1.704–1(b)(2)(iv)(*b*)(2) & (*d*).

**5.**  See I.R.C. § 168(i)(7); Prop.Reg. § 1.168–5(b).

**6.**  Reg. § 1.704–3(b)(3) Example 1(ii).

**7.**  Reg. § 1.704–3(b)(2) Example 1(iii).

depreciation was $2,000. If the partnership elects the traditional method with curative allocations, it may make a curative allocation to B of up to $400 per year of tax depreciation from another partnership asset or allocate an extra $400 of ordinary income to A (and away from B) to correct the distortion.[8]

*The Remedial Method.* Under the remedial method, ceiling rule distortions from depreciation of contributed property are corrected by a tax allocation of additional depreciation to the noncontributing partner in an amount equal to the full amount of the limitation caused by the ceiling rule and a simultaneous offsetting allocation of ordinary income to the contributing partner.[9] The timing of the remedial allocations is the tricky part. For this purpose, the calculation of book depreciation differs from the method authorized by the Section 704(b) regulations and used for purposes of the traditional methods.[10] Under the remedial method, the portion of the partnership's book basis in contributed property that equals the tax basis of the property at the time of contribution is depreciated under the same method used for tax depreciation—generally over the property's remaining recovery period at the time of contribution. The amount by which the book basis exceeds the tax basis ("the excess book basis") is depreciated using any applicable recovery period and depreciation method available to the partnership for newly acquired property.[11]

Return one last time to the example where A contributes depreciable equipment with an adjusted basis of $8,000, a fair market value of $20,000, and five years remaining on its 10–year recovery period, and B contributes $20,000 cash. The partnership's tax depreciation is still $1,600 per year. Under the remedial method,[12] the partnership's book depreciation for the next five years consists of two components: $1,600 ($8,000 tax basis divided by remaining 5 years in recovery period) plus $1,200 ($12,000 excess of book value over tax basis divided by a new 10–year recovery period), or a total of $2,800 per year. Under the partnership agreement, A and B are each allocated $1,400 of the book depreciation, B is allocated $1,400 of tax depreciation, and A is allocated the remaining $200 of tax depreciation. No remedial allocations are made because the ceiling rule has not yet caused a book allocation of depreciation to the noncontributing partner that differs from the tax allocation. For years 6 through 10, however, the partnership has $1,200 of annual book depreciation ($12,000 excess book basis divided

---

**8.** See Reg. § 1.704–3(c) especially–3(c)(4) Example 1(i) and (ii). Compare Reg. § 1.704–3(c)(4) Example 1(iii) involving an unreasonable curative allocation. The partners' shares of depreciation with respect to contributed property must be adjusted to account for any curative allocations. See Prop. Reg. § 1.1245–1(e)(2)(iii)(B). The adjustments are important for allocations of Section 1245 recapture gain. See Section B2 of this chapter, supra.

**9.** Reg. § 1.704–3(d)(1). Once again, the partners' shares of depreciation with respect to contributed property must be adjusted to account for any remedial allocations. See Prop. Reg. § 1.1245–1(e)(2)(iii)(C).

**10.** See, e.g., Reg. § 1.704–1(b)(2)(iv)(*g*)(*3*) for the generally applicable rules for determining book depreciation.

**11.** Reg. § 1.704–3(d)(2).

**12.** See Reg. § 1.704–3(d)(7) Example 1.

by new 10–year recovery period), allocated $600 each to A and B, but it has no more tax depreciation. Since B is allocated $600 of book depreciation but not tax depreciation, the partnership must make a remedial allocation of $600 of tax depreciation to B and an offsetting allocation of $600 of ordinary income to A for each of years 6 through 10. At the end of year 10, the partnership's tax and book accounts are as follows:

|  | **A** | | **B** | |
|---|---|---|---|---|
|  | **Tax** | **Book** | **Tax** | **Book** |
| On Formation | $ 8,000 | $20,000 | $20,000 | $20,000 |
| Depreciation (Yrs. 1–5) | (1,000) | (7,000) | (7,000) | (7,000) |
| Depreciation (Yrs. 6–10) |  | (3,000) |  | (3,000) |
| Remedial Allocations | 3,000 |  | (3,000) |  |
| Balance | $10,000 | $10,000 | $10,000 | $10,000 |

## 4. OTHER APPLICATIONS OF SECTION 704(c) PRINCIPLES

Regulations: § 1.704–1(b)(4)(i), –1(b)(5) Examples (14)(i)–(iv).

A problem analogous to allocations with respect to contributed property may arise when a new partner is admitted to an existing partnership. The Section 704(b) regulations require application of "Section 704(c) principles" in those situations.[1]

For example, assume partners X and Y each contribute $10,000 cash to the XY partnership, which purchases $20,000 of securities with the contributed funds. Assume further that the XY partnership agreement requires proper maintenance of capital accounts, liquidation according to positive capital account balances and restoration of deficit capital account balances upon liquidation. Finally, assume that after the securities have appreciated in value to $30,000, new partner Z makes a $15,000 cash contribution in exchange for a one-third interest in the partnership. Section 704(c) does not directly apply here because there is no contribution of property to the partnership. But the Section 704(b) regulations require application of similar principles so that the $10,000 of gain attributable to the appreciation in the securities prior to Z's entering the firm will be taxed equally to partners X and Y.[2] Allocation of the built-in gain in this manner may be accomplished by a revaluation of the securities at the time of Z's admission to the partnership along with a corresponding upward adjustment to X and Y's capital accounts.[3] If such a revaluation is made, the rules of the

**1.** Reg. §§ 1.704–1(b)(4)(i),–1(b)(5) Examples (14)(i)–(iv) & (18)(ii)–(xiii).

**2.** See Reg. § 1.704–1(b)(5) Example (14)(i). For a similar but far more complex example involving depreciation, see Reg. § 1.704–1(b)(5) Example (18).

**3.** Reg. §§ 1.704–1(b)(2)(iv)(*f*); 1.704–1(b)(4)(i). The regulations permit a revalua-tion of partnership property in connection with: (1) contributions of money or property, (2) the liquidation of the partnership or a distribution of money or property to a partner, and (3) the grant of a partnership interest in exchange for services for the benefit of the partnership. Reg. § 1.704–1(b)(2)(iv)*(f)(5)*.

regulations applicable to Section 704(c) property once again come into play[4] allowing the partnership to use any reasonable method of allocation.[5]

To illustrate, assuming the partnership uses the traditional method[6] and has no other assets, the securities would be restated at their $30,000 current value when Z joins the partnership, and each partner's capital account will be recorded at $15,000 to reflect their equal one-third interests. The "book" gain on any subsequent sale of the securities will be shared equally among the partners, and any difference between the book gain or loss and the tax gain or loss will be allocated only to X and Y. Thus, if the securities are later sold for $36,000, the $6,000 book gain is allocated $2,000 to each of the three partners for both book and tax purposes, and the remaining $10,000 of tax gain is equally divided between X and Y.[7]

The same result can be accomplished without a revaluation by a special allocation of the precontribution gain to X and Y under Section 704(b). Thus, if the securities are sold for $36,000, resulting in both a tax and book gain of $16,000, an allocation of the first $10,000 of gain to X and Y will have substantial economic effect.[8] But what if the partnership's assets are not revalued and the agreement lacks a special allocation of the built-in gain at the time of Z's admission, so that the $16,000 tax and book gain is allocated equally among the three partners? In that case, Z's capital account (and thus his entitlement in the event of a liquidation) is increased by $5,333 even though his share of appreciation is only $2,000, effectively shifting a portion of the tax gain and economic benefit of the prior appreciation from X and Y to Z. In this situation, the regulations warn that other tax consequences may arise from this capital shift, depending on its origins—e.g., the amount shifted may be treated as compensation or a gift to Z.[9]

## 5.   DISTRIBUTIONS OF CONTRIBUTED PROPERTY

Code: § 704(c)(1)(B). Skim § 737.

**4.** Reg. § 1.704–3.

**5.** Reg. § 1.704–3(a)(6). Partnerships are generally not required to use the same allocation method for reverse Section 704(c) allocations as for Section 704(c) property or to use the same allocation method each time the partnership revalues its property. Id. However, each method used must be reasonable. Id. See Rev. Rul. 2004–49, 2004–1 C.B. 939 (discussing allocation of amortization with respect to a Section 197 intangible following a revaluation of an asset upon entry of a new partner).

**6.** Reg. § 1.704–3(b).

**7.** Reg. § 1.704–1(b)(5) Example (14)(i)–(ii). If the securities dropped in value after Z's admission to the partnership and are sold at less than book value but more than their tax basis, the book loss is allocated equally among the partners but the tax gain is shared by X and Y. This is another example of the ceiling rule, which results in Z bearing an economic loss without a corresponding tax loss, understates X and Y's tax gain and fails to cure disparities between the partners' tax and book accounts. See Reg. § 1.704–1(b)(5) Example (14)(iii). Cf. Reg. § 1.704–1(b)(5) Example (18)(vi).

**8.** Reg. § 1.704–1(b)(5) Example (14)(iv).

**9.** Reg. § 1.704–1(b)(5) Example (14)(iv). See Reg. § 1.704–1(b)(1)(iv).

As originally enacted, Section 704(c) was limited to partnership sales of contributed property. As a result, a contributing partner could avoid an allocation of built-in gain or loss if the partnership distributed the contributed property to another partner rather than selling it. Since a partnership generally does not recognize gain or loss on a distribution of property,[1] the contributing partner was not taxed on the distribution, and any built-in gain was shifted to the distributee partner through a transferred basis mechanism.[2] Similarly, because a distribution of property can generally be made tax free to a contributing partner, a contributing partner also could postpone an allocation of built-in gain or loss but end up with substitute property if the partnership distributed property other than the contributed property to the contributing partner. Both of these strategies—commonly referred to as mixing bowl transactions—are now precluded by Section 704(c)(1)(B) and Section 737, respectively, if the transactions occur within seven years of the contribution of the property. Since mixing bowl transactions are interrelated with the operating distribution rules, in-depth consideration of those sections is deferred until Chapter 7.[3]

## 6. Anti-Abuse Rules for Loss Property

Code: § 704(c)(1)(C).

If a partner contributes property with a built-in loss to a partnership, that transaction may set the stage for shifting the loss to another partner or result in the partners benefiting more than once from the loss. Even though Section 704(c)(1)(A) requires precontribution loss to be allocated to the contributing partner, a weakness in that provision is that it has no effect if the contributing partner leaves the partnership. In fact, the regulations provide that if a partner transfers a partnership interest, built-in gain or loss must be allocated to the transferee partner as it would have been allocated to the transferor partner.[1] Thus, while Section 704(c)(1)(A) prevents the shift of a precontribution loss to the other partners, the current regulations *require* that a precontribution loss be shifted to a transferee of the contributing partner. Moreover, once you have mastered the intricacies of the Code provisions dealing with transfers of a partnership interest and partnership distributions,[2] you will discover that it was possible for a partner who contributed a built-in loss to a partnership in effect, to recognize the loss and also permit the remaining partners to employ the contributed property to defer their tax liability.[3]

Eventually, Congress decided to attack these tax avoidance strategies. Section 704(c)(1)(C) provides that if contributed property has a built-in loss

---

**1.** I.R.C. § 731. See Chapters 7B & 7C, infra.

**2.** I.R.C. § 732. See Chapter 7B, infra.

**3.** See Chapter 7D, infra.

**1.** Reg. § 1.704–3(a)(7).

**2.** See Chapters 6, 7, 8, and 9, *infra*.

**3.** The basic strategy involved a transfer of a partnership interest or distribution where the partnership did not make a Section 754 election to reduce the inside basis of the partnership's property under Section 734 or Section 743. See generally, Chapters 6B and 7C, infra.

(i.e., an excess of adjusted basis over fair market value at the time of the contribution) then (1) the built-in loss is to be taken into account only in determining the amount of items allocated to the contributing partner, and (2) in determining the amount of items allocated to other partners, the partnership's basis in the contributed property shall be treated as being the fair market value of the property at the time of contribution.[4] This rule will prevent partners (even a transferee partner) from benefiting from a built-in loss in property contributed by another partner.[5]

## PROBLEMS

**1**. A, B and C form an equal partnership. A contributes accounts receivable for services rendered (A.B.—$0, F.M.V.—$10,000); B, a real estate dealer, contributes lots held primarily for sale (A.B.—$5,000, F.M.V.—$10,000); and C, an investor, contributes land (A.B.—$20,000, F.M.V.—$10,000). Unless otherwise stated, the partnership is not a dealer in receivables or land, all contributed assets have been held long-term by the partners prior to contribution, and the traditional method of allocation is applied with respect to all contributed property. What tax results in the following alternative transactions:

(a) The partnership sells the receivables contributed by A for $10,000?

(b) The partnership sells the lots contributed by B for $10,600?

(c) The partnership sells the lots contributed by B for $9,100?

(d) Same as (c), above, except the partnership elects to use the remedial method of allocation.

(e) The partnership is a real estate dealer and sells the land contributed by C for $17,000?

(f) Same as (e), above, except the sale is for $7,000?

(g) Would the result in any of the above transactions change if all sales had occurred six years after the property was contributed?

**2**. A contributes $100,000 cash to the AB partnership and B contributes a building with an adjusted basis of $50,000 and a fair market value of $100,000. Unless otherwise stated, apply the traditional method with respect to all contributed property.

(a) If the building is depreciable, has a ten-year remaining recovery period and is depreciated under the straight-line method, how much tax and book depreciation will be allocated to each partner?

(b) Same as (a), above, except that B's basis in the building is $60,000?

---

**4.** The regulations may provide exceptions to this rule. The legislative history indicates that an exception should be created for a corporation succeeding to the tax attributes of a corporate partner under Section 381. H. Rep. No. 108–548, 108th Cong., 2d Sess. 283 note 312 (2004).

**5.** Sections 734 and 743 were also modified to require a reduction in the inside basis of partnership property in certain situations. See I.R.C. §§ 734(a) & (d), 743(a) & (d). These changes address situations that may not involve contributed property.

(c) Same as (a), above, except that B's basis in the building is $40,000?

(d) Same as (a), above, except that B's basis in the building is $120,000?

(e) If in (a), above, the building is sold for $90,000 after it has been held (and depreciated) by the partnership for two years, how must the partnership allocate the tax gain on the sale?

(f) Same as (e), above, except the building is sold for $60,000?

(g) What result in (c), above, if the recovery period for the building is 20 years and the partnership elects the remedial method of allocation?

**3**. A and B, both dealers in real estate, find a parcel of land to purchase for $100,000 as an investment. They believe it can be sold in two years for $200,000. They either will buy the land as tenants-in-common for $100,000 and jointly contribute it to a partnership or contribute $50,000 each to an equal partnership, which then will buy the land.

(a) How should they structure the transaction?

(b) Assume the AB partnership purchased the land for $100,000 in year one and it appreciated in value to $200,000 by the beginning of year three. At that point, C joins the partnership as an equal partner by contributing $100,000 cash to be used by the partnership to improve the land and sell it. The partners believe they can sell the land for $450,000. What results for tax and book purposes if the partnership sells the improved parcel of land for $450,000 and allocates the gain to reflect the appreciation at the time of C's entry into the partnership?

(c) What results to the partners under the facts of (b), above, if they elect to use a reverse § 704(c) allocation under Reg. § 1.704–1(b)(2)(iv)(*f*)(5) and they apply the traditional method of allocation.

(d) What results on a sale of land for $450,000 if the capital accounts of the partners are not adjusted when C joins the partnership and the agreement does not include any special allocation to reflect the built-in gain at the time C became a partner?

## D.  ALLOCATION OF PARTNERSHIP LIABILITIES

Code: §§ 704(c)(1)(A); 752(a)–(c).

Regulations: § 1.752–1; –2(a), (b), (c)(1), (f) Examples (1)–(5), (g)(1), (h), (j)(1); –3; –4(a), (b)(1), (c), (d).

## 1.  INTRODUCTION

*Background.* We have seen that Section 704(d) limits the deductibility of a partner's share of partnership losses to the partner's outside basis in

her partnership interest.[1] A partner's outside basis also measures the extent to which a cash distribution results in the recognition of gain or loss[2], as well as a partner's gain or loss on the sale of her partnership interest.[3] We also know that each partner's outside basis depends, in part, on her share of partnership liabilities.[4] It now is appropriate to explore in greater detail the rules that govern the allocation of partnership liabilities among the partners.

Since the Code itself provides no guidance, the allocation question historically has been answered in regulations and rulings issued by the Treasury. Under the regulations, recourse liabilities generally are allocated in proportion to the partners' respective shares of partnership losses[5] on the theory that loss-sharing ratios are the best indication of which partners would be responsible for paying the liabilities if the partnership is unable to do so. Nonrecourse liabilities generally are allocated by reference to the partners' respective shares of partnership profits on the assumption that those debts will be paid, if at all, from profits or assets of the partnership.[6] These rules become more complex in the case of limited partners, who by definition are not liable for partnership losses beyond their original capital contribution and any additional contributions that they are required to make under the partnership agreement. Thus, while both general and limited partners share in partnership nonrecourse liabilities, limited partners generally are not allocated partnership recourse liabilities beyond the amounts they are obligated to contribute to the partnership or pay to the creditor in the future.[7]

A laudable feature of the Section 752 regulations is their relationship to the rules governing allocations of income and losses under Section 704(b) and the rule in Section 704(d) limiting a partner from deducting losses in excess of her outside basis. The regulations allocate recourse liabilities by using the same kind of economic risk of loss analysis that is employed in testing partnership allocations under Section 704(b);[8] and in generally allocating nonrecourse liabilities by reference to the partners' profit-sharing ratios, they take into account partnership minimum gain and Section 704(c) minimum gain.[9] Coordinating these rules makes sense because a principal reason for including liabilities in a partner's outside basis is to support the deductions claimed by the partner for items attributable to those liabilities. This natural synergy will become evident soon enough. For now, it is sufficient to observe that familiarity with the Section 704(b) regulations and the treatment of contributed property under Section 704(c)(1)(A) is essential to understanding the liability allocation rules. That is why detailed coverage of Section 752 has been deferred until this point.

---

**1.** See Chapter 3C1, supra.

**2.** See I.R.C. § 731; Chapters 7B1 & 8B1, infra.

**3.** See I.R.C. § 741; Chapter 6A, infra.

**4.** See I.R.C. § 752; Chapter 2B, supra.

**5.** Reg. § 1.752–2(a); Reg. § 1.752–1(e).

**6.** Reg. § 1.752–3(a)(3); Reg. § 1.752–1(e).

**7.** Reg. § 1.752–2(a), (b).

**8.** Reg. § 1.752–2(b).

**9.** Reg. § 1.752–3(a).

*Liability Defined.* For purposes of Section 752, all legally enforceable partnership obligations are "liabilities" except accounts payable of a cash basis partnership, which are not deductible until paid,[10] and certain contingent or contested liabilities or obligations that are devoid of economic reality.[11]

## 2. RECOURSE LIABILITIES

*Economic Risk of Loss Concept.* A partnership liability is a recourse liability only to the extent that a partner or any person related to a partner[1] bears the economic risk of loss with respect to that debt.[2] To the extent that no partner or related person bears the economic risk of loss, the liability is treated as nonrecourse.[3] Thus, the economic risk of loss concept is critical in classifying a liability as recourse or nonrecourse. In the case of recourse liabilities, the extent to which a partner bears the economic risk of loss also must be determined in order to allocate the debt.[4] In general, a partner bears the economic risk of loss for a partnership liability to the extent that he ultimately would be obligated to pay the debt if all partnership assets were worthless and all partnership liabilities were due and payable.[5] In determining the risk of loss, the regulations take into account not only each partner's obligations under the partnership agreement to pay the creditor or to contribute funds to the partnership, but also all other economic arrangements or legal obligations (such as guarantees, indemnification agreements, etc.) between partners and between any partners and the partnership's creditors.[6] As a result, funds borrowed on a nonrecourse basis but personally guaranteed by a partner who has no right of reimbursement from another partner, subject the guaranteeing partner to an economic risk of loss and are recourse liabilities under the regulations.[7] Similarly, nonrecourse liabilities for which a partner or related person has pledged his own property as security subject that partner to an economic

---

**10.** See Rev.Rul. 88–77, 1988–2 C.B. 128. This is consistent with the treatment of cash basis payables in other contexts, such as corporate formations (see, e.g., I.R.C. § 357(c)(3)) and cancellation of indebtedness (see, e.g., I.R.C. § 108(e)).

**11.** See, e.g., Reg. § 1.752–2(b)(4) and Estate of Franklin v. Commissioner, 64 T.C. 752 (1975), affirmed, 544 F.2d 1045 (9th Cir. 1976).

**1.** Under the regulations, related persons are defined by reference to the relationships specified in Sections 267(b) and 707(b)(1), with some modifications. Reg. § 1.752–4(b)(1). It should be assumed that all references to a "partner" in the textual discussion of the economic risk of loss concept also encompass persons related to the partner.

**2.** Reg. § 1.752–1(a)(1).

**3.** Reg. § 1.752–1(a)(2).

**4.** Reg. § 1.752–2(b)–(j).

**5.** Reg. § 1.752–2(b)(1).

**6.** Reg. § 1.752–2(b)(3), (5).

**7.** Reg. § 1.752–2(b)(3)(i). Cf. Reg. § 1.752–2(f) Example 3. In addition, if one or more partners guarantee the payment of more than 25 percent of the total interest that accrues on an otherwise nonrecourse liability of the partnership, the loan is treated as recourse to the guaranteeing partners to the extent of the present value of the guaranteed future interest payments. Reg. §§ 1.752–2(e)(1); 1.752–2(f) Example 7. Under a safe harbor, this rule does not apply to a guarantee of interest for a period that does not exceed the lesser of five years or one-third of the term of the loan. Reg. § 1.752–2(e)(3).

risk of loss and are recourse liabilities to the extent of the value of the security.[8] Finally, nonrecourse loans from a partner to the partnership are treated as recourse liabilities because they expose the lending partner to an economic risk of loss.[9]

*Constructive Liquidation.* At the heart of the economic risk of loss analysis is the concept of a constructive liquidation of the partnership. Adopting a worst case scenario, the regulations assume that all of the partnership's liabilities become due and payable in full, any separate property pledged (directly or indirectly) by a partner to secure a partnership liability is transferred to the creditor in full or partial satisfaction of that liability,[10] and all the rest of the partnership's assets (including cash) become worthless.[11] The partnership is deemed to dispose of all of its now worthless assets in a taxable transaction for no consideration (other than the relief of any nonrecourse debt to which any asset is subject).[12] The gains and losses on these deemed dispositions, along with any actual income or loss items as of the date of the constructive liquidation, are then allocated among the partners in accordance with the partnership agreement; the partnership books and capital accounts are adjusted accordingly; and the partnership is deemed to liquidate.[13]

This doomsday scenario employed by the regulations assumes that a partner bears the economic risk of loss for the net amount that he must pay directly to creditors or contribute to the partnership at the time of the deemed liquidation. In determining a partner's payment obligation, the regulations take into account all the facts and circumstances, including contractual obligations outside the partnership agreement (such as guarantees, indemnities and reimbursement agreements running directly to creditors or to other partners, or to the partnership),[14] obligations imposed by the partnership agreement (such as obligations to make capital contributions and to restore a deficit capital account upon liquidation of the partnership),[15] obligations imposed by state law,[16] and the value of any property pledged (directly or indirectly) by the partner to secure any partnership liability.[17] The amount of a partner's gross payment obligation

---

**8.**  Reg. § 1.752–2(h)(1).

**9.**  Reg. § 1.752–2(c)(1). Under a de minimis rule, a partner who makes a nonrecourse loan to a partnership does not bear the economic risk of loss with respect to the loan if the partner owns a ten percent or less interest in each item of partnership income, gain, loss, deduction or credit, and the loan constitutes "qualified nonrecourse financing" as defined for purposes of the at-risk limitations. Reg. § 1.752–2(d)(1). See I.R.C. § 465(b)(6) and Section 3C2 of this chapter, supra.

**10.**  Reg. § 1.752–2(h). Property is considered to be pledged indirectly the extent of the value of any property that the partner contributes to the partnership solely for the

purpose of securing a partnership liability. Reg. § 1.752–2(h)(2).

**11.**  Reg. § 1.752–2(b)(1)(i)–(ii).

**12.**  Reg. § 1.752–2(b)(1)(iii). The exception for assets that secure nonrecourse liabilities is consistent with Commissioner v. Tufts, 461 U.S. 300, 103 S.Ct. 1826 (1983), rehearing denied, 463 U.S. 1215, 103 S.Ct. 3555 (1983).

**13.**  Reg. § 1.752–2(b)(1)(iv), (v).

**14.**  Reg. § 1.752–2(b)(3)(i).

**15.**  Reg. § 1.752–2(b)(3)(ii).

**16.**  Reg. § 1.752–2(b)(3)(iii).

**17.**  The value of property pledged by a partner is deemed to be the value of the

is reduced to the extent of any right to reimbursement, leaving the partner's *net* payment obligation as the ultimate measure of his potential economic risk of loss.[18] The regulations in essence seek to determine where the buck stops with respect to the responsibility for any recourse liability.

The regulations assume that recourse liabilities actually will be paid by the partners to the extent that they are personally obligated to do so even if the partner's net worth is less than the amount of the obligation, unless the facts and circumstances indicate a plan to circumvent or avoid the obligation.[19] In determining both the partner's payment obligations and rights to reimbursement, obligations that are subject to contingencies that make it unlikely that the obligation will ever be discharged are disregarded.[20] If an obligation need not be satisfied within a reasonable period of time, only its discounted present value is taken into account.[21]

*Examples.* The regulations elaborate on all these principles with several examples and, for the same reason, some examples are appropriate here. Assume that A and B are equal partners in the AB general partnership, which has an agreement that satisfies the primary test for economic effect ("The Big Three") in the Section 704(b) regulations.[22] Each partner contributes $20,000 cash, and the partnership purchases a building for $50,000, consisting of a $40,000 cash down payment and a $10,000 recourse note to the seller. In order to determine how the $10,000 liability is allocated between A and B, we must assume that the building becomes worthless and is sold for no consideration in a taxable transaction, the $10,000 debt is immediately due in full, and the partnership books are adjusted accordingly. On the sale of the worthless building, the partnership recognizes a $50,000 loss, which is allocated equally between A and B, reducing each partner's capital account by $25,000, to negative $5,000. The resulting balance sheet reveals that each partner must contribute $5,000 to the partnership to bring their respective capital accounts back to zero, and it is assumed that the partnership will use these contributions to pay off the debt. Based on these deficit restoration obligations, each partner bears a $5,000 payment obligation and thus a $5,000 economic risk of loss with respect to the liability.[23] If the partnership agreement had failed to satisfy The Big Three in these circumstances but A and B were equal general partners, each partner still would be allocated $5,000 of the liability, but their payment obligation would arise by operation of state law.[24]

The example provides a rather circuitous route to the general rule that where partners share partnership losses according to a fixed ratio (50:50 in

---

property at the time of the pledge. Reg. § 1.752–2(h)(3).

**18.**   Reg. § 1.752–2(b)(5).

**19.**   Reg. § 1.752–2(b)(6); see Reg. § 1.752–2(j).

**20.**   Reg. §§ 1.752–2(b)(4),–2(f) Example 8.

**21.**   Reg. § 1.752–2(g). There is no discount if interest that equals or exceeds the

Section 1274(d) "applicable federal rate" must be paid on the obligation. Reg. § 1.752–2(g)(2).

**22.**   See Reg. § 1.704–1(b)(2)(ii)(*b*) and Section B2 of this chapter, supra.

**23.**   Cf. Reg. § 1.752–2(f) Examples 1 and 2.

**24.**   Reg. § 1.752–2(b)(3)(iii).

the example) and their initial capital accounts reflect that same ratio, recourse debt will be allocated accordingly. But what if the loss sharing ratios do not match the ratios of the initial capital accounts? To illustrate, assume that the facts are the same as above except that losses are allocated 60 percent to A and 40 percent to B. In this situation the $50,000 loss on the deemed disposition is allocated $30,000 to A and $20,000 to B, causing A's capital account to be negative $10,000 and B's capital account to be zero. Because A would be required to contribute $10,000 to the partnership to bring his capital account to zero, A bears the economic risk of loss with respect to the liability.[25]

Now assume the same equal profit and loss sharing ratios as in the first example except that A's initial contribution and capital account was $30,000 and B's was $10,000. The constructive liquidation mandated by the regulations would generate the same $50,000 loss, allocated equally between A and B, and the allocation would reduce A's capital account to $5,000 and B's to negative $15,000. As a result, B would be required to make a contribution to the partnership of $15,000 in order to bring his capital account back to zero. Since two-thirds of this contribution would be used to pay the $10,000 partnership debt and one-third would be used to pay A his positive capital account balance on liquidation, B's payment obligation is $10,000. A has no payment obligation because his capital account is positive. Accordingly, the $10,000 liability is allocated entirely to B.[26]

The synergy between the Section 752 regulations and Section 704 should now be apparent. Although A and B divided losses equally, B began with a lower capital account and outside basis. Because B was ultimately responsible for paying the liability, the regulations consider him to be entitled to the extra basis provided by the partnership debt, which in turn supports his share of deductions under Section 704(d).

The analysis changes where at least one of the partners is a limited partner. Assume that A and B each contribute $20,000 to their equal partnership; that B is a limited partner who has no obligation to restore a capital account deficit; and the partnership agreement complies with the alternate test for economic effect.[27] As in the earlier example, the partnership purchases a $50,000 building, paying $40,000 cash and financing the $10,000 balance with a recourse note. Although losses are generally allocated equally between the two partners, only $20,000 of losses (the extent of B's initial capital account) can be allocated to B because more losses would

---

**25.** Cf. Reg. § 1.752–2(f) Examples 1 and 2. If the partnership agreement did not include The Big Three, the allocation of the liability would depend on where the ultimate economic responsibility for the debt lies under state law. The result would be the same as described in the text if, taking the partnership agreement and applicable state law into account, A would be required to contribute $10,000 to the partnership upon liquidation. But if state law required A and B each to contribute $5,000 on the deemed liquidation, the liability would be allocated $5,000 to each partner.

**26.** Cf. Reg. § 1.752–2(f) Example 1.

**27.** See Reg. § 1.704–1(b)(2)(ii).

result in an impermissible capital account deficit.[28] If the building were sold for nothing, generating a loss of $50,000, only $20,000 of that loss could be allocated to B and the remaining $30,000 loss would be allocated to A (the general partner with a deficit restoration obligation), bringing A's capital account to negative $10,000 and requiring A to make a contribution of $10,000 to the partnership on the constructive liquidation. This $10,000 would be used to pay the partnership liability. As a result, the $10,000 liability is allocated entirely to A, who bears the economic risk of loss.[29]

The preceding example illustrates the broader general rule that recourse debt is ordinarily allocated only among the general partners and not to any limited partners. The analysis changes to the extent that a limited partner contributes a promissory note to the partnership, pledges property as security, or is otherwise obligated to contribute additional unreimbursed amounts or make unreimbursed payments directly to the creditor. Assume, for example, that limited partner B contributes a $4,000 promissory note to the partnership.[30] The note does not increase B's capital account.[31] But since it represents an obligation to contribute an additional $4,000 to the partnership, B may be allocated losses that create a capital account deficit of up to $4,000.[32] On the constructive liquidation, $24,000 of the partnership's $50,000 loss can be allocated to B under Section 704(b), bringing B's capital account to negative $4,000, and B is obligated to contribute $4,000 to the partnership to pay off his note.[33] The remaining $26,000 of the partnership's loss on the deemed sale of the building must be allocated to A, giving A a capital account deficit and a payment obligation of $6,000. As a result, the $10,000 partnership liability is allocated $6,000 to A and $4,000 to B.

A final example applies the regulations to a guarantee of a nonrecourse loan by a general partner. Assume, as above, that B is a limited partner and A is the general partner in the AB partnership, and that A and B share income equally and share losses equally up to the point that B's capital account is reduced to zero. The partnership again purchases a $50,000 building, secured by a $10,000 debt that is nonrecourse as to the partnership but personally guaranteed by A. Under the now familiar doomsday liquidation scenario, the building becomes worthless and the $10,000 debt is fully due and payable. As guarantor, A is obligated to pay the debt, resulting in a $10,000 payment obligation if A has no right to reimbursement, directly or indirectly, from B.[34] A thus bears a $10,000 economic risk

---

**28.** Reg. § 1.704–1(b)(2)(ii)(*d*)(*3*).

**29.** Cf. Reg. § 1.752–2(f) Example 3. The result would be the same if A's obligation arose by operation of law.

**30.** Assume the note is due in the year the partnership liquidates so that discounting it to present value is not required. See Reg. § 1.752–2(g)(1)(i).

**31.** Reg. § 1.704–1(b)(2)(iv)(*d*)(*2*).

**32.** Reg. §§ 1.704–1(b)(2)(ii)(*c*)(*1*), (*d*).

**33.** See Reg. § 1.752–2(b)(3)(ii). Although the regulations disregard a partner's promissory note for certain other purposes unless they are readily tradeable on an established securities market (see Reg. § 1.752–2(g)(3), (h)(4)), a partner's promissory note to a partnership should be recognized as a payment obligation for purposes of the economic risk of loss test. See Reg. § 1.752–2(b)(3)(ii).

**34.** Cf. Reg. § 1.752–2(f) Example 3.

of loss, and the debt is treated as a recourse liability allocated entirely to A. The result would be the same if A did not personally guarantee the obligation but instead contributed property worth $10,000 to be used solely as security.[35]

If B rather than A had personally guaranteed the debt, the result would depend on whether or not B was entitled to reimbursement from the partnership for payments made to the creditor in satisfaction of the debt. If B were not entitled to reimbursement, he would have a $10,000 net payment obligation, and the debt would be allocated to him in its entirety. But if B were entitled to reimbursement from the partnership for payments made to the creditor, B's payment obligation would be zero ($10,000 payment obligation minus $10,000 reimbursement). The reimbursement would come from the $10,000 that A would be required to contribute as a result of operation of law or the partnership agreement.[36] Thus, A would have a $10,000 net contribution obligation, and the liability would be allocated entirely to A.[37]

## 3.   NONRECOURSE LIABILITIES

*Overview.* To the extent that no partner bears the economic risk of loss for a partnership liability, the liability is classified as nonrecourse.[1] Nonrecourse liabilities generally are allocated among the partners in accordance with their respective shares of partnership profits.[2] This general rule would suffice were it not for the complications resulting from special allocations, partnership minimum gain and Section 704(c) built-in gain.

To accommodate the more complex realities of modern partnerships, the regulations adopt a three-step approach under which a partner's share of nonrecourse liabilities is the sum of: (1) the partner's share of partnership minimum gain determined in accordance with the Section 704(b) regulations,[3] (2) in the case of nonrecourse liabilities secured by contributed property, the amount of gain that the partner would recognize under Section 704(c) if the partnership disposed of that property in a taxable transaction in full satisfaction of the liabilities and no other consideration;[4] and (3) the partner's share of any remaining ("excess") nonrecourse liabilities, determined in accordance with his share of partnership profits.[5] The third part of the formula, although labelled as the rule for "excess nonrecourse liabilities," actually governs the vast majority of situations and thus is the appropriate place to begin this discussion.

---

**35.**  Reg. § 1.752–2(h)(2).

**36.**  A would be required to contribute $10,000 to make up the $10,000 capital account deficit that would result from the allocation to A of $30,000 of the partnership's $50,000 loss. B, as a limited partner, would have no such obligation.

**37.**  See Reg. § 1.752–2(f) Example 3.

**1.**  Reg. § 1.752–1(a)(2).

**2.**  Reg. § 1.752–3(a)(3).

**3.**  Reg.  § 1.752–3(a)(1).  See  Reg. § 1.704–2(g)(1).

**4.**  Reg. § 1.752–3(a)(2).

**5.**  Reg. § 1.752–3(a)(3).

*Partner's Share of Partnership Profits.* The general rule for the allocation of nonrecourse liabilities is straightforward: nonrecourse liabilities are allocated in proportion to the partners' interests in partnership profits.[6] Absent any special allocations, nonrecourse liabilities simply are allocated in accordance with the partners' interests in the partnership. The possibilities expand considerably when the partnership agreement provides for special allocations of profits. For example, assume that A and B are equal partners, but their agreement includes allocations (that have substantial economic effect) of one significant profits item exclusively to A, and of another significant profits item exclusively to B. If the partnership purchases an asset subject to a nonrecourse liability, the regulations provide that any specification of the partners' interests in the partnership agreement will be respected for Section 752 purposes as long as it is reasonably consistent with an allocation (having substantial economic effect) of any significant item of partnership income or gain.[7] As a result, the AB partnership may allocate the nonrecourse liability exclusively to A, exclusively to B, or equally to A and B, merely by specifying "the partners' interests in partnership profits for Section 752 purposes" in the partnership agreement. Absent such a direction, the partners' interests in partnership profits are determined by taking into account all the facts and circumstances relating to the economic arrangement of the partners.[8]

The regulations also provide some alternative methods for allocating nonrecourse liabilities. Excess nonrecourse liabilities may be allocated in accordance with the manner in which it is reasonably expected that the deductions attributable to those liabilities will be allocated.[9] Additionally, in the case of contributed property subject to a nonrecourse liability, the partnership may first allocate an excess nonrecourse liability to the contributing partner to the extent that Section 704(c) gain on the property is greater than the gain resulting from the liability exceeding the basis of the property.[10] Finally, the regulations provide that the method selected for allocating excess nonrecourse liabilities may vary from year to year.[11]

*Partners' Share of Partnership Minimum Gain.* Where the partnership has generated minimum gain, the rule for allocation of nonrecourse liabilities directly follows the rule for allocation of the deductions and distributions attributable to those liabilities. The liabilities are first allocated in accordance with each partner's share of partnership minimum gain.[12] To illustrate, assume that A and B each contribute $500 cash to the AB equal partnership. The partnership purchases an asset worth $10,000 by paying

**6.** Id.

**7.** Id.

**8.** Id.

**9.** Id. See Reg. § 1.752–3(b) Example 2.

**10.** Id. If the entire amount of the excess nonrecourse liability is not allocated to the contributing partner, the remaining amount must be allocated under one of the other methods. This allocation method is also available in the case of property for which reverse Section 704(c) allocations are applicable under Reg. § 1.704–3(a)(6)(i), but it does not apply for purposes of Reg. § 1.707–5(a)(2)(ii) (disguised sales of property). Id.

**11.** Id.

**12.** Reg. § 1.752–3(a)(1). See Reg. § 1.704–2(g)(1).

$1,000 cash and taking the asset subject to a $9,000 nonrecourse liability payable in full after five years. Assume further that there is a valid special allocation of all depreciation, income, gain or loss with respect to this asset to A for the first four years,[13] followed by an equal split over the remaining life of the asset. The asset is depreciable on a straight-line basis at the rate of $500 per year. For the first two years, the partnership has no minimum gain, and the liability is allocated between A and B according to their overall interests in partnership profits, or as otherwise specified in the partnership agreement provided that agreed allocation is either reasonably consistent with: (1) some other valid allocation of a significant item of partnership income or gain, or (2) the manner in which it is reasonably expected that the deductions attributable to those nonrecourse liabilities will be allocated.[14] If we assume that the partnership agreement provides for an equal division of profits for Section 752 purposes, the liability will be allocated equally, increasing each partner's outside basis by $4,500 to $5,000.

At the end of year three, with the basis of the asset reduced to $8,500 and the liability remaining at $9,000, there is $500 of partnership minimum gain. Since all of the nonrecourse deductions that gave rise to the partnership minimum gain are allocated to A,[15] there also must be a minimum gain chargeback to A. And since A's share of partnership minimum gain is now $500, $500 of the partnership nonrecourse liability must be allocated to A.[16] The remainder of the nonrecourse liability continues to be allocated in the same proportion as it was during the first two years. As a result, the nonrecourse liability allocated to A at the end of year three will be equal to A's $500 share of partnership minimum gain plus half of the remaining $8,500, for a total of $4,750. The balance (i.e., half of $8,500, or $4,250) is allocated to B. To ensure that A has enough outside basis to be able to use the $500 nonrecourse deduction allocated to him, the basis increase attributable to the allocation of the nonrecourse liability should be deemed to occur immediately before the allocation to A of the nonrecourse deductions which caused the increase in minimum gain. This rule reflects the fact that one of the principal purposes for including partnership liabilities in the partners' outside bases is to support the deductions that will be claimed by the partners for items attributable to those liabilities.[17]

---

13. See Reg. § 1.704–2(e).

14. See supra notes 6–9 and accompanying text.

15. See Section B3 of this chapter, supra.

16. Reg. § 1.752–3(a)(1).

17. See Reg. § 1.752–3(b) Example 1. The allocation guarantees that A's outside basis is increased just when A is likely to need additional outside basis to take the deductions allocated to him. Each year that more nonrecourse deductions and minimum gain is allocated to A, more of the partnership's nonrecourse liability (and a corresponding amount of outside basis) also is allocated to A and away from B. A possibly disruptive side effect of this approach is that each partner's outside basis must be recalculated each year that partnership minimum gain is generated. If the partnership wishes to avoid this annual shifting of the liability allocation, it may elect to initially allocate the nonrecourse liability according to the manner in which it expects that the deductions attributable to that liability will be allocated—i.e., $5,500 ($2,000 plus $3,500) to A and $3,500 to B.

The minimum gain allocation rule also applies where the minimum gain is triggered by a distribution of the proceeds of a nonrecourse loan. In that event, the distributee partner, to whom the minimum gain is allocated under the Section 704(b) regulations, is the partner to whom the nonrecourse liability that generates the minimum gain will be allocated. To return to the example, assume that the AB partnership borrows another $10,000 on a nonrecourse basis secured by the asset at the end of year two (when the asset's basis was $9,000 and the asset was already encumbered by a $9,000 nonrecourse liability) and immediately distributes the loan proceeds to B. Under the Section 704(b) and Section 752 regulations, the $10,000 of partnership minimum gain generated by the borrowing is allocated to B,[18] and the $10,000 liability also is allocated to B. To ensure that the distribution of the loan proceeds does not result in the recognition of gain to B (as it would if B's outside basis were below $10,000 at the time of the cash distribution), the increase in basis that results from the allocation of partnership nonrecourse liabilities should occur before the decrease in basis from the distribution.

*Partners' Shares of Section 704(c) Gain.* When property contributed to a partnership is subject to a nonrecourse liability in excess of its adjusted basis, the property has a built-in gain (equal to the excess of liabilities over basis) similar to partnership minimum gain. Under the regulations, however, the built-in gain is not partnership minimum gain under Section 704(b) but instead is potential Section 704(c) gain.[19] The regulations provide that, to the extent of the minimum Section 704(c) gain, the nonrecourse liability secured by the contributed property is allocated to the same partner to whom this minimum built-in gain is allocated under Section 704(c).[20]

For example, assume that A and B form the equal AB partnership with A contributing $1,000 cash, and B contributing property with a value of $3,500, a basis of $1,000 and subject to a nonrecourse debt of $2,500. Also, assume A and B agree they will use the traditional method to allocate Section 704(c) gain.[21] Since a disposition of B's property for no consider-

---

**18.** Reg. § 1.704–2(h).

**19.** There is partnership minimum gain only to the extent that a nonrecourse liability to which an asset is subject exceeds the book value of the asset. Reg. § 1.704–2(d)(3). Under the regulations, contributed property is entered on the partnership's books at its fair market value at the time of the contribution. Reg. § 1.704–1(b)(2)(iv)(*d*)(*1*). As a result, there is no partnership minimum gain at the time of the contribution.

**20.** Reg. § 1.752–3(a)(2). If a partnership holds multiple properties subject to a single nonrecourse liability, it may allocate the liability among those properties under any reasonable method, and then the portion of the liability allocated to each property is treated as a separate loan for purposes of determining the minimum built-in gain in the property. Reg. § 1.752–3(b)(1). An allocation method is not reasonable if it allocates an amount of liability that, when combined with other liabilities allocated to the property, is in excess of the property's fair market value. The method of allocating a single nonrecourse liability can not be changed. But if a property becomes no longer subject to the liability, the portion of the liability allocated to that property must be reallocated to the other properties. Id. Principal payments on the liability are allocated among the multiple properties in the same proportion that the liability was allocated. Reg. § 1.752–3(b)(2).

**21.** Alternatively, the partnership could use the traditional method with curative allocations or the remedial method. If the tradi-

ation other than debt relief would generate $1,500 of gain under Section 704(c), $1,500 of the nonrecourse liability is allocated to B. The remaining $1,000 of the nonrecourse liability could be allocated between A and B in accordance with their interests in partnership profits—in this case $500 to each.[22] In these circumstances, B is relieved of $2,500 of debt but also is allocated $2,000 of the partnership's liability. The regulations allow these amounts to be netted, resulting in a net decrease in B's liabilities of $500.[23] A's share of partnership liabilities is $500.

Finally, there may be a minimum amount of gain built into an asset (as a result of nonrecourse liabilities in excess of basis) which is neither minimum gain nor Section 704(c) gain. For example,[24] when a new partner joins an ongoing partnership, the book value of partnership assets may be restated to reflect their current fair market value.[25] Thus, if the XY partnership has a building with a basis of zero and a value of $10,000 when Z becomes a partner, the building may be revalued on the partnership books at $10,000.[26] If the partnership later borrows $5,000 on a nonrecourse basis secured by the building, the partnership will have no minimum gain because the debt will not exceed the building's *book* value even though the debt exceeds the tax basis of the building by $5,000. This built-in minimum amount of gain is treated the same as Section 704(c) gain under the regulations.[27] Thus, X and Y are each allocated $2,500 of the Section 704(c)-type gain which would result if there were a sale of the property, and each is also allocated $2,500 of the $5,000 nonrecourse liability.[28]

Revenue Ruling 95–41, below, illustrates the approach of the regulations for determining a partner's share of nonrecourse liabilities. The ruling also explores how to apply the different Section 704(c) allocation methods when determining a partner's share of nonrecourse liabilities.

*Part-Recourse, Part–Nonrecourse Liabilities.* The rules for allocating part-recourse, part-nonrecourse liabilities are straightforward. After properly bifurcating the debt, the recourse portion is allocated under the rules for recourse liabilities, and the nonrecourse portion is allocated separately under the rules for nonrecourse liabilities.[29]

tional method with curative allocations is selected, the Service takes the position that curative allocations are disregarded for Section 752 purposes because those allocations cannot be determined solely from the hypothetical sale of the contributed property. Thus, there would be no difference between the traditional method and traditional method with curative allocations. See Rev. Rul. 95–41, infra page 201.

**22.** The regulations also would permit the partnership to allocate all $1,000 of the remaining excess nonrecourse liability to B because there is an additional $1,000 of Section 704(c) gain in the property. Reg. § 1.752–3(a)(3).

**23.** Reg. § 1.752–1(f).

**24.** See Section C4 of this chapter, supra.

**25.** Reg. § 1.704–1(b)(2)(iv)(*f*).

**26.** Id.

**27.** Reg. § 1.752–3(a)(2). See Reg. § 1.704–1(b)(2)(iv)(*f*)(4).

**28.** If the partnership does not revalue its assets when Z becomes a partner, the regulations require that Section 704(c) principles must nonetheless be applied in order to reach the same result. Reg. § 1.704–1(b)(2)(iv)(*f*) (flush language).

**29.** Reg. § 1.752–1(h). See also Rev.Rul. 84–118, 1984–2 C.B. 120, where the Service took the same position prior to the proposed Section 752 regulations.

To illustrate, assume that G and L form a limited partnership in which G is the general partner and L is the limited partner. Each partner contributes $20,000 and the partners agree to share profits and losses equally, except that L is not liable for losses beyond his original contribution. GL purchases a building worth $40,000, paying $5,000 down and taking the building subject to a $35,000 nonrecourse liability. G personally guarantees $15,000 of the partnership liability, and G is not entitled to reimbursement from the partnership for any part of this amount. With respect to the $15,000 of the liability which G has personally guaranteed, G will be required to pay $15,000 to the creditor if the partnership's assets are worthless. As a result, G bears the economic risk of loss with respect to $15,000 of the partnership liability. To that extent, the liability is a recourse liability and is allocated to G.[30]

With respect to the remaining $20,000, the creditor will bear the economic risk of loss if all partnership assets become worthless. As a result, the liability is a nonrecourse liability which is allocated between G and L in proportion to their equal shares of partnership profits.[31]

## Revenue Ruling 95–41

1995–1 Cum.Bull. 132.

ISSUES

How does § 704(c) of the Internal Revenue Code affect the allocation of nonrecourse liabilities under § 1.752–3(a) of the Income Tax Regulations?

FACTS

A and B form a partnership, PRS, and agree that each will be allocated a 50 percent share of all partnership items. A contributes depreciable property subject to a nonrecourse liability of $6,000, with an adjusted tax basis of $4,000 and a fair market value of $10,000. B contributes $4,000 cash.

LAW

Section 1.752–3(a) provides that a partner's share of the nonrecourse liabilities of a partnership equals the sum of the amounts specified in § 1.752–3(a)(1)–(3).

Section 1.752–3(a)(1) provides that the partner's share of the nonrecourse liabilities of a partnership includes the partner's share of partnership minimum gain determined in accordance with the rules of § 704(b) and the regulations thereunder. See § 1.704–2.

Section 1.752–3(a)(2) provides that the partner's share of the nonrecourse liabilities of the partnership includes the amount of any taxable gain that would be allocated to the partner under § 704(c) (or in the same manner as § 704(c) in connection with a revaluation of partnership proper-

---

**30.** See Reg. § 1.752–2(f) Example 5.  **31.** Id.

ty) if the partnership disposed of (in a taxable transaction) all partnership property subject to one or more nonrecourse liabilities of the partnership in full satisfaction of the liabilities and for no other consideration.

Section 1.752–3(a)(3) provides that the partner's share of the nonrecourse liabilities of the partnership includes the partner's share of the excess nonrecourse liabilities (those not allocated under § 1.752–3(a)(1) and (a)(2)) of the partnership as determined in accordance with the partner's share of partnership profits. The partner's interest in partnership profits is determined by taking into account all facts and circumstances relating to the economic arrangement of the partners. The partnership agreement may specify the partners' interests in partnership profits for purposes of allocating excess nonrecourse liabilities, provided the interests so specified are reasonably consistent with allocations (that have substantial economic effect under the § 704(b) regulations) of some other significant item of partnership income or gain. Alternatively, excess nonrecourse liabilities may be allocated among the partners in accordance with the manner in which it is reasonably expected that the deductions attributable to those nonrecourse liabilities will be allocated. [Section 1.752–3(a)(3) has been revised since this Revenue Ruling was issued. The regulation now provides that the partnership also may first allocate an excess nonrecourse liability to a partner up to the amount of built-in gain that is allocated to the partner on Section 704(c) property where such property is subject to the nonrecourse liability to the extent that such built-in gain exceeds the gain described in Reg. § 1.752–3(a)(2) with respect to such property. Ed.]

Section 704(c)(1)(A) provides that income, gain, loss, and deduction with respect to property contributed to the partnership by a partner shall be shared among the partners so as to take account of the variation between the adjusted tax basis of the property to the partnership and its fair market value at the time of contribution.

Section 1.704–3(a)(3)(i) provides that the book value of contributed property is equal to its fair market value at the time of contribution and is subsequently adjusted for cost recovery and other events that affect the basis of the property.

Section 1.704–3(a)(3)(ii) provides that the built-in gain on § 704(c) property is the excess of the property's book value over the contributing partner's adjusted tax basis in the property upon contribution. The built-in gain is thereafter reduced by decreases in the difference between the property's book value and adjusted tax basis.

ANALYSIS

Upon A's contribution of the depreciable property to PRS, there is $6,000 of § 704(c) built-in gain (the excess of the book value of the property ($10,000) over A's adjusted tax basis in the property at the time of contribution ($4,000)). As a result of the contribution, A's individual liabilities decreased by $6,000 (the amount of the nonrecourse liability which PRS is treated as having assumed). A's share of the partnership's nonrecourse liabilities is determined under § 1.752–3.

*(1) First Tier Allocations:*

Under § 1.752–3(a)(1), a partner's share of the nonrecourse liabilities of PRS includes the partner's share of partnership minimum gain determined in accordance with the rules of § 704(b) and the regulations thereunder. Section 1.704–2(d)(1) provides that partnership minimum gain is determined by computing, for each partnership nonrecourse liability, any gain the partnership would realize if it disposed of the property subject to that liability for no consideration other than full satisfaction of the liability, and then aggregating the separately computed gains. Pursuant to § 1.704–2(d)(3), partnership minimum gain is determined with reference to the contributed property's book value rather than its adjusted tax basis.

In contrast, § 704(c) requires that allocations take into account the difference between the contributed property's adjusted tax basis and its fair market value. Thus, because partnership minimum gain is computed using the contributed property's book value rather than its tax basis, allocations of nonrecourse liabilities under § 1.752–3(a)(1) are not affected by § 704(c). Moreover, because the book value of the property at the time of contribution ($10,000) exceeds the amount of the nonrecourse liability ($6,000), there is no partnership minimum gain immediately after the contribution, and neither A nor B receive an allocation of nonrecourse liabilities under § 1.752–3(a)(1) immediately after the contribution.

*(2) Second Tier Allocations:*

Under § 1.752–3(a)(2), a partner's share of the nonrecourse liabilities of the partnership includes the amount of taxable gain that would be allocated to the contributing partner under § 704(c) if the partnership, in a taxable transaction, disposed of the contributed property in full satisfaction of the nonrecourse liability and for no other consideration. If PRS sold the contributed property in full satisfaction of the liability and for no other consideration, PRS would recognize a taxable gain of $2,000 on the sale ($6,000 amount of the nonrecourse liability less $4,000 adjusted tax basis of the property). Under § 704(c) and § 1.704–3(b)(1), all of this taxable gain would be allocated to A. The hypothetical sale also would result in a book loss of $4,000 to PRS (excess of $10,000 book value of property over $6,000 amount of the nonrecourse liability). Under the terms of the partnership agreement, this book loss would be allocated equally between A and B. Because B would receive a $2,000 book loss but no corresponding tax loss, the hypothetical sale would result in a $2,000 disparity between B's book and tax allocations.

If PRS used the traditional method of making § 704(c) allocations described in § 1.704–3(b), A would be allocated a total of $2,000 of taxable gain from the hypothetical sale of the contributed property. Therefore, A would be allocated $2,000 of nonrecourse liabilities under § 1.752–3(a)(2) immediately after the contribution.

If PRS adopted the remedial allocation method described in § 1.704–3(d), PRS would be required to make a remedial allocation of $2,000 of tax loss to B in connection with the hypothetical sale to eliminate the $2,000

disparity between B's book and tax allocations. PRS also would be required to make an offsetting remedial allocation of tax gain to A of $2,000. Thus, A would be allocated a total of $4,000 of tax gain ($2,000 actual gain plus the $2,000 allocation of remedial gain) from the hypothetical sale of the contributed property. Therefore, if the partnership adopted the remedial allocation method, A would be allocated $4,000 of nonrecourse liabilities under § 1.752–3(a)(2) immediately after the contribution.

If PRS used the traditional method with curative allocations described in § 1.704–3(c), PRS would be permitted to make reasonable curative allocations to reduce or eliminate the difference between the book and tax allocations to B that resulted from the hypothetical sale. However, PRS's ability to make curative allocations would depend on the existence of other partnership items and could not be determined solely from the hypothetical sale of the contributed property. Because any potential curative allocations could not be determined solely from the hypothetical sale of the contributed property, curative allocations are not taken into account in allocating nonrecourse liabilities under § 1.752–3(a)(2). Therefore, if PRS used the traditional method with curative allocations, A would be allocated $2,000 of nonrecourse liabilities under § 1.752–3(a)(2) immediately after the contribution.

*(3) Third Tier Allocations:*

Following the allocation under § 1.752–3(a)(2), PRS has excess nonrecourse liabilities that must be allocated between A and B. Section 1.752–3(a)(3) provides several alternatives for allocating excess nonrecourse liabilities.

(a) First, PRS may choose to allocate excess nonrecourse liabilities in accordance with the partners' shares of partnership profits. The partners' interests in partnership profits are determined by taking into account all the facts and circumstances relating to the economic arrangement of the partners. The partners' agreement to share the profits of the partnership equally is one fact to be considered in making this determination. Another fact to be considered is a partner's share of § 704(c) built-in gain to the extent that the gain was not taken into account in making an allocation of nonrecourse liabilities under § 1.752–3(a)(2). This built-in gain is one factor because, under the principles of § 704(c), this excess built-in gain, if recognized, will be allocated to A. A's share of § 704(c) built-in gain that is not taken into account in making allocations under § 1.752–3(a)(2) is, therefore, one factor, but not the only factor, to be considered in determining A's interest in partnership profits.

The amount of the § 704(c) built-in gain that is not considered in making allocations under § 1.752–3(a)(2) must be given an appropriate weight in light of all other items of partnership profit. For example, if it is reasonable to expect that PRS will have items of partnership profit over the life of the partnership that will be allocated to B, PRS may not allocate all of the excess nonrecourse liabilities to A. Rather, the remaining nonre-

course liabilities must be allocated between A and B in proportion to their interests in total partnership profits.

(b) Second, the PRS partnership agreement may specify the partners' interests in partnership profits for purposes of allocating excess nonrecourse liabilities, provided that the interests specified are reasonably consistent with allocations (that have substantial economic effect under the § 704(b) regulations) of some other significant item of partnership income or gain. The partnership agreement provides that each partner will be allocated a 50 percent share of all partnership items. Assuming that such allocations have substantial economic effect, PRS can choose to allocate the excess nonrecourse liabilities 50 percent to each partner. Section 704(c) allocations, however, do not have substantial economic effect under the § 704(b) regulations. See § 1.704–1(b)(2)(iv)(d). Accordingly, under this alternative, § 704(c) allocations cannot be used as a basis for allocating excess nonrecourse liabilities.

(c) Finally, PRS may choose to allocate the excess nonrecourse liabilities in accordance with the manner in which it is reasonably expected that the deductions attributable to the excess nonrecourse liabilities will be allocated. Because A and B have agreed to allocate all partnership items 50 percent to each partner, A and B each will be entitled to allocations of book depreciation of $5,000 over the life of the contributed property. The contributed property, however, has an adjusted tax basis of $4,000 and, regardless of the method used by the partnership under § 704(c), the entire $4,000 of tax depreciation over the life of the contributed property must be allocated to B. Therefore, PRS must allocate all of the excess nonrecourse liabilities to B if it chooses to allocate the excess nonrecourse liabilities in accordance with the manner that the deductions attributable to the excess nonrecourse liabilities will be allocated.

[(d) Additionally, § 1.752–3(a)(3) now allows PRS to allocate the excess nonrecourse liabilities to a partner up to the amount of built-in gain that is allocable to the partner on Section 704(c) property where such property is subject to the nonrecourse liability to the extent that such built-in gain exceeds the gain described in § 1.752–3(a)(2). There is $6,000 of Section 704(c) built-in gain in the property contributed by A ($10,000 book value over the property's $4,000 basis). There was $2,000 of that gain described in § 1.752–3(a)(2) ($6,000 amount of nonrecourse liabilities less $4,000 adjusted basis of the property). Thus, there is $4,000 excess of total built-in gain over the gain described in § 1.752–3(a)(2). PRS may choose to use this Section 704(c) allocation as the basis for allocating excess nonrecourse liabilities to A. Ed.]

HOLDINGS

(1) Allocations of nonrecourse liabilities under § 1.752–3(a)(1) are not affected by § 704(c).

(2) Allocations of nonrecourse liabilities under § 1.752–3(a)(2) take into account remedial allocations of gain that would be made to the contributing partner under § 1.704–3(d). Allocations of nonrecourse liabili-

ties under § 1.752–3(a)(2) do not take into account curative allocations under § 1.704–3(c).

(3) Allocations of nonrecourse liabilities under § 1.752–3(a)(3) are affected by § 704(c) in the following manner:

(a) If the partnership determines the partners' interests in partnership profits based on all of the facts and circumstances relating to the economic arrangement of the partners, § 704(c) built-in gain that was not taken into account under § 1.752–3(a)(2) is one factor, but not the only factor, to be considered under § 1.752–3(a)(3).

(b) If the partnership chooses to allocate excess nonrecourse liabilities in a manner reasonably consistent with allocations (that have substantial economic effect under the § 704(b) regulations) of some other significant item of partnership income or gain, § 704(c) does not affect the allocation of nonrecourse liabilities under § 1.752–3(a)(3) because § 704(c) allocations do not have substantial economic effect.

(c) If the partnership chooses to allocate excess nonrecourse liabilities in accordance with the manner in which it is reasonably expected that the deductions attributable to the nonrecourse liabilities will be allocated, the partnership must take into account the allocations required by § 704(c) in determining the manner in which the deductions attributable to the nonrecourse liabilities will be allocated.

[(d) If the partnership chooses to allocate excess nonrecourse liabilities to a partner up to the amount of built-in gain that is allocated to the partner in excess of the gain described in § 1.752–3(a)(2), the partnership will be taking into account the allocations required by § 704(c). Ed.]

## 4. TIERED PARTNERSHIPS

The regulations provide special rules for allocation of liabilities of tiered partnerships. To illustrate, assume that A and B form the AB general partnership and agree to share profits and losses equally. A and B each contribute $5,000 to AB, which has no liabilities, and AB then contributes $10,000 cash to the ABCDEF general partnership in exchange for a one-third interest in partnership profits and losses. ABCDEF borrows $120,000 on a nonrecourse basis in order to purchase land. AB's basis in its ABCDEF partnership interest equals its $10,000 cash contribution plus its one-third share of partnership debt ($40,000), for a total outside basis of $50,000. The regulations provide that the liabilities of a subsidiary partnership that are properly allocated to an upper-tier ("parent") partnership are treated as liabilities of the upper-tier partnership for purposes of again applying Section 752 to the partners of the parent.[1] As a result, AB's $40,000 share of ABCDEF's liability is reallocated $20,000 each to A and B, increasing each partner's outside basis by $20,000 to $25,000.

---

**1.** Reg. § 1.752–4(a). See also Reg. § 1.752–2(i). This result is consistent with the law prior to the proposed regulations. See Rev.Rul. 77–309, 1977–2 C.B. 216.

## PROBLEMS

**1.** A, B and C each contribute $20,000 to form the ABC general partnership. The partnership agreement satisfies the primary test for economic effect under Section 704(b). Partnership profits and losses are allocated 40% to A, 40% to B and 20% to C. The partnership uses its $60,000 cash and borrows an additional $40,000 on a recourse basis and purchases land for $100,000.

    (a) How will the $40,000 liability be allocated and what will be each partner's outside basis?

    (b) What result in (a), above, if A, B and C had contributed $10,000, $20,000 and $30,000, respectively, to the ABC partnership?

    (c) What result in (a), above, if A and B are limited partners who are not obligated to restore a capital account deficit but the partnership agreement includes a qualified income offset?

    (d) What result in (c), above, if A contributes $15,000 of stock to the partnership as security for the liability and all income, gain or loss on the stock is allocated to A? What result if A contributes his $15,000 note as security for the liability?

    (e) What result in (c), above, if A personally guarantees the $40,000 liability?

**2.** G and L form a limited partnership. G, the general partner, contributes $10,000 and L, the limited partner, contributes $90,000. The partnership purchases a building on leased land, paying $100,000 cash and borrowing $900,000 on a nonrecourse basis from a commercial lender, securing the loan with a mortgage on the building. The terms of the loan require the payment of market rate interest and no principal for the first ten years. Assume for convenience that the building is depreciable at the rate of $50,000 per year for twenty years, and that other partnership income equals expenses for the years in question. The partnership agreement contains a qualified income offset, and G is required to make up any capital account deficit. Except as otherwise required by a minimum gain charge-back provision, the agreement allocates income 90% to L and 10% to G until such time as the partnership recognizes items of income and gain that exceed the items of deduction and loss that is has recognized over its life. Subsequent partnership income and losses are allocated equally between G and L. Assume that it is reasonably anticipated that the equal allocation will begin after ten years. The partnership agreement states that G and L each has a 50% interest in partnership profits for purposes of § 752.

    (a) How is the $900,000 liability allocated in year one?

    (b) How will the liability be allocated at the end of year three?

    (c) How will the liability be allocated at the end of years one and three if excess nonrecourse liabilities are allocated in a ratio of 90% to L and 10% to G?

(d) What result in (a), above, if the debt is guaranteed by G, who has no right to reimbursement from the partnership? Does the result change if G has a right to reimbursement from the partnership? What if G has a gross assets of only $6,000?

(e) What result in (a), above, if the debt is guaranteed by L, and L has a right to reimbursement from the partnership?

(f) What result in (a), above, if G is the lender?

**3.** The equal AB partnership's only asset is Building #1, which has a fair market value of $800,000 and an adjusted basis of $300,000. C becomes a one-third partner by contributing Building #2 with a fair market value of $700,000 and an adjusted basis of $150,000 and which is subject to a $300,000 recourse liability which the partnership assumes. At the time of C's contribution, the partnership revalues its assets under Reg. § 1.704–1(b)(2)(iv)(*f*).

(a) How is the $300,000 liability allocated?

(b) What result in (a), above, if the liability is a nonrecourse debt secured by Building #2 and the partners agree to use the traditional method to allocate § 704(c) gain?

(c) If C, instead of contributing Building #2, contributes $400,000 cash and shortly thereafter the partnership incurs a $500,000 nonrecourse loan secured by Building #1, how is the $500,000 liability allocated?

---

## E.   ALLOCATIONS WHERE PARTNERS' INTERESTS VARY DURING THE YEAR

Code: §  706(c)(2)(B) & (d).

Regulations: §  1.706–1(c)(4).

We have assumed up to now that the interests of all the partners in the partnership are the same throughout the partnership's taxable year. But if a partner sells part of his interest during the year, or if the proportionate interests of the partners change as a result of the entry of a new partner, a capital contribution by an existing partner, a partial liquidation, a gift, or for some other reason, a method must be found to determine each partner's respective share of income, losses, deductions and other partnership items.

Section 706(c)(2)(B) initially provides that if a partner disposes of less than his entire partnership interest, the partnership taxable year will not close with respect to that partner.[1] When partners' interests change during a taxable year, however, Section 706(d)(1) provides that each partner's distributive share of partnership income or loss is determined by taking into account the partners' varying interests in the partnership during the

---

**1.** The partnership year will close, however, with respect to a partner whose entire interest in the partnership terminates (whether by reason of death, liquidation, or otherwise). I.R.C. § 706(c)(2)(A). See Chapters 6A & 8A, infra.

year. In general, this means that if A is a one-third partner in the ABC Partnership for the first half of the year and a one-quarter partner for the balance, A generally must be allocated one-third of each partnership item for the first six months and one-quarter of those items for the second half of the year.[2] These rules are intended to preclude a partner who acquires his interest toward the end of the year from receiving the benefits of a retroactive allocation of deductions and losses incurred prior to his admission to the partnership.[3]

When the interests of partners change during the year, a partnership may use either of two methods to determine the distributive shares of the partners: (1) the "interim closing of the books" method, or (2) the "proration" method.[4] The interim closing method traces income and deduction items to the particular segment of the taxable year during which they are paid or incurred. Thus, a one-third partner admitted to a calendar year partnership on December 1 would be allocated only his one-third share of items paid or incurred during December. The proration method is simpler but more arbitrary. Partnership items are prorated throughout the year, and a partner's share is based on the number of days during which he was a partner. Applying the proration method to the above example, the new one-third partner admitted on December 1 would be allocated $\frac{1}{12}$ of his hypothetical one-third share of partnership items for the entire taxable year regardless of when those expenses were paid or incurred.

In response to attempts by partnerships to circumvent these general rules, Congress enacted a complex set of anti-avoidance provisions designed to prevent retroactive allocations by cash method partnerships and tiered partnership arrangements. A typical target of the reforms was the taxpayer who joined a cash method partnership toward the end of the year and sought to deduct expenses incurred prior to her admission to the firm. To illustrate, assume that B becomes a 10 percent partner in Loss Associates,

---

**2.** Of course, if the partnership agreement contains a special allocation that is valid under Section 704(b), the partners do not have to be allocated amounts corresponding exactly to their percentage interests in the partnership. See Section B2 of this chapter, supra. But an allocation that passes muster under Section 704(b) may be reallocated under Section 706(d) and related assignment of income principles in appropriate cases. See infra note 8.

**3.** See generally Staff of the Joint Committee on Taxation, General Explanation of Tax Reform Act of 1976, 94th Cong., 2d Sess. 91–94 (1976). Section 761(c), however, defines a "partnership agreement" to include any modifications made prior to the due date for filing the partnership return and, under Section 704(a), a partner's distributive share is determined by the partnership agreement. This suggests that retroactive allocations

may be permissible through an amendment to the agreement. This result clearly was not intended (cf. I.R.C. § 761(f)), but the legislative history of the Tax Reform Act of 1984 makes it clear that Section 761(c) still permits retroactive modifications to a partnership agreement that result in shifts of interests among partners who are members of the partnership for the entire taxable year, provided those shifts are not attributable to additional capital contributions. See Staff of the Joint Committee on Taxation, General Explanation of the Revenue Provisions of the Deficit Reduction Act of 1984 (hereinafter "1984 Act General Explanation"), 98th Cong., 2d Sess. 219 (1984). See Lipke v. Commissioner, 81 T.C. 689 (1983).

**4.** See 1984 Act General Explanation, supra note 3, at 217. Cf. Reg. § 1.706–1(c)(2)(ii).

a calendar year partnership, on December 1, and that Loss has a $120,000 net loss which has accrued ratably through the year. Since B has been a 10 percent partner for one-twelfth of the year, she should be entitled to deduct 10 percent of the loss accruing during her one month as a partner, or a total of $1,000 ($120,000 × $\frac{1}{12}$ × $\frac{1}{10}$). If B wished to deduct more than $1,000, and the other partners were agreeable, the partnership might allocate to B 10 percent of its losses for the entire year, including the eleven months when she was not a partner. Because Section 706 prevented such a straightforward approach, resourceful tax advisors concocted more creative techniques to achieve the effect of a retroactive allocation without its appearance. For example, with careful advance planning and an eye toward attracting year-end investors craving tax losses, Loss Associates, as a cash method taxpayer, could adopt the interim closing of the books method of allocation and simply defer payment of its deductible expenses until late in the year. In that event, even if the last minute investors were allocated only the losses incurred during the time they were partners, their allocable share would be disproportionately large in the typical case where the expenses economically accrued before the new investors became partners.[5]

To curtail this technique, Section 706(d)(2)(A) requires cash method partnerships[6] to allocate certain specified cash basis items to the time during the taxable year that these items are economically attributable, regardless of when they are paid. At the expense of simplicity, this provision puts cash basis partnerships on an accrual basis with respect to the specified items for purposes of determining distributive shares when the interests of the partners vary during the year. For this purpose, "allocable cash basis items"[7] are defined as interest, taxes, payments for

---

**5.** Prior to the enactment of Section 706(d) in the Tax Reform Act of 1984, these techniques met with mixed success. Compare Richardson v. Commissioner, 76 T.C. 512 (1981), affirmed on other issues, 693 F.2d 1189 (5th Cir.1982) (retroactive allocation upheld where payment of deductible items by cash method partnership occurred after taxpayer's admission to the partnership and interim closing of books method used) with Williams v. United States, 680 F.2d 382 (5th Cir.1982) (similar retroactive allocation rejected in an accrual method partnership).

**6.** Because this avoidance technique was not available to accrual method partnerships, Congress singled out cash method partnerships for special scrutiny. Section 706(d)(2), however, applies whether the interim closing or the proration method is used. If the partnership's "planning" involved only a single year, as in the example in the text, the rule could be further limited to partnerships using the interim closing

method because the proration method would result in an automatic accrual of the items. But if the planning extended over more than a single year (see the discussion of Section 706(d)(2)(C) below), an anti-avoidance rule is needed under both the interim and proration methods. The statute is thus not limited to interim closings.

**7.** Although Congress seemingly intended to single out *deductible* cash basis items, the statutory language seems broad enough to embrace cash method income items as well. Thus, Section 706(d)(2) might be applied to require cash method partnerships to allocate prepaid income items (e.g., interest or rent) to those who were partners at the time the item was accrued regardless of when the income was received. The relationship of Section 706(d)(2) to income items is unclear and raises enough troublesome issues to suggest that Congress should have explicitly limited application of that section to the deduction setting. See McKee, Nelson & Whitmire,

services or for the use of property, and any other items specified by the Service.[8] Thus, in the example above, even if the partnership did not pay the expenses giving rise to the $120,000 loss until after B became a partner, Section 706(d)(2) would limit B's allowable loss to $1,000 if the postponed expense was an allocable cash basis item (e.g., a rent payment).[9]

The workings of Section 706(d)(2) become more complex if the partnership pays a deductible expense in a year other than that to which the item is economically attributable. A partnership using the cash method generally may deduct an expense[10] in the year of payment. Because the deduction is ultimately passed through to the partners, it must flow to those persons who are partners in the year that the expense is deductible to the partnership. If the identity or proportionate interests of the partners in the year of payment (and, correspondingly, the year of deduction) are not identical to those that exist in the year of accrual, the deductions cannot simply be allocated according to the partners' proportionate interests at the time of accrual. Instead, they somehow must be allocated to those who are partners in the year in which the payments are deductible under the cash method.

To alleviate these problems, Section 706(d)(2)(C) provides that any allocable cash basis item which is attributable to a period before or after the year of the payment is to be assigned entirely to the first day of the year (if the payment is attributable to a prior year)[11] or entirely to the final day of the year (if the payment is attributable to a future year).[12] In addition, if the payment is attributable to a prior year and is a deductible item, the payment will be allocated to those who were partners at the time the deduction accrued in proportion to their interests at that time.[13] To the extent that some or all of the deduction would be allocable to persons who are no longer partners at the time the expense becomes deductible, that part of the payment cannot be deducted but instead must be capitalized[14]

---

Federal Taxation of Partnerships and Partners ¶ 11.03[3] (3d ed. 1996).

**8.** I.R.C. § 706(d)(2)(B). Because Section 706(d) would be ineffective if it could be overridden by a special allocation of the relevant cash basis items under Section 704, the regulations provide that an allocation valid under Section 704(b) nonetheless is subject to reallocation under Section 706(d). Reg. § 1.704–1(b)(1)(iii). Cf. Hawkins v. Commissioner, 713 F.2d 347 (8th Cir.1983) and Prop. Reg. § 1.168–2(k), both holding that depreciation accrues on a pro rata basis throughout the year.

**9.** In addition, the General Explanation of the Tax Reform Act of 1984 allows the Service to promulgate regulations which adopt conventions for determining the date of the month that a partnership interest change is deemed to occur. Use of such conventions is not permitted when the occurrence of a significant discrete event (e.g., an extraordinary gain or loss) results in significant tax avoidance. See 1984 Act General Explanation, supra note 3, at 221–222.

**10.** But see infra note 12.

**11.** I.R.C. § 706(d)(2)(C)(i).

**12.** I.R.C. § 706(d)(2)(C)(ii). This is a rare occurrence in light of current requirements of capitalization for most prepaid expenses. See Reg. § 1.263–4; compare Commissioner v. Boylston Market Ass'n, 131 F.2d 966 (1st Cir.1942), with Zaninovich v. Commissioner, 616 F.2d 429 (9th Cir.1980). See also I.R.C. § 461(i).

**13.** I.R.C. § 706(d)(2)(D)(i).

**14.** I.R.C. § 706(d)(2)(D)(ii).

and added to the basis of partnership assets.[15]

To illustrate what is going on here, assume the equal cash method ABC partnership incurs deductible interest expense of $12,000 in year one which it fails to pay until year two. Assume further that on December 31 of year one, the partnership liquidates partner A's one-third interest, and partner B buys half of one-third partner C's interest so that on January 1 of year two B owns a 75 percent interest in the partnership and C owns a 25 percent interest. Under Sections 706(d)(2)(C)(i) and (D), the $12,000 interest payment made in year two is allocated $4,000 to both B and C.[16] A cannot deduct his $4,000 share of the expense because he is no longer a partner. Instead, that $4,000 must be capitalized, added to the basis of partnership assets and allocated among them according to their relative appreciation under the principles of Section 755.[17]

Tiered partnerships also have been used to avoid the prohibition against retroactive allocations. To illustrate, assume that Loss Associates ("Loss") expects to have substantial tax losses during the year and it wishes to make those losses available to Nupartner, who will not enter the firm until just before the close of the year. The rules of Section 706(d) described above are generally adequate to prevent the parties from fulfilling their objectives. But if the promoters of Loss form new Upper Partnership ("Upper"), which in turn becomes a 95 percent partner in Loss, it may be possible to avoid Section 706(d). If both partnerships use calendar years, 95 percent of Loss's loss for the year will flow through to Upper on December 31 of Loss's taxable year. If Nupartner becomes a 50 percent partner in Upper on December 29, she will be a partner as of the time that Upper's share of Loss's loss passes through, so that a full one-half of that loss could be allocated to her if the interim closing method is used. Section 706(d)(3)[18] prohibits such arrangements by treating Upper (the "upper tier partnership")[19] as if it accrued each item of income or loss that flows through to it from Loss on the day that the item was actually accrued by Loss (the "lower tier partnership").[20] Of course, this type of allocation is necessary, and Section 706(d)(3) is applicable, only if there is a change in the proportionate ownership of the upper tier partnership during the year.

---

**15.** See I.R.C. § 755; Chapter 6B, infra.

**16.** I.R.C. § 706(d)(2)(D)(i).

**17.** See Chapter 6B, infra.

**18.** Section 706(d)(3) essentially codifies the Service's prior position in Rev.Rul. 77–311, 1977–2 C.B. 218.

**19.** Note that Section 706(d)(3) appropriately applies regardless of whether Upper is a cash or accrual method partnership.

**20.** The 1984 Act General Explanation, supra note 3, at 221, explains this provision as follows:

Effectively, under this rule, the existence of the tiered partnership arrangement is ignored for allocation purposes and the items of the lower-tier partnership "flow through" to the partners in the upper-tier partnership in accordance with their effective interests in the lower tier partnership as of the close of each day.

PROBLEMS

**1**. The ABC partnership has three partners, A, B, and C, who each has an equal interest in partnership capital, profits, and losses. To pay off losses incurred by the partnership, C contributed additional capital on October 31 of the current year. As a result of C's contribution, the partners' interests in a partnership capital, profits, and losses changed to 25% for A, 25% for B, and 50% for C. The partnership is an accrual method, calendar year taxpayer.

    (a) If the partnership loses $24,000 in the current year and the partners use the proration method of allocation, how will the losses be allocated?

    (b) What results if the facts are the same as in (a), above, except that the entire $24,000 loss was incurred during the first half of the year but the expenses that created that loss were paid on November 15 with cash contributed to the partnership by C, all other income and deductions of the partnership accrued ratably throughout the year, and the partnership uses the interim closing of the books method of allocation?

    (c) Assume the facts are the same as in (a), above, except that the partnership is a cash method taxpayer, the partnership uses the interim closing of the books method of allocation, and all income and deduction items, other than the $24,000 loss, were received or incurred ratably throughout the year. What result if:

        (i) The loss is the result of payment on November 15 of $24,000 to rent an office for the entire year?

        (ii) The partnership breaks even for the year, but the loss is the result of a settlement of a breach of contract suit brought by Plaintiff. Settlement is made on June 1 and payment is made on November 15?

        (iii) The loss in (i), above, is the result of the payment on March 1 of the current year of $24,000 rent past due from the previous year?

**2**. The AB partnership is a 75% partner in the ABC partnership, in which C owns the other 25%. Both partnerships use the calendar year as their taxable year. The ABC partnership has a tax loss of $16,000 for the year. D becomes a one-third partner in the AB partnership (with A and B owning the other two-thirds equally) on December 1 by making a cash contribution on that date. How will the ABC loss be allocated if the AB (now ABD) partnership uses the proration method? The interim closing method (assuming all income and deductions other than the $16,000 loss accrued ratably throughout the year)?

## F.  THE FAMILY PARTNERSHIP RULES

Code: § 704(e).

Regulations: § 1.704–1(e)(1) & (3)(i)(b). Skim § 1.704–1(e)(2) & (3).

    Section 704(e) governs what are commonly referred to as family partnerships. Although family limited partnerships have become a popular

estate planning technique and raise many challenging wealth transfer tax issues, this discussion is limited to income tax rules that codify familiar assignment of income principles. Section 704(e)(1) utilizes those principles to determine whether a person will be recognized as a partner in a partnership and Section 704(e)(2) applies the same principles to ascertain whether the income generated by a donated partnership interest is being taxed to the appropriate partner. For the most part, the application of these sections is straightforward but inevitably there may be some surprises.

*Section 704(e)(1).* To put Section 704(e)(1) into its proper perspective, we must glance backward at its historical development. In 1946, the Supreme Court held in two cases that a partnership would be recognized as such for federal tax purposes if the parties had a bona fide intent to create a partnership.[1] The Court added that if a party provided either "original capital" or "vital services" to the partnership, that fact would be indicative of an intent to become a member of a partnership. In the succeeding few years, the Tax Court misinterpreted the Supreme Court's message by *requiring* "original capital" or "vital services" in order to form a valid partnership.[2] As a result, the Supreme Court again discussed the issue in the *Culbertson* case,[3] where it redelivered its message:[4]

> * * * We turn next to a consideration of the Tax Court's approach to the family partnership problem. It treated as essential to membership in a family partnership for tax purposes the contribution of either "vital services" or "original capital". Use of these "tests" of partnership indicates, at best, an error in emphasis. It ignores what we said is the ultimate question for decision, namely, "whether the partnership is real within the meaning of the federal revenue laws" and makes decisive what we described as "circumstances [to be taken] into consideration" in making that determination.

> The *Tower* case thus provides no support for such an approach. We there said that the question whether the family partnership is real for income-tax purposes depends upon

>> "whether the partners really and truly intended to join together for the purpose of carrying on business and sharing in the profits or losses or both. And their intention in this respect is a question of fact, to be determined from testimony

**1.** Commissioner v. Tower, 327 U.S. 280, 66 S.Ct. 532 (1946); Lusthaus v. Commissioner, 327 U.S. 293, 66 S.Ct. 539 (1946).

**2.** Scherf v. Commissioner, 7 T.C. 346 (1946), affirmed, 161 F.2d 495 (5th Cir.1947), cert. denied, 332 U.S. 810, 68 S.Ct. 111 (1947); Monroe v. Commissioner, 7 T.C. 278 (1946).

**3.** Commissioner v. Culbertson, 337 U.S. 733, 69 S.Ct. 1210 (1949).

**4.** 337 U.S. at 741, 69 S.Ct. at 1213. (Footnotes omitted.)

disclosed by their 'agreement, considered as a whole, and by their conduct in execution of its provisions.' Drennen v. London Assurance Corp., 113 U.S. 51, 56, 5 S.Ct. 341 [343] 344; Cox v. Hickman, 8 H.L.Cas. 268. We see no reason why this general rule should not apply in tax cases where the Government challenges the existence of a partnership for tax purposes." 327 U.S. at page 287, 66 S.Ct. at page 536.

The question is not whether the services or capital contributed by a partner are of sufficient importance to meet some objective standard supposedly established by the *Tower* case, but whether, considering all the facts—the agreement, the conduct of the parties in execution of its provisions, their statements, the testimony of disinterested persons, the relationship of the parties, their respective abilities and capital contributions, the actual control of income and the purposes for which it is used, and any other facts throwing light on their true intent—the parties in good faith and acting with a business purpose intended to join together in the present conduct of the enterprise. There is nothing new or particularly difficult about such a test. Triers of fact are constantly called upon to determine the intent with which a person acted. The Tax Court, for example, must make such a determination in every estate tax case in which it is contended that a transfer was made in contemplation of death, for "The question, necessarily, is as to the state of mind of the donor." United States v. Wells, 283 U.S. 102, 117, 51 S.Ct. 446, 451 (1931). See Allen v. Trust Co. of Georgia, 326 U.S. 630, 66 S.Ct. 389 (1946). Whether the parties really intended to carry on business as partners is not, we think, any more difficult of determination or the manifestations of such intent any less perceptible than is ordinarily true of inquiries into the subjective.

But the Tax Court did not view the question as one concerning the bona fide intent of the parties to join together as partners. Not once in its opinion is there even an oblique reference to any lack of intent on the part of respondent and his sons to combine their capital and services "for the purpose of carrying on the business." Instead, the court, focusing entirely upon concepts of "vital services" and "original capital," simply decided that the alleged partners had not satisfied those tests when the facts were compared with those in the *Tower* case. The court's opinion is replete with such statements as "we discern nothing constituting what we think is a requisite contribution to a real partnership," "we find no son adding 'vital additional service' which would take the place of capital contributed because of formation of a partnership," and "the sons made no capital contribution, within the sense of the *Tower* case." 6 CCH TCM 698, 699.

Unquestionably a court's determination that the services contributed by a partner are not "vital" and that he has not partici-

pated in "management and control of the business" or contributed "original capital" has the effect of placing a heavy burden on the taxpayer to show the bona fide intent of the parties to join together as partners. But such a determination is not conclusive, and that is the vice in the "tests" adopted by the Tax Court. It assumes that there is no room for an honest difference of opinion as to whether the services or capital furnished by the alleged partner are of sufficient importance to justify his inclusion in the partnership. If, upon a consideration of all the facts, it is found that the partners joined together in good faith to conduct a business having agreed that the services or capital to be contributed presently by each is of such value to the partnership that the contributor should participate in the distribution of profits, that is sufficient. The *Tower* case did not purport to authorize the Tax Court to substitute its judgment for that of the parties; it simply furnished some guides to the determination of their true intent. Even though it was admitted in the *Tower* case that the wife contributed no original capital, management of the business, or other vital services, this Court did not say as a matter of law that there was no valid partnership. We said, instead, that "There was, thus, more than ample evidence to support the Tax Court's finding that no genuine union for partnership business purposes *was ever intended* and that the husband earned the income." 327 U.S. at page 292, 66 S.Ct. at page 538. (Italics added.)

*Third.* The Tax Court's isolation of "original capital" as an essential of membership in a family partnership also indicates an erroneous reading of the *Tower* opinion. We did not say that the donee of an intra-family gift could never become a partner through investment of the capital in the family partnership, any more than we said that all family trusts are invalid for tax purposes in Helvering v. Clifford, supra. The facts may indicate, on the contrary, that the amount thus contributed and the income therefrom should be considered the property of the donee for tax, as well as general law, purposes. In the *Tower* and *Lusthaus* cases this Court, applying the principles of Lucas v. Earl, supra; Helvering v. Clifford, supra; and Helvering v. Horst, 311 U.S. 112, 61 S.Ct. 144, found that the purported gift, whether or not technically complete, had made no substantial change in the economic relation of members of the family to the income. In each case the husband continued to manage and control the business as before, and income from the property given to the wife and invested by her in the partnership continued to be used in the business or expended for family purposes. We characterized the results of the transactions entered into between husband and wife as "a mere paper reallocation of income among the family members," noting that "The actualities of their relation to the income did not change." [327 U.S. at 292, 66 S.Ct. at 538.] This, we thought, provided

ample grounds for the finding that no true partnership was intended; that the husband was still the true earner of the income.

But application of the *Clifford-Horst* principle does not follow automatically upon a gift to a member of one's family, followed by its investment in the family partnership. It if did, it would be necessary to define "family" and to set precise limits of membership therein. We have not done so for the obvious reason that existence of the family relationship does not create a status which itself determines tax questions, but is simply a warning that things may not be what they seem. It is frequently stated that transactions between members of a family will be carefully scrutinized. But, more particularly, the family relationship often makes it possible for one to shift tax incidence by surface changes of ownership without disturbing in the least his dominion and control over the subject of the gift or the purposes for which the income from the property is used. He is able, in other words, to retain "the substance of full enjoyment of all the rights which previously he had in the property." Helvering v. Clifford, supra [at 336.] * * *

The fact that transfers to members of the family group may be mere camouflage does not, however, mean that they invariably are. The *Tower* case recognized that one's participation in control and management of the business is a circumstance indicating an intent to be a bona fide partner despite the fact that the capital contributed originated elsewhere in the family. If the donee of property who then invests it in the family partnership exercises dominion and control over that property—and through that control influences the conduct of the partnership and the disposition of its income—he may well be a true partner. Whether he is free to, and does, enjoy the fruits of the partnership is strongly indicative of the reality of his participation in the enterprise. In the *Tower* and *Lusthaus* cases we distinguished between active participation in the affairs of the business by a donee of a share in the partnership on the one hand, and his passive acquiescence to the will of the donor on the other. This distinction is of obvious importance to a determination of the true intent of the parties. It is meaningless if "original capital" is an essential test of membership in a family partnership.

The cause must therefore be remanded to the Tax Court for a decision as to which, if any, of respondent's sons were partners with him in the operation of the ranch during 1940 and 1941. As to which of them, in other words, was there a bona fide intent that they be partners in the conduct of the cattle business, either because of services to be performed during those years, or because of contributions of capital of which they were the true owners, as we have defined that term in the *Clifford, Horst,* and *Tower* cases? No question as to the allocation of income between capital and

services is presented in this case, and we intimate no opinion on that subject.

In 1951 Congress enacted Section 704(e)(1), which provides statutory guidance to validating a partnership.[5] Nevertheless, this statutory provision is not exclusive and the *Culbertson* case may still come to a taxpayer's assistance if the requirements of Section 704(e)(1) are not satisfied.

*Section 704(e)(2)*. This subsection attempts to guarantee that income generated by a family partnership is not assigned among the partners. It requires that the donor partner's services be adequately compensated and that the rate of return on the donee's capital not exceed the rate of return on the donor's capital. The section applies to all gift situations (not just family gifts) and to any interest in a partnership acquired from a "family" member by purchase.[6] Similar to Section 704(e)(1), Section 704(e)(2) is not exclusive and general assignment of income principles may apply to reallocate income.[7]

## PROBLEMS

**1**. Section 704(e)(1) recognizes a partner if he "owns a capital interest in a partnership in which capital is a material income-producing factor." Consider whether the statutory requirement is satisfied in the following situations:

(a) Father is a lawyer who makes Son (a contractor) and Daughter (a student) partners in his sole practitioner law firm.

(b) Father is a lawyer who makes Daughter (a law-school graduate who has recently passed the bar) a partner in his sole practitioner law firm.

(c) Father owns a building subject to a 10 year lease and he transfers the building along with the lease to a partnership with Son and Daughter.

(d) Father transfers just the lease in part (c), above, to the partnership.

(e) Same as part (c), above, except Father retains the right in any year to allocate the income to any of the partners and to give the building to Mother.

**2**. Father owns a group of commercial rental properties which he transfers to a partnership with Son and Daughter, who provide no consideration for their ⅓ interest in the partnership. The income from the partnership is $90,000.

---

**5.**  See generally Banoff, Long, Steele & Smith, "Family Partnerships: Capital as a Material Income–Producing Factor," 37 Tax Lawyer 275 (1984).

**6.**  Section 704(e)(3) defines "family" to include one's spouse, ancestors, lineal descendants and any trusts for the primary benefit of such persons.

**7.**  See Reg. § 1.704–1(e)(3)(i)(*b*); Woodbury v. Commissioner, 49 T.C. 180 (1967).

(a) What result if Father renders services worth $30,000 to the partnership but the partnership agreement merely calls for splitting the income ⅓ each and each partner actually receives $30,000?

(b) What result if Father renders no services but the agreement provides the income is to be divided 20% to Father and 40% to Son and Daughter?

(c) What result if Father renders services worth $30,000 and the agreement is the same as in part (b), above?

(d) What result if Son renders services worth $30,000 and the agreement is the same as in part (a), above? See Reg. § 1.704–1(e)(3)(i)(b).

(e) What results in parts (a)–(d), above, if Son and Daughter purchased their ⅓ interests from Father for fair market value?

**3**. The AB cash method, calendar year partnership is owned equally by unrelated partners A and B. During the current year, the partnership has $40,000 of net ordinary income after deductions and $20,000 of long-term capital gains. The partnership agrees to compensate B with 10% of its profits each year for his ongoing services in managing the partnership's operations. On July 1, B gives one-half of his interest in the partnership to his son, S, together with the right to all of B's non-services income from the partnership for the entire year. However, B retains the right to all of his one-half share of the partnership's depreciation deductions. Assume that the requirements of § 704(e)(1) are met and that all of the partnership's special allocations are reflected in capital accounts and satisfy the substantial economic effect standard in the § 704(b) regulations. Discuss B and S's income from the partnership for the current year as well as the allocation of the depreciation to B.

CHAPTER 5

# TRANSACTIONS BETWEEN PARTNERS AND PARTNERSHIPS

## A. PAYMENTS FOR SERVICES AND THE USE OF PROPERTY

### 1. INTRODUCTION

Code: Skim § 707(a)(1) & (c).

Regulations: § 1.707–1(a) & (c) (omit the examples).

Up to now, we have been examining how partners are taxed by focusing exclusively on their "distributive shares" of partnership income and deductions, as determined by the partnership agreement[1] and subject to the limitations of Sections 704(b), 704(c) and 706(d). Distributive shares represent the partners' annual return on their interests in the partnership and generally are based on their contributed capital and the services they may render in their capacities as partners. But partners can wear many different hats when they engage in business dealings with their partnerships. Consider, for example, Realtor, who is the general partner in a limited partnership organized to acquire and lease an apartment building. If Realtor also is a mortgage broker who helps arrange financing for the project and is paid a $50,000 fee by the partnership for his services, he may be acting other than in his capacity as a partner. To what extent should the nature of his relationship affect the tax consequences of this transaction to Realtor and the partnership? Should his fee simply be part of his distributive share (an aggregate approach), or should the transaction be treated as if it occurred between the partnership and an unrelated third party (an entity approach)?

Suppose that Realtor also performs ongoing management services for the partnership. The partnership might offer to compensate Realtor with an allocation of the first $100,000 of partnership income, leaving any remaining income or loss to be divided as agreed by all of the partners. But Realtor understandably may balk at a salary that is dependent on partnership profits, demanding instead a fixed annual fee of $100,000, payable upfront, without regard to the income of the partnership. As a general partner with day-to-day management responsibilities, Realtor likely is acting in either case as a partner, not a stranger, and even his guaranteed fee more closely resembles a distributive share than a salary paid to an

---

1. I.R.C. § 704(a).

unrelated third party. Once again, the questions are how and when should Realtor be taxed and how should that treatment affect the partnership.

Sorting out the tax consequences of payments by a partnership for services rendered by partners and a number of other partner-partnership transactions[2] has presented Congress and the courts with a conceptual challenge and offers students of Subchapter K yet another opportunity to witness the tension between the aggregate and entity theories of partnership taxation. Prior to 1954, the cases were in conflict, with a minority of courts applying an entity theory in the interests of simplicity and a majority opting for an aggregate approach.[3] In enacting the 1954 Code, Congress veered toward the entity approach by dividing partner-partnership transactions for services and the use of property into the following three broad categories:

(1) transactions between a partnership and a partner who is not acting in his capacity as a partner—treated by Section 707(a)(1) for all purposes as transactions between the partnership and an unrelated third party;

(2) "guaranteed payments"—i.e., payments to a partner in his partner capacity for services or for the use of capital, if determined without regard to the income of the partnership—treated by Section 707(c) for some purposes as payments of compensation or interest to an unrelated third party but for other purposes (principally timing) as a distributive share; and

(3) any other payments to partners in their capacity as such—e.g., payments for services rendered as a partner which are based on a percentage of partnership profits—which fall outside the ambit of Section 707 and thus are treated as part of a partner's distributive share and, when paid to the partner, are governed by the distribution rules of Section 731.[4]

Over the years, Congress has buttressed this statutory structure with rules to prevent partners from exploiting the flexibility of the partnership form by engaging in maneuvers to defer income, accelerate deductions, convert the character of income and losses and the like.[5] These anti-abuse provisions add to the challenge of planning transactions between a partnership and its partners.

---

**2.** Some other examples are sales and exchanges, loans and leases.

**3.** Compare Wegener v. Commissioner, 119 F.2d 49 (5th Cir.1941), cert. denied, 314 U.S. 643, 62 S.Ct. 84 (1941) (entity approach) with Lloyd v. Commissioner, 15 B.T.A. 82 (1929) (aggregate approach). Advocates of the aggregate approach rejected the entity theory on the ground that partners could not engage in transactions (even in part) with themselves. Those courts thus treated salaries to partners as distributive shares, an approach that engendered confusion when the salaries exceeded the income of the partnership. See, e.g., Appeal of Estate of Tilton, 8 B.T.A. 914 (1927).

**4.** See Chapter 7, infra.

**5.** See, e.g., I.R.C. § 707(a)(2)(A).

## 2. Partner Acting In Nonpartner Capacity

Code: §§ 267(a)(2), (e)(1) & (2); 707(a)(1).

## Pratt v. Commissioner

United States Tax Court, 1975.
64 T.C. 203, affirmed in part, reversed in part 550 F.2d 1023 (5th Cir.1977).

■ Scott, Judge:

[The taxpayers were general partners of two limited partnerships formed to develop and operate a shopping center. Under the partnership agreements, they were paid management fees based on a percentage of gross rentals. The Tax Court found that the fees were reasonable in amount and comparable to fees that would have been paid if an unrelated party had been employed to manage the shopping center. The partners were cash method taxpayers, but the partnership used the accrual method. The fees were accrued and deducted by the partnership but they were not actually paid to the partners during the taxable years in controversy. The issue was the proper tax classification of the fees. The parties' tax agenda was deferral—i.e., the partnership was attempting to claim a current business expense deduction when the fees were accrued but the cash method general partners wished to defer reporting the fees in income until they were received. The Service contended that the fees were for services performed as partners and thus were properly included in the partners' distributive share of partnership income. In rejecting the taxpayers' argument that they received their fees in a nonpartner capacity, the Tax Court discussed the types of transactions that are encompassed by Section 707(a)(1). Ed.]

Section 1.707–1(a) of the Income Tax Regulations with respect to a "partner not acting in capacity as partner" states that "In all cases, the substance of the transaction will govern rather than its form." Here, the record indicates that in managing the partnership petitioners were acting in their capacity as partners. They were performing basic duties of the partnership business pursuant to the partnership agreement. Although we have been unable to find cases arising under the 1954 Code concerning when a partner is acting within his capacity as such, a few cases arising under the provisions of the 1939 Code dealt with whether a payment to a partner should be considered as paid to him in a capacity other than as a partner. See Leif J. Sverdrup, 14 T.C. 859, 866 (1950); Wegener v. Commissioner, 119 F.2d 49 (5th Cir.1941), affg. 41 B.T.A. 857 (1940), cert. denied 314 U.S. 643 (1941). In *Wegener,* a joint venture was treated as a partnership for limited purposes, and the taxpayer-partner was found to be acting outside the scope of his partnership duties and in an individual capacity as an oil well drilling contractor, so that payments he received from the "partnership" for carrying out this separate and distinct activity were income to him individually as if he were an outsider. In the *Sverdrup* case, we recognized a payment to a taxpayer by a joint venture between a

partnership of which the taxpayer was a member and a third party as compensation for work done on contracts being performed by the joint venture since "This sum was not a part of the income of the partnership of which he was a member, but was paid to him as an individual for services rendered to the joint venture."

Petitioners in this case were to receive the management fees for performing services within the normal scope of their duties as general partners and pursuant to the partnership agreement. There is no indication that any one of the petitioners was engaged in a transaction with the partnership other than in his capacity as a partner. * * *

## Armstrong v. Phinney

United States Court of Appeals, Fifth Circuit, 1968.
394 F.2d 661.

■ DYER, CIRCUIT JUDGE.

Appealing from an adverse judgment in the court below, taxpayer, Tobin Armstrong, presents a novel question for our determination: Under the Internal Revenue Code of 1954 is it legally possible for a partner to be an employee of his partnership for purposes of section 119 of the Code? In granting the government's motion for summary judgment, the District Court answered this question in the negative. We disagree and reverse.

Taxpayer is the manager of the 50,000 acre Armstrong ranch located in Armstrong, Texas. Beef cattle are raised and some of the land contains certain mineral deposits. The ranch is owned by a partnership in which taxpayer has a five percent interest. In addition to his share of the partnership profits and a fixed salary for his services as manager of the ranch, the partnership provides taxpayer certain other emoluments which are the subject of this controversy. The partnership provides a home at the ranch for taxpayer and his family, most of the groceries, utilities and insurance for the house, maid service and provides for the entertainment of business guests at the ranch. Taxpayer did not include the value of these emoluments in his gross income for the years 1960, 1961 or 1962. The Internal Revenue Service determined that these items should have been included and therefore increased his taxable income by approximately $6,000 for each year involved. Taxpayer paid the assessed deficiencies, filed a refund claim, and no action having been taken thereon within the requisite period taxpayer brought this suit seeking to recover the paid deficiencies on the ground that he is an employee of the ranch and that, as such, he comes within the provisions of section 119 of the Internal Revenue Code of 1954 and is therefore entitled to exclude the value of the items in question from his gross income. Taxpayer filed an affidavit in support of his allegations and his deposition was taken. Each side moved for a summary judgment. The court granted the government's motion without an opinion and this appeal ensued.

The case law interpreting the 1939 Internal Revenue Code held that a partner could not be an employee of his partnership under any circumstances, and that therefore no partner could take advantage of the "living expense" exclusion promulgated in the regulations and rulings under the 1939 Code. Commissioner of Internal Revenue v. Robinson, 3 Cir.1959, 273 F.2d 503, 84 A.L.R.2d 1211; United States v. Briggs, 10 Cir.1956, 238 F.2d 53; Commissioner of Internal Revenue v. Moran, 8 Cir.1956, 236 F.2d 595; Commissioner of Internal Revenue v. Doak, 4 Cir.1956, 234 F.2d 704. The earlier cases, *Doak* and *Moran,* followed with little discussion by the later cases, were grounded on the theory, present throughout the 1939 Code, that a partnership and its partners are one inseparable legal unit. However, in 1954 Congress rejected this "aggregate theory" in favor of the "entity theory" in cases where "a partner sells property to, or performs services for the partnership." H.R.Rep. No. 1337, 83d Cong., 2d Sess. 67 (1954), U.S.Code Cong. & Admin.News 1954, pp. 4025, 4093. Under the entity approach "the transaction is to be treated in the same manner as though the partner were an outsider dealing with the partnership." Id. This solution to the problem of the characterization of a partner's dealings with his partnership was codified as section 707(a) of the 1954 Code, 26 U.S.C.A. § 707(a).

Considering the legislative history and the language of the statute itself, it was manifestly the intention of Congress to provide that in any situation not covered by section 707(b)–(c), where a partner sells to or purchases from the partnership or renders services to the partnership and is not acting in his capacity as a partner, he is considered to be "an outsider" or "one who is not a partner." The terms "outsider" and "one who is not a partner" are not defined by Congress; neither is the relationship between section 707 and other sections of the Code explained. However, we have found nothing to indicate that Congress intended that this section is not to relate to section 119. Consequently, it is now possible for a partner to stand in any one of a number of relationships with his partnership, including those of creditor-debtor, vendor-vendee, *and* employee-employer. Therefore, in this case the government is not entitled to a judgment as a matter of law.

Our reversal of the District Court is not dispositive of the issues upon which rest taxpayers ultimate right of recovery. On the record before us we cannot resolve these issues, nor do we express any opinion on the final outcome of the case. Among the questions which must be answered are whether taxpayer is, in fact, an employee of the partnership; whether meals and lodging are provided for the convenience of the employer; whether living at the ranch is a condition of taxpayer's employment; whether taxpayer's wife and children are also employees and, if not, how much of the $6,000 must be allocated to their meals and lodging. These questions are not meant to be exhaustive, but are merely intended to give an indication of the nature of the inquiry into the merits which must be held on remand.

Reversed and remanded.

NOTE

The questionable holding in Armstrong v. Phinney suggests that, at least for purposes of Section 119, it is possible for partners to render services to their partnerships in an employee capacity.[1] It is more common for partners who render services to partnerships in a nonpartner capacity under Section 707(a)(1) to do so as independent contractors. Similarly, partners may loan money or lease property to their partnerships in a nonpartner capacity in exchange for payments of interest or rent. In adopting an entity approach, Section 707(a)(1) encompasses not only these types of outbound payments by partnerships to partners but also inbound payments by partners to partnerships for services, or for the use of property or money.[2]

There is a dearth of authority on the question of when a partner is or is not acting in his capacity as such. In *Pratt*, the Tax Court held that a partner is acting as a partner when he performs services that are ongoing and integral to the business of the partnership.[3] Nonpartner status is more likely to exist when a partner is acting in an independent capacity, rendering services of a limited technical nature (e.g., a partner who also is an accountant prepares the partnership's tax returns) or in connection with a specific transaction. The only example of a Section 707(a)(1) transaction in the regulations involves the use by a partnership of a partner's separately owned property to obtain credit or as collateral for a partnership loan.[4] In all other cases, the regulations merely admonish that "the substance of the transaction will govern rather than its form."[5]

Does it make any difference if a payment is classified under Section 707(a)(1) or if it is treated as a distributive share? In the rare case where a partner performing services in a nonpartner capacity is able to attain employee status, exclusions from gross income for certain employee benefits may be available under Code sections outside of Subchapter K.[6] More importantly, the timing and character of the partner's and the partner-

---

**1.** But see Wilson v. United States, 376 F.2d 280 (Ct.Cl.1967), which reached a different conclusion. See also Rev. Rul. 69–184, 1969–1 C.B. 256 (partner may render services to partnership either as a partner or an independent contractor but not as an employee).

**2.** Section 707(a)(1) also applies to sales of property between partners and partnerships. Sales are covered in Section B of this chapter, infra.

**3.** Compare Wegener v. Commissioner, 119 F.2d 49 (5th Cir.1941), affirming 41 B.T.A. 857 (1940), cert. denied, 314 U.S. 643, 62 S.Ct. 84 (1941). See also Rev. Rul. 81–301, 1981–2 C.B. 144, where a partner was determined to be providing investment advisor services in a nonpartner capacity.

**4.** Reg. § 1.707–1(a).

**5.** Id. Cf. I.R.C. § 707(a)(2)(A), which codifies the substance over form approach in the case of certain payments for property or services that are disguised as allocations coupled with distributions. See Section A3 of this chapter, infra.

**6.** For example, in addition to the Section 119 meals and lodging exclusion addressed in Armstrong v. Phinney, employee status may entitle a partner to receive excludable group life insurance and death benefits. See I.R.C. §§ 79(a); 101(b). In the more common situation where partners are not treated as employees, they may be deemed to have employee status for purposes of some excludable fringe benefits. See, e.g., I.R.C. § 401(c)(1) (qualified retirement plans); Reg. § 1.132–1(b)(1) (no additional cost service fringe benefit).

ship's income or losses may be affected. The character of items that are classified as a distributive share is determined at the partnership level[7] and those items pass through to the partners in the year in which the partnership's taxable year ends.[8] In contrast, if Section 707(a)(1) applies, the partner and the partnership generally determine their character and timing consequences as if they were dealing as unrelated parties. Thus, Section 707(a)(1) payments for services or for the use of property or money are always ordinary income to the recipient and are taxed according to the recipient's method of accounting—when received or accrued, depending on whether the recipient is a cash or accrual method taxpayer. The payor ordinarily may deduct such payments as a business expense in accordance with its method of accounting subject to the capitalization requirement of Section 263.[9]

In some cases, these technical differences between Section 707(a)(1) payments and distributive shares are inconsequential. To illustrate, assume that A, B and C, all accrual method taxpayers, are equal partners in an accrual method partnership that has $10,000 of net operating income (all ordinary income) for the year. A allows the partnership to use some of her personally owned property and, in return, the partners agree to allocate $2,500 of partnership income to A and allocate any remaining net income equally among all three partners. If the $2,500 allocated to A (whether or not currently paid) is part of A's distributive share, the taxable income of the partnership is $10,000, allocated $5,000 to A and $2,500 each to B and C. But if A in substance is leasing her property in a nonpartner capacity and the $2,500 is thus a Section 707(a)(1) rent payment, the partnership's taxable income is only $7,500 ($10,000 minus $2,500 rent paid to A), of which $2,500 will be allocated to each partner, and A also must include the $2,500 rent as ordinary income. When the smoke clears, the net tax consequences are essentially the same in either case.

In more complex situations, the tax distinctions between Section 707(a)(1) payments and allocations of distributive shares may shift the character of income among the partners. For example, assume that the ABC partnership's net income for the year consisted of $6,000 long-term capital gains and $4,000 ordinary income. The effect of a $2,500 allocation to A on these facts is to increase A's distributive share of partnership net income from one-third to one-half and to correspondingly decrease the distributive shares of the other partners from one-third to one-quarter each. This results in an allocation to A of $3,000 of capital gains and $2,000 ordinary income, and allocations to B and C of $1,500 capital gains and $1,000 ordinary income. On the other hand, if A received a Section 707(a)(1) rent payment of $2,500 and each partner received an equal one-third share of partnership profits, A would recognize $2,500 of ordinary income under Section 707(a)(1), and the partnership would take a corre-

---

**7.** I.R.C. § 702(b).

**8.** I.R.C. § 706(a).

**9.** But see I.R.C. § 267(a)(2) & (e), which alter the timing of partnership deduc-

tions in certain situations where the partner and the partnership use different methods of accounting. See infra text accompanying notes 10–11.

sponding deduction. A, B and C then each would be taxed on one-third of the partnership's remaining $1,500 of ordinary income and $6,000 capital gain, for a net result of $3,000 ordinary income and $2,000 capital gains for A and $500 ordinary income and $2,000 capital gains to B and C.

To illustrate the timing differences between Section 707(a)(1) payments and distributive shares, assume that Partner A in the example is now a cash method, calendar year taxpayer while the partnership continues to use the accrual method. If the $2,500 payment for the use of A's property were subject to Section 707(a)(1), she would not be required to include the $2,500 until she received it. But if the $2,500 were treated as an allocation, A would be taxable in full at the close of the partnership's year even if actual payment (by a partnership distribution to A) were deferred until the following year.[10]

At one time, taxpayers enjoyed additional timing advantages by classifying certain payments under Section 707(a)(1) when the partnership and the partner used different accounting methods. If partner A in the example were a cash method taxpayer and the partnership used the accrual method, the partnership could accrue and deduct the $2,500 in year one but delay actual payment (and thus inclusion in A's income) until year two. To prevent taxpayers from exploiting this mismatching of income and deductions in the partnership setting, Congress extended the timing restraints of Section 267 to transactions between partners and partnerships.[11] Section 267(a)(2), in conjunction with Section 267(e), now provides that a deduction may not be taken prior to the year in which the amount is includible in the gross income of the payee. Thus, an accrual method partnership may not deduct an item owed to a cash method partner prior to the year in which the item is paid and properly included in the payee's income.[12]

## PROBLEMS

**1**. Armstrong v. Phinney holds that a partner who is compensated for services under § 707(a)(1) can achieve "employee" status outside of Subchapter K.

> (a) What types of services are within § 707(a)(1)? Are they normally the types of services rendered by "employees?"

> (b) What Code sections may come into play if a partner attains "employee" status or is deemed to be an employee?

---

**10.** The timing results are similar in the case of guaranteed payments under Section 707(c). See Section A4 of this chapter, infra.

**11.** Section 267 previously did not apply to these transactions because partnerships and partners were not treated as related parties for this purpose.

**12.** I.R.C. § 267(a)(2). Section 267 likewise would apply to defer a partner's deduc-

tion when a partner accrued an otherwise deductible expense payable to a cash method partnership in which he was a partner. If Section 707 applies to a payment of deferred compensation for services (other than pursuant to a qualified plan), Section 404(a) would defer the payor's deduction until such time as the payee included the amount in income, whether or not the parties were related.

**2.** The AB partnership is in the real estate development business. The partnership recently was involved in a lawsuit concerning the legal title to a parcel of land it acquired. The partnership paid partner B, who is a lawyer, a $5,000 fee to represent it in the legal proceedings. How should the partnership and B treat the payment for tax purposes?

## 3.   DISGUISED PAYMENTS

Code: §  707(a)(2)(A).

If a partnership pays a partner for services or the use of property in a transaction governed by Section 707(a)(1) and the expense is capital in nature (e.g., organizational fees),[1] the partnership must treat the payment for tax purposes as if it were made to an unrelated third party—i.e., as a capital expenditure which, at best, may be deducted or amortized over the applicable recovery period. The timing ramifications of structuring a payment to a partner for services or property as an allocation rather than as a payment governed by Section 707(a)(1) would be dramatic if parties could convert a capital expenditure into a currently deductible expense. Section 707(a)(2)(A) prevents taxpayers from disguising payments for services or property in order to achieve this timing advantage.[2]

To illustrate, assume the equal ABC partnership has net income of $30,000 before compensating partner A for $30,000 of services rendered in A's nonpartner capacity in connection with the acquisition of a nondepreciable asset for the firm. Because the expenditure directly relates to the creation of an asset with a life extending substantially beyond the taxable year, the partnership would be required to capitalize the payment under Section 263, and its taxable income would remain at $30,000, resulting in a $10,000 distributive share to each partner and an additional $30,000 of ordinary income to A under Section 707(a)(1).

If the parties restructured the arrangement by specially allocating $30,000 to A and followed up with a distribution of that same amount, the tax consequences would differ dramatically if the form of the arrangement were respected. The partnership's $30,000 of net income all would pass through to A, reducing A's total income from $40,000 to $30,000[3] and leaving B and C with no income. If this technique were successful, the partnership would be allowed the equivalent of a current deduction for an expense that should have been capitalized. The parties similarly might circumvent the capitalization requirement using comparable arrangements under which a partner transfers the use of property to the partnership in return for a share of profits in circumstances where the partnership would

---

**1.**  I.R.C. § 709.

**2.**  A companion provision, Section 707(a)(2)(B), attacks the related device of disguised sales. Sales between partners and partnerships are examined in Section C2 of this chapter, infra.

**3.**  The $10,000 difference is somewhat deceptive. If A were taxed on a $10,000 distributive share, he would increase his outside basis by that amount and eventually would have $10,000 less income on a sale or liquidation of his partnership interest.

be required to capitalize the payment if it were rent paid to an unrelated third party.[4]

To be sure, these maneuvers are not easily accomplished. The risk-averse service partner or lessor of property might be unwilling to accept compensation in the form of a distributive share that is dependent on partnership profits. But resourceful tax advisors devised techniques to assure partners that what might resemble a mere profit share was actually devoid of risk and thus practically guaranteed. The Service's chances of recasting these transactions[5] were impeded by the hazy line dividing the various forms of partner/partnership transactions.

Congress removed these planning opportunities when it enacted Section 707(a)(2)(A). The following excerpt from the legislative history explains the operation of this provision and surveys the factors that Congress considered most important in enforcing it:[6]

> The Act provides that, under Treasury regulations, if (1) a partner performs services for, or transfers property to, a partnership, (2) there is a related direct or indirect partnership allocation and distribution to the partner, and (3) when viewed together, the performance of such services (or the transfer of such property) and the allocation/distribution are properly characterized as a transaction between the partnership and a partner acting in a non-partner capacity, the transaction is to be treated as a transaction between the partnership and a person who is not a partner. In such a case, the amount paid to the partner in consideration for the property or services is treated as a payment for services or property provided to the partnership (as the case may be), and, where appropriate, the partnership must capitalize these amounts (or otherwise treat such amounts in a manner consistent with their recharacterization). The partnership must also treat the purported allocation to the partner performing services or transferring property to the partnership as a payment to a non-partner in determining the remaining partners' shares of taxable income or loss.

> Congress did not intend that this provision apply in every instance in which a partner acquires an interest in a partnership and also performs services for or transfers property to the partnership. In particular, Congress did not intend to repeal the general rule under which gain or loss is not recognized on a contribution of

---

**4.** For example, if property leased by a partner to a partnership were used by the partnership to create or acquire an asset which was capital in nature (e.g., equipment leased to construct a building), the rent payment would not be currently deductible but would be added to the basis of the created or acquired asset. See Commissioner v. Idaho Power Co., 418 U.S. 1, 94 S.Ct. 2757 (1974).

**5.** See, e.g., Rev.Rul. 81–301, 1981–2 C.B. 144.

**6.** Staff of the Joint Committee on Taxation, General Explanation of the Revenue Provisions of the Deficit Reduction Act of 1984, 98th Cong., 2d Sess. 226–229 (1984).

property in return for a partnership interest (section 721),[7] or to apply this new provision in cases in which a partner receives an allocation (or an increased allocation) for an extended period to reflect his contribution of property or services to the partnership and the facts and circumstances indicate that the partner is receiving the allocation in his capacity as a partner. However, Congress did intend that the provision apply to allocations which are determined to be related to the performance of services for, or the transfer of property to, the partnership and which, when viewed together with distributions, have the substantive economic effect of direct payments for such property or services under the facts and circumstances of the case.

The Act authorizes the Treasury Department to prescribe such regulations as may be necessary or appropriate to carry out the purposes of the provision. In prescribing these regulations, the Treasury should be mindful that Congress is concerned with transactions that work to avoid capitalization requirements or other rules and restrictions governing direct payments and not with nonabusive allocations that accurately reflect the various economic contributions of the partners. These regulations may apply the provision both to one-time transactions and to continuing arrangements which utilize purported partnership allocations and distributions in place of direct payments. Congress specifically intended that the provision apply to allocations used to pay partnership organization or syndication fees, subject to the general principles above.

The regulations will provide, when appropriate, that the purported partner performing services for or transferring property to the partnership is not a partner at all for tax purposes. If it is determined that the service performer or property transferor actually is a partner (because of other transactions), Congress believed that the factors described below should be considered in determining whether the partner is receiving the putative allocation and distribution in his capacity as a partner.

The first, and generally the most important, factor is whether the payment is subject to an appreciable risk as to amount. Partners extract the profits of the partnership with reference to the business success of the venture, while third parties generally receive payments which are not subject to this risk. Thus, an allocation and distribution provided for a service partner under the partnership agreement which subjects the partner to significant entrepreneurial risk as to both the amount and the fact of payment generally should be recognized as a distributive share and a partnership distribution, while an allocation and distribution pro-

---

**7.** Of course, if a partner received an interest in a partnership in exchange for services, he may recognize income upon that receipt; however, this issue arises only in situations where Rev.Proc. 93–27 does not apply. See Chapter 2C3, supra.

vided to a service partner under the partnership agreement which involve limited risk as to amount and payment should generally be treated as a fee under section 707(a). Examples of allocations that limit a partner's risk include both "capped" allocations of partnership income (i.e., percentage or fixed dollar amount allocations subject to an annual maximum amount when the parties could reasonably expect the cap to apply in most years) and allocations for a fixed number of years under which the income that will go to the partner is reasonably certain. Similarly, continuing arrangements in which purported allocations and distributions (under a formula or otherwise) are fixed in amount or reasonably determinable under all the facts and circumstances and which arise in connection with services also shield the purported partner from entrepreneurial risk. Although short-lived gross income allocations are particularly suspect in this regard, gross income allocations may, in very limited instances, represent an entrepreneurial return, which is classifiable as a distributive share under section 704. Similarly, although net income allocations appear generally to constitute distributive shares, some net income allocations may be fixed as to amount and probability of payment and should, if coupled with a distribution or payment from the partnership, be characterized as fees.

The second factor is whether the partner status of the recipient is transitory. Transitory partner status (which limits the duration of a purported joint undertaking for profit) suggests that a payment is a fee or is in return for property. The fact that partner status is continuing, however, is of no particular relevance in establishing that an allocation and distribution are received in an individual's capacity as a partner.

The third factor is whether the allocation and distribution that are made to the partner are close in time to the partner's performance of services for or transfer of property to the partnership. An allocation close in time to the performance of services, or the transfer of property, is more likely to be related to the services or property. In the case of continuing arrangements, the time at which income is scheduled to be allocated to the partner may be a factor indicating that an allocation is, in fact, a disguised payment. When the income subject to allocation arises over an extended period or is remote in time from the services or property contributed by a partner, the risk of not receiving payment (the first factor described above) may also increase.

The fourth factor is whether, under all the facts and circumstances, it appears that the recipient became a partner primarily to obtain tax benefits for himself or the partnership which would not have been available if he had rendered services to the partnership in a third party capacity. The fact that a partner also has

significant non-tax motivations in becoming a partner is of no particular relevance.

The fifth factor, which relates to purported allocations/distributions for services, is whether the value of the recipient's interest in general and continuing partnership profits is small in relation to the allocation in question (thus suggesting that the purported allocation is, in fact, a fee). This is especially significant if the allocation for services is for a limited period of time. The fact that the recipient's interest in general and continuing partnership profits is substantial does not, however, suggest that the purported partnership allocation/distribution arrangement should be recognized.

The sixth factor, which relates to purported allocations/distributions for property [see Section B3 of this chapter, infra. Ed.] is whether the requirement that capital accounts be respected under section 704(b) (and the proposed regulations thereunder) makes income allocations which are disguised payments for capital economically unfeasible and therefore unlikely to occur. This generally will be the case unless (i) the valuation of the property contributed by the partner to the partnership is below the fair market value of such property (thus improperly understating the amount in such partner's capital account), or (ii) the property is sold by the partner to the partnership at a stated price below the fair market value of such property, or (iii) the capital account will be respected at such a distant point in the future that its present value is small and there is to be no meaningful return on the capital account in the intervening period.

Congress anticipated that the Treasury Department may describe other factors that are relevant in evaluating whether a purported allocation and distribution should be respected. In applying these various factors, the Treasury and the courts should be careful not to be misled by possibly self-serving assertions in the partnership agreement as to the duties of a partner in his partner capacity but should instead seek to determine the substance of the transaction.

In the case of allocations which are only partly determined to be related to the performance of services for, or the transfer of property to, the partnership, the provision applies to that portion of the allocation which is reasonably determined to be related to the property or services provided to the partnership. Finally, it was anticipated that Treasury regulations will provide for the coordination of this provision with the preexisting rules of section 707 and other provisions of subchapter K such as section 736.

Congress did not intend to create any inference regarding the tax treatment of the transactions described above under prior law.

## PROBLEMS

**1.** A (a cash method taxpayer) is an equal partner in the ABCD partnership (an accrual method taxpayer) and has a $10,000 outside basis in her partnership interest. A owns depreciable personal property (adjusted basis—$2,000; fair market value—$15,000; fair rental value—$1,000 per year) which the partnership will use in its business. Before any of the transactions described below, the partnership has $10,000 of net income each year. What result in the following alternatives?

  (a) A leases the property to the partnership for three years. The partnership will pay A $1,000 per year for three years for the use of the property.

  (b) What result in (a), above, if the rental payments are made on January 31 of the year following accrual?

  (c) A transfers the property to the partnership, which will use it for three years and transfer it back to A at the end of that period. The partnership makes a special allocation of its first $1,000 of net income to A. What result to A? What if, instead, the first $3,000 of the first year's net income and no subsequent income in excess of her one-quarter share is allocated to A?

**2.** Consider the following example adapted from the legislative history of § 707(a)(2)(A):

A commercial office building constructed by a partnership is projected to generate gross income of at least $100,000 per year indefinitely. Architect, whose normal fee for architectural services is $40,000, contributes cash for a 25% interest in the partnership and receives both a 25% distributive share of net income for the life of the partnership and an allocation of $20,000 of partnership gross income for the first two years of partnership operations after the property is leased. The partnership expects to have sufficient cash available to distribute $20,000 to Architect in each of the first two years, and the agreement requires such a distribution.

What factors are most important in determining whether the $20,000 allocation of gross income to Architect is a share of profits or a § 707(a)(2)(A) payment?

## 4.   GUARANTEED PAYMENTS

Code: § 707(c).

Regulations: § 1.707–1(c).

Guaranteed payments are payments by a partnership to a partner for services or for the use of capital which are determined without regard to partnership income. In the services context, a guaranteed payment resembles a salary. For example, if a real estate partnership paid its general partner a fixed annual amount for ongoing management services, irrespective of partnership profits, the fee would be classified as a guaranteed

payment. A typical guaranteed payment for the use of capital would be a preferred return (e.g., 10 percent of a partner's initial cash contribution) on a partner's equity investment, payable in all events before any allocation of income or losses among the partners.

Guaranteed payments have some of the characteristics of Section 707(a)(1) payments in that they are fixed payments for services or the use of property. But they resemble distributive shares in that they relate to services or contributed capital that are an integral part of the partnership's ongoing activities. They are thus made to partners in their capacity as partners rather than as unrelated third parties. Guaranteed payments also are a hybrid for tax purposes. Like Section 707(a)(1) payments, they are treated for some purposes as made to a person who is not a member of the partnership. As such, they are taxable to the partner as ordinary income regardless of the amount or character of the partnership's taxable income, and they are deductible by the partnership under Section 162, subject to the capitalization requirement of Section 263.[1] For timing purposes, however, guaranteed payments resemble distributive shares in that they are included in income for a partner's taxable year "within or with which ends the partnership taxable year in which the partnership deducted such payments as paid or accrued under its method of accounting."[2] The partner thus must include them in income whether or not they are received.

Since a guaranteed payment is taxable whether or not it has been received, a mechanism is necessary to ensure that the partner is not taxed a second time when the payment is actually received. Perhaps the partner simply takes a tax cost basis in the guaranteed payment and thus has no further income when the payment is received.[3] On the other hand, footnote 16 of the *Gaines* case suggests that when the partner is taxed on a guaranteed payment, he simply increases his outside basis in his partnership interest, as he would when he reports his distributive share. If that is the case, receipt of the payment, like receipt of a partner's distributive share, simply would reduce the partner's outside basis under Section 705. While the language of Section 707(c) seems to imply that a guaranteed payment is treated as a distributive share for all purposes other than characterization of the partner's income and allowance of a deduction to the partnership, the section has not been construed quite so broadly by the Service. The regulations[4] state that the recipient of a guaranteed payment is treated as a partner rather than as an employee for fringe benefit purposes and also provide that a guaranteed payment is not treated as an interest in the partnership for purposes of several sections whose application varies depending on the size of the partner's interest.[5] Regrettably, there is no definitive authority on many of these issues.

---

**1.** I.R.C. § 707(c). Gaines v. Commissioner, infra. See also Cagle v. Commissioner, 63 T.C. 86 (1974), affirmed, 539 F.2d 409 (5th Cir.1976), the result of which was codified in Section 707(c) by the Tax Reform Act of 1976.

**2.** Reg. § 1.707–1(c).

**3.** See McKee, Nelson & Whitmire, Federal Taxation of Partnerships and Partners ¶ 13.03[5] (3d ed. 1996).

**4.** Reg. § 1.707–1(c).

**5.** The regulations provide that guaranteed payments are not treated as a profit share for purposes of Section 706(b)(3) (adop-

# Gaines v. Commissioner

United States Tax Court, 1982.
45 T.C.M. 363.

■ PARKER, JUDGE.

* * *

*Issue No. 2: Guaranteed Payments*

Findings of Fact

On their partnership returns for the year 1973, Lincoln Manor, Brookwood, Gaines Realty, and Riverbend each claimed as deductions certain guaranteed payments to partners. Gaines Properties was a general partner in each of these partnerships. The amounts claimed by the limited partnerships as deductions for guaranteed payments to partners and Gaines Properties' share of those guaranteed payments were as follows:

| Partnership | Amount Claimed | Gaines Properties' Share |
|-------------|----------------|--------------------------|
| Lincoln Manor | $ 74,131.26 | $ 23,750.00 |
| Brookwood | 109,666.00 | 88,666.00 |
| Gaines Realty | 125,881.00 | 91,006.00 |
| Riverbend | 216,087.00 | 104,168.50 |

Each of the four limited partnerships accrued and claimed deductions for these guaranteed payments. Lincoln Manor, Brookwood, Gaines Realty, and Riverbend all used the accrual method of accounting on their 1973 partnership returns. Gaines Properties reported its income using the cash receipts and disbursements method of accounting. Gaines Properties never received any of the guaranteed payments and did not report them in its income.

Respondent determined that Gaines Properties should have reported as income the guaranteed payments accrued and deducted by the four limited partnerships. Respondent, however, disallowed portions of the deductions that the four limited partnerships claimed for these guaranteed payments, on the ground that some portions were capital expenditures and not currently deductible.

*Issue No. 2: Guaranteed Payments*

Opinion

Lincoln Manor, Brookwood, Riverbend, and Gaines Realty accrued and claimed deductions on their partnership returns for certain "guaranteed payments," including guaranteed payments to Gaines Properties, a general partner of each limited partnership. Gaines Properties never received these guaranteed payments. Respondent disallowed to the limited partnership portions of the claimed deductions for guaranteed payments, including

tion of a partnership taxable year), Section 707(b) (disallowance of certain losses and characterization of gains) and Section 708(b) (forced termination of a partnership).

some of the deductions attributable to the guaranteed payments to Gaines Properties. Notwithstanding this partial disallowance of deductions at the partnership level, respondent determined that the *entire amount* of the guaranteed payments to Gaines Properties, including the portion disallowed as deductions at the partnership level, should be included in Gaines Properties' income. Petitioners argue that the guaranteed payments that Gaines Properties did not receive, or at least such payments to the extent that the deductions therefor were disallowed at the partnership level, were not includable in Gaines Properties' income. Respondent argues that Gaines Properties' share of these guaranteed payments was includable in its income regardless of the fact that the deduction was partially disallowed at the partnership level and regardless of the fact that Gaines Properties, which used the cash method of accounting, never received the payments. We agree with respondent.

Section 707(c), as in effect in 1973, provided:

> To the extent determined without regard to the income of the partnership, payments to a partner for services or the use of capital shall be considered as made to one who is not a member of the partnership, but only for the purposes of section 61(a) (relating to gross income) and section 162(a) (relating to trade or business expenses).

This case does in fact involve "guaranteed payments" to a partner within the meaning of section 707(c) of the Code. The fact that no actual payments were made does not affect the status of these transactions as section 707(c) guaranteed payments. "[D]espite the use of the word 'payments' in both § 707(c) and the Regulations thereunder, it is clear that no actual payment need be made; if the partnership deducts the amount under its method of accounting, the 'recipient' partner must include the amount in income in the appropriate year." W. McKee, W. Nelson and R. Whitmire, Federal Taxation of Partnerships and Partners (hereinafter McKee, Nelson and Whitmire), par. 13.03[2], pp. 13–16. See also Pratt v. Commissioner, 64 T.C. 203, 213 (1975), affd. on this point and revd. on other grounds 550 F.2d 1023 (5th Cir.1977); sec. 1.707–1(c), Income Tax Regs. The parties stipulated that each of the four limited partnerships deducted "guaranteed payments." The partnership agreements of Brookwood and Gaines Realty expressly stated that certain payments to partners "shall constitute guaranteed payments within the meaning of section 707(c) of the Code." While the descriptions of such payments in the partnership agreements are not binding upon us (Doyle v. Mitchell Bros. Co., 247 U.S. 179, 187 (1918)), the payments referred to in those two partnership agreements are clearly fixed sums determined without regard to partnership income. See Sec. 707(c); Sec. 1.707–1(c), Income Tax Regs. Furthermore, it is equally clear that the payments to the partners were for services in their capacities as partners. Respondent in his notices of deficiency determined that these payments were in fact guaranteed payments under section 707(c), and petitioners did not dispute this determination. Accordingly, we hold that the payments here were guaranteed payments within the meaning of section 707(c).

The statutory language of section 707(c) addresses only the character of the guaranteed payments and not the timing. Respondent's regulation under section 707(c), section 1.707–1(c), Income Tax Regs., addresses the timing question, as follows:

> Payments made by a partnership to a partner for services or for the use of capital are considered as made to a person who is not a partner, to the extent such payments are determined without regard to the income of the partnership. However, a partner must include such payments as ordinary income for his taxable year within or with which ends the partnership taxable year in which the partnership deducted such payments as paid or accrued under its method of accounting. See section 706(a) and paragraph (a) of § 1.706–1.

As the regulation makes clear, the statutory authority for the timing of the inclusion of these guaranteed payments is section 706(a), which provides:

> In computing the taxable income of a partner for a taxable year, the inclusions required by section 702 and section 707(c) with respect to a partnership shall be based on the income, gain, loss, deduction, or credit of the partnership for any taxable year of the partnership ending within or with the taxable year of the partner.

The separate reference of section 707(c) guaranteed payments in the timing provisions of section 706(a) was explained by the Senate Report as simply—

> to make clear that payments made to a partner for services or for the use of capital are includible in his income at the same time as his distributive share of partnership income for the partnership year when the payments are made or accrued * * *. (S.Rept. No. 1622, to accompany H.R. 8300 (Pub.L. No. 591), 83d Cong., 2d Sess. 385 (1954)).

In Cagle v. Commissioner, 63 T.C. 86 (1974), affd. 539 F.2d 409 (5th Cir.1976), we held that includability and deductibility of guaranteed payments are two separate questions, and specifically that guaranteed payments are not automatically deductible simply by reason of their being included in the recipient's income. In *Cagle,* we stated 63 T.C. at 95:

> We think that all Congress meant was that guaranteed payments should be included in the recipient partner's income in the partnership taxable year ending with or within which the partner's taxable year ends and in which the tax accounting treatment of the transaction is determined at the partnership level. S.Rept. No. 1622, supra at pp. 94, 385, 387.

We believe our statement in *Cagle* is an accurate description of the Congressional intent. We have found nothing in the statutory language, regulations, or legislative history to indicate that includability in the recipient partner's income was intended to be dependent upon deductibility at the partnership level.

Petitioners seem to argue that there is a patent unfairness in taxing them on nonexistent income, namely income that they have neither received nor benefitted from (e.g. through a tax deduction at the partnership level). Their argument has a superficial appeal to it, but on closer analysis must fail. Except for certain very limited purposes, guaranteed payments are treated as part of the partner's distributive share of partnership income and loss. Sec. 1.707–1(c), Income Tax Regs. For timing purposes guaranteed payments are treated the same as distributive income and loss. Sec. 706(a); sec. 1.706–1(a) and sec. 1.707–1(c), Income Tax Regs. A partner's distributive share of partnership income is includable in his taxable income for any partnership year ending within or with the partner's taxable year. Sec. 706(a). As is the case with a partner's ordinary distributive share of partnership income and loss, any unfairness in taxing a partner on guaranteed payments that he neither receives nor benefits from results from the conduit theory of partnerships, and is a consequence of the taxpayer's choice to do the business in the partnership form.[16] We find no justification in the statute, regulations, or legislative history to permit these petitioners to recognize their income pro rata as deductions are allowed to the partnership. See also Pratt v. Commissioner, 64 T.C. 203, 213 (1975), affd. on this ground 550 F.2d 1023 (5th Cir.1977). We hold for respondent on the guaranteed payments issue.

## Revenue Ruling 69–180

1969–1 Cum.Bull. 183.

Advice has been requested as to the proper method for computing the partners' distributive shares of the partnership's ordinary income and capital gains under the circumstances described below.

$F$ and $G$ are partners in $FG$, a two-man partnership. The partnership agreement provides that $F$ is to receive 30 percent of the partnership income as determined before taking into account any guaranteed amount, but not less than $100x$ dollars. The agreement also provides that any guaranteed amount will be treated as an expense item of the partnership in any year in which $F$'s percentage of profits is less than the guaranteed amount. The partnership agreement makes no provision for sharing capital gains.

For the taxable year in question the partnership income before taking into account any guaranteed amount, is $200x$ dollars, and consists of $120x$ dollars of ordinary income and $80x$ dollars of capital gains.

Section 707(c) of the Internal Revenue Code of 1954 provides that, to the extent determined without regard to the income of the partnership, payments to a partner for services or the use of capital shall be considered as made to one who is not a member of the partnership, but only for the

---

**16.** As part of a partner's distributive share of profit and loss, the guaranteed payments included in his income increase the partner's basis in his partnership interest. Sec. 705(a)(1) and (2).

purpose of section 61(a) (relating to gross income) and section 162(a) of the Code (relating to trade or business expenses). Section 1.707–1(c) of the Income Tax Regulations provides that for purposes of section 61(a) of the Code guaranteed payments are regarded as a partner's distributive share of ordinary income. Thus, a guaranteed payment is includible in gross income of the recipient as ordinary income, and is deductible by the partnership from its ordinary income as a business expense.

For Federal income tax purposes, $F$'s guaranteed payment, as defined under section 707(c) of the Code is $40x$ dollars, $100x$ dollars (minimum guarantee) less $60x$ dollars distributive share (30 percent of partnership income of $200x$ dollars). See Example 2 of section 1.707–1(c) of the regulations and Revenue Ruling 66–95, C.B. 1966–1, 169.

After the guaranteed payment is taken into account, the partnership's ordinary income is $80x$ dollars ($120x$ dollars of ordinary income less the $40x$ dollars guaranteed payment which is deductible by the partnership as a business expense under section 162 of the Code).

For Federal income tax purposes, the taxable income of the partnership amounts to $160x$ dollars ($80x$ dollars of ordinary income and $80x$ dollars of capital gains).

Section 704(b) of the Code and section 1.704–1(b)(1) of the regulations provide that if the partnership agreement does not specifically provide for the manner of sharing a particular item or class of items of income, gain, loss, deduction, or credit of the partnership, a partner's distributive share of any such item shall be determined in accordance with the manner provided in the partnership agreement for the division of the general profits or losses (that is, the taxable income or loss of the partnership as described in section 702(a)[8] of the Code). In applying this rule, the manner in which the net profit or loss (computed after excluding any item subject to a recognized special allocation) is actually credited on the partnership books to the accounts of the partners will generally determine each partner's share of taxable income or loss as described in section 702(a)[8] of the Code. Thus, $F$ and $G$ share the capital gains in the same ratio in which they share the general profits from business operations.

The partnership income for the taxable year, after deduction of the guaranteed payment, is $160x$ dollars. Of this amount, $F$'s distributive share, as determined above under the partnership agreement is $60x$ dollars. Therefore, $G$'s distributive share is $100x$ dollars. Hence, the effective profit sharing ratio for the year in question is 6/16 for $F$ and 10/16 for $G$. Thus, as provided by section 704(b) of the Code, the partnership capital gains as well as the partnership ordinary income are to be shared in the ratio of 6/16 for $F$ and 10/16 for $G$.

Accordingly, the amounts of ordinary income and capital gains to be reported by the partners in this case are as follows:

|                        | **F**         | **G**          | **Total**       |
| --- | --- | --- | --- |
| Ordinary income .............. | 30x dollars   | 50x dollars    | 80x dollars     |
| Guaranteed payment ......... | 40x dollars   |                | 40x dollars     |
| Total ordinary income ....... | 70x dollars   | 50x dollars    | 120x dollars    |
| Capital gains ................ | 30x dollars   | 50x dollars    | 80x dollars     |
| Total ...................... | 100x dollars  | 100x dollars   | 200x dollars    |

## NOTE

Section 707(c) apparently was enacted to make it clear that a partner realizes income as a result of receiving payments for services or capital in his partner capacity. Section 707(a) makes the same conceptual point for partners who receive similar payments while acting in a nonpartner capacity. The two provisions operate similarly except that, for timing purposes, guaranteed payments are treated as a distributive share of partnership profits. Do these differences make sense? Do they justify the need to distinguish between payments made to an individual in his partner or nonpartner capacity?

These strange distinctions have prompted commentators to urge Congress to take a closer look at Section 707(c) and possibly even repeal it.[1] In its 1997 review of partnership tax issues, the Joint Committee on Taxation floated the following proposal, which is likely to be considered if Congress should ever engage in a comprehensive review of Subchapter K:[2]

> The [Joint Committee staff's] proposal would repeal the present-law provisions governing guaranteed payments made to a partner for capital. Thus, a guaranteed payment to a partner with respect to capital would be treated according to its substance either as a deemed non-partner payment (sec. 707(a)), or as an allocation of partnership income to the recipient partner combined with a distribution (sec. 704(b)). It is expected that most guaranteed payments for capital would qualify as deemed non-partner payments that would be characterized as interest on debt for Federal tax purposes.

> The proposal would retain the present-law concept of guaranteed payments for services, but would amend the treatment of such payments to conform with non-partner service payments. For service payments, the proposal would retain the present-law concepts of both guaranteed payments for services and payments for services that are performed in a non-partner capacity. However, the proposal would treat both types of payments in the same

---

**1.** See Brannan, "The Subchapter K Reform Act of 1997," 75 Tax Notes 121, 126–129 (April 7, 1997); Banoff, "Guaranteed Payments for the Use of Capital: Schizophrenia in Subchapter K," 70 Taxes 820 (1992); Postlewaite & Cameron, "Twisting Slowly in the Wind: Guaranteed Payments After the Tax Reform Act of 1984," 40 Tax Lawyer 649 (1986).

**2.** Joint Committee on Taxation, Review of Selected Entity Classification and Partnership Tax Issues 47 (JCS–6–97), April 8, 1997.

manner, applying the present-law rules for deemed non-partner payments under section 707(a), such as inclusion of such payments in gross income under the recipient's method of accounting.

## PROBLEMS

**1**. The AB equal partnership is in a highly speculative business in which profits fluctuate widely. For the current year the partnership has profits of $20,000, of which $12,000 is ordinary income and $8,000 is long-term capital gain. A and B share profits and losses equally unless otherwise provided. A renders services to the partnership which are continuous, related to the function of the partnership and not in the nature of a capital expenditure.

    (a) What result to A, B, and AB if A worked for the partnership and was required to be paid $15,000 per year for his services regardless of the income of the partnership?

    (b) What result in (a), above, if A's services relate to improvements on land owned by the partnership?

    (c) What results if A renders the services under an agreement that he will receive $15,000 or 50% of the profits before taking into account any guaranteed payments, whichever is greater, and the profits are $20,000, consisting of $12,000 of ordinary income and $8,000 of long-term capital gain?

    (d) What result in (a) and (c), above, if A's compensation is not for services but is received as a guaranteed return on A's contributed capital to the partnership?

**2**. G, a cash method taxpayer, is a one-third partner in the FGH accrual method partnership. G is employed by the partnership and is entitled to a guaranteed payment of $10,000 for year one. G's outside basis during year one is zero. G's agreement with the partnership specifies that he will receive the $10,000 guaranteed payment on June 1 of year three. On January 1 of year two, the partnership sells an asset (basis $15,000, fair market value $15,000) and distributes $5,000 cash to each partner. What result to G?

**3**. In a situation similar to that in Revenue Ruling 69–180, supra p. 238 is it possible for amounts paid to a partner in excess of the guaranteed payment to be classified as a Section 707(a)(1) payment?

**4**. Partner renders services worth $10,000 to Partnership in which he is a partner. Without regard to Partner's services, Partnership has $75,000 of ordinary income and $25,000 of long-term capital gain for the year. Both Partner and Partnership are calendar year taxpayers, but Partner uses the cash method of accounting and Partnership uses the accrual method. Partnership makes no payment to Partner during the year, but where permitted it accrues the expense, which is currently deductible under Section 162. Determine the tax consequences of the following alternative transactions to Partner and Partnership:

(a) In recognition of his services, Partner is allocated the first $10,000 of partnership profits, which is treated as part of his distributive share.

(b) Section 707(a)(1) applies because the services are unrelated to the everyday conduct of Partnership's activities and are not continuous. See § 267(a)(2) and (e).

(c) Section 707(c) applies because the services are ongoing services related to Partnership's activities but are paid without regard to Partnership income.

(d) Partner is allocated $10,000, which is treated under § 707(a)(2)(A) as a § 707(a)(1) payment.

## B.   SALES AND EXCHANGES OF PROPERTY BETWEEN PARTNERS AND PARTNERSHIPS

Code: §§ 267(a)(1), (c), (d); 453(g); 707(a), (b); 1239(a).

Regulations: § 1.707–1(b); –3(a), (b), (c), (d); –5(a)(1), (6) & (7).

Sales and exchanges of property between partners and their partnerships raise classification issues similar to those previously encountered with services and the use of money or property. In general, a bona fide sale or exchange of property by a partner to a partnership, or vice versa, is treated for tax purposes as a Section 707(a)(1) transaction between unrelated parties. Opportunities for collusion, however, have prompted Congress to enact a number of anti-avoidance provisions which are discussed in this section.

## 1.   SALES AND EXCHANGES WITH RESPECT TO CONTROLLED PARTNERSHIPS

Partners, like family members and other related taxpayers, may seek to sell a loss asset to their partnerships in order to recognize a paper loss without parting with effective control of the asset. Section 267(a)(1), which disallows losses with respect to many transactions between related parties, does not apply to partner/partnership sales or exchanges, but Section 707(b)(1) fills the statutory gap by disallowing losses on sales or exchanges of property between partnerships and partners who own directly or indirectly[1] a more than 50 percent interest in partnership capital or profits.[2]

Partners also might be motivated to sell a depreciable asset to a related partnership to give the buyer a stepped-up basis while the selling partner

---

**1.**  For this purpose, Section 707(b) incorporates attribution rules from Section 267(c).

**2.**  Section 707(b) also applies to sales or exchanges of property between two partnerships in which the same persons own, directly or indirectly, more than 50 percent of the capital or profits interests. I.R.C. § 707(b)(1)(B).

defers gain recognition under Section 453[3] or recognizes capital gain rather than ordinary income on the sale. To prevent these abuses, Sections 707(b)(2) and 1239(a) both characterize gain on sales and exchanges of property between partners and controlled (i.e., more than 50 percent) partnerships as ordinary income. In addition, Section 453(g) disallows installment sale treatment on such sales if the property is depreciable to the transferee unless the seller can establish to the satisfaction of the Secretary that the sale did not have tax avoidance as one of its principal purposes.

## 2.   DISGUISED SALES

The provisions discussed above were aimed at timing and conversion strategies. More adventuresome taxpayers went one step further, seeking complete nonrecognition of gain by turning a sale or exchange into a contribution of property followed or preceded by a related partnership distribution. To illustrate, assume that A is an equal partner in the AB partnership and has a $100,000 outside basis. Assume further that A owns a parcel of land with a $10,000 adjusted basis and a $50,000 fair market value. A wishes to sell the land to the partnership without altering his interest in the firm. If he sells the property to the partnership for its fair market value in a transaction governed by Section 707(a)(1), A recognizes $40,000 of gain. If instead A contributes the property, he does not recognize any gain, and his outside basis is increased to $110,000.[1] If the partnership then distributes $50,000 to A and the form of the transactions is respected,[2] A would receive the cash tax-free because the amount of the distribution does not exceed his outside basis.[3]

Section 707(a)(2)(B) responds to this potential for abuse by providing that if a partner transfers money or other property to a partnership and the partnership makes a related transfer of money or other property to that partner (or another partner), the two transfers, when appropriate, shall be treated as a sale or exchange of property between the partnership and the partner acting in a nonpartner capacity, or between two partners acting as outsiders. Congress granted the Treasury broad authority to uncover disguised sales without reclassifying "non-abusive transactions that reflect the various economic contributions of the partners."[4]

The Service has issued a detailed set of regulations under Section 707(a)(2)(B). Their guiding principle is that a contribution and related

---

**3.**  But see I.R.C. § 453(i), which accelerates gain recognition of ordinary recapture income on deferred payment sales of depreciable property.

**1.**  See I.R.C. §§ 721; 722; Chapter 2A, supra.

**2.**  But see Reg. §§ 1.721–1(a) & 1.731–1(c)(3), which provide that similar transactions may be characterized as sales under a substance over form analysis. See also Rev. Rul. 57–100, 1957–1 C.B. 205. The Service met with little success, however, in applying these regulations to disguised sales.

**3.**  I.R.C. § 731. See, e.g., Otey v. Commissioner, 70 T.C. 312 (1978), affirmed per curiam, 634 F.2d 1046 (6th Cir.1980).

**4.**  H.R.Rep. No. 98–432, 98th Cong., 2d Sess. 1220 (1984).

distribution should be recast as a sale only when their combined effect is to allow a partner to withdraw all or part of his equity in the transferred property. In the case of simultaneous transfers where it is clear that the partnership would not have made a distribution if the partner had not made a contribution, the transactions are likely to be viewed as a sale.[5] But a transfer will not be treated as the first step in a disguised sale if, based on all the facts and circumstances, the transferring partner is converting equity in the property into an interest in partnership capital and the transfer is subject to the entrepreneurial risks of the enterprise.[6]

In enacting Section 707(a)(2)(B), Congress suggested that the temporal proximity of the contribution and distribution should be a significant factor in identifying a disguised sale.[7] Adopting this mechanical test of time, the regulations provide that nonsimultaneous transfers between a partnership and a partner (e.g., a contribution by a partner and a subsequent distribution by the partnership to that partner) that are made within two years of each other are presumed to be a sale[8] while transfers made more than two years apart are presumed not to be a sale.[9] Both presumptions are rebuttable based on clearly established contrary facts and circumstances.[10] The presumptions do not apply to four types of partnership distributions that historically have not been used as disguised sale vehicles.[11]

Since the presumptions are rebuttable based on facts and circumstances, the regulations provide a list of factors that may tend to prove the existence of a disguised sale. The Service is urged to raise its eyebrows, for example, if the timing and amount of a subsequent transfer are determinable with reasonable certainty at the time of an earlier transfer; if the transferring partner has a legally enforceable right to a subsequent distribution; or if that partner's right to receive money or other property for his contribution is secured.[12]

The typically compulsive drafters of the regulations included countless examples of disguised sales. In general, if the consideration treated as transferred to a partner in a sale is less than the fair market value of the property transferred to the partnership, the transaction is treated as a part sale/part contribution, and the transferring partner must pro rate his basis in the property between the sale and contribution portions. The following excerpt from the regulations illustrates the operation of this rule in the simple case of a disguised sale resulting from simultaneous transfers:[13]

---

**5.** Reg. § 1.707–3(b)(1).

**6.** Id.

**7.** See Staff of the Joint Committee on Taxation, General Explanation of the Revenue Provisions of the Deficit Reduction Act of 1984 (hereinafter "1984 Act General Explanation"), 98th Cong., 2d Sess. 232 (1984).

**8.** Reg. § 1.707–3(c)(1).

**9.** Reg. § 1.707–3(d).

**10.** Reg. § 1.707–3(c)(1), (d).

**11.** See generally Reg. § 1.707–4. Broadly categorized, the exceptions benefit guaranteed payments and other types of preferred returns on contributed capital that are reasonable in amount and payments to reimburse partners for costs they incurred prior to the formation of the partnership.

**12.** Reg. § 1.707–3(b)(2).

**13.** Reg. § 1.707–3(f) Example 1.

A transfers property X to partnership AB on April 9, 1992, in exchange for an interest in the partnership. At the time of the transfer, property X has a fair market value of $4,000,000 and an adjusted tax basis of $1,200,000. Immediately after the transfer, the partnership transfers $3,000,000 in cash to A. Assume that, under the section, the partnership's transfer of cash to A is treated as part of a sale of property X to the partnership. Because the amount of cash A receives on April 9, 1992, does not equal the fair market value of the property, A is considered to have sold a portion of property X with a value of $3,000,000 to the partnership in exchange for the cash. Accordingly, A must recognize $2,100,000 of gain ($3,000,000 amount realized less $900,000 adjusted tax basis ($1,200,000 multiplied by $3,000,000/$4,000,000)). Assuming A receives no other transfers that are treated as consideration for the sale of the property under this section, A is considered to have contributed to the partnership, in A's capacity as a partner, $1,000,000 of the fair market value of the property with an adjusted tax basis of $300,000.[14]

The legislative history of Section 707(a)(2)(B) also warned the Treasury to be on the lookout for situations where a partner or the partnership borrows against property in connection with a transfer and related distribution.[15] When the borrowed funds end up in the transferring partner's pocket, the overall transaction may be equivalent to a sale, at least to the extent that the other partners (through the partnership) assume primary responsibility for repayment of the loan. The regulations respond to the Congressional challenge with an elaborate set of special rules relating to liabilities.[16] In general, if a liability incurred by a partner in anticipation of a transfer is assumed (or taken subject to) by a partnership, the partnership is treated as transferring consideration to the partner (as part of a sale) to the extent that responsibility for repayment of the transferred liability is shifted to the other partners.[17] Liabilities incurred within two years of a transfer are presumed to be in anticipation of the transfer.[18] Liabilities incurred by a partner more than two years before a transfer are called "qualified liabilities" by the regulations.[19] The assumption of these and certain other qualified liabilities[20] are treated as consideration paid in a sale only to the extent that the transferring partner is otherwise treated as having sold a portion of the property.[21]

---

**14.** For examples of nonsimultaneous transfers and the operation of the two-year presumption, see Reg. § 1.707–3(f) Examples 2–8.

**15.** 1984 General Explanation, supra note 7 at 232.

**16.** See generally Reg. § 1.707–5.

**17.** Reg. § 1.707–5(a)(1). For rules on a partner's share of recourse and nonrecourse liabilities for this purpose, see Reg. § 1.707–5(a)(2).

**18.** Reg. § 1.707–5(a)(7).

**19.** Reg. § 1.707–5(a)(6)(i)(A).

**20.** See Reg. § 1.707–5(a)(6).

**21.** Reg. § 1.707–5(a)(7). See Reg. § 1.707–5(e).

To illustrate, assume that on the formation of the equal AB partnership A transfers a building which has a fair market value of $100,000 and is subject to a $80,000 recourse liability that A incurred immediately before the transfer, and B contributes $20,000 cash. A uses the loan proceeds to pay personal expenses. The partnership assumes the liability, which is classified as recourse under the 752 regulations,[22] and thus $40,000 of the debt is allocated to B. On these facts, the regulations treat the partnership as transferring $40,000 of consideration (the amount of the liability shifted to B) to A in connection with a sale of the property. As a result, A is treated as having sold a 40 percent interest in the building to the partnership for $40,000 and having contributed the remaining 60 percent.[23]

Finally, to give the Service a fighting chance to uncover disguised sales, the regulations require disclosure on a prescribed form when a partnership transfers money or property to a partner within two years of a transfer of property by the partner to the partnership and the partner has treated the transfer as other than a sale for tax purposes.[24]

## 3.   TRANSFERS OF PROPERTY AND RELATED ALLOCATIONS

Unlike the rendering of services or the use of property, a contribution of property to a partnership is not likely to be accompanied by an *allocation* of partnership income to the contributing partner, at least where capital accounts are maintained in accordance with the Section 704(b) regulations. Since those regulations require that a partner's capital account must be increased by the fair market value of contributed property,[1] an allocation of additional income to the contributing partner would result in double capital account credit for the contribution. This type of double dipping by the contributing partner alters the partners' economic business deal and is not likely to be accepted by the other partners.

Congress nonetheless feared that a contribution of property might be coupled with an allocation and distribution in a manner designed to avoid the capitalization requirement. For example, if the contributing partner's capital account were not properly adjusted to take account of the contribution, or the partner sells the property to the partnership at a price well below its true value, then the other partners might agree to compensate that partner through an increased allocation of partnership income. To illustrate, assume that A owns a building with a zero basis and a $10,000 fair market value. If A sells the building to the partnership, he recognizes a $10,000 gain, and the partnership takes a $10,000 basis in the building. On

---

**22.**  For Section 707(a)(2) purposes, a partner's share of recourse liabilities is determined by reference to the Section 752 regulations. Reg. § 1.707–5(a)(2)(ii). See Chapter 4D supra. Special rules are provided for allocation of nonrecourse liabilities under Section 707. See Reg. § 1.707–5(a)(2)(iii).

**23.**  Reg.   § 1.707–5(a).   See   Reg. § 1.707–5(f) Example 2.

**24.**  Reg. §§ 1.707–3(c)(2), 1.707–8. Similar disclosure requirements apply when debt is incurred within two years of a transfer of property that secures the debt and in a few other specialized situations. See, e.g., Reg. §§ 1.707–5(a)(7)(ii), 1.707–8.

**1.**  Reg. § 1.704–1(b)(2)(iv)(*b*)(2).

the other hand, assume A contributes the building to the partnership and it is reflected on the partnership books (including A's capital account) at its zero basis. If the first $10,000 of partnership income is allocated and distributed to A, A would have $10,000 of income (as on a straight sale), but the form of the transaction allows the remaining partners to escape tax on that $10,000 (resulting in the economic equivalent of a current deduction of the $10,000 paid for the building). In such an unusual[2] case, Section 707(a)(2)(A) will recast the contribution/allocation transaction into a sale between unrelated parties under Section 707(a)(1). As with payments for services or the use of property, Section 707(a)(2)(A) requires capitalization of an item that the partners were seeking to immediately expense through the ruse of an allocation of income.

## PROBLEMS

**1.** Partnership is owned 25% each by A, his wife, his wife's father and X Corporation, in which A is a 50% shareholder. What are the tax consequences to the parties involved in the following sales?

    (a) During the year the partnership sells A some land in which it has a basis of $50,000 for its fair market value of $40,000. In the succeeding year, A sells the land to B for $45,000.

    (b) Same as (a), above, except that the first sale is to a second partnership also owned by the same parties except that an unrelated party owns a 25% interest and X Corporation owns no interest in the second partnership. The second partnership then resells the land to B for $45,000.

    (c) A sells depreciable equipment in which he has an adjusted basis of $20,000 to the partnership for $30,000.

    (d) A's wife sells residential rental property held by A as a capital asset to the partnership for $120,000. She had a $100,000 basis in the property. The partnership is in the housing rental business.

    (e) Same as (d), above, except that the partnership is in the real estate sales business.

**2.** Partnership CD is owned 50% by C and 50% by D. If C sells an asset to CD and recognizes a $1,000 loss on the sale, will the loss be disallowed under § 707(b)(1)? What difference would it make if C's father, F, sells an asset to CD and recognizes a $1,000 loss? See Reg. § 1.267(b)–1(b).

**3.** A (a cash method taxpayer) is a 25% partner in the ABCD partnership (an accrual method taxpayer) and has a $30,000 outside basis in her partnership interest. A owns depreciable equipment with an adjusted basis

---

**2.** The operative word here may be "unusual." Although the fact pattern in the text is one of the few situations where Section 707(a)(2)(A) might apply to a contribution of property, it is an unlikely scenario in light of the capital account rules in the Sec-tion 704(b) regulations. Most disguised sales will be scrutinized under Section 707(a)(2)(B). See McKee, Nelson & Whitmire, Federal Taxation of Partnerships and Partners ¶ 13.02[4][a] (3d ed. 1996).

of $1,000 and a fair market value of $20,000. Before any of the following transactions, the partnership has $60,000 of net income each year. What are the tax consequences in the following alternatives?

(a) A sells the equipment to the partnership for $20,000.

(b) A contributes the equipment to the partnership. A is not allocated any additional income, but her capital account is increased by the value of the contributed property. Later in the year, A receives a distribution of $20,000.

(c) Same as (b), above, except that the distribution to A is only $15,000.

(d) Same as (b), above, except that, one month before the contribution, A borrows $15,000 on a recourse basis, securing the loan with the equipment. In connection with A's contribution, the partnership assumes the $15,000 loan. Later in the year, A receives a distribution of $5,000.

(e) A contributes the equipment to the partnership. The equipment is reflected on the books of the partnership at its $1,000 adjusted basis, and A's capital account is increased by that amount. In order to ensure that A is compensated for the full value of the equipment, the partnership allocates and distributes the first $19,000 of its income to A. The remaining $41,000 of partnership income is split equally by all four partners so that A is allocated a total of $29,250 of partnership income and the remaining partners are allocated $10,250 each.

(f) Suppose the partnership does not need A's equipment in its business but A nevertheless transfers it to the partnership. Partner B transfers similar depreciable property (adjusted basis—4,000; fair market value—$18,000) and $2,000 cash to the partnership. Two months later, the ABCD partnership distributes A's old property to B and B's old property together with $2,000 to A.

CHAPTER 6

# SALES AND EXCHANGES OF PARTNERSHIP INTERESTS

## A. CONSEQUENCES TO THE SELLING PARTNER

### 1. THE OPERATION OF SECTION 751(a)

Code: §§ 705(a); 706(c); 741; 751(a), (c), (d), (f); 752(d). Skim §§ 64; 453(b), (i), (l)(1); 708; 1031(a)(2)(D); 1060; 1245(a)(1), (2), (3)(A).

Regulations: §§ 1.706–1(c)(1), (2), (4) & (5); 1.741–1; 1.751–1(a), (c)(1)–(3), (d)(2), (g) Example (1); 1.752–1(h).

The sale or exchange of a partnership interest provides another opportunity to examine the tension between the aggregate and entity concepts of partnership taxation. The transaction might be fragmented into sales of the partner's undivided fractional interest in each asset of the partnership—an aggregate approach identical to the treatment of the sale of a sole proprietorship.[1] Alternatively, it could be viewed as the disposition of a capital asset without regard to the character of the underlying partnership assets—an entity approach resembling the treatment of sales of corporate stock. Congress settled this debate by enacting a statutory hybrid falling between these two extremes: a modified entity approach.[2] An aggregate approach would have required a cumbersome asset-by-asset fragmentation of the sale, while a pure entity approach would have facilitated the conversion of ordinary income into capital gain, forcing the Commissioner to retaliate with the usual array of vague doctrines designed to uncover and correct tax avoidance. The Congressional solution is a sensible compromise that is reminiscent of several characterization issues encountered in the basic income tax course.

Examination of the statutory scheme begins with Section 741, which provides that gain or loss from the sale or exchange of an interest in a partnership shall be considered as gain or loss from the sale of a capital asset. But unqualified capital gain treatment on the sale of a partnership interest historically led to abuse if the partnership held assets, such as inventory and accounts receivable, that gave rise to ordinary income if sold by the partnership. To curb this potential for conversion of partnership

---

**1.** Williams v. McGowan, 152 F.2d 570 (2d Cir.1945).

**2.** In adopting this approach, Congress essentially codified the result reached in litigation prior to the 1954 Code. Most courts had analogized a partnership interest to a capital asset irrespective of the underlying partnership assets. See, e.g., Commissioner v. Shapiro, 125 F.2d 532 (6th Cir.1942); Rev. Rul. 67–406, 1967–2 C.B. 420.

ordinary income into partner capital gain, Section 741 yields to Section 751(a) to the extent that the amount received by a selling partner is attributable to "unrealized receivables" or "inventory items." Working in tandem, Sections 741 and 751(a) apply whether the selling partner disposes of his entire interest or only some portion of it.[3]

The interaction between Sections 741 and 751(a) is familiar. It strongly resembles the relationship of the depreciation recapture provisions to Sections 1221 and 1231. Section 751(a) overrides Section 741 and converts what otherwise would be capital gain or loss into ordinary gain or loss. And like its recapture counterparts, Section 751(a) has priority—first carving out an appropriate amount as ordinary gain or loss and then leaving Section 741 to characterize the balance.[4]

In applying this modified entity approach to the sale of a partnership interest, the selling partner first must apply the general rules of Section 1001(a) and compute the total realized gain or loss on the sale. This requires a determination of the difference between the amount realized by the partner on the sale and the adjusted basis of the partnership interest sold. For this purpose, Section 752(d) incorporates the teachings of *Crane*[5] by including in the amount realized the selling partner's share of all partnership liabilities along with the cash and fair market value of other property received by the seller. The adjusted basis of the seller's interest is his outside basis under Section 705(a), adjusted to reflect the seller's pro-rata share of partnership income or loss from the beginning of the current taxable year up to the date of sale.

Although a partnership's taxable year generally does not close when a partner sells an interest,[6] it closes with respect to a partner immediately upon the sale or exchange of his entire interest in the partnership.[7] The income or loss arising from that short taxable period then passes through to the partner and is reflected in his outside basis. The partnership's year does not close with respect to a partner who sells only a portion of his interest. Rather, at the end of the partnership's year, the selling partner's distributive share of income or loss is determined by taking into account

---

**3.** Rev.Rul. 59–109, 1959–1 C.B. 168. See also Rev.Rul. 84–53, 1984–1 C.B. 159.

**4.** The recapture provisions, however, only characterize realized *gain* as ordinary income while Section 751(a), by considering a portion of the amount realized as resulting from the sale of a noncapital asset, encompasses both gains and losses.

**5.** Crane v. Commissioner, 331 U.S. 1, 67 S.Ct. 1047 (1947); cf. I.R.C. § 7701(g), which attempts to codify the principle of Commissioner v. Tufts, 461 U.S. 300, 103 S.Ct. 1826 (1983), rehearing denied, 463 U.S. 1215, 103 S.Ct. 3555 (1983), which holds that the full amount of the selling partner's share of partnership nonrecourse liabilities are included in the amount realized even if they

exceed the fair market value of the encumbered property at the time of disposition.

**6.** I.R.C. § 706(c)(1); but see I.R.C. § 708(b)(1)(B), considered in Chapter 8B2 infra, which terminates a partnership if there is a sale or exchange of 50 percent or more of the total capital and profits interests within a 12 month period.

**7.** I.R.C. § 706(c)(2)(A). The regulations do not require an actual closing of the partnership's books; rather, they permit the partners to estimate the selling and buying partners' share of income based on a proration using elapsed time before and after the sale or any other reasonable method. Reg. § 1.706–1(c)(2)(ii).

the partner's varying interests in the partnership during the taxable year.[8] However, the regulations require an appropriate adjustment to the outside basis of the portion sold to reflect the partner's distributive share as of the date of the exchange.[9]

The next step is to determine what portion, if any, of the seller's total realized gain or loss is characterized as ordinary income under Section 751(a).[10] Before discussing the mechanics of that computation, the categories of Section 751 assets must be defined more precisely.

Section 751 assets include "unrealized receivables" and "inventory items," as defined in Sections 751(c) and (d), respectively. Unrealized receivables generally include rights (contractual or otherwise) to payment for goods and services which have not previously been included in income, provided, in the case of goods, that the sales proceeds would be treated as received from the sale or exchange of non-capital assets.[11] In addition, unrealized receivables include certain short-term debt obligations and an array of assets to the extent that their disposition at fair market value would trigger recapture of cost recovery and certain other prior deductions.[12] Since the recapture portion would be characterized as ordinary income on a sale or other disposition of these assets, they are appropriately included in Section 751 even though it is somewhat odd to label them as "receivables."

The term "inventory items" is defined broadly, embracing not only the familiar category of non-capital assets described in Section 1221(1) but also any property which, upon sale by the partnership or the selling partner, would not be considered a capital asset or Section 1231 asset.[13] As a result of the broad definition of "inventory," an asset may constitute both an unrealized receivable and an inventory item.[14] If an asset falls within both Section 751(a)(1) and (a)(2), it will be taxed only once.[15]

Having defined the critical terms, we now may return to the computation of the selling partner's gain or loss. If part of the amount realized is attributable to Section 751 assets, the tax consequences of the sale must be

---

**8.** I.R.C. § 706(d)(1); Reg. § 1.706–1(c)(4).

**9.** Reg. § 1.705–1(a)(1).

**10.** Sales or exchanges of interests in partnerships which have Section 751 assets must be reported by the transferor partner to the partnership (I.R.C. § 6050K(c)(1)) and then by the partnership to the Service, the transferor partner and the transferee partner (I.R.C. § 6050K(a), (b) and (c)(2)). Failure to report will result in penalties. See I.R.C. §§ 6721–6724.

**11.** I.R.C. § 751(c).

**12.** The regulations generally treat a selling partner's share of recapture gain as a separate unrealized receivable with a zero basis and a value equal to the selling part-

ner's share of recapture gain. Reg. § 1.751–1(c)(4) & (5).

**13.** I.R.C. § 751(d). Prior to August 6, 1997, inventory items were treated as "ordinary income" property under Section 751(a) only if they were "substantially appreciated"—i.e., only if the aggregate fair market value of the items exceeded 120 percent of their adjusted basis to the partnership. Cf. I.R.C. § 751(b)(3).

**14.** Reg. § 1.751–1(d)(2)(ii).

**15.** If unrealized receivables fall within both Section 751(c) and (d), they are treated as Section 751(c) assets under other Code provisions. See I.R.C. §§ 735(a); 736.

bifurcated by determining the amount of income or loss from Section 751 property that would have been allocated to the selling partner if the partnership had sold all of its property in a fully taxable transaction for cash in an amount equal to the fair market value of such property.[16] The selling partner's share of income or loss from Section 751 property in this hypothetical sale takes into account special allocations and allocations required under Section 704(c), including any remedial allocations.[17] The gain or loss attributable to Section 751 property will be ordinary gain or loss.

After determining the gain or loss under Section 751(a), the final step is to determine the difference between the selling partner's total gain or loss and the ordinary gain or loss determined under section 751(a). That difference is the selling partner's section 741 capital gain or loss on the sale of the partnership interest.[18] Since this is a netting process, it is possible for the seller to have a gain under section 751(a) and a loss under Section 741 or vice versa. In keeping with the entity approach, the long or short-term character of the Section 741 capital gain or loss depends upon the partner's holding period for the partnership interest and not the partnership's holding period for its assets.[19]

The prospect of ordinary income treatment on the sale of a partnership interest has motivated sophisticated taxpayers to devise strategies to avoid the taint caused by the presence of unrealized receivables and inventory items on the partnership's balance sheet. One technique was the creation of a separate second-tier partnership to hold the "parent" partnership's Section 751 assets. A partner selling an interest in the parent then would claim that none of its assets were tainted by Section 751(a) because they were limited to the retained Section 741 assets and the parent's interest in the second partnership, which was not itself a Section 751 asset irrespective of its underlying holdings. Congress put a halt to the use of multi-tiered partnerships to avoid Section 751(a) gain by adopting an aggregate theory in Section 751(f). That section provides that in determining a partnership's Section 751 assets, the partnership "shall be treated as

---

**16.** Reg. § 1.751–1(a)(2). The determination of "fair market value" is made by taking into account Section 7701(g), which provides that the fair market value of property shall not be less than the amount of any nonrecourse debt to which the property is subject. Id. At one time, the regulations allowed the selling partner and the buyer to allocate the total purchase price for the partnership interest among the partnership's assets for purposes of the Section 751 calculations. The regulations no longer permit such an allocation to control the determination of the value of the partnership's assets. The selling partner's amount realized apparently must be allocated first to Section 751 properties based on their relative fair market values

and then to the other assets. Cf. I.R.C. § 1060.

A partner selling or exchanging any part of a partnership interest in a partnership holding Section 751 property is required to report the circumstances of the sale in a statement attached to the income tax return for the year in which the sale or exchange occurs. Reg. § 1.751–1(a)(3).

**17.** Reg. § 1.751–1(a)(2).

**18.** Id.

**19.** Gray v. Commissioner, 11 T.C.M. 17 (1952); see Section A3 of this chapter, infra., for special holding period rules in the case of a sale of a partnership interest.

owning its proportionate share of the property of any other partnership in which it is a partner." This rule applies regardless of the number of tiers between the selling partner and the ordinary income property.

The relationship of Sections 741 and 751(a) to other judicial doctrines and Code sections has evolved gradually. For example, although there once was substantial controversy over whether an exchange of partnership interests could qualify as a like-kind exchange,[20] Congress silenced the debate by disallowing nonrecognition on such exchanges.[21] Transfers of partnership interests to a controlled corporation normally qualify for non-recognition under Section 351, but problems may arise in determining the nature of the incorporation transaction.[22] The application of the Section 453 installment sales rules to the sale of a partnership interest has been somewhat hazy, but the Service has helped to clear the air with a published ruling.[23] Finally, because of the difference in tax treatment, it sometimes is necessary to distinguish the sale of a partnership interest from the liquidation of an interest. Some of these thorny questions are explored in the materials which follow; the sale vs. liquidation and incorporation issues are discussed in a later chapter.[24]

## Glazer v. Commissioner

United States Tax Court, 1965.
44 T.C. 541.

OPINION

■ RAUM, JUDGE. The Commissioner determined the following deficiencies in income tax for the year 1959:

| Taxpayer | Deficiency | Additions to tax, sec. 6654, I.R.C.1954 |
|---|---|---|
| Herman and Mollie Glazer ........ | $14,709.60 | $307.96 |
| Forrest B. Fleisher ............... | 2,368.52 | ———— |
| Estate of David Fleisher, deceased, Frances E. Fleisher, executrix, and Frances E. Fleisher ........ | 661.84 | ———— |

**20.** See Newman, "Like Kind Exchanges of Partnership Interests Under Section 1031," 18 Wake Forest L.Rev. 663 (1982) and Brier, "Like–Kind Exchanges of Partnership Interests: A Policy Oriented Approach," 38 Tax L.Rev. 389 (1983).

**21.** I.R.C. § 1031(a)(2)(D). See Reg. § 1.1031(a)–1(a)(1). The legislative history states that Congress does not intend this provision to apply to exchanges of interests in the same partnership. H.Rep. No. 98–432, 98th Cong., 2d Sess. 1234 (1984). See Rev. Rul. 84–52, 1984–1 C.B. 157, holding that a conversion of a general partnership interest into a limited partnership interest in the same partnership is treated for tax purposes as a distribution of the new partnership interest to the converting partner under Section 731 and a contribution of the old interest to the partnership under Section 721. See also I.R.C. § 1031(a)(2), flush language, making it clear that an interest in a partnership which elects under Section 761 to be excluded from Subchapter K shall be treated as an interest in each of the assets of the partnership for purposes of Section 1031.

**22.** See Rev.Rul. 84–111, infra at page 355.

**23.** See Section A3 of this chapter, infra.

**24.** See Chapters 8C and 8D1b, infra.

The only issue remaining for decision is whether the gain to the petitioners arising from the purported sale of their interests in a partnership is to be treated as ordinary income or capital gain. All of the facts have been stipulated.

Petitioners Herman Glazer (hereinafter referred to as Herman) and Mollie Glazer, husband and wife, petitioner Forrest B. Fleisher (hereinafter sometimes referred to as Forrest), and David Fleisher (hereinafter sometimes referred to as David) and petitioner Frances E. Fleisher, husband and wife, were all individuals residing in Philadelphia, Pa., during the year 1959. David was Forrest's father. The Herman Glazers and David Fleishers filed their respective joint income tax returns and Forrest E. Fleisher his individual income tax return with the district director of internal revenue in Philadelphia for the calendar year 1959. Since that time David has died and Frances E. Fleisher has been appointed executrix.

In 1957 Lowell Hills, a partnership, was formed for the purpose of constructing and selling 94 single-family dwellings on a 30–acre tract of land in Upper Merion Township, Pa. The respective partnership interests were described in the stipulation of facts as follows:

> 5.  Herman and Forrest were the active partners in the above venture. Herman was entitled to 75% of the profits of the Lowell Hills partnership. The balance of the profits accrued to the partnership Fleisher and Fleisher, which was owned two-thirds by Forrest and one-third by his father, David. Forrest had the right to represent, sign for and bind his father in all transactions pertaining to the Lowell Hills partnership.

When Lowell Hills acquired the tract of land part of it had already been subdivided. The partnership subdivided the balance and proceeded with the planned construction of the 94 single-family dwellings. The first sale by Lowell Hills occurred in 1958. In that year, 46 lots and homes were sold. Between January 1, 1959, and July 21, 1959, 24 additional lots and homes were sold. The profits therefrom were properly reported as ordinary income. As of July 21, 1959, agreements of sale had been entered into for each of the 24 remaining lots and homes and construction of these homes was approximately 80 percent completed on that date.

On July 21, 1959, Herman and Forrest (acting for himself and David), as sellers, entered into an agreement with Marvin J. Levin, purporting to sell to him their partnership interests in Lowell Hills for an aggregate amount of $172,000. The parties have stipulated that "if the twenty-four remaining lots and homes had not been under agreements of sales, the sales price of the alleged partnership interest would have been $6,000 less." Levin was an attorney for Lowell Hills, and had no experience or training in the building construction field. He thereafter not only prepared the Glazers' 1959 returns but appeared as counsel for petitioners herein.

\* \* \*

The petitioners reported as long-term capital gain their respective shares of the profit on the alleged sale of their partnership interests on their 1959 returns as follows:

| Name | Long-term gain | Gain taken into account (50 percent) |
|---|---|---|
| Herman and Mollie Glazer . . . . . . . | $36,300.37 | $18,150.18 |
| Forrest B. Fleisher . . . . . . . . . . . . . . | 8,066.76 | 4,033.38 |
| David and Frances E. Fleisher . . . . . | 4,033.37 | 2,016.68 |

All settlements on the sale of the final 24 lots and homes were effected by November 17, 1959, and a profit therefrom of $3,058.58 was reported by Levin on his Federal income tax return for 1959.

Performance under the construction contract for the period between July 21, 1959, and December 31, 1959, resulted in a profit for Herman and Forrest of $2,670.90, three-quarters of which was reported by Herman and the balance by Forrest on their respective 1959 income tax returns.

The Commissioner determined that the foregoing alleged long-term capital gains must be taxed as ordinary income,

\* \* \*

The Government contends that even if the transaction be regarded as a true sale under section 741, the Commissioner's determination must be sustained because the proceeds received by the partners were attributable to "unrealized receivables" of the partnership under section 751 and must therefore be treated as amounts "realized from the sale or exchange of property other than a capital asset."

\* \* \*

By its terms, section 741 explicitly removes from its operative scope the situations covered by section 751, and section 751(a) declares that—

any money \* \* \* received by a transferor partner in exchange for \* \* \* his interest in the partnership attributable to—

(1) unrealized receivables of the partnership \* \* \*

\* \* \*

shall be considered as an amount realized from the sale or exchange of property other than a capital asset.

The purpose of these provisions as stated in the committee reports was "to prevent the conversion of potential ordinary income into capital gain by virtue of transfers of partnership interests." S.Rept. No. 1622, 83d Cong., 2d Sess., p. 98; H.Rept. No. 1337, 83d Cong., 2d Sess., p. 70.

Under these provisions the money received by a selling partner to the extent attributable to unrealized receivables in respect of goods delivered, or to be delivered, is to be treated as received from the sale of property other than a capital asset. This is because the proceeds of the sale of such property by the partnership itself would be treated as the sale of property

other than a capital asset; and the statute was intended to require that such proceeds retain the same character in the hands of the selling partners to the extent that the selling price of their partnership interests reflected such proceeds.

In terms of the present case the partnership was in the business of selling houses, and the sales of its houses were concededly properly classified as ordinary rather than capital transactions. Accordingly, to the extent the amounts receivable from the sales of the partnership's 24 remaining houses were reflected in the amounts receivable by the selling partners the transaction may not be classified as a sale of a capital asset. In short, the amounts receivable from the sale of the 24 remaining houses fall within the term "unrealized receivables" in section 751, and therefore are denied capital gains treatment under section 741.

Petitioners do not contest the point that the agreements for the sales of the 24 houses were "unrealized receivables" within the meaning of section 751. But they argue that the money "attributable to" the unrealized receivables was only $6,000 because the parties have stipulated that if the 24 remaining lots and homes had not been under agreements of sale, the sales price would have been $6,000 less. We hold that no such limitation may fairly be read into the statutory provisions, and if such limitation were to be give effect it would defeat the very purpose of the legislation.

Stated in its simplest terms, the amount "attributable to" the unrealized receivables of a partnership is that portion of the sales price received in exchange therefor. The regulations, sec. 1.751–1(c)(3), provide that in determining the amount of the sales price attributable to unrealized receivables any arm's-length agreement between buyer and seller will generally establish the amount or value. In the absence of such an agreement full account is to be taken of the estimated cost of completing performance of the contract or agreement, and of the time between the sale and the date of payment. In the present case the existence of an arm's-length agreement is questionable, but in any event it appears that the only partnership assets of value were "unrealized receivables" so that the entire purchase price must be allocated thereto. Cf. John Winthrop Wolcott, 39 T.C. 538.

Petitioners misconstrue the meaning of the phrase "attributable to" as used in section 751(a), in making the argument that only $6,000 was *attributable* to unrealized receivables. While it is undoubtedly true that the partnership interests were more valuable because the lots and homes were under agreements of sale, the increase in the value of the partnership is not the amount "attributable to" the unrealized receivables, under the provisions of section 751.

Had petitioners retained their partnership interests there is no question that they would have realized ordinary income upon collection of amounts receivable under the agreements of sale for the 24 lots and homes. Furthermore, had construction been completed on all the houses so that all that remained for the partners to do was to collect their money at the time

of the sale of their partnership interests it is clear that the entire amounts received would be attributable to unrealized receivables. The statute was written to apply in the same manner to unrealized receivables arising out of both completed and uncompleted contracts and results should be arrived at in the same manner in both situations. Where houses are sold, although not yet completed, the cost of the lots and the cost of construction of the houses, to the extent not previously deducted as expense, would go into the basis of the unrealized receivables, and would not be totally disregarded. Sec. 1.751–1(c)(2), Income Tax Regs. Petitioners could not have disposed of anything more than bare legal title to the lots and houses since they had already been sold. The only thing of substance that petitioners had to sell was their right to receive the income from the sales upon completion of construction. Under section 751 gains resulting from amounts received therefor are to be taxed as ordinary income. *John Winthrop Wolcott,* supra.

Decisions will be entered for the respondent.

## Ledoux v. Commissioner

United States Tax Court, 1981.
77 T.C. 293, affirmed per curiam 695 F.2d 1320 (11th Cir.1983).

■ STERRETT, JUDGE. * * *

After concessions, the sole issue remaining for our decision is whether any portion of the amount received by petitioner John W. Ledoux pursuant to an agreement for the sale of a partnership interest was attributable to an unrealized receivable of the partnership and thus was required to be characterized as ordinary income under section 751, I.R.C. 1954.

FINDINGS OF FACT

* * *

[John Ledoux was a 25% partner in the Collins–Ledoux partnership, which was formed on October 1, 1955 to manage and operate a greyhound dog racing track in Seminole County, Florida. The track was owned by the Sanford–Orlando Kennel Club, Inc. and previously had been managed by a related partnership, also known as Sanford–Orlando Kennel Club. Collins–Ledoux had the right to operate the track for a period of 20 years; in return, it agreed to pay the Sanford–Orlando partnership the first $200,000 of net annual profit from track operations.

From October 1, 1955 to September 30, 1972, the Collins–Ledoux partnership operated the track pursuant to the agreement with the Sanford–Orlando group. Ledoux managed the operations of the track and received a salary along with a share of the net profits of Collins–Ledoux. During this period, Collins–Ledoux made extensive improvements to the property and acquired adjacent land for use in connection with the operation of the track. The efforts were quite successful. From 1955 to 1972, the gross income of the partnership increased from $3.6 million to $23.6 million and the net income increased from $72,000 to over $550,000.

After setting forth this background, the Tax Court went on to describe the sale of John Ledoux's 25% partnership interest. Ed.]

After the 1972 racing season two of the partners, Jerry Collins and Jack Collins, decided to purchase petitioner's 25–percent partnership interest. They agreed to allow Ledoux to propose a fair selling price for his interest. Ledoux set a price based on a price-earnings multiple of 5 times his share of the partnership's 1972 earnings. This resulted in a total value for his 25–percent interest of $800,000. There was no valuation or appraisal of specific assets at the time, and the sales price included his interest in all of the assets of the partnership.

\* \* \*

On his 1972 Federal income tax return, petitioner properly elected to report the gain from the sale of his partnership interest under the installment method as prescribed in section 453. Petitioner calculated the total gain on such sale to be as follows:

| | |
|---|---:|
| Sales price | $800,000.00 |
| Basis in partnership interest | 62,658.70 |
| Total gain on sale | 737,341.30 |

During 1972, 1973, and 1974, petitioner received payments in accordance with the October 17, 1972, agreement of sale. In each of those years, he characterized the reported gain, calculated pursuant to the installment sales method, as capital gain.

After consummation of the sale of petitioner's interest in the Collins–Ledoux partnership, the remaining partners continued to operate the dog track under the agreement of July 9, 1955, as amended.

Respondent, in his notice of deficiency, did not disagree with petitioner's calculation of the total gain. However, he determined that $575,392.50 of the gain was related to petitioner's interest in the dog track agreement and should be subject to ordinary income treatment pursuant to section 751.[2]

OPINION

The sole issue presented is whether a portion of the amount received by petitioner on the sale of his 25–percent partnership interest is taxable as ordinary income and not as capital gain. More specifically, we must decide whether any portion of the sales price is attributable to "unrealized receivables" of the partnership.

2.  Respondent determined that the value of petitioner's proportionate share of partnership assets other than the dog track agreement was as follows:

| Asset | Value |
|---|---:|
| Escrow deposit | $12,500.00 |
| Sanford–Seminole Development Co. stock | 1,000.00 |
| Fixed assets | 211,107.50 |
| | 224,607.50 |

The difference between this value and the total purchase price ($800,000) was treated by respondent as having been received by petitioner in exchange for his rights in the dog track agreement.

Generally, gain or loss on the sale or exchange of a partnership interest is treated as capital gain or loss. Sec. 741. Prior to 1954, a partner could escape ordinary income tax treatment on his portion of the partnership's unrealized receivables by selling or exchanging his interest in the partnership and treating the gain or loss therefrom as capital gain or loss. To curb such abuses, section 751 was enacted to deal with the problem of the so-called "collapsible partnership."

\* \* \*

Petitioner contends that the dog track agreement gave the Collins–Ledoux partnership the right to manage and operate the dog track. According to petitioner, the agreement did not give the partnership any contractual rights to receive future payments and did not impose any obligation on the partnership to perform services. Rather, the agreement merely gave the partnership the right to occupy and use all of the corporation's properties (including the racetrack facilities and the racing permit) in operating its dog track business; if the partnership exercised such right, it would be obligated to make annual payments to the corporation based upon specified percentages of the annual mutuel handle. Thus, because the dog track agreement was in the nature of a leasehold agreement rather than an employment contract, it did not create the type of "unrealized receivables" referred to in section 751.

Respondent, on the other hand, contends that the partnership operated the racetrack for the corporation and was paid a portion of the profits for its efforts. As such, the agreement was in the nature of a management employment contract. When petitioner sold his partnership interest to the Collinses in 1972, the main right that he sold was a contract right to receive income in the future for yet-to-be-rendered personal services. This, respondent asserts, is supported by the fact that petitioner determined the sales price for his partnership interest by capitalizing his 1972 annual income (approximately $160,000) by a factor of 5. Therefore, respondent contends that the portion of the gain realized by petitioner that is attributable to the management contract should be characterized as an amount received for unrealized receivables of the partnership. Consequently, such gain should be characterized as ordinary income under section 751.

The legislative history is not wholly clear with respect to the types of assets that Congress intended to place under the umbrella of "unrealized receivables." The House report states:

> The term "unrealized receivables or fees" is used to apply to any rights to income which have not been included in gross income under the method of accounting employed by the partnership. The provision is applicable mainly to cash basis partnerships which have acquired a contractual or other legal right to income for goods or services. \* \* \* [H.Rept. 1337, 83d Cong., 2d Sess. 71 (1954).]

Essentially the same language appears in the report of the Senate committee. S.Rept. 1622, 83d Cong., 2d Sess. 98 (1954). In addition, the regula-

tions elaborate on the meaning of "unrealized receivables" as used in section 751. Section 1.751–1(c), Income Tax Regs., provides:

> Sec. 1.751–1(c) *Unrealized receivables.* (1) The term "unrealized receivables", * * * means any rights (contractual or otherwise) to payment for—
>
> (i) Goods delivered or to be delivered (to the extent that such payment would be treated as received for property other than a capital asset), or
>
> (ii) Services rendered or to be rendered, to the extent that income arising from such rights to payment was not previously includible in income under the method of accounting employed by the partnership. Such rights must have arisen under contracts or agreements in existence at the time of sale or distribution, although the partnership may not be able to enforce payment until a later time. For example, the term includes trade accounts receivable of a cash method taxpayer, and rights to payment for work or goods begun but incomplete at the time of the sale or distribution.
>
> * * *
>
> (3) In determining the amount of the sale price attributable to such unrealized receivables, or their value in a distribution treated as a sale or exchange, any arm's length agreement between the buyer and the seller, or between the partnership and the distributee partner, will generally establish the amount or value. In the absence of such an agreement, full account shall be taken not only of the estimated cost of completing performance of the contract or agreement, but also of the time between the sale or distribution and the time of payment.

The language of the legislative history and the regulations indicates that the term "unrealized receivables" includes any contractual or other right to payment for goods delivered or to be delivered or services rendered or to be rendered. Therefore, an analysis of the nature of the rights under the dog track agreement, in the context of the aforementioned legal framework, becomes appropriate. A number of cases have dealt with the meaning of "unrealized receivables" and thereby have helped to define the scope of the term. Courts that have considered the term "unrealized receivables" generally have said that it should be given a broad interpretation. Cf. Corn Products Co. v. Commissioner, 350 U.S. 46, 52 (1955) (the term "capital asset" is to be construed narrowly, but exclusions from the definition thereof are to be broadly and liberally construed). For instance, in Logan v. Commissioner, 51 T.C. 482, 486 (1968), we held that a partnership's right in quantum meruit to payment for work in progress constituted an unrealized receivable even though there was no express agreement between the partnership and its clients requiring payment.

In Roth v. Commissioner, 321 F.2d 607 (9th Cir.1963), affg. 38 T.C. 171 (1962), the Ninth Circuit dealt with the sale of an interest in a

partnership which produced a movie and then gave a 10–year distribution right to Paramount Pictures Corp. in return for a percentage of the gross receipts. The selling partner claimed that his right to a portion of the payments expected under the partnership's contract with Paramount did not constitute an unrealized receivable. The court rejected this view, however, reasoning that Congress "meant to exclude from capital gains treatment any receipts which would have been treated as ordinary income to the partner if no transfer of the partnership interest had occurred." 321 F.2d at 611.* Therefore, the partnership's right to payments under the distribution contract was in the nature of an unrealized receivable.

A third example of the broad interpretation given to the term "unrealized receivable" is United States v. Eidson, 310 F.2d 111 (5th Cir.1962), revg. an unreported opinion (W.D.Tex.1961). The court there considered the nature of a management contract which was similar to the one at issue in the instant case. The case arose in the context of a sale by a partnership of all of its rights to operate and manage a mutual insurance company. The selling partnership received $170,000 for the rights it held under the management contract, and the Government asserted that the total amount should be treated as ordinary income. The Court of Appeals agreed with the Government's view on the ground that what was being assigned was not a capital asset whose value had accrued over a period of years; rather, the right to operate the company and receive profits therefrom during the remaining life of the contract was the real subject of the assignment. 310 F.2d at 116. The Fifth Circuit found the Supreme Court's holding in Commissioner v. P.G. Lake, Inc., 356 U.S. 260 (1958), to be conclusive:

> The substance of what was assigned was the right to receive future income. The substance of what was received was the present value of income which the recipient would otherwise obtain in the future. In short, consideration was paid for the right to receive future income, not for an increase in the value of the income-producing property. [356 U.S. at 266, cited in 310 F.2d at 115.]

In United States v. Woolsey, 326 F.2d 287 (5th Cir.1963), revg. 208 F.Supp. 325 (S.D.Tex.1962), the Fifth Circuit again faced a situation similar to the one that we face herein. The Fifth Circuit considered whether proceeds received by taxpayers on the sale of their partnership interests were to be treated as ordinary income or capital gain. There, the court was faced with the sale of interests in a partnership which held, as one of its assets, a 25–year contract to manage a mutual insurance company. As in the instant case, the contract gave the partners the right to render services for the term of the contract and to earn ordinary income in the future. In holding that the partnership's management contract constituted an unrealized receivable, the court stated:

* [The court, quoting 6 Mertens, Federal Income Taxation § 35.85 at 326, added: "The broad scope of the term unrealized receivables is limited only by the fact that it is confined to legal rights to income." Ed.]

When we look at the underlying right assigned in this case, we cannot escape the conclusion that so much of the consideration which relates to the right to earn ordinary income in the future under the "management contract," taxable to the assignee as ordinary income, is likewise taxable to the assignor as ordinary income although such income must be earned. Section 751 has defined "unrealized receivables" to include any rights, contractual or otherwise, to ordinary income from "services rendered, *or to be rendered,*" (emphasis added) to the extent that the same were not previously includable in income by the partnership, with the result that capital gains rates cannot be applied to the rights to income under the facts of this case, which would constitute ordinary income had the same been received in due course by the partnership. * * * It is our conclusion that such portion of the consideration received by the taxpayers in this case as properly should be allocated to the present value of their right to earn ordinary income in the future under the "management contract" is subject to taxation as ordinary income. * * * [326 F.2d at 291.]

Petitioner attempts to distinguish United States v. Woolsey, supra, and United States v. Eidson, supra, from the instant case by arguing that those cases involved a sale or termination of contracts to manage mutual insurance companies in Texas and that the management contracts therein were in the nature of employment agreements. After closely scrutinizing the facts in those cases, we conclude that petitioner's position has no merit. The fact that the *Woolsey* case involved sale of 100 percent of the partnership interests, as opposed to a sale of only a 25–percent partnership interest herein, is of no consequence. In addition, the fact that *Eidson* involved the surrender of the partnership's contract right to manage the insurance company, as opposed to the continued partnership operation in the instant case, also is not a material factual distinction.

The dog track agreement at issue in the instant case is similar to the management contract considered by the Fifth Circuit in *Woolsey*. Each gives the respective partnership the right to operate a business for a period of years and to earn ordinary income in return for payments of specified amounts to the corporation that holds the State charter. Therefore, based on our analysis of the statutory language, the legislative history, and the regulations and relevant case law, we are compelled to find that the dog track agreement gave the petitioner an interest that amounted to an "unrealized receivable" within the meaning of section 751(c).

Petitioner further contends that the dog track agreement does not represent an unrealized receivable because it does not require or obligate the partnership to perform personal services in the future. The agreement only gives, the argument continues, the Collins–Ledoux partnership the right to engage in a business.

We find this argument to be unpersuasive. The words of section 751(c), providing that the term "unrealized receivable" includes the right to payment for "services rendered, or to be rendered," do not preclude that

section's application to a situation where, as here, the performance of services is not required by the agreement. As the Fifth Circuit said in United States v. Eidson, supra:

> The fact that * * * income would not be received by the [partnership] unless they performed the services which the contract required of them, that is, actively managed the affairs of the insurance company in a manner that would produce a profit after all of the necessary expenditures, does not, it seems clear, affect the nature of this payment. It affects only the amount. That is, the fact that the taxpayers would have to spend their time and energies in performing services for which the compensation would be received merely affects the price at which they would be willing to assign or transfer the contract. * * * [310 F.2d at 115.]

Consequently, a portion of the consideration received by Ledoux on the sale of his partnership interest is subject to taxation as ordinary income.

Having established that the dog track agreement qualifies as an unrealized receivable, we next consider whether all or only part of petitioner's gain in excess of the amount attributable to his share of tangible partnership assets should be treated as ordinary income. Petitioner argues that this excess gain was attributable to goodwill or the value of a going concern.

With respect to goodwill, we note that petitioner's attorney drafted, and petitioner signed, the agreement for sale of partnership interest, dated October 17, 1972, which contains the following statement in paragraph 7:

> 7.  In the determination of the purchase price set forth in this agreement, the parties acknowledge no consideration has been given to any item of goodwill.

The meaning of the words "no consideration" is not entirely free from doubt. They could mean that no thought was given to an allocation of any of the sales price to goodwill, or they could indicate that the parties agreed that no part of the purchase price was allocated to goodwill. The testimony of the attorney who prepared the document indicates, however, that he did consider the implications of the sale of goodwill and even did research on the subject. He testified that he believed, albeit incorrectly, that, if goodwill were part of the purchase price, his client would not be entitled to capital gains treatment.

Petitioner attempts to justify this misstatement of the tax implications of an allocation to goodwill not by asserting mistake, but by pointing out that his attorney "is not a tax lawyer but is primarily involved with commercial law and real estate." We find as a fact that petitioner agreed at arm's length with the purchasers of his partnership interest that no part of the purchase price should be attributable to goodwill. The Tax Court long has adhered to the view that, absent "strong proof," a taxpayer cannot challenge an express allocation in an arm's-length sales contract to which he had agreed. See, e.g., Major v. Commissioner, 76 T.C. 239, 249 (1981), appeal pending (7th Cir., July 7, 1981); Lucas v. Commissioner, 58 T.C.

1022, 1032 (1972). In Spector v. Commissioner, 641 F.2d 376 (5th Cir. 1981), revg. 71 T.C. 1017 (1979), the Fifth Circuit, to which an appeal in this case will lie, appeared to step away from its prior adherence to the "strong proof" standard and move toward the stricter standard enunciated in Commissioner v. Danielson, 378 F.2d 771, 775 (3d Cir.1967), remanding 44 T.C. 549 (1965), cert. denied 389 U.S. 858 (1967). However, in this case, we need not measure the length of the step since we hold that petitioner has failed to introduce sufficient evidence to satisfy even the more lenient "strong proof" standard.

We next turn to petitioner's contention that part or all of the purchase price received in excess of the value of tangible assets is attributable to value of a going concern. In VGS Corp. v. Commissioner, 68 T.C. 563 (1977), we stated that—

> Going-concern value is, in essence, the additional element of value which attaches to property by reason of its existence as an integral part of a going concern. * * * [T]he ability of a business to continue to function and generate income without interruption as a consequence of the change in ownership, is a vital part of the value of a going concern. * * * [68 T.C. at 591–592; citations omitted.]

However, in the instant case, the ability of the dog racing track to continue to function after the sale of Ledoux's partnership interest was due to the remaining partners' retention of rights to operate under the dog track agreement. Without such agreement, there would have been no continuing right to operate a business and no right to continue to earn income. Thus, the amount paid in excess of the value of Ledoux's share of the tangible assets was not for the intangible value of the business as a going concern but rather for Ledoux's rights under the dog track agreement.

Finally, we turn to petitioner's claim that a determination of the value of rights arising from the dog track agreement has never been made and no evidence of the value of such rights was submitted in this case. We note that the $800,000 purchase price was proposed by petitioner and was accepted by Jack Collins and Jerry Collins in an arm's-length agreement of sale evidenced in the memorandum of agreement of July 19, 1972, and the agreement for sale of partnership interest of October 17, 1972. In addition, the October 17, 1972, sales agreement, written by petitioner's attorney, provided in paragraph 1 that the "Seller [Ledoux] sells to buyer [Jerry Collins and Jack Collins] all of his interest in [the partnership] * * * including but not limited to, *the seller's right to income* and to acquire the capital stock of The Sanford–Orlando Kennel Club, Inc." (Emphasis added.) Section 1.751–1(c)(3), Income Tax Regs., provides that an arm's-length agreement between the buyer and the seller generally will establish the value attributable to unrealized receivables.

Based on the provision in the agreement that no part of the consideration was attributable to goodwill, it is clear to us that the parties were aware that they could, if they so desired, have provided that no part of the consideration was attributable to the dog track agreement. No such provi-

sion was made.[8] Furthermore, the agreement clearly stated that one of the assets purchased was Ledoux's rights to future income. Considering that petitioner calculated the purchase price by capitalizing future earnings expected under the dog track agreement, we conclude that the portion of Ledoux's gain in excess of the amount attributable to tangible assets was attributable to an unrealized receivable as reflected by the dog track agreement.

Decision will be entered for the respondent.

## PROBLEMS

**1.** Partner A owns a one-third interest in the ABC cash method, calendar year general partnership, which manufactures and sells inventory. A, B and C, the original partners, each made initial cash contributions of $75,000. All income has been distributed as earned. On January 1st, A sells his interest in the partnership to D. Consider the tax consequences of the sale to A, assuming he has owned his partnership interest for several years. The balance sheet of the ABC partnership (which is to be used in all parts of this problems unless the facts indicate to the contrary) is as follows:

| Assets | A.B. | F.M.V. | Partners' Capital | A.B. | F.M.V. |
|---|---|---|---|---|---|
| Cash | $ 45,000 | $ 45,000 | A | $ 75,000 | $135,000 |
| | | | B | 75,000 | 135,000 |
| Inventory | 75,000 | 90,000 | C | 75,000 | 135,000 |
| Accounts Receivable | 0 | 45,000 | | | |
| Capital Asset | 105,000 | 225,000 | | | |
| | $225,000 | $405,000 | | $225,000 | $405,000 |

Consider the tax consequences to A on his sale in each of the following alternative situations:

(a) A sells his interest for $135,000 cash.

(b) Each partner originally contributed $150,000 cash (and assume each has an outside basis of $150,000), and the capital asset has a basis to the partnership of $330,000.

(c) Each partner originally contributed only $45,000 cash instead of $75,000, and the capital asset was purchased and held subject to a $90,000 liability. A sells his interest to D for $105,000 cash.

(d) The sale occurs on March 31, one quarter of the way through the year, at a time when A's share of partnership income through March 31 (all ordinary income) is $30,000. It is agreed that D will pay A $165,000 for his interest and also will acquire A's right to income.

---

**8.** We do not mean to imply that an opposite holding would automatically pertain if a provision had been made with respect to the dog track agreement.

**2**. Assume the same basic facts as in Problem 1, except the ABC partnership is an accrual method partnership so that the accounts receivable have an adjusted basis of $45,000 and A has an outside basis of $90,000. For each part, determine only the amount of A's Section 751(a) ordinary income:

(a) A sells his interest to D on January 1.

(b) What result in (a), above, if the partnership held the inventory as a capital asset, but A is a dealer in that type of property?

(c) What result in (a), above, if the partnership owns no inventory but has a 50% interest in another partnership (partnership #2), whose only assets are inventory with a basis of $150,000 and a value of $180,000?

(d) What result in (a), above, if in addition the partnership had a contract worth $30,000 to perform real estate management services for the next ten years?

## 2.   CAPITAL GAINS LOOK-THROUGH RULE

Code: §§  1(h)(5)(B), (9), (10).

Regulations: §§  1.1(h)–1(a), (b)(1), (2), (3)(i) & (ii).

In order to apply the Code's different rates for taxing long-term capital gains, the regulations apply a "look-through rule" for sales or exchanges of interests in a partnership, an S corporation, or a trust.[1] As a result, a partner who sells a partnership interest held for more than one year may recognize Section 751 ordinary income and up to three different types of long-term capital gains: collectibles gain (taxable at rates up to 28 percent), unrecaptured Section 1250 gain (taxable at a 25 percent maximum rate), and "residual" capital gain (taxable at a 15 percent maximum rate).[2]

Under Section 1(h)(5)(B), any gain from the sale of a partnership interest held for more than one year that is attributable to unrealized appreciation in the value of the partnership's collectibles is treated as gain from the sale or exchange of a collectible. The regulations provide that the selling partner's share of collectibles gain is the amount of the net collectibles gain (but not net loss) that would be allocated to that partner (including any residual allocation under Section 704(c)) if the partnership transferred all of its collectibles for cash equal to the fair market value of such assets in a fully taxable transaction immediately before the transfer of the partnership interest.[3] The same hypothetical sale approach is used to determine a selling partner's share of unrecaptured Section 1250 capital gain.[4] The selling partner's residual capital gain is the amount of the

---

1.  I.R.C. § 1.1(h)–1.

2.  Reg. § 1.1(h)–1(a). See I.R.C. § 1(h).

3.  Reg. § 1.1(h)–1(b)(2)(ii). If less than all of the realized gain in the partnership interest is recognized, a proportionate

amount of the gain in the collectibles is taxed. Id.

4.  Reg. § 1.1(h)–1(b)(3)(ii).

Section 741 long-term capital gain or loss minus the partner's shares of collectibles and unrecaptured Section 1250 gains.[5] Thus, the approach of the look-through rule for capital gains is quite similar to the method used to identify the amount of a selling partner's Section 751(a) gain and Section 741 gain.[6]

The following problem is adapted from examples in the regulations.[7] Use it to see if you can apply Section 751(a) in conjunction with the look-through rule for capital gains.

## PROBLEM

A and B are equal partners in a personal services partnership. Each partner acquired her partnership interest for cash several years ago. None of the partnership's assets is Section 704(c) property. The partnership has the following balance sheet:

| Assets | A.B. | F.M.V. | Liabilities and Partners' Capital | A.B. | F.M.V. |
|---|---|---|---|---|---|
| Cash | $13,000 | $13,000 | Liabilities: | | $2,000 |
| Capital Assets: | | | Capital: | | |
| Collectibles | 1,000 | 3,000 | A | $10,000 | 15,000 |
| Other | 6,000 | 2,000 | B | 10,000 | 15,000 |
| Subtotal | 7,000 | 5,000 | | | |
| | | | | | |
| Receivables | 0 | 14,000 | | | |
| Total | $20,000 | $32,000 | | $20,000 | $32,000 |

Consider the tax consequences to B on her sale in each of the following alternative situations:

(a) B sells her interest for $15,000 cash.

(b) B sells her interest for $16,000 cash and under the partnership agreement all gain from the sale of the collectibles is allocated to B.

(c) Same as (a), above, except that the collectibles have a basis of $3,000 and a fair market value of $1,000, and the other capital asset has a basis of $4,000 and a fair market value of $4,000.

## 3. COLLATERAL ISSUES

### a. HOLDING PERIOD

Regulations: §§ 1.1(h)–1(f) Example 5; 1.1223–3(a), (b), (c).

---

**5.** Reg. § 1.1(h)–1(c).

**6.** Reg. § 1.1(h)–1(e) provides that reporting rules similar to the reporting rules under Section 751(a) apply when a seller of a partnership interest recognizes collectibles gain or Section 1250 capital gain.

**7.** See Reg. § 1.1(h)–1(f) Examples 1, 2, & 3.

A partner may have a divided holding period in a partnership interest.[1] For example, assume a partner has held his partnership interest more than one year and the partner makes a cash contribution to the partnership. For the next year the partner will have a short-term holding period in the portion of the partnership interest attributable to the cash contribution.[2] Thus, if the partner sells all or a part of the partnership interest within one year of the cash contribution, any capital gain or loss has to be divided between long-term and short-term capital gain or loss in the same proportion as the long-term and short-term holding periods for the partnership interest.[3] The regulations integrate the holding period rule and the look-through rule for capital gains by first identifying the portions of the selling partner's Section 741 capital gain or loss that are long-term or short-term capital gain or loss. Then a proportionate amount of any collectibles or unrecaptured Section 1250 gain is deemed to be part of the long-term capital gain or loss. For example, assume a partner's partnership interest has a basis of $7,000 and a holding period that is 50 percent long-term and 50 percent short-term. Assume further that the partner's Section 751 ordinary income is $2,000 and the partner's allocable share of the partnership's collectibles gain is also $2,000. If the partner sells the partnership interest for $14,000, his total gain is $7,000 ($14,000 amount realized less $7,000 basis). Section 751(a) would characterize $2,000 of that gain as ordinary income and the remaining $5,000 of Section 741 capital gain would be characterized as $2,500 long-term capital gain and $2,500 short-term capital gain (50 percent each per the holding periods). The gain attributable to the collectibles that is allocable to the portion of the interest sold with a long-term holding period is $1,000 (again, 50 percent per the holding periods allocation). Thus, the partner would recognize $1,000 of collectibles gain, $1,500 of residual (i.e., 15 percent) long-term capital gain and $2,500 of short-term capital gain, in addition to $2,000 of Section 751(a) ordinary income.[4]

The regulations contain a few special rules for determining the holding period of a partner selling a partnership interest. First, if a partner both makes cash contributions and receives cash distributions during the one-year period before the sale or exchange of the partnership interest, the partner may reduce the cash contributions made during the year by the cash distributions on a last-in-first-out basis, treating all cash distributions as if they were received immediately before the sale or exchange.[5] Also, contributions of Section 751(c) unrealized receivables and Section 751(d) inventory items within one year of a sale or exchange of a partnership interest are disregarded for purposes of determining the holding period of

**1.** Reg. § 1.1223–3(a).

**2.** Reg. § 1.1223–3(b)(1).

**3.** Reg. § 1.1223–3(c)(1),(2)(ii).

**4.** See Reg. § 1.1(h)–1(f) Example 5.

**5.** Reg. § 1.1223–3(b)(2); see Reg. § 1.1223–3(f) Example 3. The cash distributions are treated as made at the time of the distribution if gain or loss is recognized under Section 731. Id. Deemed contributions of cash under Section 752(a) and deemed distributions of cash under Section 752(b) are disregarded to the extent they are disregarded in determining the selling partner's capital account. Reg. §§ 1.1223–3(b)(3); 1.704–1(b)(2)(iv)(c).

the partnership interest if the partner recognizes ordinary income or loss on such Section 751 assets in a fully taxable transaction.[6] The taxable transaction can be either a sale of all or a part of the partnership interest or a sale by the partnership of the contributed section 751 asset.[7] The theory of this exception is that the contributed section 751 asset should not both produce ordinary income to the selling partner and result in a short-term holding period in the partnership interest.

b.   INSTALLMENT SALES OF PARTNERSHIP INTERESTS

# Revenue Ruling 89–108

1989–2 Cum.Bull. 100.

ISSUE

If the property of a partnership includes inventory, to what extent may the installment method of reporting income under section 453 of the Internal Revenue Code be used to report income on the sale of an interest in that partnership?

FACTS

*P* was a partner in a partnership that held * * * inventory within the meaning of section 751(d) of the Code. A portion of this property constituted inventory within the meaning of section 453(b)(2)(B). The partnership did not hold any unrealized receivables within the meaning of section 751(c). *P* sold *P*'s partnership interest in exchange for an installment note. The gain *P* recognized from the sale was, in part, attributable to the partnership inventory. Interests in the partnership were not traded on an established market, and therefore the provisions of section 453(k) did not make the sale ineligible for installment method reporting.

LAW AND ANALYSIS

Section 453(a) of the Code states that, except as otherwise provided, income from an installment sale shall be taken into account under the installment method. Section 453(b)(1) defines an installment sale as a disposition of property where at least one payment is to be received after the close of the taxable year in which the disposition occurs. Section 453(c) defines the installment method as a method under which the income recognized for any taxable year from a disposition is that proportion of the payments received in that year which the gross profit (realized or to be realized when payment is completed) bears to the total contract price. Section 453(b)(2)(B) precludes installment method reporting in the case of a sale of personal property that is required to be included in inventory of the taxpayer if on hand at the close of the taxable year.

---

**6.**  Reg. § 1.1223–3(b)(4). This exception is not available if the partner would not otherwise be treated as holding any portion of the interest long-term (e.g., because the partner's only contributions to the partner-ship are Section 751 assets or Section 751 assets within the one year period). Id.

**7.**  Id.

Section 741 of the Code provides that, in the case of a sale or exchange of a partnership interest, gain or loss recognized to the transferor is considered gain or loss from the sale or exchange of a capital asset, except as otherwise provided in section 751.

Section 751(a) of the Code provides that the amount received by a transferor partner in exchange for all or a part of a partnership interest shall be considered as an amount realized from the sale or exchange of property other than a capital asset, to the extent such an amount is attributable to unrealized receivables or inventory items * * *.

* * * Under section 751(d)[1], inventory items include property of the partnership described in section 1221(1). Section 1221(1) refers to property which would properly be included in the inventory of the taxpayer if on hand at the close of the taxable year, and property held by the taxpayer primarily for sale to customers in the ordinary course of his trade or business. Under section 751(d)[4], inventory items also include any property held by the partnership that, if held by the selling or distributee partner, would be considered property of the type described in section 751(d)[1].

Under section 741 of the Code, the sale of a partnership interest generally is treated as the sale of a single capital asset without regard to the nature of the underlying partnership property. See H.R.Rep. No. 1337, 83d Cong., 2d Sess. 70 (1954). In this respect, the tax treatment of the sale of a partnership interest differs from that accorded the sale of a sole proprietorship. See, e.g., Williams v. McGowan, 152 F.2d 570 (2d Cir.1945), which held that the sale of an entire business as a going concern was the sale of the individual assets of the business. See also Rev.Rul. 68–13, 1968–1 C.B. 195, which holds that the installment sale of a sole proprietorship is generally considered to be a sale of individual assets of the proprietorship for purposes of applying section 453.

Section 751 of the Code was enacted to prevent the conversion of certain potential ordinary income into capital gain upon the sale or exchange of a partnership interest. This section, in effect, severs certain income items from the partnership interest. H.R.Rep. No. 1337, supra, at 70, 71, and S.Rep. No. 1622, 83d Cong., 2d Sess. 99 (1954). Thus, to the extent a partnership interest represents * * * inventory or unrealized receivables described in section 751, the tax consequences to the transferor partner are "the same tax consequences which would be accorded an individual entrepreneur." H.R.Rep. No. 1337 at 71, and S.Rep. 1622, supra, at 99. In effect, the transferor partner is treated as disposing of the property described in section 751 "independently of the rest of his partnership interest." S.Rep. No. 1622 at 98, 99. * * *

Gain recognized under section 741 of the Code on the sale of a partnership interest is reportable under the installment method. See Rev. Rul. 76–483, 1976–2 C.B. 131. However, because section 751 effectively treats a partner as if the partner had sold an interest in the section 751 property of the partnership, the portion of the gain that is attributable to section 751 property is reportable under the installment method only to the extent that income realized on a direct sale of the section 751 property

would be reportable under such method. Because the installment method of reporting income would not be available on a sole proprietor's sale of the inventory, the installment method is not available for reporting income realized on the sale of a partnership interest to the extent attributable to the * * * inventory which constitutes inventory within the meaning of section 453(b)(2)(B).

Accordingly, P's income from the sale of the partnership interest may not be reported under the installment method to the extent it represents income attributable to the partnership's * * * inventory which would not be eligible for installment sale treatment if sold directly. The balance of the income realized by P from the sale of the partnership interest is reportable under the installment method.

## HOLDING

Under section 453 of the Code, the income from the sale of a partnership interest may not be reported under the installment method to the extent it represents income attributable to the partnership's * * * inventory (within the meaning of section 751(d) of the Code) which would not be eligible for the installment sale treatment if sold directly. This holding is not to be construed as an interpretation of sections 453(k) and 453A(e).

## NOTE

The relationship of the installment sales provisions of Section 453 to the sale of a partnership interest raises a number of intriguing questions.[1] At the heart of the issue is whether an entity or aggregate approach, or some blend of the two, should be adopted in determining whether deferral of gain is permissible. The only statutory answer is found in Section 453(i)(2), which expressly denies installment sale treatment to Section 1245 and Section 1250 recapture income. "Recapture income," for this purpose, includes "so much of section 751 as relates to section 1245 or 1250."[2] This definition makes it clear that Section 751 gain on the sale of a partnership interest that is attributable to depreciation recapture must be recognized in the year of sale. In Revenue Ruling 89–108, the Service began to unravel some additional questions when it used a modified aggregate approach in ruling that installment sale reporting is not available for gain attributable to inventory that would not be eligible for installment sale treatment if the inventory were sold directly.

An interesting aspect of Revenue Ruling 89–108 is that the partnership did not own any unrealized receivables. In its analysis, however, the Service states broadly that the portion of any gain on the sale of a partnership interest that is attributable to "section 751 property" may be reported

---

**1.** This Note assumes that the seller has not elected out of installment sale treatment under Section 453(d). For discussions of this area, see McKee, Nelson & Whitmire, Federal Taxation of Partnerships and Partners ¶ 16.05 (3d ed. 1996); Willis, Pennell & Postlewaite, Partnership Taxation ¶ 12.01[12] (6th ed. 1997).

**2.** I.R.C. § 453(i)(2).

under the installment method only to the extent that the income could have been so reported on a direct sale of the property. It follows that gain attributable to unrealized receivables, other than depreciation recapture,[3] must be analyzed to determine what portion (if any) would be eligible for installment reporting if sold directly.[4] The Service's next project should be a ruling illustrating the application of the installment reporting rules on a sale of an interest in a partnership that holds unrealized receivables.[5] In keeping with its middle ground approach in Revenue Ruling 89–108, the Service presumably would rule that installment sale treatment is generally not available with respect to Section 751 gain attributable to unrealized receivables except in the rare case where a direct sale of the receivables would qualify for installment reporting under Section 453.

Revenue Ruling 89–108 also did not discuss the impact of Section 453(k)(2), which denies the installment method of reporting on the sale of stock, securities and other property regularly traded on an established securities market. Since the ruling states that Section 741 gain may be reported under the installment method, it implies that the sale of an interest in a nonpublicly traded partnership would qualify for installment reporting even if the partnership itself owned some publicly traded stock or securities. Query whether this treatment is consistent with Congress's directive to the Treasury to issue regulations disallowing use of the installment method where the rules in Section 453(k) "would be avoided through the use of related parties, pass-thru entities, or intermediaries."[6]

## PROBLEM

The ABC partnership operates a hotel and has the following balance sheet:

**3.** See supra note 2 and accompanying text.

**4.** See Town and Country Food Co. v. Commissioner, 51 T.C. 1049 (1969), acq. 1969–2 C.B. xxv, denying Section 453 treatment to a sale of receivables for inventory and services. Compare the *Ledoux* case, supra p. 257, where the taxpayer reported his gain under Section 453. Even though the partnership held unrealized receivables for services, the Service did not question the extent to which Section 453 applied to the sale.

**5.** See I.R.C. § 453(b)(2), (*l*).

**6.** I.R.C. § 453(k), flush language. In reporting its version of the Tax Reform Act of 1986, the Senate Finance Committee stated that these regulations should not deny use of the installment method if the selling partner could not have sold or caused the sale of the publicly traded securities directly. In an example, the Finance Committee indicated that a retiring partner in a large investment partnership could report a sale of his partnership interest on the installment method even though a substantial portion of the value of the interest was attributable to publicly traded stock held by the partnership, provided that the partner could not have sold or caused the sale of the partnership's assets directly. S.Rep. No. 99–313, 99th Cong., 2d Sess. 131 (1986). But this language was not included in the Conference Report or the Joint Committee on Taxation's General Explanation of the 1986 Act. The Service also has not issued regulations under Section 453A(e)(2), which permits an aggregate approach to be used when the special rules for nondealers in Section 453A are applied to a partnership interest.

| Assets | A.B. | F.M.V. | Partners' Capital | A.B.* | F.M.V. |
|---|---|---|---|---|---|
| Hotel (no recapture) | $ 30,000 | $300,000 | A | $ 38,000 | $150,000 |
| Furniture (all gain is § 1245) | 30,000 | 90,000 | B | 38,000 | 150,000 |
| Inventory (products sold by hotel shops) | 54,000 | 60,000 | C | 38,000 | 150,000 |
| | $114,000 | $450,000 | | $114,000 | $450,000 |

\* Basis figures represent each partner's outside basis including their share of liabilities

Disregarding any application of §§ 483 and 1274, what are the tax consequences to A if he sells his interest for $150,000, to be paid $50,000 per year over three years? A does not use § 453(d) to elect out of § 453 treatment.

## B.  CONSEQUENCES TO THE BUYING PARTNER

Code: §§ 742; 743; 752(a); 754; 755. Skim §§ 732(d); 734(b); 761(e); 774(a); 1060.

Regulations: §§ 1.743–1(a)–(e), (j)(1)–(3)(i); 1.754–1; 1.755–1(a), (b)(1)–(3); 1.755–1(a)(2)–(5).

*Introduction.* The general statutory rules governing the tax consequences to purchasers of partnership interests adopt the entity approach to partnership taxation. Section 742 provides that a partner takes a cost basis for a partnership interest acquired by purchase; for this purpose, cost includes the partner's share of any partnership liabilities.[1]

So far, so good.... But the above rule involves only the partner's outside basis. The rule with respect to the inside basis is initially quite surprising. Assume Buyer purchases a one-third interest in a cash method, calendar year service partnership which has as its primary asset $90,000 of accounts receivable with a zero basis and $30,000 of other assets. On December 20, Buyer pays $40,000 for the interest and thus has an outside basis of $40,000. In effect, he has paid $30,000 for his one-third interest in the receivables and $10,000 for his one-third interest in other assets. On January 1 of the following year all the receivables are collected by the partnership. One's initial reaction is to say that Buyer has no income with respect to this collection. After all, Buyer paid $30,000 for his interest in the receivables, and their collection simply results in a return of capital. Right? ... Wrong!!! Section 743(a) generally provides that "[t]he basis of partnership property shall not be adjusted as the result of a transfer of an

---

**1.** I.R.C. § 752(d). Apart from tax consequences, the purchaser of a partnership interest steps into the shoes of the selling partner. To evidence the fact that the buyer has acquired the rights to partnership assets and assumed the liabilities previously attributed to the seller, the selling partner's capital account carries over to the buyer. See Reg. § 1.704–1(b)(2)(iv)(*l*).

interest in a partnership by sale or exchange * * *.'' Thus, the partnership has $90,000 of ordinary income when the receivables are collected, and each partner, including Buyer, is taxed on his one-third distributive share, or $30,000 of ordinary income. This result occurs even though Buyer paid $30,000 for his share of the receivables and has no real gain on their collection. In addition, Seller was taxed under Section 751(a) on the $30,000 of ordinary income attributable to the receivables when he sold his partnership interest to Buyer.

In searching for relief from this result, Buyer may find solace in the fact that he may increase his outside basis by his $30,000 distributive share of partnership income under Section 705(a)(1)(A). If he later sells his partnership interest for $40,000 (still its fair market value), Buyer will have a $30,000 loss, and all will be well. Right? * * * Wrong!!! To be sure, Buyer will realize a $30,000 loss on the sale; but it will be a capital loss under Section 741, not an ordinary loss, and the timing of the loss may occur much later than when the receivables were included in income.

If you are upset and somewhat baffled by these anomalous results, join the crowd.[2] But the Code provides relief, demonstrating once again that tax equity often breeds complexity. To avoid taxing the buying partner on the appreciation of his proportionate share of partnership assets prior to the date of purchase, the partnership may elect under Section 754[3] to adjust the basis of its assets under Section 743(b). In the example above, a Section 743(b) adjustment places Buyer in the same position as if he had purchased his proportionate share of partnership assets for their fair market value at the time the partnership interest was acquired, and it gives Buyer a $30,000 inside ''cost'' basis in his share of the receivables. When the receivables are collected, the other partners each will be taxed on $30,000, just as they would be in the absence of an election, but Buyer realizes no income because of the upward adjustment of his personal inside basis.[4]

The Section 743(b) basis adjustment was desirable in the example above because it eliminated the gain that otherwise would have been realized by Buyer on the collection of the accounts receivable. But the statute works in both directions. A Section 754 election also may require a *downward* adjustment to the bases of partnership assets which have declined in value as of the time of the sale or exchange of the partnership interest. Specifically, Section 743(b)(2) requires that the partnership must decrease the adjusted bases of its assets with respect to any partner if that partner's proportionate share of the partnership's total inside basis in its

**2.** One federal district judge was equally upset. In a burst of questionable judicial legislation, he refused to allow this result to occur. See Barnes v. United States, 253 F.Supp. 116 (S.D.Ill.1966).

**3.** See Reg. § 1.754–1(b) for the time and method of making the Section 754 election. A Section 754 election triggers both the Section 743(b) basis adjustment discussed in this chapter and the basis adjustment under

Section 734(b) on a distribution of partnership property. Section 734(b) is considered in Chapter 7C, infra. Once a Section 754 election is made, it applies to all subsequent partnership distributions and transfers of partnership interests unless the Service consents to revocation of the election.

**4.** Buyer's outside basis, however, would remain at $40,000.

assets exceeds the buying partner's outside basis. The amount of the downward adjustment is the excess of that partner's proportionate share of the partnership's inside bases over the partner's outside basis in his partnership interest. The buying partner's distributive share thus will not reflect any increase or decline in value of partnership assets occurring prior to his purchase of an interest in the firm.

*Mandatory Inside Basis Adjustment for Partnership with Substantial Built-in Loss.* The Section 754 election provides a buying partner with a beneficial tax avoidance strategy. If the partnership's assets have appreciated and have built-in gains, the election will eliminate the potentially disadvantageous distortions in the timing and characterization of partnership income. But if the partnership's assets have depreciated in value and would produce losses, a savvy buyer would prefer the partnership not to make the election in order to reap the tax benefit of deducting those losses.[5] In order to reduce the "heads-I-win, tails-you-lose" aspect of the election, Section 743 *requires* an adjustment to the basis of partnership property on the transfer of a partnership interest if the partnership has a "substantial built-in loss" immediately after the transfer.[6] A partnership has a substantial built-in loss if the adjusted basis in its property exceeds the property's fair market value by more than $250,000.[7] In patrolling the $250,000 threshold for abuse, the Service has the authority to aggregate related partnerships or disregard acquisitions of property designed to avoid the limit.[8]

A special rule is provided for an "electing investment partnership,"[9] such as venture capital and buyout funds formed to raise capital from investors pursuant to a private offering and to make and hold investments for capital appreciation. Congress concluded that these types of investment partnerships "would incur administrative difficulties" if they were required to make partnership-level basis adjustments when their interests were transferred.[10] To ease the burden, an electing investment partnership is allowed to use a partner-level loss limitation instead of making basis adjustments to its assets. Under the limit, a transferee partner's share of losses (without regard to gains) from the sale or exchange of partnership property is not allowed except to the extent it is established that such losses exceed any loss recognized by the transferor on the transfer of the partnership interest.[11]

---

**5.** Of course, the recognition of partnership losses reduces the partner's outside basis and will produce more income or loss on a later sale of the partner's interest, but the distortion in the timing of income works in favor of the partner.

**6.** I.R.C. §§ 743(a), (b).

**7.** I.R.C. § 743(d)(1).

**8.** I.R.C. § 743(d)(2).

**9.** An electing investment partnership must satisfy a long list of requirements set forth in Section 743(e)(6).

**10.** H. Rep. No. 108–548, 108th Cong. 2d Sess. 283 (2004).

**11.** I.R.C. § 743(e)(1), (2). Another special rule is provided for "securitization partnerships," which generally are partnerships whose sole business is to issue securities backed by the cash flow of receivables or other financial assets. Such partnerships are deemed to not have a substantial built-in loss and thereby avoid both adjustments to the bases of property and the loss-limitation rule in Section 743(e). See I.R.C. § 743(f).

*Calculating the Section 743(b) Adjustment.* The purpose of the Section 743(b) adjustment is straightforward. It is designed to give new partners a special inside basis in their share of partnership assets and in so doing place them in roughly the same position as if they had purchased those assets directly. The mechanics of computing and allocating the adjustment are more complicated. The new partner first must determine the amount of the overall basis adjustment, which is the difference between the partner's outside basis (generally, the partner's cost plus his share of partnership liabilities) and his share of the partnership's inside basis in its assets.[12] The partner is then shuttled to Section 755, which prescribes a multi-step process for allocating the adjustment among the various partnership assets.

Keeping in mind that the basic purpose of the Section 743(b) adjustment is to produce the equivalent of a cost basis in the new partner's share of the partnership's assets, the amount of the overall Section 743(b) adjustment normally should be the difference between the new partner's outside basis and his proportionate share of the partnership's inside basis. In the garden variety partnership, one devoid of the complications presented by special allocations and Section 704(c) allocations with respect to contributed property, that intuitive formula generally will be accurate. But the workings of Subchapter K are not always intuitive and seldom are simple.

The regulations provide a complex formula for determining the transferee partner's share of the partnership's inside basis of its assets. A transferee partner's share of the adjusted basis to the partnership of its property is equal to the sum of the transferee's interest in the partnership's "previously taxed capital," plus the transferee's share of partnership liabilities. The transferee's interest in the partnership's previously taxed capital is determined by considering a hypothetical disposition by the partnership of all of its assets in a fully taxable transaction for cash equal to the fair market value of the assets. The transferee's interest in the partnership's previously taxed capital generally is equal to the cash the transferee would receive on a liquidation following the hypothetical transaction, increased by the amount of tax loss and decreased by the amount of tax gain that would be allocated to the transferee from the transaction.[13] Returning to a variation of the earlier example, assume Buyer purchases for $30,000 a one-third interest in a partnership with $90,000 of accounts receivable having a zero basis. If the partnership has a Section 754 election in effect, the Section 743(b) adjustment is equal to the difference between Buyer's outside basis ($30,000) and Buyer's share of the adjusted basis to the partnership of its property. If there were a hypothetical disposition of all the partnership's assets, Buyer would receive $30,000 cash and Buyer would be allocated $30,000 tax gain from the transaction. Buyer's interest in the partnership's previously taxed capital and his share of the adjusted

---

**12.** I.R.C. § 743(b). For the rules to determine a partner's share of the adjusted basis of partnership property, see Reg. § 1.743–1(d).

**13.** Reg. § 1.743–1(d)(1) & (2); see Reg. § 1.743–1(d)(3) Example 1.

basis to the partnership of its property would be zero ($30,000 of cash received if the partnership had liquidated immediately after the hypothetical transaction, less the $30,000 of tax gain allocable to the partner on the sale of the accounts receivable). Thus, the Section 743(b) adjustment is equal to $30,000, the difference between Buyer's $30,000 outside basis and his zero share of the adjusted basis to the partnership of its property. Note that the intuitive approach was correct here; the total Section 743(b) adjustment is equal to the difference between Buyer's outside basis and his proportionate share of the partnership's zero inside basis.

The formula in the regulations is complex because it accommodates the situation where the partnership holds contributed property subject to Section 704(c). If a partner contributes appreciated or depreciated property to the partnership and later transfers his partnership interest, built-in gain or loss is allocated to the transferee partner as it would have been allocated to the transferor partner.[14] This principle is incorporated in the calculation of the transferee's share of the adjusted basis to the partnership of its property. For example, assume A contributes land worth $1,000 with an adjusted basis of $400 in exchange for a one-third interest in the ABC partnership. B and C each contribute $1,000 cash. After the land has appreciated in value to $1,300, A sells his one-third partnership interest to T for $1,100, when a Section 754 election is in effect. The amount of the tax gain allocated to T as a result of a hypothetical disposition of the partnership's assets would be $700 ($600 of Section 704(c) gain, plus one-third of the additional $300 of gain). Thus, T's interest in the partnership's previously taxed capital is $400 ($1,100, the cash T would receive on a liquidation, decreased by $700, T's share of gain from the hypothetical disposition). T's Section 743(b) adjustment to partnership property will be $700 ($1,100, T's cost for the partnership interest, less $400, T's share of the adjusted basis to the partnership of its property).[15]

*Allocation of the Adjustment under Section 755.* Once the total Section 743(b) adjustment is determined, that adjustment must be allocated among the partnership's assets under Section 755.[16] The Section 755 regulations provide that the partnership first must determine the value of its assets.[17] Next, the partnership's assets are first divided into two classes; (1) capital assets and Section 1231(b) property (capital gain property), and (2) any other property (ordinary income property).[18] The basis adjustment is then allocated between those classes of property and within each class based on the allocations of income, gain, or loss (including remedial allocations) that the transferee partner would receive if, immediately after the transfer, all of the partnership's assets were disposed of in a fully taxable transaction

---

**14.**  Reg. § 1.704–3(a)(7).

**15.**  See Reg. § 1.743–1(d)(3) Example 2.

**16.**  I.R.C. § 743(c).

**17.**  Reg. § 1.755–1(a)(1). See the text at notes 25–28 for discussion of the valuation process.

**18.**  Reg. § 1.755–1(a). For this purpose, potential recapture gain that would be treated as an unrealized receivable under Section 751(c) is treated as separate ordinary income property. Id.

for fair market value.[19] The regulations specifically permit an increase to be made to one class or one property while a decrease is made to the other class or a different property within the class.[20] Basis is first allocated to the class of ordinary income property and then to the class of capital gain property. A decrease in basis allocated to capital gain property may not produce a negative basis in any asset. Thus, if the entire decrease allocated to capital gain property reduces the basis of those assets to zero, any excess reduces the basis of the class of ordinary income property.[21] Once again, keep in mind that the adjustment to each item of property within a class of property is designed to produce the equivalent of a cost basis for the transferee partner via the Section 743(b) adjustment.[22]

An example may be helpful in illustrating the application of these rules. Assume N buys for $90,000 a one-third interest in a partnership and is entitled to a $30,000 Section 743(b) adjustment at a time when the partnership has the following assets:[23]

| Assets | A.B. | F.M.V. |
|---|---|---|
| Accounts Receivable | $ 0 | $ 45,000 |
| Inventory | 90,000 | 105,000 |
| Capital Asset | 30,000 | 45,000 |
| Depreciable Asset (no recapture) | 60,000 | 75,000 |
| | $180,000 | $270,000 |

Under Section 755, the $30,000 Section 743(b) adjustment is first allocated between the two classes of property. If the partnership sold all of its assets in a fully taxable transaction immediately after the transfer of the interest to N, the total amount of ordinary income that would be allocated to N would be $20,000 ($15,000 in the receivables and $5,000 in the inventory) and the total amount of capital or Section 1231 gain that would be allocated to N would be $10,000 ($5,000 in the capital asset and $5,000 in the depreciable asset). Thus, the amount of the adjustment that would be allocated to the ordinary income property would be $20,000 and the amount of the adjustment allocated to the capital gain property would be $10,000.

Assuming the partnership's calculator is still functioning, the next step is to allocate the adjustments to each class of property within the class based on the amount of gain or loss that would be allocated to N from the hypothetical sale of the item.[24] In the class of ordinary income property, N would be allocated $15,000 of gain from the accounts receivable and $5,000 of gain from the inventory in the hypothetical transaction. Therefore, the amount of the adjustment to the accounts receivable is $15,000 and the

---

**19.** Reg. § 1.755–1(b)(1).

**20.** Id.

**21.** Reg. § 1. 755–1(b)(2)(i).

**22.** See Reg. § 1.755–1(b)(3).

**23.** Assume that none of the assets were contributed to the partnership by the partners and that the valuation of the assets is accurate.

**24.** Reg. § 1.755–2(b)(3). The hypothetical gain or loss is adjusted in some specialized situations not implicated by this example.

amount of the adjustment to the inventory is $5,000. In the class of capital gain property, N would be allocated $5,000 of gain from the capital asset and $5,000 of gain from the depreciable asset. Therefore, the amount of the adjustment to each of those assets is $5,000. After these adjustments, N's personal inside basis in the assets is determined as follows:

| Asset | N's Original Share of Inside Basis | + | § 743(b) Adjustment | = | New Inside Basis |
|-------|-----------------------------------|---|---------------------|---|------------------|
| Accounts Receivable | $ 0 | | $15,000 | | $15,000 |
| Inventory | 30,000 | | 5,000 | | 35,000 |
| Capital Asset | 10,000 | | 5,000 | | 15,000 |
| Depreciable Asset | 20,000 | | 5,000 | | 25,000 |
| Total | $60,000 | | $30,000 | | $90,000 |

The preceding example is relatively simple because all of the assets have appreciated in value. Problem 2 below illustrates these rules in more complicated situations.

A more practical complication results from the valuation of partnership assets that is required in the process of allocating a basis adjustment under section 755. If the assets of the partnership constitute a trade or business, the regulations provide that the valuation generally is done in accordance with the rules under Section 1060 for "applicable asset acquisitions."[25] The value of the partnership's assets other than Section 197 intangibles is first determined under an "all facts and circumstances" test.[26] The partnership then determines the gross value of all its assets, generally with reference to the basis of the transferee partner.[27] If the partnership's gross value is greater than the aggregate value of partnership property other than Section 197 intangibles, the excess is (1) first allocated to Section 197 intangibles other than goodwill and going concern value, and (2) then to goodwill and going concern value.[28]

*Effect of the Section 743(b) Adjustment.* The regulations provide that a basis adjustment under Section 743(b) is personal to the transferee partner. No adjustment is made to the common basis of the partnership property and a Section 743(b) adjustment has no effect on the partnership's computation of any Section 703 item.[29] A partnership first computes all partnership items at the partnership level and each partner, including the transferee, is allocated those items under Section 704. The partnership then adjusts the transferee's distributive share of partnership income, gain, loss or

---

**25.** Reg. § 1.755–1(a)(1) & (2). The definition of a "trade or business" for this purpose is borrowed from the active trade or business requirement under Section 355 (relating to tax-free corporate divisions). Reg. §§ 1.755–1(a)(2), 1.1060–1(b)(2). Alternatively, assets represent a trade or business if "goodwill or going concern value could under any circumstances" attach to them. Id. Although the definition is quite broad, it should not embrace partnerships engaged in purely passive investment activities.

**26.** Reg. § 1.755–1(a)(3).

**27.** Reg. § 1.755–1(a)(4).

**28.** Reg. § 1.755–1(a)(5). The buyer and seller also must comply with certain information reporting requirements. See Reg. § 1.755–1(d).

**29.** Reg. § 1.743–1(j)(1).

deduction to reflect the Section 743(b) basis adjustment. These basis adjustments do not affect the transferee's capital account.[30]

If depreciable or amortizable property acquires an upward basis adjustment under Section 743(b), the property generally is treated as two separate assets for depreciation or amortization purposes. The first asset retains the original depreciation remaining in the depreciable or amortizable property prior to the adjustment. The amount of the adjustment is treated as being attributable to a newly purchased asset for depreciation or amortization purposes.[31]

*Relationship to Section 704(c).* A principal goal of the regulations is to coordinate Sections 704(c) and 743. To that end, they generally provide that a transferee's income, gain, or loss from the sale or exchange of a partnership asset in which the transferee has a basis adjustment is equal to the transferee's share of the partnership's gain or loss from the sale of the asset (including any remedial allocations of gain or loss), minus the amount of any positive Section 743(b) basis adjustment or plus the amount of any negative Section 743(b) adjustment.[32] For example, assume A and B form an equal partnership with A contributing nondepreciable property ($100 fair market value, $50 adjusted basis) and B contributing $100 cash. The partnership uses the traditional method for making Section 704(c) allocations. A later sells her partnership interest to T for $100 when the partnership has a Section 754 election in effect. T will receive a $50 basis adjustment that is allocated to the nondepreciable property. If the partnership sells the nondepreciable property for $90 it will have a $10 book loss and a $40 tax gain. T will receive an allocation of all $40 of tax gain under Section 704(c). Because T has a $50 basis adjustment in the property, she recognizes a $10 loss from the partnership's sale of the property.[33]

In the preceding example, T stepped into A's shoes with respect to the contributed property and the ceiling rule applied under the traditional method when the partnership sold that property for a book loss.[34] Assume instead that the partnership uses the remedial method for making Section 704(c) allocations. If the partnership again sells the property for $90, the $10 book loss will be allocated equally between the partners, and the $40 of tax gain will be allocated to T under Section 704(c). To match his $5 share of book loss, B will be allocated $5 of remedial loss and T will be allocated an offsetting $5 of remedial gain. Thus, T will be allocated a total of $45 of tax gain with respect to the property. Because T has a $50 basis adjust-

---

**30.** Reg. § 1.743–1(j)(2).

**31.** Reg. § 1.743–1(j)(4)(i)(B)(1). The legislative history of Section 197 makes it clear that these same rules apply to Section 197 property, such as goodwill. H.R. Rep. No. 2141, 103d Cong., 1st Sess. 336–37 (1993). If, however, the partnership elects to use the remedial allocation method in Section 1.704–3(d) with respect to recovery property, then any Section 743(b) increase attributable to Section 704(c) built-in gain is recovered over the remaining recovery period for the partnership's excess book basis in the property under the remedial method. Reg. § 1.743–1(j)(4)(i)(B)(2); see also Reg. § 1.743–1(j)(4)(i)(C) Examples.

**32.** Reg. § 1.743–1(j)(3)(i).

**33.** See Reg. § 1.743–1(j)(3)(ii) Example 2.

**34.** See Chapter 4C, supra.

ment, she recognizes a $5 loss from the partnership's sale of the property if the remedial method is used.[35]

One other aspect of Section 704(c) may also come into play in connection with the transfer of a partnership interest. Section 704(c)(1)(C) provides that in the case of property that was contributed to a partnership with a built-in loss, no other partner may be allocated that precontribution loss.[36] Thus, the purchaser of a partnership interest may not obtain the benefit of a built-in loss contributed by the seller of the interest.

## PROBLEMS

**1**. On January 1 of year one, Nupartner purchased a one-third interest in a partnership for $40,000. At the time of purchase the partnership had the following assets:

|  | A.B. | F.M.V. |
|---|---|---|
| Accounts Receivable | $    0 | $30,000 |
| Land | 60,000 | 90,000 |

(a) If § 754 had not been elected by the partnership, what is the result to Nupartner upon collection of the receivables?

(b) What result to Nupartner in (a), above, if the partnership had made a § 754 election?

(c) Who makes a § 754 election? When and how must the election be made?

(d) Should Nupartner have conditioned his purchase of the partnership interest upon a § 754 election?

(e) Will Nupartner's purchase and the § 754 election have any immediate tax impact on the remaining old partners?

(f) Will the § 743(b) basis adjustment affect Nupartner in situations other than on collection of partnership income or sales of partnership property?

(g) At the end of year three, the partnership had earnings, all of which had been distributed, and it continued to hold the identical accounts receivable and land, each of which had the same basis and fair market value. Assuming no § 754 election, what result to Nupartner if, before the receivables are collected, he sells his partnership interest to Buyer for $40,000?

(h) What result to Nupartner in (g), above, if the partnership had made a § 754 election?

(i) What is Buyer's inside basis in (h), above?

(j) If the partnership properly maintained capital accounts and the selling partner's capital account prior to the sale of his interest was $20,000, what is Nupartner's capital account upon purchase of his one-third interest for $40,000 if:

**35.**   See Reg. § 1.743–1(j)(3)(ii) Example    **36.**   See Chapter 4C6, supra.
3.

(i) a § 754 election were in effect;

(ii) a § 754 election were not in effect.

See Reg. § 1.704–1(b)(2)(iv)(*l*), (*m*)(*1*) and (*2*).

(k) If a § 754 election is in effect, will each new purchasing partner create havoc for the partnership's accountant?

**2.** The ABC cash method general partnership, which has made a § 754 election, had the following balance sheet at the time D purchased C's interest for $60,000. None of the partnership's assets were contributed by a partner:

| Assets | A.B. | F.M.V. | Liabilities and Partners' Capital | A.B.* | F.M.V. |
|---|---|---|---|---|---|
| | | | Liabilities: | | $ 30,000 |
| | | | Capital: | | |
| Accounts Receivable | $      0 | $ 30,000 | A | $30,000 | 60,000 |
| Inventory | 30,000 | 60,000 | B | 30,000 | 60,000 |
| Land (§ 1231 asset) | 30,000 | 15,000 | C | 30,000 | 60,000 |
| Building (§ 1231 asset) | 30,000 | 105,000 | | | |
| | $90,000 | $210,000 | | $90,000 | $210,000 |

\* Basis figures represent each partner's outside basis including their share of liabilities

(a) What is D's personal inside basis in each of the assets?

(b) What is D's personal inside basis in the assets if he paid $70,000 (rather than $60,000) for C's interest?

(c) Same as (a), above (i.e., D buys C's interest for $60,000), except that C contributed the accounts receivable to the partnership at a time when the fair market value of the receivables was $30,000 and their basis was zero.

**3.** The DEF cash method general partnership, which has not made a § 754 election, had the following balance sheet at the time G purchased D's interest for $50,000. D contributed the inventory to the partnership at a time when the value of the inventory was $15,000.

| Assets | A.B. | F.M.V. | Liabilities and Partners' Capital | A.B. | F.M.V. |
|---|---|---|---|---|---|
| Cash | $ 50,000 | $ 50,000 | D | $100,000 | $ 50,000 |
| Inventory | 30,000 | 10,000 | E | 125,000 | 50,000 |
| Land | 270,000 | 90,000 | F | 125,000 | 50,000 |
| | $350,000 | $150,000 | | $350,000 | $150,000 |

(a) Will the basis of the partnership's assets be adjusted under § 743 as a result of D's sale to G? Should G urge the partnership to make a § 754 election?

(b) Assuming no adjustments are made to the basis of the partnership's assets, what will be the result to G if the partnership sells the inventory for $10,000? What result to G if the partnership sells the land for $90,000?

CHAPTER 7

# OPERATING DISTRIBUTIONS

## A. INTRODUCTION

At this point in the study of partnership taxation, a normal student might feel entrapped in an intricate jigsaw puzzle, anxiously awaiting the moment when the pieces begin to fit together. The study of operating distributions[1] provides an opportunity for that crucial breakthrough, but the promised land is attainable only by carefully dissecting the statute while keeping the broad concepts of Subchapter K clearly in focus.

Consider, at the outset, two principles that have emerged in previous chapters. Under the aggregate approach to partnership taxation, a partner is taxed on his distributive share of partnership income whether or not it is distributed.[2] A partner's outside basis includes his share of those previously taxed profits in addition to his capital contribution to the firm.[3] It follows that, to the extent of that outside basis, a partner should not be required to recognize gain on a current distribution of cash. But if a cash distribution exceeds his outside basis, the partner has received something more than his investment in the partnership and his share of previously taxed income and thus should be required to recognize gain to the extent of the excess. If a distribution consists of property other than cash, a different approach is possible. A transferred basis mechanism can be used to preserve any unrecognized gain for reckoning at a later time. We are about to discover that the treatment of partnership distributions is consistent with these principles. Congress has gone to great lengths to provide nonrecognition of gain or loss on an operating distribution by a partnership and to preserve any unrecognized gain or loss through appropriate adjustments to basis.

Another important goal of the Code has been to prevent taxpayers from converting ordinary income into capital gain. To forestall that type of potential tax avoidance in the partnership distribution setting, it is necessary to preserve the ordinary income character of certain assets in the hands of the distributee partner. Section 735 implements this policy for distributed property in a manner mirroring the treatment of contributed property under Section 724.

A third theme was introduced in the preceding chapter, where we saw that the failure to adjust the basis of partnership assets after the sale of a

---

1. "Operating" (sometimes called "current") distributions are any distributions by the partnership which are not liquidating distributions. Liquidating distributions are discussed in Chapter 8, infra.

2. I.R.C. § 701.

3. I.R.C. §§ 705; 722. Cf. I.R.C. § 752(a).

partnership interest may distort the tax treatment of the buying partner.[4] In the case of operating distributions, similar distortions may affect all the remaining partners. This chapter provides another opportunity to study a set of rules aimed at curing this imbalance through adjustments to the bases of partnership assets.

And no area of partnership tax is complete without a few complex anti-abuse provisions. Because Congress made every effort to defer the recognition of gain or loss on partnership distributions, it should come as no surprise that taxpayers have attempted to exploit these rules to achieve favorable results indirectly that could not be reached in a more straightforward manner. The final sections of this chapter examine the Congressional response to several sophisticated forms of taxpayer misbehavior. Sections 704(c)(1)(B) and 737 override the general nonrecognition rules in order to combat the "mixing bowl transaction," a strategy where a partner transfers appreciated property to a partnership and, within a seven-year period, the partnership either distributes the contributed property to another partner or distributes other property to the contributing partner. In either case, the agenda is to shift or defer the recognition of the contributing partner's precontribution gain. The purpose of Section 751(b), which also overrides the general nonrecognition rules previewed above, is to curb the potential shifting of the character of income that may result from distributions that alter the partners' interests in partnership property. Studying these provisions will be a memorable experience but the occasional pain should be accompanied by a greater appreciation of how different parts of the Subchapter K puzzle relate to one another.

Finally, while studying these *tax* rules governing partnership distributions, one must not lose sight of the attendant economic consequences. Because an operating distribution results in the withdrawal of part of a partner's equity in the partnership, the value of that partner's interest obviously is reduced. And if an operating distribution is not in accordance with the partners' respective interests in the partnership, it also will alter their future economic relationship. To properly account for these effects, the partnership allocation regulations logically require that a partner's capital account must be decreased by the amount of money and the fair market value of any property distributed to the partner.[5] If the partnership distributes property with a fair market value that differs from its book value, other adjustments—such as a restatement of the partnership assets and partner capital accounts at their current fair market values—also may be necessary to reflect accurately the respective economic interests of the partners after the distribution.[6]

**4.**  See Chapter 6B, supra.

**5.**  Reg. § 1.704–1(b)(2)(iv)(*b*)(*4*) & (*5*).

**6.**  See Reg. § 1.704–1(b)(2)(iv)(*f*)(*5*) and Section C of this chapter, infra.

## B. CONSEQUENCES TO THE DISTRIBUTEE PARTNER

## 1. NONRECOGNITION RULES ON THE DISTRIBUTION

Code: §§ 731; 732(a), (c) & (d); 733.

Regulations: §§ 1.731–1(a)(1) & (3), (c); 1.732–1(a), (c), (d)(1) & (4); 1.733–1.

*Distributions of Cash.* Section 731(a) generally provides that a partner will recognize neither gain nor loss on a current distribution of cash, and Section 733 provides that the partner's outside basis will be reduced, but not below zero, by the amount of the distribution. We have seen that the partner's outside basis represents his original investment in the partnership, adjusted upwards (or downwards) for the partner's share of profits (or losses). Consequently, to the extent of the partner's outside basis, an operating distribution represents earnings previously taxed to the partner or a return of capital. Thus, it is appropriate to confer nonrecognition of gain to the distributee partner and to require a corresponding downward adjustment to basis. On the loss side, an operating distribution does not represent a closed transaction and thus is a premature occasion for determining whether a loss has been sustained by the distributee partner.

If, however, cash distributions exceed a partner's outside basis, the partner is receiving something more than previously taxed income or a return of capital. Section 731(a)(1) thus provides, in a manner comparable to other nonrecognition provisions,[1] that the excess of cash received over the distributee partner's outside basis is treated as gain from the sale or exchange of a partnership interest—normally capital gain, unless Section 751 applies.[2] This statutory solution avoids the tax taboo of a negative basis and ensures that the partner's gain will not escape the tax collector.

The foregoing rules embrace both actual cash distributions and transactions that are treated as cash distributions. For example, recall that any reduction of a partner's share of partnership liabilities is treated as a distribution of cash to the partner.[3] Such reductions occur not only as partnership liabilities are paid off but also on various other types of transactions such as an abandonment of property,[4] a reconveyance or foreclosure,[5] a condemnation[6] or another partner's assumption of a share of liability on property.[7] A further example is provided in Revenue Ruling 79–205, which follows at page 291 in the text.

**1.** See, e.g., I.R.C. §§ 301(c)(3); 357(c).

**2.** See I.R.C. §§ 731(d); 751(b).

**3.** I.R.C. § 752(b).

**4.** Middleton v. Commissioner, 77 T.C. 310 (1981), affirmed per curiam, 693 F.2d 124 (11th Cir.1982); cf. O'Brien v. Commissioner, 77 T.C. 113 (1981).

**5.** Freeland v. Commissioner, 74 T.C. 970 (1980).

**6.** Rev.Rul. 81–242, 1981–2 C.B. 147.

**7.** Stilwell v. Commissioner, 46 T.C. 247 (1966). Cf. Rev.Rul. 74–40, 1974–1 C.B. 159.

The operating distribution rules do not apply if cash received from a partnership is not in fact a distribution. For example, if the cash is received as a loan, the transaction is governed by Section 707(a)(1) rather than Section 731(a)(1).[8] A discharge of the obligation to repay the loan, however, is treated as a distribution of cash.[9] Similarly, if the cash is a mere advance or draw against a partner's distributive share of income, it is equivalent to a loan and is not treated as a distribution until the last day of the partner's year.[10] A leading treatise suggests that the nature of the distribution as an advance or a draw will be assured if the partner is under an obligation to repay any distribution in excess of his share of partnership income for the year.[11]

*Distributions of Property.* Neither the partnership nor the distributee partner will recognize gain or loss on an operating distribution of property,[12] unless Section 704(c)(1)(B), Section 737,[13] or Section 751(b) applies,[14] or the distribution is of marketable securities. This is because a distribution of property, unlike a cash distribution, provides an opportunity for the deferral of gain. Any gain inherent in the distributed property is preserved by assigning the distributee a transferred basis under Section 732(a). Any gain inherent in the partner's interest in the partnership is preserved by Section 733, which reduces the partner's outside basis by his transferred basis in the distributed property. This scheme ensures that the sum of the partner's basis in the distributed property and his outside basis remains constant. But if the partnership's basis in the distributed assets[15] exceeds the partner's outside basis, less any cash distributed in the same transaction, the partner could not maintain his total basis unless he emerged from the distribution with a negative outside basis. Consequently, Section 732(a)(2) provides that if the partner's share of the inside basis in the distributed property exceeds his outside basis, reduced by any cash distributed in the same transaction, the transferred basis is limited to that outside basis, which then would be reduced to zero under Section 733.[16]

---

**8.** Reg. § 1.731–1(c)(2).

**9.** Id.

**10.** Reg. § 1.731–1(a)(1)(ii).

**11.** McKee, Nelson & Whitmire, Federal Taxation of Partnerships and Partners ¶ 19.03[2](3d ed. 1996).

**12.** I.R.C. § 731(a); but see I.R.C. § 731(a)(2), providing for the recognition of loss in very limited circumstances on a liquidating distribution. Section 732(f) also contains special rules for the situation where a partnership distributes corporate stock to a corporate partner which, after the distribution, controls (under Section 1504(a)(2)) the distributed corporation. The basis of the distributed corporation's assets may be reduced and the corporate partner may recognize gain. I.R.C. § 732(f)(1), (4).

**13.** Sections 704(c)(1)(B) and 737 are considered in Section D of this chapter.

**14.** See I.R.C. § 751(b), which is considered in Section E of this chapter.

**15.** This includes any special basis in the asset—for example, a Section 743(b) inside basis. In general, the holding period of the property also is tacked. See I.R.C. § 735(b), discussed in Section B2 of this chapter, infra.

**16.** In this situation, the partner's gain is preserved but the gain inherent in the distributed asset is not. Since the asset does not take a full transferred basis, the partner will recognize more gain on a sale of the asset than the partnership would have recognized had it made the sale, but this can be corrected if a Section 754 election is in effect. See

*Allocation of Basis to Distributed Properties.* If the special basis limitation rule in Section 732(a)(2) applies and several assets are distributed, the basis to be allocated (i.e., the partner's outside basis less cash received in the transaction) must be allocated among the distributed properties under Section 732(c)[17] using a multi-step process. First, any distributed unrealized receivables and inventory items are tentatively assigned a basis equal to the partnership's basis in each of those assets.[18] If the sum of the partnership's bases in the unrealized receivables and inventory items exceeds the basis to be allocated, then the partnership's bases in those properties must be decreased by the amount of the excess.[19] The reduction is achieved by first allocating basis decreases among the properties with built-in loss (i.e., properties with an assigned basis greater than their value) in proportion to the amounts of such loss and only to the extent of each property's built-in loss.[20] If needed, additional decreases are allocated in proportion to the remaining adjusted basis of the unrealized receivables and inventory items.[21] If the basis to be allocated exceeds the partnership's basis in the distributed unrealized receivables and inventory items, then each other distributed property is tentatively assigned a basis equal to the partnership's basis in that asset.[22] The partnership's bases in those properties then must be reduced so that the sum of their basis is equal to the remaining basis to be allocated.[23] Again, the reduction is accomplished by first allocating basis decreases in proportion to the built-in loss in the properties (but only to the extent of such loss) and then in proportion to the remaining adjusted bases of the properties.[24] This method of allocation is designed to preserve the partnership's basis for the unrealized receivables and inventory items and thus ensures that the partner will recognize at least the same amount of gain upon the disposition of those assets as the partnership would have recognized had they been sold at the partnership level.[25] As we will discover shortly, Section 735 preserves the ordinary income character of this gain.

*Section 732(d).* Section 732(d) provides an exception to the foregoing basis rules by permitting certain distributee partners to elect to treat any distributed properties as though the partnership had a Section 754 election

I.R.C. § 734(b)(1)(B) and Section C of this chapter.

**17.** Section 732(c) also applies to the allocation of outside basis to property received by a partner in a liquidating distribution. See I.R.C. § 732(b) and Chapter 8B, infra.

**18.** I.R.C. § 732(c)(1)(A)(i).

**19.** I.R.C. § 732(c)(1)(A)(ii).

**20.** I.R.C. § 732(c)(3)(A). These allocation rules apply to distributions after August 5, 1997. For prior distributions, basis was first allocated to any unrealized receivables and inventory items in an amount equal to the partnership's basis in each of those assets

(or, if the basis to be allocated was less than the sum of such properties' basis, in proportion to such bases) and, to the extent of any remaining basis, to any other distributed properties in proportion to their adjusted bases to the partnership.

**21.** I.R.C. § 732(c)(3)(B).

**22.** I.R.C. § 732(c)(1)(B)(i).

**23.** I.R.C. § 732(c)(1)(B)(ii).

**24.** I.R.C. § 732(c)(3).

**25.** When the Section 732(a)(2) basis limitation rule applies, the allocation method under Section 732(c) prevents to the extent possible any decrease in the basis of the ordinary income assets.

in effect when the partner purchased or inherited his interest. As a result, assets distributed to the new partner are eligible for a Section 743(b) adjustment,[26] and a special inside basis then may be used to determine the partner's basis in the distributed assets under Sections 732(a) and (c). This election is available only if the distribution is made within two years of the distributee partner's acquisition of his interest by purchase, exchange or inheritance and the partnership had no Section 754 election in effect at the time of the acquisition of his interest. The Section 732(d) election is the partner's last chance to avoid some of the distortions which may have resulted from the partnership's failure to make a Section 754 election.[27]

There are some critical differences between the effects of a Section 732(d) and Section 754 election. Section 732(d) only applies for purposes of determining the bases of distributed assets. And unlike a Section 754 election, a Section 732(d) election does not apply for purposes of partnership depreciation, depletion, or gain or loss on disposition.[28]

A Section 732(d) adjustment may be required by the Commissioner, whether or not the distribution occurs within two years from the partner's acquisition of his partnership interest, if the fair market value of the partnership property (other than money) at the time the partner acquired his interest exceeds 110 percent of its adjusted basis to the partnership.[29] The regulations limit application of this rule to cases where lack of a Section 732(d) election would cause a shift in basis from nondepreciable to depreciable property.[30]

*Distributions of Marketable Securities.* Because marketable securities are easily valued and as liquid as cash, Section 731(c) generally provides that for purposes of both Sections 731(a)(1) and 737,[31] a distribution of marketable securities is treated as a distribution of money to the extent of the fair market value of the securities at the time of the distribution.[32] "Marketable securities" are financial instruments and foreign currencies which are actively traded, including interests in a common trust fund, a mutual fund, and any financial instrument convertible into money or

---

**26.** A Section 732(d) election also is permitted with respect to liquidating distributions (I.R.C. § 732(d); see Chapter 8B1, infra) and distributions under Section 751(b) (Reg. § 1.751–1(b)(2)(iii) and (b)(3)(iii); see Section E of this chapter, infra).

**27.** The regulations permit an adjustment under Section 732(d) to be made to property which is not the same property which would have received the adjustment (e.g., property not in hand when the transferee acquired the partnership interest) if the property received is like property and the transferee, in exchange for the distributed property, relinquishes his interest in the property which would have had the special basis adjustment. Reg. § 1.732–1(d)(1)(v).

**28.** Reg. § 1.732–1(d)(1)(vi) Example. Thus, the amount of the adjustment is not reduced by depletion or depreciation because the partnership is only allowed to take depletion or depreciation if a Section 743(b) adjustment is in effect.

**29.** I.R.C. § 732(d), last sentence.

**30.** Reg. § 1.732–1(d)(4)(ii).

**31.** Section 737 may require a partner to recognize precontribution gain in contributed property when property (other than money) is distributed to the partner. See Section D2 of this chapter, infra.

**32.** I.R.C. § 731(c)(1).

marketable securities.[33] Any gain recognized by the distributee partner normally will be capital gain.[34] If a partner recognizes gain on the distribution of a marketable security, the partner's basis in the security will be its basis under Section 732, increased by the amount of gain recognized by the partner.[35]

To illustrate the operation of Section 731(c), assume A and B form the AB partnership as equal partners. A contributes property with a $1,000 fair market value and $250 basis and B contributes $1,000 cash. The partnership later purchases a marketable security for $500 and immediately distributes the security to A when A's outside basis is $250. The distribution of the security is treated as a distribution of $500 of cash, and A recognizes $250 of capital gain.[36] A's basis in the security will be its $250 basis under Section 732(a), increased by the $250 of recognized gain, for a total basis of $500.

The general rule in Section 731(c) is subject to several exceptions. For example, a distribution of a marketable security to the partner who contributed the security to the partnership generally is not subject to Section 731(c).[37] An exception is also provided for a distribution by an investment partnership to a partner who did not contribute any property to the partnership other than money or securities.[38] A partner's gain under Section 731(c) is also reduced by the excess of (1) the partner's distributive share of the net gain if all the partnership's marketable securities had been sold immediately before the distribution for their fair market value, over (2) the partner's distributive share of the net gain attributable to the partnership's marketable securities immediately after the distribution.[39] Thus, a distributee partner reduces the amount of the Section 731(c) distribution by the amount of the decrease in the partner's distributive share of the net gain in the partnership's marketable securities. For example, assume A and B form the AB partnership as equal partners. The partnership distributes marketable security X to A in a current distribution. Before the distribution, AB held marketable securities with the following fair market values, bases, and unrecognized gain or loss:

| Security | F.M.V. | A.B. | Gain (Loss) |
|----------|--------|------|-------------|
| X | $100 | $ 70 | $30 |
| Y | 100 | 80 | 20 |
| Z | 100 | 110 | (10) |

**33.**  I.R.C. § 731(c)(2).

**34.**  If the marketable security is an unrealized receivable or inventory item, the gain will be ordinary income. I.R.C. § 731(c)(6).

**35.**  I.R.C. § 731(c)(4). A basis increase attributable to gain recognized is allocated to marketable securities in proportion to their respective amounts of unrealized appreciation. Reg. § 1.731–2(f)(1)(i).

**36.**  See Reg. § 1.731–2(j) Example 1.

**37.**  I.R.C. § 731(c)(3)(A)(i).

**38.**  I.R.C. §§ 731(c)(3)(A)(iii), 731(c)(3)(C). The Service has also provided exceptions for certain securities acquired in a nonrecognition transaction and securities that were not marketable securities on the date acquired by the partnership. Reg. §§ 1.731–2(d)(1)(ii) & (iii).

**39.**  I.R.C. § 731(c)(3)(B).

If AB had sold all the securities for their fair market value immediately before the distribution to A, the partnership would have recognized $40 of net gain and A's distributive share of that gain would have been $20. If AB sold the remaining securities immediately after the distribution of security X to A, there would be $10 of net gain and A's distributive share of that gain would have been $5. The distribution reduced A's distributive share of the partnership's net gain in marketable securities by $15 ($20 net gain before distribution minus $5 net gain after distribution). Thus, the distribution of security X to A is treated as a distribution of $85 of money to A ($100 fair market value of security X minus $15 reduction).[40]

## Revenue Ruling 94–4

1994–1 Cum.Bull. 196.

ISSUE

If a deemed distribution of money under § 752(b) of the Internal Revenue Code occurs as a result of a decrease in a partner's share of the liabilities of a partnership, is the deemed distribution taken into account at the time of the distribution or at the end of the partnership taxable year?

LAW

Under § 752(b), a decrease in a partner's share of partnership liabilities is considered a distribution of money to the partner by the partnership. The partner will recognize gain under § 731(a)(1) if the distribution of money exceeds the adjusted basis of the partner's interest immediately before the distribution.

Section 1.731–1(a)(1)(ii) of the Income Tax Regulations provides that for purposes of §§ 731 and 705, advances or drawings of money or property against a partner's distributive share of income are treated as current distributions made on the last day of the partnership taxable year with respect to that partner.

Rev. Rul. 92–97, 1992–2 C.B. 124, treats a deemed distribution of money to a partner resulting from a cancellation of debt as an advance or drawing under § 1.731–1(a)(1)(ii) against that partner's distributive share of cancellation of indebtedness income.

HOLDING

A deemed distribution of money under § 752(b) resulting from a decrease in a partner's share of the liabilities of a partnership is treated as an advance or drawing of money under § 1.731–1(a)(1)(ii) to the extent of the partner's distributive share of income for the partnership taxable year. An amount treated as an advance or drawing of money is taken into account at the end of the partnership taxable year. A deemed distribution

---

**40.** Reg. § 1.731–2(j) Example 2.

of money resulting from a cancellation of debt may qualify for advance or drawing treatment under this revenue ruling and under Rev. Rul. 92–97.

## Revenue Ruling 79–205

1979–2 Cum.Bull. 255.

ISSUES

When a partnership makes a nonliquidating distribution of property, (1) is a partner permitted to offset the increase in the partner's liabilities against the decrease in the partner's liabilities in determining the extent of recognition of gain or loss, and (2) is partnership basis adjusted before or after the property distribution?

FACTS

A and B are general partners in M, a general partnership, which was formed for the purposes of owning and operating shopping centers.

On December 31, 1977, M made nonliquidating distributions in a single transaction of a portion of its property to A and B. A and B are equal partners in M. M, A and B are calendar year taxpayers. No assets of the type described in section 751(a) of the Internal Revenue Code of 1954 were distributed by M to either A or B.

Immediately prior to the distribution A had an adjusted basis for A's interest in M of 1,000x dollars, and B had an adjusted basis for B's interest in M of 1,500x dollars. The property distributed to A had an adjusted basis to M of 2,000x dollars, and was subject to liabilities of 1,600x dollars. The property distributed to B had an adjusted basis to M of 3,200x dollars and was subject to liabilities of 2,800x dollars. A's individual liabilities increased by 1,600x dollars by reason of the distribution to A. B's individual liabilities increased by 2,800x dollars by reason of the distribution to B. A's share and B's share of the liabilities of M each decreased by 2,200x dollars (1/2 of 1,600x + 1/2 of 2,800x dollars) by reason of the distributions. The basis and fair market value of the properties distributed were greater than the liabilities to which they were subject.

LAW

Section 705(a) of the Code provides, in part, that the adjusted basis of a partner's interest in a partnership shall be the basis of such interest determined under section 722 decreased (but not below zero) by partnership distributions as provided in section 733.

Section 722 of the Code provides, in part, that the basis of a partnership interest acquired by a contribution of money shall be the amount of such money.

Section 731(a)(1) of the Code provides that in the case of a distribution by a partnership to a partner gain shall not be recognized to such partner, except to the extent that any money distributed exceeds the adjusted basis

of such partner's interest in the partnership immediately before the distribution.

Section 732(a)(1) of the Code provides that the basis of property (other than money) distributed by a partnership to a partner other than in liquidation of the partner's interest shall, except as provided in section 732(a)(2), be its adjusted basis to the partnership immediately before such distribution.

Section 732(a)(2) of the Code provides that the basis to the distributee partner of property to which section 732(a)(1) is applicable shall not exceed the adjusted basis of such partner's interest in the partnership reduced by any money distributed in the same transaction.

Section 733 of the Code provides that in the case of a distribution by a partnership to a partner other than in liquidation of a partner's interest, the adjusted basis to such partner of the interest in the partnership shall be reduced (but not below zero) by the amount of any money distributed to such partner and the amount of the basis to such partner of distributed property other than money, as determined under section 732.

Section 752(a) of the Code provides that any increase in a partner's share of the liabilities of a partnership, or any increase in a partner's individual liabilities by reason of the assumption by such partner of partnership liabilities, shall be considered as a contribution of money by such partner to the partnership.

Section 752(b) of the Code provides that any decrease in a partner's share of the liabilities of a partnership, or any decrease in a partner's individual liabilities by reason of the assumption by the partnership of such individual liabilities, shall be considered as a distribution of money to the partner by the partnership.

Section 752(c) of the Code provides that for purposes of section 752 a liability to which property is subject shall, to the extent of the fair market value of such property, be considered as a liability of the owner of the property.

ANALYSIS & HOLDING

In general, partnership distributions are taxable under section 731(a)(1) of the Code only to the extent that the amount of money distributed exceeds the distributee partner's basis for the partner's partnership interest. This rule reflects the Congressional intent to limit narrowly the area in which gain or loss is recognized upon a distribution so as to remove deterrents to property being moved in and out of partnerships as business reasons dictate. See S.Rep.No. 1622, 83rd Cong., 2nd Sess., page 96 (1954). Here, since partner liabilities are both increasing and decreasing in the same transaction offsetting the increases and decreases tends to limit recognition of gain, thereby giving effect to the Congressional intent. Consequently, in a distribution of encumbered property, the resulting liability adjustments will be treated as occurring simultaneously, rather than occurring in a particular order. Therefore, on a distribution of

encumbered property, the amount of money considered distributed to a partner for purposes of section 731(a)(1) is the amount (if any) by which the decrease in the partner's share of the liabilities of the partnership under section 752(b) exceeds the increase in the partner's individual liabilities under section 752(a). The amount of money considered contributed by a partner for purposes of section 722 is the amount (if any) by which the increase in the partner's individual liabilities under section 752(a) exceeds the decrease in the partner's share of the liabilities of the partnership under section 752(b). The increase in the partner's individual liabilities occurs by reason of the assumption by the partner of partnership liabilities, or by reason of a distribution of property subject to a liability, to the extent of the fair market value of such property.

Because the distribution was part of a single transaction, the two properties are treated as having been distributed simultaneously to $A$ and $B$. Therefore, all resulting liability adjustments relating to the distribution of the two properties will be treated as occurring simultaneously, rather than occurring in a particular order.

## TREATMENT OF PARTNER A

$A$ will be deemed to have received a net distribution of $600x$ dollars in money, that is, the amount by which the amount of money considered distributed to $A$ ($2,200x$ dollars) exceeds the amount of money considered contributed by $A$ ($1,600x$ dollars). Since $600x$ dollars does not exceed $A$'s basis for $A$'s interest in $M$ immediately before the distribution ($1,000x$ dollars), no gain is recognized to $A$.

Under section 732(a) of the Code, the basis to $A$ of the property distributed to $A$ is the lesser of (i) the adjusted basis of the property to the partnership ($2,000x$ dollars), or (ii) the adjusted basis of $A$'s partnership interest ($1,000x$ dollars) reduced by the amount of money deemed distributed to $A$ ($600x$ dollars). Therefore, the basis of the property in $A$'s hands is $400x$ dollars. Under section 733, the adjusted basis of $A$'s partnership interest ($1,000x$ dollars) is reduced by the amount of money deemed distributed to $A$ ($600x$ dollars) and by the basis to $A$ of the distributed property ($400x$ dollars). The adjusted basis of $A$'s partnership interest is therefore reduced to zero.

## TREATMENT OF PARTNER B

$B$ will be deemed to have made a net contribution of $600x$ dollars, that is, the amount by which the amount of money considered contributed by $B$ ($2,800x$ dollars) exceeds the amount of money considered distributed to $B$ ($2,200x$ dollars). In applying sections 732(a) and 733 of the Code to $B$, the adjustment to $B$'s basis in $B$'s partnership interest attributable to the liability adjustments resulting from the distributions will be treated as occurring first, and the distribution of property to $B$ as occurring second. By so doing, $B$'s basis for the distributed property is increased and $B$'s basis in $B$'s partnership interest is decreased. This allocation gives greater effect to the general rule of section 732(a)(1), which provides for the partner to

have the same basis in distributed property as the partnership had for that property.

Therefore, the first step is that $B$'s basis for $B$'s partnership interest (1,500$x$ dollars) is increased under section 722 and 705(a) by the amount of the net contribution deemed made by $B$ (600$x$ dollars), and is equal to 2,100$x$ dollars. Next, under section 732(a) of the Code, the basis to $B$ of the property distributed to $B$ is the lesser of (i) the adjusted basis of the property to the partnership (3,200$x$ dollars), or (ii) the adjusted basis of $B$'s partnership interest (2,100$x$ dollars) reduced by the amount of money deemed distributed to $B$ (zero). Therefore, the basis of the property in $B$'s hands is 2,100$x$ dollars. Under section 733, the adjusted basis of $B$'s partnership interest (2,100$x$ dollars) is reduced by the amount of money deemed distributed to $B$ (zero) and by the basis to $B$ of the distributed property (2,100$x$ dollars). The adjusted basis of $B$'s partnership interest is therefore zero.

## PROBLEMS

**1**. On July 1, the ABC Partnership, a calendar year partnership, distributes to each of its equal partners $10,000 cash and land with a value of $10,000 and a basis of $5,000. A, B and C have outside bases of $20,000, $10,000 and $5,000 respectively. The partnership has the following assets prior to the distribution:

| Assets | A.B. | F.M.V. |
| --- | --- | --- |
| Cash | $50,000 | $50,000 |
| Accounts Receivable | 0 | 20,000 |
| Inventory | 20,000 | 30,000 |
| Land | 30,000 | 60,000 |
| Building | 10,000 | 50,000 |

(a) Discuss the tax consequences of the distribution to A, B, and C, each of whom has owned his partnership interest for several years.

(b) What result to C if he receives the land first and the cash in a subsequent separate distribution on October 1?

(c) What result to C in (b), above, if the cash distribution on October 1 is a draw against his share of partnership income, which is $20,000 for the year?

**2**.  Partner has a $40,000 outside basis in her partnership interest. In a pro rata operating distribution to the partners, Partner receives two assets. Asset #1 has a value of $10,000 and a basis to the partnership of $40,000. Asset #2 has a value of $10,000 and a basis to the partnership of $20,000. What basis will partner take in each property under § 732(c) if:

(a) Asset #1 is an inventory item and Asset #2 is a capital asset?

(b) Asset #2 is an inventory item and Asset #1 is a capital asset?

(c) Both properties are inventory items?

(d) Both properties are capital assets?

(e) Suppose Asset #1 has a value of $60,000 and a basis of $40,000 to the partnership and Asset #2 has a value of $50,000 and a basis of $20,000 to the partnership. What basis will Partner take in each property under § 732(c) if she receives both properties in a pro rata operating distribution and both properties are inventory items?

**3**. Nupartner purchases a one-third interest in the following three-person equal partnership for $40,000. At the time of the purchase the partnership has the following assets:

|  | A.B. | F.M.V. |
|---|---|---|
| Accounts Receivable | $ 0 | $30,000 |
| Land (capital asset) | 60,000 | 90,000 |

The partnership has made no § 754 election. It immediately distributes $10,000 of receivables to each of the three partners.

(a) What result to Nupartner on the collection of the receivables if Nupartner makes no § 732(d) election?

(b) What result to Nupartner on the collection of the receivables if he makes a § 732(d) election?

(c) If Nupartner elects § 732(d), what is his outside basis immediately after the distribution?

(d) Must the partnership approve Nupartner's election under § 732(d)?

(e) Will the § 732(d) election have any immediate effect on the basis of Nupartner's interest in the land remaining in the partnership?

## 2. CONSEQUENCES ON SUBSEQUENT SALES OF DISTRIBUTED PROPERTY

Code: §§ 735; 1245(b)(6).

Regulations: §§ 1.735–1; 1.1245–4(f)(2) & (3) Example (1).

The characterization of gain or loss on the disposition of property is generally determined by the character of the asset in the hands of the taxpayer who disposes of the property. But property acquired in a nonrecognition transaction is often subject to special rules that govern not only its basis and holding period but also the tax character of the asset.[1] So it is with property received by a partner in a distribution from a partnership. We already have seen how the Section 732 basis rules apply on an operating distribution to limit the distributee's basis for ordinary income assets to the partnership's basis in those assets. To complete the grand design and prevent the conversion of partnership ordinary income into partner capital gain, Section 735 provides additional rules to govern the character of gain or loss on the disposition of ordinary income property received by the partner in a distribution. In this respect, Section 735 is

**1.** See, e.g., I.R.C. §§ 351; 358; 362(a); 1032; 1223(1) & (2); 1245(a)(2) & (b)(3).

similar to Section 724, which preserved the ordinary income character of certain property contributed to a partnership in appropriate cases. Section 735 also provides for the tacking of the partnership's holding period in the distributed property.

*Characterization.* Under Section 735(a), gains or losses recognized by a distributee partner on the disposition of "unrealized receivables" received in a distribution are treated as ordinary income or loss,[2] and gains or losses on the sale or exchange of distributed inventory items suffer a similar character taint if they are sold or exchanged by the partner within five years from the date of their distribution.[3] In the case of unrealized receivables, the character taint remains with the assets as long as they are held by the distributee partner.[4] Since the taint is not permanent with inventory, a patient partner who holds these items as capital assets may avoid ordinary income characterization on the sale or exchange of the inventory by delaying any disposition until the expiration of five years from the date of distribution.[5] If an item is both an unrealized receivable and an inventory item, the more stringent rules governing receivables are applicable. The Section 735 taint cannot be removed in a nonrecognition transaction or a series of such transactions.[6] Except in the case of C corporation stock received in a Section 351 corporate formation, the taint carries over to the exchanged basis property received in the transaction.[7]

The Section 735(a) taint rules do not apply to recapture property.[8] But the recapture gain which the partnership would have recognized on a sale of the property carries over to the distributee partner, who recognizes ordinary income on a subsequent sale or exchange. This is accomplished through the definitions of "recomputed basis" and "additional depreciation" in the applicable recapture provisions. For example, where Section 1245 property is distributed by a partnership to a partner, the amount of Section 1245(a) ordinary income which the partnership would have recognized had it sold the recapture property at its fair market value on the date of the distribution is generally added to the distributee's adjusted basis in the property in determining his recomputed basis.[9] The legislative history

---

**2.** I.R.C. § 735(a)(1). "Unrealized receivables" are as defined in Section 751(c) except that recapture items are not included in the definition for purposes of Section 735(a).

**3.** I.R.C. § 735(a)(2). In defining inventory items under Section 735(a)(2), the long-term holding period requirement for Section 1231 property is disregarded. I.R.C. § 735(c)(1). Thus, if property would be Section 1231 property but for the fact that the partnership did not hold it long-term, it nonetheless is treated as Section 1231 property and not as an inventory item. Cf. I.R.C. § 751(d)(2).

**4.** Query whether a gift of the unrealized receivables purges the ordinary income

to the donee? See I.R.C. §§ 735(c)(2)(A) & 7701(a)(42), (43) & (45) and Problem 1(b), infra. Cf. Reg. § 1.267(d)–1(a)(3) & (4) Example (3).

**5.** For purposes of measuring this period, the holding period in the hands of the partnership does not tack. I.R.C. § 735(b), parenthetical clause.

**6.** I.R.C. § 735(c)(2)(A).

**7.** I.R.C. § 735(c)(2)(B).

**8.** See supra note 2.

**9.** I.R.C. § 1245(b)(6)(B)(i). See I.R.C. § 1245(a)(2) for the definition of "recomputed basis." Cf. § 1245(a)(1)(A). The recomputed basis must be reduced by any Section

of Section 1245 illustrates the rule as follows:[10]

> The application of this provision is illustrated as follows: A, B, and C are equal partners in a partnership whose assets consist of three pieces of section 1245 property, assets X, Y, and Z, each with a fair market value of $100,000. Asset X has an adjusted basis of $60,000 and a recomputed basis of $85,000; asset Y has an adjusted basis of $85,000 and a recomputed basis of $110,000; and asset Z has an adjusted basis of $95,000 and a recomputed basis of $100,000. Asset Y is distributed to B in complete liquidation of his partnership interest. B's basis in his partnership interest is $75,000, and under section 732 this basis is allocated to asset Y. If B later sells asset Y for [$100,000] at a time when the adjusted basis is still $75,000 and if B has not taken any depreciation deductions with respect to asset Y since the distribution, the gain to which section 1245(a) applies would be $15,000, since the recomputed basis of the property is only $90,000, that is, the adjusted basis of the property ($75,000) increased by the amount of gain ($15,000) which would have been recognized to the partnership if the asset had been sold for its fair market value at the time of distribution ($100,000 minus $85,000).[11]

*Tacked holding periods.* Section 735(b) allows the distributee partner to tack the partnership's holding period[12] with respect to property with a transferred basis from the partnership,[13] and also any distributed property which has some special type of basis.[14] Tacking is not permitted, however, in measuring the five-year taint applicable to distributed "inventory items."[15]

## PROBLEMS

**1.** A, a partner in the ABC cash method partnership, has an outside basis of $10,000. In a pro rata operating distribution to the partners, A receives a parcel of land held as inventory by the partnership with a basis of $2,000 and a value of $3,000 and zero basis accounts receivable with a value of $3,000. Both properties become capital assets in her hands. Six years later, she collects the receivables and sells the parcel for $3,000.

(a) What are the tax consequences to A on the distribution and on the collection of the receivables and the sale of the parcel? What is the justification for the different results?

751(b) gain recognized with respect to the property on the distribution. See Section E of this chapter, infra.

**10.** S.Rep. No. 1881, 87th Cong., 2d Sess. (1962), reprinted in 1962–3 C.B. 984.

**11.** Similar rules apply to other types of recapture property. Ed. See, e.g., I.R.C. § 1250(d)(6).

**12.** Tacking is not permitted, however, on property received on a Section 751(b) purchase rather than a Section 731 distribution.

**13.** Cf. I.R.C. § 1223(2).

**14.** See, e.g., I.R.C. §§ 732(a)(2), (c); 732(d); 743(b).

**15.** I.R.C.   § 735(b),   parenthetical clause.

(b) What result if, immediately after the distribution, A gives the parcel to her daughter, D, who promptly sells the parcel for $3,000? Assume the parcel is a capital asset in D's hands.

2. A and B operate a taxi business as partners. In the current year the partnership distributes to A a taxi purchased over one year ago for $5,000, which has an adjusted basis of $2,000 and a value of $3,000 when distributed. A's outside basis is $1,000. (To make § 751(b), which is considered later in the chapter, inapplicable, assume an identical distribution to B). The disposition of the taxi is not a taxable event to the partnership. see §§ 731(b) and 1245(b)(3). What are the tax consequences to A if he immediately sells the cab for $3,000?

## C.   CONSEQUENCES TO THE DISTRIBUTING PARTNERSHIP

Code: §§ 731(b); 734; 754; 755; 1245(b)(3).

Regulations: §§ 1.731–1(b); 1.734–1; 1.755–1(a) & (c).

*Nonrecognition Rule.* We have seen that Congress has done almost everything possible to ensure that a distributee partner does not recognize gain or loss on the receipt of partnership property.[1] Section 731(b) similarly provides that no gain or loss is recognized by a partnership on the distribution of money or property to a partner. Even the recapture provisions bow to nonrecognition under Section 731(b),[2] but nothing (except time) is lost because the potential ordinary income lurking in the asset carries over to the distributee partner along with its transferred basis.[3]

*Impact on Inside Basis.* Turning to the partnership's balance sheet, Section 734(a) sets forth the general rule that distributions of property do not affect the inside basis of property retained by the partnership. This "no adjustment" rule applies even though the distributee partner recognizes gain on the distribution[4] or is required to take a basis in the distributed property which differs from its basis to the partnership.[5] In these circumstances, the no adjustment rule may create distortions resembling those which occur on the sale of a partnership interest.

For example, assume the ABC partnership is an equal three-person partnership with the following balance sheet:

| Assets | A.B. | F.M.V. | Partners' Capital | A.B. | F.M.V. |
|---|---|---|---|---|---|
| Cash | $6,000 | $ 6,000 | A | $3,000 | $ 6,000 |
| Capital Asset | 3,000 | 12,000 | B | 3,000 | 6,000 |
| | | | C | 3,000 | 6,000 |
| | $9,000 | $18,000 | | $9,000 | $18,000 |

**1.** I.R.C. § 731(a).

**2.** See, e.g., I.R.C. § 1245(b)(3).

**3.** See I.R.C. §§ 735(a); 1245(b)(6); and the discussion in Section B2 of this chapter, supra.

**4.** I.R.C. § 731(a)(1).

**5.** I.R.C. § 732(a)(2), (c).

If the partnership distributes $6,000 cash to A in liquidation of her entire partnership interest, A recognizes $3,000 of gain,[6] representing the previously unrealized appreciation in A's share of the capital asset, which had an inside basis of $1,000 and a fair market value of $4,000. Under the no adjustment rule, however, the partnership's basis in that one-third portion of the asset remains $1,000, and B and C each would have a $4,500 gain on a subsequent sale of the asset for $12,000. Thus, even though A realized her $3,000 pro rata share of the gain, that same amount is left behind in the partnership to be taxed to the other partners when the asset is sold. Is this double taxation? Not necessarily. If the partnership sells the capital asset for $12,000, B and C increase their outside bases under Section 705 to reflect their respective $4,500 taxable gains, and on a subsequent liquidation of the partnership they together will recognize an offsetting $3,000 loss.[7] But a liquidation may be years away, if at all. In the meantime, B and C have a total outside basis for their partnership interests which does not equal their inside basis in the partnership's capital asset, resulting in the following distorted balance sheet:

| Assets | A.B. | F.M.V. | Partners' Capital | A.B. | F.M.V. |
|--------|------|--------|-------------------|------|--------|
| Capital Asset | $3,000 | $12,000 | B | $3,000 | $ 6,000 |
|  |  |  | C | 3,000 | 6,000 |
|  | $3,000 | $12,000 |  | $6,000 | $12,000 |

You are on the right track if you have a sense of deja vu. We have seen a similar imbalance resulting from the failure to adjust the basis of partnership property on the acquisition of a partnership interest. In the case of appreciated partnership assets, a Section 754 election allowed the partnership to make a basis adjustment under Section 743(b) and provided relief for the buying partner. In the case of both operating and liquidating distributions, a Section 754 election triggers a similar inside basis adjustment under Section 734(b) which benefits all the remaining partners and corrects the imbalance illustrated above.[8] And like Section 743, Section 734 may require a downward adjustment in the partnership's basis in its assets in order to prevent inappropriate deferral of taxes by partners following a

---

**6.**  I.R.C. § 731(a)(1).

**7.**  For example, if the capital asset is sold for $12,000, B and C each would have a $4,500 distributive share of the gain and the outside basis of each would increase by $4,500 to $7,500. If the partnership then were liquidated and the $12,000 proceeds were distributed, B and C each would receive $6,000 cash and recognize a $1,500 capital loss under Section 731(a)(2). The net effect would be a $3,000 net long-term capital gain to B and C ($4,500 gain on the sale of the capital asset less $1,500 capital loss on the liquidation of the partnership). Although the

specter of double taxation is removed, this example too conveniently assumes a prompt termination of the partnership.

**8.**  In the case of an operating distribution, the adjustment benefits all the partners, including the continuing distributee partner, unless the partnership agreement provides a special allocation of the benefits of a basis increase to the nondistributee partners who otherwise would bear the burden of the lost basis. I.R.C. § 704(b). Cf. Reg. § 1.704–1(b)(5) Example (14)(i).

liquidating distribution.[9]

Returning to the example, Section 734(b)(1)(A) permits the partnership to increase the basis of the capital asset by the $3,000 gain recognized by A, leaving the partnership with the following balance sheet:

| Assets | A.B. | F.M.V. | Partners' Capital | A.B. | F.M.V. |
|---|---|---|---|---|---|
| Capital Asset | $6,000 | $12,000 | B | $3,000 | $ 6,000 |
| | | | C | $3,000 | $ 6,000 |
| | $6,000 | $12,000 | | $6,000 | $12,000 |

Section 734(b) determines the overall adjustment. The action then shifts to Section 755, which governs the allocation of the adjustment among the partnership assets. As with Section 743(b) adjustments, the initial step is to value the partnership's assets. Next the assets of the partnership are divided into two classes: capital gain property (capital assets and Section 1231(b) property) and other property.[10] Because in the example the character of gain recognized by the distributee was capital, the regulations require the adjustment to be made only to the basis of the partnership's capital gain property.[11] At the next step, the allocation mechanism differs from the rules governing Section 743(b) adjustments, where the adjustment resulted in a special personal inside basis only for the acquiring partner. In contrast, the Section 734(b) adjustment benefits all continuing partners unless a special allocation to the contrary is made.[12]

Section 734(b) also permits an adjustment when the basis of the distributed property is limited under Section 732(a)(2) to the distributee partner's outside basis.[13] To illustrate the purpose for this second type of adjustment, assume that the ABC partnership has the following balance sheet:

| Assets | A.B. | F.M.V. | Partners' Capital | A.B. | F.M.V. |
|---|---|---|---|---|---|
| Cash | $ 3,000 | $ 3,000 | A | $ 5,000 | $ 5,000 |
| Capital Asset #1 | 9,000 | 3,000 | B | 5,000 | 5,000 |
| Capital Asset #2 | 3,000 | 9,000 | C | 5,000 | 5,000 |
| | $15,000 | $15,000 | | $15,000 | $15,000 |

At this point, each partner has a $2,000 unrealized loss represented by the decline in value of capital asset #1 and a $2,000 unrealized gain represented by the appreciation of capital asset #2. If capital asset #1 is distributed to A, A's basis in the asset will be limited to her outside basis of $5,000. When A sells the asset, she will recognize her $2,000 share of the loss, but the remaining $4,000 of predistribution capital loss inherent in the asset will disappear because $4,000 of basis evaporated at the time of distribu-

9. I.R.C. § 734(a) & (d); see Chapter 6B, supra and Chapter 8B, infra.

10. Reg. § 1.755–1(a).

11. Reg. § 1.755–1(c)(1)(ii).

12. See Problem (c), below.

13. I.R.C. § 734(b)(1)(B).

tion. Without an adjustment, the partners as a group will recognize only $2,000 of the loss on asset #1 but the entire $6,000 of gain on asset #2. To cure this distortion, Section 734(b) permits the partnership to increase its bases in the remaining assets by an amount equal to the difference between the partnership's basis in the distributed property and the basis taken by the distributee partner in that property.[14]

Section 755 once again governs the allocation of the adjustment. In order to preserve both the proper amount and character of total gain or loss, the adjustment is made to property in the same class as the distributed property whose basis was changed as a result of the distribution.[15] If there is an increase in basis allocated within a class of property, it is first allocated to properties with unrealized appreciation in proportion to their appreciation. Any remaining increase is allocated in proportion to the fair market values of the properties.[16] A decrease in basis allocated within a class of property is first allocated to properties based upon their respective amounts of unrealized depreciation before the decrease and then in proportion to the adjusted bases of the properties (after adjustment for unrealized depreciation).[17] In no event can the basis of property be reduced below zero.[18] If a partnership does not have property of the character to be adjusted or if the basis of all property of like character has been reduced to zero, the adjustment is held in abeyance until the partnership acquires property in the class to be adjusted.[19]

For purposes of cost recovery under Section 168, if the basis of a partnership's recovery property is increased under Section 734 as a result of a distribution, the increased portion of the basis is treated as newly purchased recovery property placed in service when the distribution occurs.[20] Thus, any applicable recovery period and method may be used with respect to the increased portion of the basis. No change is made in determining the cost recovery allowance for the portion of the basis for which there is no increase.[21] If a distribution triggers a decrease in the basis of a partnership's cost recovery property, the decrease is accounted for over the property's remaining recovery period, beginning with the recovery period in which the basis is decreased.[22] If a distributing partnership has a large number of assets affected by these rules, it is likely to have considerable personnel turnover in its accounting department.

---

**14.**  Id. The last sentence of Section 734(b) prohibits a partnership from adjusting the basis of its property following a distribution of an interest in another partnership if the second partnership does not have a Section 754 election in effect. This provision is intended to prevent taxpayers from achieving a net step-up in the basis of its assets by means of inconsistent elections under Section 754. For an example illustrating the type of abuse which this provision is designed to prevent, see H.R.Rep. No. 98–432, 98th Cong., 2d Sess. 1230 (1984).

**15.**  Reg. § 1.755–1(c)(1)(i).

**16.**  Reg. § 1.755–1(c)(2)(i).

**17.**  Reg. § 1.755–2(c)(2)(ii). A decrease in the bases of partnership assets can result from a distribution that liquidates a partner's interest. See I.R.C. § 734(b) and Chapter 8B1, infra.

**18.**  Reg. § 1.755–1(c)(3).

**19.**  Reg. § 1.755–1(c)(4).

**20.**  Reg. § 1.734–1(e)(1).

**21.**  Id.

**22.**  Reg. § 1.734–1(e)(2).

*Impact on Capital Accounts.* In studying the tax treatment of partnership allocations, we saw that an agreed allocation will not be respected unless, among other requirements, the partnership agreement requires "capital accounts" to be maintained throughout the life of the partnership in accordance with detailed regulations.[23] Nonliquidating distributions are among the many partnership transactions that necessitate capital account adjustments.[24]

Because a distribution reduces the distributee partner's equity in the partnership and because the function of a capital account is to measure a partner's interest in the firm at any given point in time, the regulations logically require that a partner's capital account must be reduced by any money distributed to the partner and by the fair market value of any distributed property.[25] Recall, however, that the partnership does not recognize gain or loss on distributions of property.[26] As a result, the reduction of a distributee partner's capital account by the fair market value of the distributed property would distort the partnership's balance sheet unless an additional adjustment is made to reflect the unrealized appreciation or decline in value of the property. The regulations address this problem by providing that the capital accounts of all the partners must be adjusted by their respective shares of the gain or loss that the partnership would have recognized if it had sold the distributed property for its fair market value on the date of distribution.[27]

To illustrate, assume the ABC equal partnership distributes to partner A land with a value of $10,000 and an adjusted tax basis and book value to the partnership of $4,000. For tax purposes, the partnership recognizes no gain on the distribution.[28] On the balance sheet, however, the $6,000 gain inherent in the land is treated as recognized and is allocated equally among the partners, increasing each partner's capital account by $2,000, just as if the land had been sold by the partnership for its fair market value.[29] The distributee partner (A) then reduces his capital account by $10,000, the full value of the land. When the smoke clears, A's capital account suffers a net decrease of $8,000, and the capital accounts of B and C are increased by $2,000 each.[30]

**23.** Reg. § 1.704–1(b)(2)(ii)(*b*). See Reg. § 1.704–1(b)(2)(iv) & Chapter 4B, supra.

**24.** See generally Reg. § 1.704–1(b)(2)(iv)(*b*).

**25.** Id. For special rules on the distribution of promissory notes, see Reg. § 1.704–1(b)(2)(iv)(*e*)(*2*). If the distributee partner assumes a liability connected to the property or takes the property subject to a liability, his capital account is reduced by the full value of the property less the liability. Reg. § 1.704–1(b)(2)(iv)(*b*).

**26.** I.R.C. § 731(b).

**27.** Reg. § 1.704–1(b)(2)(iv)(*e*)(*1*). The adjustment for unrealized gain or loss is only to the extent that it was not previously re-flected in capital accounts. Reg. § 1.704–1(b)(2)(iv)(*f*). For example, the built-in gain on contributed property is already reflected because the property was recorded on the partnership's books at its fair market value at the time of contribution. If the asset is later distributed, the built-in gain should not be reflected again. See Chapter 4C, supra.

**28.** I.R.C. § 731(b).

**29.** The example assumes that the partners have agreed to share profits and losses equally.

**30.** See Reg. § 1.704–1(b)(5) Example (14)(v). Note that the net decrease of $4,000 ($8,000 – $2,000 – $2,000) equals the partnership's book value for the land.

In addition, if a distribution is more than a de minimis amount and is in exchange for any portion of a partners' interest in the partnership, the partnership may elect to restate on its books all remaining assets at their current fair market value and correspondingly restate the partners' capital accounts.[31]

## PROBLEM

The ABC partnership has three equal partners, A, B, and C, and the following balance sheet:

| Assets | A.B. | F.M.V. | Partners' Capital | A.B. | F.M.V. |
|---|---|---|---|---|---|
| Cash | $ 60,000 | $ 60,000 | A | $ 70,000 | $ 80,000 |
| Capital Asset #1 | 90,000 | 60,000 | B | 70,000 | 80,000 |
| Capital Asset #2 | 40,000 | 60,000 | C | 70,000 | 80,000 |
| Capital Asset #3 | 20,000 | 60,000 | | | |
| | $210,000 | $240,000 | | $210,000 | $240,000 |

A receives capital asset #1 in an operating distribution. A has a one-ninth interest worth $20,000 in the partnership capital and profits after the distribution.

(a) What results to A and the partnership if there is no § 754 election? Reconstruct the balance sheet after the distribution.

(b) What results to A and the partnership if the partnership has made a § 754 election? Reconstruct the balance sheet after the distribution.

(c) How should any basis adjustment be allocated among the partners?

---

## D. MIXING BOWL TRANSACTIONS

Code: §§ 704(c)(1)(B) & (c)(2); 737.

Although Subchapter K does almost everything possible to provide nonrecognition of gain or loss to partners and partnerships on distributions of property,[1] Congress has enacted several exceptions to combat abuse of this lenient policy. Sections 704(c)(1)(B) and 737, the two related provisions discussed in this section, are aimed at "mixing bowl transactions," an income-shifting strategy where a partner transfers appreciated property to a partnership and the partnership later either distributes the contributed

---

**31.** Reg. § 1.704–1(b)(2)(iv)(*f*)(*5*). These adjustments must be made principally for a substantial non-tax business purpose. Id. Even absent such a revaluation, a distribution also may require adjustments to the book value of the partnership's remaining assets and the capital account of the distribu-

tee partner if the partnership adjusts the basis of its remaining property under Section 734(b) pursuant to a Section 754 election. See Reg. § 1.704–1(b)(2)(iv)(*m*)(*1*), (*4*) and (*5*).

**1.** See Sections B and C of this chapter, supra.

property to another partner or distributes substitute property to the contributing partner. The tax planning goal of this strategy is to shift or defer recognition of the contributing partner's precontribution gain by exploiting the nonrecognition rules that apply to contributions to and distributions by a partnership.[2]

## 1.   DISTRIBUTIONS OF CONTRIBUTED PROPERTY TO ANOTHER PARTNER

Under the now familiar general rule of Section 704(c)(1)(A), a partner contributing property with a built-in gain or loss to a partnership is generally allocated that gain or loss when the partnership subsequently disposes of the property.[3] As originally enacted, Section 704(c) was limited to partnership sales of contributed property. As a result, a contributing partner could avoid an allocation of precontribution gain if the partnership distributed the contributed property to another partner rather than selling it. Since a partnership generally does not recognize gain or loss on a distribution of property,[4] the contributing partner was not taxed on the distribution, and any built-in gain was shifted to the distributee partner through a transferred basis mechanism.[5]

To preclude this type of mixing bowl transaction, Section 704(c)(1)(B) provides that if property contributed by one partner is distributed to another partner within seven years of its contribution to the partnership, the contributing partner (or her successor)[6] is treated as recognizing Section 704(c) gain or loss as if the partnership had sold the property for its fair market value at the time of the distribution.[7] The character of the gain or loss is the same as if the partnership had sold the contributed property to the distributee partner.[8] Appropriately, the contributing partner's outside basis is increased or decreased by the amount of gain or loss recog-

---

**2.**   See I.R.C. §§ 721; 731.

**3.**   Reg. § 1.704–3 and Chapter 4C, supra.

**4.**   I.R.C. § 731. See Section C of this chapter, supra.

**5.**   I.R.C. § 732.

**6.**   I.R.C. § 704(c)(3). Successor partners (e.g., purchasers, donees, or legatees) thus may recognize gain under Section 704(c)(1)(B) if the contributed property is distributed to another partner within seven years of the original contribution. Section 704(c)(1)(C), however, would prevent successor partners from recognizing loss from property that was contributed with a built-in loss because the property's basis would be deemed to be equal to its fair market value at the time it was contributed to the partnership. See also I.R.C. §§ 754 and 743(b) and Section C of this chapter, supra, for the possible basis

adjustments that will eliminate built-in gain or loss on certain transfers of partnership interests.

**7.**   The seven-year time period in Section 704(c)(1)(B) applies to property contributed after June 8, 1997. The same rule, but with a five-year threshold, applies to property contributed to a partnership before June 9, 1997.

**8.**   I.R.C. § 704(c)(1)(B)(ii). As a result, Section 724 would apply in determining the character of gain or loss on contributed unrealized receivables, inventory items and capital loss property. Also, the special characterization rule in Section 707(b)(2) for a sale or exchange of property between a partnership and a more-than–50–percent partner applies. See Reg. § 1.704–4(b)(2) Example.

nized as a result of the distribution.[9] To avoid double recognition of that gain or loss, the partnership's inside basis in the property is increased or decreased prior to the distribution to reflect the gain or loss recognized by the contributing partner.[10]

To illustrate, return to the familiar example[11] where A contributes Gainacre with an adjusted basis of $12,000 and a fair market value of $20,000 and B contributes $20,000 cash to the equal AB partnership. Assume that three years later the partnership distributes Gainacre, then worth $23,000, to B. Under Section 704(c)(1)(B), A is allocated the $8,000 precontribution gain just as if the partnership had sold the property instead of distributing it,[12] and A would increase his outside basis by $8,000. In addition, Gainacre's basis would be increased to $20,000 prior to the distribution to B, who ordinarily would take the property with a $20,000 transferred basis.[13]

The general rule of Section 704(c)(1)(B) is subject to two statutory exceptions. First, it does not apply if the contributed property is distributed back to the contributing partner or her successor.[14] There is no abuse in this situation because the precontribution gain continues to lurk in the contributing partner's transferred basis in the distributed property.[15] Second, Section 704(c)(2) provides relief to a contributing partner who receives a distribution of like-kind property (within the meaning of Section 1031) within 180 days after the contributed property is distributed to another partner.[16] In that case, the contributing partner is allowed by the statute and regulations to reduce the amount of gain or loss recognized under Section 704(c)(1)(B) by the amount of built-in gain or loss in the distributed like-kind property. The effect of this exception may be to exempt from Section 704(c)(1)(B) distributions of property contributed by a partner who receives a timely distribution of like-kind property.[17] The policy here is that the contributing partner should not have to recognize gain under Section 704(c)(1)(B) if she would have qualified for nonrecognition if the transaction had taken place outside the partnership. To return to the example, where Gainacre (basis—$12,000, value—$20,000) is distributed to B three years later when it is worth $23,000, Section 704(c)(1)(B) would not apply if

---

**9.**   I.R.C. § 704(c)(1)(B)(iii). See I.R.C. § 705(a)(1)(A) & (2)(A).

**10.**   I.R.C. § 704(c)(1)(B)(iii). See I.R.C. §§ 732, 733.

**11.**   See Chapter 4C1, supra.

**12.**   If the property had been worth less than $20,000 at the time of the distribution to B and the partnership used the traditional method of making Section 704(c) allocations, A's gain would be limited by the ceiling rule. See Reg. § 1.704–3(b).

**13.**   I.R.C. § 732. This assumes that B's outside basis is at least $20,000 at the time of the distribution. I.R.C. § 732(a)(1), (b).

**14.**   I.R.C. § 704(c)(1)(B), second parenthetical.

**15.**   I.R.C. § 732(a).

**16.**   The time period is shortened to the due date for the contributing partner's tax return (with regard to extensions) if that date falls within the 180–day period. I.R.C. § 704(c)(2)(B)(ii).

**17.**   In these circumstances, the general rules of Sections 731–733 are applicable.

the partnership distributed like-kind property with at least $8,000 of built-in gain to A within 180 days of the distribution of Gainacre to B.[18]

The regulations under Section 704(c)(1)(B) also contain an anti-abuse provision under which the statute and regulations must be applied in a manner consistent with the purpose of the section and the Service can recast a transaction for federal tax purposes to achieve appropriate tax results.[19] For example, the regulations apply Section 704(c)(1)(B) to a distribution that actually takes place after the statute's time limitation (i.e., more than seven years after the contribution of property), but where the partners took steps that were the functional equivalent of a distribution before the end of that period.[20]

## 2. Distributions of Other Property to the Contributing Partner

A second potential abuse identified by Congress was a transaction where a partner contributes appreciated property to a partnership and later receives a distribution of other property while the partnership retains the contributed property. If the normal contribution and distribution rules applied in that situation, the contributing partner would be able to exchange the contributed property in a nonrecognition transaction when a similar swap outside the partnership would not have qualified for nonrecognition.[1] Section 737 prevents this type of mixing bowl transaction by requiring a contributing partner to recognize gain if she contributes appreciated property to a partnership and within seven years[2] of the contribution receives property other than money as a distribution from the partnership.[3] The amount of gain is the lesser of (1) the fair market value of the distributed property (other than money) less the partner's outside basis immediately before the distribution (reduced, but not below zero, by the amount of money received in the distribution) or (2) the "net precontribution gain" of the partner.[4] "Net precontribution gain" is the net gain that

---

**18.** See Reg. § 1.704–4(d)(3) & (4) Example. Note that while Section 704(c)(2) refers to the "value" of the distributed like-kind property the regulations base the test on the built-in gain or loss in such property. Section 704(c)(1)(B) is also inapplicable if there is a constructive termination of the partnership under Section 708(b)(1)(B). Reg. § 1.704–4(c)(3). The regulations also provide some more specialized exceptions to the application of Section 704(c)(1)(B). See Reg. § 1.704–4(c). Section 708(b)(1)(B) is considered in Chapter 8D2, infra. The interrelationship of Section 704(c)(1)(B) and 708(b)(1)(B) is considered in Hanna, "Partnership Distributions: Whatever Happened to Nonrecognition," 82 Kentucky Law J. 465 (1993), which concludes that both Sections 704(c)(1)(B) and

737 along with some other provisions of the Code are unnecessary.

**19.** Reg. § 1.704–4(f).

**20.** Reg. § 1.704–4(f)(2) Example 1.

**1.** I.R.C. §§ 731(a) 732(a), 733. But see I.R.C. § 707(a)(2)(B) considered at Chapter 5B2, supra, which would likely apply if the distribution occurred within a two-year period. Cf. Reg. § 1.704–3(a)(3).

**2.** The seven-year time period in Section 737 applies to property contributed after June 8, 1997.

**3.** I.R.C. § 737(a). The gain is in addition to any gain recognized under Section 731. Id.

**4.** For purposes of Section 737, marketable securities are treated as money to the

would have been recognized by the distributee partner under Section 704(c)(1)(B) if all of the property contributed by that partner within seven years of the current distribution had been distributed to another partner at the time of the distribution to the contributing partner.[5] The character of the gain is determined by reference to the contributed property.[6]

As under Section 704(c)(1)(B), appropriate concurrent basis adjustments are triggered when Section 737 applies. The contributing (now distributee) partner may increase her outside basis by the amount of gain recognized under Section 737.[7] This adjustment is made after measurement of the amount of Section 737(a) gain but before the distribution of the property.[8] The partnership also increases its inside basis in the contributed property by the amount of any Section 737 gain.[9]

To illustrate the operation of Section 737, assume that A again contributes Gainacre with an adjusted basis of $12,000 and a fair market value of $20,000 to the equal AB partnership. B contributes cash of $5,000 and Capital Asset with an adjusted basis and value of $15,000.[10] Within seven years of A's contribution (when A's outside basis is still $12,000), A receives the Capital Asset (still valued at $15,000) in an operating distribution. In these circumstances, A would recognize a $3,000 gain, which is the lesser of (1) $3,000, the fair market value of the Capital Asset reduced by A's outside basis ($15,000 less $12,000) or (2) $8,000, A's net precontribution gain. A also would increase his outside basis by $3,000, to $15,000, immediately prior to the distribution.[11] A would take a $15,000 transferred basis in the Capital Asset,[12] and A's outside basis after the distribution would be reduced to zero.[13] To avoid double taxation, the partnership may increase its adjusted basis in Gainacre by $3,000, to $15,000.[14]

The general rule of Section 737(a) is subject to two statutory exceptions. First, if any portion of the distributed property consists of property that was contributed by the distributee partner, that property is not taken into account in determining gain under Section 737(a)(1) or measuring the net precontribution gain under Section 737(b).[15] Second, Section 737 does

---

extent of their fair market value on the date of the distribution. I.R.C. § 731(c)(1).

**5.** I.R.C. §§ 737(a) & (b).

**6.** I.R.C. § 737(a); Reg. § 1.737–1(d). Section 724 also would apply in determining the character of gain on contributed unrealized receivables and inventory items.

**7.** I.R.C. § 737(c)(1).

**8.** Id.

**9.** I.R.C. § 737(c)(2).

**10.** If the property had been appreciated or depreciated at the time of B's contribution, Section 704(c)(1)(B) also would apply to B.

**11.** I.R.C. § 737(c)(1). The increase is after the measurement of Section 737 gain

and before the distribution of the property. Id.

**12.** I.R.C. § 732(a)(1).

**13.** I.R.C. § 733.

**14.** I.R.C. § 737(c)(2).

**15.** I.R.C. § 737(d)(1). However, if the property distributed consists of an interest in an entity that the distributee partner contributed to the partnership, the exception is inapplicable to the extent that the value of the entity is attributable to property contributed to the entity after its contribution to the partnership. Id. For example, assume A contributed C corporation stock with an adjusted basis of $12,000 and a fair market value of $20,000 to a partnership and the partnership subsequently contributed property worth

not apply to the extent that Section 751(b) applies.[16]

Section 737 is also subject to an anti-abuse rule contained in the regulations.[17] That provision requires the rules of Section 737 and the regulations to be applied in a manner consistent with the purpose of the section. The Service is also empowered to recast a transaction for federal tax purposes as appropriate to achieve tax results consistent with the purpose of Section 737. For example, the regulations disregard the basis increase attributable to a temporary contribution of property undertaken to avoid gain under Section 737.[18]

One of the most challenging aspects of Section 737 is its interrelationship with other parts of Subchapter K. Both Section 704(c)(1)(B) and Section 737 can apply to different contributing partners when there is a single distribution of contributed property. In addition, if either Section 707(a)(2)(B) or Section 704(c)(2) applies to a transaction also covered by Section 737, those sections take precedence.[19] Finally, as noted above, Section 737 does not apply to the extent that Section 751(b) overrides it. Some of these statutory interrelationships are explored in the problem below.

## PROBLEM

A, B, and C form the equal ABC partnership by contributing the following real properties, all of which are held as an investment by both the partners and the partnership:

| Partner | Property | A.B. | F.M.V. |
|---|---|---|---|
| A | #1 | $ 2,000 | $10,000 |
| B | #2 | $ 5,000 | $10,000 |
| C | #3 | $10,000 | $10,000 |

Assume that ABC uses the "traditional method" of allocation under Reg. § 1.704–3(b). What are the tax consequences to the partners in the following transactions, assuming the partners' outside bases and ABC's inside basis in the land are unchanged at the time of each transaction, if the ABC partnership:

(a) Sells property #1 for $10,000.

(b) Distributes property #1 to C six years after formation of the partnership.

$10,000 to the C corporation. If the C corporation stock is now worth $30,000 and it is distributed to A, the distribution of $10,000 of the C corporation stock would be subject to Section 737(a).

**16.** I.R.C. § 737(d)(2). See Section E of this chapter for coverage of Section 751(b). Section 737 also does not apply to a constructive termination of a partnership under Sec-

tion 708(b)(1)(B). Reg. § 1.737–2(a). Section 708(b)(1)(B) is considered in Chapter 8D2, infra. The regulations also provide some more specialized exceptions to the application of Section 737. See Reg. § 1.737–2.

**17.** Reg. § 1.737–4.

**18.** Reg. § 737–4(b) Example 1.

**19.** Reg. § 1.704–3(a)(5).

(c) Distributes property #3 to A six years after formation of the partnership.

(d) Distributes property #2 to A six years after formation of the partnership.

(e) Distributes property #2 to A one year after formation of the partnership.

(f) Simultaneously distributes property #1 to B and property #2 to A six years after formation of the partnership and the properties are like kind properties.

(g) Distributes property that is like kind to property #1 to A six years after formation of the partnership.

## E.   DISTRIBUTIONS WHICH ALTER THE PARTNERS' INTERESTS IN ORDINARY INCOME PROPERTY

Code: §§ 731(d); 732(e); 751(b). Skim § 751(a), (c) & (d).

Regulations: § 1.751–1(b). Skim § 1.751–1(g) Example (2).

*Introduction.* The operating distribution rules considered up to now reflect a typical nonrecognition scheme. Historically, life was not that simple in the partnership tax forest, where avaricious taxpayers prowled in search of the opportunity to shift ordinary income into a lower bracket or, better still, to convert ordinary income into capital gain. Congress understandably reacted by planting an imposing array of statutory trees designed to prevent income shifting and conversion. And so just as you feel that you have mastered an area, Section 751(b) appears on the scene to complicate this chapter as well as your life.

Section 751(b) overrides the nonrecognition and substituted basis rules of Section 731 and Section 732.[1] This occurs when a distribution has the effect of altering the partners' interests in Section 751 property—i.e., generally the same ordinary income assets (unrealized receivables and inventory items) that were singled out by Section 751(a) for special treatment in connection with the sale of a partnership interest but with one important caveat.[2] For purposes of Section 751(b), inventory items are treated as Section 751 property only if they have "appreciated substantially in value."[3] Section 751(b), which applies to both operating and liquidating distributions,[4] is the second feature of this ongoing horror show.

**1.** See I.R.C. §§ 731(d) & 732(e), which in essence provide that the Section 751(b) rules are to be applied prior to application of the general distribution rules. See also Reg. § 1.751–1(b)(1)(iii).

**2.** See Chapter 6A, supra. For convenience, partnership assets that do not consti-

tute Section 751 property will be referred to in this discussion as "Section 741 property."

**3.** I.R.C. § 751(b)(1)(A)(ii).

**4.** This includes distributions to a retiring partner as well as a liquidation of the partnership itself. See Rev. Rul. 77–412, 1977–2 C.B. 223 and Chapter 8D, infra.

*Substantially Appreciated Inventory Items.* Inventory items are not treated as Section 751 property for purposes of Section 751(b) unless they are substantially appreciated—i.e., unless their aggregate fair market value (meaning total value, not merely equity) exceeds 120 percent of the adjusted basis of the inventory items in the hands of the partnership.[5] This test is intended to limit the application of Section 751(b) to cases where there is a significant potential conversion of ordinary income to capital gain. Thus, in measuring appreciation, any inventory acquired for the principal purpose of avoiding the 120 percent test is excluded from consideration.[6]

Recall that the definition of inventory items includes Section 1221(1) "dealer" property as well as any property which, upon sale by the partnership or the distributee partner, would not be considered a capital asset or a Section 1231 asset.[7] As a result of the broad definition of "inventory," an asset may constitute both an unrealized receivable and an inventory item.[8] The inclusion of receivables in the inventory category is significant because they are then combined with other inventory items in determining whether those items are substantially appreciated.[9] If the aggregate inventory items are substantially appreciated, they are all treated as Section 751 assets. If an asset falls within both Section 751(b)(1)(A)(i) and (b)(1)(A)(ii), it will be taxed only once.[10] But if the inventory items, augmented by the receivables, are not substantially appreciated, then under Section 751(b)(1)(A) only the unrealized receivables (including those which also are inventory items) are treated as Section 751 assets.

The prospect of ordinary income treatment has motivated sophisticated taxpayers to devise strategies to avoid the taint caused by the presence of substantially appreciated inventory items on the partnership's balance sheet. Historically, one popular technique was to manipulate the partnership's inventory items so they would not be classified as substantially appreciated.[11] The strategy was derailed, however, by the enactment of an "anti-stuffing" rule under which any inventory acquired for "a principal purpose" of avoiding the 120 percent test is excluded in measuring appreciation.[12]

*Operation of Section 751(b).* The most productive way to master a Code section is first to understand its rationale, and that will be our approach to Section 751(b). Assume that the ABC partnership has three equal partners and the following balance sheet:

**5.** I.R.C. § 751(b)(3)(A). The test is applied to the partnership's basis and, in making the computation, special basis adjustments of any partner are disregarded. Reg. § 1.751–1(d)(1). Cf. I.R.C. §§ 732(d); 743(b).

**6.** I.R.C. § 751(b)(3)(B).

**7.** I.R.C. § 751(d).

**8.** Reg. § 1.751–1(d)(2)(ii).

**9.** I.R.C. § 751(b)(3).

**10.** If unrealized receivables fall within both Section 751(c) and (d), they are treated as Section 751(c) assets under other Code provisions. See I.R.C. §§ 735(a); 736.

**11.** See Problem 2(c), below, and McKee, Nelson & Whitmire, Federal Taxation of Partnership and Partners ¶ 16.04[2] (3d ed. 1996).

**12.** I.R.C. § 751(b)(3)(B).

| Assets | A.B. | F.M.V. | Partners' Capital | A.B. | F.M.V. |
|---|---|---|---|---|---|
| Cash | $15,000 | $15,000 | A | $ 9,000 | $15,000 |
| Inventory | 9,000 | 15,000 | B | 9,000 | 15,000 |
| Capital Asset | 3,000 | 15,000 | C | 9,000 | 15,000 |
| | $27,000 | $45,000 | | $27,000 | $45,000 |

Assume further that the partnership has held the capital asset for several years and that A receives the inventory in liquidation of his interest in the partnership.[13]

Disregarding for the moment Section 751(b), consider the tax consequences to A, B and C under the general nonrecognition rules that we have previously studied. On the distribution, A receives the inventory[14] with a $9,000 basis[15] and a $15,000 value. In effect, B and C are left with the $15,000 cash and the appreciated capital asset with a $3,000 basis and a $15,000 value. When the smoke clears from this nonrecognition transaction, A, B and C each end up with $6,000 of potential gain (A's gain lurks in the inventory, and B and C would share the $12,000 gain inherent in the capital asset). So what's the problem? It is the characterization of these potential gains. If A immediately were to sell the inventory, he would recognize $6,000 of ordinary income,[16] but if the capital asset were sold, B and C each would have $6,000 of long-term capital gain.[17] The result is an assignment of the character of the income—the very evil that Section 751(b) was designed to curb.[18] Consequently, if a current or liquidating distribution to a partner has the effect of altering the interests of the partners in Section 751 property, Section 751(b) comes into play to make things right.[19]

The *why* of Section 751(b) is perhaps easier to understand than the *how*—the mechanics of its operation. But the how also must be understood, so ... we return to the example above. Under an aggregate approach, before the distribution of inventory, A in essence held the following one-third interest in each of the partnership's assets.

**13.** Do not be concerned that this is a liquidating distribution. Section 751(b) and the other provisions discussed in this example apply with respect to both operating and liquidating distributions, and it is easier to illustrate the purpose and operation of Section 751(b) in this simplified liquidation setting.

**14.** The inventory is "substantially appreciated," as it must be for Section 751(b) to apply. I.R.C. § 751(b)(1)(A)(ii).

**15.** Under Section 732(b), which applies to liquidating distributions, the inventory receives the same substituted basis it would have under Section 732(a)(1) in the case of an operating distribution.

**16.** I.R.C. § 735(a)(2).

**17.** This is the result whether B and C sell their partnership interests, the partnership distributes the assets and B and C sell them individually (assuming they remain capital assets to B and C), or the partnership sells the assets, liquidates and distributes the proceeds.

**18.** As you will discover in Problem 4, below, Section 751(b) does not always achieve its apparent objective. It is not concerned with the *amount* of income within a class, merely assignments between classes.

**19.** Several exceptions to Section 751(b) are discussed below.

| **Assets** | **A.B.** | **F.M.V.** |
|---|---|---|
| Cash | $5,000 | $ 5,000 |
| Inventory | 3,000 | 5,000 |
| Capital Asset | 1,000 | 5,000 |
| | $9,000 | $15,000 |

By receiving all the substantially appreciated inventory, A in effect exchanged his interest in the Section 741 property—the cash and capital asset—for the remaining partners' interests in the inventory.[20] Section 751(b) requires the distributee partner to engage in this constructive exchange with the partnership, i.e., the other partners, for purposes of determining the tax consequences of the transaction to all the parties.[21]

In order for A to engage in an exchange with the partnership, A must receive property to transfer in the exchange. This is achieved under Section 751(b) by the mechanism of a phantom distribution to A of the class of property in which A was short changed on the actual distribution. Under the facts in our example, A received no Section 741 assets at a time when he had a $10,000 interest in those assets. At the same time, A received $15,000 worth of inventory when he had only a $5,000 pro rata interest prior to the distribution. He thus received too much Section 751 property to the extent of $10,000 and not enough Section 741 property to the same extent. To correct the imbalance, the partnership makes a phantom distribution to A of Section 741 property with a value of $10,000. The regulations permit the partners to specify property within the class of nondistributed assets (i.e., all cash or all capital asset in our example) but, in the absence of a specific agreement among the partners as to the properties deemed to be distributed, the phantom distribution is pro rata among the assets within the class.[22] Assuming no such agreement here, the phantom distribution to A consists of $5,000 cash and $5,000 of the capital asset.

The regular operating distribution rules of Sections 731, 732 and 733 are applied to determine the tax consequences of the phantom distribution. Recall that A receives $5,000 cash and $5,000 of the capital asset with a $1,000 basis. A recognizes no gain on the distribution[23] but reduces his outside basis by $6,000 (the amount of cash and the basis in the capital asset received).[24] The value of his interest in the partnership is reduced by the amount of the distribution ($10,000) from $15,000 to $5,000. After the phantom distribution, the ABC partnership balance sheet is as follows:

**20.** Keep in mind that Section 751(b) is only concerned with disproportionate distributions between Section 741 and 751 assets, not assets within a class. Thus, if in a subsequent liquidating distribution, B received all the cash and C received the capital asset, Section 751(b) would not apply. See Problem 4, below.

**21.** Although we say that A engages in the transaction with the partnership, the exchange is really with the other partners. This is so whether the distribution is an operating or a liquidating distribution. Reg. §§ 1.751–1(b)(2)(ii) & 1.751–1(b)(3)(ii).

**22.** Reg. § 1.751–1(g) Examples 3(c) & 4(c).

**23.** I.R.C. § 731.

**24.** I.R.C. § 733.

| Assets | A.B. | F.M.V. | Partners' Capital | A.B. | F.M.V. |
|---|---|---|---|---|---|
| Cash | $10,000 | $10,000 | A | $ 3,000 | $ 5,000 |
| Inventory | 9,000 | 15,000 | B | 9,000 | 15,000 |
| Capital Asset | 2,000 | 10,000 | C | 9,000 | 15,000 |
|  | $21,000 | $35,000 |  | $21,000 | $35,000 |

The phantom distribution provides A with the property to transfer to the partnership in exchange for the excess Section 751 property that he received on the actual distribution. On this fictional exchange, A transfers the cash and capital asset, worth $10,000, back to the partnership, which in turn transfers inventory worth $10,000 to A. A has $4,000 of capital gain on the exchange, representing the difference between his $10,000 amount realized (the fair market value of the inventory) and his $6,000 aggregate adjusted basis in the capital asset and the cash. He takes a $10,000 cost basis in the inventory. The partnership passes through $4,000 of ordinary income to B and C on the taxable exchange of the inventory ($10,000 amount realized less a $6,000 basis), and it acquires $5,000 of cash and takes a $5,000 cost basis in the capital asset. B and C thus both recognize $2,000 of ordinary income,[25] and they each increase their respective outside bases by $2,000.[26] Even if this had been an operating rather than a liquidating distribution, the gain or loss recognized by the partnership on the fictional exchanges would be allocated only to partners other than the distributee partner.[27]

After the Section 751(b) transaction, the partnership balance sheet is as follows:

| Assets | A.B. | F.M.V. | Partners' Capital | A.B. | F.M.V. |
|---|---|---|---|---|---|
| Cash | $15,000 | $15,000 | A | $ 3,000 | $ 5,000 |
| Inventory | 3,000 | 5,000 | B | 11,000 | 15,000 |
| Capital Asset | 7,000 | 15,000 | C | 11,000 | 15,000 |
|  | $25,000 | $35,000 |  | $25,000 | $35,000 |

As noted above, A has acquired $10,000 of inventory with a $10,000 cost basis.

The constructive transactions described above are only part of the picture. Section 751(b) overrides the normal distribution rules to the extent that the distribution is disproportionate. On completion of the Section 751(b) transaction, the remaining portion of A's distribution is taxed under the general rules of Sections 731, 732 and 733. A recognizes no gain on receipt of the remaining $5,000 of inventory and takes a $3,000 transferred

---

**25.**  I.R.C. § 702(a)(8).  Reg. §§ 1.751–1(b)(2)(ii) & 1.751–1(b)(3)(ii). These regulations require that this gain be allocated entirely to the nondistributee partners in accordance with their postdistribution interests in partnership profits and losses.

**26.**  I.R.C. § 705(a)(1)(A).

**27.**  Reg. §§ 1.751–1(b)(2)(ii) & 1.751–1(b)(3)(ii).

basis.[28] He thus emerges with total inventory with a value of $15,000 and an adjusted basis of $13,000 ($10,000 cost basis from the constructive exchange and $3,000 transferred basis on the normal distribution). This makes sense because A started with an outside basis of $9,000 in his $15,000 partnership interest, recognized $4,000 of gain on the fictional exchange and ended up with a total basis of $13,000. The partnership balance sheet after the distribution is as follows:

| Assets | A.B. | F.M.V. | Partners' Capital | A.B. | F.M.V. |
|---|---|---|---|---|---|
| Cash | $15,000 | $15,000 | B | $11,000 | $15,000 |
| Capital Asset | 7,000 | 15,000 | C | 11,000 | 15,000 |
| | $22,000 | $30,000 | | $22,000 | $30,000 |

The Section 751(b) rules do not apply to distributions of property which the distributee partner previously contributed to the partnership, presumably on the theory that such a distribution merely restores the status quo.[29] They also do not apply to payments governed by Section 736(a)[30] (this exception will be explained in the next chapter),[31] draws or advances received by the partner against his distributive share[32] and distributions which are gifts, payments for services or for the use of capital.[33]

Having introduced a simple Section 751(b) transaction, it is time to turn to more complex issues. The problems below, involving as they do disproportionate distributions of both Section 751 and Section 741 property, present a greater challenge because it usually is more difficult to determine the extent to which a distribution is disproportionate if it is an operating rather than a liquidating distribution. The determination is made by comparing the distributee partner's interest in either the Section 741 or 751 assets both before and after the distribution. For example, assume that the equal ABC partnership has the following balance sheet:

| Assets | A.B. | F.M.V. | Partners' Capital | A.B. | F.M.V. |
|---|---|---|---|---|---|
| Cash | $36,000 | $ 36,000 | A | $18,000 | $ 36,000 |
| Inventory | 0 | 36,000 | B | 18,000 | 36,000 |
| Capital Asset | 18,000 | 36,000 | C | 18,000 | 36,000 |
| | $54,000 | $108,000 | | $54,000 | $108,000 |

If A receives an operating distribution of $18,000 cash, he will emerge with a one-fifth interest in the partnership, and the disproportionate effect of the distribution can be measured in two different ways, either of which yields the same result. A can compare his interest in Section 751 assets

---

**28.** I.R.C. § 732(b), although under these facts this also would be A's Section 732(a)(1) carryover basis if this had been an operating distribution.

**29.** I.R.C. § 751(b)(2)(A). Cf. I.R.C. § 704(c).

**30.** I.R.C. § 751(b)(2)(B).

**31.** See Chapter 8B2, infra.

**32.** Reg. § 1.751–1(b)(1)(ii).

**33.** Id.

before and after the distribution or he can make a similar comparison of his interest in Section 741 assets. After the distribution, the balance sheet is as follows:

| Assets | A.B. | F.M.V. | Partners' Capital | A.B. | F.M.V. |
|---|---|---|---|---|---|
| Cash | $18,000 | $18,000 | A | $ 0 | $18,000 |
| Inventory | 0 | 36,000 | B | 18,000 | 36,000 |
| Capital Asset | 18,000 | 36,000 | C | 18,000 | 36,000 |
| | $36,000 | $90,000 | | $36,000 | $90,000 |

A's comparative interest in Section 751 assets is as follows:

| | | | |
|---|---|---|---|
| Before the distribution: | ⅓ of $36,000 | = | $12,000 |
| After the distribution: | ⅕ of $36,000 | = | 7,200 |
| Disproportionate share: | | | ($ 4,800) |

A similar result occurs from the following comparison of A's interest in Section 741 assets:

| | | | |
|---|---|---|---|
| Before the distribution: | ⅓ of $72,000 | = | $24,000 |
| After the distribution: | ⅕ of $54,000 ($10,800) | | |
| | plus $18,000 | = | 28,800 |
| Disproportionate share: | | | $ 4,800 |

These comparisons demonstrate that A ends up with $4,800 more than his share of Section 741 assets and $4,800 less than his share of Section 751 assets. Consequently, A must receive a phantom distribution of $4,800 of Section 751 assets. A then engages in a constructive exchange of the excess Section 751 property for an equal amount of Section 741 property. Finally, the normal distribution rules must be applied to the remainder of the distribution.

*Policy Considerations.* The purpose of Section 751(b) is to prevent shifting of the character of gain or loss among partners. To do so, it constructs hypothetical exchanges of capital and noncapital assets where no exchanges actually occurred. The complexity of Section 751(b) is so mind boggling that, even though it potentially affects many partnership distributions, it is widely believed that actual compliance is rare.

Over 50 years ago, an advisory group studying Subchapter K recommended repeal of Section 751(b), as did the American Law Institute in its 1984 partnership tax project.[1] The case for repeal is well articulated in the statement below made by a leading practitioner (and former law professor) at a 1986 House Ways and Means Committee hearing on issues relating to pass-through entities. The statement was made at a time when the distinction between capital gain and ordinary income had diminished consider-

---

**1.** See American Law Institute, Federal Income Tax Project—Subchapter K 47–55 (1984).

ably. In reading the excerpt, consider whether Mr. Rabinovitz's argument is still as compelling in light of the resurrection of a significant rate preference for long-term capital gains recognized by individuals.

### Excerpt From Statement of Joel Rabinovitz, Esq., at Hearings Before the Subcommittee on Select Revenue Measures of the House Ways and Means Committee, Issues Relating to Pass–Through Entities

99th Cong., 2d Sess. 58–65 (1986).

### Repeal of IRC 751(b)

Section 751(b) of the Internal Revenue Code should be repealed. It is not necessary to prevent one of the perceived abuses at which it is apparently aimed and ineffective to prevent the other. Moreover it is generally overlooked, frequently ignored by those aware of its application, and often applied incorrectly by those, including the Internal Revenue Service, perceptive and honest enough to make the attempt.

Apparently IRC 751(b) is intended to address two potential abuses—conversion of ordinary income to capital gain and shifting of income from high bracket to low bracket taxpayers. The first of these potential abuses, to the extent that it arises on the distribution of partnership assets to a partner, is adequately addressed by IRC 735, and to the extent that it arises on a redemption of all or part of a partner's interest for cash could be adequately dealt with by a relatively simple extension of IRC 751(a). Moreover, if the pending elimination of capital gains for individuals is enacted [as it was in the Tax Reform Act of 1986, but beginning in 1993 a significant capital gains preference began to reappear, Ed.] the abuse potential itself will largely disappear. With respect to the second perceived abuse, IRC 751(b) in its present form does nothing to prevent shifting income by distributing high basis ordinary income assets to some partners and low basis ordinary assets to others. There is no evidence, however, that this possibility is currently abused enough to justify the complexity necessary to fashion an adequate curb, and a general reduction in tax rates will reduce the likelihood of abuse still further.

In numerous situations to which IRC 751(b) applies its relevance goes unrecognized. It is likely that the vast majority of small businesses operating in partnership form are not even aware that IRC 751(b) is applicable to almost any non-pro rata distribution which they make. They are even less likely to recognize its application to the admission of a new partner to a cash method partnership. Furthermore, many large professional partnerships, aware of IRC 751(b)'s application in this situation, simply close their eyes to IRC 751(b) to avoid the disproportionate complexity and expense of having to make a large number of insignificant adjustments. And the Internal Revenue Service which, at least at the national office level, is aware of the application of IRC 751(b) to the admission of a new partner to a cash basis partnership, has applied it incorrectly in its most recent public

effort to provide guidance to taxpayers. See Revenue Ruling 84–102, 84–2 Cum.Bul. 119. There is little to be said for a statutory provision which is frequently ignored, is incapable of being applied by either the people affected by it or those charged with administering it and which is, at the same time, unnecessary or ineffective to prevent the perceived abuses at which it is purportedly aimed.

## PROBLEMS

**1**. The ABC equal partnership has the following balance sheet:

| Assets | A.B. | F.M.V. | Partners' Capital | A.B. | F.M.V. |
|---|---|---|---|---|---|
| Cash | $6,000 | $ 6,000 | A | $3,000 | $ 6,000 |
| Accounts Receivable | 0 | 3,000 | B | 3,000 | 6,000 |
| Capital Asset | 3,000 | 9,000 | C | 3,000 | 6,000 |
| | $9,000 | $18,000 | | $9,000 | $18,000 |

The partnership distributes the accounts receivable to A in an operating distribution. After the distribution, A has a one-fifth interest worth $3,000 in the remaining partnership assets.

  (a) What results to A, B, C and the partnership as a result of the distribution? Reconstruct the partnership balance sheet at the end of the transaction.

  (b) If the distribution results in an increase to the partnership's inside basis, how should that increase be allocated?

**2**. The ABC partnership has the following balance sheet, which is the same as the second hypothetical discussed above in the text:

| Assets | A.B. | F.M.V. | Partners' Capital | A.B. | F.M.V. |
|---|---|---|---|---|---|
| Cash | $36,000 | $ 36,000 | A | $18,000 | $ 36,000 |
| Inventory | 0 | 36,000 | B | 18,000 | 36,000 |
| Land (capital asset) | 18,000 | 36,000 | C | 18,000 | 36,000 |
| | $54,000 | $108,000 | | $54,000 | $108,000 |

  (a) Initially, each partner has a one-third interest in partnership capital, profits, and losses. The partnership distributes cash of $27,000 to A who then has a one-ninth interest in partnership capital, profits, and losses. A's interest is worth $9,000 after the distribution. What results to A, B, C and the partnership as a result of the distribution to A? Recompute the partnership balance sheet at the end of the transaction.

  (b) What differences in the results in (a), above, if the partnership had made a § 754 election?

  (c) Assume the inventory on the balance sheet had a basis of $24,000 instead of $0. Could the partners have avoided the application of

§ 751(b) by using the cash to purchase $36,000 worth of additional inventory?

**3.**  The § 734(b) basis adjustment is inapplicable to the extent that § 751(b) governs a distribution. Reg. § 1.734–2(b)(2). Why?

**4.**  A, B and C are equal partners in the ABC partnership which has the following balance sheet:

| Assets | A.B. | F.M.V. | Partners' Capital | A.B. | F.M.V. |
|---|---|---|---|---|---|
| Cash | $ 6,000 | $ 6,000 | A | $12,000 | $18,000 |
| Accounts Receivable | 0 | 9,000 | B | 12,000 | 18,000 |
| Inventory | 18,000 | 18,000 | C | 12,000 | 18,000 |
| Land & Building | 6,000 | 12,000 | | | |
| Equipment | 6,000 | 9,000 | | | |
| | $36,000 | $54,000 | | $36,000 | $54,000 |

The partnership distributes the $9,000 worth of accounts receivable to A and $18,000 worth of inventory equally ($9,000 each) to B and C.

(a)  Is § 751(b) applicable to this operating distribution?

(b)  What does this tell you about § 751(b)?

**5.**  A and B are individuals. The AB partnership has the following balance sheet:

| Assets | A.B. | F.M.V. | Partners' Capital | A.B. | F.M.V. |
|---|---|---|---|---|---|
| Cash | $4,000 | $ 4,000 | A | $4,000 | $ 6,000 |
| Receivables | 0 | 4,000 | B | 4,000 | 6,000 |
| Inventory | 4,000 | 4,000 | | | |
| | $8,000 | $12,000 | | $8,000 | $12,000 |

The partnership distributes all the cash to A, who thereafter owns a one-fourth interest in the partnership. If A is in the 15% tax bracket and B is in a much higher marginal bracket, how would you structure the transaction? See Reg. § 1.751–1(a)(2) and 1(g) Example 3(c) and Example 4(c). In so doing, could you fairly act as counsel to both partners?

**6.**  Should § 751(b) be repealed?

CHAPTER 8

# LIQUIDATING DISTRIBUTIONS AND TERMINATIONS

## A. INTRODUCTION

Code: §§ 736; 761(d). Skim §§ 706(c)(1) & (2)(A); 731; 732(b), (c), (d) & (e).

Our study of Subchapter K parallels the life cycle of a partner's interest in a partnership, moving from cradle to grave. Having mastered the rigors of operating distributions, we have survived the inevitable mid-life crisis and may now proceed to the closing ceremonies. The end begins with a study of liquidating distributions to a "retiring partner." For this purpose, liquidation of a partner's interest means "the termination of a partner's entire interest in a partnership by means of a distribution, or a series of distributions, to the partner by the partnership,"[1] and a "retiring partner" is one who "ceases to be a partner under local law."[2] This chapter also considers the tax consequences of partnership terminations, including complete liquidations and other events that cause a partnership to terminate for tax purposes. The special problems raised by the liquidation of a deceased partner's interest are deferred until Chapter 9.

To introduce the tax treatment of liquidating distributions, consider the choices faced by Retiring Partner ("RP"), who desires to terminate her interest in a partnership that will continue to operate after RP's withdrawal. One option would be for RP to sell her interest to the remaining partners or to a third party. As we have seen,[3] the tax consequences of the sale of a partnership interest are governed by Sections 741 and 751, and RP generally will recognize capital gain or loss except to the extent of her share of Section 751 assets. Alternatively, RP could liquidate her interest in the partnership, a transaction resembling a corporation's redemption of a shareholder's stock. In exchange, RP might receive payments for a variety of items, including her pro rata share of unrealized receivables, partnership goodwill and other assets of the partnership and perhaps an additional premium in the nature of "mutual insurance" provided by the partnership

---

**1.** I.R.C. § 761(d); Reg. § 1.761–1(d).

**2.** Reg. § 1.736–1(a)(1)(ii). The liquidation of a partner's interest in a continuing partnership does not close the partnership's taxable year where there is not a complete liquidation of the partnership (I.R.C. § 706(c)(2), see I.R.C. § 708(b)(1) and Section C of this chapter, infra), but completion

of the liquidation will result in the closing of the partnership year as to the liquidated partner (I.R.C. § 706(c)(2)(A)). These results are similar to the rules applicable to a partner who sells his partnership interest. Reg. § 1.706–1(c)(2).

**3.** See Chapter 6A, supra.

agreement. The tax consequences to RP and the remaining partners may differ depending on the manner in which RP structures her withdrawal from the partnership. A major goal of this chapter is to convey an understanding of the tax consequences involved in classifying and timing liquidating distributions and in distinguishing sales from liquidations.

Prior to the 1954 Code, the tax treatment of liquidating distributions was unsettled.[4] Congress ended much of the confusion by enacting Section 736, which in general classifies payments in liquidation of a retiring partner's interest in a continuing partnership by dividing them into two broad categories: (1) payments for the partner's interest in partnership property[5] and (2) all other payments.[6] Payments in the first category are treated by Section 736(b) as distributions in liquidation of the retiring partner's interest and thus are governed by the distribution provisions,[7] including the overriding disproportionate distribution rules in Section 751(b). Payments in the second category are characterized by Section 736(a) as either a distributive share of partnership income, if based on profits of the firm,[8] or as guaranteed payments under Section 707(c), if determined without reference to partnership income.[9]

In proceeding through this chapter, keep the function of Section 736 clearly in focus. It merely classifies payments, leaving the determination of the specific tax consequences to other provisions that you have previously encountered. Also note that the parties may have some flexibility to shape the tax consequences of a partner's withdrawal from a partnership by selecting the form of the transaction and classifying the payments in an arm's length agreement. For example, there may be significant differences in tax treatment with respect to ''premium payments'' (i.e., payments that exceed the value of the retiring partner's share of partnership property) if the transaction is structured as a liquidation rather than a sale, or if the payments in either type of transaction are made in installments.

Apart from tax consequences, also keep in mind that liquidations are inextricably linked to the capital account concept that pervades the partnership allocation regulations.[10] Capital accounts determine the amounts partners are entitled to receive on a liquidation of their interests in the partnership.[11] To properly carry out this function, they must be adjusted to reflect the book gain or loss inherent in any property distributed in liquidation of a partner's interest in a manner similar to that used in the case of operating distributions.[12]

---

**4.**  See Jackson, Johnson, Surrey, Tenen & Warren, ''The Internal Revenue Code of 1954: Partnerships,'' 54 Colum.L.Rev. 1183, 1223–1224 (1954).

**5.**  I.R.C. § 736(b).

**6.**  I.R.C. § 736(a).

**7.**  See I.R.C. §§ 731; 732; 734; 735; and Chapter 7B, 7C & 7E, supra.

**8.**  I.R.C. § 736(a)(1).

**9.**  I.R.C. § 736(a)(2).

**10.**  See Chapter 3B1, supra.

**11.**  Cf. Reg. § 1.704–1(b)(2)(ii)(*b*)(*2*).

**12.**  See Reg. § 1.704–1(b)(2)(iv)(*e*)(*1*) and Chapter 7C, supra. The liquidation of a partner's interest also is an appropriate occasion for a partnership to restate the book values of all of its remaining property and to make corresponding adjustments to the capital accounts of the continuing partners. See Reg. § 1.704–1(b)(2)(iv)(*f*).

## B.   LIQUIDATION OF A PARTNER'S INTEREST

## 1.   SECTION 736(b) PAYMENTS

Code: §§ 731; 732(b), (c), (d) & (e); 736(b). Skim §§ 734; 735; 736(a); 751(b); 754; 755.

Regulations: §§ 1.731–1(a)(2); 1.732–2(b) & (c); 1.736–1(b)(4).

*The Scope of Section 736(b).* Section 736(b) payments are liquidating distributions that are attributable to the retiring partner's interest in most types of partnership property. Two categories of property are specifically excluded from Section 736(b) and thus are taxed under Section 736(a). In the case of a retiring general partner in a partnership where capital is not a material income producing factor (e.g., a services partnership), Section 736(b) does not apply to payments for (1) the partner's share of unrealized receivables, and (2) partnership goodwill if the partnership agreement does not expressly provide for such payments.[1] For purposes of Section 736(b), recapture gain is excluded from the definition of unrealized receivables.[2] Thus, amounts paid to a retiring partner for the recapture potential in partnership property are Section 736(b) payments. The tax consequences of Section 736(b) payments are determined, with a few limited exceptions, by the same statutory scheme applicable to operating distributions. This section thus provides an opportunity to review much of the material covered in the preceding chapter.

*Tax Consequences to the Retiring Partner.* As with operating distributions, a retiring partner recognizes gain on a liquidating distribution only to the extent that the cash received exceeds the partner's outside basis.[3] If both cash and other property are distributed, Sections 731 and 732 work in tandem to treat the distribution as a nonrecognition transaction. First, the partner reduces his outside basis by the cash received[4] and then, in effect, he exchanges his remaining partnership interest for the other assets received in the distribution. Section 731 provides nonrecognition treatment to the partner and the partnership on the distribution, and Section 732(b) provides the partner with an aggregate basis in the distributed property equal to his predistribution outside basis less any cash received in the liquidation. This exchanged basis mechanism preserves any gain or loss inherent in the partner's interest for recognition when the partner disposes of the distributed assets.

If more than one asset is distributed, Section 732(c) once again prescribes the method for allocating the aggregate exchanged basis to the distributee partner.[5] If inventory items or unrealized receivables have been

---

1.  I.R.C. § 736(b)(2) & (3).

2.  I.R.C. § 751(c), flush language.

3.  I.R.C. § 731(a)(1).

4.  I.R.C. § 733.

5.  If the retiring partner received cash in excess of his outside basis, he would recognize capital gain to the extent of the excess,

distributed, those properties are first tentatively assigned a basis equal to the basis of each such property to the partnership.[6] If the sum of the partnership's bases in the distributed unrealized receivables and inventory items exceeds the basis to be allocated (the partner's outside basis less cash received in the transaction), then the partnership's bases in those properties must be reduced by the amount of the excess.[7] The reduction is achieved by first allocating basis decreases among the properties with unrealized built-in loss (i.e., properties with an assigned basis greater than their value) in proportion to the amounts of such loss and only to the extent of the built-in loss of each property.[8] If needed, additional decreases are allocated in proportion to the remaining adjusted bases of the unrealized receivables and inventory items.[9] If the basis to be allocated exceeds the partnership's basis in the distributed unrealized receivables and inventory items, then each other distributed property is next assigned a basis equal to the partnership's basis in that property.[10] Basis increases or decreases then must be allocated to the other distributed properties if the partner's remaining basis (i.e., the basis remaining after any unrealized receivables or inventory items are assigned basis equal to their bases in the hands of the partnership) is greater or less than the sum of the partnership's bases in those properties.[11] If an overall increase is required, the increase is accomplished by first allocating basis increases among the properties with unrealized appreciation in proportion to such appreciation and only to the extent of each property's unrealized appreciation.[12] Any additional increases are allocated in proportion to the respective fair market values of the properties.[13] If an overall decrease is required, the decrease is accomplished by first allocating basis decreases in proportion to the unrealized built-in loss in the properties (again, only to the extent of such loss) and then in proportion to the remaining adjusted bases of the properties.[14] In keeping with the treatment of operating distributions, the distributee partner may tack the partnership's holding period under Section 735(b), and Section 735(a) preserves the ordinary income character in the hands of the partner indefinitely for any unrealized receivables and five years for inventory items.

and any distributed assets would take a zero basis in the partner's hands.

**6.** I.R.C. § 732(c)(1)(A)(i).

**7.** I.R.C. § 732(c)(1)(A)(ii).

**8.** I.R.C. § 732(c)(3)(A). These allocation rules apply to distributions after August 5, 1997. For prior distributions, basis was first allocated to any unrealized receivables and inventory items in an amount equal to the partnership's basis in those assets (or, if the basis to be allocated was less than the sum of the bases of such properties, in proportion to such bases), and to the extent of any remaining basis, to any other distributed properties in proportion to their adjusted bas-

es to the partnership. The prior rules, by failing to take account of the fair market value of distributed property, could lead to anomalous results and put a high premium on strategic tax planning. See McKee, Nelson & Whitmire, Federal Taxation of Partnerships and Partners ¶ 19.06 (3d ed. 1996).

**9.** I.R.C. § 732(c)(3)(B).

**10.** I.R.C. § 732(c)(1)(B)(i).

**11.** I.R.C. § 732(c)(1)(B)(ii).

**12.** I.R.C. § 732(c)(2)(A).

**13.** I.R.C. § 732(c)(2)(B).

**14.** I.R.C. § 732(c)(3).

But consider the partner who receives solely cash, unrealized receivables and inventory items in a liquidating distribution.[15] In that event, unlike the case with operating distributions, Section 731(a)(2) provides that the partner recognizes a loss to the extent that his outside basis exceeds the sum of the cash distributed plus the partner's Section 732 transferred basis in the receivables and inventory items. The loss is considered as incurred on the sale or exchange of a partnership interest and thus is a capital loss under Section 741. Where a partner receives only cash, any realized gain or loss must be recognized because the partner may not defer recognition by way of an exchanged basis. If the partner also receives ordinary income assets, immediate recognition of loss is required to prevent the partner from converting a capital loss into an ordinary loss on the sale of the distributed assets.

To illustrate, assume that a retiring partner with an outside basis of $60 receives $20 cash and ordinary income assets with an inside basis of $25 in a liquidating distribution to which Sections 736(a) and 751(b) do not apply.[16] The partner first reduces his outside basis by the $20 cash received and, without more, he would be left with a $40 exchanged basis to spread among the ordinary income assets, which would result in less ordinary income or more ordinary loss when the partner sells those assets. But recall that Section 732(c)(1)(A) limits the partner's basis in ordinary income assets to the partnership's predistribution inside basis—$25 in this example. As a corollary to this rule, Section 731(a)(2) provides that the partner recognizes a $15 capital loss—the excess of his $60 outside basis over the sum of the $20 cash received and the $25 transferred basis in the ordinary income assets.

*Tax Consequences to the Partnership.* Disregarding for the moment the impact of Sections 736(a) and 751(b), a partnership generally recognizes neither gain nor loss on a liquidating distribution of property,[17] and under Section 734(a) the basis of partnership property generally is not adjusted as a result of the distribution. But as with operating distributions, a partnership with a Section 754 election in effect may adjust the basis of its assets to prevent the distortions that result from a liquidating distribution. We have seen that on certain liquidating distributions, a partner may recognize gain or loss. If gain is recognized, the partnership may increase the basis of capital assets or Section 1231 property it retains by the amount of the gain.[18] If the retiring partner recognizes a loss while a Section 754 election is in effect, Section 734(b) conversely requires the partnership to decrease the inside basis of its retained capital assets and Section 1231 property by the amount of the loss.[19] In addition, if the liquidating partner's exchanged basis in distributed capital assets or Section 1231 property exceeds the

---

**15.** This assumes no application of Sections 736(a) or 751(b).

**16.** Sections 736(a) and 751(b) are both inapplicable if the retiring partner receives a pro rata distribution of partnership properties.

**17.** I.R.C. § 731(b).

**18.** I.R.C. § 734(b)(1)(A). See Chapter 7C, supra.

**19.** I.R.C. § 734(b)(2)(A).

partnership's inside basis in those assets and a Section 754 election is in effect, the partnership must decrease its basis in retained assets of a similar class in an amount equal to the increase in the basis of the distributed assets in the hands of the retiring partner.[20]

A partnership also must decrease its basis in retained assets even if a Section 754 election has not been made whenever a liquidating distribution results in a "substantial basis reduction."[21] A substantial basis reduction occurs if the downward basis adjustment that would have been made to the partnership's assets if a Section 754 election had been made exceeds $250,000.[22] For example, if a liquidated partner recognizes a loss on the distribution that is greater than $250,000, the partnership is required to decrease the basis in its retained assets even if it has never made a Section 754 election. Similarly, a basis reduction in a partnership's retained assets is required if the basis of capital assets or Section 1231 assets that are distributed in a liquidating distribution is increased by more than $250,000 above the partnership's basis in those assets.[23] The rules for allocation of Section 734(b) basis adjustments were discussed in Chapter 7, supra.[24]

*Section 751(b).* We have seen that the disproportionate distribution rules in Section 751(b) override the general rules of Sections 731 and 732 on a partnership's operating distributions.[25] In general, Section 751(b) plays an identical role with respect to liquidating distributions. But recall that payments received by a retiring general partner for her interest in unrealized receivables or unstated goodwill of a services partnership are governed by Section 736(a). In that situation, the partner's share of unrealized receivables is disregarded in determining the partner's predistribution share of Section 751 assets,[26] and the partner's predistribution share of unstated goodwill is disregarded in determining her share of Section 741 assets.[27] As a corollary to these rules, any payments received by the partner in exchange for her share of partnership unrealized receivables or unstated goodwill or any "premium" payments received (i.e., amounts paid in excess of the fair market value of the partner's share of partnership property) are governed by Section 736(a) and thus are similarly disregarded in determining the partner's postdistribution share of Section 751 or 741 assets. Section 751(b) still applies, however, with respect to disproportionate

---

**20.** I.R.C. § 734(b)(2)(B).

**21.** I.R.C. § 734(a).

**22.** I.R.C. § 734(b)(2), (d).

**23.** The IRS is authorized to issue regulations to carry out these provisions, including regulations aggregating related partnerships and disregarding property acquired to avoid the rules. I.R.C. § 734(d)(2), 743(d)(2). A special rule exempts securitization partnerships from required downward inside basis adjustments under Section 734(a). I.R.C. § 734(e).

**24.** See I.R.C. § 755; Reg. § 1.755–1(c); Chapter 7C, supra. See also Reg. § 1.755–

1(c)(2)(ii), relating to adjustments for decreases in basis.

**25.** See Chapter 7E, supra.

**26.** Remember, however, that unrealized receivables are treated as inventory items under Section 751(d) but solely for the purpose of determining whether the inventory is substantially appreciated in value.

**27.** I.R.C. § 751(b)(2)(B); Reg. § 1.751–1(b)(4)(ii). See the discussion of the scope of Section 736(a) in Section B2 of this chapter, infra.

distributions between the remaining Section 751 assets (i.e., recapture gain and substantially appreciated inventory) and Section 741 assets.

To illustrate the operation of Section 751(b) in this context, assume the ABC services partnership has three equal general partners and the following balance sheet:[28]

| Assets | A.B. | F.M.V. | Partners' Capital | A.B. | F.M.V. |
|---|---|---|---|---|---|
| Cash | $45,000 | $45,000 | A | $15,000 | $30,000 |
| Accounts Receivable | 0 | 15,000 | B | 15,000 | 30,000 |
| Inventory | 0 | 15,000 | C | 15,000 | 30,000 |
| Goodwill | 0 | 15,000 | | | |
| | $45,000 | $90,000 | | $45,000 | $90,000 |

Assume partner A's interest is liquidated and he receives a $30,000 cash payment from the partnership with no designation that $5,000 is paid for goodwill. A would be taxed on $10,000 (the payment for A's share of the receivables and unstated goodwill) as ordinary income characterized under Section 736(a). A's share of Section 736(b) assets prior to the distribution is $15,000 of cash and $5,000 of inventory. After the distribution, A has $20,000 of cash (disregarding the $10,000 payment governed by Section 736(a)) and no further interest in the partnership inventory.[29] Under Section 751(b), A is deemed to have received a phantom distribution of $5,000 of inventory with a transferred basis of zero and to have sold the inventory to the partnership for $5,000 cash, realizing $5,000 of ordinary income on the constructive sale. The final step is to determine the tax consequences of the remaining actual distribution of $15,000 cash.[30] Since A's outside basis is $15,000, the cash distribution merely reduces his basis to zero and no gain or loss is recognized under Section 731.

If the partnership were not a services partnership or A were not a general partner, Section 736(a) would not apply and A's interest in the Section 751 assets would have been $10,000 prior to the distribution and

---

**28.** The authors know that inventory should not have a zero basis. But a zero basis for noncash assets simplifies the example and, hopefully, aids comprehension of the concepts that are being illustrated.

**29.** Using the formula above, in determining the extent of the application of § 751(b) we disregard the $10,000 of § 736(a) payments as well as the § 736(a) property being compensated—the receivables and goodwill. A's interest in the § 751 assets (other than those under § 736(a)) prior to the transaction is $5,000 and afterwards it is zero, while his interest in the § 741 assets (other than those under § 736(a)) prior to the transaction is $15,000 (one-third of the $45,000 cash) and afterwards it is $20,000.

Thus, A receives $5,000 too few § 751 assets and $5,000 too many § 741 assets.

**30.** If A had received $35,000 for his interest (the same as above except with a $5,000 premium), we would reduce the § 741 amount actually received by the $15,000 of § 736(a) payment, and we would disregard the $5,000 accounts receivable, the $5,000 for unstated goodwill and the $5,000 premium. Once again, A's interest in the cash is $15,000, and he actually receives $20,000, and his interest in the inventory is $5,000, but he actually receives no inventory. As before, § 751(b) results in a phantom distribution of $5,000 of inventory with a zero basis to A, who realizes $5,000 of ordinary income on the constructive exchange.

zero afterwards, while his interest in the Section 741 assets would have been $20,000 before and $30,000 after the distribution. Thus, A would have a $10,000 phantom distribution of Section 751 property with a zero basis, and A would realize $10,000 of ordinary income on the constructive sale and $5,000 of long-term capital gain under Section 731(a)(1).

This concludes the interlude of reminiscences. Test your understanding of these principles, with some new liquidation twists, by solving the following problems.

PROBLEMS

**1.** The ABC partnership, which has not made a § 754 election, has the following balance sheet:

| Assets | A.B. | F.M.V. | Partners' Capital | A.B. | F.M.V. |
|---|---|---|---|---|---|
| Cash | $ 90,000 | $ 90,000 | A | $ 85,000 | $ 70,000 |
| Inventory | 15,000 | 30,000 | B | 85,000 | 70,000 |
| Land | 150,000 | 90,000 | C | 85,000 | 70,000 |
| | $255,000 | $210,000 | | $255,000 | $210,000 |

(a) In liquidation of his interest, A receives one-third of the inventory and $60,000 worth of land. What are the tax consequences of this distribution to A and the partnership?

(b) In liquidation of his interest, A again receives one-third of the inventory and also receives $60,000 cash. What are the tax consequences of this distribution to A and the partnership?

(c) Why is recognized loss under § 731(a)(2) limited to liquidating distributions and further restricted with regard to the nature of the distribution?

(d) What result to A in (b), above, if the inventory were worth $120,000 rather than $30,000, A's interest were worth $100,000 and A received $60,000 of cash and his one-third of the inventory?

**2.** Partnership distributes Capital Asset #1 (inside basis—$5,000, f.m.v.—$40,000) and Capital Asset #2 (inside basis—$10,000, f.m.v.—$10,000) to Partner A in liquidation of A's interest in Partnership. Prior to the distributions, A has a $55,000 outside basis. Determine partner A's basis in the two capital assets following the liquidating distribution.

**3.** The ABC partnership has the following balance sheet:

| Assets | A.B. | F.M.V. | Partners' Capital | A.B. | F.M.V. |
|---|---|---|---|---|---|
| Cash | $3,000 | $ 3,000 | A | $3,000 | $ 6,000 |
| Inventory | 0 | 6,000 | B | 3,000 | 6,000 |
| Land #1 | 3,000 | 6,000 | C | 3,000 | 6,000 |
| Land #2 | 3,000 | 3,000 | | | |
| | $9,000 | $18,000 | | $9,000 | $18,000 |

A receives land #1 as a distribution in liquidation of his interest in the partnership. Both parcels of land are capital assets to the partnership.

(a) Disregarding § 736(a), which is inapplicable under these facts, discuss the tax consequences to A and to the partnership if there is no § 754 election in effect.

(b) What difference in result in (a), above, if the partnership had made a § 754 election?

**4.** The regulations (Reg. § 1.734–1(b)(2)) intimate that a § 734(b)(2) downward adjustment applies only to distributions in complete liquidation of a partner's interest, whereas a § 734(b)(1) upward adjustment may be applicable to both operating and liquidating distributions. Is this so? Why or why not?

## 2. SECTION 736(a) PAYMENTS

Code: § 736. Skim § 707(c).

Regulations: § 1.736–1(a), (b)(1)–(4).

*Background.* We have just seen that Section 736(b) embraces payments for a retiring partner's interest in partnership assets with some limited exceptions. To the extent that Section 736(b) is inapplicable, Section 736(a) applies. In that event, amounts received by the retiring partner are treated as Section 707(c) guaranteed payments or distributive shares of partnership income, generally resulting in ordinary income to the retiring partner and a current partnership deduction (or the equivalent) that benefits the remaining partners.

*The Scope of Section 736(a).* Section 736(a) payments are defined as all payments not falling within Section 736(b). As a practical matter, however, most payments made in liquidation of a partner's interest fall within Section 736(b), and thus the scope of Section 736(a) is very limited. Because of the exclusions in Section 736(b), Section 736(a) applies to payments received by a general partner in a partnership in which capital is not a material income-producing factor,[1] for: (1) the partner's share of unrealized receivables (not including recapture or similar gain,)[2] and (2) partnership goodwill if the partnership agreement does not expressly provide for such payments.[3] Capital is not a material income-producing factor where substantially all of the gross income of the business consists of fees, commissions, or other compensation for personal services.[4] Thus a legal, medical, dentistry, accounting, architectural or other service partnership falls within this classification even though there is a substantial investment in office plant or equipment, if that investment is merely incidental to the rendering of services.[5] Section 736(a) also applies to a third type of payment. Any

**1.** I.R.C. § 736(b)(3).

**2.** I.R.C. § 751(c) flush language.

**3.** I.R.C. § 736(b)(2).

**4.** See I.R.C. §§ 401(c)(2); 911(d).

**5.** WMCP Prt. No. 103–11, 103d Cong., 1st Sess. 345 (1993).

premium payment in excess of payments for a partner's interest in partnership property is a Section 736(a) payment regardless of the type of partnership.[6]

*Payments for Unrealized Receivables.* Section 736(b) applies to most payments for unrealized receivables. Section 736(a), however, embraces payments to compensate a liquidated general partner in a services partnership for his interest in the partnership's receivables that have not been included in income.[7] Although one would never know it from reading the statute, the regulations make it clear that only payments in excess of the partner's basis (including any special personal inside basis) in the unrealized receivables are encompassed by Section 736(a).[8] To the extent of the partner's share of the inside basis, receivables are considered as already realized and thus covered by Section 736(b).[9] Moreover, Section 736(a) only applies to *payments* for unrealized receivables. To the extent that the receivables are distributed in kind, there is no "payment," and the partner's receipt of the receivables is taxed under the Section 736(b) regime. The term "payment" does not require a cash transfer, and thus a distribution of other assets, such as land or stock, in exchange for a general partner's interest in unrealized receivables in a services partnership also is governed by Section 736(a).[10]

The scope of unrealized receivables qualifying for Section 736(a) treatment is further limited by the provision in Section 751(c) that eliminates recapture gain and other similar property held by any services or capital partnership from the definition of an unrealized receivable for purposes of Section 736.[11] Thus, payments for recapture gain automatically fall within Section 736(b).[12]

*Payments for Goodwill.* Similar to the treatment of unrealized receivables, Section 736(b) generally applies to payments for goodwill. But Section 736(a) still applies to payments to a retiring general partner for her share of goodwill in a services partnership to the extent that the payments exceed the partner's inside basis, if any, in the goodwill,[13] and the liquidation agreement does not specifically state that the payment is for

---

**6.** Reg. § 1.736–1(a)(3).

**7.** I.R.C. § 736(b)(2)(A) & (3).

**8.** Reg. § 1.736–1(b)(2). Cf. §§ 736(d); 743(b).

**9.** Reg. § 1.736–1(b)(1) and (2).

**10.** See Willis, Pennell & Postlewaite, Partnership Taxation ¶ 15.06 (6th ed. 1997). When Section 736(a) liquidating "payments" are made with property other than cash, the usual Subchapter K distribution rules do not apply and thus the partnership is required to recognize gain or loss if the property is appreciated or has declined in value.

**11.** I.R.C. § 751(c) flush language.

**12.** Recapture gain continues to be an unrealized receivable for purposes of the distribution rules in Section 731, and the partnership sale provisions of Sections 741 and 751, including the infamous Section 751(b) regime. See I.R.C. § 751(c) flush language.

**13.** Reg. § 1.736–1(b)(3). Again, any special basis adjustment of the retiring partner is used to determine his share of appreciation. Cf. I.R.C. §§ 732(d), 743(b). Goodwill normally would have a zero basis unless the partnership previously acquired a business and allocated a portion of the purchase price to goodwill or unless the basis of goodwill was increased under Sections 743(b) or 734(b).

goodwill.[14] Thus, the parties in this situation may remove goodwill from Section 736(a) and include it in Section 736(b) by including a specific provision in the agreement governing the liquidation.[15] The "agreement," for this purpose, includes any written and oral modifications to the original partnership agreement made in any year prior to the date of filing an income tax return for the year of the liquidation.[16] To fall within Section 736(b), payments allocated to goodwill must be "reasonable," but a valuation normally will be accepted by the Service if it is the product of an arm's length agreement between the parties.[17] It should now be apparent that the flexibility in classifying payments for goodwill places a premium on careful drafting. The *Smith* and *Jackson Investment* cases, which follow in the text, consider the issue of whether a partnership agreement sufficiently "provides for" a payment for goodwill.

*Premium Payments.* In addition, because Section 736(b) applies only to payments for a retiring partner's interest in partnership *assets* (other than payment for unrealized receivables and unstated goodwill made to a general partner of a services partnership), any premium payments to a liquidated partner (in either a services or capital partnership) also are taxed under Section 736(a).[18] To determine whether there is a premium, one must first determine the amount of the partner's share of the partnership's property. Any payments in excess of that amount in the form of cash or other property are governed by Section 736(a), regardless of the nature of the partnership. These payments often are in the nature of mutual insurance provided by a separate buy-sell agreement or in the partnership agreement itself.

*The Method of Taxing Section 736(a) Payments.* Section 736(a) payments are taxed either as a distributive share of partnership income or as a guaranteed payment, depending upon whether they are determined with or without regard to the income of the partnership.[19] To the extent that the payments are based on income of the firm, they are treated as a distributive share of partnership income to the recipient and correspondingly reduce the distributive shares of partnership income allocable to the remaining partners.[20] To the extent that Section 736(a) payments are

---

14. I.R.C. §§ 736(b)(2)(B) & (3).

15. I.R.C. § 736(b)(2)(B); Reg. § 1.736–1(b)(3). Cf. I.R.C. § 197.

16. I.R.C. § 761(c); Reg. § 1.761–1(c); Commissioner v. Jackson Investment Co., 346 F.2d 187 (9th Cir.1965).

17. Reg. § 1.736–1(b)(1) & (3). If the agreed allocation reflects only the partner's net interest in the Section 736(b) property (i.e., total assets less liabilities), it must be adjusted so that both the value of the partner's interest in the property and the basis for his interest take into account the partner's share of partnership liabilities. Reg. § 1.736–1(b)(1).

18. Reg. § 1.736–1(a)(3).

19. I.R.C. § 736(a)(1) & (2).

20. Reg. § 1.736–1(a)(3)(i) & (a)(4). The retiring partner must include a Section 736(a)(1) distributive share in his taxable year with or within which ends the partnership taxable year for which the payment is a distributive share irrespective of when actual distributions are made. Reg. § 1.736–1(a)(5). If the payment is made by a distribution in kind, the partnership will recognize gain or loss.

determined without regard to partnership income, they are considered to be guaranteed payments under Section 707(c) and are taxed as ordinary income to the retiring partner and are deductible in computing the partnership's taxable income.[21] Whether or not the payments are made with regard to partnership income is determined in the same manner used to resolve this issue for purposes of Section 707(c).[22]

## Smith v. Commissioner

United States Court of Appeals, Tenth Circuit, 1962.
313 F.2d 16.

■ HILL, CIRCUIT JUDGE.

This case is here on the Smiths' Petition To Review a decision of the Tax Court of the United States which was adverse to them.

The facts necessary for our disposition of the case are not in dispute. In January, 1947, V. Zay Smith (petitioner) and three other individuals formed a partnership known as Geophoto Services (Geophoto) for the purpose of engaging in the business of evaluating geological structures based upon aerial photography, which was to be used in the search for petroleum and petroleum reserves. Petitioner, at the time of World War II, was a geologist and, from his experience as a photo intelligence officer in the Navy, conceived the idea of using aerial photography for evaluating geological structures in the search for oil and petroleum.

The original partnership agreement was for a period of five years. Immediately prior to its expiration and on December 31, 1952, the articles of partnership were revised to provide a means of expelling one of the partners.

The partnership prospered during the next four years of the 5 year period of the partnership agreement, with petitioner receiving substantial net income for his share. In January, 1957, the other three partners voted to expel petitioner as a partner in Geophoto. In accordance with paragraph 25 of the revised articles, petitioner received the consideration agreed upon therein. The total amount of $77,000.00 was paid to petitioner in the form of a check for $72,740.71 and an automobile of an agreed upon value of $4,259.29. It was stipulated, however, that the book value of petitioner's interest in the partnership on the date in question was $53,264.61, thereby leaving a payment to him of $2,045.45 as salary and a payment of $21,689.94 as a "premium", for a total payment over and above his partnership interest of $23,735.39.

---

**21.** Reg. § 1.736–1(a)(3)(ii), (4) & (5). Guaranteed payments are taxable to the distributee for his taxable year with or within which the partnership is entitled to deduct the payment. Reg. § 1.736–1(a)(5). The partnership always may deduct Section 736(a)(2) payments; they never are treated as capital expenditures. The partnership will recognize gain or loss if it uses appreciated or depreciated property to make a guaranteed payment.

**22.** See Chapter 5A4, supra.

In their income tax return for the year 1957, petitioners reported the excess over and above his partnership interest in the amount of $23,735.39 as a capital gain—this figure includes the salary payment of $2,045.45. The Commissioner of Internal Revenue determined that the entire excess of $23,735.39 was ordinary income and, accordingly, made a deficiency assessment of $6,992.20 in their income tax for 1957.

Petitioners thereafter filed a petition with the Tax Court alleging that the Commissioner, in determining taxable income for the year 1957, erroneously included the $23,735.39 payment as ordinary income and requested the Tax Court to determine that there was no deficiency due on the 1957 income tax. The Commissioner's position before the Tax Court was that the $23,735.39 payment to petitioner was in liquidation of his interest in the partnership and, accordingly, it was taxable as ordinary income under Section 736(a) of the Internal Revenue Code of 1954, 26 U.S.C. § 736(a). Specifically, the Commissioner contended that the $2,045.45 salary payment should be taxed as a guaranteed payment under paragraph (2) of subsection (a) and the remainder as a distributive share of partnership income under paragraph (1) thereof.

Petitioners argued that the questioned amount was a payment for "good will" and should be treated as a capital gain under Section 736(b) of the Act, 26 U.S.C. § 736(b). Specifically, they urged that paragraph (2)(B) of subsection (b) applied. Beyond any question, the $2,045.45 was ordinary income and no further discussion of that item is necessary.

The Tax Court rejected petitioners' contention and, in holding that the questioned amount should be treated as ordinary income, acknowledged this was a case of first impression. The provisions of Section 736 first became embodied in the tax law by the enactment of the 1954 Internal Revenue Code. This was the first time the Congress attempted to specifically cover by statute the tax situation arising when a partnership interest is in fact liquidated by payments from the partnership to the retiring or withdrawing partner. The situation here is not that of a partner selling his interest to another partner or a third party. If that was the situation, the government concedes, and we agree, that Section 741 of the Internal Revenue Code of 1954, 26 U.S.C. § 741, would be applicable, as contended by the taxpayer. We agree with the Tax Court that under the facts Section 736 provides the proper tax treatment.

From a careful reading of Section 736 and consideration of the Senate Finance Report[7] made at the time the new legislation was before the

**7.** 3 U.S.Cong. & Adm.News (1954) p. 5037 states:

"Special rules are provided in subsection (b)(2) so as to exclude certain items from the application of subsection (b). Thus, payments for an interest in partnership property under subsection (b) do not include amounts paid for unrealized receivables of the partnership. Also excluded from subsection (b) are payments for an interest in partnership goodwill, except to the extent that the partnership agreement provides for payments with respect to goodwill. Where the partnership agreement provides for payments with respect to goodwill, such payments may not

Congress, the intended scope of such Section appears clear. Paragraph (2)(B) of subsection (b) exempts from ordinary income treatment payments made for good will only when the partnership agreement so provides specifically and does not permit an intent to compensate for good will to be drawn from the surrounding circumstances as the taxpayer here urges us to do. In fact, the partnership agreement here specifically states " * * * In determining the value or the book value of a deceased or retiring partner's interest, no value shall be assigned to good will, * * *."

The discussion in 6 Mertens, Law of Federal Income Taxation, § 35.81, pp. 232–233, of the questioned statute supports the position of the government:

> "Partnership good will has an ambivalent character under Section 736 of the 1954 Code. Because of the difficulties on the one hand of valuing good will and on the other hand the inequities which might result if good will were required to be disregarded in every case, Section 736(b)(2), in effect, permits an election as to the treatment of partnership good will.

> "If the partnership agreement provides for a specific payment as to good will and such amount is not in excess of the reasonable value of the partner's share of good will, good will is considered a partnership asset and payments with respect thereto are treated as 'Section 736(b) Payments.' The capitalizing of good will may be desirable from the point of view of the retiring partner or deceased partner's successor. The retiring partner is entitled to capital gain treatment on the amount of the payments allocable to good will. The deceased partner's successor will have a basis equal to the date of death valuation for payments allocable to good will. While this treatment is beneficial to the retiring partner or deceased partner's successor, the continuing partners will not be allowed a deduction or exclusion for such payments.

> "On the other hand, if the partnership agreement does not treat good will as partnership property under Section 736(b), the payments relating thereto fall under Section 736(a). Such payments are taxable as ordinary income to the recipient, and may be excluded from the current income of the partnership or deducted therefrom. The treatment of good will under Section 736(a) is favorable to continuing partners since they are permitted to expense the cost of acquiring the withdrawing partner's interest in partnership good will.

> "The treatment of good will under the 1954 Code would appear to be one of the principal tax factors to be taken into account in drafting partnership agreements. In most cases it would be desirable for the partners to agree in advance as to whether

exceed the reasonable value of the partner's share of partnership good-will.''

partnership good will is to be capitalized or not. If the partnership agreement fails to provide for the treatment of good will, the agreement may be so amended at the time of termination of an interest. Section 761(d) of the 1954 Code also permits a partnership agreement to be modified up to the time for filing the partnership return for the taxable year. It is doubtful, however, that the remaining partners could act adversely to the interest of the withdrawing partner after he had left the partnership."

\* \* \*

The case of Commissioner of Internal Revenue v. Lester, 366 U.S. 299, 81 S.Ct. 1343, 6 L.Ed.2d 306, is analogous to this case. It involved a situation where a divorced taxpayer and his former wife entered into a written agreement for periodic payments by him to his former wife. The agreement provided that in the event any of the parties' three children should marry, become emancipated or die, the payments should "be reduced in a sum equal to one-sixth of the payments which would thereafter otherwise accrue." The taxpayer deducted the whole of these periodic payments in the taxable years of 1951 and 1952. The government sought to recover tax deficiencies for those years equal to one-half of the periodic payments made contending that the quoted language of the written agreement sufficiently identified ½ of the periodic payments as having been "payable for the support" of the taxpayer's minor children under § 22(k)[8] of the Internal Revenue Code of 1939 and therefore, not deductible by him under § 23(u) of the Code. The Supreme Court held "that the Congress intended that, to come within the exception portion of § 22(k), the agreement providing for the periodic payments must specifically state the amounts or parts thereof allocable to the support of the children" (366 U.S. at page 301, 81 S.Ct. at page 1345) and said that by this statute "the Congress was in effect giving the husband and wife the power to shift a portion of the tax burden from the wife to the husband by the use of a simple provision in the settlement agreement which fixed the specific portion of the periodic payment made to the wife as payable for the support of the children. Here the agreement does not so specifically provide." (366 U.S. at 304, 81 S.Ct. at 1347). The court also noted that "It [the statute] does not say that 'a sufficiently clear purpose' on the part of the parties would satisfy" but "It says that the written instrument must 'fix' that amount, or 'portion of the payment' which is to go to the support of the children." (366 U.S. at page 305, 81 S.Ct. at page 1347).

This reasoning would appear to be particularly applicable here and we think the payment in question should be treated as ordinary income rather than capital gain since the articles of partnership do not specifically provide

---

**8.** The pertinent portion of § 22(k) reads as follows:

"\* \* \* This subsection [allowing deductions] shall not apply to that part of any such periodic payment *which the terms of the \* \* \* written instru-* *ment fix,* in terms of \* \* \* a portion of the payment, as a sum which is payable for the support of minor children of such husband. \* \* \* "(Emphasis supplied.)

that the payment is for good will. If intent is to be determined by something other than the plain language of the partnership agreement, uncertainty and confusion will becloud the issue and the efforts of Congress to clarify a complex situation will go for naught. Important, also, is the fact that this result treats fairly both the expelled partner and the remaining partners as the tax consequences are determined in advance by the contract to which they all agreed.

The decision of the Tax Court is Affirmed.

## Commissioner v. Jackson Investment Co.

United States Court of Appeals, Ninth Circuit, 1965.
346 F.2d 187.

■ BARNES, CIRCUIT JUDGE.

The Commissioner of Internal Revenue has brought this petition to review decisions of the Tax Court (41 T.C. 675 (1964)) involving federal income taxes for the taxable years 1956 through 1958. The amounts in controversy involve distributions made by respondents, Jackson Investment Company and West Shore Company, partners in George W. Carter Company, to a retiring partner, Ethel M. Carter. Petitioner concluded that the distributions were not deductible expenses, and, consequently, assessed deficiencies against Jackson in the aggregate amount of $9,848.18 and against West Shore in the aggregate amount of $15,577.85. The Tax Court, however, rendered a decision adverse to the Commissioner. The Commissioner subsequently petitioned for review, invoking this court's jurisdiction under Section 7482 of the Internal Revenue Code of 1954.

The question presented for our consideration involves the construction of Section 736 of the Internal Revenue Code of 1954.

* * *

The intended purpose of this provision was to permit the participants themselves to determine whether the retiring partner or the remaining partners would bear the tax burdens for payments in liquidation of a retiring partner's interest. Thus, under the general approach of subsection (a), the tax burden is borne by the retiring partner—he recognizes the payments as taxable income, and the remaining partners are allowed a commensurate deduction from partnership income. Under subsection (b), the general rule conceives an approach of nonrecognition of ordinary income to the retiring partner, but places the tax burden on the partnership by denying a deduction from income for the payments. This latter subsection, however, adopts a special rule—(b)(2)(B)—in an express effort to assist the participants to decide *inter sese* upon the allocation of the tax burden. This special rule lies at the heart of the present controversy. Under this rule, payments for the good will of the partnership are deductible by the partnership (and hence recognizable as ordinary income to the retiring partner) "except to the extent that the partnership agreement provides for a payment with respect to good will." If the partnership agreement pro-

vides for a payment with respect to good will, the tax burden is allocated to the partnership—no deduction is allowed and the retiring partner need not recognize the payments as ordinary income. In the present case, petitioner contends that this exception under Section 736(b)(2)(B) applies, and thus the deductions taken by the partnership should be disallowed. We must determine, therefore, whether the parties intended to place the tax burden on the partnership by expressly incorporating into the partnership agreement a provision for payment to the retiring partner with respect to good will.

It is undisputed that the original Partnership Agreement did not contain a provision for partnership good will or a payment therefor upon the withdrawal of a partner. On May 7, 1956, however, the three partners executed an instrument entitled "Amendment of Limited Partnership Agreement of George W. Carter Co." * * * This instrument provided for Ethel Carter's retirement, and bound the partnership to compensate Ethel in the amount of $60,000.00 in consideration for her withdrawal. After the necessary adjustment of the figures, it was determined that $19,650.00 of the amount was in return for Ethel's "15% interest in the fair market value of all the net assets of the partnership." The other $40,350.00, the amount in controversy here, was referred to as "a guaranteed payment, or a payment for good will." * * * The $40,350.00 was paid by the partnership in three annual parts, and deductions were made for good will expense in the partnership net income for each of the years. It is these deductions that petitioner challenges.

The decision of the Tax Court (six judges dissenting), concluded that the document entitled "Amendment of Limited Partnership Agreement of George W. Carter Co." was not a part of the partnership agreement, and therefore, the exception of Section 736(b)(2)(B) was not applicable. As a result, the court held that the amounts in question were legitimate deductions from the partnership income under the terms of Section 736(a)(2). The court founded its conclusion on the fact that the "Amendment" was solely designed to effect a withdrawal of one of the partners; it was not at all concerned with any continued role for Ethel in the partnership affairs.

We cannot agree with the interpretation of the majority of the Tax Court. We find this view unduly interferes with the clear objective of the statute, i.e., to permit and enable the partners to allocate the tax burdens as they choose, and with a minimum of uncertainty and difficulty. If a partnership agreement such as the one involved here, had no provision regarding the withdrawal of a partner, and the partners negotiated to compensate the retiring partner with payments that could be treated by the recipient at capital gain rates, the statutory scheme should not be read to frustrate the parties' efforts. An amendment to the partnership agreement which incorporates the plan of withdrawal and which designates the amount payable as being in consideration for the partnership good will seems clearly to be an attempt to utilize Section 736(b)(2)(B), affording capital gain rates to the retiring partner but precluding an expense deduction for the partnership. Simply because the subject matter of the amend-

ment deals only with the liquidation of one partner's interest, we should not thwart whatever may be the clear intent of the parties by holding the amendment is not part of the partnership agreement. The Internal Revenue Code of 1954 expressly touches upon modifications of partnership agreements, and it gives no support to the thesis that an amendment dealing with the withdrawal of a partner cannot be considered a part of the partnership agreement. Section 761(c) provides:

> *"Partnership Agreement.*—For purposes of this subchapter, a partnership agreement includes any modifications of the partnership agreement made prior to, or at, the time prescribed by law for the filing of the partnership return for the taxable year (not including extensions) which are agreed to by all the partners, or which are adopted in such other manner as may be provided by the partnership agreement."

We hold, therefore, in harmony with the intent of the parties to the partnership, that the "Amendment of Limited Partnership Agreement of George W. Carter Co." was a modification of the partnership agreement within the meaning of Section 761(c). As such, the requirement of a provision in the partnership agreement as specified in Section 736(b)(2)(B) is satisfied.

There remains, however, an additional requirement to call into operation Section 736(b)(2)(B), viz., that the provision for payment in the partnership agreement be *with respect to good will.* As noted above, the payment of the $40,350.00 was inartistically described in the Amendment as a "guaranteed payment, or a payment for good will." The "guaranteed payment" terminology seems to expressly incorporate Section 736(a)(2), which would permit an expense deduction to the partnership, while recognizing the payments as ordinary income to the retiring partner. The "good will" language, on the other hand, would appear directed to Section 736(b)(2)(B), which results in the opposite tax consequences. In resolving this conflict, we feel the most helpful guide is to pay deference to what we may determine was the revealed intent of the parties. An examination of the entire amendment leads us to conclude that, notwithstanding the use of the words "guaranteed payment," the parties intended to invoke Section 736(b)(2)(B), not Section 736(a)(2). The Amendment expressly states the following (which we find impossible to harmonize with the majority opinion of the Tax Court or the arguments advanced by respondents in their brief):

> "It is recognized by all the parties hereto that the prior agreements among the partners do not provide for any payment to any partner *in respect to good will* in the event of the retirement or withdrawal of a partner, but George W. Carter Company will nevertheless make a payment to Ethel M. Carter *in respect to good will* as herein provided in consideration of her entering into this agreement and her consent to retire from the partnership upon the terms herein expressed." (Tr. 66.) (Emphasis added.)

The meaning of this language as well as the words chosen to express it leads to the conclusion that the $40,350.00 was to be a payment "in respect

to good will," with the parties intending to be governed by the tax consequences of Section 736(b)(2)(B). The concluding paragraph of Judge Raum's dissenting opinion in the Tax Court, joined in by five other judges, expresses in our judgment sound reasoning, and we incorporate it here as a summary statement of our viewpoint:

> "To fail to give effect to the plain language thus used by the parties is, I think, to defeat the very purpose of the pertinent partnership provisions of the statute, namely, to permit the partners themselves to fix their tax liabilities *inter sese.* Although the May 7, 1956, agreement may be inartistically drawn, and indeed may even contain some internal inconsistencies, the plain and obvious import of its provisions in respect of the present problem was to amend the partnership agreement so as to provide specifically for a goodwill payment. This is the kind of thing that section 736(b)(2)(B) dealt with when it allowed the partners to fix the tax consequences of goodwill payments to a withdrawing partner. And this is what the partners clearly attempted to do here, however crude may have been their effort. I would give further effect to that effort, and would not add further complications to an already overcomplicated statute." (41 T.C. at 685.)

The decision of the Tax Court is reversed, and the matter is remanded to that court for further proceedings consistent with this opinion.

## 3. ALLOCATION AND TIMING OF SECTION 736 PAYMENTS

Regulations: § 1.736–1(b)(5)–(7).

If a retiring partner receives a single lump sum liquidating distribution, the Section 736 tax consequences occur in the year of payment. It is more typical, however, to receive a series of installment payments over more than one year. In that event, the aggregate payments first must be allocated between Sections 736(a) and (b) and then each year's installment payments similarly must be allocated.[1]

Absent an agreed allocation between the parties, the rules for reporting installment payments under Section 736 differ depending on whether or not the payments are fixed in amount. If the retiring partner receives a fixed amount over a fixed number of years, the portion of each annual payment allocated to Section 736(b) is determined by the following formula:[2]

$$\S\ 736(b)\ \text{Portion} = \frac{\text{Total Fixed Agreed Payments for Taxable Year}}{} \times \frac{\text{Total Fixed § 736(b) Payments}}{\text{Total Fixed § 736(a) and (b) Payments}}$$

---

**1.** Reg. § 1.736–1(b)(5) & (6).

**2.** Reg. § 1.736–1(b)(5)(i). Note that the Section 736(b) ratio is applied to the total fixed agreed payments for the year as distinguished from the amount actually received. If less than the agreed payment is made in any year, the amount actually paid is first deemed to be a Section 736(b) payment to the extent such payment is due. Id.

The balance, if any, of the amount received is treated as a Section 736(a) payment.[3] If the retiring partner receives payments which are not fixed (e.g., contingent payments), the payments are first treated as Section 736(b) payments to the full extent of the partner's interest in partnership property and thereafter as Section 736(a) payments.[4]

Alternatively, the parties may avoid all this trouble by negotiating an agreement apportioning Section 736(a) and (b) payments, provided that the total amount allocated to Section 736(b) property may not exceed its total value at the date of the partner's retirement.[5] This once again illustrates the latitude accorded the parties to tailor the tax treatment of Section 736 payments to their own needs and objectives.[6]

The foregoing allocation rules are accompanied by an equally awesome array of timing options for Section 736 payments. Section 736(a) payments are taxable to the distributee in his taxable year with or within which ends the partnership's taxable year for which the payment is a distributive share or in which the partnership may deduct the amount as a guaranteed payment.[7] The treatment of Section 736(b) payments is far more flexible. Under the general rule, each installment is treated as a separate distribution decreasing the partner's outside basis. The partner does not recognize gain until he receives actual and constructive distributions of cash in excess of his outside basis.[8] This gives the partner the advantage of reporting the distribution as an open transaction, a method that normally is unavailable for deferred payment arrangements.[9] Recognition of loss, if any, is deferred until the year in which the final distribution is made.[10] Alternatively, a partner who is to receive a fixed amount of Section 736(b) payments may elect to annually report a pro rata portion of his gain or loss over the distribution period, in effect treating the transaction in a manner similar to the installment method under Section 453.[11]

At the risk of turning this note into one of the first published excerpts on the intersection of tax law and cosmology, consider the timing rules applicable to Section 751(b) disproportionate distribution transactions which fall within Section 736(b). The nature of this transaction is different because each installment distribution by the partnership, when viewed in

---

3. Id.

4. Reg. § 1.736–1(b)(5)(ii). The regulations also prescribe the consequences of receiving some fixed and some contingent payments. See Reg. § 1.736–1(b)(5)(i).

5. Reg. § 1.736–1(b)(5)(iii).

6. All the parties must agree. To avoid controversies, the agreement should include covenants that all the parties will report the liquidation payments consistently with their agreed allocation. Query, should the partners retain independent counsel in negotiating such an agreement?

7. Reg. § 1.736–1(a)(5).

8. I.R.C. § 731(a)(1); Reg. §§ 1.731–1(a)(1), 1.736–1(b)(6), (7) Example (1).

9. Open transaction treatment is available because Section 736(b) payments are treated as distributions. The result arguably would be different if there were a "disposition," in which event the installment sale rules in Section 453 would apply and ordinarily foreclose open transaction reporting.

10. Reg. § 1.731–1(a)(2).

11. Reg. § 1.736–1(b)(6).

isolation, may be disproportionate even if the entire transaction is not.[12] The Section 751(b) consequences presumably should be determined as if all the payments were made at one time, and all the resulting gain or loss then should be prorated over the life of the payments.[13]

## PROBLEM

**1.** A has owned a one-third general partnership interest in the ABC partnership for several years. The partnership is one in which capital is a material income-producing factor. A has an outside basis of $12,000. The partnership, which has not made a § 754 election, has the following balance sheet:

| Assets | A.B. | F.M.V. | Partners' Capital | A.B. | F.M.V. |
|---|---|---|---|---|---|
| Cash | $24,000 | $24,000 | A | $12,000 | $18,000 |
| Accounts Receivable | 0 | 9,000 | B | 12,000 | 18,000 |
| Capital Assets | 9,000 | 15,000 | C | 12,000 | 18,000 |
| Goodwill | 3,000 | 6,000 | | | |
| | $36,000 | $54,000 | | $36,000 | $54,000 |

(a) What tax consequences to A and the partnership (i.e., B and C) if A receives a $20,000 cash payment for his interest and the agreement makes no provision as to goodwill? Assume the goodwill is not an amortizable § 197 intangible.

(b) What result to A and the partnership in (a), above, if substantially all of the income of the partnership consists of fees for personal services rendered by the partners?

(c) What result to A and the partnership in (b), above, if A agrees to receive $10,000 cash in year one and $1,000 cash per year in each of the next ten years?

(d) What different result in (c), above, if A has an outside basis of $16,000?

(e) What result in (c), above, if A receives $10,000 cash and one-tenth of each year's profits in each of the next ten years, assuming profits are $10,000 per year?

**12.** For example, assume a retiring partner has an interest in $100 worth of Section 751 assets and $100 worth of Section 741 assets. He will receive his proportionate share of both by taking $100 of Section 751 assets in year one and $100 of Section 741 assets in year two. Although the entire distribution is proportionate, if we look at each year separately the partner has received too many Section 751 assets in year one and too few in year two, resulting in the application of the Section 751(b) disproportionate distribution rule in both years!

**13.** For a discussion of this question and other timing issues under Section 736(b), see McKee, Nelson & Whitmire, Federal Taxation of Partnerships and Partners ¶ 22.02[4] (3d ed. 1996) and Willis, Pennell & Postlewaite, Partnership Taxation ¶ 15.05 (6th ed. 1997).

(f)  What result in (b), above, if the agreement provides that $2,000 is being received for A's interest in partnership goodwill? Would A prefer to include this provision in the agreement?

2.  The ABC partnership has the following balance sheet:

| Assets | A.B. | F.M.V. | Partners' Capital | A.B. | F.M.V. |
|---|---|---|---|---|---|
| Cash | $30,000 | $30,000 | A | $13,000 | $20,000 |
| Accounts Receivable | 0 | 15,000 | B | 13,000 | 20,000 |
| Inventory | 9,000 | 15,000 | C | 13,000 | 20,000 |
| | $39,000 | $60,000 | | $39,000 | $60,000 |

(a)  Discuss the results to A, B and C if A receives $10,000 cash, $5,000 of receivables, and $5,000 of inventory in liquidation of his interest. Reconstruct the partnership balance sheet after the distribution.

(b)  Discuss the results to A, B and C and reconstruct the partnership balance sheet after the liquidation of A's interest if, instead, A receives $24,000 cash in liquidation of his interest in the partnership in which capital is a material income-producing factor.

(c)  What result in (b), above, to A if he receives $12,000 in the current year and $12,000 in the succeeding year?

3.  The ABC partnership has the following balance sheet:

| Assets | A.B. | F.M.V. | Partners' Capital | A.B. | F.M.V. |
|---|---|---|---|---|---|
| Cash | $15,000 | $ 15,000 | A | $25,000 | $ 55,000 |
| Accounts Receivable | 0 | 30,000 | B | 25,000 | 55,000 |
| Inventory | 30,000 | 60,000 | | | |
| Equipment ($15,000 of § 1245 recapture) | 15,000 | 30,000 | C | 25,000 | 55,000 |
| Land | 15,000 | 30,000 | | | |
| | $75,000 | $165,000 | | $75,000 | $165,000 |

The partnership distributes all the inventory to A in liquidation of his interest.

(a)  Discuss the tax consequences to A, B and C and reconstruct the partnership balance sheet after the distribution. Assume capital is a material income-producing factor in the partnership.

(b)  Would there have been any difference in the result in (a), above, if the partnership had made a § 754 election?

---

## C.  LIQUIDATION VS. SALE OF A PARTNERSHIP INTEREST

Code: Skim §§ 731; 732; 736; 741; 751.

# Foxman v. Commissioner

United States Court of Appeals, Third Circuit, 1965.
352 F.2d 466.

■ WILLIAM F. SMITH, CIRCUIT JUDGE.

This matter is before the Court on petitions to review decisions of the Tax Court, 41 T.C. 535, in three related cases consolidated for the purpose of hearing. The petitions of Foxman and Grenell challenge the decision as erroneous only as it relates to them. The petition of the Commissioner seeks a review of the decision as it relates to Jacobowitz only if it is determined by us that the Tax Court erred in the other two cases.

The cases came before the Tax Court on stipulations of fact, numerous written exhibits and the conflicting testimony of several witnesses, including the taxpayers. The relevant and material facts found by the Tax Court are fully detailed in its opinion. We repeat only those which may contribute to an understanding of the narrow issue before us.

As the result of agreements reached in February of 1955, and January of 1956, Foxman, Grenell and Jacobowitz became equal partners in a commercial enterprise which was then trading under the name of Abbey Record Manufacturing Company, hereinafter identified as the Company. They also became equal shareholders in a corporation known as Sound Plastics, Inc. When differences of opinion arose in the spring of 1956, efforts were made to persuade Jacobowitz to withdraw from the partnership. These efforts failed at that time but were resumed in March of 1957. Thereafter the parties entered into negotiations which, on May 21, 1957, culminated in a contract for the acquisition of Jacobowitz's interest in the partnership of Foxman and Grenell. The terms and conditions, except one not here material, were substantially in accord with an option to purchase offered earlier to Foxman and Grenell. The relevant portions of the final contract are set forth in the Tax Court's opinion.

The contract, prepared by an attorney representing Foxman and Grenell, referred to them as the "Second Party," and to Jacobowitz as the "First Party." We regard as particularly pertinent to the issue before us the following clauses:

"Whereas, the parties hereto are equal owners and the sole partners of ABBEY Record Mfg. Co., a partnership, * * *, and are also the sole stockholders, officers and directors of SOUND PLASTICS, INC., a corporation organized under laws of the State of New York; and

"WHEREAS, the first party is desirous of selling, conveying, transferring and assigning all of his right, title and interest in and to his one-third share and interest in the said ABBEY to the second parties; and

"WHEREAS, the second parties are desirous of conveying, transferring and assigning all of their right, title and interest in and to their combined two-thirds shares and interest in SOUND PLASTICS, INC., to the first party;

"Now, Therefore, It Is Mutually Agreed as Follows:

"*First*: The second parties hereby purchase all the right, title, share and interest of the first party in ABBEY and the first party does hereby sell, transfer, convey and assign all of his right, title, interest and share in ABBEY and in the moneys in banks, trade names, accounts due, or to become due, and in all other assets of any kind whatsoever, belonging to said ABBEY, for and in consideration of the following. * * * "

The stated consideration was cash in the sum of $242,500; the assignment by Foxman and Grenell of their stock in Sound Plastics; and the transfer of an automobile, title to which was held by the Company. The agreement provided for the payment of $67,500 upon consummation of the contract and payment of the balance as follows: $67,500 on January 2, 1958, and $90,000 in equal monthly installments, payable on the first of each month after January 30, 1958. This balance was evidenced by a series of promissory notes, payment of which was secured by a chattel mortgage on the assets of the Company. This mortgage, like the contract, referred to a sale by Jacobowitz of his partnership interest to Foxman and Grenell. The notes were executed in the name of the Company as the purported maker and were signed by Foxman and Grenell, who also endorsed them under a guarantee of payment.

The down payment of $67,500 was by a cashier's check which was issued in exchange for a check drawn on the account of the Company. The first note, in the amount of $67,500, which became due on January 2, 1958, was timely paid by a check drawn on the Company's account. Pursuant to the terms of an option reserved to Foxman and Grenell, they elected to prepay the balance of $90,000 on January 28, 1958, thereby relieving themselves of an obligation to pay Jacobowitz a further $17,550, designated in the contract as a consultant's fee. They delivered to Jacobowitz a cashier's check which was charged against the account of the Company.

In its partnership return for the fiscal year ending February 28, 1958, the Company treated the sum of $159,656.09, the consideration received by Jacobowitz less the value of his interest in partnership property, as a guaranteed payment made in liquidation of a retiring partner's interest under § 736(a)(2) of the Internal Revenue Code of 1954, Title 26 U.S.C.A. This treatment resulted in a substantial reduction of the distributive shares of Foxman and Grenell and consequently a proportionate decrease in their possible tax liability. In his income tax return Jacobowitz treated the sum of $164,356.09, the consideration less the value of his partnership interest, as a long term capital gain realized upon the sale of his interest. This, of course, resulted in a tax advantage favorable to him. The Commissioner determined deficiencies against each of the taxpayers in amounts not relevant to the issue before us and each filed separate petitions for redetermination.

The critical issue before the Tax Court was raised by the antithetical positions maintained by Foxman and Grenell on one side and Jacobowitz on the other. The former, relying on § 736(a)(2), supra, contended that the transaction, evidenced by the contract, constituted a liquidation of a retiring partner's interest and that the consideration paid was accorded

correct treatment in the partnership return. The latter contended that the transaction constituted a sale of his partnership interest and, under § 741 of the Code, 26 U.S.C.A., the profit realized was correctly treated in his return as a capital gain. The Tax Court rejected the position of Foxman and Grenell and held that the deficiency determinations as to them were not erroneous; it sustained the position of Jacobowitz and held that the deficiency determination as to him was erroneous. The petitioners Foxman and Grenell challenge that decision as erroneous and not in accord with the law.

It appears from the evidence, which the Tax Court apparently found credible, that the negotiations which led to the consummation of the contract of May 21, 1957, related to a contemplated sale of Jacobowitz's partnership interest to Foxman and Grenell. The option offered to Foxman and Grenell early in May of 1957, referred to a sale and the execution of "a bill of sale" upon completion of the agreement. The relevant provisions of the contract were couched in terms of "purchase" and "sale." The contract was signed by Foxman and Grenell, individually, and by them on behalf of the Company, although the Company assumed no liability thereunder. The obligation to purchase Jacobowitz's interest was solely that of Foxman and Grenell. The chattel mortgage on the partnership assets was given to secure payment.

Notwithstanding these facts and the lack of any ambiguity in the contract, Foxman and Grenell argue that the factors unequivocally determinative of the substance of the transaction were: the initial payment of $67,500 by a cashier's check issued in exchange for a check drawn on the account of the Company; the second payment in a similar amount by check drawn on the Company's account; the execution of notes in the name of the Company as maker; and, the prepayment of the notes by cashier's check charged against the Company's account.

This argument unduly emphasizes form in preference to substance. While form may be relevant "[t]he incidence of taxation depends upon the substance of a transaction." Commissioner of Internal Revenue v. Court Holding Co., 324 U.S. 331, 334, 65 S.Ct. 707, 708, 89 L.Ed. 981 (1945); United States v. Cumberland Pub. Serv. Co., 338 U.S. 451, 455, 70 S.Ct. 280, 94 L.Ed. 251 (1950). The "transaction must be viewed as a whole, and each step, from the commencement of negotiations" to consummation, is relevant. Ibid. Where, as here, there has been a transfer and an acquisition of property pursuant to a contract, the nature of the transaction does not depend solely on the means employed to effect payment. Ibid.

It is apparent from the opinion of the Tax Court that careful consideration was given to the factors relied upon by Foxman and Grenell. It is therein stated, 41 T.C. at page 553:

> "These notes were endorsed by Foxman and Grenell individually, and the liability of [the Company] thereon was merely in the nature of security for their primary obligation under the agreement of May 21, 1957. The fact that they utilized partnership resources to discharge their own individual liability in such man-

ner can hardly convert into a section 736 'liquidation' what would otherwise qualify as a section 741 'sale'."

\* \* \*

" \* \* \* the payments received by Jacobowitz were in discharge of their [Foxman's and Grenell's] obligation under the agreement, and not that of [the Company.] It was they who procured those payments in their own behalf from the assets of the partnership which they controlled. The use of [the Company] to make payment was wholly within their discretion and of no concern to Jacobowitz; his only interest was payment."

We are of the opinion that the quoted statements represent a fair appraisal of the true significance of the notes and the means employed to effect payment.

When the members of the partnership decided that Jacobowitz would withdraw in the interest of harmony they had a choice of means by which his withdrawal could be effected. They could have agreed inter se on either liquidation or sale. On a consideration of the plain language of the contract, the negotiations which preceded its consummation, the intent of the parties as reflected by their conduct, and the circumstances surrounding the transaction, the Tax Court found that the transaction was in substance a sale and not a liquidation of a retiring partner's interest. This finding is amply supported by the evidence in the record. The partners having employed the sale method to achieve their objective, Foxman and Grenell cannot avoid the tax consequences by a hindsight application of principles they now find advantageous to them and disadvantageous to Jacobowitz.

The issue before the Tax Court was essentially one of fact and its decision thereon may not be reversed in the absence of a showing that its findings were not supported by substantial evidence or that its decision was not in accord with the law. Cleveland v. C.I.R., 335 F.2d 473, 477 (3d Cir.1964), and the cases therein cited. There has been no such showing in this case.

The decisions of the Tax Court will be affirmed.

## Revenue Ruling 93–80

1993–2 Cum.Bull. 239.

ISSUE

Is a loss incurred on the abandonment or worthlessness of a partnership interest a capital or an ordinary loss?

FACTS

*Situation 1.* PRS is a general partnership in which *A, B,* and *C* were equal partners. During 1993, *PRS* became insolvent, and *C* abandoned *C's* partnership interest. *C* took all steps necessary to effect a proper abandonment, including written notification to *PRS. PRS's* partnership agreement

was amended to indicate that *C* was no longer a partner. At the time *C* abandoned the partnership interest, *PRS's* only liabilities were nonrecourse liabilities of 120*x* dollars, shared equally by *A*, *B*, and *C*. *C* had a remaining adjusted basis in the partnership interest of 180*x* dollars. *C* did not receive any money or property on leaving the partnership.

*Situation 2. LP* is a limited partnership in which *D* and *E* were general partners and *F* was one of the limited partners. During 1993, *LP* became insolvent, and *F* abandoned *F*'s limited partnership interest. *F* took all steps necessary to effect a proper abandonment, including written notification to *LP*. *LP*'s partnership agreement was amended to indicate that *F* was no longer a partner. At the time *F* abandoned the partnership interest, *F* had a remaining adjusted basis of 200*x* dollars in the partnership interest. *F* did not bear the economic risk of loss for any of the partnership liabilities and was not entitled to include a share of the partnership liabilities in the basis of *F*'s partnership interest. *F* did not receive any money or property on leaving the partnership.

LAW

Section 165(a) of the Internal Revenue Code allows a deduction for any loss sustained during the taxable year and not compensated for by insurance or otherwise. Section 165(b) provides that the basis for determining the amount of a deduction for any loss is the adjusted basis provided in section 1011 for determining the loss from the sale or other disposition of property. Section 1.165–1(b) of the Income Tax Regulations provides that a loss must be evidenced by closed and completed transactions, fixed by identifiable events, and actually sustained during the taxable year.

Section 165(f) of the Code provides that losses from sales or exchanges of capital assets are allowed only to the extent allowed in sections 1211 or 1212. Under section 1.165–2 of the regulations, however, absent a sale or exchange a loss that results from the abandonment or worthlessness of non-depreciable property is an ordinary loss even if the abandoned or worthless asset is a capital asset (such as a partnership interest).

To establish the abandonment of an asset, a taxpayer must show an intent to abandon the asset, and must overtly act to abandon the asset. * * *

Section 731(a) of the Code provides that in the case of a distribution by a partnership to a partner, loss is recognized by the partner only upon distribution in liquidation of the interest in a partnership, and only where no property other than money, unrealized receivables, and inventory is distributed to that partner. Loss is recognized by the partner to the extent the adjusted basis of the partner's partnership interest exceeds the money distributed and the basis to the distributee partner in any unrealized receivables and inventory items distributed. Any loss recognized under section 731(a) is considered a loss from the sale or exchange of the partnership interest of the distributee partner.

Section 741 of the Code provides that in the case of a sale or exchange of a partnership interest, gain or loss is recognized to the transferor partner. The gain or loss is considered gain or loss from the sale or exchange of a capital asset, except as otherwise provided in section 751 (relating to inventory items that have appreciated substantially in value and unrealized receivables).

Section 752(b) of the Code provides that any decrease in a partner's share of the liabilities of a partnership, or any decrease in a partner's individual liabilities by reason of the assumption by the partnership of the individual liabilities, is considered a distribution of money to the partner by the partnership.

In Rev.Rul. 70–355, 1970–2 C.B. 51, a taxpayer paid cash for an interest as a limited partner in a partnership, and the taxpayer's capital account was credited with an amount less than the cash paid. The partnership agreement provided that losses would first be allocated against each partner's capital account and any balance would be shared only by the general partners. In a subsequent taxable year, the partnership sustained a loss in its business operations, entered into bankruptcy, and dissolved. The taxpayer's distributive share of the partnership loss for the taxable year reduced the taxpayer's capital account to zero. In addition, the taxpayer's adjusted basis in the partnership interest, which was greater than the taxpayer's capital account, was reduced by the taxpayer's distributive share of the loss. However, the taxpayer's adjusted basis in the partnership interest was not reduced to zero. The taxpayer did not receive any cash or other consideration in liquidation of the taxpayer's partnership interest.

Rev.Rul. 70–355 concludes that the taxpayer's loss is deductible as an ordinary loss under section 165(a) of the Code. The taxpayer's loss was composed of the taxpayer's distributive share of the partnership loss equal to the taxpayer's capital account and the balance of the taxpayer's adjusted basis in the partnership interest.

In Rev.Rul. 76–189, 1976–1 C.B. 181, *D* purchased a one-third interest in the *ABC* partnership from taxpayer *A*. *ABC* sustained a net loss from its business operations for the taxable year and terminated at the end of that taxable year. At termination, *ABC* had no remaining assets or liabilities. *D*'s distributive share of the partnership loss did not reduce *D*'s basis in *D*'s partnership interest to zero.

Rev.Rul. 76–189 concludes that *D* has an ordinary loss deduction for *D*'s distributive share of the partnership loss under section 702(a) of the Code and a capital loss deduction for any remaining adjusted basis in *D*'s partnership interest under section 731(a) on the date the partnership terminated. This was so even though there was no actual or deemed distribution from the partnership.

ANALYSIS

The abandonment or worthlessness of a partnership interest may give rise to a loss deductible under section 165(a) of the Code. Whether a loss

from the abandonment or worthlessness of a partnership interest is capital or ordinary depends on whether or not the loss results from the sale or exchange of a capital asset.

Sections 731 and 741 of the Code apply to any transaction in which the partner receives an actual distribution of money or property from the partnership. These provisions likewise apply to any transaction in which a partner is deemed to receive a distribution from the partnership (*e.g.*, section 752(b)). Thus, whether there is an actual distribution or a deemed distribution, the transaction is treated as a sale or exchange of the partnership interest, and any loss resulting from the transaction is capital (except as provided in section 751(b)). Such a transaction is not treated for tax purposes as involving a loss from the abandonment or worthlessness of a partnership interest regardless of the amount of the consideration actually received or deemed received in the exchange.

Any decrease in a partner's share of partnership liabilities is deemed to be a distribution of money to the partner under section 752(b). The section 752(b) deemed distribution triggers the distribution on liquidation rule of section 731(a) for recognition of loss. For purposes of determining whether or not section 752(b) applies to create a deemed distribution upon abandonment or worthlessness, liability shifts that take place in anticipation of such event are treated as occurring at the time of the abandonment or worthlessness under general tax principles. See also section 1.731–1(a)(2) of the regulations providing that the liquidation of a partner's interest in a partnership may take place by means of a series of distributions.

A loss from the abandonment or worthlessness of a partnership interest will be ordinary if there is neither an actual nor a deemed distribution to the partner under the principles described above. Even a *de minimis* actual or deemed distribution makes the entire loss a capital loss. Citron v. Commissioner, 97 T.C. 200, 216 n. 14 (1991). In addition, the loss will be ordinary only if the transaction is not otherwise in substance a sale or exchange. For example, a partner's receipt of consideration from another partner (or a party related thereto) may, depending upon the facts and circumstances, establish that a purported abandonment or worthlessness of a partnership interest is in substance a sale or exchange.

Partner *D* in Rev.Rul. 76–189 satisfied all of the requirements for ordinary loss treatment. Partner *D* did not receive any actual distributions, and *D* was not deemed to receive any distributions under section 752(b) of the Code as a result of liability shifts. Nevertheless, Rev.Rul. 76–189 denied *D* ordinary loss treatment because the Service concluded that for partnership terminations section 731 applied as if an actual distribution had taken place. The Service will no longer follow Rev.Rul. 76–189.

The taxpayer in Rev.Rul. 70–355 also satisfied all of the requirements for ordinary loss treatment. Unlike Rev.Rul. 76–189, however, Rev.Rul. 70–355 concludes that the taxpayer's loss is ordinary without discussing the relevance of partnership liabilities in determining whether a partner has an ordinary loss under section 165(a) of the Code upon the abandonment or worthlessness of a partnership interest. Further, some taxpayers have

interpreted the partnership's bankruptcy as an essential fact in Rev.Rul. 70–355. Thus, although the conclusion in Rev.Rul. 70–355 is consistent with the conclusion in this revenue ruling, to avoid further confusion, Rev.Rul. 70–355 is clarified and superseded.

In *Situation 1,* when *C* abandons the interest in *PRS,* which has liabilities in which *C* shares, a deemed distribution of 40*x* dollars is made to *C* under section 752(b) of the Code. The deemed distribution reduces the basis of *C*'s interest to 140*x* dollars (180*x* − 40*x* = 140*x*). Because there is a deemed distribution to *C,* section 731(a) applies and any loss allowed is capital. Thus, *C*'s entire 140*x* dollars loss from abandoning the *PRS* interest is a capital loss even though the deemed distribution under section 752(b) is only 40*x* dollars. The results would be the same if *C*'s interest in *PRS* were found to be worthless. Because *C* shares in the liabilities of *PRS,* a deemed distribution is made to *C* on a finding of worthlessness, section 731 applies, and any loss allowed is capital.

In *Situation 2, F* permanently abandons *F*'s interest in *LP.* Section 731 of the Code does not apply because *F* did not receive any actual or deemed distribution from the partnership. *F* received nothing in exchange for *F*'s interest in *LP.* Accordingly, *F* realizes an ordinary loss of 200*x* dollars for the adjusted basis of *F*'s partnership interest, which may be deducted under section 165(a) as an ordinary loss subject to all other applicable rules of the Code. The results would be the same if *F*'s partnership interest in *LP* had become worthless.

## HOLDING

A loss incurred on the abandonment or worthlessness of a partnership interest is an ordinary loss if sale or exchange treatment does not apply. If there is an actual or deemed distribution to the partner, or if the transaction is otherwise in substance a sale or exchange, the partner's loss is capital (except as provided in section 751(b)).

\* \* \*

## NOTE

Revenue Ruling 93–80 is a variation of the liquidation vs. sale issue where the tax stakes (ordinary vs. capital loss) may be high. The effect of the ruling is that any partner whose share of partnership liabilities is reduced on abandonment of a partnership interest will recognize a capital loss. Otherwise, if the partner takes all steps necessary to effect a proper abandonment, the transaction will yield a more valuable ordinary loss.

## PROBLEM

The ABC general partnership, a law firm, has the following unusual but pedagogically useful balance sheet:

| Assets | A.B. | F.M.V. | Partners' Capital | A.B. | F.M.V. |
|--------|------|--------|-------------------|------|--------|
| Cash | $60,000 | $ 60,000 | A | $20,000 | $ 50,000 |
| Goodwill | 0 | 90,000 | B | 20,000 | 50,000 |
|  |  |  | C | 20,000 | 50,000 |
|  | $60,000 | $150,000 |  | $60,000 | $150,000 |

A is leaving the firm and retiring. He will receive $50,000 cash, which will be his only income for the year.

(a) What results if the transaction is structured as a sale of A's interest to B and C?

(b) What results if the transaction is structured as a sale of A's interest to B and C but the payment is made by the partnership rather than by B and C?

(c) What result if the transaction is structured as a liquidation? Should goodwill be stated?

(d) How can the parties be sure that their chosen structure will be respected by the Service so that they can avoid litigation?

---

## D. LIQUIDATION OF A PARTNERSHIP

## 1. VOLUNTARY LIQUIDATION

### a. IN GENERAL

Code: Skim §§ 708(b)(1)(A); 731; 732; 736; 751(b).

Up to this point, we have been considering the liquidation of a retiring partner's interest in a continuing partnership. If the entire partnership is liquidated, the tax consequences are somewhat different. Section 736(a) is inapplicable when there is a single distribution of assets to the parties on a complete dissolution of the partnership.[1] The essence of Section 736(a) is that payments are made by the partnership, but the partnership is hardly in a position to make payments if it no longer exists. This is distinguishable from a situation where a partner receives a series of payments and then, upon termination of the payments, the partnership is liquidated. Section 736(a) would apply to the first partner on liquidation of his interest, but it would not apply to the remaining partners on liquidation of the partnership.[2]

---

**1.** Cf. Yourman v. United States, 277 F.Supp. 818 (S.D.Cal.1967). See McKee, Nelson & Whitmire, Federal Taxation of Partnerships and Partners ¶ 22.01 [1] (3d ed. 1996).

**2.** The Service applies Section 736(a) to the first partner even in the case of a two-person partnership. Reg. § 1.736–1(a)(6). But see Phillips v. Commissioner, 40 T.C. 157 (1963), and Swihart, "Tax Problems Raised

Since Section 736(a) is inapplicable to a liquidation of the entire partnership, the next question is whether Section 751(b) applies on a disproportionate distribution in connection with a complete liquidation. Revenue Ruling 77–412, which follows in the text, answers this question in the affirmative. It involves a two-person firm, but its principles also apply to larger partnerships.

If a liquidation of a partnership results in a pro rata or at least a nondisproportionate distribution of all the partnership assets to the partners, Sections 736(a) and 751(b) are both inapplicable, and the Sections 731, 732 and 735 distribution rules apply.[3]

## Revenue Ruling 77–412

1977–2 Cum. Bull. 223.

Advice has been requested concerning the Federal income tax consequences upon the complete liquidation of a two person partnership involving the non-pro rata distribution of "section 751 property" to the partners.

Section 751 of the Internal Revenue Code of 1954 governs the treatment of unrealized receivables of the partnership (as defined in section 751(c)) and inventory items of the partnership that have appreciated substantially in value (as defined in section 751(d)), insofar as they affect sales or exchanges of partnership interests and certain distributions by a partnership. Unrealized receivables and substantially appreciated inventory items are referred to as "section 751 property."

Under section 751(a) of the Code, the amount of any money, or the fair market value of any property, received by a transferor partner in exchange for all or a part of such partner's interest in the partnership attributable to section 751 property, is considered an amount realized from the sale or exchange of property other than a capital asset. Thus, any gain or loss attributable to the sale or exchange of section 751 property would be ordinary income or loss.

Section 751(b)(1) of the Code provides that where a partner receives, in a distribution, partnership section 751 property in exchange for all or a part of such partner's interest in other partnership property (including money), or receives other partnership property (including money) in exchange for all or a part of an interest in partnership section 751 property, such transaction shall be considered as a sale or exchange of such property between the distributee and the partnership (as constituted after the distribution). Consequently, section 751(b) of the Code applies to that part of the distribution to a partner that consists of the non-pro rata distribution of the partnership section 751 property in exchange for other property,

by Liquidations of Partnership Interests," 44 Texas L.Rev. 1209, 1235 (1966), questioning the validity of this regulation. See also I.R.C. § 708(b)(1)(A) and Reg. § 1.708–1(b)(1)(i).

**3.** See Problem 1 at page 326 the text for an example of such a situation.

or the non-pro rata distribution of other partnership property in exchange for section 751 property.

In Yourman v. United States, 277 F.Supp. 818 (S.D.Calif.1967), the court held that section 751 of the Code applied to a non-pro rata distribution of section 751 property of a partnership even though the partnership did not continue in existence after the distribution.

Accordingly in the case of a two person partnership, to the extent that a partner either receives section 751 property in exchange for relinquishing any part of such partner's interest in other property, or receives other property in exchange for relinquishing any part of the interest in section 751 property, the distribution is treated as a sale or exchange of such properties between the distributee partner and the partnership (as constituted after the distribution), even though after the distribution the partnership consists of a single individual.

For example, the non-pro rata distribution by a two person partnership of section 751 property to its partners, A and B, as part of a distribution resulting in a complete liquidation of the partnership, can be viewed in two ways, both of which result in the same tax consequences to each party to the transaction. In the non-pro rata distribution, partner A receives more partnership section 751 property than A's underlying interest in such property, while partner B receives more partnership other property than B's interest in such property. Partner A may be treated as the distributee partner who has exchanged part of an interest in partnership property other than section 751 property with the partnership as constituted after the distribution (partner B) for section 751 property. Partner A would be treated as realizing gain or loss on a sale or exchange of the property other than section 751 property, and the partnership as constituted after the distribution would realize ordinary income or loss on the exchange of the section 751 property.

Partner B may be treated as the distributee partner who has exchanged part of an interest in the partnership section 751 property with the partnership as constituted after the distribution (partner A) for other property. Partner B would be treated as realizing ordinary income or loss on the exchange of the section 751 property, and the partnership as constituted after the distribution would realize gain or loss on a sale or exchange of the other property. However, regardless of which partner is considered to be the distributee and which is considered to be the remaining partner, the Federal income tax consequences are the same to each partner.

## Revenue Ruling 99–6

1999–1 Cum. Bull. 432.

ISSUE

What are the federal income tax consequences if one person purchases all of the ownership interests in a domestic limited liability company (LLC)

that is classified as a partnership under § 301.7701–3 of the Procedure and Administration Regulations, causing the LLC's status as a partnership to terminate under § 708(b)(1)(A) of the Internal Revenue Code?

## FACTS

In each of the following situations, an LLC is formed and operates in a state which permits an LLC to have a single owner. Each LLC is classified as a partnership under § 301.7701–3. Neither of the LLCs holds any unrealized receivables or substantially appreciated inventory for purposes of § 751(b). For the sake of simplicity, it is assumed that neither LLC is liable for any indebtedness, nor are the assets of the LLCs subject to any indebtedness.

*Situation 1.* A and B are equal partners in AB, an LLC. A sells A's entire interest in AB to B for $10,000. After the sale, the business is continued by the LLC, which is owned solely by B.

*Situation 2.* C and D are equal partners in CD, an LLC. C and D sell their entire interests in CD to E, an unrelated person, in exchange for $10,000 each. After the sale, the business is continued by the LLC, which is owned solely by E.

After the sale, in both situations, no entity classification election is made under § 301.7701–3(c) to treat the LLC as an association for federal tax purposes.

## LAW

Section 708(b)(1)(A) and § 1.708–1(b)(1) of the Income Tax Regulations provide that a partnership shall terminate when the operations of the partnership are discontinued and no part of any business, financial operation, or venture of the partnership continues to be carried on by any of its partners in a partnership.

Section 731(a)(1) provides that, in the case of a distribution by a partnership to a partner, gain is not recognized to the partner except to the extent that any money distributed exceeds the adjusted basis of the partner's interest in the partnership immediately before the distribution.

Section 731(a)(2) provides that, in the case of a distribution by a partnership in liquidation of a partner's interest in a partnership where no property other than money, unrealized receivables (as defined in § 751(c)), and inventory (as defined in § 751(d)(2)) is distributed to the partner, loss is recognized to the extent of the excess of the adjusted basis of the partner's interest in the partnership over the sum of (A) any money distributed, and (B) the basis to the distributee, as determined under § 732, of any unrealized receivables and inventory.

Section 732(b) provides that the basis of property (other than money) distributed by a partnership to a partner in liquidation of the partner's interest shall be an amount equal to the adjusted basis of the partner's interest in the partnership, reduced by any money distributed in the same transaction.

Section 735(b) provides that, in determining the period for which a partner has held property received in a distribution from a partnership (other than for purposes of § 735(a)(2)), there shall be included the holding period of the partnership, as determined under § 1223, with respect to the property.

Section 741 provides that gain or loss resulting from the sale or exchange of an interest in a partnership shall be recognized by the transferor partner, and that the gain or loss shall be considered as gain or loss from a capital asset, except as provided in § 751 (relating to unrealized receivables and inventory items).

Section 1.741–1(b) provides that § 741 applies to the transferor partner in a two-person partnership when one partner sells a partnership interest to the other partner, and to all the members of a partnership when they sell their interests to one or more persons outside the partnership.

Section 301.7701–2(c)(1) provides that, for federal tax purposes, the term "partnership" means a business entity (as the term is defined in § 301.7701–2(a)) that is not a corporation and that has at least two members.

In Edwin E. McCauslen v. Commissioner, 45 T.C. 588 (1966), one partner in an equal, two-person partnership died, and his partnership interest was purchased from his estate by the remaining partner. The purchase caused a termination of the partnership under § 708(b)(1)(A). The Tax Court held that the surviving partner did not purchase the deceased partner's interest in the partnership, but that the surviving partner purchased the partnership assets attributable to the interest. As a result, the surviving partner was not permitted to succeed to the partnership's holding period with respect to these assets.

Rev. Rul. 67–65, 1967–1 C.B. 168, also considered the purchase of a deceased partner's interest by the other partner in a two-person partnership. The Service ruled that, for the purpose of determining the purchaser's holding period in the assets attributable to the deceased partner's interest, the purchaser should treat the transaction as a purchase of the assets attributable to the interest. Accordingly, the purchaser was not permitted to succeed to the partnership's holding period with respect to these assets. See also Rev. Rul. 55–68, 1955–1 C.B. 372.

## ANALYSIS AND HOLDINGS

*Situation 1.* The AB partnership terminates under § 708(b)(1)(A) when B purchases A's entire interest in AB. Accordingly, A must treat the transaction as the sale of a partnership interest. Reg. § 1.741–1(b). A must report gain or loss, if any, resulting from the sale of A's partnership interest in accordance with § 741.

Under the analysis of McCauslen and Rev. Rul. 67–65, for purposes of determining the tax treatment of B, the AB partnership is deemed to make a liquidating distribution of all of its assets to A and B, and following this

distribution, B is treated as acquiring the assets deemed to have been distributed to A in liquidation of A's partnership interest.

B's basis in the assets attributable to A's one-half interest in the partnership is $10,000, the purchase price for A's partnership interest. Section 1012. Section 735(b) does not apply with respect to the assets B is deemed to have purchased from A. Therefore, B's holding period for these assets begins on the day immediately following the date of the sale. See Rev. Rul. 66–7, 1966–1 C.B. 188, which provides that the holding period of an asset is computed by excluding the date on which the asset is acquired.

Upon the termination of AB, B is considered to receive a distribution of those assets attributable to B's former interest in AB. B must recognize gain or loss, if any, on the deemed distribution of the assets to the extent required by § 731(a). B's basis in the assets received in the deemed liquidation of B's partnership interest is determined under § 732(b). Under § 735(b), B's holding period for the assets attributable to B's one-half interest in AB includes the partnership's holding period for such assets (except for purposes of § 735(a)(2)).

*Situation 2.* The CD partnership terminates under § 708(b)(1)(A) when E purchases the entire interests of C and D in CD. C and D must report gain or loss, if any, resulting from the sale of their partnership interests in accordance with § 741.

For purposes of classifying the acquisition by E, the CD partnership is deemed to make a liquidating distribution of its assets to C and D. Immediately following this distribution, E is deemed to acquire, by purchase, all of the former partnership's assets. Compare Rev. Rul. 84–111, 1984–2 C.B. 88 (Situation 3), which determines the tax consequences to a corporate transferee of all interests in a partnership in a manner consistent with McCauslen, and holds that the transferee's basis in the assets received equals the basis of the partnership interests, allocated among the assets in accordance with § 732(c).

E's basis in the assets is $20,000 under § 1012. E's holding period for the assets begins on the day immediately following the date of sale.

PROBLEM

The AB partnership has the following balance sheet:

| Assets | A.B. | F.M.V. | Partners' Capital | A.B. | F.M.V. |
|---|---|---|---|---|---|
| Cash | $20,000 | $ 20,000 | A | $35,000 | $ 60,000 |
| Accounts Receivable | 0 | 20,000 | B | 35,000 | 60,000 |
| Inventory | 20,000 | 40,000 | | | |
| Capital Asset | 30,000 | 40,000 | | | |
| | $70,000 | $120,000 | | $70,000 | $120,000 |

A and B liquidate the partnership. A receives the accounts receivable and the capital asset, while B receives the cash and the inventory. Consider the tax consequences to A, B and the partnership on the liquidation.

b. INCORPORATION OF A PARTNERSHIP

# Revenue Ruling 84–111

1984–2 Cum.Bull. 88.

ISSUE

Does Rev.Rul. 70–239, 1970–1 C.B. 74, still represent the Service's position with respect to the three situations described therein?

FACTS

The three situations described in Rev.Rul. 70–239 involve partnerships *X*, *Y*, and *Z*, respectively. Each partnership used the accrual method of accounting and had assets and liabilities consisting of cash, equipment, and accounts payable. The liabilities of each partnership did not exceed the adjusted basis of its assets. The three situations are as follows:

*Situation 1*

*X* transferred all of its assets to newly-formed corporation *R* in exchange for all the outstanding stock of *R* and the assumption by *R* of *X*'s liabilities. *X* then terminated by distributing all the stock of *R* to *X*'s partners in proportion to their partnership interests.

*Situation 2*

*Y* distributed all of its assets and liabilities to its partners in proportion to their partnership interests in a transaction that constituted a termination of *Y* under section 708(b)(1)(A) of the Code. The partners then transferred all the assets received from *Y* to newly-formed corporation *S* in exchange for all the outstanding stock of *S* and the assumption by *S* of *Y*'s liabilities that had been assumed by the partners.

*Situation 3*

The partners of *Z* transferred their partnership interests in *Z* to newly-formed corporation *T* in exchange for all the outstanding stock of *T*. This exchange terminated *Z* and all of its assets and liabilities became assets and liabilities of *T*.

In each situation, the steps taken by *X*, *Y*, and *Z*, and the partners of *X*, *Y*, and *Z*, were parts of a plan to transfer the partnership operations to a corporation organized for valid business reasons in exchange for its stock and were not devices to avoid or evade recognition of gain. Rev.Rul. 70–239 holds that because the federal income tax consequences of the three situations are the same, each partnership is considered to have transferred its assets and liabilities to a corporation in exchange for its stock under section 351 of the Internal Revenue Code, followed by a distribution of the stock to the partners in liquidation of the partnership.

LAW AND ANALYSIS

Section 351(a) of the Code provides that no gain or loss will be recognized if property is transferred to a corporation by one or more persons solely in exchange for stock * * * in such corporation and immediately after the exchange such person or persons are in control (as defined in section 368(c)) of the corporation.

Section 1.351–1(a)(1) of the Income Tax Regulations provides that, as used in section 351 of the Code, the phrase "one or more persons" includes individuals, trusts, estates, partnerships, associations, companies, or corporations. To be in control of the transferee corporation, such person or persons must own immediately after the transfer stock possessing at least 80 percent of the total combined voting power of all classes of stock entitled to vote and at least 80 percent of the total number of shares of all other classes of stock of such corporation.

Section 358(a) of the Code provides that in the case of an exchange to which section 351 applies, the basis of the property permitted to be received under such section without the recognition of gain or loss will be the same as that of the property exchanged, decreased by the amount of any money received by the taxpayer.

Section 358(d) of the Code provides that where, as part of the consideration to the taxpayer, another party to the exchange assumed a liability of the taxpayer or acquired from the taxpayer property subject to a liability, such assumption or acquisition (in the amount of the liability) will, for purposes of section 358, be treated as money received by the taxpayer on the exchange.

Section 362(a) of the Code provides that a corporation's basis in property acquired in a transaction to which section 351 applies will be the same as it would be in the hands of the transferor.

Under section 708(b)(1)(A) of the Code, a partnership is terminated if no part of any business, financial operation, or venture of the partnership continues to be carried on by any of its partners in a partnership. Under section 708(b)(1)(B), a partnership terminates if within a 12–month period there is a sale or exchange of 50 percent or more of the total interest in partnership capital and profits.

Section 732(b) of the Code provides that the basis of property other than money distributed by a partnership in a liquidation of a partner's interest shall be an amount equal to the adjusted basis of the partner's interest in the partnership reduced by any money distributed. Section 732(c) of the Code provides rules for the allocation of a partner's basis in a partnership interest among the assets received in a liquidating distribution.

Section 735(b) of the Code provides that a partner's holding period for property received in a distribution from a partnership (other than with respect to certain inventory items defined in section 751(d)(2)) includes the partnership's holding period, as determined under section 1223, with respect to such property.

Section 1223(1) of the Code provides that where property received in an exchange acquires the same basis, in whole or in part, as the property surrendered in the exchange, the holding period of the property received includes the holding period of the property surrendered to the extent such surrendered property was a capital asset or property described in section 1231. Under section 1223(2), the holding period of a taxpayer's property, however acquired, includes the period during which the property was held by any other person if that property has the same basis, in whole or in part, in the taxpayer's hands as it would have in the hands of such other person.

Section 741 of the Code provides that in the case of a sale or exchange of an interest in a partnership, gain or loss shall be recognized to the transferor partner. Such gain or loss shall be considered as a gain or loss from the sale or exchange of a capital asset, except as otherwise provided in section 751.

Section 751(a) of the Code provides that the amount of money or the fair value of property received by a transferor partner in exchange for all or part of such partner's interest in the partnership attributable to unrealized receivables of the partnership, or to inventory items of the partnership that have appreciated substantially in value, shall be considered as an amount realized from the sale or exchange of property other than a capital asset.

Section 752(a) of the Code provides that any increase in a partner's share of the liabilities of a partnership, or any increase in a partner's individual liabilities by reason of the assumption by the partner of partnership liabilities, will be considered as a contribution of money by such partner to the partnership.

Section 752(b) of the Code provides that any decrease in a partner's share of the liabilities of a partnership, or any decrease in a partner's individual liabilities by reason of the assumption by the partnership of such individual liabilities, will be considered as a distribution of money to the partner by the partnership. Under section 733(1) of the Code, the basis of a partner's interest in the partnership is reduced by the amount of money received in a distribution that is not in liquidation of the partnership.

Section 752(d) of the Code provides that in the case of a sale or exchange of an interest in a partnership, liabilities shall be treated in the same manner as liabilities in connection with the sale or exchange of property not associated with partnerships.

The premise in Rev.Rul. 70–239 that the federal income tax consequences of the three situations described therein would be the same, without regard to which of the three transactions was entered into, is incorrect. As described below, depending on the format chosen for the transfer to a controlled corporation, the basis and holding periods of the various assets received by the corporation and the basis and holding periods of the stock received by the former partners can vary.

Additionally, Rev.Rul. 70–239 raises questions about potential adverse tax consequences to taxpayers in certain cases involving collapsible corporations defined in section 341 of the Code, personal holding companies

described in section 542, small business corporations defined in section 1244, and electing small business corporations defined in section 1371. Recognition of the three possible methods to incorporate a partnership will enable taxpayers to avoid the above potential pitfalls and will facilitate flexibility with respect to the basis and holding periods of the assets received in the exchange.

HOLDING

Rev.Rul. 70–239 no longer represents the Service's position. The Service's current position is set forth below, and for each situation, the methods described and the underlying assumptions and purposes must be satisfied for the conclusions of this revenue ruling to be applicable.

*Situation 1*

Under section 351 of the Code, gain or loss is not recognized by $X$ on the transfer by $X$ of all its assets to $R$ in exchange for $R$'s stock and the assumption by $R$ of $X$'s liabilities.

Under section 362(a) of the Code, $R$'s basis in the assets received from $X$ equals their basis to $X$ immediately before their transfer to $R$. Under section 358(a), the basis to $X$ of the stock received from $R$ is the same as the basis to $X$ of the assets transferred to $R$, reduced by the liabilities assumed by $R$, which assumption is treated as a payment of money to $X$ under section 358(d). In addition, the assumption by $R$ of $X$'s liabilities decreased each partner's share of the partnership liabilities, thus, decreasing the basis of each partner's partnership interest pursuant to sections 752 and 733.

On distribution of the stock to $X$'s partners, $X$ terminated under section 708(b)(1)(A) of the Code. Pursuant to section 732(b), the basis of the stock distributed to the partners in liquidation of their partnership interests is, with respect to each partner, equal to the adjusted basis of the partner's interest in the partnership.

Under section 1223(1) of the Code, $X$'s holding period for the stock received in the exchange includes its holding period in the capital assets and section 1231 assets transferred (to the extent that the stock was received in exchange for such assets). To the extent the stock was received in exchange for neither capital nor section 1231 assets, $X$'s holding period for such stock begins on the day following the date of the exchange. See Rev.Rul. 70–598, 1970–2 C.B. 168. Under section 1223(2), $R$'s holding period in the assets transferred to it includes $X$'s holding period. When $X$ distributed the $R$ stock to its partners, under sections 735(b) and 1223, the partners' holding periods included $X$'s holding period of the stock. Furthermore, such distribution will not violate the control requirement of section 368(c) of the Code.

*Situation 2*

On the transfer of all of $Y$'s assets to its partners, $Y$ terminated under section 708(b)(1)(A) of the Code, and, pursuant to section 732(b), the basis

of the assets (other than money) distributed to the partners in liquidation of their partnership interests in $Y$ was, with respect to each partner, equal to the adjusted basis of the partner's interest in $Y$, reduced by the money distributed. Under section 752, the decrease in $Y$'s liabilities resulting from the transfer to $Y$'s partners was offset by the partners' corresponding assumption of such liabilities so that the net effect on the basis of each partner's interest in $Y$, with respect to the liabilities transferred, was zero.

Under section 351 of the Code, gain or loss is not recognized by $Y$'s former partners on the transfer to $S$ in exchange for its stock and the assumption of $Y$'s liabilities, of the assets of $Y$ received by $Y$'s partners in liquidation of $Y$.

Under section 358(a) of the Code, the basis to the former partners of $Y$ in the stock received from $S$ is the same as the section 732(b) basis to the former partners of $Y$ in the assets received in liquidation of $Y$ and transferred to $S$, reduced by the liabilities assumed by $S$, which assumption is treated as a payment of money to the partners under section 358(d).

Under section 362(a) of the Code, $S$'s basis in the assets received from $Y$'s former partners equals their basis to the former partners as determined under section 732(c) immediately before the transfer to $S$.

Under section 735(b) of the Code, the partners' holding periods for the assets distributed to them by $Y$ includes $Y$'s holding period. Under section 1223(1), the partners' holding periods for the stock received in the exchange includes the partners' holding periods in the capital assets and section 1231 assets transferred to $S$ (to the extent that the stock was received in exchange for such assets). However, to the extent that the stock received was in exchange for neither capital nor section 1231 assets, the holding period of the stock began on the day following the date of the exchange. Under section 1223(2), $S$'s holding period of the $Y$ assets received in the exchange includes the partner's holding periods.

*Situation 3*

Under section 351 of the Code, gain or loss is not recognized by $Z$'s partners on the transfer of the partnership interests to $T$ in exchange for $T$'s stock.

On the transfer of the partnership interests to the corporation, $Z$ terminated under section 708(b)(1)(A) of the Code.

Under section 358(a) of the Code, the basis to the partners of $Z$ of the stock received from $T$ in exchange for their partnership interests equals the basis of their partnership interests transferred to $T$, reduced by $Z$'s liabilities assumed by $T$, the release from which is treated as a payment of money to $Z$'s partners under sections 752(d) and 358(d).

$T$'s basis for the assets received in the exchange equals the basis of the partners in their partnership interests allocated in accordance with section 732(c). $T$'s holding period includes $Z$'s holding period in the assets.

Under section 1223(1) of the Code, the holding period of the $T$ stock received by the former partners of $Z$ includes each respective partner's holding period for the partnership interest transferred, except that the holding period of the $T$ stock that was received by the partners of $Z$ in exchange for their interests in section 751 assets of $Z$ that are neither capital assets nor section 1231 assets begins on the day following the date of the exchange.

* * *

NOTE

Revenue Ruling 84–111 announces that for tax purposes the Service will respect the form adopted to incorporate a partnership. But what if the incorporation does not follow one of the patterns described in Revenue Ruling 84–111? For example, some states have laws that permit the conversion of a partnership into a corporation without the actual transfer of the partnership's assets or interests. How should the basis and holding period issues be sorted out in that type of incorporation? In Revenue Ruling 2004–59,[1] the Service analogizes an incorporation under such a statute to the situation where a partnership elects to be classified as a corporation for federal tax purposes. Thus, the transaction is taxed like Situation 1 in Revenue Ruling 84–111—i.e., the partnership is deemed to contribute all of its assets and liabilities to the corporation for stock and, immediately thereafter, the partnership liquidates by distributing the stock to its partners.[2]

PROBLEM

The AC partnership has the following balance sheet:

| Assets | A.B. | F.M.V. | Partners' Capital | A.B. | F.M.V. |
|---|---|---|---|---|---|
| Inventory | $ 80,000 | $100,000 | A | $ 60,000 | $100,000 |
| Capital Asset | 40,000 | 100,000 | C | 100,000 | 100,000 |
| | $120,000 | $200,000 | | $160,000 | $200,000 |

The difference between the partnership's aggregate inside basis in its assets and the partners' outside bases in their interests is attributable to the fact that C purchased her interest from B three years ago. For convenience, assume that the balance sheet remained unchanged over that period of time.

A and C wish to incorporate the partnership. Several alternative forms of incorporation are available: (1) the partnership could distribute its assets in complete liquidation, and A and C could transfer those assets to the corporation in exchange for its stock; (2) A and C could transfer their

---

**1.**   2004–2 C.B. 1050.

**2.**   See Reg. § 301.7701–3(g)(1)(i).

partnership interests to the corporation in exchange for its stock and the corporation would in essence liquidate the partnership; or (3) the partnership could transfer its assets to the corporation in return for stock and the partnership then could liquidate, distributing the stock to A and C.

(a) Consider the tax consequences of each alternative approach to incorporation of the partnership. See §§ 351, 358, 362.

(b) Does Revenue Ruling 84–111 correctly conclude that the results are different?

## c.  PARTNERSHIP MERGERS AND DIVISIONS

Code: § 708(b)(2)

*Partnership Mergers.* Section 708(b)(2)(A) provides that if two or more partnerships merge or consolidate into one partnership, the resulting partnership is considered the continuation of the merging or consolidating partnership whose members own an interest of more than 50 percent in the capital and profits of the resulting partnership.[1] When partnerships merge or combine, the transaction may take one of three forms: (1) the terminated partnership may transfer its assets and liabilities to the resulting partnership in exchange for a partnership interest which is distributed to the partners of the terminated partnership (assets-over form); (2) the terminating partnership may liquidate by distributing its assets and liabilities to its partners who then contribute the assets and liabilities to the resulting partnership (assets-up form); or (3) the partners in the terminating partnership may transfer their partnership interests to the resulting partnership in exchange for interests in that partnership, and the terminating partnership liquidates into the resulting partnership (interest-over form).[2]

The tax results of a merger of partnerships may vary depending upon the form selected for the transaction. For example, the adjusted basis of assets contributed to the resulting partnership may vary depending upon the form of transaction selected when the partners' aggregate outside bases do not equal the terminating partnership's inside basis. In an assets-over transaction, the resulting partnership's basis in the assets will be the same as the terminating partnership's basis under Section 723. In contrast, in an assets-up transaction the adjusted basis of the assets will first be determined under Section 732 on the liquidation of the terminating partnership

---

**1.** If the resulting partnership can be considered a continuation of more than one partnership under this rule, it is considered a continuation of the partnership contributing the assets with the greatest fair market value (net of liabilities), unless the Service permits otherwise. If the members of none of the merging or consolidating partnerships have an interest of more than 50 percent in the capital and profits of the resulting partnership, all of the merged or consolidated partnerships are terminated, and a new partnership results. Reg. § 1.708–1(c)(1).

**2.** A similar choice is presented when partners decide to incorporate a partnership. See Rev. Rul. 84–111, at page 355 of the text; see also Preamble to Proposed Regulations on Partnership Mergers and Divisions (hereinafter "Preamble"), 2000–1 C.B. 455.

and then under Section 723 on the contribution to the resulting partnership.

The regulations under Section 708 provide partners with a great deal of flexibility when they merge partnerships. Under those regulations, the form of the merger will be respected if the partners select the assets-over or assets-up form for the transaction.[3] If the merger is accomplished without undertaking a particular form or takes an interest-over form, the merger is treated as undertaking the assets-over form for federal tax purposes.[4]

Two special rules relating to mergers of partnerships deserve a brief mention. The regulations provide that increases and decreases in partnership liabilities associated with a merger or consolidation are netted by the partners in the terminating partnership and the resulting partnership to determine the effect of the merger under Section 752.[5] This rule prevents the terminating partnership from recognizing gain under section 752 when it becomes a momentary partner in the resulting partnership in an assets-over transaction.[6] Another potential problem is raised if a partner in the terminating partnership does not want to become a partner in the resulting partnership and wishes to receive money or property instead of a partnership interest. If to facilitate the buyout, the resulting partnership transfers money or other consideration to the terminating partnership in addition to the resulting partnership interests in an assets-over transaction, the terminating partnership could be treated as selling part of its property under Section 707(a)(2)(B).[7] The regulations, however, provide that the partner's sale of the interest will be respected as a sale if the merger agreement (or similar document) specifies (1) that the resulting partnership is purchasing an interest from a particular partner in the merging partnership, and (2) the consideration that is transferred for each interest sold.[8]

*Partnership Divisions.* Section 708(b)(2)(B) provides that if a partnership divides into two or more partnerships, a resulting partnership shall be considered a continuation of the prior partnership if members of the resulting partnership had a more than 50 percent interest in the capital and profits of the prior partnership.[9] Partnership divisions, like mergers,

---

**3.** Reg. § 1.708–1(c)(3).

**4.** Reg. § 1.708–1(c)(3)(i). The assets-over form is selected for an interest-over transaction to avoid application of Sections 704(c) and 737. Since the resulting partnership receives all of the partnership interests in the terminated partnership in an interest-over transaction, it is the sole member and would be deemed to receive the assets (a partnership cannot have one partner), thereby potentially bringing Sections 704(c) and 737 into play. Characterization of an interest-over merger as an assets-over transaction avoids this potential problem. Preamble, supra note 2.

**5.** Reg. § 1.752–1(f); see Reg. § 1.752–1(g) Example 2.

**6.** Preamble, supra note 2.

**7.** Id.

**8.** Reg. § 1.708–1(c)(4). The resulting partnership and its partners thus inherit the selling partner's capital account and Section 704(c) liability. If the terminating partnership has a Section 754 election in effect, the resulting partnership will have a special basis adjustment under Section 743. Preamble, supra note 2.

**9.** Any other resulting partnership is considered a new partnership. Reg. § 1.708–1(d)(1).

may be accomplished using either an assets-over or assets-up form. The regulations respect for federal tax purposes whichever of these two forms that is selected for the transaction.[10] If, however, the division takes place without a form or does not employ the assets-up form, it will be characterized under the assets-over form for federal tax purposes.[11]

*Application of the Mixing–Bowl Rules.* The operation of the mixing bowl rules, Sections 705(c)(1)(B) and 737, is an important issue when partnerships merge or divide. How will preexisting built-in gains and losses be treated? Will a merger trigger the beginning of a new seven-year period under the mixing bowl rules? Revenue Ruling 2004–43,[12] which follows, expresses the Service's views on how the mixing bowl rules apply to a partnership merger following the assets-order form. Revenue Ruling 2004–43 has been revoked but the Service announced that it intends to issue regulations implementing its principles.[13] Until those regulations are issued, the ruling is the best guidance that is available. Read it carefully to see if you agree with the government's analysis.

A partnership division also potentially raises issues under Sections 704(c)(1)(B) and 737. In a division following the assets-up form, the distribution of partnership assets to the partners could trigger either of those sections. In an assets-over division, the partnership interest in the resulting partnership is treated as Section 704(c) property to the extent that the interest is received in exchange for Section 704(c) property.[14] Thus, the distribution of interests in the resulting partnership will trigger Section 704(b)(1)(B) to the extent that interests are received by partners other than the partner who contributed the Section 704(c) property. Section 737 also may be triggered if a partner who contributed Section 704(c) property receives an interest in the resulting partnership that is not attributable to Section 704(c) property.[15]

# Revenue Ruling 2004–43

2004–1 Cum. Bull. 842.

ISSUES

1) Does § 704(c)(1)(B) of the Internal Revenue Code apply to § 704(c) gain or loss that is created in an assets-over partnership merger?

10. Reg. § 1.708–1(d)(3). The regulations permit the momentary ownership by the prior partnership of all interests in the new partnership when the assets-over form is used. Preamble, supra note 2.

11. Reg. 1.708–1(d)(3)(i).

12. 2004–1 C.B. 842.

13. Rev. Rul. 2005–10, 2005–1 C.B. 492.

14. Reg. 1.704–4(d)(1).

15. Preamble, supra note 2. The Section 737 regulations contain one exception for a partnership division. Section 737 does not apply when a partnership transfers all of the Section 704(c) property contributed by a partner to a second partnership, followed by a distribution of an interest in the second partnership in complete liquidation of the interest of the partner who originally contributed the section 704(c) property. Reg. § 1.737–2(b)(2). No similar rule is available under Section 704(c)(1)(B). The Service has asked for comments on whether the exceptions to Sections 704(c)(1)(B) and 737 should be expanded in certain circumstances relating to divisive transactions. Preamble, supra note 2.

2) For purposes of § 737(b), does net precontribution gain include § 704(c) gain or loss that is created in an assets-over partnership merger?

## FACTS

*Situation 1.* On January 1, 2004, A contributes Asset 1, with a basis of $200x and a fair market value of $300x to partnership AB in exchange for a 50 percent interest. On the same date, B contributes $300x of cash to AB in exchange for a 50 percent interest. Also on January 1, 2004, C contributes Asset 2, with a basis of $100x and a fair market value of $200x to partnership CD in exchange for a 50 percent interest. D contributes $200x of cash to CD in exchange for a 50 percent interest.

On January 1, 2006, AB and CD undertake an assets-over partnership merger in which AB is the continuing partnership and CD is the terminating partnership. At the time of the merger, AB's only assets are Asset 1, with a fair market value of $900x, and $300x in cash, and CD's only assets are Asset 2, with a fair market value of $600x and $200x in cash. After the merger, the partners have capital and profits interests in AB as follows: A, 30 percent; B, 30 percent; C, 20 percent; and D, 20 percent.

The partnership agreements for AB and CD provide that the partners' capital accounts will be determined and maintained in accordance with § 1.704–1(b)(2)(iv) of the Income Tax Regulations, distributions in liquidation of the partnership (or any partner's interest) will be made in accordance with the partners' positive capital account balances, and any partner with a deficit balance in the partner's capital account following the liquidation of the partner's interest must restore that deficit to the partnership (as set forth in § 1.704–1(b)(2)(ii)(b)(2) and (3)). AB and CD both have provisions in their partnership agreements requiring the revaluation of partnership property upon the entry of a new partner. AB would not be treated as an investment company (within the meaning of § 351) if it were incorporated. Neither partnership holds any unrealized receivables or inventory for purposes of § 751. AB and CD do not have a § 754 election in place. Asset 1 and Asset 2 are nondepreciable capital assets.

On January 1, 2012, AB has the same assets that it had after the merger. Each asset has the same value that it had at the time of the merger. On this date, AB distributes Asset 2 to A in liquidation of A's interest in AB.

*Situation 2.* The facts are the same as in Situation 1, except that on January 1, 2012, Asset 1 has a value of $275x, and AB distributes Asset 1 to C in liquidation of C's interest in AB.

## LAW

Under § 704(b) and the regulations thereunder, allocations of a partnership's items of income, gain, loss, deduction, or credit provided for in the partnership agreement will be respected if the allocations have substantial economic effect. Allocations that fail to have substantial economic effect will be reallocated according to the partners' interests in the partnership.

Section 1.704–1(b)(2)(iv)(*f*) provides that a partnership may, upon the occurrence of certain events (including the contribution of money to the partnership by a new or existing partner), increase or decrease the partners' capital accounts to reflect a revaluation of the partnership property.

Section 1.704–1(b)(2)(iv)(*g*) provides that, to the extent a partnership's property is reflected on the books of the partnership at a book value that differs from the adjusted tax basis, the substantial economic effect requirements apply to the allocations of book items. Section 704(c) and § 1.704–1(b)(4)(i) govern the partners' distributive shares of tax items.

Section 1.704–1(b)(4)(i) provides that if partnership property is, under § 1.704–1(b)(2)(iv)(*f*), properly reflected in the capital accounts of the partners and on the books of the partnership at a book value that differs from the adjusted tax basis of the property, then depreciation, depletion, amortization, and gain or loss, as computed for book purposes, with respect to the property will be greater or less than the depreciation, depletion, amortization, and gain or loss, as computed for federal tax purposes, with respect to the property. In these cases the capital accounts of the partners are required to be adjusted solely for allocations of the book items to the partners (see § 1.704–1(b)(2)(iv)(*g*)), and the partners' shares of the corresponding tax items are not independently reflected by further adjustments to the partners' capital accounts. Thus, separate allocations of these tax items cannot have economic effect under § 1.704–1(b)(2)(ii)(*b*)(*1*), and the partners' distributive shares of tax items must (unless governed by § 704(c)) be determined in accordance with the partners' interests in the partnership. These tax items must be shared among the partners in a manner that takes account of the variation between the adjusted tax basis of the property and its book value in the same manner as variations between the adjusted tax basis and fair market value of property contributed to the partnership are taken into account in determining the partners' shares of tax items under § 704(c).

Section 704(c)(1)(A) provides that income, gain, loss, and deduction with respect to property contributed to the partnership by a partner shall be shared among the partners so as to take account of the variation between the basis of the property to the partnership and its fair market value at the time of contribution.

Section 1.704–3(a)(2) provides that, except as provided in § 1.704–3(e)(2) and (3), § 704(c) and § 1.704–3 apply on a property-by-property basis.

Section 1.704–3(a)(3)(i) provides that property contributed to a partnership is § 704(c) property if at the time of contribution its book value differs from the contributing partner's adjusted tax basis. For purposes of § 1.704–3, book value is determined as contemplated by § 1.704–1(b). Therefore, book value is equal to fair market value at the time of contribution and is subsequently adjusted for cost recovery and other events that affect the basis of the property.

Section 1.704–3(a)(3)(ii) provides that the built-in gain on § 704(c) property is the excess of the property's book value over the contributing partner's adjusted tax basis upon contribution. The built-in gain is thereafter reduced by decreases in the difference between the property's book value and adjusted tax basis.

Section 1.704–3(a)(6) provides that the principles of § 1.704–3 also apply to "reverse § 704(c) allocations" which result from revaluations of partnership property pursuant to § 1.704–1(b)(2)(iv)(*f*).

Section 1.704–3(a)(7) provides that, if a contributing partner transfers a partnership interest, built-in gain or loss must be allocated to the transferee partner as it would have been allocated to the transferor partner. If the contributing partner transfers a portion of the partnership interest, the share of built-in gain or loss proportionate to the interest transferred must be allocated to the transferee partner.

Section 704(c)(1)(B) provides that if any property contributed to the partnership by a partner is distributed (directly or indirectly) by the partnership (other than to the contributing partner) within seven years of being contributed: (i) the contributing partner shall be treated as recognizing gain or loss (as the case may be) from the sale of the property in an amount equal to the gain or loss which would have been allocated to the partner under § 704(c)(1)(A) by reason of the variation described in § 704(c)(1)(A) if the property had been sold at its fair market value at the time of the distribution; (ii) the character of the gain or loss shall be determined by reference to the character of the gain or loss which would have resulted if the property had been sold by the partnership to the distributee; and (iii) appropriate adjustments shall be made to the adjusted basis of the contributing partner's interest in the partnership and to the adjusted basis of the property distributed to reflect any gain or loss recognized under § 704(c)(1)(B).

Section 1.704–4(c)(4) provides that § 704(c)(1)(B) and § 1.704–4 do not apply to a transfer by a partnership (transferor partnership) of all of its assets and liabilities to a second partnership (transferee partnership) in an exchange described in § 721, followed by a distribution of the interest in the transferee partnership in liquidation of the transferor partnership as part of the same plan or arrangement. Section 1.704–4(c)(4) also provides that a subsequent distribution of § 704(c) property by the transferee partnership to a partner of the transferee partnership is subject to § 704(c)(1)(B) to the same extent that a distribution by the transferor partnership would have been subject to § 704(c)(1)(B).

Section 1.704–4(d)(2) provides that the transferee of all or a portion of the partnership interest of a contributing partner is treated as the contributing partner for purposes of § 704(c)(1)(B) and § 1.704–4 to the extent of the share of built-in gain or loss allocated to the transferee partner.

Section 708(a) provides that, for purposes of subchapter K, an existing partnership shall be considered as continuing if it is not terminated.

Section 708(b)(2)(A) provides that in the case of the merger or consolidation of two or more partnerships, the resulting partnership shall, for purposes of § 708, be considered the continuation of any merging or consolidating partnership whose members own an interest of more than 50 percent in the capital and profits of the resulting partnership.

Section 1.708–1(c)(3)(i) provides that when two or more partnerships merge or consolidate into one partnership under the applicable jurisdictional law without undertaking a form for the merger or consolidation, or undertake a form for the merger or consolidation that is not described in § 1.708–1(c)(3)(ii), any merged or consolidated partnership that is considered terminated under § 1.708–1(c)(1) is treated as undertaking the assets-over form for federal income tax purposes. Under the assets-over form, the merged or consolidated partnership that is considered terminated under § 1.708–1(c)(1) contributes all of its assets and liabilities to the resulting partnership in exchange for an interest in the resulting partnership, and immediately thereafter, the terminated partnership distributes interests in the resulting partnership to its partners in liquidation of the terminated partnership.

Section 737(a) provides that, in the case of any distribution by a partnership to a partner, the partner shall be treated as recognizing gain in an amount equal to the lesser of (1) the excess (if any) of (A) the fair market value of property (other than money) received in the distribution over (B) the adjusted basis of the partner's interest in the partnership immediately before the distribution reduced (but not below zero) by the amount of money received in the distribution, or (2) the net precontribution gain of the partner. Gain recognized under the preceding sentence shall be in addition to any gain recognized under § 731. The character of the gain shall be determined by reference to the proportionate character of the net precontribution gain.

Section 737(b) provides that for purposes of § 737, the term "net precontribution gain" means the net gain (if any) which would have been recognized by the distributee partner under § 704(c)(1)(B) if all property which (1) had been contributed to the partnership by the distributee partner within seven years of the distribution, and (2) is held by the partnership immediately before the distribution, had been distributed by the partnership to another partner.

Section 1.737–1(c)(1) provides that the distributee partner's net precontribution gain is the net gain (if any) that would have been recognized by the distributee partner under § 704(c)(1)(B) and § 1.704–4 if all property that had been contributed to the partnership by the distributee partner within seven years of the distribution and is held by the partnership immediately before the distribution had been distributed by the partnership to another partner other than a partner who owns, directly or indirectly, more than 50 percent of the capital or profits interest in the partnership.

Section 1.737–1(c)(2)(iii) provides that the transferee of all or a portion of a contributing partner's partnership interest succeeds to the transferor's

net precontribution gain, if any, in an amount proportionate to the interest transferred.

Section 1.737–2(b)(1) provides that § 737 and § 1.737–2 do not apply to a transfer by a partnership (transferor partnership) of all of its assets and liabilities to a second partnership (transferee partnership) in an exchange described in § 721, followed by a distribution of the interest in the transferee partnership in liquidation of the transferor partnership as part of the same plan or arrangement.

Section 1.737–2(b)(3) provides that a subsequent distribution of property by the transferee partnership to a partner of the transferee partnership that was formerly a partner of the transferor partnership is subject to § 737 to the same extent that a distribution from the transferor partnership would have been subject to § 737.

ANALYSIS

Section 1.704–4(c)(4) describes the effect of an assets-over partnership merger on pre-existing § 704(c) gain or loss for purposes of § 704(c)(1)(B). Under § 1.704–4(c)(4), if the transferor partnership in an assets-over merger holds contributed property with § 704(c) gain or loss, the seven year period in § 704(c)(1)(B) does not restart with respect to that gain or loss as a result of the merger. Section 1.704–4(c)(4) does not prevent the creation of new § 704(c) gain or loss when assets are contributed by one partnership to another partnership in an assets-over merger. Section 704(c)(1)(B) applies to this newly created § 704(c) gain or loss if the assets contributed in the merger are distributed to a partner other than the contributing partner (or its successor) within seven years of the merger.

Section 1.737–2(b)(1) and (3) describes the effect of an assets-over partnership merger on net precontribution gain that includes pre-existing § 704(c) gain or loss. Under § 1.737–2(b)(3), if the transferor partnership in an assets-over merger holds contributed property with § 704(c) gain or loss, the seven year period in § 737(b) does not restart with respect to that gain or loss as a result of the merger. Section 1.737–2(b)(3) does not prevent the creation of new § 704(c) gain or loss when assets are contributed by one partnership to another partnership in an assets-over merger. This gain or loss must be considered in determining the amount of net precontribution gain for purposes of § 737 if the continuing partnership distributes other property to the contributing partner (or its successor) within seven years of the merger.

Section 1.704–3(a)(6)(i) provides that the principles of § 1.704–3 apply to reverse § 704(c) allocations. In contrast, the regulations under § 704(c)(1)(B) and § 737 contain no similar rule requiring that the principles of § 704(c)(1)(B) and § 737 apply to reverse § 704(c) allocations. Under those regulations, § 704(c)(1)(B) and § 737 do not apply to reverse § 704(c) allocations.

In both of the situations described above, on the date of the partnership merger, CD contributes cash and Asset 2 to AB in exchange for an

interest in AB. Immediately thereafter, CD distributes, in liquidation, interests in AB to C and D. Asset 2 has a basis of $100x and a fair market value of $600x upon contribution. Of the $500x of built in gain in Asset 2, $100x is pre-existing § 704(c) gain attributable to C's contribution of Asset 2 to CD, and $400x is additional § 704(c) gain created as a result of the merger. As the transferees of CD's partnership interest in AB, C and D each succeed to one-half of CD's $400x of § 704(c) gain in Asset 2 (each $200x). Section 1.704–3(a)(7). Thus, C's share of § 704(c) gain is $300x, and D's share of § 704(c) gain is $200x.

The entry of CD as a new partner of AB causes partnership AB to revalue its property. When CD enters as a new partner of AB, Asset 1 has a basis of $200x and a fair market value of $900x. Of the $700x of built-in gain in Asset 1, $100x is pre-existing § 704(c) gain attributable to the contribution of Asset 1 by A. The revaluation results in the creation of $600x of reverse § 704(c) gain in Asset 1. This layer of reverse § 704(c) gain is shared equally by A and B ($300x each). Thus, A's share of § 704(c) gain is $400x, and B's share of § 704(c) gain is $300x. The calculation of § 704(c) gain in each asset is summarized in the following table.

| | Adjusted Tax Basis | Value on Date of Contribution | § 704(c) Gain on Date of Contribution | Value on Date of Merger | § 704(c) Gain Created by Merger | Total § 704(c) Gain After Merger |
|---|---|---|---|---|---|---|
| Asset 1 | $200x | $ 300x | $100x | $ 900x | $ 600x | $ 700x |
| Asset 2 | $100x | $ 200x | $100x | $ 600x | $ 400x | $ 500x |
| Cash | $500x | $ 500x | $ 0x | $ 500x | $ 0x | $ 0x |
| Total | $800x | $1,000x | $200x | $2,000x | $1,000x | $1,200x |

The partners' share of § 704(c) gain in each of AB's assets after the merger is summarized in the following table.

| | A's Share of § 704(c) Gain | B's Share of § 704(c) Gain | C's Share of § 704(c) Gain | D's Share of § 704(c) Gain | Total § 704(c) Gain |
|---|---|---|---|---|---|
| Asset 1 | $400x | $300x | $ 0x | $ 0x | $ 700x |
| Asset 2 | $ 0x | $ 0x | $300x | $200x | $ 500x |
| Cash | $ 0x | $ 0x | $ 0x | $ 0x | $ 0x |
| Total | $400x | $300x | $300x | $200x | $1,200x |

In Situation 1, the distribution of Asset 2 to A occurs more than seven years after the contribution of Asset 2 to CD. Therefore, § 704(c)(1)(B) does not apply to the $100x of pre-existing § 704(c) gain attributable to that contribution. However, the distribution of Asset 2 to A occurs within seven years of the contribution of Asset 2 by CD to AB. The contribution of Asset 2 by CD to AB creates § 704(c) gain of $400x. As the transferees of CD's partnership interest in AB, C and D each succeed to one-half of the $400x of § 704(c) gain created by the merger. Section 1.704–3(a)(7). Section 704(c)(1)(B) applies to that § 704(c) gain, causing C and D each to recognize $200x of gain.

The distribution of Asset 2 to A occurs more than seven years after the contribution of Asset 1 to AB, and A made no subsequent contributions to

AB. Therefore, A's net precontribution gain for purposes of § 737(b) at the time of the distribution is zero. AB's $600x of reverse § 704(c) gain in Asset 1, resulting from a revaluation of AB's partnership property at the time of the merger, is not net precontribution gain. Accordingly, A will not recognize gain under § 737 as a result of the distribution of Asset 2.

In Situation 2, § 704(c)(1)(B) does not apply to the distribution by the continuing partnership of Asset 1 to C on January 1, 2012. The distribution of Asset 1 to C occurs more than seven years after the contribution of Asset 1 to AB, and § 704(c)(1)(B) does not apply to the reverse § 704(c) gain in Asset 1 resulting from a revaluation of AB's partnership property at the time of the merger. Accordingly, neither A nor B will recognize gain under § 704(c)(1)(B) as a result of the distribution of Asset 1 to C.

The distribution of Asset 1 to C occurs more than seven years after the contribution of Asset 2 to CD. Therefore, C's net precontribution gain at the time of the distribution does not include C's $100x of pre-existing § 704(c) gain attributable to that contribution. However, the distribution of Asset 1 to C occurs within seven years of the contribution of Asset 2 by CD to AB. The contribution of Asset 2 by CD to AB creates net precontribution gain of $400x. As the transferees of CD's partnership interest in AB, C and D each succeed to one-half of CD's $400x of net precontribution gain in Asset 2. Section 1.737–1(c)(2)(iii). Thus, C's portion of CD's net precontribution gain created by the merger is $200x. The excess of Asset 1's fair market value, $275x, over the adjusted tax basis of C's interest in AB immediately before the distribution, $100x, is $175x, which is less than C's $200x of net precontribution gain. Therefore, C will recognize $175x of capital gain under § 737 as a result of the distribution. Because no property is distributed to D and none of the property treated as contributed by D is distributed to another partner, D recognizes no gain under § 737 or § 704(c)(1)(B).

HOLDINGS

1) Section 704(c)(1)(B) applies to newly created § 704(c) gain or loss in property contributed by the transferor partnership to the continuing partnership in an assets-over partnership merger, but does not apply to newly created reverse § 704(c) gain or loss resulting from a revaluation of property in the continuing partnership.

2) For purposes of § 737(b), net precontribution gain includes newly created § 704(c) gain or loss in property contributed by the transferor partnership to the continuing partnership in an assets-over partnership merger, but does not include newly created reverse § 704(c) gain or loss resulting from a revaluation of property in the continuing partnership.

## 2. PARTNERSHIP TERMINATIONS FORCED BY STATUTE

Code: § 708(b)(1)(B). Skim §§ 721; 722; 723; 731; 732; 743(b); 755; 761(e)(1); 774(c).

Regulations: § 1.708–1(b)(2), (4), (5).

*Introduction.* A partnership is considered to continue for tax purposes if it is not "terminated," but termination does not result solely from the cessation of business activity. Section 708(b)(1)(B) provides that a partnership, other than an electing large partnership, is terminated if "within a 12–month period there is a sale or exchange of 50 percent or more of the total interest in partnership capital and profits."[1] The regulations make it clear that this requires a sale of different interests of 50 percent or more of partnership capital and profits within the period and not a sale of the same 25 percent interest twice.[2] Sales between partners are considered for purposes of the 50 percent test. The section does not apply, however, to dispositions by gift, inheritance or liquidation of a partnership interest.[3]

The regulations also prescribe the consequences of a Section 708(b)(1)(B) termination. A termination occurs on the date of the sale of an interest that puts sales at or over the 50 percent level,[4] and on that date the partnership year closes.[5] The regulations further provide that if a partnership is terminated by a sale or exchange of an interest, it is deemed to contribute all of its assets and liabilities to a new partnership in exchange for an interest in that new entity.[6] The terminated partnership is then deemed to liquidate by distributing interests in the new partnership to the purchasing partner and the other remaining partners, either for the continuation of the business of the new partnership or for its dissolution and winding up.[7] Because the reconstituted partnership is treated as a new entity, it must make new elections relating to accounting methods, depreciation, and other matters.

In order to prevent an involuntary termination of a partnership resulting from a sale or exchange, many carefully drafted partnership agreements include a provision forbidding any sale or exchange that would cause a termination. If the partners balk at such a restriction, another technique to avoid a termination is for a selling partner to dispose of his interest over more than a 12 month period or to sell only a portion of his interest (e.g., in capital but not profits) and defer the sale of the remaining portion beyond the 12–month statutory window.

*Collateral Consequences of a Section 708(b)(1)(B) Termination.* The regulations go to great lengths to make a termination of a partnership

---

**1.** The regulations provide that this requires a sale or exchange of 50 percent or more of the total interest in partnership capital plus 50 percent or more of the total interest in partnership profits. Reg. § 1.708–1(b)(2). Section 774(c) excludes electing large partnerships from application of Section 708(b)(1)(B).

**2.** Reg. § 1.708–1(b)(2).

**3.** Id. It also would appear that Section 708 is inapplicable to a charitable contribution of a partnership interest, at least if it is not converted into a part gift/part sale as a result of relief of the partner's share of liabilities. Changes of ownership as a result of contributions to capital also do not constitute a sale or exchange. Id. See Rev.Rul. 75–423, 1975–2 C.B. 260. However, corporate distributions of partnership interests are treated as exchanges of those interests for purposes of Section 708. I.R.C. § 761(e)(1).

**4.** Reg. § 1.708–1(b)(3)(ii).

**5.** Reg. § 1.708–1(b)(3).

**6.** Reg. § 1.708–1(b)(4).

**7.** Id.

under Section 708(b)(1)(B) as painless as possible from a tax perspective. First, the capital account of any transferee partner and the capital accounts of the other partners of the terminated partnership carry over to the new partnership and the constructive liquidation of the terminated partnership is disregarded in the maintenance and computation of the partners' capital accounts.[8] If the terminated partnership has a Section 754 election (including one made on its final return) in effect for the taxable year in which the sale occurs, the election applies to any incoming partner. Therefore, the bases of the partnership assets are adjusted pursuant to Sections 743 and 755 before the deemed contribution to the new partnership.[9] In addition, a partner with a special basis adjustment in property held by the terminated partnership continues to have the same special basis adjustment with respect to property deemed contributed to the new partnership, regardless of whether that partnership makes its own Section 754 election.[10] Subchapter K's "mixing bowl" provisions (Sections 704(c)(1)(B) and 737) are also applied with some mercy. Because a Section 708(b)(1)(B) termination does not result in a distribution of partnership properties to the partners, the mixing bowl rules do not apply to the deemed distribution of interests in the new partnership caused by the termination.[11] Also, the regulations say that a new seven-year period under Sections 704(c)(1)(B) and 737 does not begin with respect to the built-in gain and built-in loss property contributed to the new partnership.[12] However, a later distribution of Section 704(c) property by the new partnership is subject to both Sections 704(c)(1)(B) and 737 to the same extent that a distribution by the terminated partnership would have been subject to those sections.[13]

*Tiered Partnerships.* The Section 708 regulations prescribe special rules for tiered partnerships. If the sale of an upper-tier partnership results in its termination, the upper-tier partnership is treated as exchanging its entire interest in the capital and profits of any lower-tier partnership.[14] This deemed exchange could terminate the lower-tier partnership or be combined with actual sales or exchanges of interests in the lower-tier partnership to cause a termination. But if a sale or exchange of an interest in an upper-tier partnership does not result in a termination, the transaction is not treated as a sale or exchange of a proportionate share of the upper-tier partnership's interest in the lower-tier partnership.[15]

---

**8.** Reg. §§ 1.704–1(b)(2)(iv)(*l*),–1(b)(5) Example 13(v). Because the termination and deemed contribution do not change capital accounts or the books of the partnership, the deemed contribution does not create new book/tax disparities under Section 704(c).

**9.** Reg. § 1.708–1(b)(5).

**10.** Reg. § 1.743–1(h)(1). Additionally, a downward inside basis adjustment could be required under Section 743(a) if the partnership has a substantial built-in loss.

**11.** Reg. §§ 1.704–4(c)(3); 1.737–2(a); see Reg. § 1.708–(b)(4) Example.

**12.** Reg. §§ 1.704–4(a)(4)(ii); 1.737–2(a). The new partnership is not required to use the same method as the terminated partnership with respect to Section 704(c) property. Reg. § 1.704–3(a)(2).

**13.** Reg. §§ 1.704–4(c)(3); 1.737–2(a).

**14.** Reg. § 1.708–1(b)(2).

**15.** Id.

# McCauslen v. Commissioner

United States Tax Court, 1966.
45 T.C. 588.

## OPINION

■ MULRONEY, JUDGE. Respondent determined a deficiency in petitioners' income tax for 1959 in the amount of $20,738.86. The only issue is whether the gain realized by petitioners from a sale of certain partnership properties acquired by them under a buy-sell agreement is taxable as a long-term or short-term capital gain, which turns upon whether petitioners are entitled to use the partnership's holding period with respect to such properties.

All of the facts were stipulated and they are so found.

Edwin E. and Frances E. McCauslen, husband and wife, are residents of Steubenville, Ohio. They filed their joint Federal income tax return for 1959 with the district director of internal revenue at Cleveland, Ohio.

In 1946 petitioner Edwin E. McCauslen and his brother, William T. McCauslen, formed a two-man partnership to engage in the nursery, greenhouse, wholesale, and retail flower business. Both men were equal, active partners in the business until William died on March 7, 1959, and after William's death the floral business was continued by the petitioner. The partnership had a fiscal year ending May 31 for tax and accounting purposes.

On October 17, 1956, petitioner and William (together with their wives) executed an agreement which provided, in part [for the surviving partner to buy out the decedent partner's interest at his death. Ed.]

William died on March 7, 1959, and pursuant to the agreement of October 17, 1956, petitioner acquired William's partnership interest. On May 28, 1959, petitioner sold for $200,000 a greenhouse and greenhouse equipment which had previously been owned by the partnership for a period of longer than 6 months.

Petitioner and his wife reported the sale on their 1959 return as follows:

### Sale of Greenhouse Business

| | | |
|---|---:|---:|
| Sold to Dieckmann Bros., May 28, 1959 | | $200,000.00 |
| Less commission to broker | | 8,000.00 |
| Net sale price | | 192,000.00 |
| Less cost of assets sold: | | |
| Land | | $35,172.75 |
| Greenhouse and equipment .. $185,388.32 | | |
| Less depreciation to date .... 155,316.16 | 30,072.16 | 65,244.91 |
| Long-term capital gain | | 126,755.09 |

Respondent in his statutory notice of deficiency increased petitioners' taxable income for 1959 and explained the adjustment as follows:

During the taxable year ended December 31, 1959 you sold a greenhouse and equipment for $200,000.00. You reported the gain realized of $126,755.09 as a long-term capital gain on Schedule D of your income tax return. Since one-half of your interest in these assets was acquired by you within 6 months before their sale, it is held that under Section 1222 of the Internal Revenue Code, the gain on this portion is a short-term capital gain. * * *

Section 741 of the Internal Revenue Code of 1954 recognizes a partnership interest as a capital asset which may be sold or exchanged with capital gain or loss treatment. When petitioner purchased the decedent's interest in the partnership from the estate pursuant to the October 17, 1956, agreement, the partnership was terminated. Sec. 708(b). At that point petitioner owned all of the partnership assets, i.e., the assets attributable to his own one-half partnership interest since 1946 in the two-man partnership, as well as the assets attributable to the decedent's partnership interest acquired by petitioner in 1959.

There does not now appear to be any dispute between the parties as to the proper bases to be applied to the partnership assets in petitioner's hands after the termination of the partnership. Moreover, as to the proper holding period of these assets, respondent recognizes that petitioner acquired by distribution that portion of the partnership assets relating to his own partnership interest and that with respect to such assets the petitioner is entitled to include the partnership's holding period. Therefore, when petitioner in May 1959 (less than 6 months after decedent's death) sold some of the former partnership assets which had previously been held by the partnership for more than 6 months, the partnership's holding period could be tacked on to petitioner's holding period for that portion of the assets attributable to his own partnership interest, entitling him to long-term capital gains treatment of a portion of the gain realized.[3]

Petitioner argues that he is also entitled to tack on the holding period of the partnership to the portion of the partnership assets he acquired when he purchased the partnership interest of the decedent partner from the estate. Petitioner relies upon section 735, the pertinent portions of which we have set forth in a footnote, and which in section 735(b) provides that in determining the period for which a partner has held property received in a distribution from a partnership (excluding certain inventory items), there shall be included the holding period of the partnership with respect to such property.

We believe that petitioner's reliance upon section 735(b) is misplaced. Sections 731 through 735 represent an attempt to deal comprehensively with the whole problem of partnership distributions of property. Generally, the statutory sections allow tax-free distributions of property by a partner-

---

**3.** Respondent, in his statutory notice of deficiency, allowed $60,633.38 of petitioner's reported gain of $126,755.09 from the May 28, 1959, sale as long-term capital gain, treating the balance of the reported gain as short-term capital gain.

ship, with provisions for a carryover basis or a substituted basis, depending upon the type of distribution, and for adjustments to the basis of a distributee partner's interest in the partnership. Section 735 merely follows the distributed partnership property into the hands of the partner and describes the character of the gain or loss when the partner disposes of such distributed property, and in section 735(b) provides that the holding period of the partnership for the distributed property may be tacked on to the holding period in the hands of the partner. The emphasis throughout these sections is upon distributions to a partner in connection with an existing partnership interest.

Much of the complexity of the partnership provisions in the 1954 Code arises because they are based upon conflicting concepts of the nature of a partnership, i.e., the entity approach and the aggregate approach, as well as from Congress' desire to introduce a certain amount of flexibility in this area of partnership taxation. See David A. Foxman, 41 T.C. 535, affd. 352 F.2d 466. Thus, as we indicated in the *Foxman* case, drastic tax differences can result depending upon the categorization of a transaction (for example, as a "sale" of a partnership interest rather than a "liquidation" of such interest), even though the ultimate economic effect is much the same. Therefore, it would seem that concepts which might be meaningful under one section might prove misleading under another section.

The provision for tacking on the partnership's holding period is entirely consistent with the general statutory scheme of postponing recognition of gain or loss until the distributee partner finally disposes of the distributed partnership property. But where, as here, a partner acquires another partner's share by purchase and, as a consequence of the termination of the partnership resulting from such purchase, acquires the partnership assets relating to such purchased interest, the statute has no application. The statute cannot be construed as permitting the purchaser to tack on the partnership's holding period of such assets. In effect, petitioner is contending that he purchased assets belonging to another with a built-in holding period. Neither logic nor necessity supports such an argument and we do not believe that section 735(b) calls for such a result.

Since petitioner's purchase of the decedent's partnership interest resulted in a termination of the partnership under section 708(b), it is our view that petitioner acquired the partnership assets relating to such interest by purchase, rather than by any distribution from the partnership, and that petitioner's holding period for such assets begins from the date of such purchase. See 6 Mertens Law of Federal Income Taxation, sec. 35.60. Consequently, we agree with respondent's determination that petitioner's holding period for the assets attributable to the purchased interest was less than 6 months at the time of their sale by petitioner on May 28, 1959, with the result that the portion of the gain attributable to such assets is taxable as short-term capital gain.

Reviewed by the Court.

## Revenue Ruling 95–37

1995–1 Cum. Bull. 130.

ISSUES

(1) Do the federal income tax consequences described in Rev. Rul. 84–52, 1984–1 C.B. 157, apply to the conversion of an interest in a domestic partnership into an interest in a domestic limited liability company (LLC) that is classified as a partnership for federal tax purposes?

(2) Does the taxable year of the converting domestic partnership close with respect to all the partners or with respect to any partner?

(3) Does the resulting domestic LLC need to obtain a new taxpayer identification number?

LAW AND ANALYSIS

In Rev. Rul. 84–52, a general partnership formed under the Uniform Partnership Act of State M proposed to convert to a limited partnership under the Uniform Limited Partnership Act of State M. Rev. Rul. 84–52 generally holds that (1) under section 721 of the Internal Revenue Code, the conversion will not cause the partners to recognize gain or loss under sections 741 or 1001, (2) unless its business will not continue after the conversion, the partnership will not terminate under section 708 because the conversion is not treated as a sale or exchange for purposes of section 708, (3) if the partners' shares of partnership liabilities do not change, there will be no change in the adjusted basis of any partner's interest in the partnership, (4) if the partners' shares of partnership liabilities change and cause a deemed contribution of money to the partnership by a partner under section 752(a), then the adjusted basis of such a partner's interest will be increased under section 722 by the amount of the deemed contribution, (5) if the partners' shares of partnership liabilities change and cause a deemed distribution of money by the partnership to a partner under section 752(b), then the basis of such a partner's interest will be reduced under section 733 (but not below zero) by the amount of the deemed distribution, and gain will be recognized by the partner under section 731 to the extent the deemed distribution exceeds the adjusted basis of the partner's interest in the partnership, and (6) under section 1223(*l* ), there will be no change in the holding period of any partner's total interest in the partnership.

The conversion of an interest in a domestic partnership into an interest in domestic LLC that is classified as a partnership for federal tax purposes is treated as a partnership-to-partnership conversion that is subject to the principles of Rev. Rul. 84–52.

Section 706(c)(1) provides that, except in the case of a termination of a partnership and except as provided in section 706(c)(2), the taxable year of a partnership does not close as the result of the death of a partner, the entry of a new partner, the liquidation of a partner's interest in the partnership, or the sale or exchange of a partner's interest in the partnership.

Section 706(c)(2)(A)(i) provides that the taxable year of a partnership closes with respect to a partner who sells or exchanges the partner's entire interest in a partnership. Section 706(c)(2)(A)(ii) provides that the taxable year of a partnership closes with respect to a partner whose interest is liquidated, except that the taxable year of a partnership with respect to a partner who dies does not close prior to the end of the partnership's taxable year. [Section 706(c)(2) has been amended with respect to a partner who dies. Ed.]

In the present case, the conversion of an interest in a domestic partnership into an interest in a domestic LLC that is classified as a partnership for federal tax purposes does not cause a termination under section 708. See Rev. Rul. 84–52. Moreover, because each partner in a converting domestic partnership continues to hold an interest in the resulting domestic LLC, the conversion is not a sale, exchange, or liquidation of the converting partner's entire partnership interest for purposes of section 706(c)(2)(A). See Rev. Rul. 86–101, 1986–2 C.B. 94 (the taxable year of a partnership does not close with respect to a general partner when the partnership agreement provides that the general partner's interest converts to a limited partnership interest on the general partner's death because the decedent's successor continues to hold an interest in the partnership). Consequently, the conversion does not cause the taxable year of the domestic partnership to close with respect to all the partners or with respect to any partner.

Because the conversion of an interest in a domestic partnership into an interest in a domestic LLC that is classified as a partnership for federal tax purposes does not cause a termination under section 708, the resulting domestic LLC does not need to obtain a new taxpayer identification number.

## HOLDINGS

(1) The federal income tax consequences described in Rev. Rul. 84–52 apply to the conversion of an interest in a domestic partnership into an interest in a domestic LLC that is classified as a partnership for federal tax purposes. The federal tax consequences are the same whether the resulting LLC is formed in the same state or in a different state than the converting domestic partnership.

(2) The taxable year of the converting domestic partnership does not close with respect to all the partners or with respect to any partner.

(3) The resulting domestic LLC does not need to obtain a new taxpayer identification number.

The holdings contained herein would apply in a similar manner if the conversion had been of an interest in a domestic LLC that is classified as a partnership for federal tax purposes into an interest in a domestic partnership. The holdings contained herein apply regardless of the manner in which the conversion is achieved under state law.

This revenue ruling does not address the federal tax consequences of a conversion of an organization that is classified as a corporation into an organization that is classified as a partnership for federal tax purposes. See, e.g., sections 336 and 337.

EFFECT ON OTHER REVENUE RULINGS

Rev. Rul. 84–52 and Rev. Rul. 86–101 are amplified.

NOTE

The Service has extended the principles of Revenue Ruling 95–37 to the conversion of a general partnership into a limited liability partnership. Revenue Ruling 95–55[1] holds that: (1) a New York general partnership registered as a New York limited liability partnership is a partnership for federal tax purposes, and (2) the registration does not terminate the partnership under Section 708(b).

PROBLEMS

**1**. The ABCD partnership has been operating for several years. Each partner has an equal interest in capital and profits. On January 1 of the current year, C sold his interest to E, and on July 1 of the current year, D sold her interest to F. At the time of both sales, the asset side of the partnership balance sheet was as follows:

| **Assets** | **A.B.** | **F.M.V.** |
|---|---|---|
| Cash | $ 4,000 | $ 4,000 |
| Accounts Receivable | 8,000 | 8,000 |
| Inventory | 8,000 | 12,000 |
| | $20,000 | $24,000 |

The partnership at no time had any liabilities and has never filed an election under § 754. At all relevant times, A and B each had a $4,000 basis for their respective partnership interests, and the bases of E and F, representing in each instance the price paid to C and D, respectively, were each $6,000.

Discuss the tax consequences to Partners A, B, E and F and the partnership. Reconstruct the ABEF partnership balance sheet after D's sale in the following alternative situations:

(a) Assume no elective basis adjustments.

(b) Assume a § 754 election had been made by the partnership.

(c) Assume no § 754 election had been made but E and F both invoked § 732(d).

---

**1.** 1995–2 C.B. 313.

(d) Does § 708(b)(1)(B) apply if, instead of selling her interest to F, D liquidates the interest for $6,000 cash, and F contributes $6,000 to the partnership for a ⅙ interest?

**2.** A, B, C, D and E have been equal 20% partners in the ABCDE partnership for several years. The partnership, which has made no § 754 election, owns many assets including some AT & T stock with a basis of $5,000 and a value of $25,000 which it has held for several years. B buys out A's 20% interest, and one week later in an operating distribution the partnership distributes 40% of the stock, worth $10,000, to B and 60% of it equally to C, D, and E. One month later B sells his share of the stock for $12,000, its then fair market value.

(a) What are the tax consequences to B on the sale if a § 754 election had not been in effect when B purchased A's interest and a § 732(d) election were not made by B?

(b) What result in (a), above, if either a § 754 or a § 732(d) election were in effect?

CHAPTER 9

# THE DEATH OF A PARTNER

## A. INTRODUCTION

When a partner dies, there is no repose for her partnership interest, which remains in the purgatory that we have come to know as Subchapter K. At a partner's death, her interest in the partnership can: survive and be acquired by her successor in interest; be sold pursuant to a buy-sell agreement taking effect at the partner's death; or be liquidated by the partnership under a preexisting agreement. There are different tax consequences applicable to each of these alternatives.[1]

This chapter examines the special tax problems that arise on the death of a partner, focusing on: (1) the treatment of the deceased partner's distributive share of partnership income or loss for the year of death; (2) the inclusion and valuation of the partnership interest in the decedent's gross estate for federal estate tax purposes and the collateral basis and income in respect of a decedent consequences to the decedent's successor in interest; and (3) the tax consequences of a sale or liquidation of the deceased partner's interest at her death.

## B. TREATMENT OF INCOME IN YEAR OF PARTNER'S DEATH

Code: §§ 706(c); 708(b).

In general, a partnership's taxable year does not close on the death of a partner.[1] As to the deceased partner, however, the partnership year closes at the date of the decedent's death under each of the three scenarios described above.[2] As a result, a partner's distributive share of income or loss for all or part of any partnership year is included on the decedent's final income tax return. In addition, a partner's distributive share of partnership income or loss from a partnership year ending prior to her death and within the decedent's final taxable year is included on the decedent's final return.[3] For example, assume Partner, a calendar-year taxpayer, has an interest in a partnership with a fiscal year ending April

---

**1.** It is possible that the successor in interest will enter into a sale or liquidation agreement *subsequent* to the decedent's death. In that event, the tax consequences of the first alternative will be governed by the general principles of Sections 741 and 751 (on a sale) or Section 736 (on a liquidation).

**1.** I.R.C. § 706(c)(1).

**2.** I.R.C. § 706(c)(2)(A).

**3.** I.R.C. § 706(a).

30. Partner dies on October 31 of year one. The distributive share of partnership income or loss for the fiscal year ending April 30 of year one must be included on Partner's final income tax return, which will cover the period from the beginning of the calendar year through the date of death. Partner's year also terminates on October 31 of year one, with the result that income for both years is bunched on Partner's final income tax return.[4]

The foregoing rules apply even if the decedent was a member of a two-person partnership, provided that her successor continues to share in the profits and losses of the firm.[5] Moreover, the partnership does not terminate under Section 708(b) even if the decedent was a 50 percent or more partner because a disposition by gift, bequest, or inheritance is not considered a "sale or exchange" for purposes of triggering a partnership termination.[6] But the partnership year does close with respect to the 50–percent-or-more deceased partner at the time of death if, as a result of a pre-existing buy-sell agreement, a sale of the deceased partner's entire interest occurs at the time of death.[7]

## C. ESTATE TAXATION OF PARTNERSHIP INTERESTS, TREATMENT OF "IRD" ITEMS AND BASIS CONSEQUENCES

Code: §§ 691(a)–(c); 753; 1014(a) & (c); 2033.

Regulations: §§ 1.742–1; 1.753–1(a).

*Inclusion in Gross Estate and Valuation.* The fair market value of a decedent's interest in a partnership, including the partner's distributive share of income earned prior to death, is included in the decedent's gross estate for federal estate tax purposes.[1] As with other closely held businesses, the valuation of a partnership interest is an inexact science. In theory, the fair market value is what a willing buyer would pay to a willing seller, neither being compelled to buy or sell and both having reasonable knowledge of the relevant facts.[2] More certainty can be achieved if the decedent enters into a bona fide, arm's length buy-sell or liquidation agreement that is binding both during the decedent's life and at death. In that event, the sale or liquidation price, which often is determined by a

---

**4.** Since all of the income is taxed on Partner's final income tax return, none of it constitutes income in respect of a decedent. See I.R.C. § 691 and Chapter 9B, infra.

**5.** Reg. § 1.708–1(b)(1)(i); Estate of Skaggs v. Commissioner, 75 T.C. 191 (1980). However, if the decedent's successor in interest does not continue to share in profits and losses, a two-person partnership is considered to terminate upon the death of one partner.

**6.** Reg. § 1.708–1(b)(2).

**7.** I.R.C. § 706(c)(2)(A); Reg. § 1.706–1(c)(3)(iv) & (vi) Example (2).

**1.** I.R.C. §§ 2031; 2033.

**2.** Reg. § 20.2031–3. The valuation may include discounts for a minority interest or for lack of marketability, or a premium for control. See Bogdanski, Federal Tax Valuation, Ch. 4 (Warren, Gorham & Lamont, 1996).

formula in the agreement, may determine the value of the partnership interest for estate tax purposes.[3]

Even a brief discussion of valuation of partnership interests for wealth transfer tax purposes would be incomplete without mentioning two fashionable estate planning vehicles, the family limited partnership ("FLP") and the family limited liability company ("FLLC").[4] Many legitimate nontax goals may motivate a family to form an FLP or FLLC to conduct an operating business or hold family investment assets such as real estate or securities. Centralized management, protection from the claims of creditors, and achieving economies of scale are among the well-accepted business purposes for these popular business or investment vehicles. Many FLPs and FLLCs, however, are created primarily, if not exclusively, to obtain substantial wealth transfer tax valuation discounts. These entities are typically structured to maximize discounts for minority interests and illiquidity, causing value to disappear from the transfer tax base. The Service has mounted challenges in the most egregious cases, with mixed success, and legislative proposals to curtail aggressive valuation strategies have not been embraced by Congress. Detailed consideration of the ongoing transfer tax policy debate over FLPs and FLLCs is well beyond the scope of this text, but it is worth noting that the proliferation of these business and investment entities will stimulate greater interest in some of the income tax issues discussed in this chapter.

*Income in Respect of a Decedent ("IRD").* Fundamental to a thorough understanding of the tax consequences of a partner's death is some familiarity with an income tax concept known as income in respect of a decedent ("IRD"). A brief explanation of IRD is included here for the uninitiated.[5]

In general, property owned at death is included in the decedent's gross estate and takes a "date-of-death" basis in the hands of the successor in interest equal to its fair market value on the date of the decedent's death.[6] The date-of-death basis rule creates special problems in connection with items that have been earned but not yet taxed as of the date of death. For example, assume that Attorney, a cash method taxpayer, dies holding a $3,000 receivable for services rendered. Attorney would not have been taxed on this amount during his life because he never received cash or its equivalent. If the basis of the receivable were stepped-up to its $3,000 date-of-death value, the decedent's successor in interest would realize no income on its subsequent sale or collection. Compare the treatment of Physician, an accrual method taxpayer, who dies holding a similar $3,000 claim for

**3.** See I.R.C. § 2703 (especially § 2703(b)); Reg. § 20.2031–2(h); Reg. § 25.2703–1(b)(3); Stephens, Maxfield, Lind & Calfee, Federal Estate and Gift Taxation ¶ 19.04 (8th ed. 2002).

**4.** See generally Henkel, Estate Planning and Wealth Preservation ch. 16 (1997).

**5.** For a more detailed discussion, see Freeland, Lathrope, Lind and Stephens, Fundamentals of Federal Income Taxation, Chapter 24E (13th ed. 2004).

**6.** At least until the new carryover basis regime of Section 1022 goes into effect in 2010, the basis of property acquired from a decedent is its fair market value on the date of death or the Section 2032 alternate valuation date. I.R.C. §§ 1014; 2033. Cf. I.R.C. §§ 2032, 2032A.

services rendered. Since the right to receive the amount was fixed, Physician would have included the $3,000 in income prior to her death. Thus, the "ripe" income of a cash method decedent would be exempt from the income tax while similar items held by an accrual method taxpayer would be taxed. A cash *or* accrual method decedent reporting a deferred payment transaction under Section 453 would enjoy a similar advantage over a decedent who elected out of installment sale reporting under Section 453(d).

To correct these inequities, Congress devised the present "neutralization" approach under which several sections of the Code combine to require the decedent's successor in interest eventually both to report the amount and to retain the character of income which previously escaped tax in the hands of the decedent. First, Section 451(a) provides that amounts included in income on the decedent's final return are determined by his regular accounting method. Consequently, a cash method taxpayer who dies holding a $3,000 account receivable for services would not include the $3,000 on his final income tax return.[7] To preserve the income for later recognition by the decedent's successor in interest, Section 1014(c) denies a date-of-death basis to IRD items and instead requires the successor to take a transferred basis—zero in the case of a cash method decedent's receivables. Finally, Section 691(a)(1) provides that the IRD item will be taxable when it is actually received or collected by the decedent's estate or distributees,[8] and Section 691(a)(3) completes the picture by characterizing the IRD items to the recipient in the same manner as if they had been received by the decedent. Applying these provisions to the example above, the decedent's successor in interest would realize $3,000 of ordinary income on collection of the receivables.

The IRD concept is more involved than this brief introduction suggests, but the additional nuances are not essential for an understanding of this chapter.[9] It is sufficient to recall that IRD typically includes income items that already have been earned by, but not yet taxed to, the decedent prior to death, such as cash method receivables and Section 453 obligations. On the other hand, mere asset appreciation, including the built-in recapture income, generally is not subject to the IRD regime.

*Outside Basis Consequences.* In general, the basis of a partnership interest in the hands of the successor is the fair market value of the interest as of the date of death, increased by the successor's share of

---

**7.** Under Section 443(a)(2), the taxable year of a deceased taxpayer closes as of the date of death. The decedent's final return covers the period from the beginning of the taxable year through the date of death.

**8.** But see I.R.C. § 691(a)(2), which treats the transfer of a right to receive an IRD item by the successor in interest as an event triggering immediate recognition of income. Compare I.R.C. § 453B, which triggers

similar recognition of gain on the disposition of an installment obligation.

**9.** For example, Section 691(b) passes through certain deductions of the decedent related to the IRD items which were not deductible on the decedent's final return, and Section 691(c) allows the recipient of an IRD item to take an income tax deduction for the federal estate tax attributable to the item.

partnership liabilities and decreased by any IRD items.[10] The relationship of the IRD concept to the decedent's interest in partnership assets is somewhat more complex. The consequences vary, depending on whether the partnership interest continues in the hands of the decedent's successor, is sold, or is liquidated.

*Treatment of IRD Items.* If the decedent's interest is liquidated pursuant to an agreement effective as of the date of death, Section 753 provides that amounts classified under Section 736(a) are considered IRD under Section 691.[11] The role of Section 753 is limited to characterizing Section 736(a) payments received by a deceased partner's successor in interest as IRD. It does not apply if the partner's interest continues in the hands of a successor or is sold pursuant to a pre-existing buy-sell agreement. In both those situations, however, the decedent may have an interest in the partnership's zero basis accounts receivables. These receivables would constitute IRD if the decedent held them directly, and there is no logical reason for treating them otherwise if they are held by a partnership. To the consternation of strict constructionists of the Code,[12] the Service has contended that Section 753 is not the exclusive means of classifying the decedent's interest in partnership assets as IRD. Applying an aggregate theory, the courts have concurred with the Service, in effect creating an additional category of IRD that is not specifically contemplated by Section 753. The *Quick's Trust* and *Woodhall* cases, below, adopted this approach with respect to a continuation of a partnership interest and a sale situation, respectively. This judicially created category of IRD should be extended to other types of partnership assets[13] and to zero basis accounts receivable of a liquidated partnership interest that are within Section 736(b).[14]

*Property Contributed by the Decedent with a Built–In Loss.* If the deceased partner had contributed property to the partnership with a built-in loss (i.e., the property's basis exceeded its fair market value at the time of contribution), Section 704(c)(1)(C) provides that (1) the built-in loss can only be allocated to the contributing partner and (2) the property's basis is deemed to be its fair market value at the time of contribution for purposes

---

**10.** Reg. § 1.742–1. See I.R.C. § 1014(c).

**11.** Reg. § 1.753–1(a). Recall that Section 736(a) payments are payments to a general partner in a services partnership for appreciation on the partner's share of unrealized receivables and unstated goodwill as well as any premium payments to any liquidated partner of either a services or capital partnership. See Chapter 8B, supra. Also keep in mind that Section 753 should apply only to Section 736(a) payments made pursuant to a liquidation agreement in effect at the decedent partner's death and not to payments negotiated by the executor or beneficiary after the date of death. See McKee, Nelson &

Whitmire, Federal Taxation of Partnerships and Partners ¶ 23.03[2][a] (3d ed. 1996). But see Rev.Rul. 66–325, below, which suggests that a post-death liquidation agreement also is subject to Section 753.

**12.** See, e.g., Willis, Little & McDonald, "Problems on Death, Retirement, or Withdrawal of a Partner," 17 N.Y.U. Inst. on Fed. Tax'n 1033, 1042 (1959).

**13.** For example, a partnership Section 453 installment sales obligation should be treated as an IRD item. See McKee, Nelson & Whitmire, Federal Taxation of Partnerships and Partners ¶ 23.03[2][c] (3d ed. 1996).

**14.** See I.R.C. § 736(b)(2) and (3).

of making allocations to other partners. Thus, the built-in loss is eliminated when the partnership interest passes from the decedent.

*Inside Basis Consequences.* The death of a partner also may have an impact on the inside bases of partnership assets. Since the decedent's successor in interest takes a date-of-death outside basis (except for IRD items), the successor's outside basis may not be the same as his share of the inside basis. To correct the imbalance, Sections 743(b) and 732(d) are potentially applicable to allow an adjustment to the inside bases of partnership assets if there is a Section 754 election in effect or if a liquidation occurs within two years of the decedent's death and the successor in interest makes a Section 732(d) election.[15] The question whether a portion of the adjustment may be allocated to IRD items is considered in Revenue Ruling 66–325, which follows the cases below. Additionally, Section 743 will require a downward adjustment to the inside basis of partnership assets if the partnership has a substantial built-in loss (i.e., the adjusted basis of its assets exceeds the fair market value of those assets by more than $250,000) immediately after the transfer of the decedent's partnership interest.[16]

## Quick's Trust v. Commissioner

United States Tax Court, 1970.
54 T.C. 1336, affirmed per curiam, 444 F.2d 90 (8th Cir.1971).

■ TANNENWALD, JUDGE:

* * *

## OPINION

When Quick died he was an equal partner in a partnership which had been in the business of providing architectural and engineering services. In 1957, the partnership had ceased all business activity except the collection of outstanding accounts receivable. These receivables, and some cash, were the only assets of the partnership. Since partnership income was reported on the cash basis, the receivables had a zero basis.

Upon Quick's death in 1960, the estate became a partner with Maguolo and remained a partner until 1965 when it was succeeded as a partner by petitioner herein. The outstanding accounts receivable were substantial in amount at that time. In its 1960 return, the partnership elected under section 754 to make the adjustment in the basis of the partnership property provided for in section 743(b) and to allocate that adjustment in accordance with section 755. On the facts of this case, the net result of this adjustment was to increase the basis of the accounts receivable to the partnership from zero to an amount slightly less than one-half of their face value. If such treatment was correct, it substantially reduced the amount of the taxable

---

**15.** An adjustment under Section 732(d) applies only for purposes of distributions and not for purposes of gain or loss on a disposition. See Reg. § 1.732–1(d)(1)(vi) Example.

**16.** I.R.C. § 743(a), (d).

income to the partnership from the collection of the accounts receivable under section 743(b) and the estate and the petitioner herein were entitled to the benefit of that reduction.

The issue before us is whether the foregoing adjustment to basis was correctly made. Its resolution depends upon the determination of the basis to the estate of its interest in the partnership, since section 743(b)(1) allows only an "increase [in] the adjusted basis of the partnership property by the excess of *the basis to the transferee partner of his interest in the partnership* over his proportionate share of the adjusted basis of the partnership property." (Emphasis added.) This in turn depends upon whether, to the extent that "the basis to the transferee partner" reflects an interest in underlying accounts receivable arising out of personal services of the deceased partner, such interest constitutes income in respect of a decedent under section 691(a)(1) and (3). In such event, section 1014(c) comes into play and prohibits equating the basis of Quick's partnership interest with the fair market value of that interest at the time of his death under section 1014(a).

Petitioner argues that the partnership provisions of the Internal Revenue Code of 1954 adopted the entity theory of partnership, that the plain meaning of those provisions, insofar as they relate to the question of basis, requires the conclusion that the inherited partnership interest is separate and distinct from the underlying assets of the partnership, and that, therefore, section 691, and consequently section 1014(c), has no application herein.

Respondent counters with the assertion that the basis of a partnership interest is determined under section 742 by reference to other sections of the Code. He claims that, by virtue of section 1014(c), section 1014(a) does not apply to property which is classified as a right to receive income in respect of a decedent under section 691 and that the interest of the estate and of petitioner in the proceeds of the accounts receivable of the partnership falls within this classification. He emphasizes that, since the accounts receivable represent money earned by the performance of personal services, the collections thereon would have been taxable to the decedent, if the partnership had been on the accrual basis, or to the estate and to petitioner if the decedent had been a cash basis sole proprietor. Similarly, he points out that if the business had been conducted by a corporation, the collections on the accounts receivable would have been fully taxable, regardless of Quick's death. Respondent concludes that no different result should occur simply because a cash basis partnership is interposed.

The share of a general partner's successor in interest upon his death in the collections by a partnership on accounts receivable arising out of the rendition of personal services constituted income in respect of a decedent under the 1939 Code. United States v. Ellis, 264 F.2d 325 (C.A.2, 1959); Riegelman's Estate v. Commissioner, 253 F.2d 315 (C.A.2, 1958), affirming 27 T.C. 833 (1957). Petitioner ignores these decisions, apparently on the ground that the enactment of comprehensive provisions dealing with the taxation of partnerships in the 1954 Code and what it asserts is "the plain

meaning" of those provisions render such decisions inapplicable in the instant case. We disagree.

The partnership provisions of the 1954 Code are comprehensive in the sense that they are detailed. But this does not mean that they are exclusive, especially where those provisions themselves recognize the interplay with other provisions of the Code. Section 742 specifies: "The basis of an interest in a partnership acquired other than by contribution shall be determined under part II of subchapter O (sec. 1011 and following)." With the exception of section 722, which deals with the basis of a contributing partner's interest and which has no applicability herein, this is the only section directed toward the question of the initial determination of the basis of a partnership interest. From the specification of section 742, one is thus led directly to section 1014 and by subsection (c) thereof directly to section 691. Since, insofar as this case is concerned, section 691 incorporates the provisions and legal underpinning of its predecessor (sec. 126 of the 1939 Code), we are directed back to a recognition, under the 1954 Code, of the decisional effect of *United States v. Ellis,* supra, and *Riegelman's Estate v. Commissioner,* supra.

Thus, to the extent that a "plain meaning" can be distilled from the partnership provisions of the 1954 Code, we think that it is contrary to petitioner's position.[11] In point of fact, however, we hesitate to rest our decision in an area such as is involved herein exclusively on such linguistic clarity and purity. See David A. Foxman, 41 T.C. 535, 551 fn. 9 (1964), affd. 352 F.2d 466 (C.A.3, 1965). However, an examination of the legislative purpose reinforces our reading of the statute. Section 751, dealing with unrealized receivables and inventory items, is included in subpart D of subchapter K, and is labeled "Provisions Common to Other Subparts." Both the House and Senate committee reports specifically state that income rights relating to unrealized receivables or fees are regarded "as severable from the partnership interest and as subject to the same tax consequences which would be accorded an individual entrepreneur." See H. Rept. No. 1337, 83d Cong., 2d Sess., p. 71 (1954); S. Rept. No. 1622, 83d Cong., 2d Sess., p. 99 (1954). And the Senate committee report adds the following significant language.

> *The House bill provides that a decedent partner's share of unrealized receivables are* [sic] *to be treated as income in respect of a decedent.* Such rights to income are to be taxed to the estate or heirs when collected, with an appropriate adjustment for estate taxes. * * * *Your committee's bill agrees substantially with the House in the treatment described above* but also provides that other income apart from unrealized receivables is to be treated as income in respect of a decedent. [See S. Rept. No. 1622, supra at 99; emphasis added.]

---

**11.** We note that petitioner's position has been the subject of extensive legal analysis and that it has some support among the legal pundits. See Willis, Handbook of Part- nership Taxation, 389–395 (1957); Ferguson, "Income and Deductions in Respect of Decedents and Related Problems," 25 Tax L.Rev. 5, 100 et seq.

In light of the foregoing, the deletion of a provision in section 743 of the House bill which specifically provided that the optional adjustment to basis of partnership property should not be made with respect to unrealized receivables is of little, if any, significance. H.R. 8300, 83d Cong., 2d Sess., sec. 743(e) (1954) (introduced print). The fact that such deletion was made without comment either in the Senate or Conference Committee reports indicates that the problem was covered by other sections and that such a provision was therefore unnecessary. Similarly, the specific reference in section 753 to income in respect of a decedent cannot be given an exclusive characterization. That section merely states that certain distributions in liquidation under section 736(a) shall be treated as income in respect of a decedent. It does not state that no other amounts can be so treated.

Many of the assertions of the parties have dealt with the superstructure of the partnership provisions—assertions based upon a technical and involuted analysis of those provisions dealing with various adjustments and the treatment to be accorded to distributions after the basis of the partnership has been determined. But, as we have previously indicated * * *, the question herein involves the foundation, not the superstructure, i.e., what is the basis of petitioner's partnership interest?

Petitioner asserts that a partnership interest is an "asset separate and apart from the individual assets of the partnership" and that the character of the accounts receivable disappears into the character of the partnership interest, with the result that such interest cannot, in whole or in part, represent a right to receive income in respect of a decedent. In making such an argument, petitioner has erroneously transmuted the so-called partnership "entity" approach into a rule of law which allegedly precludes fragmentation of a partnership interest. But it is clear that even the "entity" approach should not be inexorably applied under all circumstances. See H. Rept. No. 2543, 83d Cong., 2d Sess., p. 59 (1954). Similarly, the fact that a rule of nonfragmentation of a partnership interest (except to the extent that the statute otherwise expressly provides) may govern sales of such an interest to third parties (cf. Donald L. Evans, 54 T.C. 40 (1970)) does not compel its application in all situations where such an interest is transferred. In short, a partnership interest is not, as petitioner suggests, a unitary res, incapable of further analysis.

A partnership interest is a property interest, and an intangible one at that. A property interest can often be appropriately viewed as a bundle of rights. Indeed, petitioner suggests this viewpoint by pointing out that the partnership interest herein is "merely a right to share in the profits and surplus of the Partnership." That partnership interest had value only insofar as it represented a right to receive the cash or other property of the partnership. Viewed as a bundle of rights, a major constituent element of that interest was the right to share in the proceeds of the accounts receivable as they were collected. This right was admittedly not the same as the right to collect the accounts receivable; only the partnership had the latter right. But it does not follow from this dichotomy that the right of the estate to share in the collections merged into the partnership interest.

Nothing in the statute compels such a merger. Indeed, an analysis of the applicable statutory provisions points to the opposite conclusion.

Accordingly, we hold that section 691(a)(1) and (3) applies and that the right to share in the collections from the accounts receivable must be considered a right to receive income in respect of a decedent. Consequently, section 1014(c) also applies and the basis of the partnership interest must be reduced from the fair market value thereof at Quick's death. The measure of that reduction under section 1014 is the extent to which that value includes the fair market value of a one-half interest in the proceeds of the zero basis partnership accounts receivable. See sec. 1.742–1, Income Tax Regs. It follows that the optional adjustment to basis made by the partnership under section 743(b) must be modified accordingly and that respondent's determination as to the amount of additional income subject to the tax should be sustained.[14] See Rev.Rul. 66–325, 1966–2 C.B. 249.

Petitioner would have us equate the absence of statutory language specifically dealing with the problem herein and purported inferences from tangential provisions with an intention on the part of Congress entirely to relieve from taxation an item that had previously been held subject to tax. We would normally be reluctant to find that Congress indirectly legislated so eccentrically. See separate opinion in Henry McK. Haserot, 46 T.C. 864, 877 (1966), affirmed sub nom. Commissioner v. Stickney, 399 F.2d 828 (C.A.6, 1968). In any event, as we have previously indicated, we think the enacted provisions prevent us from so doing herein.

* * *

## Woodhall v. Commissioner

United States Court of Appeals, Ninth Circuit, 1972.
454 F.2d 226.

■ Choy, Circuit Judge.

W. Lyle Woodhall died on January 20, 1964, leaving Mrs. Woodhall as his sole heir and executrix. For 1964, Mrs. Woodhall filed a joint income tax return as surviving spouse. She also filed a fiduciary income tax return for the estate for part of 1964. For 1965, she filed an individual tax return and a fiduciary return.

The Commissioner of Internal Revenue determined deficiencies against Mrs. Woodhall for the years 1964 and 1965. The ground was that she had not declared as income certain amounts which came to her from the sale of her husband's interest in a partnership. Mrs. Woodhall petitioned the Tax Court for a declaration that she did not owe the deficiencies. The Tax Court upheld the Commissioner's determination and Mrs. Woodhall appeals. We affirm.

---

**14.** We reached a similar result in Chrissie H. Woodhall, T.C.Memo. 1969–279; that case involved a sale of the partnership interest by the decedent's successor in interest.

From January 1958 until his death, Woodhall was equal partner with his brother, Eldon Woodhall, in a lath and plaster contracting business known as Woodhall Brothers.

In December 1961, the brothers executed a written buy-sell agreement, which provided that "upon the death of either partner the partnership shall terminate and the survivor shall purchase the decedent's interest in the partnership." The price was to be determined according to a formula set out in the agreement. The formula defined accounts payable and included certain valuations for fixed assets, inventory, accounts receivable and other assets. It is the accounts receivable item that generates this controversy over Mrs. Woodhall's income for 1964 and 1965.

Because the partnership reported income on a cash basis, Woodhall had not paid taxes on his share of the accounts receivable which were outstanding at the time of his death. Mrs. Woodhall, in filing her tax returns as an individual and as executrix of her husband's estate, did not report as income the amounts allocated to the accounts receivable. Instead Mrs. Woodhall's tax returns stated that no gain had been realized by the sale of her husband's partnership interest because the tax basis of the interest was the fair market value at the time of death and this was the same as the sale price.

The issue presented is whether portions of payments received by Mrs. Woodhall, as executrix of the estate and as surviving spouse, constitute income in respect of a decedent under § 691(a)(1) of the Internal Revenue Code and are therefore subject to income taxes to the extent that such portions are allocable to unrealized receivables.

Generally, the sale of a partnership interest is an occasion for determining the character of gain or loss "to the transferor partner" as provided by § 741. In the case at bar, however, there was technically no "transferor partner" to accomplish the sale. The Woodhall Brothers partnership terminated automatically upon the death of Woodhall by operation of the buy-sell agreement, as well as under common law. Mrs. Woodhall, as executrix of the estate and as holder of a community property interest, was the transferor.

A tax regulation [Reg. § 1.741–1(b). Ed.] recognizes that § 741 applies when the sale of the partnership interest results in a termination of the partnership. The question arises whether a termination of the partnership by operation of a written agreement of the parties upon the death of one partner has the same effect.

The legislative history of § 741 explicitly deals with this question. The House report reads as follows:

"Transfer of an interest in a partnership (§§ 741–743, 751)

(1) General rules.—Under present decisions the sale of a partnership interest is generally considered to be a sale of a capital asset, and any gain or loss realized is treated as capital gain or loss. It is not clear whether the sale of an interest whose value is attribut-

able to uncollected rights to income gives rise to capital gain or ordinary income * * *.

\* \* \*

(2) Unrealized receivables or fees * * * In order to prevent the conversion of potential ordinary income into capital gain by virtue of transfers of partnership interests, certain rules have been adopted * * * which will apply to *all* dispositions of partnership interests.

\* \* \*

A decedent partner's share of unrealized receivables and fees will be treated as income in respect of a decedent. Such rights to income will be taxed to the estate or heirs when collected * * *.

\* \* \*

The term "unrealized receivables or fees' is used to apply to any rights to income which have not been included in gross income under the method of accounting employed by the partnership. The provision is applicable mainly to cash basis partnerships which have acquired a contractual or other legal right to income for goods or services." House Report No. 1337, to accompany H.R. 8300 (Pub.L. 591), 83rd Cong., 2d Sess., pp. 70–71 (1954) (emphasis added); U.S.Code Cong. & Admin.News, p. 4096.

The Senate report is similar, with only technical amendments which do not alter the basic statement of purpose in the House report. Senate Report No. 1622, to accompany H.R. 8300 (Pub.L. 591), 83rd Cong., 2d Sess., p. 396 (1954).

Mrs. Woodhall's approach to the issue was much different. On the sale of her husband's partnership interest, she attempted to elect to establish the tax basis as the fair market value on the date of her husband's death. By this means, the sale price would be the same as the fair market value; there would be no gain and so no income to be taxed.

Mrs. Woodhall contends that the payments she received for the accounts receivable do not come within § 691(a), pertaining to income in respect of a decedent. Section 691(f) [now (e), Ed.] she points out, makes cross-reference to § 753, for application of § 691 to income in respect of a deceased partner. Section 753, in turn, refers to § 736 which provides that payments by a partnership for a deceased partner's interest in unrealized receivables shall be considered income in respect of a decedent under § 691. Mrs. Woodhall argues that a payment by a surviving partner is distinct from a payment by a partnership. Thus, she would have us interpret § 753, in conjunction with § 736, exclusively. In effect, this means that no payment other than one by a partnership which continues after one partner's death could constitute income in respect of a deceased partner. We reject this reading of the statutes.

The approach suggested by Mrs. Woodhall is not an appropriate characterization of the transfer of funds to her. Reading § 691 in the light of § 741, it is clear that Congress intended that the money Mrs. Woodhall received as an allocation from the unrealized accounts receivable be treated as income in respect of a decedent.

The Court of Appeals for the Eighth Circuit has just recently ruled that accounts receivable of a partnership shared in by a successor in interest of a deceased partner constituted income in respect of a decedent. Quick's Trust v. Commissioner of Internal Revenue, 444 F.2d 90 (8th Cir.1971.) The instant case is substantially the same.

We hold that the Commissioner rightly determined deficiencies against Mrs. Woodhall in the tax years 1964 and 1965.

* * *

## Revenue Ruling 66–325

1966–2 Cum. Bull. 249.

Advice has been requested whether, in the circumstances described below, sections 754 and 743 of the Internal Revenue Code of 1954 may be applied so as to give the estate of a deceased member of a personal service partnership the benefit of an adjustment to the basis of the partnership's accounts receivable existing at the date of the decedent's death.

The decedent was a member of a two-man partnership engaged in the practice of medicine. The partnership reported its income on the cash basis method of accounting. At the time of the decedent's death, the firm had a substantial amount of accounts receivable, a small bank account and in addition, furniture and fixtures having only a nominal value. The partnership was continued in existence for well over a year after the decedent's death for the purpose of collecting its accounts receivable, paying its debts, and liquidating the interests of the two partners.

Under the terms of the liquidation agreement executed by the surviving partner and the estate of the deceased partner, after the payment of the firm's debts, the surviving partner was to receive a specified amount in cash and the estate was to receive the remaining proceeds of the partnership bank account and collections on the accounts receivable, together with the partnership furniture and fixtures.

The partnership filed a timely election under section 754 of the Code in respect to optional adjustment to basis of partnership property provided by section 743 of the Code.

Under the circumstances involved, the partnership is considered as having continued in existence during the liquidation period until the winding up of its affairs was completed. (See sections 1.708–1(b)(1)(i)(a) and 1.708–1(b)(1)(iii)(a) of the Income Tax Regulations.) Furthermore, since under the terms of the liquidation agreement payments were made to the deceased partner's estate in liquidation of the decedent's partnership

interest, section 736 of the Code is applicable. Section 1.736–1(a)(6) of the regulations states that if a partner in a two-man partnership dies, and his estate or other successor in interest receives payments under section 736 of the Code the partnership shall not be considered to have terminated upon the death of the partner but shall terminate as to both partners only when the entire interest of the decedent is liquidated.

Since the payments to the decedent's estate which were attributable to the collection of the firm's accounts receivable were determined with reference to the income of the partnership, such payments must be considered as a distributive share to the recipient of partnership income within the scope of section 736(a) of the Code. Section 753 of the Code provides that the amount includible in the gross income of a successor in interest of a deceased partner under section 736(a) of the Code shall be considered income in respect of a decedent under section 691 of the Code.

The payments to the decedent's estate which were attributable to the collection of the firm's accounts receivable must be considered distributive share payments within the scope of section 736(a) of the Code, and hence income in respect of a decedent under section 753 of the Code. Consequently the value of the estate's right to receive them had to be excluded from its basis for the partnership interest acquired from the decedent, by reason of section 1.742–1 of the regulations. (Also see section 1014(c) of the Code.)

Accordingly, where the collection of accounts receivable represents income in respect of a decedent, the provisions of section 743 of the Code may not be applied so as to give the estate of a deceased member of a personal service partnership the benefit of an adjustment to the basis of the partnership's accounts receivable existing at the date of the decedent's death.

## PROBLEM

D is a one-third general partner in the DEF partnership. Both D and the partnership are cash method, calendar year taxpayers. D dies at a time when the partnership has earned $15,000 for the current year, and his share of the untaxed and undistributed partnership income for the year is $5,000. Under all of the sale or liquidation agreements described below, D is to be paid $30,000 for his interest, which includes his share of income. Immediately prior to D's death, the DEF partnership has the following balance sheet:

| Assets | A.B. | F.M.V. | Partners' Capital | A.B. | F.M.V. |
|---|---|---|---|---|---|
| Cash | $ 9,000 | $ 9,000 | D | $3,000 | $30,000 |
| Cash (not yet in D, E, and F's income) | 15,000 | 15,000 | E | 3,000 | 30,000 |
| Receivables for services | 0 | 45,000 | F | 3,000 | 30,000 |
| Depreciable § 1245 property | 0 | 3,000 | | | |
| Goodwill | 0 | 18,000 | | | |
| | $24,000 | $90,000 | | $9,000* | $90,000 |

\* The $9,000 basis does not include the $15,000 not previously taken into income.

Assume, alternatively, that D's interest: (1) passes to his estate; (2) is subject to a buy-out agreement at his death; (3) is liquidated by the partnership (which is a services partnership); or (4) is liquidated by the partnership in which capital is a material income-producing factor. Under each alternative, consider the following questions:

(a)  Does the partnership's taxable year close as to D's estate?

(b)  What is the amount included in D's gross estate?

(c)  To what extent does the interest included in D's gross estate constitute income in respect of a decedent?

(d)  What outside basis does D's estate take in the partnership interest immediately following D's death?

## D.   Consequences of a Sale or Liquidation of a Deceased Partner's Interest at Death

Code: Review §§ 691(a), 736 and other sections dealing with liquidations; 741, 751 and other sections dealing with sales; 1014(c).

Regulations: §§ 1.736–1(b)(3).

The preceding sections of this chapter involved the special problems raised by the death of a partner. This section adds nothing new but provides you with an opportunity to review much of the material covered in Chapters 6 through 8, to combine it with the concept of IRD, and to put it all together in solving the problems below. The problems disregard any consideration of income earned by the partnership at the death of the decedent's death by assuming that the date of death is immediately after the end of the partnership year.

PROBLEMS

In each of the problems below, the ABC partnership has three equal partners, A, B, and C and the following balance sheet:

| Assets | A.B. | F.M.V. | Partners' Capital | A.B. | F.M.V. |
|---|---|---|---|---|---|
| Cash | $60,000 | $ 60,000 | A | $30,000 | $ 45,000 |
| Receivables | 0 | 15,000 | B | 30,000 | 45,000 |
| Inventory | 15,000 | 30,000 | C | 30,000 | 45,000 |
| Goodwill | 15,000 | 30,000 | | | |
| | $90,000 | $135,000 | | $90,000 | $135,000 |

**1.** Partner A dies on the first day of the current year and under a buy-sell agreement his executor sells his interest to D for $45,000. What result to A's estate if:

    (a)  the partnership has made a § 754 election?

    (b)  the partnership has made no § 754 election?

    (c)  the partnership has made no § 754 election but the executor elects under § 732(d)?

**2.** Partner A dies on the first day of the current year and, in an agreement arranged prior to his death, Services Partnership liquidates A's general partnership interest for $45,000 of cash. What result to A's estate if:

    (a)  there is a specific provision in the agreement that $10,000 is for A's interest in the goodwill and either a § 754 or a § 732(d) election is in effect?

    (b)  same as (a), above, but neither a § 754 nor a § 732(d) election is in effect?

    (c)  the agreement is silent as to goodwill but either a § 754 or a § 732(d) election is in effect?

    (d)  the agreement is silent as to goodwill and neither a § 754 nor a § 732(d) election is in effect?

    (e)  the agreement is silent as to goodwill and neither a § 754 nor a § 732(d) election is in effect and the partnership is one in which capital is a material income-producing factor?

**3.** Prepare the partnership's balance sheet after the liquidation in Problem 2(a), above. See Reg. § 1.734–2(b)(1).

# CHAPTER 10

# THE PARTNERSHIP ANTI–ABUSE REGULATIONS

## A. INTRODUCTION

Subchapter K was designed to permit businesses organized for joint profit to be conducted with "simplicity, flexibility, and equity as between the partners."[1] Some creative tax advisors have exploited this flexible statutory regime by concocting abusive transactions to reduce the taxes of their clients. To combat this practice, the Treasury promulgated a controversial set of anti-abuse regulations[2] that are the subject of this culminating chapter.

The partnership anti-abuse regulations contain two distinct rules. The first permits the Service to recast an abusive transaction for federal tax purposes as appropriate to achieve tax results that are consistent with the intent of Subchapter K.[3] The second rule allows the Service to disregard the partnership entity and treat a partnership as an aggregate of its partners (in whole or in part) as appropriate to carry out the purpose of any provision of the Code or regulations.[4] In addition to these "global" anti-abuse regulations, the Service has begun to incorporate specific anti-abuse rules in regulations interpreting specific sections of the Code.[5]

The partnership anti-abuse regulations reflect several familiar "common law" principles that have long pervaded the tax law, such as the business purpose, substance over form, sham transaction, and step transaction doctrines. The regulations do not purport to be exclusive, however, and these doctrines and other statutory and regulatory authorities still may apply independently to challenge a transaction.[6]

When the partnership anti-abuse regulations first surfaced on the horizon in proposed form, their unknown breadth and application struck fear in the hearts and minds of tax practitioners.[7] The Service attempted to

---

**1.** S.Rep. No. 1622, 83d Cong., 2d Sess. 89 (1954); H.R. Rep. No. 1337, 83d Cong., 2d Sess. (1954) (cited in Preamble to proposed partnership anti-abuse regulations).

**2.** Reg. § 1.701–2.

**3.** Reg. §§ 1.701–2(a)–(c).

**4.** Reg. § 1.701–2(e).

**5.** See, e.g., Reg. § 1.704–4(f); § 1.737–4.

**6.** Reg. § 1.701–2(i); see Reg. § 1.701–2(d) Example 11.

**7.** See Gouwar, "The Proposed Partnership Anti–Abuse Regulation: Treasury Oversteps its Authority," 11 J. Partnership Tax'n 287 (1994); Lipton, "Controversial Partnership Anti–Abuse Prop. Reg. Raise Many Questions," 81 J.Tax'n 68 (1994).

allay these concerns by announcing:[8]

> The anti-abuse rule in the final regulation is expected primarily to affect a relatively small number of partnership transactions that make inappropriate use of the rules of Subchapter K. The regulation is not intended to interfere with bona fide joint business arrangements conducted through partnerships.

In a further narrowing of the scope of their application, the regulations state that they apply solely with respect to income taxes, and not to any wealth transfer or excise tax consequences.[9]

## B.   ABUSIVE USE OF SUBCHAPTER K

Regulations: § 1.701–2(a)–(c).

The regulations begin on a reassuringly positive note by stating that the intent of Subchapter K is to permit taxpayers to conduct joint business or investment activities through a flexible economic arrangement without incurring entity level tax.[10] They then state that implicit in the intent of Subchapter K are the following requirements:[11]

(1) The partnership must be bona fide and each partnership transaction or series of related transactions must be entered into for a substantial business purpose;

(2) The form of each partnership transaction must be respected under the doctrine of substance over form; and

(3) The tax consequences under Subchapter K to each partner of partnership operations and partner-partnership transactions must accurately reflect the partners' economic agreement and clearly reflect the partners' income.

The regulations add a caveat to the third requirement. If a transaction passes muster under the business purpose and substance over form doctrines, the clear reflection of income requirement does not need to be met if a provision of Subchapter K or its regulations clearly contemplates a lack of clear reflection of income in order to promote administrative convenience or other policy objectives.[12] For example, the regulations provide that the failure by a bona fide partnership to make a Section 754 election satisfies the test even though the effect is that the partnership retains a higher basis in its assets than if a Section 754 election had been made. Even though there is not a proper reflection of income because the election is not made, that result is contemplated by Subchapter K so the transaction is treated as satisfying the proper reflection of income standard.[13] This rule

---

**8.** T.D. 8588, 60 Fed. Reg. 23 (Jan. 3, 1995), promulgating Reg. § 1.701–2.

**9.** Reg. § 1.701–2(h).

**10.** Reg. § 1.701–2(a).

**11.** Reg. §§ 1.701–2(a)(1)–(3).

**12.** Reg. § 1.701–2(a)(3).

**13.** Reg. § 1.701–2(d) Example (9); see also Reg. § 1.701–2(d) Example (6) (the value-equals-basis presumption of Reg. § 1.704–1(b)(2)(iii)(C) satisfies this test).

has been tempered by legislative changes made since the anti-abuse regulations were issued. Sections 734 and 743 now require downward adjustments to be made to the basis of a partnership's assets when the failure to do so would provide the partners with significant timing advantages through the use of partnership losses.[14]

The regulations go on to provide that if a partnership is formed or availed of in connection with a transaction a principal purpose of which is to substantially[15] reduce the present value of the partners' aggregate federal tax liability in a manner that is inconsistent with the intent of Subchapter K, the Commissioner can recast the transaction for federal tax purposes to achieve tax results that are consistent with the intent of Subchapter K.[16] Since tax savings are often a principal motivation for the use partnerships, the centerpiece of the anti-abuse rule presumably is whether a transaction is "inconsistent with the intent of Subchapter K"— i.e., whether the three requirements set forth above are satisfied.[17]

*Facts and Circumstances Analysis.* To assist in determining whether the Subchapter K anti-abuse rule applies, the regulations employ a facts and circumstances analysis that considers a series of factors, including a comparison of the purported business purpose for a transaction with the claimed resulting tax benefits.[18] The list of factors in the regulations is not exclusive and the weight given any factor depends upon the facts and circumstances.[19] The presence or absence of a factor does not create a presumption that the partnership was (or was not) used in an abusive manner.[20] The specific factors include:[21]

(1) The present value of the partners' federal income tax liability is substantially less than had the partners owned the partnership assets directly;

(2) The present value of the partners' federal income tax liability is substantially less than it would be if purported separate transactions are integrated and treated as steps in a single transaction;

(3) There are partners who have a nominal interest or who are substantially protected from any risk of loss;

(4) The partners are related;

(5) There are Section 704(b) allocations that are inconsistent with the purpose of Section 704(b);

(6) The ownership of property nominally contributed to the partnership is effectively retained by the contributing partner; or

---

**14.** See I.R.C. §§ 734(a), (d); 743(a), (d).

**15.** This requirement in effect creates a de minimis exception where the tax reduction is not significant. T.D. 8588, supra note 8.

**16.** Reg. § 1.701–2(b).

**17.** See Reg. §§ 1.701–2(a)(1)–(3).

**18.** Reg. § 1.701–2(c).

**19.** Id.

**20.** Id.

**21.** Reg. §§ 1.701–2(c)(1)–(7).

(7) The benefits and burdens of ownership of partnership property are effectively shifted to a distributee partner other than at the time of distribution.

*Examples.* Assistance in interpreting the Subchapter K anti-abuse rule is provided in a series of examples that illustrate circumstances in which the rule will or will not be applied. A summary of the most basic examples is instructive as to the scope of the regulations. In the context of a choice of entity decision, for example, the anti-abuse rules will not be applied in the following situations: a limited partnership is organized with a 1% corporate general partner and a 99% individual limited partner to obtain limited liability and pass-through tax treatment;[22] an S corporation and a nonresident alien, who would not be an eligible S corporation shareholder, form a partnership to conduct their bona fide business without losing pass-through tax treatment because of the nonresident alien's participation in the venture;[23] and a partnership rather than a corporation is used to avoid recognition of gain under Sections 351(e) and 357(c) on a contribution of encumbered real estate.[24] In each of these situations, the use of the partnership form is consistent with Subchapter K's intent "to permit taxpayers to conduct joint business activity through a flexible economic arrangement without incurring an entity-level tax."[25]

In the operational setting, the examples indicate that there is no abuse when a bona fide partnership makes a valid Section 704(b) special allocation of a floating rate of return to one partner;[26] uses a Section 704(b) special allocations of real estate depreciation deductions and credits to partners to whom there would be an immediate tax benefit and away from a partner who could not immediately use them;[27] or fails to make a Section 754 election, resulting in a higher basis in property retained in a partnership after a liquidating distribution to a partner.[28]

The anti-abuse rules are violated in the following situations: a transitory partner involved in a series of transactions where the purported business purpose is insignificant compared to the tax benefits;[29] and creation of a double loss with respect to contributed loss property where the partnership fails to make a Section 754 election.[30]

*Commissioner's Authority.* If the Subchapter K anti-abuse rule is violated, the Commissioner may recast the transaction in a manner that achieves results consistent with the intent of Subchapter K.[31] This includes disregarding the partnership in whole or in part by treating the partnership assets as held directly by the partners; disregarding one or more partners—treating them as non-partners; changing accounting methods to

---

**22.** Reg. § 1.701–2(d) Example 1.

**23.** Reg. § 1.701–2(d) Example 2. See I.R.C. § 1361(b).

**24.** Reg. § 1.701–2(d) Example 4.

**25.** Reg. § 1.701–2(a).

**26.** Reg. § 1.701–2(d) Example 5.

**27.** Reg. § 1.701–2(d) Example 6.

**28.** Reg. § 1.701–2(d) Example 9. However, Section 734 would now require that a downward basis adjustment be made if there is a substantial basis reduction. § 734(a), (d).

**29.** Reg. § 1.701–2(d) Example 7.

**30.** Reg. § 1.701–2(d) Example 8.

**31.** Reg. § 1.701–2(b).

clearly reflect income; or reallocating partnership income, gain, loss, deductions, or credits.[32] In the abusive examples provided by the regulations, the Treasury does not specifically state how the transactions are to be recast.[33]

## PROBLEM

A (a C corporation), and B and C, both individuals, are partners in a limited partnership. A is the general partner and B and C are limited partners owning 10%, 45%, and 45% interests in the partnership, respectively. The balance sheet is as follows:

| Assets | A.B. | F.M.V. | Partners' Capital | A.B. | F.M.V. |
|---|---|---|---|---|---|
| Cash | $10,000 | $ 10,000 | A | $ 5,000 | $ 10,000 |
| Depreciable real estate (no § 1250 gain) | 32,000 | 45,000 | B | 22,500 | 45,000 |
| Cap. Asset #1 | 8,000 | 45,000 | C | 22,500 | 45,000 |
| | $50,000 | $100,000 | | $50,000 | $100,000 |

The partnership, which has not made a § 754 election, distributes Capital Asset #1 to C in liquidation of her interest.

(a) What are the tax consequences to the parties?

(b) Do the anti-abuse regulations apply to the transaction? See Reg. § 1.701–2(d) Examples 1, 8 and 9; see also § 734(a) & (d).

## C. ABUSIVE TREATMENT OF A PARTNERSHIP AS AN ENTITY

Regulations: §§ 1.701–2(e), (h), & (i).

The second anti-abuse rule allows the Commissioner to treat a partnership as a mere aggregate of its partners in whole or in part when the use of the partnership vehicle under Subchapter K is designed to frustrate any Code provision or regulation.[1] This rule is aimed primarily at use of the partnership entity to frustrate other parts of the income tax Code in transactions involving partnerships.[2] No showing of the intent of the parties is necessary in applying this rule.[3] To illustrate, assume two corporations form a partnership to issue high yield discount obligations on which the interest is currently deductible by the partnership, but would not be currently deductible by the corporations.[4] An example in the regulations applies the abuse-of-entity-treatment rule in this situation to disregard the

**32.** Id.

**33.** But see Reg. § 1.701–2(d) Examples 7 and 8, which suggest that disregard of a partner seems to be the appropriate remedy.

**1.** Reg. § 1.701–2(e)(1). The rule is effective for all transactions involving a partnership that occur on or after December 29, 1994. Reg. § 1.701–2(g).

**2.** T.D. 8588, 60 Fed. Reg. 23 (Jan. 3, 1995), promulgating Reg. § 1.701–2.

**3.** Id.

**4.** See I.R.C. § 163(e)(5).

partnership entity and disallow a current interest deduction.[5] In a second example, a corporate partnership is set aside because the corporate partners are attempting to avoid a stock basis reduction rule under Section 1059(a).[6] The regulations, however, provide an exception to the partnership entity rule if (1) a Code provision or regulation prescribes the treatment of a partnership as an entity in whole or in part; and (2) that treatment and the ultimate tax results taking into account all relevant facts and circumstances, are clearly contemplated by that provision.[7]

5.  Reg. § 1.701–2(f) Example 1.
6.  Reg. § 1.701–2(f) Example 2.
7.  Reg.  § 1.701–2(e)(2).  See  Reg. § 1.701–2(f) Example 3 applying the exception to a situation involving Section 904(d)(3), which involves the operation of the foreign tax credit in the case of a controlled foreign corporation.

\*

# Taxation of Other Pass-Through Entities

CHAPTER 11   S Corporations and Their Shareholders

CHAPTER 11

# S CORPORATIONS AND THEIR SHAREHOLDERS*

## A. INTRODUCTION

We have seen that partnerships and limited liability companies are treated for tax purposes as conduits whose income and deductions pass through to their partners or members as they are realized, with various items retaining their tax character in the process.[1] Because income is taxed at the partner level, partnership distributions of cash and property generally do not produce any tax liability.[2] A "C" corporation, on the other hand, has a tax existence separate and apart from its shareholders and is subject to tax on its net income at rates ranging from 15 to 35 percent.[3] Because dividends generally are taxable to the shareholders but not deductible by the corporation, earnings withdrawn from a corporate enterprise are taxed at both the corporate and shareholder levels before finally coming to rest in the shareholders' pockets.[4] Although many techniques have been devised to avoid the double tax, it nonetheless remains the principal feature distinguishing the taxation of incorporated and unincorporated businesses.

It is not surprising that taxpayers have sought to obtain the state law benefits of the corporate form (limited liability, centralized management, etc.) without the sting of the double tax. Congress attempted to accommodate this desire in 1958 when it enacted Subchapter S, which then permitted the shareholders of a "small business corporation" to elect to avoid a corporate level tax in most situations. The stated purpose of Subchapter S was to permit a business to select its legal form "without the necessity of taking into account major differences in tax consequence."[5]

As originally adopted, Subchapter S was a modified corporate scheme of taxation rather than a partnership-like pass-through regime. This early version was a strange hybrid of corporate and partnership concepts, laden with complexity. In these formative years, an electing small business necessarily depended on skilled lawyers and accountants to avoid Subchapter S's many technical traps. Calls for reform began with a 1969 Treasury

---

* See generally Eustice and Kuntz, Federal Income Taxation of Subchapter S Corporations (4th ed. 2001).

**1.** I.R.C. § 702(a), (b).

**2.** I.R.C. § 731(a).

**3.** I.R.C. § 11. See generally Lind, Schwarz, Lathrope & Rosenberg, Fundamentals of Corporate Taxation (6th ed. 2005).

**4.** I.R.C. §§ 61(a)(7); 301.

**5.** S.Rep. No. 1983, 85th Cong., 2d Sess. § 68 (1958), reprinted in 1958–3 C.B. 922.

Department study, which in general proposed a liberalization of the eligibility requirements and the adoption of a conduit approach more closely conforming to the tax treatment of partnerships.[6] Congress gradually relaxed the eligibility requirements through piecemeal legislation, most notably the Subchapter S Revision Act of 1982.[7] The 1982 Act greatly reduced the tax disparities between S corporations and partnerships by replacing the modified corporate structure of Subchapter S with a statutory scheme which is similar but not identical to the tax treatment of partnerships and partners under Subchapter K. The Act also introduced the terminology now used in the Code. Electing small business corporations are called "S corporations" while other corporations are known as "C corporations."[8]

Subsequent legislation, culminating with the American Jobs Creation Act of 2004, further liberalized the Subchapter S eligibility requirements and eliminated technical traps for corporations seeking to elect and maintain S corporation status. As a result of these reforms, the tax differences between partnerships and S corporations have narrowed, making operation as an S corporation a viable, albeit less flexible, alternative for some closely held businesses. But significant differences in tax treatment remain between S corporations and unincorporated businesses. For example, Subchapter S status is available only for corporations that satisfy the statutory definition of "small business corporation" in Section 1361(b). This definition restricts eligibility to corporations with 100 or fewer shareholders; prohibits more than one class of stock; and limits the types of permissible shareholders. Moreover, partners' bases in their partnership interests are increased by their share of partnership liabilities,[9] while debts incurred by an S corporation have no effect on the bases of the corporation's shareholders in their stock. This difference may have an impact upon the ability of investors to utilize losses generated by the enterprise and the treatment of distributions.[10] Subchapter K also offers partners more flexibility in determining their individual tax results from partnership operations. Partnership allocations of specific items of income or deduction to a particular partner will be respected as long as the allocation has substantial economic effect, while shareholders of an S corporation are required to report a pro rata share of each corporate item.[11]

For a brief time, the inverted rate structure introduced by the Tax Reform Act of 1986 expanded the role of S corporations by reducing the top individual rate below the maximum rate for C corporations and broadening the corporate tax base. As a result, many closely held businesses requiring the corporate form and able to meet the eligibility requirements chose to

---

**6.** See U.S. Treasury Department, Technical Explanation of Treasury Tax Reform Proposals: Hearings Before the House Comm. on Ways and Means, 91st Cong., 1st Sess. 5228–5275 (April 22, 1969).

**7.** Pub.L. No. 97–354 (1982), reprinted in 1982–2 C.B. 702.

**8.** I.R.C. § 1361(a).

**9.** I.R.C. § 752(a).

**10.** See also I.R.C. § 469, limiting the current deductibility of losses from certain passive activities.

**11.** Compare I.R.C. § 704(b)(2) with I.R.C. §§ 1366(a) & 1377(a).

operate as S corporations. The current maximum individual rate on ordinary income now equals the top corporate rate. More importantly, the emergence of the limited liability company, with its far greater flexibility, and the Service's willingness to allow any unincorporated business entity to elect partnership status for tax purposes, have profoundly influenced the choice of entity decision.[12] At least for newly formed businesses, many predicted that these developments would threaten to send S corporations to the sidelines, despite the more liberal eligibility requirements introduced by Congress. Many existing S corporations remain on the scene, however, and the S corporation tax regime and governance structure are relatively simple and familiar. In fact, S corporations became the most common corporate entity type in 1997 and, for taxable year 2001, 58.2 percent of all corporations filing tax returns were S corporations.[13] Thus, S corporations continue to be an important option for investors and a study of the fundamentals of Subchapter S continues to be essential for a comprehensive understanding of business enterprise taxation. It also is instructive to compare the provisions of Subchapters S and K and to consider which of these pass-through taxation models is preferable from a policy standpoint.[14]

## B. ELIGIBILITY FOR S CORPORATION STATUS

Code: § 1361.

Eligibility to make a Subchapter S election is limited to a "small business corporation," defined in Section 1361(b) as a domestic corporation[1] which is not an "ineligible corporation" and which has: (1) no more than 100 shareholders, (2) only shareholders who are individuals, estates, and certain types of trusts and tax-exempt organizations, (3) no nonresident alien shareholders, and (4) not more than one class of stock. The 100–shareholder limit disqualifies publicly traded corporations from S status, and the one-class-of-stock rule shuts the door to corporations with complex capital structures. Significantly, however, a "small business corporation" need not be small when measured by income or value as a going concern, and some very large enterprises operate as S corporations.

Some remaining aspects of the S corporation eligibility requirements are summarized below.

*Ineligible Corporations and Subsidiaries.* An "ineligible corporation" may not qualify as a "small business corporation."[2] Certain types of corporations, such as banks and insurance companies, are "ineligible" because they are governed by other specialized tax regimes.[3] At one time,

---

**12.** See Chapter 1C, supra.

**13.** Bennett, "S Corporation Returns, 2001, 23 SOI Bulletin 47 (2004)."

**14.** See Section H of this chapter, infra.

**1.** I.R.C. § 1361(b)(1). A domestic corporation is defined as a corporation created or organized in the United States or under the laws of the United States or of any state or territory. Reg. §§ 1.1361–1(c); 301.7701–5.

**2.** I.R.C. § 1361(b)(1).

**3.** I.R.C. § 1361(b)(2).

any corporation that was a member of an "affiliated group" also was ineligible to be an S corporation—a rule that effectively precluded S corporations from owning 80 percent or more of the stock of another C or S corporation.[4] Under current law, S corporations may hold subsidiaries under certain conditions. C corporation subsidiaries generally are permitted,[5] and parent-subsidiary relationships between two S corporations also are allowed if the parent elects to treat its offspring as a "qualified subchapter S subsidiary" ("QSSS"), which generally is defined as a 100 percent owned domestic corporation that is not an "ineligible corporation" and otherwise would qualify for S status if all of its stock were held by the shareholders of its parent.[6] If this QSSS election is made, the subsidiary is disregarded for tax purposes, and all of its assets, liabilities, income, deductions, and credits are treated as belonging to its S parent.[7] The regulations provide detailed procedures to govern revocation and other terminations of a QSSS election. In general, they treat a terminating event as a deemed incorporation of a new subsidiary that is governed by general tax principles.[8]

*Number of Shareholders.* Congress has made S corporations more widely available by gradually increasing the number of permissible shareholders. The current 100–shareholder limit[9] is nearly triple an earlier 35–shareholder cap. For purposes of this limit, a husband and wife (and their estates) are counted as one shareholder regardless of their form of ownership.[10] If stock is jointly owned (e.g., as tenants in common or joint tenants) by other than a husband and wife, each joint owner is considered a separate shareholder.[11] In the case of a nominee, guardian, custodian, or agent holding stock in a representative capacity, the beneficial owners of the stock are counted toward the 100–shareholder limit.[12]

In addition to the special rule for a husband and wife, all the members of a "family" may elect to be treated as a single shareholder for purposes of the 100–shareholder limit.[13] A family is defined as the lineal descendants (and their spouses and former spouses) of a common ancestor who is no more than six generations removed from the youngest generation shareholder at the time the election is made.[14] The election to be treated as one

---

**4.** I.R.C. § 1361(b)(2)(A)(pre–1997).

**5.** I.R.C. § 1504(b)(8). The S parent, however, may not join in a consolidated return with the C corporation.

**6.** I.R.C. § 1361(b)(3)(B). For election procedures, see Reg. § 1.1361–3(a).

**7.** I.R.C. § 1361(b)(3)(A). See Reg. § 1.1361–4(a)(1). If a subsidiary was in existence and had a prior tax history, the QSSS election triggers a deemed liquidation of the subsidiary under Sections 332 and 337 as of the day before the election is effective. Reg. § 1.1361–4(a).

**8.** See Reg. § 1.1361–5(b).

**9.** I.R.C. § 1361(b)(1)(A).

**10.** I.R.C. § 1361(c)(1)(A)(i); Reg. § 1.1361–1(e)(2).

**11.** I.R.C. § 1.1361–1(e)(2).

**12.** Reg. § 1.1361–1(e)(1).

**13.** I.R.C. § 1361(c)(1)(A)(ii). If a husband and wife are part of an electing family they are counted as part of that family. I.R.C. § 1361(c)(1)(A)(i).

**14.** I.R.C. § 1361(c)(1)(B). Adopted children and foster children are treated as children by blood. I.R.C. § 1361(c)(1)(C) (mistakenly citing I.R.C. § 152(b)(2).). A spouse is considered to be of the same generation as the individual to whom the spouse is married. I.R.C. § 1361(c)(1)(B)(ii).

shareholder may be made by any member of the family and remains in effect until terminated as provided in regulations that will be issued by the Service.[15]

*Eligible Shareholders.* Congress also has gradually expanded the eligible S corporation shareholder pool. Once limited to individuals who were U.S. citizens or resident aliens, the permissible shareholder list now also includes decedent's and bankruptcy estates,[16] certain types of trusts discussed in more detail below,[17] qualified pension trusts, and charitable organizations that are exempt from tax under Section 501(c)(3).[18] A corporation still may not make an S election if any of its shareholders are C corporations, partnerships, ineligible trusts, or nonresident aliens.[19]

When Subchapter S was first enacted, trusts were not eligible shareholders, primarily because of Congress's desire for a relatively simple one-tier corporate tax regime where all beneficial owners were clearly identifiable. In response to the pleas of tax advisors to closely held businesses, Congress gradually relented by permitting various widely used types of trusts to be S corporation shareholders if certain conditions are met. Under current law, the trusts that are permissible shareholders include:

(1) Voting trusts, in which case each beneficial owner is treated as a separate shareholder;[20]

(2) Grantor trusts—i.e., domestic trusts treated for tax purposes as owned by their grantor—provided the grantor is an individual who is a U.S. citizen or resident.[21] An example would be the commonly used revocable living trust created to provide for continuity of asset management in the event of the grantor's disability and to avoid probate administration on death. For purposes of the 100–shareholder limit, the deemed owner of the trust is treated as the shareholder.[22]

(3) Former grantor trusts that continue as testamentary trusts, but only for the two-year period following the grantor's death.[23] The former deemed owner's estate is treated as the S corporation shareholder.[24]

(4) Testamentary trusts that receive S corporation stock under the terms of a will, but again only for the two-year period after the

---

**15.** I.R.C. § 1361(c)(1)(1). Regulations may also change the rule that the election may be made by one family member.

**16.** I.R.C. §§ 1361(b)(1)(B), (c)(3).

**17.** See infra text accompanying notes 20–35.

**18.** I.R.C. §§ 1361(b)(1)(B), (c)(6). The trade-off for tax-exempt pension trusts and Section 501(c)(3) organizations is that their interest in the S corporation is treated as an interest in an "unrelated trade or business," and any net income is generally taxable at the trust or corporate rates. I.R.C. § 512(e)(1).

**19.** I.R.C. § 1361(b)(1)(B).

**20.** I.R.C. § 1361(c)(2)(A)(iv), (B)(iv).

**21.** I.R.C. § 1361(c)(2)(A)(i). Foreign grantor trusts are not eligible shareholders. I.R.C. § 1361(c)(2)(A), flush language.

**22.** I.R.C. § 1361(c)(2)(B)(i).

**23.** I.R.C. § 1361(c)(2)(A)(ii).

**24.** I.R.C. § 1361(c)(2)(B)(ii).

date of transfer of the stock to the trust.[25] The testator's estate continues to be treated as the S corporation shareholder.[26]

(5) Qualified Subchapter S trusts ("QSSTs"), defined generally as trusts all of the income of which is actually distributed or must be distributed currently to one individual who is a U.S. citizen or resident.[27] A QSST may only have one current income beneficiary, who must elect QSST status and, as a result, is treated as the owner for tax purposes of the portion of the trust consisting of the S corporation stock with respect to which the election was made.[28] Among other things, the QSST definition permits a Qualified Terminable Interest Property ("QTIP") Trust,[29] the most widely used type of estate tax marital deduction trust created for the benefit of a surviving spouse, to hold S corporation stock.

(6) Electing small business trusts ("ESBTs"), a statutory creation that potentially expands the usefulness of S corporations in estate planning for a family business. All the beneficiaries of an ESBT must be individuals or estates who are eligible S corporation shareholders, or charitable organizations holding contingent remainder interests.[30] The beneficial interests in an ESBT must have been acquired by gift or bequest, not purchase,[31] and the trust must elect ESBT status to qualify as an S corporation shareholder.[32] Each potential current beneficiary of the trust is treated as a shareholder for purposes of the 100–shareholder limit,[33] but the trust's pro rata share of S corporation income is taxable to the trust at the highest individual marginal rates under rules specially designed for this purpose.[34] The significance of the ESBT category is that it permits inter vivos and testamentary trusts with more than one beneficiary—e.g., a "sprinkling" trust where the trustee has discretion to determine whether and how much income or corpus to distribute among several beneficiaries—to qualify as an S corporation shareholder.

The legislative history of the rule treating a family as one shareholder for the 100–shareholder limit explains that the rule applies to family members who own stock directly as well as those who are shareholders because they are beneficiaries of a QSST or ESTB.[35]

**25.** I.R.C. § 1361(c)(2)(A)(iii).

**26.** I.R.C. § 1361(c)(2)(B)(iii).

**27.** I.R.C. § 1361(d).

**28.** Id.

**29.** See I.R.C. § 2056(b)(7).

**30.** I.R.C. § 1361(e)(1)(A)(i). Charitable remainder trusts, however, may not be S corporation shareholders. I.R.C. § 1361(e)(1)(B)(iii). See also Rev. Rul. 92–48, 1992–1 C.B. 301.

**31.** I.R.C. § 1361(e)(1)(A)(ii).

**32.** I.R.C. § 1361(e)(1)(A)(iii). Trusts that already have made a QSST election or are wholly exempt from tax do not qualify as ESBTs. I.R.C. § 1361(e)(1)(B).

**33.** I.R.C. § 1361(c)(2)(B)(v). If there are no potential current income beneficiaries, then the trust is treated as the shareholder for that period. Id.

**34.** I.R.C. § 641(d).

**35.** H.Rep. No. 108–755, 108th Cong., 2d Sess. 34 (2004).

*One-Class-of-Stock Requirement.* An S corporation may issue both stock and debt, but it may not have more than one class of stock.[36] The purpose of this rule is to simplify the allocation of income and deductions among an S corporation's shareholders and prevent "special allocations" and their potential for income shifting. The one-class-of-stock requirement has spawned many controversies over its history, but the issuance of final regulations has resolved the most contentious issues.

An S corporation generally is treated as having one class of stock if all of its outstanding shares confer identical rights to distributions and liquidation proceeds.[37] Significantly, differences in voting rights among classes of common stock are disregarded, permitting an S corporation to issue both voting and nonvoting common stock.[38] In determining whether outstanding stock confers identical rights to distribution and liquidation proceeds, the regulations look to the corporate charter, articles of incorporation, bylaws, applicable state law, and binding shareholders' agreements.[39]

Commercial contractual arrangements, such as leases, employment agreements, or loan agreements, are disregarded in determining whether a second class of stock is present unless a principal purpose of the agreement is to circumvent the one class of stock requirement.[40] For example, differences in salary or fringe benefits paid to employee-shareholders under compensation agreements will not result in a second class of stock if the agreements are not designed to circumvent the requirement.[41] Bona fide agreements to redeem or purchase stock at the time of death, divorce, disability or termination of employment also are disregarded in determining whether an S corporation has a second class of stock.[42] Other shareholder buy-sell, stock transfer and redemption agreements are disregarded in determining whether a corporation's outstanding shares confer identical distribution and liquidation rights unless: (1) a principal purpose of the agreement is to circumvent the one-class-of-stock requirement, and (2) the purchase price under the agreement is significantly in excess of or below the fair market value of the stock. Agreements that provide for a purchase or redemption of stock at book value or at a price between book value and fair market value satisfy the purchase price standard.[43]

---

**36.**  I.R.C. § 1361(b)(1)(D).

**37.**  Reg. § 1.1361–1(*l*)(1). "Outstanding stock" generally does not include stock that is subject to a substantial risk of forfeiture under Section 83 unless the holder has made the Section 83(b) election. Reg. § 1.1361–1(*l*)(3).

**38.**  I.R.C. § 1361(c)(4); Reg. § 1.1361–1(*l*)(1).

**39.**  Reg. § 1.1361–1(*l*)(2)(i).

**40.**  Reg. § 1.1361–1(*l*)(2)(i).

**41.**  Reg. § 1.1361–1(*l*)(2)(v) Examples (3) & (4). Any distributions (actual, constructive or deemed) that differ in timing or amount are given appropriate tax treatment.

For example, even though an employment agreement does not result in a second class of stock, excessive compensation paid under the agreement is not deductible. Reg. § 1.1361–1(*l*)(2)(i), (v) Example (3).

**42.**  Reg. § 1.1361–1(*l*)(2)(iii)(B).

**43.**  Reg. § 1.1361–1(*l*)(2)(iii)(A). A good faith determination of fair market value is respected unless it is substantially in error and was not determined with reasonable diligence. Id. A determination of book value is respected if it is determined in accordance with generally accepted accounting principles or used for any substantial nontax purpose. Reg. § 1.1361–1(*l*)(2)(iii)(C).

Unless the straight debt safe harbor applies,[44] any instrument, obligation or arrangement issued by a corporation (other than outstanding stock) is treated as a second class of stock if: (1) it constitutes equity under general tax principles, and (2) a principal purpose of issuing or entering into the instrument, obligation or arrangement is to circumvent the distribution and liquidation rights of outstanding shares or the limitation on eligible shareholders.[45] Safe harbors from reclassification are provided for short-term unwritten advances to the corporation that do not exceed $10,000 and obligations held proportionately among the shareholders.[46] The existence of various corporate instruments that give holders the right to acquire stock (e.g., call options or warrants) also may create a second class of stock depending upon whether the right is substantially certain to be exercised by the holder.[47]

*Straight Debt Safe Harbor.* The interaction of the one-class-of-stock limitation with the debt vs. equity classification issues encountered under Subchapter C[48] historically presented some knotty problems for S corporations with outstanding debt. In the formative years of Subchapter S, the Service adopted a practice of reclassifying nominal S corporation debt owed to shareholders as a second class of stock, causing the corporation to lose its S status.[49] This threat has diminished considerably by a safe harbor provision in Section 1361(c)(5) under which "straight debt" is not treated as a disqualifying second class of stock. "Straight debt" is defined as any written unconditional promise to pay on demand or on a specified date a sum certain in money if: (1) the interest rate and payment dates are not contingent on profits, the borrower's discretion or similar factors; (2) the instrument is not convertible (directly or indirectly) into stock; and (3) the creditor is an individual (other than a nonresident alien), an estate or trust that would be a qualifying shareholder in an S corporation, or a person that is actively and regularly engaged in the business of lending money.[50] The fact that an obligation is subordinated to other debt of the corporation does not prevent it from qualifying as straight debt.[51]

Obligations that qualify as straight debt are not classified as a second class of stock even if they would be considered equity under general tax principles and they generally are treated as debt for other purposes of the Code.[52] Thus, interest paid or accrued on straight debt is treated as such by the corporation and the recipient and does not constitute a distribution

---

**44.**  See I.R.C. § 1361(c)(5) and notes 48–55, infra, and accompanying text.

**45.**  Reg. § 1.1361–1(*l*)(4)(ii)(A).

**46.**  Reg. § 1.1361–1(*l*)(4)(ii)(B).

**47.**  Reg. § 1.1361–1(*l*)(4)(iii). Exceptions are provided for certain call options in connection with loans or to employees and independent contractors. If the strike price of a call option is at least 90 percent of its fair market value at its issuance, it is not substantially certain to be exercised. Reg. § 1.1361–1(*l*)(4)(iii)(B)–(C).

**48.**  See generally I.R.C. § 385.

**49.**  The courts, however, usually were not receptive to this argument. See, e.g., Portage Plastics Co. v. United States, 486 F.2d 632 (7th Cir.1973).

**50.**  I.R.C. § 1361(c)(5)(B).

**51.**  Reg. § 1.1361–1(*l*)(5)(ii).

**52.**  I.R.C. § 1361(c)(5)(A);  Reg. § 1.1361–1(*l*)(5)(iv).

governed by Section 1368.[53] But if a straight debt instrument bears an unreasonably high rate of interest, the regulations provide than an "appropriate" portion may be recharacterized and treated as a payment that is not interest.[54] If a C corporation has outstanding debt obligations that satisfy the straight debt definition but may be classified as equity under general tax principles, the safe harbor ensures that the obligation will not be treated as a second class of stock if the C corporation elects to convert to S status. The conversion and change of status also is not treated as an exchange of the debt instrument for stock.[55]

## PROBLEM

Unless otherwise indicated, Z Corporation ("Z") is a domestic corporation which has 120 shares of voting common stock outstanding. In each of the following alternative situations, determine whether Z is eligible to elect S corporation status:

(a) Z has 99 unrelated individual shareholders, each of whom owns one share of Z stock. The remaining 21 shares are owned by A and his brother, B, as joint tenants with right of survivorship.

(b) Same as (a), above, except that A and B are married and own 11 of the 21 shares as community property. The remaining 10 shares are owned 5 by A as her separate property and 5 by B as his separate property.

(c) In (b), above, assume that the shareholders of Z elected S corporation status. What will be the effect on Z's election if one year later A dies and bequeaths her interest in Z stock to F, her long-time friend?

(d) Same as (a), above, except that the remaining 21 shares are held by a voting trust which has three beneficial owners.

(e) Same as (a), above, except that the remaining 21 shares are owned by a revocable living trust created by an individual, the income of which is taxed to the grantor under § 671.

(f) Same as (a), above, except that the remaining 21 shares are owned by a testamentary trust under which the surviving spouse has the right to income for her life, with the remainder passing to her children. The trust is a "qualified terminable interest trust" (see § 2056(b)(7)).

(g) Assume Z has 100 individual shareholders and forms a partnership with two other S corporations, each of which also have 100 individual shareholders, for the purposes of jointly operating a business. Z's one-third interest in this partnership is its only asset.

---

**53.** Id.

**54.** Id. Such a reclassification does not result in a second class of stock.

**55.** Reg. § 1.1361–1(*l*)(5)(v).

(h) Z has 100 shares of Class A voting common stock and 50 shares of Class B nonvoting common stock outstanding. Apart from the differences in voting rights, the two classes of common stock have equal rights with regard to dividends and liquidation distributions. Z also has an authorized but unissued class of nonvoting stock which would be limited and preferred as to dividends. The Class A common stock is owned by four individuals and the Class B common stock is owned by E and F (a married couple) as tenants-in-common.

(i) Same as (h), above, except that Z enters into a binding agreement with its shareholders to make larger annual distributions to shareholders who bear heavier state income tax burdens. The amount of the distributions is based on a formula that will give the shareholders equal after-tax distributions.

(j) Z has four individual shareholders each of whom own 100 shares of Z common stock for which each paid $10 per share. Each shareholder also owns $25,000 of 15–year Z bonds. The bonds bear interest at 3% above the prime lending rate established by the Chase Manhattan Bank, adjusted quarterly, and are subordinated to general creditors of Z.

## C.   ELECTION, REVOCATION AND TERMINATION

Code: §§ 1362 (omit (e)(5)–(6)); 1378. Skim §§ 444(a), (b), (c)(1), (e); 7519(a), (b), (d)(1), (e)(4).

*Electing S Corporation Status.* An otherwise eligible corporation may elect S corporation status under Section 1362 if all the shareholders consent.[1] Once made, an election remains effective until it is terminated under Section 1362(d).[2] An election is effective as of the beginning of a taxable year if it is made either during the preceding taxable year or on or before the fifteenth day of the third month of the current taxable year.[3] If the election is made during the first 2½ months of the year, the S corporation eligibility requirements must have been met for the portion of the taxable year prior to the election, and all shareholders at any time during the pre-election portion of the year must consent to the election.[4] If the eligibility requirements are not met during the pre-election period or if

---

**1.** I.R.C. § 1362(a). For rules and procedures on shareholders' consent to an S election, see Reg. § 1.1362–6.

**2.** I.R.C. § 1362(c). See generally Reg. § 1.1362–2.

**3.** I.R.C. § 1362(b)(1). Elections made not later than 2 months and 15 days after the first day of the taxable year are deemed made during the year even if the year is shorter than 2 months and 15 days. I.R.C.

§ 1362(b)(4). For rules on how to count months and days for this purpose, see Reg. § 1.1362–6(a)(2)(ii). For the Service's authority to treat a late election as timely if there was reasonable cause for the tardiness, see I.R.C. § 1362(b)(5). See Rev. Proc. 2004–48, 2004–2 C.B. 272, for the procedures to obtain relief for a late election.

**4.** I.R.C. § 1362(b)(2).

any shareholder who held stock during that period does not consent, the election does not become effective until the following taxable year.[5] In some cases, however, such as where an election is technically invalid because of the corporation's inadvertence or failure to obtain all the requisite shareholder consents on time, the Service may grant dispensation and waive the defect if there is reasonable cause.[6]

*Revocation of Election.* An S corporation election may be revoked if shareholders holding more than one-half of the corporation's shares (including nonvoting shares) consent to the revocation.[7] The revocation may specify a prospective effective date.[8] If a prospective effective date is not specified, a revocation made on or before the fifteenth day of the third month of the taxable year is effective on the first day of the taxable year and a revocation made after that date is effective on the first day of the following taxable year.[9]

*Termination of Election.* Apart from revocation, an S corporation election may be terminated if the corporation ceases to satisfy the definition of a small business corporation or, in certain circumstances, if the corporation earns an excessive amount of passive investment income.[10] The first ground for termination is easily illustrated. Terminating events include: (1) exceeding 100 shareholders; (2) issuance of a second class of stock; or (3) transfer of stock to an ineligible shareholder. In all those cases, the corporation will cease to be a small business corporation and its S corporation election will terminate on the day after the disqualifying event.[11] To prevent or cure transfers that may jeopardize a corporation's S corporation status, the shareholders will be well advised at the outset to enter into an agreement restricting stock transfers.

The limitation on passive investment income is more complex. Under Section 1362(d)(3), an election to be an S corporation will terminate if for three consecutive taxable years the corporation's "passive investment income" exceeds 25 percent of its gross receipts and the corporation has Subchapter C earnings and profits.[12] A termination triggered by excess passive investment income is effective beginning on the first day of the taxable year following the three year testing period.[13] It is important to note that the Subchapter C earnings and profits requirement has the effect

---

**5.** I.R.C. § 1362(b)(2)(B).

**6.** I.R.C. § 1362(f). An ineffective election to treat (1) a subsidiary as a qualified subchapter S subsidiary or (2) a family as one shareholder may also be salvaged under Section 1362(f).

**7.** I.R.C. § 1362(d)(1)(B). See Reg. § 1.1362–2(a).

**8.** I.R.C. § 1362(d)(1)(D).

**9.** I.R.C. § 1362(d)(1)(C). If the revocation is effective on a day other than the first day of a taxable year (e.g., because a prospective date is selected in the middle of the year), the taxable year will be an "S termi-

nation year," and the corporation will be taxed pursuant to rules in Section 1362(e). See Reg. § 1.1362–3 and infra text accompanying notes 19–21.

**10.** I.R.C. § 1362(d)(2), (3).

**11.** I.R.C. §§ 1361(b)(1)(A)–(D); 1362(d)(2)(B).

**12.** See Reg. § 1.1362–2(c). Prior years in which the corporation was not an S corporation are not considered for purposes of the passive investment income component of this test. I.R.C. § 1362(c)(3)(A)(iii)(II).

**13.** I.R.C. § 1362(c)(3)(A)(ii).

of rendering this limitation inapplicable to a corporation that has always been an S corporation or which has been purged of its earnings and profits.[14] Passive investment income generally is defined as gross receipts from royalties, rents, dividends, interest, annuities and gains from sales or exchanges of stock or securities,[15] but it does not include dividends received by an S corporation from a C corporation subsidiary to the extent they are attributable to earnings and profits of the subsidiary that are derived from the active conduct of a trade or business.[16] Gross receipts from sales or exchanges of stock or securities are considered only to the extent of gains.[17] For purposes of the overall gross receipts definition, gross receipts on the disposition of capital assets other than stock or securities are taken into account only to the extent of the excess of capital gains over capital losses from such dispositions.[18]

When an S corporation election terminates during the S corporation's taxable year, the corporation experiences an "S termination year," which is divided into two short years: an S short year and a C short year.[19] Income, gains, losses, deductions and credits for an S termination year generally may be allocated between the two short years on a pro rata basis or the corporation may elect to make the allocation under its normal accounting rules.[20] The corporation's tax liability for the short taxable year as a C corporation is then computed on an annualized basis.[21]

*Inadvertent Terminations.* If an S corporation election is terminated, the corporation generally is not eligible to make another election for five taxable years unless the Treasury consents to an earlier election.[22] Section 1362(f) provides relief if a termination is caused by the corporation ceasing to be a small business corporation or by excessive passive investment income. The corporation will be treated as continuing as an S corporation and the terminating event will be disregarded if: (1) the Service determines that the termination was inadvertent, (2) the corporation takes steps within a reasonable time to rectify the problem, and (3) the corporation and

---

**14.**   An S corporation, however, may acquire earnings and profits under Section 381 in a corporate acquisition.

**15.**   I.R.C.   § 1362(d)(3)(C)(i).   Losses from sales or exchanges of stock or securities do not offset gains for purposes of determining passive investment income. Id. The statute also contains rules for certain specialized items. See I.R.C. § 1362(d)(3)(C)(ii)–(iv).

**16.**   I.R.C.   § 1362(d)(3)(E).

**17.**   I.R.C.   § 1362(d)(3)(C)(i).

**18.**   I.R.C.   § 1362(d)(3)(B).

**19.**   I.R.C.   § 1362(e)(1). The C short year begins on the first day the termination is effective. I.R.C. § 1362(e)(1)(B).

**20.**   See Reg. § 1.1362–3. To use normal accounting rules, an election must be filed by all persons who are shareholders during the S short year and all persons who are shareholders on the first day of the C short year. I.R.C.   § 1362(e)(3). The pro rata allocation method may not be used in an S termination year if there is a sale or exchange of 50 percent or more of the stock in the corporation during the year. I.R.C. § 1362(e)(6)(D). For more rules on taxing an S termination year, see I.R.C. § 1362(e)(6).

**21.**   I.R.C.   § 1362(e)(5)(A).

**22.**   I.R.C.   § 1362(g). As a special act of amnesty, Section 1317(b) of the Small Business Job Protection Act of 1996 permits an automatic reelection after the date of enactment of the Act without regard to the five-year limit if the termination occurred in a taxable year beginning before January 1, 1997.

its shareholders agree to make whatever adjustments are required by the Service.[23] The corporation has the burden of establishing that under the relevant facts and circumstances the Commissioner should determine that the termination was inadvertent. Under the regulations, inadvertence may be established by showing that the terminating event was not reasonably within the control of the corporation and was not part of a plan to terminate the election, or that the event took place without the knowledge of the corporation notwithstanding its due diligence to prevent the termination.[24] For example, if a corporation in good faith determines that it has no Subchapter C earnings and profits but the Service later determines on audit that the corporation's S election terminated because it had excessive passive investment income for three consecutive years while it also had accumulated earnings and profits, it may be appropriate for the Service to find that the termination was inadvertent.

*Taxable Year of an S Corporation.* To preclude S corporations from using fiscal years to achieve a deferral of the shareholders' tax liability, S corporations must use a "permitted year," which is defined as either a calendar year or an accounting period for which the taxpayer establishes a business purpose.[25] The Service has ruled that the business purpose requirement may be satisfied if the desired tax accounting period coincides with a "natural business year"[26] and has quantified the concept with the same 25–percent test applicable to partnerships seeking to use a natural business fiscal year.[27] Under this test, a natural business year exists if 25 percent or more of the S corporation's gross receipts for the selected 12–month period are earned in the last two months. This 25–percent test must be met in each of the preceding three 12–month periods that correspond to the requested fiscal year.[28]

Section 1378 makes it clear that tax deferral for shareholders does not constitute a business purpose for a fiscal year. The legislative history also identifies several factors which generally do not support a claim of business purpose:[29]

> The conferees intend that (1) the use of a particular year for regulatory or financial accounting purposes; (2) the hiring patterns of a particular business, e.g., the fact that a firm typically hires staff during certain times of the year; (3) the use of a particular year for administrative purposes, such as the admission or retirement of partners or shareholders, promotion of staff, and compensation or retirement arrangements with staff, partners, or shareholders; and (4) the fact that a particular business involves the use

---

**23.**  I.R.C. § 1362(f).

**24.**  Reg. § 1.1362–4(b).

**25.**  I.R.C.    § 1378(b).   See   Reg. § 1.1378–1.

**26.**  Rev.Proc. 74–33, 1974–2 C.B. 489.

**27.**  Rev.Proc. 2002–38; §§ 2.02, 2.06, 5.05; 2002–1 C.B. 1037. See Chapter 3A3, supra.

**28.**  If the taxpayer does not have the required period of gross receipts, it cannot establish a natural business year under the revenue procedure. Rev. Proc. 87–32, supra note 27.

**29.**  H.R.Rep. No. 99–841, 99th Cong., 2d Sess. II–319 (1986).

of price lists, model year, or other items that change on an annual basis ordinarily will not be sufficient to establish that the business purpose requirement for a particular taxable year has been met.

*Fiscal Year Election.* Congress has modified these strict taxable year requirements by allowing S corporations to elect to adopt, retain or change to a fiscal year under certain conditions, including the payment of an entity-level tax designed to represent the value of any tax deferral to the shareholders that would result from the use of the fiscal year. The rules governing the fiscal year election and the required entity-level payment are found in Sections 444 and 7519 and are similar to the rules applicable to partnerships.[30]

Section 444 permits a newly formed S corporation to elect to use a taxable year other than the calendar year required by Section 1378 provided that the year elected results in no more than a three-month deferral of income to the shareholders.[31] An election and the Section 7519 payment is not required, however, for any S corporation that has established a business purpose for a fiscal year under Section 1378(b)(2).[32]

The trade-off for a Section 444 fiscal year election is that the corporation must make a "required payment" under Section 7519 for any taxable year for which the election is in effect. The mechanics of the required payment are annoyingly complex, but the concept is clear. An electing S corporation must pay and keep "on deposit" an amount roughly approximating the value of the tax deferral that the shareholders would have achieved from the use of a fiscal year. Thus, if an S corporation whose shareholders all used calendar years elected a fiscal year ending September 30, the corporation would be required to pay a tax that supposedly equalled the tax benefit from the three months deferral received by the shareholders.[33] Under a de minimis rule, no payment is required if the amount due is less than $500,[34] and a payment made in one year generates a balance "on deposit" that may be used in subsequent years.[35]

## PROBLEM

Snowshoe, Inc. ("Snowshoe"), a ski resort located in Colorado, was organized by its four individual shareholders (A, B, C and D) and began operations on October 3 of the current year. A owns 300 shares of Snowshoe voting common stock and B, C and D each own 100 shares of Snowshoe nonvoting common stock. Each share of common stock has equal

---

**30.** See Chapter 3A3, supra.

**31.** I.R.C. § 444(a), (b)(1). S corporations formed or electing prior to 1987 also were permitted to retain a taxable year that was the same as the entity's last taxable year beginning in 1986. I.R.C. § 444(b)(3).

**32.** See I.R.S. Notice 88–10, 1988–1 C.B. 478.

**33.** We say "supposedly" because the Section 7519 "required payment" is determined mechanically, without regard to amounts actually deferred by the shareholders. See I.R.C. §§ 7519(b), (c) and (d) for the details.

**34.** I.R.C. § 7519(a)(2).

**35.** I.R.C. § 7519(b)(2), (e)(4).

rights with respect to dividends and liquidation distributions. Consider the following questions in connection with the election and termination of Snowshoe's S corporation status:

(a) If the shareholders wish to elect S corporation status for Snowshoe's first taxable year, who must consent to the election? What difference would it make if, prior to the election, B sold her stock to her brother, G? What difference would it make if B is a partnership which, prior to the election, sold its stock to H, an individual?

(b) What is the last day an effective Subchapter S election for Snowshoe's first taxable year is permitted?

(c) If the shareholders elect S corporation status, what taxable year will Snowshoe be allowed to select?

In the following parts of the problem, assume that Snowshoe elected S corporation status during its first taxable year.

(d) Can A revoke Snowshoe's Subchapter S election without the consent of B, C or D?

(e) If C sold all of his stock to Olga, a citizen of Sweden living in Stockholm, what effect would the sale have on Snowshoe's status as an S corporation?

(f) Same as (e), above, except that C only sold five shares to Olga and had no idea that the sale might adversely affect Snowshoe's S corporation status.

(g) Would it matter if Snowshoe's business is diversified and 45% of its gross receipts come from real estate rentals, dividends and interest?

## D.   TREATMENT OF THE SHAREHOLDERS

Code: §§ 1363(b), (c); 1366(a)–(e); 1367. Skim §§ 1366(f); 1371(b); 1377.

### 1.   PASS-THROUGH OF INCOME AND LOSSES: BASIC RULES

*Entity Treatment.* Although an S corporation is generally exempt from tax,[1] it nonetheless must determine its gross income,[2] deductions and other tax items in order to establish the amounts which pass through to the shareholders. Like a partnership, an S corporation computes its "taxable income" in the same manner as an individual except that certain deductions unique to individuals (e.g., personal exemptions, alimony, medical and moving expenses) are not allowed.[3] In addition, deductions normally available only to corporations, such as the dividends received deduction, are not

---

**1.** For the few limited exceptions, see Section F of this chapter, *infra.*

**2.** Section 1366(c) provides that a shareholder's pro rata share of the S corpora-

tion's gross income is used to determine the shareholder's gross income.

**3.** I.R.C. § 1363(b)(2).

allowed,[4] but an S corporation may elect to deduct and amortize its organizational expenses under Section 248.[5] Finally, a wide variety of items, ranging from charitable contributions and capital gains to depletion, must be separately computed in order to preserve their special tax character for purposes of the pass-through to the shareholders.[6] Thus, an S corporation is not entitled to any charitable deduction, but corporate charitable gifts may pass through to the shareholders without regard to the normal 10 percent limit on corporate contributions.

Although an S corporation is not a *taxable* entity, it is treated as an entity for various purposes. For example, tax elections affecting the computation of items derived from an S corporation (e.g., to defer recognition of gain on an involuntary conversion under Section 1033) generally are made at the corporate level.[7] Likewise, limitations on deductions (e.g., the dollar limitation under Section 179 on expensing the cost of certain recovery property) apply at the corporate level and often at the shareholder level as well.[8] And like a partnership, an S corporation is treated as an entity for filing tax returns and other procedural purposes.[9]

*Pass-Through of Income and Deductions.* Once the S corporation's tax items have been identified, the next step is to determine the manner in which they pass through to the shareholders. The pass-through scheme applicable to S corporations will have a familiar ring to a student who has endured the rigors of Subchapter K. First, income and deductions are characterized at the corporate level.[10] Section 1366(a)(1)(A) provides that items which may have potentially varying tax consequences to the individual shareholders must be separately reported. The most common separately stated items are capital and Section 1231 gains and losses, dividends taxed as net capital gains, interest and other types of "portfolio income" under the Section 469 passive loss limitations, tax-exempt interest, charitable contributions, investment interest, foreign taxes, intangible drilling expenses and depletion on oil and gas properties.[11] Thus, Section 1231 gains and losses do not fall into any corporate hotchpot; rather, they pass through and are aggregated with each shareholder's other Section 1231 gains and losses in order to determine their ultimate character. All the nonseparately stated items are aggregated and the resulting lump sum passes through as ordinary income or loss.

---

**4.** S.Rep. No. 97–640, 97th Cong., 2d Sess. 15 (1982), reprinted in 1982–2 C.B. 718, 724.

**5.** I.R.C. § 1363(b)(3).

**6.** I.R.C. §§ 1363(b)(1); 1366(a)(1)(A).

**7.** I.R.C. § 1363(c)(1).

**8.** See, e.g., I.R.C. § 179(d)(8).

**9.** I.R.C. § 6037. Cf. I.R.C. §§ 6221–6255.

**10.** I.R.C. § 1366(b). See Reg. § 1.1366–1(b). If shareholders are utilizing an S corporation for the principal purpose of converting ordinary income to capital gain or capital loss into ordinary loss on the sale or exchange of property, the regulations generally provide for the character of the gain or loss to be determined at the shareholder level. Reg. § 1.1366–1(b)(2), (3).

**11.** See generally Reg. § 1.1366–1(a)(2). See also Rev.Rul. 84–131, 1984–2 C.B. 37, where the Service ruled that a shareholder's share of an S corporation's investment interest is a separately stated item.

The timing of the shareholders' income and the allocation of pass-through items also is virtually a mirror image of the partnership rules. The shareholders of an S corporation take into account their respective pro rata shares of income, deductions and other separately stated items on a pro rata, per share daily basis.[12] These items are reported in the shareholder's taxable year in which the corporation's taxable year ends.[13] For example, if an S corporation with a natural business year uses a fiscal year ending January 31, 2006, the shareholders will report the respective pass-through items on their 2006 calendar year tax returns, thus achieving a healthy deferral of any gains or an unfortunate delay in recognizing any losses. A deceased shareholder's Subchapter S items are allocated on a daily basis between the shareholder's final income tax return and the initial return of the decedent's estate.[14]

*Basis Adjustments.* Section 1367 requires S corporation shareholders to increase the basis of their stock by their respective shares of income items (including tax-exempt income) and to reduce basis (but not below zero) by losses, deductions, and non-deductible expenses which do not constitute capital expenditures, and by tax-free distributions under Section 1368. Under the Code's ordering rules, basis is first increased by current income items, then decreased by distributions, and finally decreased (to the extent permitted) by any losses for the year.[15] Any additional losses in excess of a shareholder's stock basis must be applied to reduce the shareholder's basis (again, not below zero) in any corporate indebtedness to the shareholder.[16] If the basis of both stock and debt is reduced, any subsequent upward adjustments must first be applied to restore the basis in the indebtedness to the extent that it was previously reduced before increasing the basis of the stock.[17] These basis adjustments are generally made as of the close of the S corporation's taxable year unless a shareholder disposes of stock during the year, in which case the adjustments with respect to the transferred stock are made immediately prior to the disposition.[18]

## 2. LOSS LIMITATIONS

### a. IN GENERAL

Section 1366(d) limits the amount of losses or deductions that may pass through to a shareholder to the sum of the shareholder's adjusted basis in the stock plus his adjusted basis in any indebtedness of the corporation to the shareholder. Losses disallowed because of an inadequate basis may be carried forward indefinitely and treated as a loss in any subsequent year in which the shareholder has a basis in either stock or

---

**12.** I.R.C. § 1366(a)(1). See § 1377(a)(1) for the method of determining each shareholder's "pro rata share."

**13.** I.R.C. § 1366(a)(1).

**14.** Id. See also Reg. § 1.1366–1(a)(1).

**15.** I.R.C. §§ 1366(d)(1)(A); 1368(d), last sentence. For other details on stock and debt basis adjustments, see Reg. § 1.1367–1,–2.

**16.** I.R.C. § 1367(b)(2)(A).

**17.** I.R.C. § 1367(b)(2)(B).

**18.** Reg. § 1.1367–1(d)(1).

debt.[1] A special rule also provides that if a shareholder's stock is transferred under Section 1041 to a spouse or former spouse incident to a divorce, any suspended loss or deduction may be carried forward indefinitely by the transferee-spouse.[2] As illustrated by the *Harris* case, which follows this Note, one of the most litigated issues to arise under Subchapter S has involved the determination of a shareholder's basis in S corporation stock and debt for purposes of applying the general loss limitation rules in Section 1366(d).

Losses that pass through to a shareholder of an S corporation also may be restricted by the at-risk limitations in Section 465 and the passive activity loss limitations in Section 469.[3] The at-risk rules are applied on an activity-by-activity basis, except that activities constituting a trade or business generally are aggregated if the taxpayer actively participates in the management of the trade or business and at least 65 percent of the losses are allocable to persons actively engaged in the management of the trade or business.[4] The passive activity loss limitations cast a wider net and may delay an investor's ability to deduct legitimate start-up losses passing through from a new business operating as an S corporation unless the investor also materially participates in the activity.[5]

# Harris v. United States

United States Court of Appeals, Fifth Circuit, 1990.
902 F.2d 439.

■ GARWOOD, CIRCUIT JUDGE:

Facts and Proceedings Below

In June 1982, Taxpayers contracted with Trans–Lux New Orleans Corporation to purchase for $665,585 cash a New Orleans pornographic theater that they intended to convert into a wedding hall. The Taxpayers' obligations under the contract were conditioned on their being able to secure from a third party a loan for not less than $600,000 repayable in fifteen to twenty years.[1] Shortly before this time, Taxpayers had contacted John Smith (Smith), a real estate loan officer with Hibernia National Bank (Hibernia), to discuss the possibility of obtaining financing for the impending acquisition. Smith orally committed to lend Taxpayers $700,000.[2]

---

**1.** I.R.C. §§ 1366(d)(2)(A), 1366(a)(1).

**2.** I.R.C. § 1366(d)(2)(B).

**3.** See generally Chapter 3C2 and 3C3, supra. These limitations apply on a shareholder-by-shareholder basis rather than at the corporate level. I.R.C. §§ 465(a)(1)(A); 469(a)(2)(A).

**4.** I.R.C. § 465(c)(3)(B).

**5.** I.R.C. § 469(c)(1).

**1.** As part of the contract, Taxpayers deposited with the seller $32,500, all of which was to be applied to the purchase price. In the event Taxpayers were unable to procure the loan, the purchase contract called for their deposit to be refunded.

**2.** Smith asserted in his deposition that he did not know the purpose of the borrowed funds in excess of the purchase price, but he surmised that the money was intended for improvements to the theater. No written loan commitment was ever issued.

Subsequently, to shield themselves from the potential adverse publicity that could follow from the purchase of the pornographic theater, as well as to limit their personal liability and enhance their chances of qualifying for industrial revenue bonds to finance the theater's renovation, in July 1982 Taxpayers formed Harmar (Harmar), a Louisiana corporation, which elected to be taxed pursuant to Subchapter S of the Internal Revenue Code, to purchase and operate the subject property. Harris and Martin each initially contributed $1,000 to the corporation, receiving its stock in return, and each also loaned Harmar $47,500 to satisfy operating expenses. Harris and Martin were the sole shareholders of Harmar, each owning half of its stock.

The purchase of the theater closed on November 1, 1982, and the theater was conveyed to Harmar on that date. Hibernia furnished the $700,000 necessary to close the transaction. In borrowing the funds necessary to acquire the subject property, Harmar executed two promissory notes payable to Hibernia for $350,000 each, each dated November 1, 1982. One of these notes was secured by a $50,322.09 Hibernia certificate of deposit in Harris' name and another $304,972.49 certificate of deposit in the name of his wholly-owned corporation, Harris Mortgage Corporation. Harmar secured the other note, in accordance with its collateral pledge agreement, by its $3,000,000 note (which was unfunded apart from the $700,000) and its collateral mortgage on the theater, each executed by Harmar in favor of Hibernia and dated November 1, 1982. Under the terms of the collateral pledge agreement executed by Harmar in reference to the $3,000,000 note and mortgage, the mortgage secured "not only" Harmar's $350,000 note to Hibernia, "but also any and every other debts, liabilities and obligations" (other than consumer credit debt) of Harmar to Hibernia whether "due or to become due, or whether such debts, liabilities and obligations" of Harmar "are now existing or will arise in the future." Thus, the collateral mortgage secured the full $700,000 loan from Hibernia. Additionally, Taxpayers each executed personal continuing guarantees of Harmar indebtedness in the amount of $700,000 in favor of Hibernia. Smith testified in his deposition that the transaction was structured so that half the loan, as represented by one of the $350,000 notes, would be primarily secured by the certificates of deposit and the other half, represented by the other $350,000 note, primarily by the mortgage on the property purchased, with the entire amount also secured by Taxpayers' individual guarantees.

On its income tax return for the year ending December 31, 1982, Harmar reported a net operating loss of $104,013. Pursuant to [the predecessor of Section 1366], Taxpayers each claimed half of the loss as a deduction on their 1982 individual returns,[5] concluding that their bases in Harmar were in fact greater than Harmar's net operating loss for that year and that they therefore were entitled to deduct the entire loss on their personal returns. On audit, the Internal Revenue Service (IRS) found to

---

**5.** Harris and Martin claimed deductions for Harmar's loss of $52,006 and $52,007, respectively.

the contrary and determined that Harris and Martin each had a basis of $1,000 in his Harmar stock and an adjusted basis in Harmar's indebtedness to each of them as shareholders of $47,500. Pursuant to I.R.C. [§ 1366(d)], the IRS limited Taxpayers' deductions of the net operating loss to what it considered to be their bases in Harmar, $48,500 each. The IRS's disallowance of a portion of the deductions claimed by Taxpayers[6] resulted in additional tax liability, including interest, for Martin of $3,150.58 and for Harris of $1,280. Taxpayers paid the tax in dispute and now appeal the district court's summary judgment dismissing their suit for refund.

Discussion

Taxpayers contend on appeal that in determining the deduction allowable for Harmar's net operating loss, the IRS should have included in Taxpayers' bases in their Harmar stock the full value of the $700,000 Hibernia loan they guaranteed. I.R.C. [§ 1366] permits a Subchapter S shareholder to deduct from his personal return a proportionate share of his corporation's net operating loss to the extent that the loss does not exceed the sum of the adjusted basis of his Subchapter S corporation stock and any corporate indebtedness to him. See section [1366(d)(1)]. To arrive at their basis figure, Taxpayers seek to recast the transaction in question. They in essence urge that we disregard the form of the Hibernia loan—one from Hibernia to Harmar—in favor of what Taxpayers consider as the substance of the transaction—a $700,000 loan from Hibernia to them, the $700,000 proceeds of which they then equally contributed to Harmar's capital account. As evidence of their view of the substance of the transaction, Taxpayers point to the deposition testimony of Smith indicating that Hibernia looked primarily to Taxpayers, rather than to Harmar, for repayment of the loan, and they call attention to the $700,000 guarantees they each provided Hibernia as well as the $355,294.58 in certificates of deposit that Harris pledged to Hibernia as part of the November 1, 1982 loan transaction.

In its summary judgment memorandum, the district court declared that Brown v. Commissioner, 706 F.2d 755 (6th Cir.1983), was "on all fours" with the instant case and therefore resolved it. In *Brown*, the Sixth Circuit rejected shareholders' substance over form argument in ruling that the shareholders' guarantees of loans to their Subchapter S corporation could not increase their bases in their stock in the corporation unless the shareholders made an economic outlay by satisfying at least a portion of the guaranteed debt. Id. at 757. Without such an outlay, the *Brown* court concluded that " 'the substance matched the form' "of the transaction before it. Id. at 756. The reasoning of *Brown* was followed by the Fourth Circuit in Estate of Leavitt v. Commissioner, 875 F.2d 420 (4th Cir.1989), *aff'g*, 90 T.C. 206 (1988). There, the court, affirming the en banc Tax Court, held that shareholder guarantees of a loan to a Subchapter S corporation did not increase shareholders' stock basis because such guarantees had not "cost" shareholders anything and thus did not constitute an

---

**6.** The IRS disallowed $4,506 of Harris' deduction and $4,507 of Martin's.

economic outlay. *Leavitt,* 875 F.2d at 422 & n. 9.[7] In reaching this conclusion, the Fourth Circuit affirmed as not clearly erroneous a finding of the Tax Court that the loan, in form as well as in substance, was made to the corporation rather than to the shareholders.[8] Id. at 424. The court rejected appellants' suggestion that it employ the debt/equity principles espoused in Plantation Patterns, Inc. v. Commissioner, 462 F.2d 712 (5th Cir.1972), in determining whether the shareholders had actually made an economic outlay,[9] instead choosing to employ a debt/equity analysis only after making a finding that an economic outlay had occurred. *Leavitt,* 875 F.2d at 427. The *Leavitt* court reasoned that the legislative history of section [1366] limiting the basis of a Subchapter S shareholder to his corporate investment or outlay could not be circumvented through the use of debt/equity principles. Id. at 426 & n. 16. See generally Bogdanski, Shareholder Guarantees, Interest Deductions, and S Corporation Stock Basis: The Problems with Putnam, 13 J.Corp.Tax'n 264, 268–89 (1986).

Taxpayers press this Court to follow the contrary holding of Selfe v. United States, 778 F.2d 769 (11th Cir.1985). There, the Eleventh Circuit ruled that a shareholder's guaranty of a Subchapter S corporation loan could result in an increase in equity or debt basis even though the shareholder had not satisfied any portion of the obligation. *Selfe,* 778 F.2d at 775. The court remanded the case to the district court for it to employ debt/equity principles in determining if the loan in question was in substance one to the shareholder rather than to the corporation. Id.

The courts have uniformly ruled that a shareholder must make an economic outlay to increase his Subchapter S corporation stock basis. Taxpayers assert that if we look beyond the form of the transaction at what they contend is its substance—a loan from Hibernia to them, which in turn they contributed to Harmar as capital—we must find that a $700,000 outlay occurred and that their stock bases therefore correspondingly increased. They contend that use of debt/equity principles will lead us to such a conclusion.

---

**7.** In reasoning that the shareholders had not increased their stock bases as a result of their guarantees, the court turned to I.R.C. § 1012, which defines basis of property as its cost. Id. at 422 n. 9. Cost of property, in turn, is defined in the Treasury Regulations as the "amount paid for such property in cash or other property." 26 C.F.R. § 1.1012-1(a).

**8.** The court noted that the loan in question had been made by the bank directly to the corporation, the loan payments were made by the corporation directly to the bank, and neither the corporation nor the shareholders reported the payments as constructive dividends. Id.

Under *Leavitt,* the presumption is that the form will control and that presumption will not be surmounted absent the shareholder's satisfying the higher standard applicable to a taxpayer's seeking to disavow the form he selected and recast a transaction. See Bowers, Building Up an S Shareholder's Basis through Loans and Acquisitions, J. Tax'n S Corp., Fall 1989, at 22, 29.

**9.** In *Plantation Patterns,* this Court considered whether a Subchapter C corporation could deduct interest payments made on its debt and whether its shareholders had resulting dividend income. The Court, using a debt/equity analysis, affirmed a Tax Court finding that a corporation's interest payments on debentures were constructive dividends and could not be deducted as interest payments. Id. at 723–24. * * *

Ordinarily, taxpayers are bound by the form of the transaction they have chosen; taxpayers may not in hindsight recast the transaction as one that they might have made in order to obtain tax advantages. * * * The IRS, however, often may disregard form and recharacterize a transaction by looking to its substance. Higgins v. Smith, 308 U.S. 473, 60 S.Ct. 355, 357, 84 L.Ed. 406 (1940). The Tax Court has recognized an exception to the rule that a taxpayer may not question a transaction's form in cases such as this one in which the shareholder argues that guaranteed corporate debt should be recast as an equity investment on the shareholder's part. Blum v. Commissioner, 59 T.C. 436, 440 (1972).

In this case we find that the transaction as structured did not lack adequate substance or reality and that an economic outlay justifying the basis claimed by Taxpayers never occurred.

The summary judgment evidence reflects that the parties to this transaction intended that the Hibernia loan be one to the corporation. Each of the two $350,000 promissory notes was executed by and only in the name of Harmar. The notes have been renewed and remain in the same form, namely notes payable to Hibernia in which the sole maker is Harmar. Hibernia, an independent party, in substance earmarked the loan proceeds for use in purchasing the subject property to which Harmar took title, Harmar contemporaneously giving Hibernia a mortgage to secure Harmar's debt to Hibernia. The bank sent interest due notices to Harmar, and all note payments were made by checks to Hibernia drawn on Harmar's corporate account. Harmar's books and records for all years through the year ended December 31, 1985, prepared by its certified public accountant, reflect the $700,000 loan simply as an indebtedness of Harmar to Hibernia. They do not in any way account for or reflect any of the $700,000 as a capital contribution or loan by Taxpayers to Harmar, although they do reflect the $1,000 capital contribution each Taxpayer made and Harmar's indebtedness to Taxpayers for the various cash advances Taxpayers made to it. The Harmar financial statements for the year ended December 31, 1986, are the first to show any contributed capital attributable to the Hibernia loan. Further, Hibernia's records showed Harmar as the "borrower" in respect to the $700,000 loan and the renewals of it. Harmar's 1982 tax return, which covered August 15 through December 31, 1982, indicates that Harmar deducted $12,506 in interest expenses. Because only the Hibernia loan generated such expenses for that period, it is reasonably inferable that the deduction corresponded to that loan. The 1982 Harmar return showed no distribution to Taxpayers, as it should have if the $700,000 Hibernia loan on which Harmar paid interest was a loan to the Taxpayers. Further, the return shows the only capital contributed as $2,000 and the only loan from stockholders as $68,000, but hows other indebtedness of $675,000. In short, Harmar's 1982 income tax return is flatly inconsistent with Taxpayers' present position. Moreover, there is no indication that Taxpayers treated the loan as a personal one on their individual returns by reporting Harmar's interest payments to Hibernia as constructive dividend income. In sum, the parties' treatment of the transaction, from the time it was entered into and for years thereafter, has been

wholly consistent with its unambiguous documentation and inconsistent with the way in which Taxpayers now seek to recast it. Hibernia was clearly an independent third party, and the real and bona fide, separate existence of Harmar is not challenged. The parties did what they intended to do, and the transaction as structured did not lack adequate reality or substance.

Moreover, if the transaction is to be "recast," it is by no means clear that it should be recast in the form sought by Taxpayers, namely as a cash loan to them from Hibernia followed by their payment of the cash to Harmar as a contribution to its capital, and Harmar's then using the cash to purchase the building. Such recasting does not account for Hibernia's mortgage on the building. In any event, if the transaction is to be recast, why should it not be recast as a loan by Hibernia to Taxpayers, with the Taxpayers using the funds to themselves purchase the building, giving Hibernia a mortgage on the building to secure their debt to it, and then transferring the building, subject to the mortgage, to Harmar as a contribution to capital? Presumably in that situation Taxpayers' bases in their Harmar stock would be reduced by the amount of the debt secured by the mortgage under I.R.C. § 358(d). See Wiebusch v. Commissioner, 59 T.C. 777, aff'd per curiam "on the basis of the opinion of the Tax Court," Wiebusch v. Commissioner, 487 F.2d 515 (8th Cir.1973).[15] While section 358(d) likely does not affect stockholder basis in the debt of the Subchapter S corporation to the stockholder, Taxpayers have not sought to recast the transaction as a loan by Hibernia to them followed by their loan of the proceeds to Harmar; indeed even after Harmar's books were rearranged starting with the year ending December 31, 1986, the books do not show any indebtedness in this respect of Harmar to Taxpayers and do continue to show Harmar as owing the money in question to Hibernia. There is simply no evidence of Harmar indebtedness to Taxpayers in respect to these funds.

Taxpayers' guarantees and Harris' pledge of certificates of deposit do not undermine the intent of the parties that Harmar be the borrower in this transaction. It certainly is not difficult to fathom that a careful lender to a new, small, closely held corporation such as Harmar would seek personal guarantees from all of its shareholders. See Bogdanski, supra, at 269. Moreover, the wholly unperformed guarantees do not satisfy the requirement that an economic outlay be made before a corresponding increase in basis can occur. See generally *Underwood,* 535 F.2d at 312. In

---

**15.**   See also Megaard, No Stock Basis for Shareholder Guarantee of S Corporation Debt, 15 J.Corp.Tax'n 340 (1989). Megaard explains that "[u]nder Section 358(d), the assumption by a corporation of its shareholder's debt is treated as money received which reduces the shareholder's basis in the stock." Id. at 349. Cf. id. at 350 ("Having the corpo- ration's assets encumbered by the shareholder's personal debt runs the risk of a basis reduction under Section 358 should the Service argue that the transaction was a purchase by the shareholder of the * * * assets followed by a contribution of the assets to the corporation subject to the debt.").

the same light, Harris' pledge to Hibernia of some $355,000 in certificates of deposit of his (and Harris Mortgage Corporation) does not provide such an outlay.[16]

We conclude that the transaction must be treated as it purports to be and as the parties treated it—namely as a loan by Hibernia to Harmar, all payments on which through the relevant time have been made by Harmar to Hibernia. For any funds or other assets Taxpayers have actually provided to Harmar as loans or contributions, Taxpayers are, of course, entitled to basis additions as of the time such contributions or loans were furnished by them to Harmar, but they are not entitled to a 1982 basis addition for Hibernia's 1982 $700,000 loan to Harmar, notwithstanding that it was also secured by Taxpayers' execution of guarantees and Harris' pledge to Hibernia of his and Harris Mortgage Corporation's certificates of deposit in the total face amount of some $355,000.

Conclusion

There was no genuine dispute as to any material fact necessary to sustain the Government's summary judgment motion. The district court's judgment is correct and it is therefore

Affirmed.

NOTE

In *Harris,* the Fifth Circuit joined several other circuits[1] and the Tax Court[2] in holding that the guarantee of an S corporation's loan by its shareholders may not be treated as an additional investment in the corporation which will increase the shareholders' bases for purposes of the loss limitation rule in Section 1366(d). In conflict with this line of authority is the Eleventh Circuit's decision in Selfe v. United States.[3] In *Selfe,* the court reasoned that debt-equity principles under Subchapter C were applicable in determining whether a shareholder-guaranteed debt should be characterized as a capital contribution. In remanding the case for a determination of whether the shareholder's guarantee amounted to either an equity investment or a shareholder loan to the corporation, the court directed the district court to apply the principles of *Plantation Patterns,* a Subchapter C case discussed in *Harris.*

**16.** Taxpayers would have us, in effect, convert this pledge to Hibernia into a $700,000 cash contribution made to Harmar by Taxpayers equally. But that did not happen. Taxpayers do not contend that the certificates of deposit were contributed to Harmar's capital.

**1.** Brown v. Commissioner, 706 F.2d 755 (6th Cir.1983); Estate of Leavitt v. Commissioner, 875 F.2d 420 (4th Cir.1989), cert. denied, 493 U.S. 958, 110 S.Ct. 376 (1989); Uri v. Commissioner, 949 F.2d 371 (10th Cir.1991); Sleiman v. Commissioner, 187 F.3d 1352 (11th Cir. 1999); Grojean v. Commissioner, 248 F.3d 572 (2001).

**2.** Estate of Leavitt v. Commissioner, 90 T.C. 206 (1988); Hitchins v. Commissioner, 103 T.C. 711 (1994).

**3.** 778 F.2d 769 (11th Cir.1985).

Despite the seeming conflict among the circuits, the Supreme Court has declined to add this fascinating tax issue to its docket.[4]

### b.   SUBCHAPTER S LOSSES AND SECTION 362(e)(2)

Code: § 362(e)(2)

The rules for allocating and characterizing gains and losses that are inherent in property contributed to a partnership ("precontribution gains and losses") are one of the principal features of the Subchapter K partnership tax regime. Under Section 704(c)(1)(A), precontribution gains and losses generally must be taxed to the contributing partner, and Section 724 prevents partners from gaining a tax advantage by converting precontribution ordinary income into capital gain and precontribution capital loss into ordinary loss. Other provisions buttress these rules by preventing shifting of precontribution gains and losses through partnership distributions and dispositions of partnership interests.[1] In short, Subchapter K has an array of provisions designed to ensure that a partner who contributes property with a precontribution gain will be taxed on that gain and that precontribution losses may not be shifted to other partners.[2]

Subchapter S is relatively primitive compared to its Subchapter K cousin in the treatment of precontribution gains and losses. Under Section 1377, precontribution gains and losses are taxed like any other gain or loss under a per-share, per-day allocation method.[3] Precontribution gains and losses in an S corporation are thus routinely shifted to other shareholders.

As part of the American Jobs Creation Act of 2004,[4] Congress decided to attack various schemes by taxpayers to duplicate losses by way of transactions involving corporations. Section 362(e)(2) was one of the provisions enacted to curb those abuses. That section provides that if a shareholder transfers property with an aggregate built-in loss to a corporation in a Section 351 transaction, the corporation's basis in the property must be reduced to the fair market value of such property.[5] If more than one asset is contributed, the basis reduction is allocated among the property in proportion to their respective built-in losses immediately before the transaction.[6] As an alternative to reducing the property's basis, the shareholder and the corporation may elect to reduce the basis of the stock that was received for the property to the stock's fair market value immediately after the transfer.[7]

---

**4.** The Court denied the taxpayer's petition for certiorari in the *Estate of Leavitt* case, supra note 1.

**1.** I.R.C. §§ 704(c)(1)(B); 737; 751(a).

**2.** Section 704(c)(1)(C) prevents a shift of precontribution losses to other partners, even a transferee partner.

**3.** The regulations hold out the possibility of attacking plans to alter the character of precontribution gains and losses in an S corporation. See Reg. § 1366–1(b)(2) & (3).

**4.** Pub. L. No. 108–357, 108th Cong., 2d Sess. (2004).

**5.** I.R.C. § 362(e)(2)(A).

**6.** I.R.C. § 362(e)(2)(B).

**7.** I.R.C. § 362(e)(2)(C).

Section 362(e)(2) potentially will defer or limit precontribution losses in an S corporation, sometimes in a very unusual way. For example, assume that an individual decides to form an S corporation by contributing property with a $20,000 basis and $12,000 fair market value for all of the corporation's stock in a Section 351 exchange. Under Section 362(e)(2), the property's basis will be reduced to $12,000 and the precontribution loss in the property will disappear. If the corporation were to sell the property for $12,000, there would be no gain or loss recognized by the corporation. The shareholder's basis in the stock, however, would still be $20,000 so the loss would remain in the shares. The timing of the loss, however, would be deferred until the shareholder either liquidates the corporation or sells the stock. Alternatively, assume that the shareholder and the corporation elect to reduce the basis of the shareholder's stock to $12,000. In that case, the basis of the property in the corporation would remain at $20,000. If the corporation were to sell the property, it would recognize its $8,000 loss, which would pass through to the shareholder. The shareholder's stock basis would then be reduced by the loss down to $4,000, putting the shareholder in a position where a sale of the stock for its $12,000 fair market value would result in an $8,000 gain. Over time, the shareholder would report an $8,000 loss and an $8,000 gain, the net result being that the loss essentially disappeared. Finally, assume that the shareholder also contributed property with a $10,000 built-in gain to the S corporation at the same time as the transfer of the property with the built-in loss. In that case, no reduction in the basis of the loss property or the stock would be required under Section 362(e)(2) because the two properties that were transferred did not have an aggregate built-in loss.

It is hard to believe that Congress considered the effects on Subchapter S when it enacted Section 362(e)(2). That section now lurks as a trap for those who either receive poor advice or are not initiated in the ways of Subchapters C and S. Until Congress fixes this problem, taxpayers planning a new venture involving property with a built-in loss will be well advised to consider structuring the venture as a limited liability company or partnership governed by Subchapter K. Alternatively, another strategy for preserving a built-in loss in property would be to offer to make the property available to an S corporation through a leasing arrangement.

## 3.   Sale of S Corporation Stock

Code: § 1(h).

The tax consequences of a sale of S corporation stock are determined by regulations promulgated under the "look-through" rules of Section 1(h). In general, S corporation stock is treated as a capital asset that gives rise to capital gain or loss on sale. Unlike the more complex approach taken by Subchapter K to the sale of a partnership interest, Subchapter S historically has not required selling shareholders to characterize a portion of their gain or loss on a stock sale by reference to the types of assets (e.g., ordinary income property) held by the corporation at the time of the sale. When

Congress enacted the Section 1(h) capital gains rate regime, however, it authorized the Service to prescribe appropriate regulations to apply the various maximum capital gains rates to the sale of interests in pass-through entities.[1]

The Section 1(h) regulations apply a partial capital gains "look-through" rule for sales and exchanges of interests in an S corporation.[2] Shareholders who sell S corporation stock held for more than one year may recognize collectibles gain (taxable at a maximum rate of 28 percent) and residual capital gain, which is generally taxable at a maximum rate of 15 percent.[3] The selling shareholder's share of collectibles gain is defined as the amount of the net collectibles gain (but not net collectibles loss) that would be allocated to that shareholder if the S corporation transferred all of its collectibles in a fully taxable transaction immediately before the transfer of the stock.[4] The selling shareholder's residual capital gain is the amount of long-term capital gain or loss that the shareholder would recognize on the sale of the stock ("pre-look-through capital gain or loss") minus the partner's share of collectibles gain.[5] The look-through rules do not extend to other corporate assets, such as inventory or depreciable real estate, that would generate ordinary income, or to real estate that would produce unrecaptured (i.e., 25–percent) Section 1250 gain on a corporate-level sale. What is the policy justification for this "pick and choose" look-through approach for S corporations?

The regulations illustrate these rules with the following example.[6] Assume that X, Inc., which always has been an S corporation and is owned equally by individuals A, B, and C, invests in antiques. After they were purchased, the antiques appreciated in value by $300. A owned one-third of the X stock and has held the stock for more than one year. A's adjusted basis in the X stock is $100. If A were to sell all of the X stock to T for $150, A would recognize $50 of pre-look-through long-term capital gain. If X were to sell all of the antiques in a fully taxable transaction immediately before the transfer to T, A would be allocated $100 of collectibles gain on account of the sale. Therefore, A will recognize $100 of collectibles gain on account of the collectibles held by X. The difference between A's pre-look-through capital gain or loss ($50) and the collectibles gain ($100) is A's residual long-term capital gain or loss on the sale of the X stock. Thus, A will recognize $100 of collectibles gain and $50 of residual long-term capital loss on the sale of A's X stock.

---

**1.** I.R.C. § 1(h)(11).

**2.** Reg. § 1.1(h)–1.

**3.** Reg. § 1.1(h)–1(a). In limited situations (e.g., where a transaction is governed by provisions of Subchapter C that treat gain on a sale or redemption of stock as ordinary income), shareholders also may recognize ordinary income on a sale of their S corporation stock. See, e.g., I.R.C. §§ 304, 306, 341.

**4.** Reg. § 1.1(h)–1(b)(2)(ii). A shareholder's share of collectibles gain is limited to the amount attributable to the portion of the stock transferred that was held for more than one year.

**5.** Reg. § 1.1(h)–1(c).

**6.** Reg. § 1.1(h)–1(f) Example 4.

## PROBLEMS

**1.** S Corporation is a calendar year taxpayer which elected S corporation status in its first year of operation. S's common stock is owned by A (200 shares with a $12,000 basis) and B (100 shares with a $6,000 basis). During the current year, S will have the following income and expenses:

| | |
|---|---|
| Business income | $92,000 |
| Tax-exempt interest | 1,000 |
| Salary expense | 44,000 |
| Depreciation | 8,000 |
| Property taxes | 7,000 |
| Supplies | 4,000 |
| Interest expense paid on a margin account maintained with S Corp.'s stock broker | 6,000 |
| Gain from the sale of equipment held for two years: | |
| § 1245 gain | 7,000 |
| § 1231 gain | 12,000 |
| STCG from the sale of AT & T stock | 7,500 |
| LTCG from the sale of Chrysler stock held for two years | 15,000 |
| LTCL from the sale of investment real estate held for two years | 9,000 |
| Bribe of government official | 6,000 |
| Recovery of a bad debt previously deducted | 4,500 |

(a) How will S Corporation, A and B report these events? Compare § 704(b)(2) and (c).

(b) What is A's basis in his S stock at the end of the current year?

(c) Whose accounting method will control the timing of income and deductions?

(d) If S realizes a gain upon an involuntary conversion, who makes the election under § 1033 to limit recognition of gain?

(e) Would it matter if the equipment would have been property described in § 1221(1) if held by A?

**2.** D, E and F each own one-third of the outstanding stock of R Corporation (an S corporation). During the current year, R will have $120,000 of net income from business operations. The net income is realized at a rate of $10,000 per month. Additionally, in January of this year R sold § 1231 property and recognized a $60,000 loss.

(a) Assume D's basis in her R stock at the beginning of the year is $10,000. If D sells one-half of her stock to G midway through the year for $25,000, what will be the tax results to D and G?

(b) What difference would it make in (a), above, if D sold all of her stock to G for $50,000?

**3**. The Ace Sporting Goods Store (an S corporation) is owned by Dick and Harry. Dick and Harry each own one-half of Ace's stock and have a $2,000 basis in their respective shares. At incorporation, Dick loaned $4,000 to Ace and received a five year, 12% note from the corporation.

(a) If Ace has an $8,000 loss from business operations this year, what will be the results to Dick and Harry? Do you have any suggestions for Harry? Would it matter if on December 15 Ace borrowed $4,000 from its bank on a full recourse basis? What if Dick and Harry personally guaranteed the loan? Compare §§ 752(a) and 722.

(b) If Ace has $6,000 of net income from business operations next year, what will be the results to Dick and Harry?

(c) What difference would it make in (a), above, if the $8,000 loss was made up of $2,000 of losses from business operation and a $6,000 long-term capital loss? See Reg. § 1.704–1(d)(2).

(d) What would be the effect in (a), above, if Ace's S corporation status was terminated at the end of the current year?

**4**. Allied Technologies, an S corporation, is owned by Betty (25%), Chuck (35%) and Diana (40%). Betty and Chuck also each own one-half of the stock of the Portland Exporting Corporation, also an S corporation.

(a) If Allied sells investment real estate which it purchased two years ago for $40,000 to Portland for $20,000, what will be the result to Allied? See § 267.

(b) What difference would it make in (a), above, if Portland were a C corporation?

(c) Assume Allied is an accrual method taxpayer and owes $1,500 to Betty (a cash method taxpayer) for her December salary. If Allied pays the salary on January 15 of the following year, what will be the tax results to Allied and Betty (assuming both are calendar year taxpayers?) See § 267(e).

## E.   DISTRIBUTIONS TO SHAREHOLDERS

Code: §§ 311(b); 1368; 1371(a)(1), (c), (e); Skim § 301(a), (b) & (d).

Under the double tax regime governing C corporations and their shareholders, nonliquidating distributions are taxable as dividends to the extent that they are made out of the C corporation's current or accumulated earnings and profits.[1] "Earnings and profits" is a special tax concept that seeks to measure a C corporation's economic income, both during the current taxable year and over the corporation's lifetime. Earnings and

---

**1.**   I.R.C. §§ 301(c)(1); 316.

profits have long served as the benchmark for determining whether distributions by C corporations to their shareholders are taxable dividends. As discussed below, the tax consequences of S corporation distributions may be influenced by these Subchapter C concepts.

*S Corporations Without Earnings and Profits.* If an S corporation has no accumulated earnings and profits, distributions to shareholders are treated as a tax-free return of capital which is first applied to reduce the shareholder's stock basis.[2] Any distribution in excess of basis is treated as gain from the sale or exchange of property—capital gain if the stock is a capital asset.[3] Virtually all S corporations formed after 1982 do not generate earnings and profits[4] and are governed by this simple regime. This basic taxing pattern for distributions by S corporations also governs any distribution of property to which Section 301(c) would apply.[5] Thus, the tax consequences of transactions treated as Section 301 distributions by other Code provisions, such as Sections 302 (redemptions) and 305 (stock dividends), are determined under Section 1368.

*S Corporations With Earnings and Profits.* S corporations with earnings and profits present more challenging problems because of the need to harmonize the Subchapter S rules with the corporation's prior C history. Some S corporations may have accumulated earnings and profits attributable to prior years when they were governed by Subchapter C. In addition, an S corporation may have inherited the earnings and profits of another company in a corporate acquisition subject to Section 381. In all these cases, the undistributed earnings have not been taxed at the shareholder level and represent an irresistible temptation for a tax-free bailout. There is no free lunch, however, and it thus becomes necessary to identify those distributions which should be taxed at the shareholder level because they are made out of accumulated earnings and profits.

The drafters of the 1982 Act devised a new tax concept—the "accumulated adjustments account" ("AAA")—to serve as the reference point for determining the source of distributions by an S corporation with accumulated earnings and profits. The AAA represents the post–1982 undistributed net income of the corporation. It begins at zero and is increased and decreased annually in a manner similar to the adjustment of the basis in a shareholder's stock.[6] Any distribution by an S corporation with accumulated earnings and profits is treated as a tax-free return of capital to the extent it does not exceed the AAA.[7] A distribution in excess of the AAA is

---

**2.** I.R.C. § 1368(b)(1).

**3.** I.R.C. § 1368(b)(2).

**4.** I.R.C. § 1371(c)(1). An S corporation formed after 1982 may generate earnings and profits for any year in which it is not an S corporation and may acquire earnings and profits under Section 381 in a corporate acquisition.

**5.** I.R.C. § 1368(c).

**6.** I.R.C.    § 1368(e)(1)(A);    Reg. § 1.1368–2. Unlike a shareholder's basis,

however, the AAA is not increased by tax-exempt income items and is not decreased for expenses related to tax-exempt income. The adjustments also may result in a negative AAA. Reg. § 1.1368–2(a)(3)(ii). In addition, no adjustment is made for federal taxes attributable to any taxable year in which the corporation was a C corporation. Id.

**7.** I.R.C. § 1368(c)(1). Except to the extent provided in regulations, the AAA is allocated proportionately among distributions if

treated as a dividend to the extent of accumulated earnings and profits,[8] and any portion of the distribution still remaining after both the AAA and accumulated earnings and profits are exhausted is treated first as a recovery of basis and then as gain from the sale of property.[9]

One might reasonably ask at this point: what is the purpose of this statutory scheme? The answer is more straightforward than it first appears. The function of the AAA is to identify the source of distributions by those few S corporations with accumulated earnings and profits. It permits the corporation to make a tax-free distribution of the net income recognized during its S corporation era which already was taxed at the shareholder level. Only after these previously taxed earnings are exhausted will a distribution be considered as emanating from accumulated earnings and profits.[10]

*Distributions of Appreciated Property.* At the shareholder level, the Section 1368 distribution rules make no distinction between distributions of cash and other property. At the corporate level, however, an S corporation that distributes appreciated property (other than its own obligations) recognizes gain in the same manner as if the property had been sold to the shareholder at its fair market value.[11] This rule is borrowed from Subchapter C, and it applies to liquidating and nonliquidating distributions of property by an S corporation.[12] The gain is not taxed to the corporation but, like other corporate-level income, it passes through to the distributee shareholder, who takes a fair market value basis in the distributed property.[13] The shareholder's basis in his S corporation stock is reduced by the fair market value (not the adjusted basis) of the distributed property.[14] These rules are required to prevent the appreciation from escaping tax through a distribution which is tax-free at both the corporate and shareholder levels followed by a tax-free sale by the shareholder, who would take the property with a fair market value basis.

the distributions exceed the AAA. See Reg. § 1.1368–2(b), (c).

**8.** I.R.C. § 1368(c)(2).

**9.** I.R.C. § 1368(c)(2), (3). For lots of details about the AAA, see Reg. § 1.1368–2.

**10.** In lieu of these rules, an S corporation may elect, with the consent of all shareholders who have received distributions during the year, to treat distributions as a dividend to the extent of accumulated earnings and profits. I.R.C. § 1368(e)(3); Reg. § 1.1368–1(f)(2). There normally is little incentive to make this election. One possible motivation would be to enable the corporation to sweep its Subchapter C earnings and profits account clean and thus avoid the corporate level tax and possible termination of S corporation status that would result from

the co-existence of Subchapter C earnings and profits and excessive passive investment income. See I.R.C. § 1375. A similar election is provided during a post-termination transition period. I.R.C. § 1371(e)(2).

**11.** I.R.C. § 311(b). An S corporation may not recognize loss, however, on a distribution of property that has declined in value. I.R.C. § 311(a).

**12.** See I.R.C. § 1371(a), which provides that, except as otherwise provided in Subchapter S, the provisions of Subchapter C apply to S corporations and their shareholders.

**13.** I.R.C. § 301(d)(1).

**14.** I.R.C. §§ 1367(a)(2)(A), 1368.

PROBLEMS

**1**. Ajax Corporation is a calendar year taxpayer which was organized two years ago and elected s corporation status for its first taxable year. Ajax's stock is owned one-third by Dewey and two-thirds by Milt. At the beginning of the current year, Dewey's basis in his Ajax shares was $3,000 and Milt's basis in his shares was $5,000. During the year, Ajax will earn $9,000 of net income from operations and have a $3,000 long-term capital gain on the sale of 100 shares of Exxon stock. What results to Dewey, Milt and Ajax in the following alternative situations?

  (a) On October 15, Ajax distributes $5,000 to Dewey and $10,000 to Milt.

  (b) On October 15, Ajax distributes $8,000 to Dewey and $16,000 to Milt.

  (c) Ajax distributes a parcel of land with a basis of $9,000 and a fair market value of $8,000 to Dewey and a different parcel with a basis of $13,000 and fair market value of $16,000 to Milt.

  (d) On October 15, Ajax distributes its own notes to Dewey and Milt. Dewey receives an Ajax five year, 12% note with a face amount and fair market value of $8,000 and Milt receives an Ajax five year, 12% note with a face amount and fair market value of $16,000.

**2**. P Corporation was formed ten years ago by its two equal shareholders, Nancy and Opal, and elected S corporation status at the beginning of the current year. On January 1, Nancy had a $1,000 basis in her P stock and Opal had a $5,000 basis in her stock. P has $6,000 of accumulated earnings and profits from its prior C corporation operations and has the following results from operations this year:

| | |
|---|---|
| Gross Income | $32,000 |
| Long-term capital gain | 4,000 |
| Salary Expense | 18,000 |
| Depreciation | 8,000 |

What are the tax consequences to Nancy, Opal and P Corporation in the following alternative situations.

  (a) On November 1, P distributes $5,000 to Nancy and $5,000 to Opal.

  (b) Same as (a), above, except that P distributes $10,000 to Nancy and $10,000 to Opal.

  (c) What difference would it make in (a), above, if P also received $4,000 of tax-exempt interest during the year and distributed $2,000 of the interest to Nancy and $2,000 to Opal?

  (d) During the current year P makes no distributions. On January 1 of next year Nancy sells her P stock to Rose for $6,000. If P breaks even on its operations next year, what will be the result to Rose if P distributes $6,000 to each of its shareholders next February 15?

  (e) During the current year P makes no distributions. Nancy and Opal revoke P's Subchapter S election effective January 1 of next year.

Assume P Co. has $5,000 of earnings and profits next year. What results to Nancy and Opal if P distributes $7,000 to each of them on August 1 of next year?

**3**. How do the tax rules governing distributions of appreciated property by an S corporation differ from the rules governing similar distributions by partnerships? Why? Which approach is preferable?

---

## F.   TAXATION OF THE S CORPORATION

Code: §§ 1363; 1374; 1375.

The major benefit of a Subchapter S election is the elimination of tax at the corporate level. But this immunity from tax is not absolute. As part of its continuing mission to patrol abuse, Congress has provided that in certain limited situations an S corporation may be subject to tax under Section 1374 on certain built-in gains inherent in corporate property and under Section 1375 on a portion of its passive investment income.

*Tax on Certain Built-in Gains: Section 1374.* Throughout our tax history, the principal feature of the taxation of corporations and their shareholders under Subchapter C of the Code has been the double taxation of corporate income. Corporate profits are subject to tax at the corporate level and a second tax at the shareholder level when they are distributed as dividends. But the double tax regime has never been absolute. Historically, one of the principal refuges from the corporate income tax was the so-called *General Utilities* doctrine, which emanated from an early Supreme Court decision[1] and was codified in various provisions allowing corporations to make in-kind distributions of appreciated property to their shareholders without incurring a corporate level tax.[2] Long criticized by tax reformers, the *General Utilities* doctrine was the subject of considerable legislative attention from the time it was codified in the 1954 Code. After many years of piecemeal erosion, "the General" finally met his death in the Tax Reform Act of 1986.

In repealing the *General Utilities* doctrine, Congress recognized that the shareholders of a C corporation might elect S corporation status in order to avoid the corporate level tax imposed on in-kind distributions of appreciated property. For example, assume Liquidating Co. is a C corporation which holds highly appreciated assets. Liquidating is owned by shareholders A and B, who would realize substantial taxable gains if they sold their stock or liquidated the company. If A and B caused Liquidating to sell its assets and liquidate, or to distribute the assets in complete liquidation, the corporation would be taxed on its asset gains, and A and B likewise

---

**1.** General Utilities & Operating Co. v. Helvering, 296 U.S. 200, 56 S.Ct. 185 (1935). See generally Lind, Schwarz, Lathrope & Rosenberg, Cases and Materials on Fundamentals of Corporate Taxation, Chapters 4D1, 5E1 and 7B2 (6th ed. 2005); Bittker & Eustice, Federal Income Taxation of Corporations and Shareholders ¶ 8.20 (7th ed. 2000).

**2.** See, e.g., I.R.C. §§ 311; 336; 337 (pre–1987).

would be taxed on their stock gains.[3] But if Liquidating qualified as a "small business corporation," A and B could elect S corporation status in order to reduce the double tax burden on the sale or liquidation. The company then could sell its assets and the gains would pass through to A and B, whose stock bases would be correspondingly increased. If successful, the S corporation/liquidation strategy would avoid the full impact of the double tax.

Section 1374 blocks this opportunity by taxing an S corporation that has a "net recognized built-in gain" at any time within ten years of the effective date of its S corporation election.[4] At the outset, two important limitations on this tax should be noted. First, Section 1374 applies only if the corporation's S election was made after December 31, 1986.[5] Second, it does not apply to a corporation that always has been subject to Subchapter S.[6]

In general, Section 1374 is designed to tax an S corporation on the net gain that accrued while it was subject to Subchapter C if that gain is subsequently recognized on sales, distributions and other dispositions of property within a ten-year "recognition period" beginning with the first taxable year in which the corporation was an S corporation. For this purpose, any gain recognized during the recognition period, including income from "ripe" items such as cash-basis accounts receivable or Section 453 installment obligations, is a "recognized built-in gain" unless the corporation establishes either that it did not hold the asset at the beginning of its first S taxable year or the recognized gain exceeds the gain inherent in the asset at that time.[7] Conversely, any loss recognized during the recognition period, including deductible items attributable to the corporation's pre-S life, is a "recognized built-in loss" to the extent that the S corporation establishes that it held the asset at the beginning of its first S year and the loss does not exceed the loss inherent in the asset at that time.[8] Since the taxpayer has the burden of proof under these definitions, a C corporation making an S election should obtain an independent appraisal of its assets to establish their value on the relevant date in order to avoid being taxed on gain arising under the S regime and to benefit from the losses that accrued during the corporation's C years.

The Section 1374 tax is computed by applying the highest rate applicable to C corporations (currently 35 percent) to the S corporation's "net recognized built-in gain," which is defined as the corporation's taxable income computed by taking into account only recognized built-in gains and losses but limited to the corporation's taxable income computed generally

---

3. See I.R.C. §§ 331(a); 336(a); 1001(a).

4. I.R.C. § 1374(a), (d)(7).

5. Tax Reform Act of 1986, P.L. No. 99–514, 99th Cong., 2d Sess. § 633(b) (1986).

6. I.R.C. § 1374(c)(1). This exemption may not apply, however, if the S corporation had a "predecessor" that was a C corpora-

tion. Id. This could occur, for example, where a C corporation was acquired by the S corporation in a tax-free reorganization.

7. I.R.C. § 1374(d)(3), (5)(A).

8. I.R.C. § 1374(d)(4), (5)(B).

as if it were a C corporation.[9] The purpose of the taxable income limitation is to ensure that Section 1374 does not tax the corporation on more income than it actually realizes during the taxable year. To prevent taxpayers from avoiding the tax by manipulating the timing of post-conversion losses, Section 1374(d)(2)(B) provides that any net recognized built-in gains not taxed because of the taxable income limitation are carried forward and treated as recognized built-in gain in succeeding years in the recognition period.[10] Finally, the amount of net recognized built-in gain taken into account for any taxable year may not exceed the net unrealized built-in gain at the time the corporation became an S corporation reduced by any net recognized built-in gains which were subject to Section 1374 in prior taxable years.[11]

The Section 1374 tax easily could be avoided if it applied only to built-in gains recognized on the disposition of assets that were held by the S corporation at the beginning of its first S taxable year. For example, assume that a C corporation converting to S status holds an asset (Oldacre) with a built-in gain which it subsequently exchanges for property of like kind (Newacre) in a Section 1031 nonrecognition transaction. The gain inherent in Oldacre is preserved in Newacre's exchanged basis under Section 1031(d). If the corporation disposes of Newacre within ten years after switching to S status, the Section 1374 tax should apply to the built-in "C gain" even though Newacre was not held on the first day that the corporation was subject to Subchapter S. Section 1374(d)(6) ensures this result by providing that an asset taking an exchanged basis from another asset held by the corporation at the time it converted to S status shall be treated as having been held as of the beginning of the corporation's first S year. In the above example, the built-in gain inherent in Oldacre on the conversion from C to S status is recognized under Section 1374 if the corporation disposes of Newacre at a gain during the recognition period.

Section 1374(d)(8) is another testament to Congress's protective attitude toward the double tax. It ensures that built-in gain in assets acquired by an S corporation from a C corporation in a tax-free reorganization does not escape a corporate level tax. For this purpose, the recognition period commences as of the date the asset is acquired rather than on the beginning of the first taxable year for which the corporation was an S corporation.[12]

Tax advisors began to plot strategies to reduce the impact of Section 1374 soon after it was enacted. For example, it was suggested that the tax might be avoided if an S corporation sold an asset with built-in gain during

---

**9.** I.R.C. § 1374(b)(1), (d)(2). Taxable income, as defined in Section 63(a), is modified by disregarding certain deductions (e.g., the dividends received deduction) and net operating losses. I.R.C. §§ 1374(d)(2)(A)(ii); 1375(b)(1)(B). Net operating loss and capital loss carryforwards from prior years as a C corporation are taken into account in com-

puting the amount subject to tax under Section 1374. I.R.C. § 1374(b)(2).

**10.** The carryover rule applies only to corporations that elected S status on or after March 31, 1988. I.R.C. § 1374(d)(2)(B).

**11.** I.R.C. § 1374(c)(2), (d)(1).

**12.** I.R.C. § 1374(d)(8).

the 10–year recognition period on the installment method but delayed receipt of any payments (and thus any recognized gain) until after the recognition period had expired.[13] Not surprisingly, the Service has expressed its displeasure with this gambit. The regulations provide that the built-in gain rules will continue to apply to income recognized under the installment method during taxable years ending after the expiration of the recognition period. The gain, when recognized, will be subject to tax under Section 1374.[14]

*Tax on Passive Investment Income.* When it widened the gates to Subchapter S, Congress became concerned that a C corporation with earnings and profits might make an S election and redeploy substantial amounts in liquid assets yielding passive investment income such as dividends and interest. Left unchecked, this strategy would enable a profitable C corporation to move to the single-tax regime of Subchapter S and pass through the investment income to its shareholders, who might delay, perhaps forever, paying any shareholder-level tax on the Subchapter C earnings and profits. This plan had particular allure when a C corporation sold all of its operating assets and was seeking an alternative to the shareholder-level tax that would be imposed under Section 331 on a distribution of the proceeds in complete liquidation.[15]

The Code includes two weapons to foil the Subchapter S/passive income ploy. As discussed earlier, an S corporation with accumulated earnings and profits from its prior life as a C corporation will lose its S status if it has passive investment income that exceeds 25 percent of its gross receipts for three consecutive taxable years.[16] In addition, even before its S status is terminated, the corporation will be subject to a corporate-level tax under Section 1375. The tax, which equals 35 percent of the corporation's "excess net passive income," is imposed if an S corporation has earnings and profits from a taxable year prior to its S election and more than 25 percent of the corporation's gross receipts for the taxable year consist of "passive investment income."

For purposes of the Section 1375 tax, "passive investment income" is defined as gross receipts from royalties, rents, dividends, interest, and annuities, together with gains from sales or exchanges of stock or securities.[17] Interest earned on obligations acquired from the sale of inventory, the gross receipts of certain lending and finance institutions, and gains received as a result of the liquidation of a more than 50% controlled corporation are not passive investment income.[18] To prevent easy manipulation of the gross receipts test, only the excess of gains over losses from

**13.** See, e.g., Taggart, "Emerging Tax Issues in Corporate Acquisitions," 44 Tax L.Rev. 459, 481 (1989).

**14.** Reg. § 1.1374–4(h)(1). For the relationship of this rule to other aspects of Section 1374, see Reg. § 1.1374–4(h)(2)–(5).

**15.** Under Section 331(a), liquidating distributions received by a C corporation

shareholder are treated as in full payment in exchange for the stock.

**16.** I.R.C. § 1362(d)(3). See Section C of this chapter, supra.

**17.** I.R.C.                §§ 1375(b)(3); 1362(d)(3)(D)(i).

**18.** I.R.C. § 1362(d)(3)(D)(ii)–(iv).

dispositions of capital assets (other than stock and securities) is included in gross receipts, and gross receipts from the sales or exchanges of stock or securities are taken into account only to the extent of gains.[19] The term "stock or securities" is interpreted expansively and includes stock rights, warrants, debentures, partnership interests, and "certificates of interest" in profit-sharing arrangements.[20]

The computation of the Section 1375 tax is a technician's dream (and a student's nightmare?). The base for the Section 1375 tax, "excess net passive income," is a percentage of the corporation's "net passive income," which is generally equal to passive investment income less deductions directly connected with the production of such income.[21] To arrive at excess net passive income, net passive income is multiplied by a ratio, which has a numerator equal to the excess of passive investment income over 25 percent of gross receipts for the year, and a denominator equal to passive investment income for the year.[22] There is one final caveat: excess net passive income cannot exceed the corporation's taxable income for the year computed with the special changes described in Section 1374(d)(4).[23]

An example may help control the pollution. Assume that X Corporation made a Subchapter S election last year and will have accumulated earnings and profits from prior C corporation operations at the end of its current taxable year, in which X has $50,000 of income from its regular business operations and $35,000 of business deductions. X also receives $15,000 of interest income and $10,000 of dividends and incurs $5,000 of expenses directly related to the production of the investment income.

Is X subject to the Section 1375 tax? The corporation will have Subchapter C earnings and profits at the close of its taxable year and more than 25 percent of its gross receipts are passive investment income ($25,000 out of $75,000 of gross receipts), so the tax is potentially applicable. X's net passive income is $20,000 ($25,000 of passive investment income less directly connected expenses), and it will have $5,000 of excess net passive income ($20,000 of net passive income multiplied by a ratio having $6,250 as the numerator ($25,000 of passive investment income reduced by 25 percent of gross receipts) and $25,000 as the denominator (passive investment income)). Since excess net passive income does not exceed X's taxable income as determined under Section 1374(d)(4), the corporation's tax liability will be $1,750 ($5,000 × 35 percent).

Section 1375(d) offers one avenue for relief from the Section 1375 tax. The tax may be waived if the S corporation establishes to the satisfaction of the Service that it determined, in good faith, that it had no earnings and profits at the close of a taxable year and, within a reasonable period after discovering earnings and profits, they were distributed. The addition of an

**19.**  I.R.C. §§ 1375(b)(3); 1362(d)(3)(C); 1222(9).

**20.**  See Reg. § 1.1362–3(d)(4)(ii)(B).

**21.**  I.R.C. § 1375(b)(2).

**22.**  I.R.C. § 1375(b)(1)(A).

**23.**  I.R.C. § 1375(b)(1)(B).

"anti-blunder" provision to this complex area is a welcome sign and one hopes the Service will be merciful in its administration of Section 1375(d).

Because the definition of passive investment income includes gross receipts from sales or exchanges of stock or securities, the same gain might be taxed under both Sections 1374 and 1375. To prevent this possibility, Congress provided in Section 1375(b)(4) that the amount of passive investment income taken into account under Section 1375 is reduced by any recognized built-in gain or loss of the S corporation for any taxable year in the recognition period. Congress also considered the interaction of Sections 1374 and 1375 with the provisions taxing the shareholders of an S corporation. Any Section 1374 tax is treated as a loss (characterized according to the built-in gain subject to tax) sustained by the S corporation which will pass through to the shareholders, and each item of passive investment income is reduced by its proportionate share of the Section 1375 tax.[24]

It is important to keep the application of Sections 1374 and 1375 in perspective. A new corporation making a Subchapter S election generally does not have to be concerned with either provision. Section 1374(c)(1) will protect the corporation from the Section 1374 tax and, since the corporation's activities will not generate earnings and profits,[25] Section 1375 cannot apply to the corporation. Therefore, Sections 1374 and 1375 normally will not play a role in deciding whether to utilize a partnership or an S corporation for a new venture.

Additional considerations come into play if a C corporation is considering a move to a single tax regime. An operating C corporation must consider the impact of Sections 1374 and 1375 on a possible Subchapter S election. Weighed against these penalty provisions is the fact that a shift from C corporation status to partnership status requires a liquidation of the corporation, which may result in significant current corporate and shareholder tax liability.[26] The immediate tax cost of moving to a partnership format may be significant enough to tip the balance in favor of a Subchapter S election and force an accommodation with Sections 1374 and 1375, if planning cannot successfully eliminate their impact.

## PROBLEMS

**1.** Built-in Corporation ("B") was formed in 2000 as a C corporation. The shareholders of B elected S corporation status effective as of January 1, 2004, when it had no Subchapter C earnings and profits and the following assets:

| Asset | Adj. Basis | F.M.V. |
|---|---|---|
| Land | $30,000 | $20,000 |
| Building | 10,000 | 35,000 |
| Machinery | 15,000 | 30,000 |

**24.**  I.R.C. § 1366(f)(2), (3).

**25.**  I.R.C. § 1371(c)(1).

**26.**  See I.R.C. §§ 331; 336; 1001.

For purposes of this problem, disregard any cost recovery deductions that may be available to B. Consider the shareholder and corporate level tax consequences of the following alternative transactions:

(a) B sells the building for $50,000 in 2005; its taxable income for 2005 if it were not an S corporation would be $75,000.

(b) Same as (a), above, except that B's taxable income for 2005 if it were not an S corporation would be $20,000.

(c) Same as (a), above, except that B also sells the machinery for $40,000 in 2006, when it would have substantial taxable income if it were not an S corporation.

(d) B trades the building for an apartment building in a tax-free § 1031 exchange and then sells the apartment building for $50,000 in 2005, when it would have substantial taxable income if it were not an S corporation.

(e) B sells the building for $90,000 in 2014.

**2.** S Corporation elected S corporation status beginning in 2001 and will have Subchapter C earnings and profits at the close of the current taxable year. This year, S expects that its business operations and investments will produce the following tax results:

| | |
|---|---|
| Gross income from operations | $75,000 |
| Business deductions | 60,000 |
| Tax-exempt interest | 5,000 |
| Dividends | 12,000 |
| Long-term capital gain from the sale of investment real property | 35,000 |
| Long-term capital gain from the sale of IBM stock | 18,000 |
| Long-term capital loss from the sale of General Motors stock | 8,000 |

(a) Is S Corporation subject to the § 1375 tax on passive investment income? If so, compute the amount of tax.

(b) Same as (a), above, except that S receives an additional $5,000 of tax-exempt interest.

**3.** The San Diego Bay Boat Storage and Marina Corporation ("Bay") was formed in 1999 as a C corporation and has substantial accumulated earnings and profits. Bay's business consists of three primary activities. About one-third of Bay's gross receipts are derived from marine service and repair work conducted by its two mechanics. Another one-third of Bay's total receipts come from the rental of berths to boat owners. Berthing fees vary depending upon the size of the particular boat. A boat owner renting a berth from Bay must pay a separate charge to have Bay's employees launch or haul out his boat. However, if given advance notice, Bay employees will fuel an owner's boat, charging only for the fuel. The remainder of bay's receipts come from dry storage of boats. Owners pay $200 per month for dry storage in Bay's warehouse where a Bay employee is on duty 24 hours a day. For this fee, Bay employees will launch, fuel (with a charge for fuel)

and haul out the boat whenever requested by the owner. Bay's mechanics also will perform a free engine analysis every other year for owners of power boats in dry storage.

Bay is considering the possibility of making a Subchapter S election and has requested your advice concerning any problems which it may have. What difference would it make if Bay were a newly formed corporation?

---

## G.   Coordination with Subchapter C

Code: §§ 1371; 1372.

It is important to remember that an S corporation is still a corporation for many tax purposes. It is organized in the same manner as other corporations, and it may engage in most of the transactions and experience the corporate adjustments encountered throughout this text. After incorporating or escaping from Subchapter C, S corporations may make nonliquidating distributions of property or stock, engage in redemptions, or acquire other businesses in either taxable or tax-free transactions. They may sell their assets and liquidate, be acquired by another corporation, or divide up into two or more separate corporations. The tax consequences of these and other events in an S corporation's life cycle are determined by a patchwork quilt of Code sections pieced together from Subchapters C and S. The resulting product provides a challenging opportunity to study the uneasy relationship between a double tax regime and a pass-through scheme.

Section 1371(a) begins the statutory snake dance with the deceptively simple general rule that the provisions of Subchapter C apply to an S corporation and its shareholders. This broad admonition is subject to two related exceptions. First, any provision in the Code specifically applicable to S corporations naturally will apply. Second, if the provisions of Subchapter C are "inconsistent with" Subchapter S, the S rules are controlling. Reliable authority is sparse on precisely how Congress intended to harmonize the rules, but the Service gradually has offered guidance. The details are best raised in the context of specific transactions.

*Formation of a Corporation.* The same rules governing transfers of property to a C corporation apply to newly formed S corporations.[1] Shareholders who comprise the founding 80 percent or more "control" group do not recognize gain or loss on the transfer of property to the corporation if the requirements of Section 351(a) are met, but realized gain is recognized to the extent the shareholder receives boot[2] or if the transferred liabilities exceed the shareholder's basis for the transferred property.[3] Shareholders determine their basis in stock, debt obligations and other boot received under Section 358. The corporation takes a transferred basis in any contributed assets under Section 362(a). Organizational expenditures may

---

**1.**  I.R.C. § 351(a).                    **3.**  I.R.C. § 357(c).

**2.**  I.R.C. § 351(b).

be deducted and amortized if the corporation elects to do so under Section 248, and the benefit of the deductions passes through to the shareholders.

Several other formation issues, most relating to the "small business corporation requirements," are unique to S corporations. To qualify for the S election, the corporation must be mindful of the 100–shareholder limit and the prohibition against certain types of shareholders (e.g., nonresident aliens, partnerships). As for capital structure, an S corporation is limited to one class of stock and thus may not issue preferred stock, but it is free to issue debt, preferably in a form that qualifies for the straight debt safe harbor.[4] Unlike a corporation facing the double tax, an S corporation has no particular incentive to issue pro rata debt to its shareholders.[5]

*S Corporations as Shareholders.* At one time, an S corporation in its capacity as a shareholder of another corporation was treated as an individual for purposes of Subchapter C. The purpose of this rule was to ensure that an S corporation would not qualify for the Section 243 dividends received deduction, which is designed to prevent double taxation at the corporate level and thus should not be available to a pass-through entity.[6] As drafted, however, the rule had a ripple effect on other transactions, leading Congress to repeal it in 1996 and clarify the tax consequences of many of the transactions discussed below. The legislative history includes a reminder that S corporations, like individuals, may not claim a dividends received deduction or treat any item of income or deduction in a manner inconsistent with the treatment accorded to individual taxpayers.[7]

*Distributions and Liquidating Sales.* As discussed earlier,[8] Subchapter S generally preempts Subchapter C in determining the tax consequences of nonliquidating distributions. Section 1368 specifically provides that it shall apply to any distribution to which Section 301(c) otherwise would apply. This means that Section 1368 is the reference point not only for routine nonliquidating distributions but also other transactions, such as dividend-equivalent redemptions and taxable stock distributions, which are classified under Subchapter C as distributions to which Section 301 applies.[9] We have seen that an S corporation recognizes gain under Section 311(b) on a distribution of appreciated property but, unless Section 1374 applies, that gain is not taxed at the corporate level. Instead, the gain passes through to the shareholders, who may increase their stock basis by their respective shares of the gain.

In the case of liquidating distributions and sales, Subchapter C reassumes center stage. Liquidating distributions generally trigger recognition

---

**4.** I.R.C. § 1361(c)(5).

**5.** For the advantages and disadvantages of issuing debt in the S corporation setting, see Eustice & Kuntz, Federal Income Taxation of S Corporations ¶ 6.03[1] (4th ed. 2001).

**6.** See, e.g., S.Rep. No. 640, 97th Cong., 2d Sess. 15, reprinted in 1982–2 C.B. 718, 724–725.

**7.** See H.R. Rep. 104–737, 104th Cong., 2d Sess. 56 (1996).

**8.** See Section E of this chapter, supra.

**9.** See, e.g., I.R.C. §§ 302(d); 305(b). Section 306 is unlikely to apply in the S setting, however, because an S corporation may not issue preferred stock.

of gain or loss to an S corporation under Section 336 in the same manner as if the corporation were subject to Subchapter C. Sales of assets pursuant to a plan of complete liquidation also are taxable. In either case, however, these gains will pass through to the shareholders and be subject to a single shareholder-level tax unless Section 1374 intercedes. An S corporation also may make a liquidating sale on the installment method. Under certain conditions, these installment obligations may be distributed without triggering corporate-level gain (unless Section 1374 applies), and the shareholders may use the installment method to report the gain.[10] The *character* of the shareholder's gain in this situation is not determined by reference to their stock, which ordinarily would be a capital asset, but rather "in accordance with the principles of Section 1366(d)"[11]—i.e., as if the corporate-level gain on the sale of the asset had been passed through to the shareholders.[12]

Subchapter C also governs the shareholder-level consequences of a complete liquidation. An S corporation shareholder treats distributions in complete liquidation as in full payment in exchange for the stock under Section 331. Although liquidating distributions and sales result in only one level of tax to an S corporation and its shareholders,[13] variations between the shareholder's stock basis and the corporation's basis in its assets may have an impact on the character of the shareholder's gain or loss. For example, assume A owns all of the stock of S, Inc. (an S corporation with no prior C history) and has a $2,000 basis in her S stock. Assume S owns one ordinary income asset which has a $10,000 fair market value and a $1,000 adjusted basis. If S sells the asset, it will recognize $9,000 of ordinary income. The gain passes through to A, and her stock basis is increased by $9,000, to $11,000, under Section 1367. When S liquidates and distributes $10,000 cash to A, she recognizes a $1,000 long-term capital loss. Alternatively, if the ordinary income asset had a $2,000 basis, S would recognize $8,000 of ordinary income on its sale which would pass through to A, increasing her stock basis to $10,000. When S liquidates and distributes $10,000 cash to A, she would recognize no additional gain or loss.

*Taxable Acquisitions of S Corporations.* An acquisition of an S corporation may be structured as either a purchase of stock from the shareholders or a purchase of assets from the corporation. The method chosen affects not only the amount, character and timing of gain but also may have an impact on the tax status of the S corporation and perhaps even the acquiring party if it also is an S corporation.

---

**10.** See I.R.C. § 453B(h). To qualify for corporate-level nonrecognition, the S corporation must distribute the obligation in complete liquidation. In addition, the obligations must result from sales of assets (other than nonbulk sales of inventory) during the 12–month period following the adoption of the liquidation plan. See I.R.C. § 453(h).

**11.** I.R.C. § 453B(h).

**12.** Thus, if the installment sale would have given rise to ordinary income, that character will pass through to the shareholders when they collect the installment obligations.

**13.** This is because the corporate-level gain on a liquidating distribution or sale results in upward basis adjustments to the shareholder's stock under Section 1367. A double tax would be imposed, however, if Section 1374 applies.

An asset acquisition often is preferable because the purchaser will obtain a cost basis in the S corporation's assets at the cost of only a shareholder-level tax.[14] For example, assume P, Inc. wishes to acquire T, Inc. (an S corporation with no prior C history). If P purchases T's assets, any gain or loss recognized by T on the sale will pass through to its shareholders, and P will obtain a cost basis in the assets. T's shareholders will increase their stock basis by any gain recognized on the sale under Section 1367, thus avoiding a second tax on the same economic gain when T liquidates.

If P is a C corporation and purchases a controlling interest in the T stock, the T shareholders recognize gain or loss on the sale, and P takes a cost basis in the stock it acquires. T's S election will terminate, however, because an S corporation may not have any C corporation shareholders.[15] If P does not make a Section 338 election, T retains its historic bases in its assets, and as a new C corporation it will face the prospect of a corporate-level tax on any built-in gain. If P makes a Section 338 election to obtain a cost basis in T's assets, T—which loses its S status on the acquisition—must pay a corporate-level tax as a result of the deemed asset sale.[16] If P and T make a joint Section 338(h)(10) election, the regulations provide that old T (still considered an S corporation at this point) recognizes gain or loss on the deemed sale of its assets and then is deemed to have distributed those assets in complete liquidation.[17] The gain or loss on the deemed asset sale passes through to T's shareholders, with resulting basis adjustments to their T stock. Those adjustments then may be taken into account in determining the shareholders' gain or loss under Section 331 on the deemed complete liquidation of old T.[18]

*Taxable Acquisitions by S Corporations.* When the purchasing corporation ("P") is an S corporation, the primary concern usually is the preservation of P's S status. If P purchases the assets of T, the mix of consideration used in the transaction must be tailored to the S corporation eligibility requirements. P thus should avoid using its own stock or hybrid debt in order to avoid running afoul of the 100–shareholder limit or the prohibition against having more than one class of stock.[19]

When an S corporation acquires the stock of T, the acquisition will not necessarily result in a loss of the acquiring corporation's S status because S

---

**14.** Once again, this assumes that the corporation has no built-in gains that would be taxed under Section 1374. In contrast, an acquisition of assets from a C corporation generates tax at both the corporate and shareholder levels if the target liquidates. See Chapter 16B, supra.

**15.** I.R.C. §§ 1362(d)(2); 1361(b)(1)(B). After 1996, two or more S corporations may have a parent-subsidiary relationship in which case they are treated as one S corporation for tax purposes. I.R.C. § 1361(b)(3).

**16.** T's S election terminates when P acquires T's stock, and its short C year in-

cludes the day of the terminating event. Thus, the gain on the deemed asset sale must be reported on a one-day return for old T's "short C year." See I.R.C. §§ 1362(e)(1)(B); 338(a)(1). The economic burden of the corporate-level tax is borne by P unless it is reflected in the price paid for the stock.

**17.** Reg. §§ 1.338(h)(10)–1(h)(10),–1(d)(3)(i),–1(d)(4)(i).

**18.** See Reg. § 1.338(h)(10)–1(d)(5)(i).

**19.** See generally I.R.C. § 1361(b).

corporations may have controlled C corporation subsidiaries. In addition, an acquiring S corporation is eligible to make a Section 338 election, which will trigger immediate recognition of all T's gains and losses. Finally, if an S corporation acquires 80 percent or more of T's stock and liquidates T, the liquidation will be tax free to both corporations under Sections 332 and 337. Following that liquidation, however, any of T's built-in gains while it was a C corporation may later be subject to tax under Section 1374 upon a subsequent disposition.[20]

*Tax-Free Reorganizations.* An S corporation may be either the target or the acquiring corporation in a tax-free acquisitive reorganization. Looking first to situations where an S corporation is the target, it will lose its S status if it remains in existence as an 80 percent or more subsidiary following a tax-free acquisition of its stock by a C corporation in a Type B reorganization or reverse triangular merger. If an S corporation-target's assets are acquired in a merger or Type C reorganization, the transaction may proceed on a tax-free basis, and the target will terminate its existence as a result of the merger or the liquidation that necessary must follow a Type C reorganization.

If an S corporation is the acquiring corporation in a tax-free reorganization, it necessarily must issue new stock to the target shareholders. Whatever form of acquisition is used, care must be exercised to avoid termination of the election by exceeding the 100–shareholder limit or inheriting an ineligible shareholder. Now that S corporations may have subsidiaries, a Type B stock-for-stock acquisition, once impossible without losing S status, is now a feasible alternative. Similarly, acquisition of the assets of a C corporation in a Type A or C reorganization should not adversely affect the acquirer's S election, but the earnings and profits from the target's C years could jeopardize the acquiring corporation's S status or subject it to the Section 1375 tax if it has substantial passive investment income.[21] Moreover, an S corporation that is the acquiring corporation in a Type A or C reorganization or a forward triangular merger will inherit the target's tax attributes, including its earnings and profits, under Section 381, and its accumulated adjustments account if the target is an S corporation with a prior C history.[22] Finally, any assets acquired from a C corporation in a tax-free reorganization trigger a new ten-year recognition period for purposes of the Section 1374 tax on built-in gains.[23]

*Corporate Divisions.* An S corporation may divide itself into separate corporations in a transaction that is tax-free at both the corporate and shareholder levels if all the requirements of Section 355 are met. Even when S corporations were not permitted to have subsidiaries, the Service

**20.** As to built-in gains, see I.R.C. § 1374(d)(8); Reg. § 1.1374–8. Many of these results were in doubt prior to repeal of the statutory rule treating S corporations in their shareholder capacities as individuals for Subchapter C purposes. See generally Bittker & Eustice, Federal Income Taxation of Corpora-

tions and Shareholders ¶ 6.09[2]-[3] (7th ed. 2000).

**21.** I.R.C. § 1362(b)(3); 1375.

**22.** For rules on AAA carryovers, see Reg. § 1.1368–2(d)(2).

**23.** I.R.C. § 1374(d)(8).

was tolerant in this area, ignoring the transitory nature of a subsidiary formed in preparation for a division.[24] After the division, the new corporation (or corporations, in the case of a split-up) may immediately make an S election.[25]

PROBLEMS

**1**. Hi–Flying Co. is an aggressive growth company which was formed as a C corporation many years ago to develop new innovative technology. Hi–Flying has been successful and expects to receive inquiries concerning possible taxable and tax-free takeovers in the next few years. Can Hi–Flying's shareholders improve their tax situation in a future takeover by making an S election? In general, if Hi–Flying makes an S election, would you advise a potential corporate purchaser desiring a cost basis in Hi–Flying's assets to structure its acquisition as a purchase of stock or assets?

**2**. Target Corporation ("T") is a C corporation which has substantially appreciated assets and is a takeover candidate being pursued by several suitors. Purchasing corporation ("P") has a Subchapter S election in effect and is considering making a bid for T. Consider the tax consequences of the following acquisition offers by P:

> (a) P will offer to purchase T's stock for cash or a combination of cash and P notes.
>
> (b) P will acquire T in a Type C reorganization.

---

## H.  COMPENSATION ISSUES

S corporation shareholders also commonly serve as officers, directors and employees of their corporation. Individuals with this multiple status may have a choice as to whether to withdraw cash as compensation or as a shareholder distribution. Payments of salary are deductible by the corporation as a business expense (with the benefit of the deduction passing through to the shareholders), and are includible in the employee's gross income. Employee wages also are subject to various federal and state employment taxes imposed on both the employer and the employee (e.g., federal social security and medicare taxes).[1] Distributions, by contrast, generally may be received tax-free by shareholders to the extent of their stock basis, but they do not give rise to a deduction at the corporate level.

---

**24.**  See, e.g., G.C.M. 39678 (1988).

**25.**  For other issues, such as how to divide up the accumulated adjustments account, see Eustice & Kuntz, supra note 5, at ¶ 12.10.

**1.**  In 2005, for example, both the employer and employee must pay social security taxes of 6.2% of the first $90,000 of an employee's taxable wages. I.R.C. §§ 3101; 3111; 3121. An additional medicare tax of 1.45%, again payable by both the employer and employee, is imposed on all of an employee's wages. I.R.C. § 3121(b). See generally Raby & Raby, "New Incentives for Avoiding SE and FICA Tax," 81 Tax Notes 1389 (Oct. 14, 1998).

Because the payment of salaries to shareholders usually results in a tax "wash" in the case of a profitable corporation (the compensation deduction reduces the operating income that passes through to the shareholders), the *income* tax consequences of salaries and distributions may be identical.[2] The escalating employment tax base has influenced some S corporation shareholders to avoid this additional federal levy by foregoing salaries in lieu of larger shareholder distributions. The *Radtke* case, below, is one court's hostile reaction to this maneuver.

# Joseph Radtke, S.C. v. United States

United States District Court, Eastern District of Wisconsin, 1989.
712 F.Supp. 143, affirmed 895 F.2d 1196 (7th Cir.1990).

## ORDER

■ TERENCE T. EVANS, DISTRICT JUDGE.

* * *

## FACTS

None of the facts are disputed.

Joseph Radtke received his law degree from Marquette University in 1978. The Radtke corporation was incorporated in 1979 to provide legal services in Milwaukee. Mr. Radtke is the firm's sole incorporator, director, and shareholder. In 1982, he also served as the unpaid president and treasurer of the corporation, while his wife Joyce was the unpaid and nominal vice-president and secretary. The corporation is an electing small business corporation, otherwise known as a subchapter S corporation. This means that it is not taxed at the corporate level. All corporate income is taxed to the shareholder, whether or not the income is distributed.

In 1982, Mr. Radtke was the only full-time employee of the corporation, though it employed a few other persons on a piece-meal and part-time basis. Under an employment contract executed between Mr. Radtke and his corporation in 1980, he received "an annual base salary, to be determined by its board of directors, but in no event shall such annual salary be less than $0 per year * * *. Employee's original annual base salary shall be $0." This base salary of $0 continued through 1982, a year in which Mr. Radtke devoted all of his working time to representing the corporation's clients.

Mr. Radtke received $18,225 in dividends from the corporation in 1982. Whenever he needed money, and whenever the corporation was showing a profit—that is, when there was money in its bank account—he would do what was necessary under Wisconsin corporate law to have the board declare a dividend, and he would write a corporate check to himself.

---

**2.** The tax results are more complex, however, if the S corporation has losses for the taxable year. See Eustice & Kuntz, Feder-al Income Taxation of S Corporations ¶ 11.02[2] (4th ed. 2001).

Mr. Radtke paid personal income tax on the dividends in 1982. The Radtke corporation also declared the $18,225 on its form 1120S, the small business corporation income tax return. But the corporation did not file a federal employment tax form (Form 941) or a federal unemployment tax form (Form 940). In other words, it did not deduct a portion of the $18,225 for Social Security (FICA) and unemployment compensation (FUTA). The IRS subsequently assessed deficiencies as well as interest and penalties. The Radtke corporation paid the full amount that IRS demanded under FUTA—$366.44—and it also paid $593.75 toward the assessed FICA taxes, interest, and penalties. Then the corporation sued here after a fruitless claim for refunds.

DISCUSSION

\* \* \*

The Radtke corporation acknowledges that wages are subject to FICA and FUTA taxes, but it argues that the Internal Revenue Code nowhere treats a shareholder-employee's dividends as wages for the purpose of employment taxes. The government, on the other hand, contends that "since Joseph Radtke performed substantial services for Joseph Radtke, S.C., and did not receive reasonable compensation for such services other than 'dividends', the 'dividends' constitute 'wages' subject to federal employment taxes." The government does not allege that the Radtke corporation is a fiction that somehow failed to comply with Wisconsin statutes governing corporations.

The Federal Insurance Contributions Act defines "wages" as "all remuneration for employment," with various exceptions that are not relevant to this dispute. 26 U.S.C. § 3121(a). Similarly, the Federal Unemployment Tax Act defines "wages" as "all remuneration for employment," with certain exceptions that are not relevant. 26 U.S.C. § 3306(b). (Dividends are not specifically excepted in either act, and "remuneration" is not defined.) Mr. Radtke was clearly an "employee" of the Radtke corporation, as the plaintiff concedes. *See* 26 U.S.C. §§ 3121(d) and 3306(i). Likewise, his work for the enterprise was obviously "employment." *See* 26 U.S.C. §§ 3121(b) and 3306(c).

According to the Radtke corporation, not all "income" can be characterized as "wages." I agree. See Royster Company v. United States, 479 F.2d 387, 390 (4th Cir.1973) (free lunches did not constitute "wages" subject to FICA and FUTA); Central Illinois Public Service Co. v. United States, 435 U.S. 21, 25, 98 S.Ct. 917, 919, 55 L.Ed.2d 82 (1978) (reimbursement for lunches not "wages" subject to withholding tax; Court says in dicta that dividends are not wages).

At the same time, however, I am not moved by the Radtke corporation's connected argument that "dividends" cannot be "wages." Courts reviewing tax questions are obligated to look at the substance, not the form, of the transactions at issue. Transactions between a closely held corporation and its principals, who may have multiple relationships with

the corporation, are subject to particularly careful scrutiny. Whether dividends represent a distribution of profits or instead are compensation for employment is a matter to be determined in view of all the evidence.

In the circumstances of this case—where the corporation's only director had the corporation pay himself, the only significant employee, *no* salary for substantial services—I believe that Mr. Radtke's "dividends" were in fact "wages" subject to FICA and FUTA taxation. His "dividends" functioned as remuneration for employment.

It seems only logical that a corporation is required to pay employment taxes when it employs an employee. See Automated Typesetting, Inc. v. United States, 527 F.Supp. 515, 519 (E.D.Wis.1981) (corporation liable for employment taxes on payments to officers who performed more than nominal services for corporation); C.D. Ulrich, Ltd. v. United States, 692 F.Supp. 1053, 1055 (D.Minn.1988) (discussing case law defining who is an "employee"; court refuses to enjoin IRS from collecting employment taxes from S corporation that paid dividends but no salary to sole shareholder and director, a certified public accountant who worked for the firm). See also Rev.Rul. 73–361, 1973–2 C.B. 331 (stockholder-officer who performed substantial services for S corporation is "employee," and his salary is subject to FICA and FUTA tax); Rev.Rul. 71–86, 1971–1 C.B. 285 (president and sole stockholder of corporation is "employee" whose salary is subject to employment taxes, even though he alone fixes his salary and determines his duties).

An employer should not be permitted to evade FICA and FUTA by characterizing *all* of an employee's remuneration as something other than "wages." Cf. Greenlee v. United States, 87–1 U.S.T.C. Para. 9306 (corporation's interest-free loans to sole shareholder constituted "wages" for FICA and FUTA where loans were made at shareholder's discretion and he performed substantial services for corporation). This is simply the flip side of those instances in which corporations attempt to disguise profit distributions as salaries for whatever tax benefits that may produce. See, e.g., Miles–Conley Co. v. Commissioner, 173 F.2d 958, 960–61 (4th Cir.1949) (corporation could not deduct from its gross income excessive salary paid to president and sole stockholder).

Accordingly, the plaintiff's motion for summary judgment is DENIED, and the defendant's motion for summary judgment is GRANTED. The plaintiff is ORDERED to pay the remaining deficiency on its 1982 FICA taxes along with the assessed interest, penalties, and fees.

## NOTE

*Subsequent Developments.* In accord with *Radtke* are Fred R. Esser, P.C. v. United States,[1] Dunn & Clark, P.A. v. Commissioner,[2] and Spicer Accounting, Inc. v. United States.[3] A contrary result was reached in Davis

---

**1.**   750 F.Supp. 421 (D.Ariz.1990).          **2.**   57 F.3d 1076 (9th Cir.1995).

**3.**   918 F.2d 90 (9th Cir.1990).

v. United States,[4] where the court declined to recharacterize S corporation distributions as taxable wages. *Davis* is distinguishable, however, because the shareholders performed only minor services on behalf of the S corporation.

*Fringe Benefits.* Fringe benefits paid by an S corporation to its shareholder-employees also are subject to special treatment. Section 1372 provides that an S corporation shall be treated as a partnership for purposes of employee fringe benefits, and any shareholder owning either more than two percent of the corporation's outstanding stock or more than two percent of the total voting power of all stock will be treated as a partner. As a result, an S corporation seldom can provide benefits, such as a medical reimbursement plan or group-term life insurance, which are deductible by the corporation and excludable from gross income of its shareholder-employees.[5]

---

## I.   TAX POLICY ISSUES: SUBCHAPTER K VS. SUBCHAPTER S*

The check-the-box elective classification regime discussed in Chapter 1 has made it easier for virtually any closely held business to obtain pass-through taxation treatment. This has resurrected the longstanding debate on the most desirable structure for a pass-through system. The excerpt below, from a study by the Joint Committee on Taxation, compares the tax treatment of partnerships and S corporations and surveys the competing views on the need to retain two different pass-through regimes.

### Excerpt From Review of Selected Entity Classification and Partnership Tax Issues

Staff of Joint Committee on Taxation (JCS–6–97) 23–25 (April 8, 1997).

*Need for multiple sets of rules for pass-through entities*

[The issuance of final check-the-box classification regulations raises a set of issues regarding] whether there is a continuing need in the tax law for parallel pass-through systems for general business activities.[42] Although S corporations (and their shareholders) generally are treated similarly to partnerships (and their partners), significant differences exist, some of which favor S corporations while others favor partnerships.

---

**4.**   74 AFTR 2d 5618 (D.Colo.1994).

**5.**   For special rules relating to health insurance, see I.R.C. § 162(*l*)(1), (5), and Rev. Rul. 91–26, 1991–1 C.B. 184.

\* See generally Eustice, "Subchapter S Corporations and Partnerships: A Search for the Pass Through Paradigm (Some Preliminary Proposals)," 39 Tax L.Rev. 345 (1984).

**42.**   Eliminating the two-tier corporate tax system, perhaps through some form of corporate integration, could also minimize the need for multiple sets of rules for pass-through entities, but is beyond the scope of this discussion.

For example, the items of income, gain, loss, deduction or credit of a partnership generally are taken into account by a partner pursuant to the partnership agreement (or in accordance with the partners' interest in the partnership if the agreement does not provide for an allocation) so long as such allocation has substantial economic effect.[43] Because of the one-class-of-stock rule for S corporations (sec. 1361(b)(1)(D)), the items of income, gain, loss, deduction or credit of an S corporation cannot be separately allocated to a particular shareholder, but are taken into account by all the shareholders on a per-share, per-day basis. Thus, partnerships generally are considered to be a more flexible vehicle for purposes of allocating particular entity-level items to investors.

Another important difference making partnerships more flexible than S corporations is the treatment of entity-level debt, for purposes of the owner's basis in his interest. A partner includes partnership-level debt in the basis of his interest (sec. 752), whereas an S corporation shareholder does not (sec. 1367). The amount of the partner's or S corporation shareholder's basis in his interest serves as a limit on the amount of losses that can be passed through (secs. 704(d), 1366(d)), which makes increases in basis for entity-level debt important.

The sale of stock in an S corporation generally results in capital gain or loss to the selling shareholder. The sale of an interest in a partnership also generally gives rise to capital gain or loss, but gives rise to ordinary income to the selling partner to the extent attributable to unrealized receivables and certain inventory items (sec. 751).

The distribution of appreciated property by an S corporation to a shareholder (as a dividend, in redemption of shares, or in liquidation) is treated as a taxable sale of such property. Any gain is allocated to all the shareholders on a per-share, per day basis and increases the shareholder's adjusted bases in their shares. The distributee shareholder then reduces his basis by the amount of the distribution (i.e., fair market value of the distributed property) and takes a fair market value basis in the property. By contrast, the distribution of appreciated property by a partnership to a partner generally is not treated as a taxable sale of the property (sec. 731).

An existing C corporation may elect to be treated as an S corporation on a tax-free basis, subject to certain special rules. Converting C corporations are subject to corporate-level tax on the recapture of LIFO benefits,[44] on certain built-in gains recognized within a 10–year period after conversion,[45] and on certain passive investment income earned while the corpora-

**43.** Sections 704(a) and (b). The determination of whether an allocation has substantial economic effect is complex (Treas. Reg. sec. 1.704–1(b)(2)).

**44.** Sec. 1363(d).

**45.** Section 1374. For a discussion of how section 1374 allows the conversion of a C corporation to S corporation to be treated more favorably than the liquidation of a C corporation into a sole proprietorship or a partnership, despite the economic equivalence of the transactions, see letter to Chairman Dan Rostenkowski from Ronald A. Pearlman, Chief of Staff of the Joint Committee on Taxation, recommending several simplification proposals, reprinted in Committee on Ways and Means, Written Proposals on Tax Simplification (WMCP 101–27), May 25,

tion retains its former C corporate earnings and profits.[46] The conversion of a C corporation to a partnership (or sole proprietorship) is treated as a liquidation of the entity, taxable to both the corporation and its shareholders.

The rules of subchapter C generally apply to an S corporation and its shareholders. Thus, for example, an S corporation may merge into a C corporation (or vice versa) on a tax-free basis. Similar rules do not apply to combinations of C corporations and partnerships.

Individual partners treated as general partners generally are subject to self-employment tax on their distributive shares of partnership income. Shareholders of an S corporation are not subject to self-employment tax on S corporation earnings, but are subject to payroll tax to the extent they receive salaries or wages from the corporation.

Partnerships, LLCs treated as partnerships, and S corporations may be treated differently for State income or franchise tax purposes.

### Continuing utility of S corporations

If an LLC can provide limited liability to all owners and achieve pass-through status as a partnership under the check-the-box regulations (or under the Service's prior revenue rulings on LLCs), the need for S corporations could be questioned. Particularly in light of the growing use of LLCs, it could be argued that the great flexibility of the partnership tax rules outweigh the principal advantage of S corporations: relative simplicity. Thus, it is argued that the rules for S corporations could be repealed without detriment to taxpayers.[47]

Others say the continued existence of subchapter S is worthwhile. A corporate charter is a prerequisite imposed by regulators for some trades or businesses (e.g., for depository institutions or to hold certain licenses), and LLCs may not meet such regulatory requirements. Moreover, the corporate form is a familiar, time-tested format, while the LLC form is new and unfamiliar (particularly where a business undertakes interstate commerce). Subchapter S supporters further point out that the rules of subchapter S are much simpler than the rules of subchapter K.[48] Others point to specific

---

1990, p. 24. In his 1995 and 1997 budget messages to the Congress, President Clinton recommended that section 1374 be repealed for C corporations above a certain size. [Later proposals made by the Clinton administration would have repealed Section 1374 for C-to-S conversions of corporations with a value of more than $5 million at the time of conversion and treated the transaction as a taxable liquidation of the C corporation followed by a contribution of the assets to an S corporation by the recipient shareholders. Ed.]

**46.**   Section 1375.

**47.**   W. Schwidetzky, "Is It Time to Give the S Corporation a Proper Burial?" 15 Virginia Tax Review 591 (1996).

**48.**   However, it must be pointed out that partners of a partnership may opt for a simple, subchapter-S like structure if they so desire. It could be said that the check-the-box regulations expand the appeal of subchapter S, because prior to those regulations, only entities structured as corporations for State law purposes could elect S corporation status, whereas now, a State-law partnership or LLC can be classified as a corporation for tax purposes and elect S status (provided applicable requirements are met).

advantages of subchapter S over the partnership tax rules (primarily the ability to convert from C to S corporation status generally without current corporate tax on appreciation, and the availability of tax-free reorganization rules for business combinations and reorganizations). At least until LLC interests are as easily issued in capital markets as traditional corporate stock, the S corporation may continue to be an attractive vehicle in which to start a business, if it is anticipated that it will later go public. Finally, any repeal of subchapter S would require rules providing for the treatment of existing S corporations.[49]

Whether or not it is advisable to retain both the partnership rules and the S corporation rules, some argue that the complexity of either regime is excessive for small businesses, and a new, much simpler pass-through system should be provided for small businesses that would be consistent with the new simplicity for choice of entity under the check-the-box regulations.[50] A significant question, under such an approach, is the definition of a small business, which could depend on the number of owners, the value of the entity's assets, the amount of its gross or net income (if any), or some combination of these or other factors. Related questions involve the treatment of businesses that grow (or fluctuate in size), crossing the definitional line, and the treatment of tax attributes imported from a more complex tax regime. Weighing of simplicity against accuracy of income measurement and allocation would be a factor in designing a simpler regime.

Others would argue that there is nothing inherently complex in the application of the partnership tax rules to most small business transactions. Small businesses today can achieve the effect of a simplified partnership regime for most common business arrangements. Mandating the use of specific rules for small business would deny them the flexibility of present law partnership rules and, it could be argued, would represent a competitive disadvantage relative to larger businesses.

---

**49.** See, for example, the letter of July 25, 1995, from Leslie B. Samuels, Assistant Treasury Secretary (Tax Policy) to Senator Orin Hatch, suggesting possible legislative proposals to allow S corporations to elect partnership status or to apply the check-the-box regulations to S corporations.

**50.** American Law Institute, Federal Income Tax Project—Taxation of Pass-Through Entities, Memorandum No. 2 96–105 (Sept. 2, 1996) (G. Yin and D. Shakow, reporters).

\*

# FORM 1065, SCHEDULE K–1

6511

| | | | |
|---|---|---|---|
| ☐ Final K-1 | ☐ Amended K-1 | | OMB No. 1545-0099 |

**Schedule K-1**
**(Form 1065)**

20**04**

Department of the Treasury
Internal Revenue Service

Tax year beginning _____ , 2004
and ending _____ , 20 __

**Partner's Share of Income, Deductions,**
**Credits, etc.**   ► See back of form and separate instructions.

| Part I | Information About the Partnership |
|---|---|

**A**   Partnership's employer identification number

**B**   Partnership's name, address, city, state, and ZIP code

**C**   IRS Center where partnership filed return

**D** ☐ Check if this is a publicly traded partnership (PTP)
**E** ☐ Tax shelter registration number, if any _____
**F** ☐ Check if Form 8271 is attached

| Part II | Information About the Partner |
|---|---|

**G**   Partner's identifying number

**H**   Partner's name, address, city, state, and ZIP code

**I** ☐ General partner or LLC member-manager   ☐ Limited partner or other LLC member

**J** ☐ Domestic partner   ☐ Foreign partner

**K**   What type of entity is this partner? _____

**L**   Partner's share of profit, loss, and capital:

| | Beginning | Ending |
|---|---|---|
| Profit | _____ % | _____ % |
| Loss | _____ % | _____ % |
| Capital | _____ % | _____ % |

**M**   Partner's share of liabilities at year end:

Nonrecourse   $ _____
Qualified nonrecourse financing   $ _____
Recourse   $ _____

**N**   Partner's capital account analysis:

Beginning capital account   $ _____
Capital contributed during the year   $ _____
Current year increase (decrease)   $ _____
Withdrawals & distributions   $ ( _____ )
Ending capital account   $ _____

☐ Tax basis   ☐ GAAP   ☐ Section 704(b) book
☐ Other (explain)

| Part III | Partner's Share of Current Year Income, Deductions, Credits, and Other Items |
|---|---|

| | | | |
|---|---|---|---|
| 1 | Ordinary business income (loss) | 15 | Credits & credit recapture |
| 2 | Net rental real estate income (loss) | | |
| 3 | Other net rental income (loss) | 16 | Foreign transactions |
| 4 | Guaranteed payments | | |
| 5 | Interest income | | |
| 6a | Ordinary dividends | | |
| 6b | Qualified dividends | | |
| 7 | Royalties | | |
| 8 | Net short-term capital gain (loss) | | |
| 9a | Net long-term capital gain (loss) | 17 | Alternative minimum tax (AMT) items |
| 9b | Collectibles (28%) gain (loss) | | |
| 9c | Unrecaptured section 1250 gain | | |
| 10 | Net section 1231 gain (loss) | 18 | Tax-exempt income and nondeductible expenses |
| 11 | Other income (loss) | | |
| | | 19 | Distributions |
| 12 | Section 179 deduction | | |
| 13 | Other deductions | | |
| | | 20 | Other information |
| 14 | Self-employment earnings (loss) | | |

*See attached statement for additional information.

For IRS Use Only

For Privacy Act and Paperwork Reduction Act Notice, see Instructions for Form 1065.   Cat. No. 11394R   Schedule K-1 (Form 1065) 2004

This list identifies the codes used on Schedule K-1 for all partners and provides summarized reporting information for partners who file Form 1040. For detailed reporting and filing information, see the separate Partner's Instructions for Schedule K-1 and the instructions for your income tax return.

1. **Ordinary business income (loss).** You must first determine whether the income (loss) is passive or nonpassive. Then enter on your return as follows:

| | *Enter on* |
|---|---|
| Passive loss | See the Partner's Instructions |
| Passive income | Schedule E, line 28, column (g) |
| Nonpassive loss | Schedule E, line 28, column (h) |
| Nonpassive income | Schedule E, line 28, column (j) |

2. **Net rental real estate income (loss)** — See the Partner's Instructions

3. **Other net rental income (loss)**
| Net income | Schedule E, line 28, column (g) |
|---|---|
| Net loss | See the Partner's Instructions |

4. **Guaranteed payments** — Schedule E, line 28, column (j)

5. **Interest income** — Form 1040, line 8a

6a. **Ordinary dividends** — Form 1040, line 9a

6b. **Qualified dividends** — Form 1040, line 9b

7. **Royalties** — Schedule E, line 4

8. **Net short-term capital gain (loss)** — Schedule D, line 5, column (f)

9a. **Net long-term capital gain (loss)** — Schedule D, line 12, column (f)

9b. **Collectibles (28%) gain (loss)** — 28% Rate Gain Worksheet, line 4 (Schedule D Instructions)

9c. **Unrecaptured section 1250 gain** — See the Partner's Instructions

10. **Net section 1231 gain (loss)** — See the Partner's Instructions

11. **Other income (loss)**

Code
| A | Other portfolio income (loss) | See the Partner's Instructions |
|---|---|---|
| B | Involuntary conversions | See the Partner's Instructions |
| C | Sec. 1256 contracts & straddles | Form 6781, line 1 |
| D | Mining exploration costs recapture | See Pub. 535 |
| E | Cancellation of debt | Form 1040, line 21 or Form 982 |
| F | Other income (loss) | See the Partner's Instructions |

12. **Section 179 deduction** — See the Partner's Instructions

13. **Other deductions**
| A | Cash contributions (50%) | Schedule A, line 15 |
|---|---|---|
| B | Cash contributions (30%) | Schedule A, line 15 |
| C | Noncash contributions (50%) | Schedule A, line 16 |
| D | Noncash contributions (30%) | Schedule A, line 16 |
| E | Capital gain property to a 50% organization (30%) | Schedule A, line 16 |
| F | Capital gain property (20%) | Schedule A, line 16 |
| G | Deductions—portfolio (2% floor) | Schedule A, line 22 |
| H | Deductions—portfolio (other) | Schedule A, line 27 |
| I | Investment interest expense | Form 4952, line 1 |
| J | Deductions—royalty income | Schedule E, line 18 |
| K | Section 59(e)(2) expenditures | See Partner's Instructions |
| L | Amounts paid for medical insurance | Schedule A, line 1 or Form 1040, line 31 |
| M | Educational assistance benefits | See the Partner's Instructions |
| N | Dependent care benefits | Form 2441, line 12 |
| O | Preproductive period expenses | See the Partner's Instructions |
| P | Commercial revitalization deduction from rental real estate activities | See Form 8582 Instructions |
| Q | Penalty on early withdrawal of savings | Form 1040, line 33 |
| R | Pensions and IRAs | See the Partner's Instructions |
| S | Reforestation expense deduction | See the Partner's Instructions |
| T | Other deductions | See the Partner's Instructions |

14. **Self-employment earnings (loss)**
*Note. If you have a section 179 deduction or any partner-level deductions, see the Partner's Instructions before completing Schedule SE.*
| A | Net earnings (loss) from self-employment | Schedule SE, Section A or B |
|---|---|---|
| B | Gross farming or fishing income | See the Partner's Instructions |
| C | Gross non-farm income | See the Partner's Instructions |

15. **Credits & credit recapture**
| A | Low-income housing credit (section 42(j)(5)) | Form 8586, line 5 |
|---|---|---|
| B | Low-income housing credit (other) | Form 8586, line 5 |
| C | Qualified rehabilitation expenditures (rental real estate) | Form 3468, line 1 |
| D | Qualified rehabilitation expenditures (other than rental real estate) | Form 3468, line 1 |
| E | Basis of energy property | Form 3468, line 2 |
| F | Qualified timber property | Form 3468, line 3 |
| G | Other rental real estate credits | See the Partner's Instructions |
| H | Other rental credits | See the Partner's Instructions |

Code
| I | Undistributed capital gains credit | Form 1040, line 69, box a |
|---|---|---|
| J | Work opportunity credit | Form 5884, line 3 |
| K | Welfare-to-work credit | Form 8861, line 3 |
| L | Disabled access credit | Form 8826, line 7 |
| M | Empowerment zone and renewal community employment credit | Form 8844, line 3 |
| N | New York Liberty Zone business employee credit | Form 8884, line 3 |
| O | New markets credit | Form 8874, line 2 |
| P | Credit for employer social security and Medicare taxes | Form 8846, line 5 |
| Q | Backup withholding | Form 1040, line 63 |
| R | Recapture of low-income housing credit (section 42(j)(5)) | Form 8611, line 8 |
| S | Recapture of low-income housing credit (other) | Form 8611, line 8 |
| T | Recapture of investment credit | See Form 4255 |
| U | Other credits | See the Partner's Instructions |
| V | Recapture of other credits | See the Partner's Instructions |

16. **Foreign transactions**
| A | Name of country or U.S. possession | Form 1116, Part I |
|---|---|---|
| B | Gross income from all sources | Form 1116, Part I |
| C | Gross income sourced at partner level | Form 1116, Part I |

*Foreign gross income sourced at partnership level*
| D | Passive | Form 1116, Part I |
|---|---|---|
| E | Listed categories | Form 1116, Part I |
| F | General limitation | Form 1116, Part I |

*Deductions allocated and apportioned at partner level*
| G | Interest expense | Form 1116, Part I |
|---|---|---|
| H | Other | Form 1116, Part I |

*Deductions allocated and apportioned at partnership level to foreign source income*
| I | Passive | Form 1116, Part I |
|---|---|---|
| J | Listed categories | Form 1116, Part I |
| K | General limitation | Form 1116, Part I |

*Other information*
| L | Total foreign taxes paid | Form 1116, Part II |
|---|---|---|
| M | Total foreign taxes accrued | Form 1116, Part II |
| N | Reduction in taxes available for credit | Form 1116, line 12 |
| O | Foreign trading gross receipts | Form 8873 |
| P | Extraterritorial income exclusion | Form 8873 |
| Q | Other foreign transactions | See the Partner's Instructions |

17. **Alternative minimum tax (AMT) items**
| A | Post-1986 depreciation adjustment | |
|---|---|---|
| B | Adjusted gain or loss | See the Partner's Instructions and the Instructions for Form 6251 |
| C | Depletion (other than oil & gas) | |
| D | Oil, gas, & geothermal—gross income | |
| E | Oil, gas, & geothermal—deductions | |
| F | Other AMT items | |

18. **Tax-exempt income and nondeductible expenses**
| A | Tax-exempt interest income | Form 1040, line 8b |
|---|---|---|
| B | Other tax-exempt income | See the Partner's Instructions |
| C | Nondeductible expenses | See the Partner's Instructions |

19. **Distributions**
| A | Cash and marketable securities | See the Partner's Instructions |
|---|---|---|
| B | Other property | See the Partner's Instructions |

20. **Other information**
| A | Investment income | Form 4952, line 4a |
|---|---|---|
| B | Investment expenses | Form 4952, line 5 |
| C | Fuel tax credit information | Form 4136 |
| D | Look-back interest—completed long-term contracts | Form 8697 |
| E | Look-back interest—income forecast method | Form 8866 |
| F | Dispositions of property with section 179 deductions | |
| G | Recapture of section 179 deduction | |
| H | Special basis adjustments | |
| I | Section 453(l)(3) information | |
| J | Section 453A(c) information | |
| K | Section 1260(b) information | See the Partner's Instructions |
| L | Interest allocable to production expenditures | |
| M | CCF nonqualified withdrawals | |
| N | Information needed to figure depletion—oil and gas | |
| O | Amortization of reforestation costs | |
| P | Unrelated business taxable income | |
| Q | Other information | |

# INDEX

References are to Pages

459

†

D0630816